T0189581

Communications
in Computer and Information Science   1749

More information about this series at https://link.springer.com/bookseries/7899

Rabindra Nath Shaw · Marcin Paprzycki ·
Ankush Ghosh (Eds.)

Advanced Communication and Intelligent Systems

First International Conference, ICACIS 2022
Virtual Event, October 20–21, 2022
Revised Selected Papers

Editors
Rabindra Nath Shaw ⓘ
Global Power Energy
Melbourne, Australia

Marcin Paprzycki ⓘ
Systems Research Institute
Warsaw, Poland

Ankush Ghosh ⓘ
The Neotia University
Sarisha, India

ISSN 1865-0929   ISSN 1865-0937 (electronic)
Communications in Computer and Information Science
ISBN 978-3-031-25087-3   ISBN 978-3-031-25088-0 (eBook)
https://doi.org/10.1007/978-3-031-25088-0

This Springer imprint is published by the registered company Springer Nature Switzerland AG
The registered company address is: Gewerbestrasse 11, 6330 Cham, Switzerland

Preface

The book features selected high-quality papers presented at the International Conference on Advanced Communication and Intelligent Systems (ICACIS 2022), organized by Warsaw Management University, Poland during October 20–21, 2022, in online mode. The conference got an overwhelming response and received more than 250 papers from all around the world. All submitted papers went through a single-blind review process. The acceptance rate was less than 30%. The accepted papers are published in this volume. It focuses on current development in the fields of communication and intelligent systems. Advances in artificial intelligence and machine learning have spawned fresh research activities all around the world in the last few years, as we examine novel approaches to constructing intelligent systems and smart communication technologies. The book covers topics such as Wireless Communication, Artificial Intelligence and Machine Learning, Robotics and Automation, Data Science, IoT, and Smart Applications. The book includes both focused and multidisciplinary research on these topics, providing up-to-date information in one place. It will be beneficial for readers from both academia and industry.

We are grateful to all authors who submitted papers for keeping the quality of ICACIS at a high level. The editors of this book would like to acknowledge all the authors for their contributions and the reviewers. We received invaluable help from the members of the International Program Committee and the chairs responsible for different aspects of the conference. We also appreciate the role of the special session organizers. Thanks to all of them, we were able to collect many papers on interesting topics, and during the conference we had very interesting presentations and stimulating discussions.

We hope that the volume will provide useful information to professors, researchers, and graduate students in the areas of Computer Science Engineering, Electronics, and Communication Engineering and Technologies, and also AI and IoT Applications. They will all find this collection of papers inspiring, informative, and useful. We also hope to see you at a future ICACIS event.

February 2023

Rabindra Nath Shaw
Marcin Paprzycki
Ankush Ghosh

Organization

Honorary Chair

Lakhmi C. Jain   KES International

General Chairs

Marcin Paprzycki   Polish Academy of Sciences, Warsaw, Poland
Monica Bianchini   University of Siena, Italy

General Co-chair

Sanjoy Das   Indira Gandhi National Tribal University,
                              Manipur, India

Conference Chair and Chair of Oversight Committee

Rabindra Nath Shaw   Global Power Energy, Australia

Conference Secretary

Saravanan D.   Galgotias University, India

Technical Chair

Ankush Ghosh   TNU, India

Publication Chair

Vincenzo Piuri   University of Milan, Italy

Publicity Chair

Prashant R. Nair   Amrita Vishwa Vidyapeetham, India

Advisory Committee

Bimal K. Bose	University of Tennessee, USA
Muhammad H. Rashid	University of West Florida, USA
Muhammet Koksal	Halic University, Turkey
Nasrudin Bin Abd Rahim	University of Malaysia, Malaysia
Hamid Ali Abed Al-Asadi	University of Basra, Iraq
Tarek Bouktir	University of Setif, Algeria
Subramaniam Ganesan	Oakland University, USA
Claudio Moraga Roco	European Centre for Soft Computing, Spain
Suganthan P. N.	Nanyang Technological University, Singapore
Sanjib Kumar P.	National University of Singapore, Singapore
Ralph Kennel	Technische Universität München, Germany
Udaya Madawala	University of Auckland, New Zealand
Dylan Lu	University of Sydney, Australia
Yeap Peik Foong	Multimedia University, Malaysia
Terence Karran	University of Lincoln, UK
B. Chitti Babu	University of Nottingham, Malaysia
Jyh-Horng Chou	NKUAS, Taiwan
Yurii Boreisha	Minnesota State University, USA
Herbert H. C. Lu	University of Western Australia, Australia

Contents

Towards 6G-Enabled Edge-Cloud Continuum Computing – Initial Assessment

Jaydip Kumar[1], Jitendra K Samriya[2], Marek Bolanowski[3],
Andrzej Paszkiewicz[3], Wiesław Pawłowski[4], Maria Ganzha[5],
Katarzyna Wasielewska-Michniewska[5(✉)], Bartłomiej Solarz-Niesłuchowski[5],
Marcin Paprzycki[5,6], Ignacio Lacalle Úbeda[7], and Carlos E. Palau[7]

[1] Babasaheb Bhimrao Ambedkar University (A Central University), Lucknow, India
[2] Sanskrit University, Mathura, India
jitendras.cse@sanskriti.edu.in
[3] Rzeszów University of Technology, Rzeszów, Poland
[4] University of Gdańsk, Gdańsk, Poland
[5] Systems Research Institute Polish Academy of Sciences, Warszawa, Poland
katarzyna.wasielewska@bspan.waw.pl
[6] Warsaw Management University, Warsaw, Poland
[7] University Politechnica Valencia, Valencia, Spain

Abstract. While actual deployments of fifth generation (5G) networks
are in their initial stages and the actual need for 5G in our daily
lives remains an open question, their potential to deliver high speed,
low latency, and dependable communication services remains promising.
Nevertheless, sixth generation (6G) networks have been proposed as a
way to enhance the 5G solutions. Moreover, their potential is claimed
to facilitate further development of intelligent Internet of Things solutions. This work outlines the main aspects, and proposed applications,
of 6G technology. Moreover, the role that 6G networks can play in the
transition from the IoT, as we know it, to the Edge-Cloud continuum is
considered. Applicability to deep learning techniques and security aspects
of 6G deployments are also noted.

Keywords: 6G network · 5G networks · Security · Artificial
intelligence · Internet of Things · Edge-cloud continuum

1 Introduction

In the post-pandemic era, the transformation of human experience that links the
physical, digital, and biological worlds is likely to bring about novel possibilities as
well as serious challenges. In this context it is often claimed that advanced features
and new communication architectures provided by the sixth generation (6G) network technology will help realizing the vision of a "connected globe" and support
growth, sustainability, and the idea of complete digital access. However, in order
for this optimistic vision to be realized an ambitious 6G strategy is needed [1]. Such

R. N. Shaw et al. (Eds.): ICACIS 2022, CCIS 1749, pp. 1–15, 2023.
https://doi.org/10.1007/978-3-031-25088-0_1

strategy should allow realization of scenarios in which 6G technology dramatically boosts and enhances human potential and capacities, going beyond digitalization of the 2020s [2]. Here, high quality digital (virtual) worlds that are disconnected from geographical locations may attract people, delivering new experiences. Bearing this in mind, it also becomes clear that processing needs to be performed closer to the data sources (often smart devices), in an effort to minimise latency, save bandwidth, improve security, guarantee privacy and increase autonomy leveraging the IoT-edge-cloud continuum of computation. For instance, when next generation of devices with user-friendly interfaces, and new sensing capabilities will materialize, humans commanding their "avatars", will be able to activate different aspects of the physical world. Here, the interconnection will be provided/realized through a portfolio of biological and mechanical sensing devices accessible through futuristic human-computer interfaces. The 6G techniques bring also promise for the next generation of industrial applications, as they are to offer substantial performance boost and new dimensions of interactions between physical, biological and digital environments. Recent articles [3–7], discuss the relevant 6G vision(s) and technologies. However, one has to keep in mind that deep-dive analysis must wait till about 2030, when the start of actual adoption of 6G is to materialize. This assumption is based on the fact that current duration of each network generation is around ten years. In this context, outline presented here should be seen as an attempt to outline potential of 6G infrastructures for future Edge-Cloud deployments more than hard-facts based prediction.

In this context, the birds-eye view allows one to state that while there will be an increase in demand for mobile broadband from both consumers and businesses, the actual adoption of 6G-based ultra-reliable and low latency connections will primarily be driven by specialized and local use cases in conjunction with private networks. Moreover, such "local deployments" will frequently involve support for various forms of artificial intelligence. Here, automobiles, industrial machinery, appliances, watches, and clothing are just a few examples of objects that will use 6G networks to automatically adapt behaviour, environment, and business operations, in order to learn and organise themselves to meet demands of (domain) specific use cases. Another important design consideration for 6G is going to be energy efficiency, because the amount of energy that can be found in each architectural domain will determine how well the network performs.

1.1   Historical Perspective

Since the first appearance of analogue communications networks in the 1980s, mobile communication networks have developed phenomenally. The progress has been made in subsequent generations, each with its own standards, capabilities, and methodologies. Nearly every ten years, a new generation has been introduced [8]. Figure 1 depicts the evolution of the mobile network.

(1–3)G Networks. The first generation mobile network, which had a data rate of up to 2.4 kbps and was built for voice services, was initially introduced in

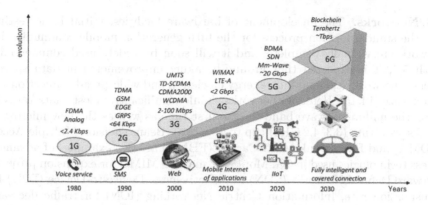

Fig. 1. Evolution of mobile networks [8]

the 1980s. Due to the analogue signal, utilised for transmission, and the lack of a global wireless standard, there were numerous limitations, including difficult hand-offs, ineffective transmission, and no security [9]. The second-generation systems, sometimes referred to as 2G systems, were constructed on digitally modulated techniques such Time Division Multiple Access (TDMA) and Code Division Multiple Access (CDMA). They supported enhanced audio services as well as services like Short Message Service (SMS) and had a data rate of up to 64 kbps. Throughout the 2G period, the GSM (Global System for Mobile Communication) was the dominant mobile communication system [10]. The third generation was introduced in 2000, with the intention of facilitating high-speed data transport. High-speed Internet access and data transmission rates of at least 2 Mbps were provided by the 3G network [11]. This enabled the use of services like Web browsing, TV streaming, navigational mapping, and video services that were not supported by 1G/2G networks. During this time frame, the Third Generation Partnership Project (3GPP) was created to conceptualize the technical requirements and carry on the process of developing mobile standards and technologies in order to achieve global roaming [12].

4G Networks. The 4G network infrastructure, which has been launched in the late 2000s, was an all-IP network capable of transmitting data at speeds of up to 1 Gbps in the download, and 500 Mbps in the upload. In order to meet the requirements of applications like video chat, High Definition TV, and Digital Video Broadcasting, it boosted spectral efficiency and minimised latency. Additionally, 4G enabled terminal mobility to offer wireless services, whenever and wherever they were needed, through autonomous roaming across wireless network boundaries. Long Term Evolution-Advanced (LTE-A) and Wireless Interoperability for Microwave Access are examples of the 4G technology (WiMAX) [13].

5G Networks. The development of hardware facilities, initial basic testing, and the standardization process for the fifth generation mobile communication network are virtually complete, and it will soon be widely used commercially. With 5G, it is expected that ground-breaking improvements in data speeds, latency, network dependability, energy efficiency, and widespread connection will materialize [14,15]. Here, 5G networks should significantly boosts data rates by using the millimeter-wave band for the first time as well as the new microwave band's spectrum (3.3–4.2 GHz) (up to 10 Gbps). Beam Division Multiple Access (BDMA) and Filter Bank Multi-Carrier (FBMC) are two examples of advanced access technologies used in 5G. Moreover, massive MIMO for expansion projects, Software Defined Networks (SDN) for effectiveness, Device-to-Device (D2D) for transmission rate, Information Centric Networking (ICN) for traffic decrease, and Network Slicing for rapid deployment of different services are a few of the cutting-edge innovations that 5G combines to improve the performance [16]. Enhanced mobile broadband (eMBB), Ultra-reliable and low latency communications (URLLC), and mMTC (Massive Machine-Type Communications) were the three main 5G utilisation scenarios that have been suggested and are still considered to be valid (and waiting to be practically validated).

2   Architecture of 6G Networks – Current Vision

As 5G networking moved into the commercial deployment stage, research institutions started to focus on theoretical foundations and early-stage laboratory-based experiments with 6G networking. In 6G network, it is postulated that the peak data rates of 1 Tbps and exceptionally low latency measured in microseconds can be delivered. This means that 6G is expected to seriously enhance the performance of data transmission. Specifically, it is to offer up to a thousand times greater bandwidth than 5G technology, because of terahertz frequency transmission and spatial multiplexing. Moreover, by combining satellite network connectivity with underwater communications, 6G aims to provide ubiquitous connectivity and global coverage [17]. To illustrate the progress of communication capabilities of 4G, 5G and expected 6G networks, Table 1 summarizes their main characteristics.

Table 1. Performance evaluation of 4G, 5G, and 6G [18]

Characteristics	4G	5G	6G
Peak data rate of the device	1 Gbps	10 to 20 Gbps	1 Tbps
Latency	100 ms	5–10 ms	10 to 100 μs
Highest possible spectral efficiency	15 bps/Hz	30 bps/Hz	100 bps/Hz
Mobility	350 km/h	500 km/h	Up to 1000 km/h
Energy efficiency of a network	1x	10–100x of 4G	10–100x of 5G

In addition to a safe and automated coordination design, the 6G architecture comprises building blocks that cross key architectural areas of a telecommunications network, beginning at the physical layer and going all the way up to the service layer (see, [19]). As shown in Fig. 2, the main building components for the 6G architecture have already been defined. The Nokia Bell Labs 6G architectural breakdown consists of four key interconnected components that offer an open and distributed reference architecture. The "Net-Cloud" component of the 6G architectural cloud shift includes notions such an information circulation run-time architecture, accessible, flexible, and agnostic hardware-accelerated, and more. It effectively acts as the architecture's infrastructure platform. The functional part of the architecture is covered by the "functions" component, which also covers RAN-CORE converge, cell free and mesh connection, link building, and AI. The development of specialized networks and related functional characteristics is a key transformational aspect of the 6G-based ecosystems. Devices that will join 6G networks are becoming ever smarter in collecting, processing and transmitting data, posing new challenges, thus it will be key for 6G implementations to achieve increasingly demanding levels of reconfigurability, self-* and automation, in order to scale efficiently, manage resources, and optimise operation while handling multi-vertical traffic with distinct demands. Consequently, architecture elements that affect performance, such as adjustable offload, extreme chopping and subnetting, are presented as parts of the "specialized" core component. For a business to succeed, the "automation" component of the change to the 6G architecture, which will offer an open service allowing for environment engagement, domain resource monetizing, in addition to cognitively closed system and mechanisation, is essential.

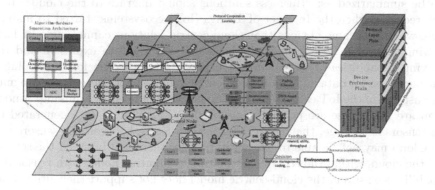

Fig. 2. Architecture of 6G network [19]

2.1   B5G Networks

Before moving to the visions of advances that are to be brought by 6G networking let us focus, for a moment, on the time when movement towards 6G will materialize. Here, as a metaphor one can consider 5G networks realized "on top of 4G". This is known as "beyond 5G" (B5G) and just a few of the B5G applications include robotic communications, e-health, human-robot interaction, multimedia, e-learning, public security, e-governance, logistics and transportation manufacturing, and transportation technologies. In order to enable Internet of Things, wireless communication technologies are essential. They refer to environmentally responsible, energy-efficient, sustainable, and intelligent technologies [20]. Future commercial and non-terrestrial wireless communications networks will need multi-beam antennas as essential components. These antennas' many beams will make it possible for different terrestrial, airborne, and space-based network nodes to dynamically connect with one another. When the operating frequency for sixth-generation (6G) and beyond 5G (B5G) systems increases to the high millimetre wave (mmWave) and terahertz (THz) bands, relatively few techniques are anticipated to dominate in the design of high gain multi-beam antennas [21].

3   Selected Application Areas of 6G Networking

Let us now "move forward" and consider where 6G networking could be useful. Here, only few areas of particular interest to our research have been selected. Let us start from the reflection concerning changes of the leading paradigm for development and deployment of large distributed ecosystems.

3.1   Towards Edge-Cloud Continuum Computing

The beginning of 21st century has been characterized by a general trend that can be summarized as: "Business solutions should migrate to the cloud". It is only recently, when the Internet of Things (IoT) ecosystems started to materialize, when it became obvious that cloud-centric solutions cannot support fast-growing sizes of IoT deployments. The unprecedented data explosion and the evolving capabilities of virtual infrastructures, set the scene for developing a new paradigm for data and compute resource management. Here, there are multiple aspects of the IoT ecosystems that do not fit cloud-centric thinking. Among them are (and these are just few examples): (a) amount of data generated by the sensors is so large, that networking infrastructure between the sensors and the Cloud may not be able to efficiently transfer them, (b) between the sensors and the cloud, within the ecosystem, multiple computing nodes with reasonable capabilities exist and the cloud-centric model does not support their utilization, (c) large IoT ecosystems may require extremely time-constraint decision loops, which cannot be realized in cloud-centric deployments, (d) privacy and security of travelling data is put at stake.

In response to these issues, a novel approach to performing computational tasks, based on the concept of the *edge-cloud continuum* has been proposed. It advocates consuming and processing data along the whole "architectural spectrum" – from the edge devices up to the cloud. In this approach, computing and/or storage "nodes" can be located anywhere across the network (ecosystem), offering a "computational fabric" spanning (any fragment of) the path from (constrained) devices to the powerful cloud systems. Devices will be able to unload their activities and offer (possibly pre-processed) data to the nodes constituting the distributed infrastructure of the "fabric." The decentralized computing model, as compared to the centralised one, provided by the cloud alone, is a key advantage of the edge-cloud continuum approach. Additionally, as data and tasks may be processed and evaluated close to their "point of origin", latency is reduced. Furthermore, the edge-cloud continuum approach aims at increasing the network capacity and the frequency spectrum use. The highly distributed node placement improves computation and storage capacities "in places where they are needed", which may also have a beneficial effect on system reliability [22]. However, the challenge of seamlessly integrating various edge technologies into a homogeneous "continuum" remains open, since current centralised deployments store and process long-term data, relying on the cloud, but lack capabilities needed to handle key open challenges, such as (i) cloud-centricity by default in most legacy in-place systems, (ii) latency, (iii) cost, (iii) network congestion, (iv) heterogeneous smart devices - posing heterogeneous access concerns- and (v) the lack of a security and privacy reference implementation considering CI/CD and DevOps procedures.

Here, it is relatively easy to realize that support for the edge-cloud continuum based computational model has a potential to become a major application of the massive data handling capabilities that are to be provided by the 6G technology. Given the high number of devices exchanging data and (concurrently) running large number of applications, the computing and storage services provided by the nodes placed within the edge-cloud continuum will be crucial; and thus becomes a potential 6G deployment-driving use case. Additionally, 6G infrastructure will offer a number of useful features like geo-distributed data, for example. The 6G communications will enable interconnectivity of the nodes and allow for achieving an extremely low latency and efficient bandwidth usage [23]. Here, it is worthy realizing that large scale edge-cloud continuum ecosystems will not require 6G infrastructure "everywhere". Rather, it will be possible to obtain expected performance characteristics by deploying 6G infrastructures in selected "regions" (parts of) the ecosystem. Worth noting, the decision on whether or not to apply 6G features to a specific vertical (or continuum deployment) will rely on the collaboration of such networks with the governance implemented by the next generation meta-operating system that will orchestrate the IoT-edge-cloud continuum (some examples are appearing as European-funded initiatives in the meta-OS program of the EC, where the project aerOS promises to be a reference [24].

The ever increasing number of edge devices in use requires the provision of a stable communications platform that can exchange large amounts of data with low latency [25, 26]. Through a 6G wireless communication network, the edge-cloud continuum can achieve its full potential and enable a variety of physical and virtual nodes to exchange information in a very efficient way. Effective methods to increase the spectrum and energy efficiency include simultaneous wireless information and power transfer (SWIPT) and cooperative spectrum sharing.

With significantly increased data rates and spectral efficiency, 6G wireless communication and networks will continue to shift to higher frequency and larger bandwidth. Given the diversity and density of the edge-cloud continuum deployments, it may be necessary to expand the 6G wireless network to support modern random access (RA) for applications distributed across the "continuum". In such a distributed data and compute scenario, the so-called network compute fabric, the network should host computing intertwined with communication for the highest level of efficiency, to support heterogeneous systems, ranging from simple terminals to performance-sensitive robots and augmented reality nodes. This can be done by designing smart protocols and using signal processing and communication technologies. A good possibility is provided by contemporary RA techniques such massive multiple-input multiple-output (MIMO), OFDMA, nonorthogonal multiple access (NOMA), sparse signal processing, or innovative orthogonal design methodologies. Grant-free transmission for distributed architecture should be planned for a successful implementation of 6G-based computational continuum, where applications frequently take part in self-organizing decision-making.

Nevertheless, it should be also realized that the implementation of the paradigm of "computing continuum", based on capabilities of 6G networking, will not be without its problems. In particular, difficulties involving resource allocation, work offloading, energy efficiency, delay minimization, justice, and security will emerge [27]. They will be further magnified as the deployments will become part of large-scale edge-cloud ecosystems. Here, 6G "patches" will have to be managed not only taking into account their "internal needs", but also to "understand the context" of their role within the ecosystem. For instance, while internally (within the 6G patch) some energy saving measures may seem appropriate, they may be prohibited by the needs of a workflow that is being realized to deliver user-defined service. Hence, 6G in edge-cloud continuum may need be reactive to the dynamically changing, context of the "outside world".

3.2   Artificial Intelligence in Edge-Cloud Ecosystems

It is easy to observe that mobile applications, driven by artificial intelligence, are being developed as a result of the widespread use of smart mobile devices. In multiple application areas, such as computer vision, natural language processing, and autonomous driving, AI has made remarkable successes. AI activities require a lot of computing and are typically trained, developed, and used in data centers with specialized servers. However, with growing power of mobile devices, significant number of intelligent applications are anticipated to be implemented at the edges of cellular connections [28]. AI at the edge of the network promises to be beneficial not just at functional but also at business level, allowing the realisation of federated/distributed AI scenarios and adjusting to the capabilities of the continuum applying techniques such as frugal AI. To support "intelligent applications" at different edge handheld devices with extremely heterogeneous communication, compute, hardware, and energy resources, the 6G wireless network may deliver the needed infrastructure [29]. Here, the 6G network is expected to provide adaptable platforms to enable ubiquitous mobile AI services. In addition, it will provide a thorough method for optimizing telecommunication, computing, and storage infrastructure to accommodate modern AI functions across end-devices, networking boundaries, and cloud data centres [30].

Nevertheless, it is easy to see that the extreme heterogeneity of devices "roaming within the 6G network infrastructure" will, again bring the need for edge-cloud continuum thinking. While some devices may be able to get involved directly into AI/ML activities, such as mode training or use, others may "need help" (provided by devices that are somewhere within the continuum). It is at this point where novel approaches (such as the one brought by project aerOS [24]) will come into place, materializing federated AI in a dynamic and smart way (adapting the sharing of models/data depending on the needs and network and node capabilities). This being the case, it is easy to realize that the 6G networking by itself, regardless how fast it becomes will not be enough to facilitate deployment of intelligence across the continuum.

3.3 Distributed Ledger Technologies and 6G Networking

Globally, multiple business and research groups have adopted distributed ledger technology (DLT; [31]). In what follows we will, however, use the term blockchain to represent all DLT solutions. One of key advantages of blockchain is decentralisation, which eliminates the need for middlemen and "trusted-centralised" third parties; another is transparency with anonymity; a third is provenance and non-repudiation of the transactions made; a fourth is immutability and tamper-proofing of the distributed ledger's content; a fifth is the removal of single points of failure (improving adaptability and resistance to attacks like DDoS).

Given that blockchain technology has been designated as one of the key enabling technologies for 6G mobile networks, it is essential to look into the various benefits, opportunities, and difficulties related to its application [32,33].

The 6G vision includes a wide range of applications that can be made possible or enhanced by using blockchain. The idea behind using blockchain, to provide or enhance these applications in 6G, comes from the possibilities stemming from their key characteristics, namely decentralisation, transparency, immutability, availability, and security [34].

Moreover, the 6G infrastructure itself offers a wealth of application potential for utilising blockchain to improve performance or enable new services/use-cases. Particularly, Service Level Agreement (SLA) Management, Authentication, Authorization and Accounting (AAA), Decentralized Network Management Structures, Network Service Pricing, Billing and Charging, and Spectrum Sharing. Here, it is worthy noting that majority of these use cases naturally belong to the IoT deployments. Hence, they are also going to find their way into edge-cloud continuum deployments.

3.4   Industry 4.0 and Beyond

The use of the expected 6G capabilities will be significantly influenced by the industrial applications in 6G. Industrial environments adapt themselves particularly well to the problems and important characteristics of blockchain technology. Holographic communication, for instance, require decentralised systems that are also trustworthy in order to support industrial use-cases like remote maintenance or widespread networking of industrial manufacturing equipment [35]. From another perspective, 6G and the realization of an actual IoT-edge-cloud orchestrated continuum will allow the creation of highly flexible, sustainable (green) modular digital production lines and manufacturing of a new product in a low-volume production (high customisation). The previous will unleash implementation of smart rapid response features in connection with self-optimisation, re-configurations ramp-up, adaptation of the production line and the operations, driving manufacturing closer to Industry 5.0 principles [36].

3.5   Healthcare Applications

The number of chronic patients will rise in the future, and the medical resources needed to give them the care they will be in short supply. These issues will have to be addressed by healthcare systems [37,38]. Adoption of ICT is essential for the upcoming health services. The ability to measure some health indicators in real-time and assess the patient's overall condition, along with the automatic sharing of the collected clinical data among all members of the care team, is vital for the personalised management of the patient's health. This is especially true for patients who have multiple chronic diseases. 6G can alter the future wireless healthcare system which will allow the implementation of new healthcare services and essentially change the current telecare paradigm. The specification of 6G future communication application scenarios and the associated enabling communications technologies is the main are of the ongoing work and the 6G vision, which also includes significant drivers, research requirements, obstacles, and critical research problems [39].

To address enduring challenges in 5G networks, smart healthcare in 6G will need to develop. Here, it is worthy noting that future healthcare systems may be based on blockchain technologies. Here, the privacy concern is the next in line for these technical issues. Furthermore, the immutability feature offered by blockchains makes it possible to maintain the integrity of healthcare data. Blockchains particularly can provide user-controlled privacy and safe data storage without the need for a centrally trusted third party. Here, as noted above, there is a direct applicability of 6G networks and blockchains.

3.6   Environment Protection and Monitoring

Environmental sensing applications that are decentralised and cooperative may need blockchains to store trusted data, and they may be possible by 6G on a global scale. These capabilities can be put to use in applications like smart cities, transportation, and environmental preservation for the green economy.

In summary, it can be clearly seen that there is a direct connection between the (1) vision and theory underlying future development of 6G based networks, (2) multiple application areas and tools that need them, and (3) edge-cloud continuum that will be used to realize practical use cases, delivering actual (and needed) services to the users.

4   Security of 6G Networks

Many innovations and developments in terms of architecture, applications, technologies, regulations, and standardization are being researched to be included in the 6G network concept. Similar to generic 6G vision, which adds intelligence to 5G networks' cloud infrastructure and software, 6G security vision closely integrates AI to produce security automation (Fig. 3). Here, one has to realize that the "adversaries" also work non-stop to produce new kinds of security risks. For instance, identifying zero-day attacks is never easy, but stopping them from spreading is the most practical defense. Therefore, integrating intelligent and adaptable security methods will be more crucial than ever for predicting, detecting, reducing, and preventing security threats as well as restricting the spread of such vulnerabilities in the 6G networks. Ensuring trust and privacy in the relevant areas and among participants is also important. Particularly, security, privacy and trust are themes that are closely related to one another, with security relating to the protection of the data itself, privacy assuring the hiding of the identities associated with that data, and trust bringing meta level reflection influencing interactions between (semi-)intelligent entities. While privacy and security are mutually exclusive, the reverse is not true: in order to protect privacy, there should always be security measures in place to protect data. At the same time, trust goes beyond privacy and security. Here, it should be noted that an entity can be secure and may preserve privacy. However, in the context of large-scale IoT ecosystem it may not be trusted that it will deliver required service within the contracted time (see, also [40]).

To be able to assess the value of 6G deployments (including security-related aspects), Key Performance Indicators (KPIs) and Key Value Indicators (KVIs) are needed to properly account for the aspects of the impact that are outside the reach of deterministic performance measures, and will help determine the limits of 6G [32]. It is anticipated that 6G systems will include unique components such embedded devices, local computer and storage, integrated sensing, and artificial intelligence [41]. These aspects will necessitate development of new KPIs and KVIs, such as, for instance, slightly more accurate, computation round-trip period, and AI model time complexity, as well as improvements to existing KPIs. This being the case, the UN Sustainable Development Goals' principles of sustainability, security, inclusivity, and reliability may be used to measure the value of future 6G-related technologies [42]. Therefore, it is anticipated that the new features, brought by 6G network-based systems (e.g. edge-cloud ecosystems), will

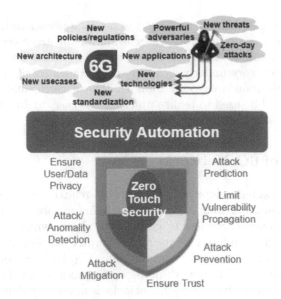

Fig. 3. Security vision of 6G network [32]

significantly affect also how security KPIs are developed and assessed. A set of KPI where proposed in [43] were: level of protection, time to respond, coverage, autonomicity level, AI robustness, Secure AI model convergence time, security function chain round-trip-time, deployment cost for security functions. Moreover, several factors, including PLS, network information security, and security-related to AI/ML, should be taken into account when characterizing security [44].

5   Concluding Remarks

The successful launch of 6G architectural research marks the beginning of the path towards the 6G connected worlds. At the same time, commercial 5G installations are currently underway, or will start soon in the majority of markets worldwide. The architectural conceptualization of 6G is still ongoing and is expected to continue for at least another eight years. Beyond that, the future holds enormous potential for a fundamentally new human experience due to real-time connectivity and synchronisation across the physical, digital, and biological worlds. Physical can be broadly referred to as physical and analysis focus from the perspective of a network, digital is all about upcoming software architecture and sophisticated automated representation, and biological includes unique human-machine interfaces and biosensors. To accomplish the adaptability, simplicity, dependability, security, efficiency, and automation required to fulfil the multiplicity of future applications, they will all be closely interconnected. Analysis performed on the basis of current knowledge indicates that the implementation of 5G and, in the future, 6G technology on a massive scale will result in a revolution, with a large number of leapfrogging changes in the area of engineering fundamentals of entire information systems. The currently dominant microservices architecture, requiring highly interconnected functional components [45], will be an additional impetus forcing faster mass deployment of 6G networks.

At the same time, cloud-centric solutions will start to be replaced by edge-cloud deployments. The so-called computing continuum is an active field of research that aims at governing nodes spanning across IoT to edge to cloud, forming a fabric that will be closely tied to the performance (and further capabilities of 6G) networks improving features like latency and availability. This process will be particularly important for large-scale, highly heterogeneous ecosystems. Here, to be able to deliver services to the users, 6G based networks will be needed. However, 6G networking, even if it will achieve all of its currently predicted properties will not be enough. Since, for a long time into the future, 5G and 6G will be available locally, while edge-cloud deployments will have to encompass highly heterogeneous networking, additional software layer will be needed. Such software layer will treat 5G/6G network patches as parts of "global ecosystem" and provide "context information" needed to realize user-requested workflows. Development of this software layer (meta-operating system governing the orchestration) is the goal of the aerOS project. We will report on our progress in subsequent publications.

Acknowledgements. Work of Marek Bolanowski and Andrzej Paszkiewicz was supported by the project financed by the Minister of Education and Science of the Republic of Poland within the "Regional Initiative of Excellence" program for years 2019–2023. Project number 027/RID/2018/19, amount granted 11 999 900 PLN. Work of Wiesław Pawłowski, Maria Ganzha, Katarzyna Wasielewska-Michniewska, Bartłomiej Solarz-Niesłuchowski and Marcin Paprzycki was funded in part by the European Commission, under the Horizon Europe project aerOS, grant number 101069732.

References

1. Ziegler, V., Viswanathan, H., Flinck, H., Hoffmann, M., Räisänen, V., Hätönen, K.: 6G architecture to connect the worlds. IEEE Access **8**, 173508–173520 (2020)
2. Viswanathan, H., Mogensen, P.E.: Communications in the 6G era. IEEE Access **8**, 57063–57074 (2020)
3. Rappaport, T.S., et al.: Wireless communications and applications above 100 GHz: opportunities and challenges for 6G and beyond. IEEE Access **7**, 78729–78757 (2019)
4. Heath, R.W., Jr., Sayed, A.H., González-Prelcic, N.: 3 from the editor going toward 6G. IEEE Signal Process. Mag. **36**, 2 (2019)
5. Zhang, J., Kang, K., Huang, Y., Shafi, M., Molisch, A.F.: Millimeter and THz wave for 5G and beyond. China Commun. **16**(2), iiii–vi (2019)
6. Yrjola, S., et al.: White paper on business of 6G. arXiv preprint arXiv:2005.06400 (2020)
7. Ziegler, V., Yrjola, S.: 6G indicators of value and performance, pp. 1–5 (2020)
8. Tongyi Huang, W., Yang, J.W., Ma, J., Zhang, X., Zhang, D.: A survey on green 6G network: architecture and technologies. IEEE Access **7**, 175758–175768 (2019)

9. Gupta, A., Jha, R.K.: A survey of 5G network: architecture and emerging technologies. IEEE Access **3**, 1206–1232 (2015)
10. David, K., Berndt, H.: 6G vision and requirements: Is there any need for beyond 5G? IEEE Veh. Technol. Mag. **13**(3), 72–80 (2018)
11. Sharma, P.: Evolution of mobile wireless communication networks - 1G to 5G as well as future prospective of next generation communication network. Int. J. Comput. Sci. Mob. Comput. **2**(8), 47–53 (2013)
12. Gawas, A.U.: An overview on evolution of mobile wireless communication networks: 1G–6G. Int. J. Recent Innov. Trends Comput. Commun. **3**(5), 3130–3133 (2015)
13. Parikh, J., Basu, A.: LTE advanced: the 4G mobile broadband technology. Int. J. Comput. Appl. **13**(5), 17–21 (2011)
14. Shafi, M., et al.: 5G: a tutorial overview of standards, trials, challenges, deployment, and practice. IEEE J. Sel. Areas Commun. **35**(6), 1201–1221 (2017)
15. Sepczuk, M., Kotulski, Z., Niewolski, W., Nowak, T.: Low-complexity access control scheme for MEC-based services, pp. 673–681 (2022)
16. Zhou, Z., Dong, M., Ota, K., Wang, G., Yang, L.T.: Energy-efficient resource allocation for D2D communications underlaying cloud-ran-based LTE-A networks. IEEE Internet Things J. **3**(3), 428–438 (2015)
17. Yastrebova, A., Kirichek, R., Koucheryavy, Y., Borodin, A., Koucheryavy, A.: Future networks 2030: architecture & requirements. In: 2018 10th International Congress on Ultra Modern Telecommunications and Control Systems and Workshops (ICUMT), pp. 1–8. IEEE (2018)
18. Akbar, M.S., Hussain, Z., Sheng, Q.Z., Mukhopadhyay, S.: 6G survey on challenges, requirements, applications, key enabling technologies, use cases, AI integration issues and security aspects. arXiv preprint arXiv:2206.00868 (2022)
19. Letaief, K.B., Chen, W., Shi, Y., Zhang, J., Zhang, Y.-J.A.: The roadmap to 6G: AI empowered wireless networks. IEEE Commun. Mag. **57**(8), 84–90 (2019)
20. Alsamhi, S.H.: Green IoT using UAVs in B5G networks: a review of applications and strategies. arXiv preprint arXiv:2103.17043 (2021)
21. Jay Guo, Y., Ansari, M., Ziolkowski, R.W., Fonseca, N.J.G.: Quasi-optical multi-beam antenna technologies for B5G and 6G mmWave and THz networks: a review. IEEE Open J. Antennas Propag. **2**, 807–830 (2021)
22. Siqi Luo, X., Chen, Z.Z., Chen, X., Weigang, W.: Incentive-aware micro computing cluster formation for cooperative fog computing. IEEE Trans. Wirel. Commun. **19**(4), 2643–2657 (2020)
23. Aggarwal, S., Kumar, N.: Fog computing for 5G-enabled tactile internet: research issues, challenges, and future research directions. Mobile Netw. Appl., 1–28 (2019). https://doi.org/10.1007/s11036-019-01430-4
24. aerOS project website. https://aeros-project.eu/. Accessed 27 Oct 2022
25. Verma, J.: Enabling internet of things through sensor cloud: a review. Scalable Comput. Pract. Exp. **22**(4), 445–462 (2021)
26. Chinh, H.D., Anh, H., Hieu, N.D., Radhakrishnan, K.K.: An IoT based condition monitoring system of biogas electrical generator for performance evaluation, pp. 7–11 (2021)
27. Malik, U.M., Javed, M.A., Zeadally, S., ul Islam, S.: Energy efficient fog computing for 6g enabled massive IoT: recent trends and future opportunities. IEEE Internet Things J. **9**, 14572–14594 (2021)
28. Li, Q.: A survey on federated learning systems: vision, hype and reality for data privacy and protection. IEEE Trans. Knowl. Data Eng., 1 (2021)

29. McMahan, B., Moore, E., Ramage, D., Hampson, S., Aguera y Arcas, B.: Communication-efficient learning of deep networks from decentralized data. In: Artificial Intelligence and Statistics, pp. 1273–1282. PMLR (2017)
30. Yang, K., Shi, Y., Ding, Z.: Low-rank optimization for data shuffling in wireless distributed computing. In: 2018 IEEE International Conference on Acoustics, Speech and Signal Processing (ICASSP), pp. 6343–6347. IEEE (2018)
31. Chang, Y., Xu, J., Ghafoor, K.Z.: An IoT and blockchain approach for the smart water management system in agriculture. Scalable Comput. Pract. Exp. **22**(2), 105–116 (2021)
32. Latva-aho, M., Leppänen, K., Clazzer, F., Munari, A.: Key drivers and research challenges for 6G ubiquitous wireless intelligence (2020)
33. Zhang, Z., et al.: 6G wireless networks: vision, requirements, architecture, and key technologies. IEEE Veh. Technol. Mag. **14**(3), 28–41 (2019)
34. Hewa, T., Gür, G., Kalla, A., Ylianttila, M., Bracken, A., Liyanage, M.: The role of blockchain in 6G: Challenges, opportunities and research directions. In: 2020 2nd 6G Wireless Summit (6G SUMMIT), pp. 1–5 (2020)
35. Mahmood, N.H., Alves, H., López, O.A., Shehab, M., Osorio, D.P.M., Latva-aho, M.: Six key enablers for machine type communication in 6G. arXiv e-prints, arXiv-1903 (2019)
36. Nahavandi, S.: Industry 5.0-a human-centric solution. Sustainability **11**(16), 4371 (2019)
37. Syed Rameem Zahra and Mohammad Ahsan Chishti: Assessing the services, security threats, challenges and solutions in the internet of things. Scalable Comput. Pract. Exp. **20**(3), 457–484 (2019)
38. Samriya, J.K., Kumar, M., Ganzha, M., Paprzycki, M., Bolanowski, M., Paszkiewicz, A.: An energy aware clustering scheme for 5G-enabled edge computing based IoMT framework. In: Groen, D., de Mulatier, C., Paszynski, M., Krzhizhanovskaya, V.V., Dongarra, J.J., Sloot, P.M.A. (eds.) ICCS 2022. LNCS, vol. 13351, pp. 169–176. Springer, Cham (2022). https://doi.org/10.1007/978-3-031-08754-7_23
39. Mucchi, L., et al.: How 6G technology can change the future wireless healthcare. In: 2020 2nd 6G Wireless Summit (6G SUMMIT), pp. 1–6. IEEE (2020)
40. Ganzha, M., Paprzycki, M., Lirkov, I.: Trust management in an agent-based grid resource brokering system-preliminary considerations. In: AIP Conference Proceedings, vol. 946, PP. 35–46 (2007). https://doi.org/10.1063/1.2806037
41. Pouttu, A., et al.: 6G white paper on validation and trials for verticals towards 2030's. 6G Research Visions, 4 (2020)
42. Ziegler, V., Yrjola, S.: 6G indicators of value and performance. In: 2020 2nd 6G wireless summit (6G SUMMIT), pp. 1–5. IEEE (2020)
43. Porambage, P., Gür, G., Osorio, D.P.M., Liyanage, M., Gurtov, A., Ylianttila, M.: The roadmap to 6G security and privacy. IEEE Open J. Commun. Soc. **2**, 1094–1122 (2021)
44. Gui, G., Liu, M., Tang, F., Kato, N., Adachi, F.: 6G: opening new horizons for integration of comfort, security, and intelligence. IEEE Wirel. Commun. **27**(5), 126–132 (2020)
45. Bolanowski, M., et al.: Efficiency of REST and gRPC realizing communication tasks in microservice-based ecosystems. In: Fujita, H., Watanobe, Y., Azumi, T. (eds.) Frontiers in Artificial Intelligence and Applications. IOS Press, September 2022

Experiments with Big Semi-Structured Data Analytics for Digital Marketing

Andreea Liliana Bădică[1], Kumar Nalinaksh[2](✉), and Agnieszka Król[3]

[1] Faculty of Economics and Business Administration, University of Craiova,
A.I. Cuza 13, 200585 Craiova, Romania
[2] QuickAssist Technology, Network Platforms Group, Intel Technology Poland,
Juliusza Słowackiego 173, 80-298 Gdańsk, Poland
kumar.nalinaksh@intel.com
[3] Institute of Management and Technical Sciences, Warsaw Management University,
Kawęczyńska 36, 03-772 Warsaw, Poland
agnieszka.krol@mans.org.pl

Abstract. This research aims to examine the Big Semi-Structured Data Analytics approach in a commercial environment. Quantitative digital marketing research was chosen as the application domain. The proposed methodology is constructed using Turi's GraphLab Create framework and its application on publicly available marketing data sets is described. The research is focused on Big Semi-Structured Data pre-processing and the experiments highlight some of the possible difficulties usually encountered when dealing with real data sets, as well as potential practical solutions. Each solution is supported by a working pre-processing Python script. The experimental results, the associated problems and the encountered difficulties, as well as the proposed solutions are highlighted and explained.

Keywords: Analytics · Data science · Big Data · Digital marketing

1 Introduction

There is a huge practical interest in the application of Analytics & Data Mining methods and technologies in many problem domains, including: tourism, logistics, health care, mobility, marketing, management (and business in general), social media, manufacturing, cybersecurity, environment & sustainability, a.o. Moreover, the application of quantitative models (also known as econometric models) has a long tradition in business in general and marketing research in particular [7].

Data Mining can be thought of as a collection of advanced computational methods for quantitative research, leveraging on Machine Learning approaches

K. Nalinaksh—The views expressed in this chapter are those of the author and do not necessarily represent or reflect the positions, strategies or opinions of his employer, Intel Corporation.

from Artificial Intelligence and Data Base technologies from Computer Science. The rapid advancement of ICT technologies, including data storage, high-performance and distributed computing, networking, and the Internet of Things, enabled massive volumes of heterogeneous and unstructured data production, transmission, and acquisition. This phenomenon is currently known and ubiquitously referred to as Big Data. Consequently, the Data Mining approaches are currently being upgraded to enable their functioning under the Big Data paradigm [18].

Digital marketing can be concisely defined as the result of the digital transformation of traditional marketing. Digital marketing subsumes digitisation, which involves the automation of organisational processes based on direct human interaction and manual processing of classic documents on paper by digitising information, i.e., transforming documents from physical or analogue format to digital format. According to [16], world society is currently witnessing an era of digital disruption that is causing an unprecedented increase in companies in various industries. Marketing research is profoundly transformed by new marketing practises supported by information and communication technologies such as: artificial intelligence, mixed reality (virtual and augmented, which involves enriching the real world by combining elements of physical and virtual reality with digital technologies), and block-chains based on distributed decentralised peer-to-peer databases. Marketing practises are embracing more and more other technologies with digital transformation potential, such as the Internet of Things (IoT) and cyber-physical systems.

Recent bibliographic studies revealed a significant increase in the trend of scientific research in Big Data marketing [17]. The unique characteristics of Big Data on Social Networks, usually captured by multiple Vs patterns, raise many challenges for Big Data analytics [15]. One particular aspect relates to the insufficient ability of contemporary technologies to deal with mixtures of structured and unstructured data, sometimes referred to as semi-structured data [5].

The chapter considers the preliminary experiments with Big Semi-Structured Data Analytics in marketing research. There are many software tools to support data mining tasks in an educational or industrial context [2]. GraphLab Create framework [13] has been chosen motivated by the focus on scalability aspects that are required in experiments with large data sets, as typically encountered under the Big Data setting.

The chapter is structured as follows. Section 2 begins with a brief overview of some related works. Section 3 introduces the experimental environment and the data sources used in the preliminary experiments. In this work, the focus is solely on the tabular data, although GraphLab Create supports also graph data and time series. Section 4 presents some results of data manipulation and visualisation. tasks. A practical approach is followed by first introducing the problem, then presenting the solution, and finally discussing the results. Section 5 discusses the conclusions derived and points to future work.

2   Related Work

There are many frameworks, packages, and libraries providing Analytics support, including Machine Learning and Data Mining algorithms. They can be classified according to diverse criteria, including their purpose – academic/educational or business/industrial, or programming language/software platform integration – for example Python-based, Java-based, C/C++-based, or R-based [2].

In this body of work the unanimous choice was GraphLab Create – a robust and scalable Data Mining framework written in C++ and available from a Python platform, supporting Big Data of tabular, graph, and time series types [13]. Python is currently a leading programming language used in academic education and quantitative scientific research [1]. GraphLab Create enables the facile development of Big Data Mining applications with Python using a variety of algorithms for data manipulation, analysis and mining. Other Python packages that offer similar functionalities are Pandas [25], Scikit-learn [26], and NetworkX [24]. Pandas offers support for the manipulation of tabular and time series data [3], Scikit-learn provides machine learning algorithms [10], while NetworkX is a library for analysing graphs and networks [11].

GraphLab Create, Pandas, Scikit-learn, and NetworkX are rather similar in the functionalities they provide. However, GraphLab Create has the advantage of scalability, being able to properly scale to use available disk space, as well as to take advantage of specialised multithreaded and GPU-based hardware, while Pandas, Scikit-learn, and NetworkX use in-memory only data structures. On the other hand, Pandas, Scikit-learn, and NetworkX are open source and can be used in commercial applications without any fee, while GraphLab Create requires one to purchase a licence for commercial application. However, the supporting Turi company provides a one-year licence to academic users for free use of GraphLab Create in academic projects.

Another approach for increasing the performance of Data Mining applications is to combine existing Data Mining algorithms and frameworks with high-performance computing architectures, like, for example, Grid and Cloud Computing. One notable proposal employs Grid Services for mining fuzzy association rules [8]. A good and recent overview of computational and data base technologies and their supporting methodologies to exploit Big Data analytics for marketing decisions is provided by [5].

Quantitative marketing research has triggered a lot of interest in Data Mining applications during the last decades. A complete review of this work would go far beyond the scope of this research note. For example, it is worth mentioning the rather early reference [14] that provides a comprehensive review of Data Mining applications in Customer Relationship Management, including Customer Identification, Customer Attraction, Customer Retention, and Customer Development.

Moreover, classical Data Mining approaches are currently being reconsidered in the context of the rapid spread of Big Data characterised by large volume, heterogeneity, and autonomy of distributed data sources with decentralised control, as well as by complexity and evolution of relationships between data [18]. A very recent overview of Big Data frameworks is presented in [12]. In particular, Big Data Analytics raised a high interest in education [6].

3   System Development

This section outlines the steps taken to build the experimental system.

3.1   Environment Setup

The process for experimental data analysis starts by setting up the working environment. Tutorial introduction is followed that is available on Turi's Web site [28] to set up and configure a suitable working environment. The steps followed are presented below.

- Anaconda [19] platform was downloaded and installed. This solution was chosen rather than for a basic Python installation, since Anaconda already provides many Python packages for numerical and scientific computations that will be needed in future work.
- A special Anaconda environment was created that was required for the installation of GraphLab Create. In particular this environment was setup to use Python 2.7 – as this is the Python version that is currently required for creating and running the GraphLab Create framework.
- The registration as an academic user was carried out at Turi [27], the private company that currently supports the development of GraphLab Create.
- Finally GraphLab Create was installed in the newly created Anaconda environment, using the license key provided while registering with Turi.

3.2   Data Sources

It was decided to start the work using publicly available marketing research data. Therefore, during the next step, suitable open data sets were identified and downloaded in the field of marketing research. It should be noted that GraphLab Create tutorials are already using publicly available data, in particular, data relevant for marketing research; see, for example, the Yelp data set [30]. Nevertheless, it was decided to use data sets not provided by Turi, in order to face as realistic as possible scenarios, as one typically might encounter when working with real and independently available data.

Following this decision, appropriate data sources were sought using a simple Google search with the following search query: "marketing data sets". Choosing the first answer, 16 marketing data sets available at *data.world* [21] were discovered. From this repository, two data sets provided by *datafiniti*, in the shoe sales business, were selected:

- *Men's Shoe Prices* data set [23] – MSP in what follows.
- *Women's Shoe Prices* data set [29] – WSP in what follows.

Then, the data sets were downloaded, available as two large ZIP archives, and those archives were unpacked into a local directory. Each archive included CSV files with tabular data, as follows: file *7004_1.csv* containing the first data set with a size on disk of approximately 49.6 MB, and file *7003_1.csv* containing the second data set with a size on disk of approximately 41.8 MB.

Before data import, an initial examination of the data format was performed using available text editors and data processing tools. The basic data format was text, which allowed us to perform a basic data visualisation using a text editor. Moreover, the *.csv* format was appropriate to do a preliminary import of the data using a spreadsheet processing tool. Preliminary visual examination of the data revealed the following aspects:

- Meta-data is available in the file header. It consists of a list of attributes, enabling an initial flat tabular data visualization (e.g. `id`, `asins`, `brand`, `categories`, `colors`, `count`, `dateadded`, ...).
- Many attributes have missing information in the data sets observed as multiple consecutive commas (e.g. `46.26, , , new, , USD,2016-06-14T04: 29:57Z, ...`).
- Preliminary tabular visualisation is limited. A careful examination with the help of a text editor revealed a deeper structure of the data, going beyond the strict tabular model. The data contain a mixture of hierarchically structured and text data, revealing the true semi-structured nature of the data sets. Therefore, the data items contain attribute data (that is, comma-separated text values of the attributes present in the meta-data), as well as key-value pairs, similar to those encountered in the definitions of objects using the JSON format [22]. Comma-separated attributes are sometimes hierarchically nested with key-value object representations leading to complex hierarchical structures (e.g. `GameDay Boots, ,"[""dateSeen"":[""2017-01-27T01: 34:26Z""], ""name"": ""Big Deal Hunter"", ""dateSeen"": [""2017-01-27T01: 34:26Z""], ""name"":""Viomart""]"`, ...).
- Many data items contain mixtures of data with meta-data. For example, it was noticed that for some data items, price information could contain the price value mixed with the currency value and other information (e.g., `REDUCED USD 37.01`), while size information might contain the size values mixed with the unit values of measurement (e.g., `Dimensions 3'' H x 275'' W x 575''`).

3.3   Data Importing

At this stage, the data sets were imported into the GraphLab Create working environment using the Python script shown in the Listing 1. A data set is represented in GraphLab Create using an object of class *SFrame*.

While undertaking the import experiment, the operation resulted in the MSP data set successfully importing 19,240 rows, from 19,387 available in the original data set, while 147 rows failed to parse correctly. Similarly, for the WSP data set were successfully imported 19,036 rows from 19,045 available in the original data, while 9 rows failed to parse correctly.

Listing 1. Importing the data set in GraphLab Create

```
import graphlab as gl
# The complete path to the local directory with the data files
path = '...'
man_fname = path + '7004_1.csv'
woman_fname = path + '7003_1.csv'
man_shoe_prices=gl.SFrame.read_csv(man_fname)
woman_shoe_prices=gl.SFrame.read_csv(woman_fname)
man_shoe_prices.show()
woman_shoe_prices.show()
```

An important observation is that GraphLab Create performs automatic type inference based on inspection of the first *nrows_to_infer* rows of the table. The default value (used in this experiment) of the *nrows_to_infer* parameter is 100. Increasing the value of this parameter resulted in the import of more rows, while, on the other hand, the parsing of those imported rows was not always correct. For example, increasing the number of rows used for inference to 5,000 resulted in successfully importing all the data set into GraphLab Create environment. However, a careful analysis of the imported data revealed that some rows may not have been correctly mapped to the inferred schema of the table. This phenomenon was observed using data inspection tools already available at *data.world*. Nevertheless, the detailed examination and discussion of these issues was considered outside the scope of this chapter and therefore it was not included here.

4   Experiments and Results

4.1   Basic Visualisation

The *show()* method of the *SFrame* class was used to visualize some useful summary information regarding the data sets. For example, the imported MSP data set has 19,240 rows and 48 columns, while the imported WSP data set has 19,036 rows and 47 columns. Moreover, the GraphLab Create canvas can also visualize some useful summary information about the data sets. The canvas provides three types of visualizations: summary, tabular, and plots.

An interesting observation resulting from the analysis of summary information of each data set is that the most expensive pair of sold luxury shoes recorded in the MSP data set was valued to 16,949 USD, while the most expensive pair of sold luxury shoes in the ASP data set was priced at the incredible price of 104,350 USD. Other interesting observations refer to the most popular brands (reflected as most frequent items): 'Nike', 'Ralph Lauren', and 'PUMA' for the MSP data set, and 'Ralph Lauren', 'Nike', and 'TOMS' for the WSP data set.

Moreover, Fig. 1 contains a graph presenting the mean minimum prices and the number of products sold for a selection of brands of the MSP data set. Carefully examining this figure shows that, among the displayed brands (note that only a few part of the total number of brands are displayed), the maximum of the mean of minimum price was obtained for the 'AIR JORDAN' brand, for which only 6 products were sold, while the minimum of the mean of minimum price of 4.25 USD was obtained for 'Argyle Culture' brand, for which only a single product was sold. Furthermore, a more popular brand was observed as ASICS for which 102 products were sold at a mean of the minimum price of 86.568 USD.

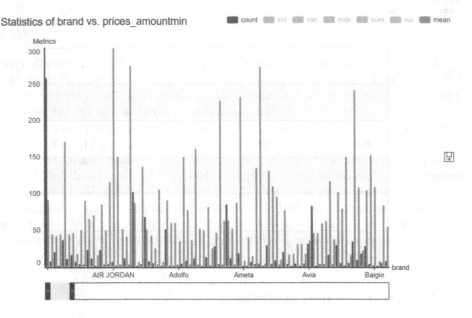

Fig. 1. Mean of minimum prices (in yellow) and number of sold products (in blue) for each brand of the MSP data set. Brands (shown on X-axis) are alphabetically ordered, and only a small subset is considered to fit the width of a page. (Color figure online)

Finally, the tabular visualisation provides a spreadsheet-style presentation of the data. Apart from entirely browsing a data set, which is of limited value for really large volumes of data, the user has the possibility to explore in detail each column of the data set. This feature was useful, for example, to extract histograms showing the brands most frequently sold, both for MSP and WSP. This information is presented in Fig. 2.

4.2 Data Manipulation

GraphLab Create provides many functionalities for data manipulation, including working with separate columns of a data set, as well as various options for data aggregation, grouping, and filtering.

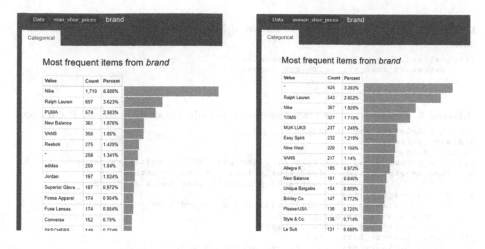

Fig. 2. Most popular brands determined by counting the most frequently sold items of a given brand.

Listing 2. Converting columns of MSP data set from string to date and time format

```
man_shoe_prices['dateadded']=man_shoe_prices['dateadded'].str_to_datetime()
man_shoe_prices['dateupdated']=man_shoe_prices['dateupdated'].str_to_datetime()
```

The analysis of the imported data revealed that two columns were imported as strings, while in fact the data represents date and time values – the columns '*dateadded*' and '*dateupdated*'. Converting these two columns to date and time format can be done using column manipulation operations of the *SFrame* class, using the script presented in Listing 2.

Comparing women's shoe brands with men's shoes was another area of interest. The Python script from Listing 3 determines that the data sets contain 2,144 unique women shoes brand names, 1,951 unique men shoes brand names, while 1,582 brands occur only for women, while 1,389 brands occur only for men. In addition, 562 brands are common to men and women.

The final interest was to automatically determine the additional column which is present in the MSP data set, as compared with the WSP data set.

Listing 3. Analyzing the number of unique brand names in each data set

```
len(woman_shoe_prices['brand'].unique())
len(man_shoe_prices['brand'].unique())
len(set(woman_shoe_prices['brand'].unique()) -
    set(man_shoe_prices['brand'].unique()))
len(set(man_shoe_prices['brand'].unique()) -
    set(woman_shoe_prices['brand'].unique()))
len(set(woman_shoe_prices['brand'].unique()) &
    set(man_shoe_prices['brand'].unique()))
```

Listing 4. Determining the column names of MSP data set, not present in the WSP data set

```
list(set(man_shoe_prices.column_names()) -
    set(woman_shoe_prices.column_names()))
```

Listing 5. Determining the price histograms of ordinary shoes in the MSP data set

```
import matplotlib.pyplot as plt
ordinary_price = 200
no_hist_bins = 50
man_shoe_prices = man_shoe_prices.filter_by(['USD'],'prices_currency')
man_shoe_average_prices = (man_shoe_prices['prices_amountmin'] +
                           man_shoe_prices['prices_amountmax'])/2
man_show_average_prices =
    man_shoe_average_prices.filter(lambda x: x<ordinary_price)
print len(man_shoe_average_prices)
y = man_shoe_average_prices.to_numpy()
plt.hist(y,bins=no_hist_bins)
plt.title('Ordinary price histogram for MSP data set')
plt.xlabel('Price')
plt.ylabel('No. of products')
plt.show()
```

Using the simple Python command shown in Listing 4 revealed that this is column *'vin'*.

In what follows, the focus was on determining the price histograms for ordinary shoes, in both the MSP and the WSP data sets. Shoes that were sold with an average price below $200 USD were considered ordinary. The average price is computed as the arithmetic average of the *'prices_ amountmin'* and *'prices_ amountmax'* columns. Note that according to the description of the product schema used by the MSP and WSP data sets [20], the values of these two fields are generally equal, except in situations where a price range is provided.

The construction and visualisation of the histograms for the MSP data set are presented in Listing 5. Note that not all (but the majority of) shoes prices are expressed in USD. Therefore, it was necessary to first filter out the shoes with prices expressed in USD. It was found that there are 18,460 products in the MSP data set and 18,199 products in the WSP data set with prices expressed in USD. Moreover, 16,425 products in the MSP data set and 16,719 products in the WSP data set that were sold at an average price below 200 USD. It was observed that the histogram presented in Fig. 3 resembles the logarithmic normal distribution (a statistical distribution of a random variable whose logarithm has a corresponding normal distribution) A logarithmic normal distribution is commonly used to describe distributions of financial assets, such as stock prices [4]. Note that the values of a log-normal distribution are positive, so they are appropriate for capturing the prices of the assets.

The definition of each histogram uses 50 bins of equal size. The resulting visualisations of these histograms are presented in Fig. 3.

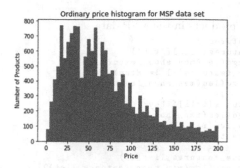
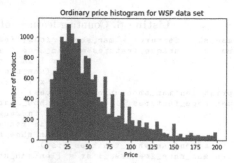

Fig. 3. Ordinary price histograms for both data sets.

4.3 Big Data Characteristics

Big Data has been informally described as possessing a number of characteristics that are usually not present in classical data, as found for example in ordinary relational data bases. One characteristic is heterogeneity, understood as covering also the variability of data formats and schema in a data set.

The heterogeneity aspect was explored in the context of the MSP data set. Each product has been described by a set of characteristics captured using the *'features'* column of type *list*. According to *datafiniti*, this field collects specific features available on different sections on product listings.

In fact, a closer investigation reveals that each such set of features is represented as a list of 2-field key-value dictionaries. The key represents the feature name, while the value represents the value of that feature. Using this observation, it became possible to explore the feature set of each product recorded in the MSP data set. The first finding was that not all of the products have values for the *'features'* column. Of the 18,460 products with a price in USD: (i) only 13,300 products were found to contain a nonempty value for this column; (ii) the total number of unique features of these products is 492; and (iii) the minimum, average, and maximum number of features of an MSP product is 1, 7.69, respectively 49. These values suggest a high heterogeneity of the data set, compared to a relational data base, where all the tuples of a table share the same set of attributes (or features in this case), captured by the database schema.

The Python script to obtain these results is shown in Listing 6. At first the determination of the 'features' column takes place. Then, for each row i with the 'feature field equal to a proper list (i.e. not equal to *None*), for each pair of keys and values x of this list, and for each 'key of x, the value of the 'key field is collected into a Python set (to ensure uniqueness) using Python set comprehension. Note that this script can be easily extended to extract also the values of each feature for each product of the MSP data set.

A simple analysis reveals that the computational cost incurred by the script from Listing 6 is quite high. If there are n rows in the data set and if the 'feature field is a list with k elements on average, then the average asymptotic computational cost of the script is $O(n \cdot k)$.

Listing 6. Counting features of products in the MSP data set

```
man_shoe_features = man_shoe_prices['features']
man_shoe_unique_features = {man_shoe_features[i][x]['key']
                    for i in range(len(man_shoe_features))
                    if (man_shoe_features[i] != None)
                    for x in range(len(man_shoe_features[i]))}
print len(man_shoe_unique_features)
man_shoe_features_list = [[man_shoe_features[i][x]['key']
                    for x in range(len(man_shoe_features[i]))]
                    for i in range(len(man_shoe_features))
                    if (man_shoe_features[i] != None)]
print len(man_shoe_features_list)
len_man_shoe_features_list = [len(man_shoe_features_list[i])
                    for i in range(len(man_shoe_features_list))]
print sum(len_man_shoe_features_list) / float(len(len_man_shoe_features_list))
print max(len_man_shoe_features_list)
print min(len_man_shoe_features_list)
```

Listing 7. Counting frequencies of features present in the '*features*' column of the MSP data set

```
man_shoe_prices_notnone = man_shoe_prices[man_shoe_prices['features'] != None]
key_counter =
    [{'key': key.lower(),
      'counter': len(man_shoe_prices_notnone[man_shoe_prices_notnone.apply(
         lambda x: len([x['features'][i]
                    for i in range(0,len(x['features']))
                    if key.lower() ==
                        x['features'][i]['key'].lower()])>0)])}
    for key in man_shoe_unique_features_list]
```

Based on the initial findings, a deeper investigation of the nature of the product features recorded in the '*features*' column takes place. In what follows, some of the problems encountered are highlighted. In particular these findings suggest that deeper domain knowledge is needed for the preliminary selection of the relevant features of each product recorded in the data set.

The number of products that contain each specific feature in the '*features*' column was counted using the script presented in Listing 7. The result is saved into a list of key-value pairs that associates each feature to its number of occurrences.

Then the number of occurrences of each characteristic occurring in more than 300 products was plotted using the script presented in Listing 8. Most of the features were observed to occur only in a few products, while some features have a significantly higher frequency of occurrence than all other features (see Fig. 4). More specifically, 39 features of 492 (that is, 7.92%) occur in more than 300 products, while 318 features (that is, 64.63%) occur in less than 20 products.

Note that if there are n records in the data set, if the total number of unique keys is m, and if the average number of features per record is k, then the time complexity of the script from Listing 7 is $O(n \cdot m \cdot k)$, that is, quite high.

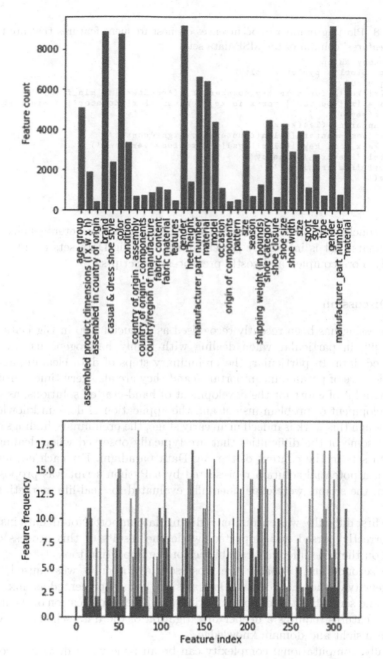

Fig. 4. Features of the *'features'* column occurring in more than 300 products (top) and in less than 20 products (bottom) of the MSP data set. Feature names are not presented on the X axis of the bottom figure for readability reasons.

Listing 8. Plotting number of occurrences of most frequent features that are present in the '*features*' column of the MSP data set

```
import numpy as np
import matplotlib.pyplot as plt
min_freq = 300
keys = [x['key'] for x in key_counter if x['counter'] > min_freq]
counters = [x['counter'] for x in key_counter if x['counter'] > min_freq]
print len(keys)
x_pos = np.arange(len(keys))
plt.bar(x_pos,counters[0:len(counters)],align='center')
plt.xticks(x_pos, keys[0:len(keys)], rotation='vertical')
plt.ylabel('Feature frequency')
plt.xlabel('Feature index')
plt.show()
```

The conclusion of this section is that dealing with the heterogeneity of the data formats that is inherently present in real-life Big Data sets results in considerably more complex and costly preprocessing scripts.

4.4   Discussion

Pre-processing has been recently recognised as a crucial step in Big Data applications [9], in particular when dealing with highly heterogeneous and semi-structured data. In particular, the preliminary steps of data cleaning and normalization are of paramount importance and they are also very time consuming, requiring a lot of effort for the development of hand-crafted solutions, as well as the development of problem insight and the application of domain knowledge.

Although this work is indeed in an early stage, the preliminary findings clearly revealed some of the difficulties that are typically observed when dealing with real data sets in the context of the Big Data paradigm. For each encountered problem, a potential solution represented by a Python script was proposed. In addition, the scripts were experimentally evaluated for real-life marketing data sets.

The first difficulty was encountered during data import. Not all data instances were correctly parsed and imported, while the results of this process clearly depend on the type-inference capabilities of the importing tool.

The second (and probably the most severe) difficulty was caused by the heterogeneity of the data format. Data sets are usually presented as mixtures of tabular and semi-structured representations, and the identification of the initially relevant features requires a deeper investigation of the data schema, as well as problem insight and domain knowledge.

Finally, computational complexity can be an issue when designing complex scripts and queries, in particular, when large data sets cannot be entirely fit to the computer store. The scripts and experiments clearly show that the computational complexity can increase significantly when processing complex Big Semi-Structured Data sets.

5 Conclusions

The GraphLab Create framework for Big Semi-Structured Data Analytics in quantitative marketing applications was introduced. Two data sets from the shoe business were considered. A series of Python scripts for data import, basic manipulation, and data visualisation were proposed. The results obtained were discussed in some detail, highlighting challenges and achievements. As future work,the results could be extended in several directions: i) to expand the analysis of these two data sets by considering more complex tasks, eventually requiring more sophisticated Data Mining algorithms; ii) to apply the current approach on other, possibly significantly larger, data sets in the marketing domain; iii) to consider the application of other data models available in GraphLab Create – graphs and time series, to appropriately chosen and publicly available marketing data sets.

References

1. Bădică, C., Bădică, A., Ivanović, M., Muraretu, I.D., Popescu, D., Ungureanu, C.: On the role of Python in programming-related courses for computer science and engineering academic education. In: Rocha, Á., Adeli, H., Reis, L.P., Costanzo, S., Orovic, I., Moreira, F. (eds.) WorldCIST 2020. AISC, vol. 1161, pp. 192–202. Springer, Cham (2020). https://doi.org/10.1007/978-3-030-45697-9_19
2. Bello-Orgaz, G., Jung, J.J., Camacho, D.: Social big data: recent achievements and new challenges. Inf. Fusion **28**, 45–59 (2016)
3. Chen, D.Y.: Pandas for Everyone: Python Data Analysis. Addison-Wesley, Reading (2018)
4. Cohen, A., Levy, H.: The log normal asset pricing model (LAPM). Ann. Financ. Econ. **1**(1), 0550002 (2005)
5. Ducange, P., Pecori, R., Mezzina, P.: A glimpse on big data analytics in the framework of marketing strategies. Soft Comput. **22**, 325–342 (2018)
6. Eckroth, J.: A course on big data analytics. J. Parallel Distrib. Comput. **118**(Part 1), 166–176 (2018)
7. Franses, P.H., Paap, R.: Quantitative Models in Marketing Research. Cambridge University Press, Cambridge (2004)
8. Gabroveanu, M., Iancu, I., Coşulschi, M., Constantinescu, N.: Towards using grid services for mining fuzzy association rules. In: Proceedings of the Ninth International Symposium on Symbolic and Numeric, Algorithms for Scientific Computing, SYNASC 2007, pp. 507–513 (2007)
9. García, S., Ramírez-Gallego, S., Luengo, J., Benítez, J.M., Herrera, F.: Big data preprocessing: methods and prospects. Big Data Anal. **1**, 9 (2016)
10. Géron, A.: Hands-On Machine Learning with Scikit-Learn and TensorFlow. O'Reilly Media, Sebastopol (2017)
11. Hagberg, A.A., Schult, D.A., Swart, P.J.: Exploring network structure, dynamics, and function using NetworkX. In: Varoquaux, G., Vaught, T., Millman, J. (eds.) Proceedings of the 7th Python in Science conference (SciPy 2008), pp. 11–15 (2008)
12. Inoubli, W., Aridhi, S., Mezni, H., Maddouri, M., Nguifo, E.M.: An experimental survey on big data frameworks. Future Gener. Comput. Syst. **86**, 546–564 (2018)

13. Low, Y., Gonzalez, J., Kyrola, A., Bickson, D., Guestrin, C., Hellerstein, J.: GraphLab: a new framework for parallel machine learning. In: Grunwald, P., Spirtes, P. (eds.) Proceedings of the Twenty-Sixth Conference on Uncertainty in Artificial Intelligence (UAI 2010), Arlington, Virginia, USA, pp. 340–349. AUAI Press (2010)

14. Ngai, E.W.T., Xiu, L., Chau, D.C.K.: Application of data mining techniques in customer relationship management: a literature review and classification. Expert Syst. Appl. **36**(2, Part 2), 2592–2602 (2009)

15. Saura, J.R.: Using Data Sciences in Digital marketing: framework, methods, and performance metrics. J. Innov. Knowl. **6**(2), 92–102 (2021)

16. Shah, D., Murthi, B.P.S.: Marketing in a data-driven digital world: implications for the role and scope of marketing. J. Bus. Res. **125**, 772–779 (2020)

17. Viloria, A., et al.: Big data marketing during the period 2012–2019: a bibliometric review. In: Pandian, A., Ntalianis, K., Palanisamy, R. (eds.) Intelligent Computing, Information and Control Systems. ICICCS 2019, Advances in Intelligent Systems and Computing, vol 1039, pp. 186–193. Springer, Cham (2019)

18. Wu, X., Zhu, X., Wu, G.-Q., Ding, W.: Data mining with big data. IEEE Trans. Knowl. Data Eng. **26**(1), 97–107 (2014)

19. Anaconda. https://anaconda.org/. Accessed 6 Oct 2022

20. Datafiniti Product Data Schema. https://datafiniti-api.readme.io/docs/product-data-schema. Accessed 6 Oct 2022

21. Data World. https://data.world/. Accessed 6 Oct 2022

22. Introducing JSON. https://www.json.org. Accessed 6 Oct 2022

23. Men's Shoe Prices data set. https://data.world/datafiniti/mens-shoe-prices. Accessed 6 Oct 2022

24. NetworkX. https://networkx.org/. Accessed 6 Oct 2022

25. Pandas. https://pandas.pydata.org/. Accessed 6 Oct 2022

26. Scikit-learn. http://scikit-learn.org/. Accessed 6 Oct 2022

27. Turi. https://github.com/apple/turicreate/. Accessed 6 Oct 2022

28. Turi Machine Learning Platform User Guide. https://github.com/apple/turicreate/tree/main/userguide. Accessed 6 Oct 2022

29. Women's Shoe Prices data set. https://data.world/datafiniti/womens-shoe-prices. Accessed 6 Oct 2022

30. Yelp Data Set. https://www.yelp.com/dataset. Accessed 6 Oct 2022

Stratification of White Blood Cells Using Optimized DenseNet201 Model

Kanwarpartap Singh Gill[1(✉)], Vatsala Anand[1], Sheifali Gupta[1], and Paweł Figat[2]

[1] Chitkara University Institute of Engineering and Technology, Chitkara University, Chandigarh, Punjab, India
{kanwarpartap.gill,vatsala.anand,sheifali.gupta}@chitkara.edu.in
[2] Institute of Management and Technical Sciences, WMU, Warsaw, Poland
pfigat@wp.pl

Abstract. White blood cells, that shape the preface of the safe system, guarantee the body from exterior interlopers and irresistible illnesses. Though the number and essential highlights of WBCs can deliver imperative information nearly the prosperity of people, the extent of the subtypes of these cells and discernible mis-happenings are an extraordinary marker inside the innovative arrangement. The affirmation of cells of the sort of Eosinophil, Lymphocyte, Monocyte and Neutrophil is basic. In this chapter, Significant Learning based CNN models illustrate proposed classification of cell types such as eosinophils, lymphocytes, monocytes, and neutrophils WBCs. The exhibit shown is based on pre-trained models. To choose the predominance of the proposed methodology, the classification was additionally performed and compared utilizing pre-trained DenseNet121, DenseNet201, EfficientNetB0, EfficientNetB7, ResNet50 and ResNet152V2 models individually. The accuracies and losses of these six models are compared in this research and the most excellent result is found on DenseNet201 CNN model which shows with the accuracy of 86% on Adam optimizer utilizing 30 epoch value and 32 batch size. DenseNet201 show gives higher precision than other pre-trained models.

Keywords: WBC · Transfer learning · Classification · Biomedical · Optimization

1 Introduction

White blood cells are crucial building pieces of the safe system that offer help fight malady and guarantee the body against inaccessible substances such as diseases. Determination of diseases such as blood cancer, Makes a difference from WBCs is imperative for hematologists [1]. Segregating WBC cells into subtypes is troublesome due to contrasts in cell shape in pictures amid development. The different stages of picture preparing is utilized to attain more quality and precision in recognizing blood cancers. The exactness depends upon the influenced zone of the blood test image [2]. Deep Learning could be a modern field to inquire about. The learning bends and disarray network are made with the assistance of profound learning calculations by making utilize of the different organize structures. Mechanized frameworks like this may well be accommodating in sparing time and moving forward effectiveness in clinical settings [3]. Manufactured insights to white blood cell (WBC) classification tend to be a wasteful expansion to therapeutic determination frameworks owing to moderate picture division, loss include extraction and low classification precision [4]. In any case, manual WBC review is time-consuming and labor-intensive for specialists, which implies mechanized classification strategies are required for WBC acknowledgment. Another issue is that the conventional programmed acknowledgment framework needs a huge sum of clarified restorative pictures for preparing, which is exceedingly expensive. In this regard, the semi-supervised learning system has as of late been broadly utilized for therapeutic conclusion due to its specificity, which can investigate significant data from gigantic unlabeled information.

2 Literature

A forward strategy of stratification of WBCs utilizing a blend of preprocessing, convolutional neural systems, highlight determination calculations, and classifiers must be exhausted. Preprocessing, versatile equalization is connected to the input images. A CNN is outlined and prepared to be utilized for conjunction with CNN systems. As Jung, C. proposed five WBC sorts for advance benefits and engineered WBC pictures were produced utilizing Generative Ill-disposed Organize to be utilized for instruction and investigate purposes through sharing. [5]. Patel, K.A. proposed to distinguish distinctive sorts of WBC in befuddling pictures of neural arrange arrangement. The test was conducted on the WBC database [6]. Cheuque, C. displayed a two-stage half breed multi-level plot that productively classified four cell bunches [7]. Considering a colossal potential within the meaning of characterization of WBCs, Begum A utilized a significant learning procedure Convolution Neural Systems (CNN) which orchestrated the pictures of WBCs into its subtypes [8]. Zhai, proposed that limit division prepare can find and fragment all conceivable WBC districts rapidly. The accuracy is improved by amassing the highlights of diverse layers to make way better coordinated spatial and semantic data. Tests included a real-world dataset that proposed the calculation accomplishment on normal WBC classification accuracy of 98.43%. In expansion, the accuracy calculation is executed with state-of-the-art calculations [9]. A semi-supervised WBC classified strategy was put forwarded by Ha, Y. who named the strategy as Intelligent Consideration Learning. It comprised of an Intelligent Consideration component [10]. Khalil utilized python dialect and profound learning model to distinguish maladies. The proposed learning model is prepared, approved and tried [11]. Ruby EK. Investigated the execution of three methods. Superior division and location precision compared to other peer delicate computing calculations is accomplished. The outcomes should be recipient for hematologists as demonstrative [12]. Monteiro created a cognitive approach situated towards DL, accomplishing accuracy of value 84.1 percent, utilizing a dataset of restorative computerized pictures of human blood cells. The AI-oriented approach is pointed so that dependable and reasonable strategy can be actualized as a third strategy for blood tests [13]. Ana Carolina Borges, et al. utilized an artificial intelligent approach that accomplished an accuracy which utilized Python with a dataset of 12,500 restorative computerized pictures of human blood cells [14]. Afriyie, Y. proposed a variation capsule arrangement to compensate for the nearness of lacks within the convolutional neural systems (CNNs) [15]. Xiao, Shuhan, et al. built the blood cell acknowledgment framework to distinguish diverse sorts of blood cells. The structure of this framework is a CNN based on EfficientNet model, with the optimization of altering parameter [16]. Jiang, L. proposed a profound neural organize for WBC classification by means of discriminative locale discovery helped highlight accumulation (DRFA-Net), which can precisely find the WBC region to boost last classification execution [17]. Alharbi proposed a novel demonstration that employs the ResNet and UNet systems to extricate highlights and after that fragments leukocytes from blood tests [18]. Wang, Ziyi, et al. proposed a Profound Convolutional Neural Arrangement with highlighted combination methodologies, for classification. To get consideration of CNN, the combination highlights of the primary and the final convolutional layer are extricated [19]. Gothai, E., et al. proposed a modern strategy for recognizing distinctive sorts of White Blood Cells, such as monocytes, lymphocytes, eosinophils, and neutrophils. Convolutional neural systems are utilized to extricate WBC highlights, and the CCA is utilized to expel cores from overlaying cells and learn from them. The proposed CNN with Canonical Relationship Examination decides more exactness than the past approaches, concurring to test information [20].

This chapter contributes majorly as follows:

- Utilizing information sets of Eosinophil, Lymphocyte, Monocyte and Neutrophil WBC pictures and comparing them on six CNN Models to be specific DenseNet121, DenseNet201, EfficientNetB0, EfficientNetB7, ResNet50 and ResNet152V2.
- The dataset is utilized to discover the accuracy on diverse CNN Models utilizing distinctive components for best yield.
- The leading models having distinctive accuracies are at that point compared on distinctive epochs and batch sizes.
- Considering both the writing and the results obtained, Blood Cell classification was performed with exact accurate procedures on DenseNet201 Demonstration.

The rest of the chapter is organized in the systematic procedure. The structure of the strategy proposed in Sect. 3 is point by point. The results and dialog obtained in Sect. 4 are displayed. Within the final area, a brief assessment of the proposed strategy is given.

3 Proposed Methodology

The number of blood-based illnesses regularly includes recognizing and characterizing understanding blood tests. Mechanized strategies to distinguish and classify blood cell subtypes have critical restorative applications.

3.1 Input Dataset

This dataset consist of 12,500 extended pictures of blood cells going with cell sort names. It has around 3,000 pictures for each of 4 particular cell sorts collected into 4 unmistakable envelopes (concurring to cell sort). The cell sorts that are used are namely

Eosinophil, Lymphocyte, Monocyte, and Neutrophil. This dataset is accumulated with an additional dataset containing the initial 410 pictures that are pre-augmented. Conjoint boxes for each cell is made for each of these 410 pictures in this dataset. More especially, the organizer contained 410 pictures of blood cells with subtype names, though the envelope contained 2,500 extended pictures. There are generally 3,000 expanded pictures for each course of the 4 classes as compared to 88, 33, 21, and 207 pictures of each in the main data file (Fig. 1).

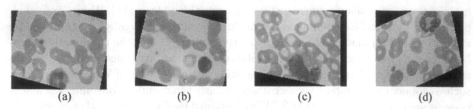

(a)   (b)   (c)   (d)

Fig. 1. Input images of (a) Eosinophil (b) Lymphocyte (c) Monocyte (d) Neutrophil

The flowchart is used to depict count for augmented and pre-augmented images of cell sorts of Eosinophil, Lymphocyte, Monocyte, and Neutrophil. In order to display the exact count of number of images, the Fig. 2 shows that the cell sorts contain 3000 images each and the segregation of pre-augmented images is further segmented to Jpeg and xml format for user convenience.

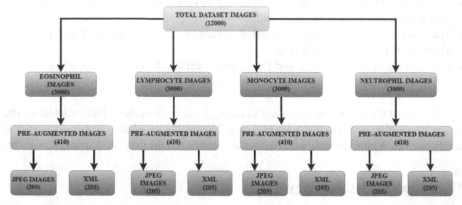

Fig. 2. Flowchart depicting count for images in eosinophil, lymphocyte, monocyte, and neutrophil

3.2 Data Augmentation

The CNN models require a huge amount of information source for ideal preparing to illustrate progressed execution on bigger datasets. Since there's as it were a little dataset being utilized, usually utilized to misleadingly improve the dataset [20]. Figure 3 gives an outline of the strategies utilized in this work to improve the preparing pictures.

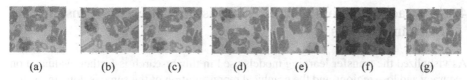

(a)   (b)   (c)   (d)   (e)   (f)   (g)

Fig. 3. Data augmentation of dataset images for enhancement: (a) original image (b) random rotation (c) horizontal rotation (d) vertical rotation (e) zoom (f) random brightness (g) resize

3.3 White Blood Cells Prediction Using Pre-trained Models

When an expansive dataset is regularly prepared on a wide scale picture classification assignment at that point that spared arrangement is named as a pre-trained demonstration. The show can be customized whereas utilizing either pre-trained demonstrate or exchange learning concurring to the information enlargement errand as appeared in Fig. 3. For deep learning the concept is that in case an exhibit is ready on a colossal and common dataset, at that point at that point the picture classification can be done with the help of the highlight maps without having to hustle from scratch by planning a tremendous exhibit on a colossal dataset [21, 22].

Figure 4 shows all the pre-trained models utilized in this research. One of the foremost powerful profound neural networks, ResNet, exceeded expectations within the 2015 ILSVRC classification challenge, accomplishing incredible execution results. ResNet too illustrated solid generalization execution on other distinguishing proof assignments. The ResNet engineering has different varieties, all of which utilize the same fundamental thought but a diverse number of layers. In this chapter ResNet50 and ResNet152V2 models are utilized. Each ResNet arrange utilizes 77 and 33 bit sizes for the basic convolution and max-pooling, independently. The chart underneath outlines the ResNet50 design, that comprises of 4 stages. The expected input measure is 224 x 224 x 3 for the reason of clarification. In ResNet50 and ResNet152v2, an add up of three layers are heaped on best of one another for each leftover work. Convolutions (1, 3, and 1) make up the three levels.

EfficientNet-B0 to EfficientNet-B7 may be a convolutional neural arrangement that's prepared on more than a million pictures from the Image Net database. The network can classify pictures into 1000 question categories. As a result, the arrangement has learned wealthy highlight representations for a wide extend of pictures. The arrangement has a picture input estimate of 224-by-224.

In DenseNet, the input picture is convolutional various times to supply high-level highlights. Each layer in DenseNet gets extra data from all levels that came some time recently and it possess maps to all layers that came after it. Concatenation is utilized. Each layer is getting "collective information" from the levels that came some time recently it. It employs two sorts of DenseNet models. These are DenseNet121 and DenseNet201.Apart from the basic convolutional and pooling layers, DenseNet is made up of two noteworthy building components. They comprise of the move layers and Thick Squares. A fundamental convolution and pooling layer frame the establishment of DenseNet. MobileNet show is utilizing significance quick unmistakable convolution layers. When compared to an organized nets, the number of parameters is significantly decreased. Lightweight profound neural systems are conveyed as a result from this.

4   Accuracy and Loss Curves Analysis for Different Transfer Learning Models

As visualized the transfer learning models used in this research is further evaluated on accuracy and loss regions and the graphical representation of the same is done in further sections. The transfer learning models need to be calculated on the accuracy and loss basis so that proper results are obtained and the best observation is made for the cell sorts that are being taken for consideration.

4.1   Analysis for DenseNet121 Model

In Table 1 the evaluations show the accuracy of 67% when dataset is input in DenseNet121 CNN Model.

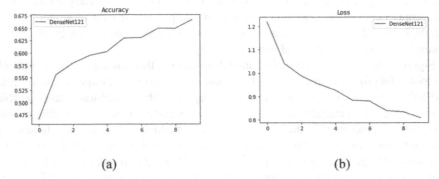

(a)   (b)

Fig. 4. (a) Accuracy chart for DenseNet121 (b) Loss chart for DenseNet121

The Accuracy graph shows an increment in DenseNet121 CNN Model as shown in Fig. 4 (a) and the Loss Graph shows a decrement in Fig. 4 (b) when displayed on x-y format with the increase in epoch value. The accuracy is starting from epoch value 0 and keeps on increasing at epoch value 8.

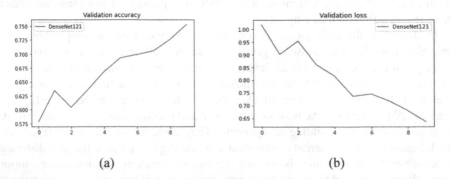

(a)   (b)

Fig. 5. (a) Validation accuracy chart for DenseNet121 (b) validation loss chart for DenseNet121

In Fig. 5 (a) the value of validation Accuracy decreases first on 0.630 then increases after passing the 2 epoch and increases constantly. The Validation loss keeps on decreasing although it has some upward trend at some point at epoch value 3 but after that keeps on decreasing as shown in Fig. 5 (b).

4.2 Analysis for DenseNet201 Model

In Table 1 the assessments show the Accuracy of value 77% when dataset is input in DenseNet201 CNN Demonstration.

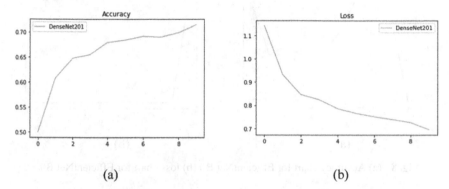

(a)   (b)

Fig. 6. (a) Accuracy chart for DenseNet 201 (b) loss chart for DenseNet 201

The Accuracy chart appears an increase in DenseNet201 CNN Model as appeared in Fig. 6 (a) and the Loss Chart appears a decrement in Fig. 6 (b) when arranged on graphical format. The loss is decreasing with increase in epoch value and accuracy is of value 77 percent at epoch value 8.5.

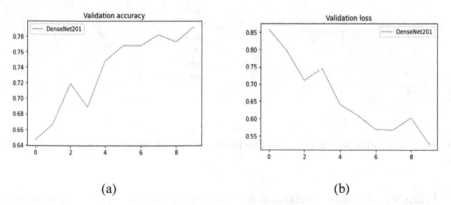

(a)   (b)

Fig. 7. (a) Validation accuracy chart for DenseNet 201 (b) validation loss chart for DenseNet 201

In Fig. 7 (a) the accuracy validation diminishes at start on 0.68 and at that point increments after passing the epoch value 3 and increments always. The loss validation keeps on diminishing in spite of the fact that it has a few upward drift at a few point at age esteem 3 but after that keeps on diminishing as appeared in Fig. 7 (b).

4.3 Analysis for EfficientNetB0 Model

The accuracy of 24% is obtained in Table 1 when dataset is input in EfficientB0 CNN Model.

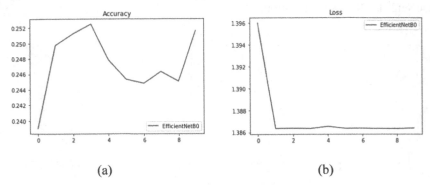

(a)   (b)

Fig. 8. (a) Accuracy chart for EfficientNet B0 (b) loss chart for EfficientNet B0

The increment in accuracy is depicted in Graph of Accuracy in EfficientB0 CNN Model as shown in Fig. 8 (a) and the decrease in value is shown in Fig. 8 (b) which shows Loss when displayed on Accuracy- epoch format.

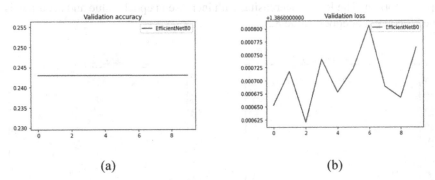

(a)   (b)

Fig. 9. (a) Validation accuracy chart for EfficientNet B0 (b) validation loss chart for EfficientNet B0

In Fig. 9 (a) the value of validation Accuracy increases constantly in a straight line at value 0.243 value. The Validation loss keeps on decreasing although it has some upward trend at some point at epoch value 6 but after that keeps on decreasing as shown in Fig. 9 (b).

4.4   Analysis for EfficientNetB7 Model

When dataset is input in EfficientB7 CNN model, the evaluations show the accuracy of 24% as it is shown in Table 1. The Macro and Weighted Avg is also a major factor while calculating exact values.

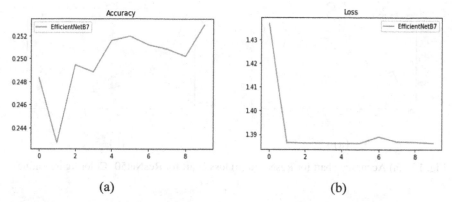

	(a)		(b)

Fig. 10. (a) Accuracy chart for EfficientNet B7 (b) loss chart for EfficientNet B7 (Color figure online)

The blue colored line shows an increased movement in Accurate Graph of EfficientB7 CNN Model as shown in Fig. 10 (a) and the Loss Graph also uses the same blue line to show a decrease in Fig. 10 (b).

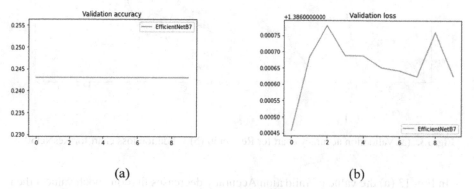

	(a)		(b)

Fig. 11. (a) Validation accuracy chart for EfficientNet B7 (b) validation loss chart for EfficientNet B7

The Approval loss keeps on diminishing in spite of the fact that it has a few upward slant at a few point at epoch values 2 and 8 but after that keeps on diminishing as shown in Fig. 11 (b). In Fig. 11 (a) the value of Accuracy increments in a straight line at value of 0.243.

4.5 Analysis for ResNet50 Model

For the record first the Precision, Recall, F1- score and Support are used in the accuracy prediction, as in Table 1 the evaluations show the accuracy of percentage value 31% when dataset entered in ResNet50 CNN Model.

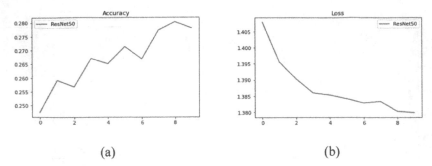

(a)   (b)

Fig. 12. (a) Accuracy chart for ResNet50 (b) loss chart for ResNet50 (Color figure online)

The Accuracy graph shows a red -colored zig-zag increased movement in ResNet50 CNN Model as shown in Fig. 12 (a) and the Loss Graph shows a decrement in Fig. 12 (b) when the results are taken. The accuracy shows value of 27 percent when it is at epoch value 5 and loss shows value of 13 percent when value of epoch is 7.

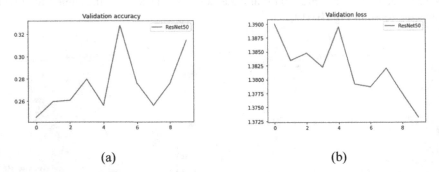

(a)   (b)

Fig. 13. (a) Validation accuracy chart for ResNet50 (b) validation loss chart for ResNet50

In Fig. 13 (a) the value of validation Accuracy decreases first on epoch value 4 then monumentally increases at the epoch value 5 and keeps on increases constantly. The loss validation keeps on decreasing although it has also has some upward trend at epoch value 4 but after that keeps on decreasing as shown in Fig. 13 (b).

4.6 Analysis for ResNet152V2 Model

Similarly to all models the ResNet152V2 CNN Model shows the accuracy of 66% in Table 1 when dataset is used for augmentation.

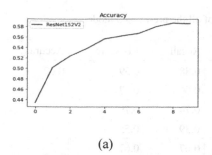
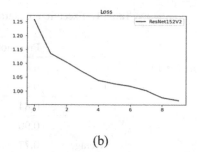

(a)   (b)

Fig. 14. (a) Accuracy chart for ResNet152V2 (b) loss chart for ResNet152V2 (Color figure online)

The graph of accuracy very precisely shows the increment in ResNet152V2 CNN Model as shown in Fig. 14 (a) using the blue colored line. In the same manner the Loss Graph shows a drop in Fig. 14 (b) as epochs are increasing.

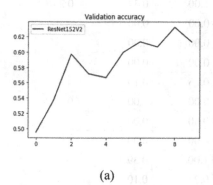
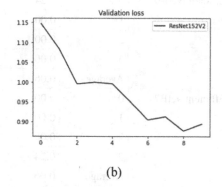

(a)   (b)

Fig. 15. (a) Validation accuracy chart for ResNet152V2 (b) validation loss chart for ResNet152V2

In Fig. 15 (a) the value of validation Accuracy declines first on value of epoch 2 then escalate at the epoch value 4 and then keeps on escalating constantly. The Validation loss keeps on diminishing although it shows some upward trend at some point but after that keeps on decreasing as shown in Fig. 15 (b). All the results received utilizing the proposed demonstrations are described in a systematic way. The CNN models are tried utilizing kaggle dataset. Different execution criteria such as Support, F1- Score, Precision and Recall are taken under consideration when analyzing the proposed model. An exploratory examination is carried out utilizing different variables, which are depicted underneath.

4.7 Confusion Matrix Parameters Analysis of all Transfer Learning Models

The exploratory setup in Table 1 indicates that the pre-trained models are prepared and the execution of each is delineated on different components. The representation of preparing exhibitions of distinctive CNN Models utilizing parameters such as Precision, Recall, F1-score and Support is tired Table. Utilizing these parameters, the forecast of

Table 1. Execution preparation of all the pre-trained models.

		Precision	Recall	F1- score	Accuracy
DenseNet121	0	0.45	0.88	0.59	0.67
	1	0.91	0.66	0.77	
	2	0.84	0.74	0.79	
	3	0.90	0.39	0.55	
	Average	0.77	0.67	0.67	
DenseNet201	0	0.70	0.65	0.68	0.77
	1	0.96	0.84	0.90	
	2	0.68	0.97	0.80	
	3	0.79	0.61	0.69	
	Average	0.79	0.77	0.77	
EfficientNetB0	0	0.24	1.00	0.39	0.24
	1	0.00	0.00	0.00	
	2	0.00	0.00	0.00	
	3	0.00	0.00	0.00	
	Average	0.06	0.25	0.10	
EfficientNetB7	0	0.00	0.00	0.00	0.24
	1	0.00	0.00	0.00	
	2	0.00	0.00	0.00	
	3	0.24	1.00	0.39	
	Average	0.06	0.25	0.10	
ResNet50	0	0.27	0.09	0.14	0.31
	1	0.47	0.37	0.41	
	2	0.59	0.02	0.04	
	3	0.26	0.77	0.39	
	Average	0.40	0.31	0.24	
ResNet152V2	0	0.57	0.50	0.54	0.66
	1	0.72	0.67	0.69	
	2	0.76	0.77	0.77	
	3	0.57	0.67	0.61	
	Average	0.66	0.65	0.65	

the finest CNN show is done. The numbers 0 represents as Eosinophil, 1 as Lymphocyte, 2 as Monocyte, and 3 as Neutrophil.

The dataset is utilized to discover the accuracy on distinctive CNN Models. The accuracy are compared on six CNN Models to be specific DenseNet121, DenseNet201,

EfficientNetB0, EfficientNetB7, ResNet50 and ResNet152V2. Distinctive parameters are utilized to form the perceptions. It can be clearly seen that DenseNet201 Model shows the best accuracy with value of 77% when augmented.

5   Analysis of Best DenseNet201 Model on Five Different Optimizers with Different Epochs

The graph on every specific input is displayed beside the specific optimizers. In Figures above, the DenseNet201 model is used on five different optimizers namely Adam, SGD, Adadelta, Adagrad and RMSProp. Different epochs of value 10, 20, 30 is used on batch size 32. Depiction of the best accuracy output in done in the form of chart for the specific CNN model.

5.1   Analysis of Adam Optimizer

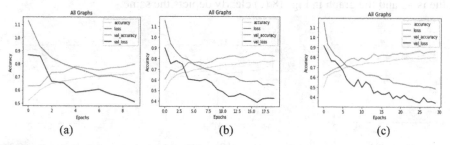

(a)   (b)   (c)

Fig. 16. Graph for Adam optimizer on 32 batch size using (a) 10 epoch value (b) 20 epoch value (c) 30 epoch value

Figure 16 (a) reveals the epoch accuracy prediction in the case of Adam optimizer. The value of accuracy is constant after the epoch value 3. The value of loss is decreasing with the increase in the value of epochs. Validation accuracy value is 0.8 at epoch value 7.5 and it remains consistent thereafter as shown in Fig. 16 (b). The values of Adam optimizer are compared for predicting accuracy on DenseNet201 model using batch size of 32 value in Fig. 16 (c). The best value is found on epoch value 30 and it shows the accuracy value of percentage as 86. The other epochs show value of accuracy as 81 on 10 epoch value and 83 on epoch value 20 respectively.

5.2   Analysis of SGD Optimizer

Linear representation of loss and validation loss is depicted in Fig. 17 (a) where the value of accuracy is 0.82 at epoch value 8. The graph is showing zig zag representation on the four parameters where the validation accuracy shows value of 0.74 at epoch value in Fig. 17 (b). Figure 17 (c) shows the graphical representation of SGD optimizer on value of epoch 30 where the best accuracy is found of percentage value 83.

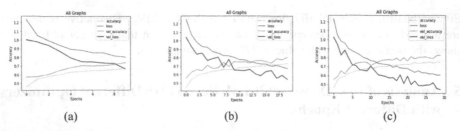

(a)   (b)   (c)

Fig. 17. Graph for SGD optimizer on 32 batch size using (a) 10 epoch value (b) 20 epoch value (c) 30 epoch value

5.3 Analysis of Adadelta Optimizer

On the value of epoch 7 the accuracy shows the value of as 0.34 and the loss shows the value 1.5 as exhibited in Fig. 18 (a). In Fig. 18 (b) the blue and green lines showing the validation loss and loss have the value of accuracy as 1.45 at epoch of value 17.5. The best accuracy on Adadelta optimizer is found on epoch value 30 where the percentage value is 42 and the graph in Fig. 18 (c) clearly depicts the same.

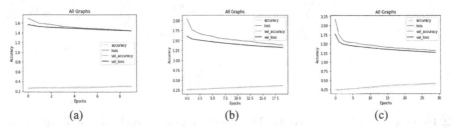

(a)   (b)   (c)

Fig. 18. Graph for Adadelta optimizer on 32 batch size using (a) 10 epoch value (b) 20 epoch value (c) 30 epoch value

5.4 Analysis of Adagrad Optimizer

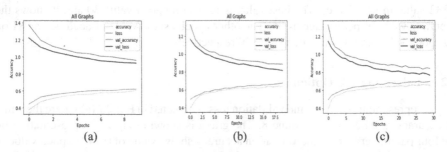

(a)   (b)   (c)

Fig. 19. Graph for Adagrad optimizer on 32 batch size using (a) 10 epoch value (b) 20 epoch value (c) 30 epoch value

The V- shaped graph shows the four parameters very evidently where the accuracy increases very precisely and the loss keeps on decreasing constantly in Fig. 19 (a). The lines of validation accuracy and accuracy are merging at the epoch value 2.5 in Fig. 19 (b). Although the graphs seem to be same in Fig. 19 (c) if seen roughly but when evaluated in depth it is found that the best accuracy of Adagrad optimizer is on value of epoch as 30 whereas at value of epoch 10 and 20 it shows accuracy of percentage value 62 and 68.

5.5   Analysis of RMSProp Optimizer

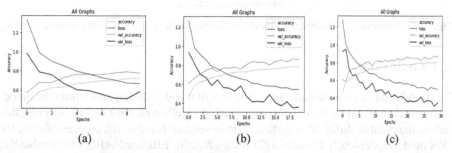

Fig. 20. Graph for RMSProp optimizer on 32 batch size using (a) 10 epoch value (b) 20 EPoch value (c) 30 epoch value (Color figure online)

The validation loss and validation accuracy lines as blue and red colored are meeting at a common point at epoch value of 2 in Fig. 20 (a) where it has accuracy of value 0.7. Accuracy of validation going with red line in the graph shows accuracy of value 0.7 at epoch of value 5.0 as shown in Fig. 20 (b). There is a tough competition between Adam and RMSProp optimizer since there accuracies are the maximum of all where in Fig. 20 (c) RMSProp optimizer shows the accuracy of percentage value 86 on epoch of value 30.

5.6   Comparison on Different Optimizers on DenseNet201 Model

In Fig. 21, the DenseNet201 show is utilized on five distinctive optimizers specifically Adam, SGD, Adadelta, Adagrad and RMSProp. Distinctive epochs of value 10, 20, 30 is utilized on batch size 32 for all optimizers to delineate the finest accuracy obtained for the particular CNN model. On Adam optimizer the finest accuracy of value 86% is on epoch of value 30. On SGD optimizer the maximum accuracy is of value 83% is on epoch of value 30. On Adadelta optimizer the leading accuracy of value 42% is obtained on epoch of value 30. On Adagrad optimizer the finest accuracy of value 70% is on epoch of value 30. On RMSProp optimizer the leading accuracy of value 86% is on value of epoch 30.

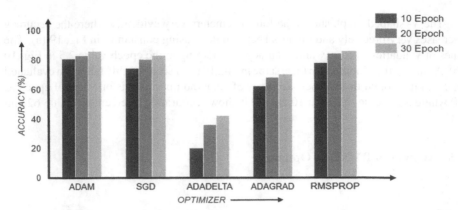

Fig. 21. Accuracies of DenseNet201 model on five different optimizers with different epochs.

6   Conclusion

The Blood cell test give the data almost the sum of blood cells displays within the blood. On the off chance that the number of particular blood cells is exterior the ordinary run, this leads to the event of different maladies. So in its respect this research is done utilizing six CNN models specifically DenseNet121, DenseNet201, EfficientNetB0, EfficientNetB7, ResNet50 and ResNet152V2 that are prepared utilizing exchange learning to overcome this issue. The displayed models have been analyzed profoundly on different parameters in a nitty gritty way. The accuracies and losses of these six models are compared and the most excellent result was found on DenseNet201 show with the exactness of 86% on Adam optimizer utilizing 30 epoch value and 32 batch size when it was compared on five diverse optimizers to be specific Adam, SGD, Adadelta, Adagrad and RMSProp. Considering both the literature and the results obtained, it moreover depicts that DenseNet201 CNN model's perceptions can be utilized as important input amid application of medical diagnostics of blood cells.

References

1. Shahzad, A., Raza, M., Shah, J.H., Sharif, M., Nayak, R.S.: Categorizing white blood cells by utilizing deep features of proposed 4B-AdditionNet-based CNN network with ant colony optimization. Complex Intell. Syst. **8**(4), 3143–3159 (2022). https://doi.org/10.1007/s40747-021-00564-x
2. Sujithraa, G.S., Karthigaiveni, S., Janani, S.: Use of alexnet architecture in the detection of bone marrow white blood cancer cells. ECS Trans. **107**(1), 5587 (2022)
3. Cengil, E., Çınar, A., Yıldırım, M.: A hybrid approach for efficient multi-classification of white blood cells based on transfer learning techniques and traditional machine learning methods. Concurr. Comput.: Pract. Exp. **34**(6), e6756 (2022)
4. Sharma, S., et al.: Deep learning model for the automatic classification of white blood cells. Comput. Intell. Neurosci. **2022** (2022)
5. Jung, C., Abuhamad, M., Mohaisen, D., Han, K., Nyang, D.: WBC image classification and generative models based on convolutional neural network. BMC Med. Imaging **22**(1), 1–16 (2022)

6. Patel, K.A., Gandhi, K.K., Vyas, A.K.: An effective approach to classify white blood cell using CNN. In: Thakkar, F., Saha, G., Shahnaz, C., Hu, Y.C. (eds.) Proceedings of the International e-Conference on Intelligent Systems and Signal Processing, vol. 1370, pp. 633–641. Springer, Singapore (2022). https://doi.org/10.1007/978-981-16-2123-9_49

7. Cheuque, C., Querales, M., León, R., Salas, R., Torres, R.: An efficient multi-level convolutional neural network approach for white blood cells classification. Diagnostics **12**(2), 248 (2022)

8. Begum, A., Biradar, V., Nase, G.: Blood cell classification using CNN. J. Adv. Res. Appl. Artif. Intell. Neural Netw. **5**(2), 10–17 (2022)

9. Zhai, Q., Fan, B., Zhang, B., Li, J.-H., Liu, J.-Z.: Automatic white blood cell classification based on whole-slide images with a deeply aggregated neural network. J. Med. Biol. Eng. **42**(1), 126–137 (2022). https://doi.org/10.1007/s40846-022-00683-x

10. Ha, Y., Du, Z., Tian, J.: Fine-grained interactive attention learning for semi-supervised white blood cell classification. Biomed. Sign. Process. Control **75**, 103611 (2022)

11. Khalil, A.J., Abu-Naser, S.S.: Diagnosis of blood cells using deep learning. Int. J. Acad. Eng. Res. (IJAER), **6**(2) (2022)

12. Ruby, E.K.: Automatic detection of white blood cancer from blood cells using novel machine learning techniques. In: 2022 8th International Conference on Advanced Computing and Communication Systems (ICACCS), vol. 1, pp. 79–85. IEEE (2022)

13. Monteiro, A.C.B., França, R.P., Arthur, R., Iano, Y.: AI approach based on deep learning for classification of white blood cells as a for e-healthcare solution. In: Tyagi, A.K., Abraham, A., Kaklauskas, A. (eds.) Intelligent Interactive Multimedia Systems for e-Healthcare Applications, pp. 351–373. Springer, Singapore (2022). https://doi.org/10.1007/978-981-16-6542-4_18

14. Monteiro, A.C.B., França, R.P., Arthur, R., Iano, Y.: An artificial intelligent cognitive approach for classification and recognition of white blood cells employing deep learning for medical applications. In: Deep Learning for Medical Applications with Unique Data, pp. 53–69. Academic Press (2022)

15. Afriyie, Y., A Weyori, B., A Opoku, A.: Classification of blood cells using optimized capsule networks. Neural Process. Lett. 54, 1–20 (2022). https://doi.org/10.1007/s11063-022-10833-6

16. Xiao, S., Toe, T.T., Ran, Z., Yang, A.: The optimization of white blood cell classification based on EfficientNet model. In: 2022 4th International Conference on Advances in Computer Technology, Information Science and Communications (CTISC), pp. 1–5. IEEE (2022)

17. Jiang, L., Tang, C., Zhou, H.: White blood cell classification via a discriminative region detection assisted feature aggregation network. Biomed. Opt. Express **13**(10), 5246–5260 (2022)

18. Alharbi, A.H., Aravinda, C.V., Lin, M., Venugopala, P.S., Reddicherla, P., Shah, M.A.: Segmentation and classification of white blood cells using the UNet. Contrast Media Mol. Imaging **2022** (2022)

19. Wang, Z., Xiao, J., Li, J., Li, H., Wang, L.: WBC-AMNet: automatic classification of WBC images using deep feature fusion network based on focalized attention mechanism. PLoS ONE **17**(1), e0261848 (2022)

20. Gothai, E., Natesan, P., Rajalaxmi, R.R., Kumar, N.N., Prasad, T.N., Jhothith, K.G.: Image classification of white blood cells with canonical correlation. In: 2022 International Conference on Computer Communication and Informatics (ICCCI), pp. 01–08. IEEE (2022)

21. Anand, V., Gupta, S., Nayak, S.R., Koundal, D., Prakash, D., Verma, K.D.: An automated deep learning models for classification of skin disease using dermoscopy images: a comprehensive study. Multimedia Tools Appl. **81**, 1–23 (2022)

22. Anand, V., Gupta, S., Koundal, D., Nayak, S.R., Barsocchi, P., Bhoi, A.K.: Modified U-NET architecture for segmentation of skin lesion. Sensors **22**(3), 867 (2022)

Generating Functions and Approximations of the Caputo Fractional Derivative

Yuri Dimitrov[1,3], Venelin Todorov[1,2(✉)] [iD], Radan Miryanov[4],
Stefka Fidanova[2][iD], and Jan Rusinek[5][iD]

[1] Institute of Mathematics and Informatics, Bulgarian Academy of Sciences,
Department of Information Modeling, Acad. Georgi Bonchev Str., Block 8,
1113 Sofia, Bulgaria
yuri.dimitrov@ltu.bg, vtodorov@math.bas.bg
[2] Institute of Information and Communication Technologies,
Bulgarian Academy of Sciences, Department of Parallel Algorithms,
Acad. G. Bonchev Str., Block 25 A, 1113 Sofia, Bulgaria
{venelin,stefka}@parallel.bas.bg
[3] Department of Mathematics, Physics and Informatics, University of Forestry,
Sofia 1756, Bulgaria
[4] Department of Statistics and Applied Mathematics, University of Economics,
77 Knyaz Boris I Blvd., Varna 9002, Bulgaria
miryanov@ue-varna.bg
[5] Warsaw Management University (MANS), Warsaw, Poland
j-rusinek@o2.pl

Abstract. The present chapter is a continuation of the work in [6]. We construct an approximation of order 2-α of the Caputo derivative. The approximation is related to the midpoint sum of the integral in the definition of the Caputo derivative. The generating functions of the approximation involves the polylogarithm function of order α. The weights of the approximation have similar properties as the weights of the L1 approximation. We construct induced shifted approximations of order 2-α of the Caputo derivative and the second-order shifted Grünwald difference formula approximations. The optimal shift values of the approximations are determined, where the approximations have second and third order accuracy respectively. We study also some applications of the approximations for the two-term equation' numerical solutions. The developed reliable approximations will be important for applications in intelligent robot systems, control theory and signal processing.

Keywords: Caputo derivative · Generating functions · L1 approximation

Y. Dimitrov—is supported by the BNSF under Project KP-06-M32/2 - 17.12.2019. The work is also supported by the BNSF under the Projects KP-06-N52/5, KP-06-N62/6 and KP-06-Russia/17.

1 Introduction

Nowadays the development of effective methods for solution of ordinary and partial fractional differential equations (PDFEs) is a key research area. In recent years, the FDEs are widely used in intelligent robot systems, signal processing and control theory. Particularly there is a great interest in high order convergent numerical methods for evaluating some intelligent robot systems, which are described by the nonlinear fractional variable coefficient reaction diffusion equations with delay [16].

The Caputo derivative (CD) of order α, $0 < \alpha < 1$ is defined by

$$y^{(\alpha)}(t) = \frac{1}{\Gamma(1-\alpha)} \int_0^t \frac{y'(x)}{(t-x)^\alpha} dx.$$

The L1 approximation (L1A) of the CD is an important and widely used approximation for numerical solution of FDEs [1,2,8,9,11]. The L1A has an order $2-\alpha$ and an expansion formula of second order [4,5]

$$\frac{1}{h^\alpha} \sum_{k=0}^n \sigma_k^{(\alpha)} y_{n-k} = y_n^{(\alpha)} + C_1(\alpha) y_n'' h^{2-\alpha} + O\left(h^2\right), \tag{1}$$

where $C_1(\alpha) = \zeta(\alpha - 1)/\Gamma(2-\alpha)$ and

$$\sigma_0^{(\alpha)} = \frac{1}{\Gamma(2-\alpha)}, \quad \sigma_n^{(\alpha)} = \frac{(n-1)^{1-\alpha} - n^{1-\alpha}}{\Gamma(2-\alpha)},$$

$$\sigma_k^{(\alpha)} = \frac{(k+1)^{1-\alpha} - 2k^{1-\alpha} + (k-1)^{1-\alpha}}{\Gamma(2-\alpha)}, \quad (2 \le k \le n-1).$$

The L1A (1) has a generating function (GF)

$$G_1(x) = \sum_{k=0}^\infty \sigma_k^{(\alpha)} x^k = \frac{(1-x)^2 \mathrm{Li}_{\alpha-1}(x)}{x \Gamma(2-\alpha)},$$

where $\mathrm{Li}_\alpha(x)$ is the polylogarithm function with order α

$$\mathrm{Li}_\alpha(x) = \sum_{k=1}^\infty \frac{x^k}{k^\alpha} = x + \frac{x^2}{2^\alpha} + \frac{x^3}{3^\alpha} + \cdots + \frac{x^k}{k^\alpha} + \cdots$$

The series expansion of the function $\mathrm{Li}_\alpha\left(e^{-x}\right)$ is

$$\mathrm{Li}_\alpha\left(e^{-x}\right) = \Gamma(1-\alpha)x^{\alpha-1} + \sum_{k=0}^\infty \frac{\zeta(\alpha-k)}{k!}(-x)^k.$$

In [7] we develop quadrature formulas whose generating functions involve secant and tangent. In [2,14] we develop approximations of the first and second derivative with exponential and logarithmic generating functions. In [6] we derive approximations of order $2 - \alpha$ of the CD

$$\frac{1}{h^\alpha} \sum_{k=0}^n \sigma_k^{(\alpha)} y_{n-k} = y_n^{(\alpha)} + C_2(\alpha) y_n'' h^{2-\alpha} + O\left(h^2\right), \tag{2}$$

$$\sigma_0^{(\alpha)} = \frac{\zeta(\alpha) - \zeta(1 + \alpha)}{\Gamma(-\alpha)}, \ \sigma_1^{(\alpha)} = \frac{1 - \zeta(\alpha)}{\Gamma(-\alpha)},$$

$$\sigma_k^{(\alpha)} = \frac{1}{\Gamma(-\alpha)k^{1+\alpha}}, \ C_2(\alpha) = \frac{\zeta(\alpha) - \zeta(\alpha - 1)}{2\Gamma(-\alpha)}$$

and

$$\frac{1}{h^\alpha} \sum_{k=0}^{n} \sigma_k^{(\alpha)} y_{n-k} = y_n^{(\alpha)} + C_3(\alpha) y_n'' h^{2-\alpha} + O\left(h^2\right), \tag{3}$$

$$C_3(\alpha) = \frac{\zeta(\alpha) - 2\zeta(\alpha - 1)}{2\Gamma(1 - \alpha)},$$

$$\sigma_0^{(\alpha)} = \frac{1 - 2\zeta(\alpha)}{2\Gamma(1 - \alpha)}, \ \sigma_1^{(\alpha)} = \frac{1 + 2^{1+\alpha}\zeta(\alpha)}{2^{1+\alpha}\Gamma(1 - \alpha)},$$

$$\sigma_k^{(\alpha)} = \frac{1}{2\Gamma(1 - \alpha)}\left(\frac{1}{(k+1)^\alpha} - \frac{1}{(k-1)^\alpha}\right).$$

Approximations (2), and (3) hold when the function y satisfies $y(0) = y'(0) = y''(0) = 0$. In [7] we extend (2) and (3) to the class C^2 by assigning values to the last three weights. Approximations (2) and (3) have generating functions

$$G_2(x) = \frac{\text{Li}_{1+\alpha}(x) - \zeta(1 + \alpha)}{\Gamma(-\alpha)}, G_3(x) = \frac{(1 - x)^2 \text{Li}_\alpha(x)}{2\Gamma(1 - \alpha)x}.$$

The generating functions $G_i(x)$ of approximations (1), (2) and (3) satisfy the condition

$$\lim_{x \to 1} \frac{G_i(x)}{(1 - x)^\alpha} = 1.$$

In Sect. 2 we construct an approximation of order $2 - \alpha$ of the CD

$$\frac{1}{h^\alpha} \sum_{k=0}^{n} \sigma_k^{(\alpha)} y_{n-k} = y_n^{(\alpha)} + C_4(\alpha) y_n'' h^{2-\alpha} + O\left(h^2\right), \tag{4}$$

$$C_4(\alpha) = \frac{(2 - 2^\alpha)\zeta(\alpha - 1) - (2^\alpha - 1)\zeta(\alpha)}{2\Gamma(1 - \alpha)},$$

$$\sigma_0^{(\alpha)} = \frac{2^\alpha - (2^\alpha - 1)\zeta(\alpha)}{\Gamma(1 - \alpha)}, \sigma_1^{(\alpha)} = \frac{2^\alpha - 6^\alpha + 3^\alpha(2^\alpha - 1)\zeta(\alpha)}{3^\alpha\Gamma(1 - \alpha)},$$

$$\sigma_k^{(\alpha)} = \frac{2^\alpha}{\Gamma(1 - \alpha)}\left(\frac{1}{(2k+1)^\alpha} - \frac{1}{(2k-1)^\alpha}\right).$$

Approximation (4) has a generating function

$$G_4(x) = \frac{1 - x}{\sqrt{x}\Gamma(1 - \alpha)}\left(2^\alpha \text{Li}_\alpha\left(\sqrt{x}\right) - \text{Li}_\alpha(x)\right).$$

In Sect. 3 we construct the induced shifted approximations (ISA) of order $2 - \alpha$ of approximations (1–4).

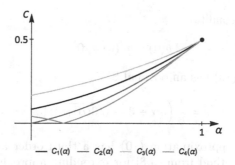

Fig. 1. Absolute values of $C_1(\alpha)$, $C_2(\alpha)$, $C_3(\alpha)$, $C_4(\alpha)$ presented as a graph.

The coefficients $C_i(\alpha)$, $i = 1, 2, 3, 4$ of the terms of order $2 - \alpha$ in the formulas of the approximations satisfy the inequalities (Fig. 1)

$$|C_2(\alpha)| < |C_1(\alpha)| < |C_3(\alpha)|, \quad |C_4(\alpha)| < |C_1(\alpha)|. \tag{5}$$

The weights of the L1A (1) and approximations (2), (3) and (4) have properties

$$\sigma_0^{(\alpha)} > 0, \ \sigma_1^{(\alpha)} < \sigma_2^{(\alpha)} < \cdots < \sigma_k^{(\alpha)} < \cdots < \sigma_{n-1}^{(\alpha)} < 0. \tag{6}$$

The Grünwald difference approximation (GDA) of the CD has a first order accuracy

$$\mathcal{G}_n^{(\alpha)}[y] = \frac{1}{h^\alpha} \sum_{k=0}^{n} (-1)^k \binom{\alpha}{k} y_{n-k} = y_n^{(\alpha)} + O(h) \tag{7}$$

when y satisfies $y(0) = 0$. The generation function of the Grünwald difference formula (11) is $G(x) = (1 - x)^\alpha$ and the expansion formula of third order

$$\frac{1}{h^\alpha} \sum_{k=0}^{n} (-1)^k \binom{\alpha}{k} y_{n-k} = y_n^{(\alpha)} - \frac{\alpha}{2} h y_n^{(1+\alpha)} \tag{8}$$

$$+ \frac{\alpha + 3\alpha^2}{24} h^2 y_n^{(2+\alpha)} + O(h^3),$$

The GDA formula of the CD has an accuracy of order two with the shift value (SV) equal to $\alpha/2$

$$\mathcal{G}_n^{(\alpha)}[y] = \frac{1}{h^\alpha} \sum_{k=0}^{n} (-1)^k \binom{\alpha}{k} y_{n-k} = y_{n-\alpha/2}^{(\alpha)} + O(h^2). \tag{9}$$

In Sect. 4 we construct the ISA of the GDA

$$\mathcal{C}_n^{(\alpha)}[y] = \mathcal{G}_n^{(\alpha)}[y] - (s - \alpha/2) h \mathcal{G}_n^{(1+\alpha)}[y]. \tag{10}$$

$\mathcal{C}_n^{(\alpha)}[y]$ is a SA of second order of the CD with SV s

$$\mathcal{C}_n^{(\alpha)}[y] = y_{n-s}^{(\alpha)} + O(h^2)$$

when y satisfies the condition

$$y(0) = y'(0) = 0.$$

The approximation (10) has an optimal SV

$$s = \frac{1}{6}\left(3\alpha + 3 - \sqrt{3(\alpha+3)}\right).$$

At the optimal SV, approximation (10) has a third order accuracy $O\left(h^3\right)$. In Sect. 4 we use the method from [6,8] for extending approximation (10) to the class $C^2[0,t]$ by assigning values to the last two weights. When the SV $s = 0$ we derive an approximation of the second order of the CD

$$\frac{1}{h^\alpha}\sum_{k=0}^{n} w_k^{(\alpha)} y_{n-k} = y_n^{(\alpha)} + O\left(h^2\right), \tag{11}$$

$$w_k^{(\alpha)} = (-1)^k \binom{\alpha+1}{k}\frac{\alpha^2 + 3\alpha + 2 - 2k}{2(\alpha+1)},$$

$$w_{n-1}^{(\alpha)} = \frac{n^{1-\alpha}}{\Gamma(2-\alpha)} + \frac{(-1)^n C_1}{2(\alpha-1)(n-2)}\binom{\alpha-1}{n-3},$$

$$w_n^{(\alpha)} = \frac{(-1)^n C_2}{2(\alpha-1)(n-2)}\binom{\alpha-1}{n-3} - \frac{n^{1-\alpha}}{\Gamma(2-\alpha)},$$

where

$$C_1 = 4n + 5an + a^2 n - 2n^2 - 6a - 4a^2 - 2a^3,$$
$$C_2 = 4 + 4a + 3a^2 + a^3 - 6n - 3an - a^2 n + 2n^2.$$

The numerical solutions (NSs) of the two-term equation (TTE) are developed in [3,10,12,13,15].

$$y^{(\alpha)}(t) + Ly(t) = F(t), \quad y(0) = y_0. \tag{12}$$

Let $h = 1/n$ and

$$\frac{1}{h^\alpha}\sum_{k=0}^{m} \lambda_k^{(\alpha)} y_{m-k} = y_m^{(\alpha)} + O\left(h^{2-\alpha}\right) \tag{*}$$

be an approximation of the CD. By approximating the CD in (12) at $t_m = mh$ with (*) we find

$$\frac{1}{h^\alpha}\left(\lambda_0^{(\alpha)} y_m + \sum_{k=1}^{m} \lambda_k^{(\alpha)} y_{m-k}\right) + Ly_m = F_m + O\left(h^{2-\alpha}\right).$$

The sequence $\{u_m\}_{m=0}^n$, where u_m is an approximation of the solution $y_m = y(mh)$ is evaluated with the recursive formula

$$u_n = \frac{1}{\lambda_0^{(\alpha)} + h^\alpha L} \left(h^\alpha F_n - \sum_{k=1}^n \lambda_k^{(\alpha)} y_{n-k} \right). \qquad (NS1(*))$$

Numerical solution NS1(*) has initial conditions $u_0 = y_0$ and

$$u_1 = \frac{y_0 + h^\alpha \Gamma(2-\alpha) F(h)}{1 + L h^\alpha \Gamma(2-\alpha)},$$

$$u_2 = \frac{y_0 + (2h)^\alpha \Gamma(2-\alpha) F(2h)}{1 + L(2h)^\alpha \Gamma(2-\alpha)}.$$

The initial conditions u_1, u_2 are approximations of second order of the values of the solution $y(h)$ and $y(2h)$ of Eq. (12). The TTE

$$y^{(\alpha)}(t) + Ly(t) = \frac{2t^{2-\alpha}}{\Gamma(3-\alpha)} + Lt^2, \; y(0) = 0 \qquad (13)$$

has a solution $y(t) = t^2$. The obtained numerical results for the error (E) and the order (O) of NS1(1–4) and second order NS1(11) of Eq. (13) are given in Tables 1, 2, 3, 4 and 5. The experimental results suggest a relation between inequalities (5) for the coefficients $C_i(\alpha)$ and the errors of the NSs (Fig. 1). The errors of NS1(2) and NS1(4) of Eq. (13) are smaller than the errors of NS1(1). One can also see that the errors of NS1(3) are larger than the errors of NS1(1).

Table 1. Order and Maximum error of NS1(1).

h	$\alpha = 0.25, L = 1$		$\alpha = 0.75, L = 2$	
	E	O	E	O
0.00125	1.1751×10^{-6}	1.7219	6.6280×10^{-5}	1.2498
0.000625	3.5505×10^{-7}	1.7267	2.7870×10^{-5}	1.2498
0.0003125	1.0698×10^{-7}	1.7306	1.1719×10^{-5}	1.2498

Table 2. Order and Maximum error of NS1(2).

h	$\alpha = 0.25, L = 1$		$\alpha = 0.75, L = 2$	
	E	O	E	O
0.00125	7.4064×10^{-7}	1.9542	6.0564×10^{-5}	1.2506
0.000625	1.9032×10^{-7}	1.9603	2.5458×10^{-5}	1.2503
0.0003125	5.4607×10^{-8}	1.8013	1.0702×10^{-5}	1.2501

Table 3. Order and Maximum error of NS1(3).

h	$\alpha = 0.25, L = 1$		$\alpha = 0.75, L = 2$	
	E	O	E	O
0.00125	1.7437×10^{-6}	1.7118	7.2352×10^{-5}	1.2491
0.000625	5.2980×10^{-7}	1.7186	3.0432×10^{-5}	1.2494
0.0003125	1.6036×10^{-7}	1.7241	1.2798×10^{-5}	1.2496

Table 4. Order and Maximum error of NS1(4).

h	$\alpha = 0.25, L = 1$		$\alpha = 0.75, L = 2$	
	E	O	E	O
0.00125	8.9326×10^{-7}	1.7318	6.3321×10^{-5}	1.2502
0.000625	2.6839×10^{-7}	1.7347	2.6622×10^{-5}	1.2501
0.0003125	8.0501×10^{-8}	1.7372	1.1193×10^{-5}	1.2500

Table 5. Order and Maximum error of NS1(11).

h	$\alpha = 0.25, L = 1$		$\alpha = 0.75, L = 2$	
	E	O	E	O
0.00125	7.4064×10^{-7}	1.9542	3.7200×10^{-6}	1.9718
0.000625	1.9032×10^{-7}	1.9603	9.4110×10^{-7}	1.9829
0.0003125	4.8723×10^{-8}	1.9657	2.3695×10^{-7}	1.9897

2   Approximations of the Caputo Derivative

Let $\mathcal{M}_n[y]$ be the midpoint approximation (MA) of the integral in the definition of CD

$$\mathcal{M}_n[y] = \frac{h}{\Gamma(1-\alpha)} \sum_{k=1}^{n} \frac{y'_{k-1/2}}{(x - t_{k-1/2})^\alpha}.$$

By approximation of $y'_{k-1/2}$ with $(y_k - y_{k-1})/2$ we find

$$\begin{aligned}
\mathcal{M}'_n[y] &= \frac{h^{1-\alpha}}{\Gamma(1-\alpha)} \sum_{k=1}^{n} \frac{y_k - y_{k-1}}{(n - k + 1/2)^\alpha} \\
&= \frac{2^\alpha h^{1-\alpha}}{\Gamma(1-\alpha)} \sum_{k=1}^{n} \frac{y_k - y_{k-1}}{(2n - 2k + 1)^\alpha} \\
&= \frac{2^\alpha h^{1-\alpha}}{\Gamma(1-\alpha)} \left(\sum_{k=0}^{n-1} \frac{y_{n-k}}{(2k + 1)^\alpha} - \sum_{k=1}^{n} \frac{y_{n-k}}{(2k - 1)^\alpha} \right).
\end{aligned}$$

Approximation $\mathcal{M}'_n[y]$ has a generating function

$$G_4(x) = \frac{2^\alpha(1-x)}{2\sqrt{x}\Gamma(1-\alpha)}\left(\mathrm{Li}_\alpha\left(\sqrt{x}\right) - \mathrm{Li}_\alpha\left(-\sqrt{x}\right)\right).$$

The polylogarithm function satisfies

$$\mathrm{Li}_\alpha(x) + \mathrm{Li}_\alpha(-x) = 2^{1-\alpha}\mathrm{Li}_\alpha(x^2),$$

$$\mathrm{Li}_\alpha(\sqrt{x}) + \mathrm{Li}_\alpha(-\sqrt{x}) = 2^{1-\alpha}\mathrm{Li}_\alpha(x).$$

Then

$$G_4(x) = \frac{1-x}{\sqrt{x}\Gamma(1-\alpha)}\left(2^\alpha\mathrm{Li}_\alpha\left(\sqrt{x}\right) - \mathrm{Li}_\alpha\left(x\right)\right).$$

From the expansion formulas of the functions $G_4(x)$ and $G_4(e^{-x})$ we obtain an approximation (4) of order $2-\alpha$. By substituting y''_n in (4) with a second-order backward difference approximation we derive approximation of second order of the CD

$$\mathcal{A}_{14,n}[1] = \frac{1}{\Gamma(1-\alpha)h^\alpha}\sum_{k=0}^{n}\sigma_k^{(\alpha)}y_{n-k} = y_n^{(\alpha)} + O\left(h^2\right), \tag{14}$$

$$\sigma_0^{(\alpha)} = 2^\alpha + \frac{3}{2}\left(1-2^\alpha\right)\zeta(\alpha) + \left(2^{\alpha-1}-1\right)\zeta(\alpha-1),$$

$$\sigma_1^{(\alpha)} = \left(\frac{2}{3}\right)^\alpha - 2^\alpha - 2\left(1-2^\alpha\right)\zeta(\alpha) - 2\left(2^{\alpha-1}-1\right)\zeta(\alpha-1),$$

$$\sigma_2^{(\alpha)} = \left(\frac{2}{5}\right)^\alpha - \left(\frac{2}{3}\right)^\alpha + \frac{1-2^\alpha}{2}\zeta(\alpha) + \left(2^{\alpha-1}-1\right)\zeta(\alpha-1),$$

$$\sigma_k^{(\alpha)} = \frac{2^\alpha}{\Gamma(1-\alpha)}\left(\frac{1}{(2k+1)^\alpha} - \frac{1}{(2k-1)^\alpha}\right).$$

Approximations (1–4) and (14) hold when y satisfies

$$y(0) = y'(0) = y''(0) = 0.$$

Now we extend the approximations to the class of functions $C^2[0,t]$ by assigning values to the last three weights. Approximations (1–4) and (14) have exact values for the functions $1, t$ and t^2 when

$$\mathcal{A}_{i,n}[1] = 0, \mathcal{A}_{i,n}[t] = \frac{t^{1-\alpha}}{\Gamma(2-\alpha)}, \mathcal{A}_{i,n}[t^2] = \frac{2t^{2-\alpha}}{\Gamma(3-\alpha)}. \tag{15}$$

From (14) we obtain a system of equations for the last three weights $\sigma_{n-2}^{(\alpha)}, \sigma_{n-1}^{(\alpha)}$ and $\sigma_n^{(\alpha)}$.

$$\sigma_n^{(\alpha)} + \sigma_{n-1}^{(\alpha)} + \sigma_{n-2}^{(\alpha)} = -\sum_{k=0}^{n-3} \sigma_k^{(\alpha)}, \tag{16}$$

$$\sigma_{n-1}^{(\alpha)} + 2\sigma_{n-2}^{(\alpha)} = \frac{n^{1-\alpha}}{\Gamma(2-\alpha)} - \sum_{k=0}^{n-3}(n-k)\sigma_k^{(\alpha)},$$

$$\sigma_{n-1}^{(\alpha)} + 4\sigma_{n-2}^{(\alpha)} = \frac{2n^{2-\alpha}}{\Gamma(3-\alpha)} - \sum_{k=0}^{n-3}(n-k)^2\sigma_k^{(\alpha)}.$$

The system of equations (16) has solutions

$$\sigma_{n-2}^{(\alpha)} = \frac{n^{1-\alpha}(2n+\alpha-2)}{2\Gamma(3-\alpha)} - \frac{1}{2}\sum_{k=0}^{n-3}(n-k)(n-k-1)\sigma_k^{(\alpha)},$$

$$\sigma_{n-1}^{(\alpha)} = \frac{2n^{1-\alpha}(2-\alpha-n)}{\Gamma(3-\alpha)} + \sum_{k=0}^{n-3}(n-k)(n-k-2)\sigma_k^{(\alpha)},$$

$$\sigma_n^{(\alpha)} = \frac{n^{1-\alpha}(2n+3\alpha-6)}{2\Gamma(3-\alpha)} - \frac{1}{2}\sum_{k=0}^{n-3}(n-k-1)(n-k-2)\sigma_k^{(\alpha)}.$$

The weights $\sigma_{n-2}, \sigma_{n-1}$ and σ_n are evaluated with $O(n)$ operations because the sums

$$\sum_{k=0}^{n-3}\sigma_k^{(\alpha)}, \quad \sum_{k=0}^{n-3}k\sigma_k^{(\alpha)}, \quad \sum_{k=0}^{n-3}k^2\sigma_k^{(\alpha)}$$

are evaluated with $O(n)$ operations. The TTE

$$y^{(\alpha)}(t) + Ly(t) = t^{1-\alpha}E_{1,2-\alpha}(t) + Le^t, \quad y(0) = 1 \tag{17}$$

has a solution $y(t) = e^t$. The obtained numerical results for the order (O) and the maximal error (E) of NS1(1–4) and NS1(14) of Eq. (17) are given in Tables 6, 7, 8, 9 and 10.

Table 6. Order and Maximum error of NS1(1).

h	$\alpha = 0.25, L = 1$		$\alpha = 0.75, L = 2$	
	E	O	E	O
0.00125	7.5916×10^{-7}	1.7114	1.9558×10^{-5}	1.2685
0.000625	2.3057×10^{-7}	1.7191	8.1558×10^{-6}	1.2618
0.0003125	6.9743×10^{-8}	1.7251	3.4115×10^{-6}	1.2574

Table 7. Order and Maximum error of NS1(2).

h	$\alpha = 0.25, L = 1$		$\alpha = 0.75, L = 2$	
	E	O	E	O
0.00125	4.1631×10^{-7}	1.7894	1.8176×10^{-5}	1.2717
0.000625	1.2352×10^{-7}	1.7529	7.4633×10^{-6}	1.2639
0.0003125	3.6646×10^{-8}	1.7530	3.1191×10^{-6}	1.2639

Table 8. Order and Maximum error of NS1(3).

h	$\alpha = 0.25, L = 1$		$\alpha = 0.75, L = 2$	
	E	O	E	O
0.00125	1.1096×10^{-6}	1.6960	2.1298×10^{-5}	1.2658
0.000625	3.3991×10^{-7}	1.7069	8.8920×10^{-6}	1.2601
0.0003125	1.0351×10^{-7}	1.7152	3.7222×10^{-6}	1.2563

Table 9. Order and Maximum error of NS1(4).

h	$\alpha = 0.25, L = 1$		$\alpha = 0.75, L = 2$	
	E	O	E	O
0.00125	5.8551×10^{-7}	1.7259	1.8710×10^{-5}	1.2701
0.000625	1.7638×10^{-7}	1.7309	7.7971×10^{-6}	1.2628
0.0003125	5.2999×10^{-8}	1.7347	3.2601×10^{-6}	1.2580

Table 10. Order and Maximum error of NS1(14).

h	$\alpha = 0.25, L = 1$		$\alpha = 0.75, L = 2$	
	E	O	E	O
0.00125	7.4064×10^{-7}	1.9542	3.8126×10^{-6}	1.9713
0.000625	1.9032×10^{-7}	1.9603	9.6460×10^{-7}	1.9827
0.0003125	4.8723×10^{-8}	1.9657	2.4287×10^{-7}	1.9897

3 Optimal Shifted Approximations

Shifted approximations of integer and fractional order derivatives are studied in [1,4,8,14]. Denote by $\mathcal{A}_{i,n}^{(\alpha)}[y]$ approximations (1), (2), (3) and (4), where $i = 1, 2, 3, 4$. Consider the approximations

$$\mathcal{B}_{i,n}^{(\alpha)}[y] = \mathcal{A}_{i,n}^{(\alpha)}[y] - sh\mathcal{A}_{i,n}^{(\alpha+1)}[y].$$

Approximation $\mathcal{B}_{i,n}^{(\alpha)}[y]$ has a second order expansion

$$\mathcal{B}_{i,n}^{(\alpha)}[y] = y_n^{(\alpha)} - shy_n^{(\alpha+1)} + D_i(\alpha)y_n''h^{2-\alpha} + O\left(h^2\right),$$

where $D_i(\alpha) = C_i(\alpha) - sC_i(\alpha + 1)$. Then

$$\mathcal{B}_{i,n}^{(\alpha)}[y] = y_{n-s}^{(\alpha)} + D_i(\alpha)y_n''h^{2-\alpha} + O\left(h^2\right).$$

Approximation $\mathcal{B}_{i,n}^{(\alpha)}[y]$ is the induced shifted approximation of $\mathcal{A}_{i,n}^{(\alpha)}[y]$ with a shift parameter s. Approximation $\mathcal{B}_{i,n}^{(\alpha)}[y]$ has a second order accuracy when $D_i(\alpha) = 0$.

$$C_i(\alpha) - sC_i(\alpha + 1) = 0, \quad s = \frac{C_i(\alpha)}{C_i(\alpha + 1)}.$$

The L1A has an induced SA

$$\frac{1}{\Gamma(2 - \alpha)h^\alpha} \sum_{k=0}^{n} w_k^{(\alpha)} y_{n-k} = y_{n-s}^{(\alpha)} + O\left(h^{2-\alpha}\right), \tag{18}$$

where $w_0^{(\alpha)} = 1 + s(\alpha - 1)$ and

$$w_1^{(\alpha)} = 2^{1-\alpha} + s(\alpha - 1)2^{-\alpha} - 2(s(\alpha - 1) + 1),$$

$$w_k^{(\alpha)} = (k+1)^{1-\alpha} - 2k^{1-\alpha} + (k-1)^{1-\alpha}$$
$$+ s(\alpha - 1)\left((k+1)^{-\alpha} - 2k^{-\alpha} + (k-1)^{-\alpha}\right),$$

$$w_n^{(\alpha)} = (n-1)^{1-\alpha} - n^{1-\alpha} + s(\alpha - 1)\left((n-1)^{-\alpha} - n^{-\alpha}\right).$$

Approximation (18) has a shift value which is optimal

$$s = S_{18}(\alpha) = \frac{\zeta(\alpha - 1)}{(1 - \alpha)\zeta(\alpha)}.$$

When $s = S_{18}(\alpha)$ shifted approximation (18) has a second order accuracy $O(h^2)$. Approximation (2) has an induced shifted approximation

$$\frac{1}{\Gamma(-\alpha)h^\alpha} \sum_{k=0}^{n} w_k^{(\alpha)} y_{n-k} = y_{n-s}^{(\alpha)} + O\left(h^{2-\alpha}\right), \tag{19}$$

where

$$w_0^{(\alpha)} = \zeta(\alpha) + ((\alpha + 1)s - 1)\zeta(\alpha + 1) - (\alpha + 1)s\zeta(\alpha + 2),$$

$$w_1^{(\alpha)} = 1 + (\alpha + 1)s - \zeta(\alpha) - (\alpha + 1)s\zeta(\alpha + 1),$$

$$w_k^{(\alpha)} = \frac{1}{k^{1+\alpha}} + \frac{s(1 + \alpha)}{k^{2+\alpha}}, \quad (k = 2, \cdots, n).$$

SA (19) has $2 - \alpha$ order when $y(t)$ satisfies

$$y(0) = y'(0) = 0.$$

Now (19) has accuracy of order two at the optimal SV

$$s = S_{19}(\alpha) = \frac{\zeta(\alpha) - \zeta(\alpha - 1)}{(1 + \alpha)(\zeta(\alpha) - \zeta(1 + \alpha))}.$$

Approximation (3) has an ISA

$$\frac{1}{2\Gamma(1 - \alpha)h^\alpha} \sum_{k=0}^{n} w_k^{(\alpha)} y_{n-k} = y_{n-s}^{(\alpha)} + O\left(h^{2-\alpha}\right), \tag{20}$$

where

$$w_0^{(\alpha)} = 1 + \alpha s - 2\alpha s \zeta(\alpha + 1) - 2\zeta(\alpha),$$

$$w_1^{(\alpha)} = \frac{1}{2^\alpha} + \frac{\alpha s}{2^{\alpha+1}} + 2\alpha s \zeta(\alpha + 1) + 2\zeta(\alpha),$$

$$w_k^{(\alpha)} = \frac{1}{(k+1)^\alpha} - \frac{1}{(k-1)^\alpha} + \frac{\alpha s}{(k+1)^{\alpha+1}} - \frac{\alpha s}{(k-1)^{\alpha+1}},$$

for $2 \leq k \leq n$. SA (20) has an optimal SV

$$s = S_{20}(\alpha) = \frac{2\zeta(\alpha - 1) - \zeta(\alpha)}{\alpha(\zeta(\alpha + 1) - 2\zeta(\alpha))}.$$

Approximation (4) has an induced shifted approximation

$$\frac{1}{\Gamma(1 - \alpha)h^\alpha} \sum_{k=0}^{n} w_k^{(\alpha)} y_{n-k} = y_{n-s}^{(\alpha)} + O\left(h^{2-\alpha}\right), \tag{21}$$

where

$$w_0^{(\alpha)} = 2^\alpha(2\alpha s + 1) - \alpha s \left(2^{\alpha+1} - 1\right)\zeta(\alpha + 1) - (2^\alpha - 1)\zeta(\alpha),$$

$$w_1^{(\alpha)} = 2^\alpha \left(2\alpha s \left(3^{-\alpha-1} - 1\right) + 3^{-\alpha} - 1\right)$$
$$+ \alpha s \left(2^{\alpha+1} - 1\right)\zeta(\alpha + 1) + (2^\alpha - 1)\zeta(\alpha),$$

$$w_k^{(\alpha)} = \frac{2^\alpha}{(2k+1)^\alpha} - \frac{2^\alpha}{(2k-1)^\alpha} + \frac{\alpha s 2^{\alpha+1}}{(2k+1)^{\alpha+1}} - \frac{\alpha s 2^{\alpha+1}}{(2k-1)^{\alpha+1}}$$

for $2 \leq k \leq n$. Now (21) has an optimal SV

$$s = S_{21}(\alpha) = \frac{(2^\alpha - 1)\zeta(\alpha) - (2^\alpha - 2)\zeta(\alpha - 1)}{\alpha((2^{\alpha+1} - 2)\zeta(\alpha) - (2^{\alpha+1} - 1)\zeta(\alpha + 1))}.$$

Furthermore we compute the NSs of the TTE

$$y^{(\alpha)}(t) + Ly(t) = F(t), \quad y(0) = y_0 \tag{22}$$

which use approximations (18–21) of the CD. Let $h = 1/n$, where $n > 0$ is an integer and

$$\frac{1}{h^\alpha} \sum_{k=0}^{m} \lambda_k^{(\alpha)} y_{m-k} = y_{m-s}^{(\alpha)} + O\left(h^{\beta(\alpha)}\right) \qquad (**)$$

be a SA of the CD of order $\beta(\alpha) \leq 3$. By approximation of the CD of (22) at $t_{m-s} = (m-s)h$ satisified (**) we find

$$\frac{1}{h^\alpha} \sum_{k=0}^{m} \lambda_k^{(\alpha)} y_{m-k} + y_{m-s} = F_{m-s} + O\left(h^{\beta(\alpha)}\right).$$

In [3] we showed that

$$\frac{s(s-1)}{2} y_{m-2} + s(2-s)y_{m-1} + \frac{(s-1)(s-2)}{2} y_m = y_{m-s} + O(h^3).$$

Let $\{u_m\}_{m=0}^{n}$ be the NS of TTE (22), where u_m is an approximational value of $y_m = y(mh)$. Then

$$\frac{1}{h^\alpha} \sum_{k=0}^{m} \lambda_k^{(\alpha)} u_{m-k} + \frac{s(s-1)L}{2} u_{m-2}$$

$$+ s(2-s)Lu_{m-1} + \frac{(s-1)(s-2)L}{2} u_m = F_{m-s},$$

$$\left(\lambda_0^{(\alpha)} + 0.5(s-1)(s-2)Lh^\alpha\right) u_m + 0.5\,h^\alpha s(s-1)Lu_{m-2}$$

$$+ 0.5\,h^\alpha s(2-s)Lu_{m-1} + \sum_{k=1}^{m} \lambda_k^{(\alpha)} u_{m-k} = h^\alpha F_{m-s}.$$

The NS of the TTE is computed with the recursive formula

$$u_m = \frac{h^\alpha \left(F_{m-s} - Ls\left(0.5(s-1)u_{m-2} + (2-s)u_{m-1}\right)\right) - S_m}{\lambda_0^{(\alpha)} + 0.5L(s-1)(s-2)h^\alpha}, \qquad (NS2(**))$$

where $S_m = \sum_{k=1}^{m} \lambda_k^{(\alpha)} u_{m-k}$. NS2(*) has initial conditions $u_0 = y_0$ and [8]

$$u_1 = \frac{y_0 + h^\alpha \Gamma(2-\alpha)F(h)}{1 + Lh^\alpha \Gamma(2-\alpha)},$$

$$u_2 = \frac{y_0 + (2h)^\alpha \Gamma(2-\alpha)F(2h)}{1 + L(2h)^\alpha \Gamma(2-\alpha)},$$

The TTE

$$y^{(\alpha)}(t) + Ly(t) = t^3 + \frac{6Lt^{3-\alpha}}{\Gamma(4-\alpha)}, \quad y(0) = 0 \qquad (23)$$

has a solution $y = t^3$. The numerical results for the error (E) and the order (O) of NS2(18–21) of Eq. (23) are given in Tables 11, 12, 13 and 14.

Table 11. Order and Error of NS2(18) and $L = 1$.

h	$\alpha = 0.5, s = 0.1$		$\alpha = 0.5, s = S_{10}(0.5)$	
	E	O	E	O
0.00125	1.7509×10^{-5}	1.7219	2.2252×10^{-7}	1.9993
0.000625	6.2329×10^{-6}	1.7267	5.5659×10^{-8}	1.9992
0.0003125	2.2143×10^{-6}	1.7306	1.3921×10^{-8}	1.9993

Table 12. Order and error of NS2(19) and $L = 2$.

h	$\alpha = 0.25, s = 0.3$		$\alpha = 0.25, S_{11}(0.25)$	
	E	O	E	O
0.00125	8.5957×10^{-6}	1.2831	3.7123×10^{-6}	1.9901
0.000625	3.5705×10^{-6}	1.2674	9.3188×10^{-7}	1.9941
0.0003125	1.4917×10^{-6}	1.2592	2.3353×10^{-7}	1.9964

Table 13. Order and error of NS2(20) and L = 1.

h	$\alpha = 0.75, s = 0.4$		$\alpha = 0.75, S_{12}(0.75)$	
	E	O	E	O
0.00125	5.8520×10^{-6}	1.3335	3.7123×10^{-6}	1.9901
0.000625	2.4411×10^{-6}	1.2613	9.3188×10^{-7}	1.9941
0.0003125	1.0230×10^{-6}	1.2547	2.3353×10^{-7}	1.9965

Table 14. Order and error of NS2(21) and $L = 2$.

h	$\alpha = 0.25, s = 0.5$		$\alpha = 0.25, s = S_{13}(0.25)$	
	E	O	E	O
0.00125	3.4442×10^{-6}	1.7285	9.7630×10^{-8}	2.0035
0.000625	1.0369×10^{-6}	1.7319	2.4379×10^{-8}	2.0016
0.0003125	3.1152×10^{-7}	1.7348	6.0918×10^{-9}	2.0007

4   Shifted Grünwald Difference Approximation

In this section we construct the second order SA of the GDA. Let

$$\mathcal{C}_n^{(\alpha)}[y] = \mathcal{G}_n^{(\alpha)}[y] - (s - \alpha/2)h\mathcal{G}_n^{(1+\alpha)}[y]. \qquad (24)$$

Shifted approximation (24) has a GF

$$G(x) = (1 - x)^\alpha (2 - 2s + \alpha + (2s - \alpha)x)/2.$$

Now we find a formula of the weights of (24). Let

$$C_n^{(\alpha)}[y] = \frac{1}{h^\alpha} \sum_{k=0}^{n} w_k^{(\alpha)} y_{n-k},$$

and $g_k^{(\alpha)} = (-1)^k \binom{\alpha}{k}$ be the Grünwald formula approximation (GFA)' weights. From (24)

$$
\begin{aligned}
w_k^{(\alpha)} &= g_k^{(\alpha)} - (s - \alpha/2) g_k^{(\alpha+1)} \\
&= (-1)^k \binom{\alpha}{k} - (-1)^k (s - \alpha/2) \binom{\alpha+1}{k}, \\
w_k &= (-1)^k \binom{\alpha+1}{k} \left(\frac{\alpha^2 + 3\alpha + 2 - 2k}{2(\alpha+1)} - s \right).
\end{aligned}
$$

Lemma 1. *Let $y(0) = y'(0) = 0$. Then*

$$C_n^{(\alpha)}[y] = y_{n-s}^{(\alpha)} + O(h^2).$$

Proof. The GFA of the CD has a first accuracy order

$$G_n^{(1+\alpha)}[y] = \frac{1}{h^{1+\alpha}} \sum_{k=0}^{n} \binom{1+\alpha}{k} y_{n-k} = y_n^{(1+\alpha)} + O(h).$$

Now $y(t)$ satisfies $y(0) = y'(0) = 0$ and

$$(s - \alpha/2) h G_n^{(1+\alpha)}[y] = (s - \alpha/2) h \frac{d}{dt} y_n^{(\alpha)} + O(h^2).$$

Hence

$$C_n^{(\alpha)}[y] = y_n^{(\alpha)} - sh \frac{d}{dt} y_n^{(\alpha)} + O(h^2) = y_{n-s}^{(\alpha)} + O(h^2).$$

The weights of the Grünwald approximation satisfy [13]

$$\sum_{k=0}^{n-2} g_k^{(\alpha)} = (-1)^n \binom{\alpha-1}{n-2}, \tag{25}$$

$$\sum_{k=0}^{n-2} k g_k^{(\alpha)} = (-1)^n \alpha \binom{\alpha-2}{n-3}. \tag{26}$$

Denote by S_0 and S_1 the sums

$$S_0 = \sum_{k=0}^{n-2} w_k^{(\alpha)}, \qquad S_1 = \sum_{k=0}^{n-2} k w_k^{(\alpha)}.$$

Claim 2.

$$S_0 = (-1)^n \binom{\alpha - 1}{n - 3} \frac{(\alpha^2 + 2\alpha + 4 - 2m - 2s\alpha)}{2(n - 2)}.$$

Proof.

$$S_0 = \sum_{k=0}^{n-2} w_k^{(\alpha)} = \sum_{k=0}^{n-2} g_k^{(\alpha)} - (s - \alpha/2) \sum_{k=0}^{n-2} g_k^{(\alpha+1)}.$$

From (17)

$$S_0 = (-1)^n \binom{\alpha - 1}{n - 2} - (s - \alpha/2)(-1)^n \binom{\alpha}{n - 2}$$

$$= (-1)^n \binom{\alpha - 2}{n - 2} \left(\frac{\alpha - n + 2}{\alpha} + \frac{\alpha}{2} - s \right) \frac{\alpha}{n - 2}$$

$$= \frac{(-1)^n}{2(n - 2)} \binom{\alpha - 1}{n - 3} (\alpha^2 + 2\alpha + 4 - 2m - 2s\alpha).$$

Claim 3.

$$S_1 = (-1)^n \binom{\alpha - 1}{n - 3} \frac{(\alpha^3 + 2\alpha^2 + 3\alpha - 2\alpha m + 2s - 2s\alpha^2)}{2(\alpha - 1)}.$$

Proof.

$$S_1 = \sum_{k=0}^{n-2} k w_k^{(\alpha)} = \sum_{k=0}^{n-2} k g_k^{(\alpha)} - (s - \alpha/2) \sum_{k=0}^{n-2} k g_k^{(\alpha+1)}.$$

From (18)

$$S_1 = (-1)^n \alpha \binom{\alpha - 2}{n - 3} - (s - \alpha/2)(-1)^n (\alpha + 1) \binom{\alpha - 1}{n - 3}$$

$$= (-1)^n \binom{\alpha - 1}{n - 3} \left(\frac{\alpha(\alpha - n + 2)}{\alpha - 1} + (\alpha + 1) \left(\frac{\alpha}{2} - s \right) \right)$$

$$= \frac{(-1)^n}{2(\alpha - 1)} \binom{\alpha - 1}{n - 3} (\alpha^3 + 2\alpha^2 + 3\alpha - 2\alpha m + 2s - 2s\alpha^2).$$

Now we extend SA (24) to the class of functions $C^2[0, t]$. From the conditions

$$C_n^{(\alpha)}[1] = 0, \qquad C_n^{(\alpha)}[t] = \frac{(t - s)^{1-\alpha}}{\Gamma(2 - \alpha)}$$

we derive the following system of equations for the weights $w_{n-1}^{(\alpha)}$, $w_n^{(\alpha)}$

$$w_n^{(\alpha)} + w_{n-1}^{(\alpha)} = -S_0,$$

$$w_{n-1}^{(\alpha)} = \frac{(n - s)^{1-\alpha}}{\Gamma(2 - \alpha)} - nS_0 + S_1.$$

The system of equations has a solution

$$w_{n-1}^{(\alpha)} = \frac{(n-s)^{1-\alpha}}{\Gamma(2-\alpha)} + S_1 - nS_0,$$

$$w_n^{(\alpha)} = (n-1)S_0 - S_1 - \frac{(n-s)^{1-\alpha}}{\Gamma(2-\alpha)}.$$

From Claim 2 and Claim 3

$$w_{n-1}^{(\alpha)} = \frac{(n-s)^{1-\alpha}}{\Gamma(2-\alpha)} + \frac{(-1)^n C_1}{2(\alpha-1)(m-2)}\left(\frac{\alpha-1}{n-3}\right),$$

$$w_n^{(\alpha)} = \frac{(-1)^n C_2}{2(\alpha-1)(m-2)}\left(\frac{\alpha-1}{n-3}\right) - \frac{(n-s)^{1-\alpha}}{\Gamma(2-\alpha)}$$

where

$$C_1 = 4n + 5an + a^2 n - 2n^2 - 6a - 4a^2 - 2a^3$$
$$- 4s + 4a^2 s + 2ns - 2ans,$$
$$C_2 = 4 + 4a + 3a^2 + a^3 - 6n - 3an - a^2 n + 2n^2$$
$$+ 4s - 2as - 2a^2 s - 2ns + 2ans.$$

From (6) we find the third order expansion formula of (24)

$$\mathcal{C}_n^{(\alpha)}[y] = y_{n-s}^{(\alpha)} - \frac{C(\alpha,s)}{24}h^2 y_n^{(2+\alpha)} + O(h^3), \tag{27}$$

where

$$C(\alpha,s) = 12\,s^2 - 12\,s(\alpha+1) + 3\alpha^2 + 5\alpha.$$

Approximation (24) has an accuracy of third order when the coefficient in the second order term of (27) is 0, $C(\alpha,s) = 0$. Approximation (24) has an optimal SV

$$s = S_{24}(\alpha) = \frac{1}{6}\left(3\alpha + 3 - \sqrt{3(\alpha+3)}\right).$$

The TTE

$$y^{(\alpha)}(t) + Ly(t) = t^{1-\alpha}E_{1,2-\alpha}(t) + Le^t, \quad y(0) = 1 \tag{28}$$

has a solution $y = e^t$. The experimental results of second order NS2(24) of (28) are given in Tables 15, 16. The experimental results of third order NS2(24) of (23) with $s = S_{24}(\alpha)$ are given in Table 17.

Table 15. Order and Error of NS2(24) and $L = 2$.

h	$\alpha = 0.25, s = 0.25$		$\alpha = 0.75, s = 0.5$	
	E	O	E	O
0.00125	3.1684×10^{-7}	1.9246	1.8406×10^{-6}	1.9828
0.000625	8.3001×10^{-8}	1.9325	4.6353×10^{-7}	1.9894
0.0003125	2.1626×10^{-8}	1.9403	1.1640×10^{-7}	1.9936

Table 16. Order and Error of NS2(24) and $L = 1$.

h	$\alpha = 0.25, s = 0$		$\alpha = 0.75, s = 0$	
	E	O	E	O
0.00125	2.9565×10^{-7}	1.9992	1.2525×10^{-6}	1.9986
0.000625	7.3933×10^{-8}	1.9996	3.1327×10^{-7}	1.9993
0.0003125	1.8485×10^{-8}	1.9998	7.8334×10^{-8}	1.9997

Table 17. Order and Error of NS2(24) and $L = 1$.

h	$\alpha = 0.25, s = S_{24}(0.25)$		$\alpha = 0.75, s = S_{24}(0.75)$	
	E	O	E	O
0.00125	3.1982×10^{-9}	2.9542	1.7531×10^{-8}	2.9901
0.000625	4.1092×10^{-10}	2.9603	2.2003×10^{-9}	2.9941
0.0003125	5.2599×10^{-11}	2.9657	2.7570×10^{-10}	2.9964

5   Conclusions

In this chapter we construct approximations of of order $2 - \alpha$ for the Caputo derivative whose weights have properties which are identical to the properties of the L1 approximation. The experimental results in the chapter suggest a relation between the properties (5) of the coefficients of the terms of order $2 - \alpha$ in the approximations' expansion formulas and the errors of numerical solutions. The weights of the approximations have properties (6). In Sects. 3 and 4 we obtain the shifted approximations of the approximations studied in the chapter. The order of the induced shifted approximations is higher at their optimal shift values. In future work we will use properties (6) of the approximations for analyzing the convergence of the fractional differential equations' numerical solutions which use the studied Caputo derivative' approximations.

References

1. Alikhanov, A.A.: A new difference scheme for the time fractional diffusion equation. J. Comput. Phys. **280**, 424–438 (2015). https://doi.org/10.1016/j.jcp.2014.09.031

2. Apostolov, S., Dimitrov, Y., Todorov, V.: Constructions of second order approximations of the Caputo fractional derivative. In: Lirkov, I., Margenov, S. (eds.) LSSC 2021. LNCS, vol. 13127, pp. 31–39. Springer, Cham (2022). https://doi.org/10.1007/978-3-030-97549-4_3

3. Diethelm, K.: The Analysis of Fractional Differential Equations: An Application-oriented Exposition Using Differential Operators of Caputo Type. LNM, vol. 2004, 1st edn. Springer, Heidelberg (2010). https://doi.org/10.1007/978-3-642-14574-2

4. Dimitrov, Y.: A second order approximation for the Caputo fractional derivative. J. Fract. Calc. App. **7**(2), 175–195 (2016)

5. Dimitrov, Y.: Three-point approximation for the Caputo fractional derivative. Commun. Appl. Math. Comput. **31**(4), 413–442 (2017)

6. Dimitrov, Y.: Approximations for the Caputo derivative (I). J. Fract. Calc. App. **9**(1), 15–44 (2018)

7. Dimitrov, Y., Miryanov, R., Todorov, V.: Quadrature formulas and Taylor series of secant and tangent. Econ. Comput. Sci. **4**, 23–40 (2017)

8. Dimitrov, Y., Miryanov, R., Todorov, V.: Asymptotic expansions and approximations of the Caputo derivative. Comp. Appl. Math. **37**, 5476–5499 (2018). https://doi.org/10.1007/s40314-018-0641-3

9. Jin, B., Lazarov, R., Zhou, Z.: An analysis of the L1 scheme for the subdiffusion equation with nonsmooth data. IMA J. Numer. Anal. **36**(1), 197–221 (2016). https://doi.org/10.1093/imanum/dru063

10. Li, C., Chen, A., Ye, J.: Numerical approaches to fractional calculus and fractional ordinary differential equation. J. Comput. Phys. **230**(9), 3352–3368 (2011).https://doi.org/10.1016/j.jcp.2011.01.030

11. Lin, Y., Xu, C.: Finite difference/spectral approximations for the time-fractional diffusion equation. J. Comput. Phys. **225**(2), 1533–1552 (2007). https://doi.org/10.1016/j.jcp.2007.02.001

12. Ma, Y.: Two implicit finite difference methods for time fractional diffusion equation with source term. J. Appl. Math. Bioinform. **4**(2), 125–145 (2014)

13. Podlubny, I.: Fractional Differential Equations. Academic Press, San Diego (1999)

14. Todorov, V., Dimitrov, Y., Dimov, I.: Second order shifted approximations for the first derivative. In: Dimov, I., Fidanova, S. (eds.) HPC 2019. SCI, vol. 902, pp. 428–437. Springer, Cham (2021). https://doi.org/10.1007/978-3-030-55347-0_36

15. Zeng, F., Zhang, Z., Karniadakis, G.E.: Second-order numerical methods for multi-term fractional differential equations: smooth and non-smooth solutions. Comput. Methods Appl. Mech. Eng. **327**, 478–502 (2017). https://doi.org/10.1016/j.cma.2017.08.029

16. Zhou, B., Gu, W.: Numerical study of some intelligent robot systems governed by the fractional differential equations. IEEE Access **7**, 138548–138555 (2019). https://doi.org/10.1109/ACCESS.2019.2943089

Real-Time 3D Reconstruction for Mixed Reality Telepresence Using Multiple Depth Sensors

Shafina Abd Karim Ishigaki$^{(\boxtimes)}$ and Ajune Wanis Ismail

Mixed and Virtual Reality Research Lab, ViCubeLab, School of Computing,
Universiti Teknologi Malaysia, 81310 Johor, Malaysia
`shafina@graduate.utm.my`, `ajune@utm.my`

Abstract. In recent years, there has been a great development in real-time three-dimensional (3D) scene reconstruction from depth sensor data, as well as the study of such data in Virtual Reality (VR) and Augmented Reality (AR) contexts. Although it has been extensively investigated and has attracted the attention of many researchers, the challenge of real-time 3D reconstruction remains a difficult research task. The majority of current techniques, target real-time 3D reconstruction for the single-view-based system rather than multi-view. In order to provide multi-view 3D reconstruction for Mixed Reality (MR) telepresence, this chapter aims to propose a multiple depth sensor capture using a marching square approach to produce a single full 3D reconstruction surface of a moving user in real-time. The chapter explains the design stage that involves setup from multiple depth sensors, surface reconstruction and merging of 3D reconstruction data for MR Telepresence. The chapter ends with results and a conclusion.

Keywords: Real-time · 3D reconstruction · MR telepresence · Depth sensor

1 Introduction

Globalization has boosted demand for immersive telepresence solutions, which are a type of technology that allows individuals who are physically separated to collaborate as if the user were in the same room [1]. By giving an alternative to travelling to presential meetings, this technology can save time and money while also decreasing environmental impact [2]. It enables users to present at a remote location through a virtual projection. The idea of telepresence arises from Marvin Minsky, one of the first to coin the term "telepresence" as the feeling of remote existence when using a teleoperator [3]. Since Marvin Minsky stated the principle, several systems have been developed to accomplish telepresence [4].

In early telepresence, due to limitations in the technology available at that time, telepresence systems were unable to acquire and transmit high-quality real-time three-dimensional (3D) reconstruction objects to distant users [5]. However, following the introduction of inexpensive commodity depth sensors such as the Microsoft Kinect

© The Author(s), under exclusive license to Springer Nature Switzerland AG 2023
R. N. Shaw et al. (Eds.): ICACIS 2022, CCIS 1749, pp. 67–80, 2023.
https://doi.org/10.1007/978-3-031-25088-0_5

became more widely available, many 3D reconstructions at the room size were developed, such as room2room life-size telepresence [6]. The capability of 3D reconstruction that is able to capture and reconstruct real-world elements makes significant advances in telepresence [7].

However, implementing 3D reconstruction for telepresence requires real-time rendering for moving object since telepresence capture user movement in real-time. Real-time 3D reconstruction for moving objects is challenging in computer vision and computer graphics [7, 8]. The majority of current techniques target real-time 3D reconstruction for a single-view-based system, from a single depth sensor rather than multiple-view from multiple depth sensors.

With the use of a Head-mounted-display (HMD), 3D reconstruction can be viewed with a wider Field-of-View (FoV) compared to a standard phone or monitor [9]. This allows users to interact with virtual environments in a manner that is similar to being physically present in those environments [10]. Mixed Reality (MR) refers to a new category of experiences in which a layer of computer-graphics-based interaction tied to a certain activity is superimposed on top of the real environment [11]. It allows users to experience the actual world as a more integrated and better environment. The user of an MR interface sees the actual world through a portable HMD that coats graphics on the surroundings [12]. [13] were the first to demonstrate HMD, which gave rise to the concept of MR. According to [14], an MR system brings together physical and digital objects in the same space, allows for two-way communication between them, and keeps track of their location and state in real-time.

In this chapter, a depth sensor is proposed to capture real-world objects and reconstruct the data in 3D. However, the FoV of a depth sensor is insufficient to capture a full 3D object and physically impossible to gather all the input data for the object or scene at once [15]. Therefore, to produce a full 3D reconstruction, most researchers use the fusion Kinect method, which moves the depth sensor around the real-world object to capture the data by frame. This method, however, is very computationally intensive and can only be run in an offline mode [16]. Furthermore, more than half of the picture is obscured at any given time when employing a single depth sensor to reconstruct non-rigid motion, and continuous motion creates large frame-to-frame fluctuations, which may lead to inconsistency in the scene's topological structures [17].

As a result, multiple depth sensors are required to be positioned at different angles to obtain unobstructed data from the sides of the object in order to complete the full 3D reconstruction in real-time [18]. According to [19], multiple depth sensors, enable users to get visual information that may not be available from a certain perspective when using a single depth sensor. From the previous studies, multiple depth sensors often consist of more than two depth sensor devices. However, based on recent studies in [20–22], multiple depth sensors and multiple cameras can be achieved by utilizing two depth sensors or two cameras. Therefore, this chapter proposes a real-time 3D reconstruction method with multiple depth sensors for MR telepresence. The related work for this chapter is further discussed in the next section. The methodology of the proposed method is described in Sect. 3, and in Sect. 4 we presented the result.

2   Related Work

Real-world 3D reconstruction has long been an aim of computer vision. Numerous instruments, including as stereo cameras, laser range finders, monocular cameras, and depth sensors, have been used to correctly perceive the 3D environment [23]. With the advancement of depth sensor devices such as Microsoft Kinect and Intel RealSense, many new and exciting applications is developed. However, due to issues like noisy depth data, poor registration, camera tracking drift, and a lack of precise surface details, 3D models reconstructed by depth consumer cameras are not yet widely employed in applications. Table 1 represents the summary of related work on 3D reconstruction for MR telepresence which are utilizing depth sensor devices to enable 3D reconstruction.

Table 1. Related work of 3D reconstruction for MR telepresence using a depth sensor

Year	Researchers	Proposed method	No. of depth sensors	Drawbacks
2022	Lin et al. [24]	OcclusionFusion: calculate occlusion-aware 3D motion to guide the reconstruction	1	Unable to handle topology change
2022	Sun et al. [25]	Propose a hybrid voxel- and surface-guided sampling technique which leads to significant improvements in reconstruction quality	1	Inaccurate camera registration can affect final reconstruction quality
2021	Muhlenbrock et al. [21]	Propose a combination of a custom 3D registration with a feature detection algorithm	2	Slight distortions due to the depth camera in a larger volume
2020	Fadzli et al. [26]	Explores a robust real-time 3D reconstruction method for MR telepresence	1	MR wearable headset is heavy and has a face distortion issue

(continued)

Table 1. (*continued*)

Year	Researchers	Proposed method	No. of depth sensors	Drawbacks
2019	Prokopetc & Dupont [27]	Present a comparative study with an evaluation of four depth map-based Multi-View Stereo methods for dense 3D reconstruction against brand-new deep learning models	1	Dataset is hard to achieve in the settings of real medical environments due to the vast amount of specular materials and weakly-textured surfaces
2018	Papaefthymiou et al. [28]	Present a comparison of the most recent hardware and software methods for the speedy reconstruction of actual people using RGB or RGB-D images as input	1	Does not provide an evaluation of the proposed method
2017	Joachimczak et al. [10]	Proposed to render 3D reconstructions directly (real-time), inside HoloLens in MR Telepresence	2	Require stable internet connection
2016	Sing & Xie [29]	Garden: enables the player to transform their environment into a virtual garden of 3D reconstruction in MR	1	Improvements in drift correction are required

Sun et al. [25] have presented a real-time 3D reconstruction in MR by discretizing the world space into 10 cm voxels which are grouped into $8 \times 8 \times 8$ chunks. Voxels that have points that fall within its boundaries are marked occupied and rendered as cubes, like in Minecraft. While engaging with a virtual environment, the user is free to move through wide areas in the actual world without running into any barriers.

Meanwhile, Joachimczak et al. [10] highlighted the real-time 3D reconstruction in MR Telepresence in their study. They utilized HoloLens with Kinect devices as a depth sensor for the 3D reconstruction purpose as shown in Fig. 1. However, their study provides limited information as they did not perform the evaluation of the proposed method for further discussion. In the research carried out by Fadzli et al. [26], the authors provided a discovery on the MR framework that might be used to transmit a full-body human from a nearby region to a more distant one. Therefore, they introduced a user telepresence capability for 3D reconstruction, allowing people to interact with an accurate 3D model of a remote user. The depth data from the depth sensor is captured and processed in real-time for the 3D reconstruction with the point cloud rendering process.

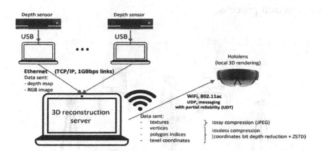

Fig. 1. Real-time 3D reconstruction using HoloLens and Kinect [10].

3   Real-Time 3D Reconstruction Method

This section elaborates on the real-time 3D reconstruction method, which consists of multiple depth sensor setup, surface reconstruction and merging of 3D reconstruction data for MR telepresence. This is explained in the next subsection.

3.1   Multiple Depth Sensor Setup

In order to produce the 3D reconstruction, depth information is required to generate the data. The conventional camera is only capable of producing two-dimensional (2D) red, green and blue (RGB) data, including photos and videos. The conventional camera is unable to collect depth data into the programmed device, the output is insufficient to enable and capture an item in 3D data. Therefore, a depth sensor is required in this chapter for capturing and converting real-world objects into 3D data. The depth sensor proposed in this chpater is the Microsoft Kinect sensor.

Microsoft Kinect sensor is a low-cost depth sensor known as a skeleton tracker that is used with the Microsoft software development kit [30]. It allows users to communicate with computers and game consoles intuitively via gestures and spoken commands without any additional peripherals [31]. It can also extract data about the subject's 3D joint locations [32].

Microsoft offers not one but two Kinect models. The first generation of Kinect sensors (Kinect v1) debuted in 2010. They were based on structured light coding technology. Following that, Microsoft made it Windows-compatible using a standard development kit (SDK) and a power conversion adaptor. Based on the time-of-flight (ToF) technology, the second generation of Kinect sensors (Kinect v2) was released in 2014 with improved specs in comparison to the first Kinect in terms of speed, accuracy, and field of vision.

However, the FoV of the Kinect sensor is constrained and physically impossible to gather all the point cloud data for the 3D object at once. Therefore, this chapter proposes two Kinect sensors, to acquire the data front and back of the user simultaneously. The setup for multiple depth sensors is shown in Fig. 2. Based on Fig. 2, the distance between the Kinect sensor and the user is fixed at 2.1 m. While the height of the Kinect sensor from the floor is fixed at 1.1 m. This setup for the multiple Kinect sensors is based on [33] research. This setup will ensure the Kinect sensor able to track the user's full body for the 3D reconstruction process.

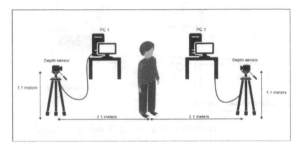

Fig. 2. Setup for multiple depths

3.2 Surface Reconstruction

Surface reconstruction is one of the steps in this chapter's real-time 3D reconstruction technique. Surface reconstruction is the process of acquiring 3D real-world object input data from a depth sensor in order to produce a mesh from the input data. For surface reconstruction, there are two methods available, explicit and implicit methods. The implicit method is proposed in this chapter to reconstruct the surface. When one of the isocontours is available near the input data, it is defined as an implicit surface. In the depiction of the reconstructed surfaces, the implicit technique employs the triangulation method.

The most intuitive form of triangulated surfaces for surface reconstruction uses k-nearest neighbours of a point to generate the connection between linked triangles made from the input points [34]. To generate the triangulated surface from the implicit method, the Marching Squares algorithm is by far the most well-known technique.

Marching Squares is a computer graphics approach for recovering 2D isocontours from a grid of sample points. The goal is to analyze each grid cell individually and to calculate the contours that pass through it depending on the values at its corners. The initial stage in this procedure is to identify the edges that are linked by contours depending on whether the corners are above or below the contour value. To keep things simple, the evaluation is only considering contours along with the value 0, focusing on the positive or negative corners. The Marching Squares lookup table is shown in Fig. 3 Based on Fig. 3, there is a total of $2^4 = 16$ distinct examples which consists of Case 0 until Case 15.

Look-up table contour lines

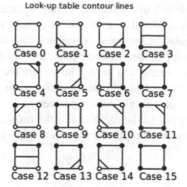

Fig. 3. Marching squares lookup table

The pseudocode for the marching square algorithm is shown in Table 2 as referred to [35]. Based on the Marching Squares algorithm the triangulation process is implemented by including the process of searching for vertex candidates from the value of the contour based on the Marching Squares lookup table. Hence, the triangulation is formed according to the vertex candidates lists.

Table 2. Marching squares algorithm

Marching Squares algorithm
1. function TRIANGULATION
2.   for all vertex candidates do
3.   current disparity coordinate ß visited
4.   block size = 2 x 2 FIND_BLOCK (current
5.   disparity coordinate, block size, current four
6.   vertex candidates per block)
7.   four vertex candidates ß current four vertex
8.   candidates per block
9.   FIND_TRIANGLE_CANDIDATE (four vertex
10.   candidates, current triangle candidate lists)
11.   triangle candidate lists ß current triangle
12.   candidates lists
13.   CREATE_TRIANGLE (triangle candidate lists,
14.   triangle)
15.   triangle lists ß triangle
16.   end for
17. end function

This process of triangulation using the Marching Squares algorithm is performed after the point cloud data is acquired from the depth sensor as shown in Fig. 4. Based on Fig. 4. After the triangulation has been completed and successfully produced the mesh. The mesh will be mapped with texture mapping. Texture mapping is the final stage to complete the 3D reconstruction look. The texture for the mesh is generated by composing the segmented images from the depth sensor as shown in Fig. 4. The images contain vertices that consist of a single colour per vertex. The colours are acquired to produce the texture and mapped to the mesh. After the texture has been mapped to the mesh, the 3D reconstruction final output is ready to display as a 3D representation for MR telepresence.

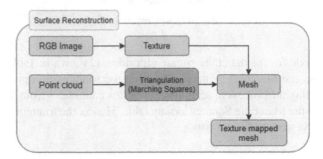

Fig. 4. Surface reconstruction process

3.3 Merging of 3D Reconstruction Data for MR Telepresence

After the mapped mesh texture has been completed, the next phase is to merge the 3D reconstruction data from multiple depth sensors for MR telepresence. The drawback of the Kinect sensor is one personal computer (PC) can only connect to one Kinect sensor. Therefore, a network is required to merge the data between the multiple Kinect sensors. The network used for this chapter is a local network. The local network will transmit the 3D reconstruction data from each Kinect at the remote user site to the receiver site, which is the local user. Figure 5 shows the process of merging 3D reconstruction data for the MR telepresence system.

Based on Fig. 5, before the 3D reconstruction data is transmitted through the network, the 3D reconstruction data that consists of vertices, triangles, colours and UVs will undergo compression to reduce the data size. Reducing the data size can reduce the bandwidth required for data transmission. After the receiver PC has received the 3D reconstruction data from both sender PC, the 3D reconstruction data will decompress and reconstruct the 3D data. The merging of 3D reconstruction data is then executed at the receiver site to be displayed at the MR telepresence. We manually adjust the position and rotation of the 3D reconstruction data from sender 1 and sender 2 using unity tools software, to be aligned in a full 3D reconstruction.

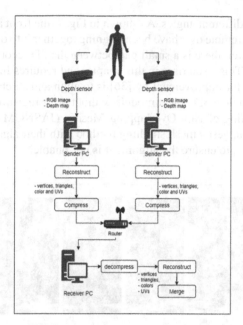

Fig. 5. Merging process at the receiver

4 Results

This section continues to discuss the results of the proposed method using multiple depth sensors for 3D reconstruction in real-time for MR Telepresence. Figure 6 shows the final setup for the remote user workspace. Based on Fig. 6, the remote user is placed in between the Kinect sensor and the setup for the Kinect sensor is as discussed in the previous section.

Fig. 6. Final setup for the remote user using multiple depth sensors

Next, Fig. 7 shows the results after the 3D reconstruction data has been merged from multiple depth sensors. In Fig. 7, we present a full real-time 3D reconstruction view of the remote user at six different angles. As shown in Fig. 7, the front and behind views of the 3D reconstruction remote user have been aligning together into one complete full 3D reconstruction. However, there is a small gap between the 3D reconstruction data from the front and behind. This issue rises in this chapter and requires further improvement. The recommendation for improvement by [36] is to align and stitch two 3D meshes by the boundaries to complete 3D object models without prior registration using the Joint Alignment and Stitching of Non-Overlapping Meshes (JASNOM) algorithm. Recent studies by [37], also suggest a mesh stitching method with their algorithm that includes pre-processing process, to ensure the alignment is reasonable.

Fig. 7. Results of merging 3D reconstruction data at the receiver site

Furthermore, Fig. 8 shows the final output for real-time 3D reconstruction for the MR telepresence system using multiple depth sensors. Figure 8 is a captured image from the local user's point-of-view (POV). In Fig. 8, the remote user appears in 3D reconstruction in the MR environment. The interaction between the local user and the remote user is in real-time. The local user is able to interact and move around the MR telepresence simultaneously with the remote user.

Fig. 8. Final output real-time 3D reconstruction for MR telepresence

During the real-time interaction, the data that has been compressed which consists of vertices, triangles, colors and UVs from the remote user are transmitted to the local user using a stable local network. Since the data transmitted is required a local network, the bandwidth of the local network may influence the speed of the data transmission. The higher, the bandwidth of the local network, the faster the compressed data can be transmitted to the local user. However, if the local network bandwidth is low, network latency will occur and reduce the speed of the data transmission which can affect the real-time performance. Figure 9(a) shows the local user view of the remote user from the side. While Fig. 9(b) shows the side of the remote user in closer range.

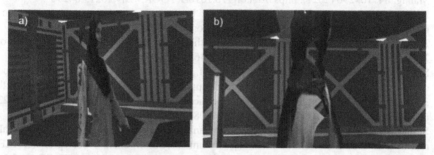

Fig. 9. Local user view of the remote user (a) side view (b) closer range of the side view

5   Conclusion

Based on the literature study, real-time 3D reconstruction technology and MR HMDs may now be used to enable a new potential for telepresence and teleoperation systems. Users can interact with a distant individual or operate remote devices by perceiving their 3D virtual representations as a part of their nearby surroundings.

In this chapter, we suggest employing multiple depth sensors to provide a real-time 3D reconstruction for MR telepresence. We utilized two depth sensors to produce depth data for the 3D reconstruction process. First, we captured depth data to form triangulation using a marching square algorithm and produce a surface reconstruction. The process continues with generating texture from the RGB image captured by the depth sensor to be mapped on the mesh. As the process is completed, the 3D reconstruction of the remote user is presented in real-time within the MR environment that was enabled on the HMD worn by the local user.

As for future work, we suggest addressing the gap issues that we found during the merging of the 3D reconstruction from multiple depth sensors to produce a more realistic and volumetric presentation. Other than that, enhancement for the interaction between the local user and remote user can be studied and improved by adding whiteboard interaction, pointing ray and object manipulation in MR telepresence.

Acknowledgement. We deeply appreciate the Mixed and Virtual Reality Laboratory (mivielab), and ViCubeLab at Universiti Teknologi Malaysia (UTM) for the equipment and technical assistance. This work has been funded by the Ministry of Higher Education under FRGS, Registration Proposal No: FRGS/1/2020/ICT10/UTM/02/1.

References

1. Itani, O.S., Hollebeek, L.D.: Light at the end of the tunnel: visitors' virtual reality (versus in-person) attraction site tour-related behavioral intentions during and post-COVID-19. Tour. Manag. **84**, 104290 (2021). https://doi.org/10.1016/J.TOURMAN.2021.104290
2. Luevano, L., Lopez de Lara, E., Quintero, H.: Professor avatar holographic telepresence model. Hologr. Mater. Appl. (2019). https://doi.org/10.5772/INTECHOPEN.85528
3. Zahorik, P., Jenison, R.L.: Presence as being-in-the-world. Presence Teleop. Virtual Environ. **7**, 78–89 (1998). https://doi.org/10.1162/105474698565541
4. Sakashita, M., Minagawa, T., Koike, A., Suzuki, I., Kawahara, K., Ochiai, Y.: You as a puppet: evaluation of telepresence user interface for puppetry. In: UIST 2017 - Proceedings of the 30th Annual ACM Symposium on User Interface Software and Technology, pp. 217–228 (2017). https://doi.org/10.1145/3126594.3126608
5. Stotko, P., Krumpen, S., Hullin, M.B., Weinmann, M., Klein, R.: SLAMCast: large-scale, real-time 3D reconstruction and streaming for immersive multi-client live telepresence. IEEE Trans. Vis. Comput. Graph. **25**, 2102–2112 (2019). https://doi.org/10.1109/TVCG.2019.2899231
6. Pejsa, T., Kantor, J., Benko, H., Ofek, E., Wilson, A.: Room2Room: enabling life-size telepresence in a projected augmented reality environment. In: Proceedings of ACM *Conference on Computer Supported Cooperative Work*, CSCW, vol. 27, pp. 1716–1725 (2016). https://doi.org/10.1145/2818048.2819965
7. Ingale, A.K.: Real-time 3D reconstruction techniques applied in dynamic scenes: a systematic literature review. Comput. Sci. Rev. **39**, 100338 (2021). https://doi.org/10.1016/J.COSREV.2020.100338
8. Cai, H., Feng, W., Feng, X., Wang, Y., Zhang, J.: Neural Surface Reconstruction of Dynamic Scenes with Monocular RGB-D Camera (2022)
9. Teo, T., Hayati, A.F., Lee, G.A., Billinghurst, M., Adcock, M.: A technique for mixed reality remote collaboration using 360 panoramas in 3D reconstructed scenes. In: Proceedings of ACM Symposium on Virtual Reality Software and Technology, VRST, vol. 11 (2019). https://doi.org/10.1145/3359996.3364238
10. Joachimczak, M., Liu, J.: Real-time mixed-reality telepresence via 3D reconstruction with HoloLens and commodity depth sensors (2017). https://doi.org/10.1145/3136755.3143031
11. John, B., Wickramasinghe, N.: A review of mixed reality in health care. In: Wickramasinghe, N., Bodendorf, F. (eds.) Delivering Superior Health and Wellness Management with IoT and Analytics. HDIA, pp. 375–382. Springer, Cham (2020). https://doi.org/10.1007/978-3-030-17347-0_18
12. Harborth, D.: A systematic literature review on augmented reality augmented reality in information systems research: a systematic literature review (2017)
13. Sutherland, I.E.: A head-mounted three dimensional display (1968)
14. Azuma, R.T.: A survey of augmented reality. Presence Teleop. Virtual Environ. **6**, 355–385 (1997)
15. Li, J., Huang, S., Cui, H., Ma, Y., Chen, X.: Automatic point cloud registration for large outdoor scenes using a priori semantic information. Remote Sens. **13**, 3474–3474 (2021). https://doi.org/10.3390/RS13173474

16. Jia, Q., et al.: Real-time 3D reconstruction method based on monocular vision. Sensors **21**, 5909–5909 (2021). https://doi.org/10.3390/S21175909
17. Nor'a, M.N.A., Fadzli, F.E., Ismail, A.W.: A review on real-time 3D reconstruction methods in dynamic scene. Int. J. Innov. Comput. **12**, 91–97 (2022). https://doi.org/10.11113/IJIC.V12 N1.317
18. Clark, R.A., Mentiplay, B.F., Hough, E., Pua, Y.H.: Three-dimensional cameras and skeleton pose tracking for physical function assessment: a review of uses, validity, current developments and Kinect alternatives. Gait Posture. **68**, 193–200 (2019). https://doi.org/10.1016/J. GAITPOST.2018.11.029
19. Meruvia-Pastor, O.: Enhancing 3D capture with multiple depth camera systems: a state-of-the-art report. In: Rosin, P.L., Lai, Y.-K., Shao, L., Liu, Y. (eds.) RGB-D Image Analysis and Processing. ACVPR, pp. 145–166. Springer, Cham (2019). https://doi.org/10.1007/978-3-030-28603-3_7
20. Mühlenbrock, A., Fischer, R., Schröder-Dering, C., Weller, R., Zachmann, G.: Fast, accurate and robust registration of multiple depth sensors without need for RGB and IR images. Vis. Comput. **38**, 3995–4008 (2022). https://doi.org/10.1007/s00371-022-02505-2
21. Muhlenbrock, A., Fischer, R., Weller, R., Zachmann, G.: Fast and robust registration of multiple depth-sensors and virtual worlds. In: Proceedings of 2021 International Conference on Cyberworlds, CW 2021, pp. 41–48 (2021). https://doi.org/10.1109/CW52790.2021.00014
22. Espinosa, R., Ponce, H., Gutiérrez, S., Martínez-Villaseñor, L., Brieva, J., Moya-Albor, E.: Application of convolutional neural networks for fall detection using multiple cameras. Stud. Syst. Decis. Control **273**, 97–120 (2020). https://doi.org/10.1007/978-3-030-38748-8_5/COVER
23. Li, J., Gao, W., Wu, Y., Liu, Y., Shen, Y.: High-quality indoor scene 3D reconstruction with RGB-D cameras: a brief review. Comput. Vis. Media **83**(8), 369–393 (2022)
24. Lin, W., Zheng, C., Yong, J.-H., Xu, F.: OcclusionFusion: occlusion-aware motion estimation for real-time dynamic 3D reconstruction. In: Proceedings of the IEEE/CVF Conference on Computer Vision and Pattern Recognition, pp. 1736–1745 (2022)
25. Sun, J., Chen, X., Wang, Q., Li, Z., Averbuch-Elor, H., Zhou, X., Snavely, N.: Neural 3D reconstruction in the wild. In: Special Interest Group on Computer Graphics and Interactive Techniques Conference Proceedings, pp. 1–9 (2022)
26. Fadzli, F.E., Ismail, A.W.: A robust real-time 3D reconstruction method for mixed reality telepresence. Int. J. Innov. Comput. **10**, 15–20 (2020). https://doi.org/10.11113/IJIC.V10 N2.265
27. Mandal, S., et al.: Lyft 3D object detection for autonomous vehicles. In: Artificial Intelligence for Future Generation Robotics, pp. 119–136 (2021). https://doi.org/10.1016/B978-0-323-85498-6.00003-4
28. Papaefthymiou, M., Kanakis, M.E., Geronikolakis, E., Nochos, A., Zikas, P., Papagiannakis, G.: Rapid reconstruction and simulation of real characters in mixed reality environments. In: Ioannides, M. (ed.) Digital Cultural Heritage. Lecture Notes in Computer Science, vol. 10605, pp. 267–276. Springer, Cham (2018). https://doi.org/10.1007/978-3-319-75826-8_22
29. Das, S., et al.: Advance machine learning and artificial intelligence applications in service robot. In: Artificial Intelligence for Future Generation Robotics, pp. 83–91 (2021). https://doi.org/10.1016/B978-0-323-85498-6.00002-2
30. Moon, S., Park, Y., Ko, D.W., Suh, I.H.: Multiple kinect sensor fusion for human skeleton tracking using Kalman filtering. **13** (2017). https://doi.org/10.5772/62415
31. Mukhopadhyay, M., et al.: Facial emotion recognition based on textural pattern and convolutional neural network. In: 2021 IEEE 4th International Conference on Computing, Power and Communication Technologies (GUCON), pp. 1–6 (2021). https://doi.org/10.1109/GUC ON50781.2021.9573860

32. Mocanu, C., Mocanu, I.: Human body posture recognition using a kinect sensor (2015)
33. Fadzli, F.E., Ismail, A.W., Ishigaki, S.A.K., Nor'a, M.N.A., Aladin, M.Y.F.: Real-time 3D reconstruction method for holographic telepresence. Appl. Sci. **12**, 4009–4009 (2022). https://doi.org/10.3390/APP12084009
34. Khatamian, A., Arabnia, H.R.: Survey on 3D surface reconstruction (2016). https://doi.org/10.3745/JIPS.01.0010
35. Jang, G.R., et al.: Real-time polygon generation and texture mapping for tele-operation using 3D point cloud data. J. Inst. Control Robot. Syst. **19**, 928–935 (2013). https://doi.org/10.5302/J.ICROS.2013.13.8012
36. Brandão, S., Costeira, J., Costeira, J.P., Veloso, M.: Effortless Scanning of 3D Object Models by Boundary Aligning and Stitching mobile phone dataset analysis View project Point matching View project Effortless Scanning of 3D Object Models by Boundary Aligning and Stitching (2014)
37. Naik, R., Singh, P., Kalra, P.: Putting jewellery and accessories on a 3D face model generated from 2D image. In: Babu, R.V., Prasanna, M., Namboodiri, V.P. (eds.) NCVPRIPG 2019. CCIS, vol. 1249, pp. 229–238. Springer, Singapore (2020). https://doi.org/10.1007/978-981-15-8697-2_21

A Robust Data Hiding Scheme Using Singular Value Decomposition and Wavelet Transform

Sudhir Singh(✉) and Buddha Singh

School of Computer and Systems Sciences, Jawaharlal Nehru University Delhi, Delhi, India
sidsingh73@gmail.com

Abstract. Due to latest development in computing and communication technologies, there are various kinds of digital contents on the internet in terms of audio, video, and images. Also, there are many freely available softwares that can modify a given digital object. These softwares have created a challenge for the owners of the original contents. Digital image watermarking secret data hiding may be helpful in addressing this problem digital contents. This chapter discusses a data hiding scheme by using the singular value decomposition (SVD) and digital wavelet transform (DWT). Our scheme performs better than the recent methods for the quality and the extracted watermark image.

Keywords: Data hiding · DWT · SVD · Frequency band · PSNR

1 Introduction

Latest developments in computational and communication technologies have made multimedia contents over the internet quite rich and easily accessible [1]. These contents can be easily copied and distributed, reducing the control of their ownership by the freely available softwares. To protect this ownership of a digital content, secret data hiding or digital watermarking schemes can be useful. A watermark may be considered as a secret data/code, which consists of the identification information for the creator/owner of the original contents that can be used to prove the ownership of contents, if required. A watermark must be unobtrusive, that is, it should not degrade the visual quality of an image in a perceptible manner, and should be robust, that is, it should be resistant to the intentional as well as unintentional attacks, specifically geometric distortions, collusion attacks, and compression distortion. Watermarking can be blind and non-blind. The hybrid form of these two is semi-blind watermarking in which some extra information is to be provided to help a detector in the detection process. The watermark can be visible as well as invisible. An invisible watermark is an image that cannot be seen but can be detected algorithmically, whereas a visible watermark is a transparent picture that is placed on the cover image. In this chapter, we go over a method for watermarking that is both invisible and semi-blind. Typically, a watermarking technique is used in the transform (frequency) and spatial domains. Some of the bits of the pre-specified pixels are adjusted in the spatial domain-based approaches, such as the last two bits of high pixel values.

The spatial domain techniques are simpler to use and easier to construct, but they have less capacity and are more vulnerable to the attacks. In [2, 3] some of the watermarking techniques in spatial domain are discussed. For transform domain, the unitary transforms are applied on the blocks of the intended cover image and the pre-specified frequency coefficients are modified. A watermarking technique is mainly assessed based on the perceptibility, robustness, and security parameters [4, 5]. Perceptibility signifies the visibility and invisibility of the watermark. Robustness refers to the strength of the technique, and the security to resist various attacks. Another important parameter is time needed for embedding the watermark and its detection process. In this chapter, we present a 2-D DWT and SVD-based method for digitally watermarking images. The matrix is essentially divided into 4 bands by the DWT: LL, LH, HL, and HH. The LL band maintains the most of the image's information, while the HH band maintains the most of its details. In-between details about the image are contained in the final two bands. A matrix of dimension (m x n) is factorised into three matrices (U, S, and V) using the singular value decomposition method. U is a matrix of dimension (m x r), S is of dimension (r x r), and V is of dimension (r x n), where r is the rank of the original matrix. S is a diagonal matrix, U and V are the unitary transform matrices. Compared to the approaches [2, 6], our scheme performs better.

2   Related Work

With its first academic conference held in the year 1996, digital watermarking is considered relatively a young research area. Since then a large number of watermarking techniques have been proposed. Recently, SVD based techniques [1, 2] have become popular. The basic reason for using SVD is that the diagonal matrix obtained after decomposition of the original matrix governs different luminous levels. The modification done on this diagonal matrix has very little effect on the perceptibility of the image. Based on the combination of DCT, SVD, and CNT Tian [5] has proposed a method. In this, the host image is created using a one level CNT and the embedding process uses its low frequency coefficients. It offers imperceptibility 42.77 dB and strengthens resistance to numerous threats. Zhang et al. [2] have discussed a data hiding scheme on the basis of SVD by exploring horizontal variation in the image intensity, that is U matrix, for hiding the watermark. It modifies the absolute variation of two consecutive rows of U matrix to preserve positive relationships between its rows even after performing JPEG encoding. But, this method does not provide error-free watermark extraction. Another issue with this method is complex block selection.

Salehnia et.al. [6] proposed an algorithm by using SVD and lifting wavelet transform (LWT). The LWT gives 4 sub-images, namely LL, LH, HL, HH, when applied on an image. Three LH, HL, and HH sub-bands have lower resolution than the LL sub-band. This method solves both the issues of method [2]. The first issue is addressed by considering the diagonal matrix using LWT and Three Module Redundancy (TMR) technique. The second one is addressed by considering the complex blocks on the basis of the number of edges. But this algorithm has a disadvantage that it does not work correctly when all the edges are confined to one particular area of the image. Therefore, there is a need to resolve this problem. Our scheme resolves this issue by using the watermark made of a binary image and embedding it in the high-high frequency region of the DWT coefficients. Our proposed method is highly robust and has better perceptibility as compared to the methods discussed in [2, 6]. The proposed method is introduced in Sect. 3 and Sect. 4 provides its experimental results. The chapter is concluded in Sect. 5.

3 Proposed Scheme

Before introducing our proposed method, we briefly discuss SVD and DWT as these are the basic concepts used to develop our proposed scheme.

3.1 Singular Value Decomposition (SVD)

The singular value decomposition (SVD) factorizes a rectangular matrix, which can be real or complex into tree matrices. Consider a matrix X of dimension mxn. On applying SVD on X, we get three matrices as shown below.

$$X = USV^T \tag{1}$$

The matrix U refers to horizontal variation in intensity in X, S is a diagonal matrix that contains singular values of X, and V refers to vertical variation in intensity in X.

3.2 Discrete Wavelet Transform

The discrete wavelet transform (DWT) splits a 1-dim signal into two parts: low and high frequency components. The low frequency component consists of maximum information of the signal, whereas the detailed information such as edges is confined to the high frequency component. On applying DWT on an image (2-dim signal), we get for components, denoted as low-low (LL) frequency band, low-high (LH) frequency band, high-low (HL) frequency band, and high-high (HH) frequency band as shown in Fig. 1. Generally LL sub-image is used to hide the secret data.

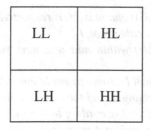

Fig. 1. Various bands into which image is decomposed.

We now discuss our proposed scheme. We first apply the DWT to the cover image and then apply SVD to LL sub-image. We use diagonal matrix for hiding the secret data that is obtained by SVD from LL sub-image. For maintaining the perceptibility of the resultant image, we select the complex blocks of the LL sub-image for embedding. The algorithm for embedding the watermark in an image is given below.

1. *Load image to be watermarked (Fig. 2).*
2. *Take its discrete wavelet transformation.*
3. *Choose LL band to work upon.*
4. *Take a 32 × 32 block (for 512 × 512 image) watermark image and convert it into binary image.*
5. *Reshape binary image to 1x1024.*
6. *Group 256 × 256 pixels of LL matrix obtained, into 32 × 32 groups of 8 × 8 each.*
7. *On each 8 × 8 block, apply SVD and store S(1, 1) element/coefficients in an array (denoted by b(i)).*
8. *Store indices of min(b(i)) and max(b(i)) respectively as j and k and set jth and kth bit in 1 × 1024 (W) to either 0 or 1.*
9. *Group the intervals of b(i) within min and max values with 1024 intervals as max(b(i))-min(b(i))/1024.*
10. *Modify the values of S(1, 1) by adding 1/4 from lower bound if watermark bit is '1' and by subtracting 1/4 from upper bound if watermark bit is '0'.*
11. *Replace them in b(i) array and take SVD inverse with new SVD(1, 1) values to form the watermarked LL.*
12. *Take inverse dwt with this changed LL and previous HH, HL, LH to get the watermarked image.*

The algorithm for extracting the watermark from the resultant (watermarked) image is given below.

1. *Load watermarked image (Fig. 5).*
2. *Take its discrete wavelet transformation.*
3. *Choose LL band to work upon.*
4. *Since we have set jth (min value index) and kth (max value index) bits either 1 or 0, we know the deviation of the min and max values in original b(i) array.*
5. *Group 256 × 256 pixels of LL matrix obtained, into 32 × 32 groups of 8 × 8 each.*
6. *On each 8 × 8 block, apply SVD and store S(1, 1) element/coefficients in an array (denoted by b(i)).*
7. *Store the indices of min(b(i)) and max(b(i)) respectively as j and k and set jth and kth bit in 1 × 1024 (W) to either 0 or 1.*
8. *Group the intervals of b(i) within min and max value with 1024 intervals as max(b(i))-min(b(i))/1024.*
9. *The interval boundaries will be same as while embedding, so we can check which S(1, 1) or b(i) value has changed and thus we can obtain the watermark pattern.*
10. *Since we store the bit as 0 or 1 according to the shift observed in b(i) values.*
11. *After extracting the watermark and comparing with the original, the authenticity of image can be ascertained.*

Fig. 2. 512 × 512 Lena (host image)

Fig. 3. Watermark image

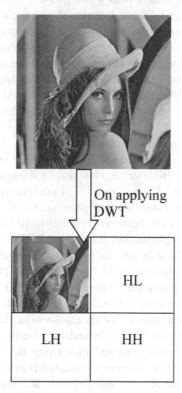

On applying DWT

HL

LH

HH

Fig. 4. Decomposition of the host image

Fig. 5. Watermarked image

4 Watermark Attacks

By conducting numerous tests, such as image attacks utilising the Lena Picture (512 × 512) as the host image—which is depicted in Fig. 2—we assess the effectiveness of our system. The watermark has a binary size of 24 × 24 and an additional two key data bits, as illustrated in Fig. 3. Figure 4 depicts the image's breakdown following the use of DWT, and Fig. 5 depicts the watermarked Lena image. The resilience of the watermark to attacks such as row-column blanking, row-column copying, rotation, low pass filtering, scaling, cropping, salt & pepper noise, and picture manipulation. With the exception of image tampering and JPEG2000 attacks, all attacks are conducted using MATLAB R2021a. The MORGAN JPEG2000 toolkit is used for the JPEG2000 attack, while PAINTBRUSH is used for picture tampering. A good PSNR of 53.36 dB is present in the watermarked image.

The watermarked image is rotated at various angles (10, 20, 30 degrees) up to which exactly the same watermark is detected with the correlation factor of 1, but the rotation attack shows great similarity. However, it maintains its strength at various angles except in the vicinity of 40 degrees. Using lossy JPEG compression the watermark image is compressed with various quality factors such as 30, 40, 60, and 100. The JPEG compression value ranges from 0 (best compression) to 100 (best quality). Our scheme stands outstanding even for high compression and has 0.9792 value for the quality factor of 30. The higher values of the quality factor show great level of similarity with the original watermark. Due to the extremely strong presence of watermark in the upper region of the image cropping attack does not show great results but for cropping in the lower region good results are obtained. A 3 × 3 mask with intensity values of 0.9 is considered for low pass filtering attack. Our scheme shows great resilience to the low pass filtering attack as can be seen in Table 1. In resizing, we first reduce the watermarked image by half in both the dimensions and then using the bicubic interpolation it is enlarged to the original size. The watermark extracted is exactly same to the embedded watermark. A certain number of rows and columns are eliminated in a row column blanking attack, including 10, 30, 40, 70, 100, 120, and 140 rows and columns. In a row-column copy attack, several rows and columns are copied to randomly chosen or relatively neighbouring locations, for example, 10th row is copied to 30th one, 40th to

70th, 100th to 120th and 140th to 160th. As can be seen from Table 1, the watermark extracted from the row column blanking and copying attacks has good similarity with the original watermark. The watermarked image is corrupted by salt & pepper noise with density of 0.001, 0.002, 0.003, and 0.004. The watermarks from the corrupted images are clearly visible, which justifies that our scheme is resilient to the noise attacks. Finally, the proposed scheme shows good results for bit plane removal and image tampering attacks. The NC (normalized cross-correlation) value helps to compare the robustness of the proposed scheme. Table 1 summarizes the performance parameters.

Table 1. Proposed scheme comparison and their performance

Parameters	Zhang et al.[2]	Salehnia et al. [6]	Proposed method
Image quality (in dB)	49.07	50.3453	53.3612
Type of attack	NC values		
Rotation (in degrees) (10, 20, 40, 60)	0.5333		1
	0.4988		1
	0.4712		0.02
	0.4856		0.9965
Low pass filtering 3 × 3 kernel	0.9386	0.9862	0.9896
Resizing 512-256-512	0.9538	0.8155	1
JPEG Compression (Quality factor) 30, 40, 60, 100	0.9295	0.9211	0.9792
	0.9793	0.9711	0.9965
	0.9986	0.9961	1.0000
	1.0000	1.0000	1.0000
JPEG2000 Compression (Quality factor) 5,10,30,50	0.3323	0.6502	1.0000
	0.2819	0.9953	1.0000
	0.8765	1.0000	1.0000
	0.8989	1.0000	1.0000
Salt & pepper Noise (Noise density) .1%,.2%,.3%,.4%	0.9923	0.9624	0.9896
	0.9566	0.9512	0.9757
	0.9255	0.9102	0.9515
	0.9148	0.9184	0.9202

(continued)

Table 1. (*continued*)

Parameters	Zhang et al.[2]	Salehnia et al. [6]	Proposed method
Bit plane removal 1st, 2nd and 3rd	0.9802	1.0000	1.0000
	0.9802	0.9009	0.1099
	0.4354	0.8076	0.1696
Image tampering	0.9353	0.9907	0.9688

5   Conclusion

In this chapter, we provide an SVD and DWT-based data hiding technique. It is strong and able to fend off numerous attacks. Peak-to-signal ratio, which is 53.3612, and perceptibility are both good indicators of the image's quality. Additionally, it is immune to JPEG compression, scaling, row column blanking, rotation, cropping, low pass filtering, row column copying, bit plane removal, salt and pepper noise, and tampering. The linked techniques are better for specific parameters when it comes to rotation and cropping attack. The proposed approach outperforms the existing algorithms used for comparison in all other attacks.

References

1. Altay, ŞY., Ulutaş, G.: Self-adaptive step firefly algorithm based robust watermarking method in DWTSVD domain. Multimedia Tools Appl. **80**, 23457–23484 (2021)
2. Zhang, H., Wang, C., Zhou, X.: A robust image watermarking scheme based on SVD in the spatial domain. Future Internet **9**, 45 (2017). https://doi.org/10.3390/fi9030045
3. Bartolini, F., Tefas, A., Barni, M., Pitas, I.: Image authentication techniques for surveillance applications. Proc. IEEE **89**(10), 1403–1418 (2001). https://doi.org/10.1109/5.959338
4. Kim, W.-H., Nam, S.-H., Kang, J.-H., Lee, H.-K.: Robust watermarking in curvelet domain for preserving cleanness of high-quality images. Multimedia Tools Appl. **78**(12), 16887–16906 (2019). https://doi.org/10.1007/s11042-018-6879-3
5. Tian, C., Wen, R.H., Zou, W.P., Gong, L.H.: Robust and blind watermarking algorithm based on DCT and SVD in the contourlet domain. Multimedia Tools Appl. **79**, 7515–7541 (2020). https://doi.org/10.1007/s11042-019-08530-z
6. Salehnia, T., Fathi, A.: Fault tolerance in LWT-SVD based image watermarking systems using three module redundancy technique. Expert Syst. Appl. **179** (2021). https://doi.org/10.1016/j.eswa.2021.115058

Simulation Experiments of a Distributed Fault Containment Algorithm Using Randomized Scheduler

Anurag Dasgupta[1](✉), David Tan[1], and Koushik Majumder[2]

[1] Valdosta State University, Valdosta 31698, USA
adasgupta@valdosta.edu
[2] Maulana Abul Kalam Azad University of Technology, West Bengal, Kolkata 700064, India
koushik@ieee.org

Abstract. Fault containment is a critical component of stabilizing distributed systems. A distributed system is termed stabilizing (or self-stabilizing) if it exhibits two properties – a) convergence: a finite sequence of moves leading to a stable configuration, and b) closure: the system remains in that legitimate state unless another fault hits. In today's world, the likelihood of several failures is quite low, and a single fault is far more likely to occur. The results of simulation experiment we did for single failure instances are presented in this study. For node selection, we employed a randomized scheduler. The results show that the fault containment mechanism we used restores valid configurations after a transient fault. The studies took into account variations in the number of nodes and the degree of the malfunctioning node. The results were graphically and numerically presented to provide relevant information. We can learn about the efficiency of our method by analyzing the simulation outcomes.

Keywords: Stabilization · Simulation · Distributed systems · Fault containment · Algorithm

1 Introduction

Fault containment is a critical feature of stabilizing distributed systems. Random illegitimate configurations can occur because of transient failures that can disrupt the system state. A distributed system is said to be stabilizing, when from any given configuration, there exists a sequence of moves, using which the system can reach a legitimate configuration, and once it reaches that configuration, it stays in that state unless any other fault occurs in the system [1, 2].

In most modern day systems, the probability of a massive failure is considered low and single fault is much more likely to occur compared to multiple failures. Containing single failures is more important these days because of improved system reliability. Local transient faults are likely to give rise to almost legal states, instead of arbitrary states. To make sure that non- faulty processes mostly stay unaffected by such local failures, some algorithms allow just a small section of the network around the faulty node to make state changes. The authors in [3, 4] describe how fault containment followed by recovery is achieved using this strategy.

In our fault containment algorithm, weak stabilization is considered. Weak stabilization is defined in the following way starting from an arbitrary configuration, there exists at least one computation that leads the system to a legal configuration. Weak stabilization algorithms are best implemented using a randomized scheduler [5, 6]. Therefore, our algorithm is going to be implemented using a randomized scheduler to guarantee eventual recovery.

In this chapter, the authors wrote programs to implement a fault containment algorithm and run simulation experiments. The simulations provided insight regarding the efficiency of the algorithm. The authors experimented by varying the number of nodes and by changing the faulty node's degree.

A fundamental understanding of graph theory is assumed and relevant notations are used throughout the chapter to discuss the algorithm of self-stabilization and its results. The readers are recommended to consult [7] for an overview of graph theory and the notations and definitions used in this chapter.

2 Background

2.1 Motivation

The occurrence of a transient fault could be catastrophic in certain systems and conditions and it can be very expensive to fix the fault. Sometimes it could be almost impossible too to manually rectify the fault. Consider the example of a commercial satellite orbiting around the Earth. If the shuttle's power supply were to fail due to some electrical malfunction, a major investment of time, effort, and resources would be wasted. A few such examples are – submarine communications cable system under the ocean [8], systems in satellite or space stations [9], sensors in battle fields [10] etc.

One way to resolve the above problem is to design the system in such a way so that the satellite or the cable network would self-stabilize in response to the fault. In other words, this means after a certain period of time the system would get back to what is known as legal states and resume its normal operations without any outside intervention. This is the general idea of autonomous fault containment and because of the nature of the solution, its practical implications are of great significance.

We can generalize this concept to hold for any random configuration of any such system. To continue with our examples, consider the satellite or the cable network at any stage in their state-space tree, and after self-stabilization, we end up with a *legal configuration* of the system. This is the main advantage of self-stabilizing algorithms and it is for this characteristic that self-stabilization is a much-sought property in modern distributed systems.

Related Work. Dijkstra's landmark paper on stabilization in 1974 was the first paper in the field of self-stabilization [2]. Since then, stabilization research has come a long way. Lately stabilization research not only is limited to computer science alone, but also combines other fields such as mathematics, biology, engineering, physics etc. For the interested readers, some important applications like the construction of stabilizing spanning trees in a graph [11], stabilizing maximum flow trees in network topology [12], construction of stabilizing rooted shortest path tree [13], stabilizing maximal matching algorithm [14], stable path problem [15] etc. are suggested. For readers who need an introduction and basic understanding of the subject, an excellent and lucid introduction might be the book written by Dolev [1]. The probabilistic fault containment algorithm based on which we conducted our experiments in this paper was derived by Dasgupta et al. [16]. In this paper, a thorough and elaborate explanation of the stabilization algorithm is provided along with formal proofs of correctness and other important results. The current paper features programs written in Java of the proposed algorithm and tested on varying instances of number of nodes and the degree of the faulty node. We record the time taken, and cite interesting observations made from the results along with implementation details.

Model and Notation. For the sake of simplicity, we only considered simple connected graphs, i.e., graphs without parallel edges and self- loops. Definitions: Given a graph $G = (V, E)$, the *neighborhood* N_i of a vertex, $v_i \in V$, is defined to be $\{v_j \in V \mid \exists (v_i, v_j) \in E\}$, $i \neq j$, i.e., the neighborhood of a vertex constitutes all vertices that share an edge with the vertex. Each vertex $v_i \in V$ holds two variable values: a primary variable value, $v(i)$, and a secondary variable value, $x(i)$. The primary value of the vertices can be either 0 or 1, i.e., $v(i) \in \{0, 1\}$ whereas the secondary value $x(i) \in \mathbb{Z}^+$. This approach helps model our system to elect local leaders as described in [16]. The *local leader* is defined as the vertex with the largest secondary variable value amongst all vertices in its neighborhood. Formally, the local leader is a vertex $v_k \in N_i \cup v_i$ such that $\forall v_j \in N(i) \cup v_i$, $x(j) \leq x(k)$. For our fault containment algorithm, a constant arbitrarily large positive integer, $m \in \mathbb{Z}^+$ is required. This is used to increase the weight of the local leader. This variable acts like a fence and hence helps in containing the fault. Only when some other node in its neighborhood is chosen more than a certain value determined by m, a possible new leader is elected.

3 Algorithm

The algorithm assumes a randomized scheduler which picks a node or a process represented by a vertex i and compares the state of i with the state of its neighbors, $N(i)$. This is known as the shared memory model. If the selected vertex satisfies one of the algorithm rules, the state of the vertex is *updated*. If the chosen vertex does not match a rule, the state of the vertex remains the same.

$$\forall j \in N(i), \ v(i) \neq v(j) \Rightarrow \text{Update } v(i) \tag{1}$$

Rule (1) states that if all neighboring vertices have a different primary variable value than the selected vertex, the primary variable value of the vertex will be updated to match that of its neighbors.

$$\exists j \in N(i) \text{ s.t. } v(i) \neq v(j) \wedge \neg (\forall j \in N(i), \ v(i) \neq v(j)) \wedge i \text{ is}$$
$$\text{the local leader} \Rightarrow \text{Update } v(i) \wedge x(i) = x(i) + m \tag{2}$$

Rule (2) states that if there is a neighbor with a different primary variable value than the chosen vertex, and Rule 1 is not satisfied, and the chosen vertex is the local leader - then the chosen vertex's primary variable value is updated and the secondary variable value of the vertex is increased by *m*.

$$\exists j \in N(i) \text{ s.t. } v(i) \neq v(j) \wedge \neg(\forall j \in N(i),\ v(i) \neq v(j)) \wedge i \text{ is not the local leader} \Rightarrow x(i) = x(i) + 1 \quad (3)$$

Rule (3) states that if there is a neighbor with a different primary variable value than the chosen vertex, and Rule 1 is not satisfied, and the vertex is not the local leader - then the secondary variable value of the vertex is increased by 1 but the primary variable value of the vertex remains unchanged.

Rule (2) increases the secondary variable value of the local leader by *m* while flipping the leader's primary variable value. But if all the neighbors have a different primary variable value, in that case the algorithm flips the vertex's primary variable value without increasing the secondary variable value. The methodology of increasing a chosen vertex's secondary variable value ensures that the probability of the fault propagation is very low and constitutes the heart of the algorithm.

4 Methodology

The approaches and strategies utilized to construct the code in the research experiment and simulations will be covered in this part.

Eclipse was our IDE (integrated development environment). Due to the faster buffer time when executing the code, we decided to switch to Intelli J [17] throughout the experiments. The overarching goal was to record the time spent within the fault gap, which is defined as the shortest interval after which the system was ready to handle the next single failure with the same level of efficiency [16]. Other resources we used to build this sophisticated application include Coursera [18] and edx [19].

We created code for a random graph generator in the application since we had to construct any random graph with provided node counts. Figure 1 illustrates a piece of code that demonstrates our program's "Graph" class.

```java
public class Graph {

    public static void main(String[] args) {
        ArrayList<Integer> x_values = new ArrayList<>();
        int size = 21;
        for (int i = 0; i < size; i++) {
            x_values.add(i);
        }
        Collections.shuffle(x_values);
        ArrayList<Node> nodes = new ArrayList<>();
        // generate 20 nodes
        for (int i = 0; i < size; i++) {
            nodes.add(new Node(x_values.get(i)));
        }
        // link them randomly
        linking(nodes);

        long start = System.currentTimeMillis();
        String firstTime = java.time.LocalTime.now().toString();

        Node finalNode = processing(nodes);

        System.out.println("Time start: " + firstTime);
        System.out.println("Time end: " + java.time.LocalTime.now());
        System.out.println("Total time taken for execution: "
                + (System.currentTimeMillis() - start) + " milli second");

        System.out.println("node " + finalNode.getNumber() + " was selected.");
        System.out.println(finalNode.connection());

    }
```

Fig. 1. Code snippet showing the main method of the program.

The program outputs how much time it takes, when the code started, and ended. We added an x value for the secondary variable in the algorithm for all the nodes and their neighbors. The x values are randomized from 0 to 20. Next, we created the randomize scheduler and the scheduler picked any node at random. Then it checks whether the three conditions (rules) of the algorithm for that node are satisfied or not.

This set the stage for the fault containment algorithm. In the end, the stabilization time was recorded. In Fig. 2, the true and false values act as the primary variable. By achieving stabilization, we were able to record the time within the fault gap.

```
 98
 99     public static boolean isAllTrue(ArrayList<Node> nodes) {
100         for (Node node : nodes) {
101             if (node.getState() == false) {
102                 return false;
103             }
104         }
105         return true;
106     }
107
```

Fig. 2. The Boolean method that contains the primary variable of the nodes.

There are three ways for the code to achieve stabilization: first whatever node is selected to be the faulty node, if it is the local leader in the list then the Boolean variable will automatically turn true and this will rectify the fault right away but if it is not the local leader then it will move to step 2 or 3. Step 2 suggests that if one of the neighboring node's primary variable is not equal to that of the faulty node, then its x value will increase by m and the primary variable will flip (if it is true then it flips to false and vice versa) until the faulty node becomes the local leader. Step 3 suggests that if the neighboring node's x value is less than or equal to that of the faulty node then the neighboring node's x value will increase by 1 and its primary variable value stays unchanged. This will go on until the faulty node becomes the local leader and thus eventually its primary variable value flips to the same value as its neighbors.

5   Results

This section presents the results and the inferences we made from the results.

Figure 3 displays the different numbers of nodes ranging from 20 to 200 in increments of 20. In our tests, we changed the numbers of nodes to display the scalability of the program. Each time we ran the program, it displayed the stabilization time within the fault gap. Also, we wanted to know the average time it took overall so we ran the code ten times for each of the numbers and thus calculated the average time. What we can infer from the tests is that as predicted – while the scale became larger so did the average time it took for stabilization to occur.

Figure 4 shows the stabilization time for the faulty node's deviation in degrees 2, 3, and 4 for total number of nodes 20 to 200, by increments of 20. As mentioned previously, the average time was found by producing 10 experimental run times for each

Node Number	20	40	60	80	100	120	140	160	180	200
	265579	55572	72356	110259	132021	153226	210065	223569	243962	277231
	4207	41235	55465	63569	124436	110363	196362	206654	223651	256213
	3477	22578	52365	72569	105569	128554	153265	215565	241623	263316
	8791	32152	12258	82246	113659	151235	206543	213328	235663	271621
	9274	38426	36542	100698	98625	138854	192236	196354	243316	243165
	80	42315	39569	95562	105378	110369	206321	205698	233656	269563
	853	21589	71125	73256	121369	146550	194563	220364	237128	275863
	819	37856	46589	83465	115639	142396	186336	199856	231236	265436
	17971	51582	44569	103356	126963	152646	201136	200656	229633	256312
	29	26539	253349	756233	110639	134886	204563	211566	240361	273165
Total	72080	369844	456187	1541313	1154298	1362088	1951390	2091608	2360229	2651385
Average	7208	36984.4	45618.7	154121.3	115429.8	136208.8	195139	209160.8	236022.9	265138.5

Fig. 3. Average stabilization time (milliseconds) with increase in node number.

Fig. 4. Average stabilization time with deviation in faulty node's degrees 2 to 4 and the increase of nodes.

Fig. 5. Average stabilization time with deviation in faulty node's degree 5 to 8 and the increase of nodes.

of the selected node numbers and averaging ten runs for each node. The value for each degree was randomly generated (in Fig. 4, 5, and 6; indicated within curly braces are the node numbers selected by the program) as described in the methodology portion of the research. The randomized values for each degree was used to run the program and produce 10 experimental run times for each degree. The 10 run times for each degree were averaged as well.

Figure 5 depicts the data for the deviation in degrees 5, 6, 7, and 8 for number of nodes varied from 20 to 200, by increments of 20. Figure 6 depicts the data for the deviation in degrees 9 and 10 for number of nodes varied from 20 to 200, by increments of 20. We noticed that the stabilization time increased with the increase in degrees. This was also expected as the program had to check through more neighbors as the degree increased and therefore the stabilization took longer to occur.

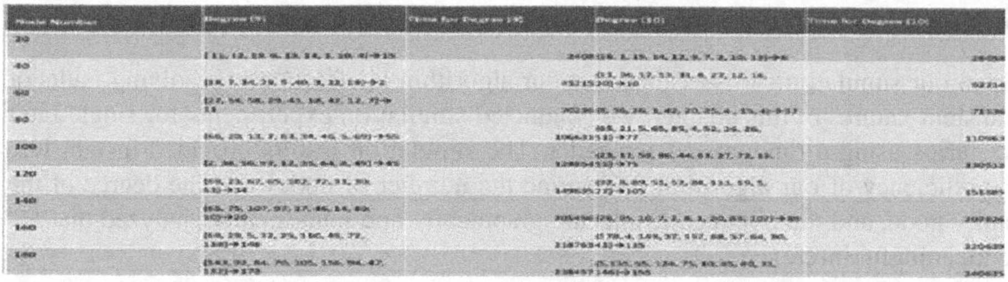

Fig. 6. Average stabilization time with deviation in faulty node's degrees 9, 10 and the increase of nodes.

In Fig. 7, the trend of average time with increase of number of nodes is demonstrated. The relationship shown in the figure appeared to be a positive linear relationship between node number and average run time. The relationship indicates that as the node number increases so does the average stabilization time. The graph also revealed some spikes between 60 and 80 and again in the range of 140–150. Besides those deviations, it shows the increase in the average time, when scaling to higher nodes, follows approximately a linear trend. We observe that this positive linear relation ties along with the node numbers as we scale the node numbers higher and higher.

Figure 8 shows the trend in deviation in degrees of node 20 to 200, by increments of 20. The relationship shown in the figure appeared to be a positive linear relationship between node number and run time for each degree. The relationship indicates that as the node number increases so does the run time for each degree. As we expected, when we increase the degrees of the faulty node, the algorithm takes more time to fully execute because it takes longer time to compare and run through the algorithm rules.

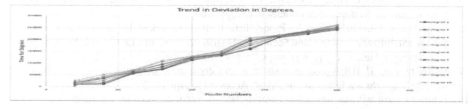

Fig. 7. Trend in average time of selective node numbers.

Fig. 8. Trends in deviation in degrees of selective node numbers.

6 Conclusion

From our simulations it is evident that our algorithm is effective in resolving faults of transient nature. In this chapter, we conducted simulation experiments for single fault scenarios using a randomized scheduler. The simulation results provided insight into the efficiency of our algorithm. We varied the number of nodes and the degree of the faulty node, and the obtained results are graphically and numerically analyzed that led to meaningful inference.

References

1. Dolev, S.: Self-stabilization. MIT Press, Cambridge (2000)
2. Dijkstra, E.W.: Self-stabilizing systems in spite of distributed control. Comm. ACM **17**, 643–644 (1974)
3. Gupta, A.: Fault-containment in self-stabilizing distributed systems, PhD Thesis, Department of Computer Science, The University of Iowa, Iowa City, IA (1997)
4. Dasgupta, A.: Extensions and refinements of stabilization, PhD Thesis, Department of Computer Science, The University of Iowa, Iowa City, IA (2009)
5. Devismes, S., Tixeuil, S., Yamashita, M.: Weak vs. self vs. probabilistic stabilization. In: Distributed Computing Systems, International Conference, Los Alamitos, CA, pp. 681–688 (2008)
6. Dasgupta, A., Ghosh, S., Xiao, X.: Fault-containment in weakly- stabilizing systems, Special Issue: Self-* Systems of Theoretical Computer Science (2011)
7. Deo, N.: Graph Theory with Applications to Engineering and Computer Science. Prentice-Hall, Hoboken (1974)
8. Andres, J., Fang, T., Nedbal, M.: Cable route planning and installation control: recent advances. Sub Optic 2007: Baltimore, Maryland (2007)
9. Fayyaz, M., Vladimirova, T.: Fault-tolerant distributed approach to satellite on-board computer design. In: IEEE Aerospace Conference, Big Sky, Montana (2014)
10. Dalichaouch, Y., Czipott, P.V., Perry, A.R.: Magnetic sensors for battlefield applications. Aerospace/Defense Sensing, Simulation, and Controls, Orlando, Florida (2001)
11. Chen, N.S., Yu, H.P., Huang, S.T.: A self-stabilizing algorithm for constructing spanning trees. Inf. Process. Lett. **39**, 147–151 (1991)
12. Dasgupta, A.: Selfish stabilization of maximum flow tree for two colored graphs. The Pennsylvania Association of Computer and Information Science Educators, California, PA (2014)
13. Cohen, J., Dasgupta, A., Ghosh, S., Tixeuil, S.: An exercise in selfish stabilization. ACM TAAS **3**(4), 1–12 (2008)
14. Hsu, S., Huang, S.: A self-stabilizing algorithm for maximal matching. Inf. Process. Lett. **43**(2), 77–81 (1992)
15. Cobb, J.A., Gouda, M.G., Musunari, R.: A stabilizing solution to the stablepath problem. Self-Stabilizing Systems, San Francisco, CA, pp. 169–183 (2003)
16. Dasgupta, A., Ghosh, S., Xiao, X.: Probabilistic fault-containment. In: Masuzawa, T., Tixeuil, S. (eds.) Stabilization, Safety, and Security of Distributed Systems. LNCS, vol. 4838, pp. 189–203. Springer, Heidelberg (2007). https://doi.org/10.1007/978-3-540-76627-8_16
17. JetBrains IntelliJ IDEA coding assistance and ergonomic design developer productivity website. https://www.jetbrains.com/idea/. Accessed30 Apr 2022
18. Coursera learn without limits from world-class universities website. https://www.coursera.org/. Accessed 30 Apr 2022
19. Edx the next era of online learning from world's best institutions website. https://www.edx.org/. Accessed30 Apr 2022

Novel Computer Vision Approach for Scale-Specific Generative Stick Figure as Synthetic Tribal Art Works

Suman Deb[1](✉), Debosmit Neogi[1], Nataraj Das[1], Partha Pratim Das[2],
Bappaditya Sarkar[3], and Chinu Mog Choudhari[4]

[1] National Institute of Technology Agartala, Agartala, India
sumandebcs@gmail.com
[2] Women's Polytechnic, Agartala, India
[3] ETCE Department Women's Polytechnic Hapania Agartala, Agartala, India
[4] Department of Computer Science and Engineering, Tripura Institute of Technology,
Narsingarh, West Tripura, India

Abstract. A detailed methodology of generation of figures of Warli art (an ancient tribal art) using precise computational geometry, advanced trigonometry and intelligent computer vision techniques, has been presented in this chapter. The figures have been generated for both the genders- male and female. The visual variances between the genders are attributed to carefully chosen phenotypic traits and differences in anatomical structures, that have been incorporated during generation of the images. A total of 60,000 images have been generated in multiple batches, with both genders in almost equal proportions. The batches of images generated are properly labelled and annotated and finally split into training and validation data. The whole directory structure has been carefully formatted so that it can be used effectively as data set for future model training. In-fact, the data set generated has been used to train Generative Adversarial Networks (GAN) based models and has produced promising results. The entire work is done using spherical polar coordinates, instead of complex fractal geometry. All the sequential steps of the closed loop operation have been performed to generate aesthetically pleasing figures, viable for multi facet uses in the future.

Keywords: Warli-art · Computer vision · Computational geometry · Human anatomy · Synthetic-art · Color-space

1 Introduction

Warli art is an ancient tribal art that dates back to early 10 century AD [1]. This style of art is associated with the Warli tribe who inhabited the western coastal regions of India, especially in Maharashtra-Gujarat region. This ancient art form has an unique distinguished style of art. The paintings, discovered from the caves often showcased male and female figures in their natural habitat. The paintings provide an unique experience taking viewers on a visual journey through time. In this digital age, our work focuses on

R. N. Shaw et al. (Eds.): ICACIS 2022, CCIS 1749, pp. 97–110, 2023.
https://doi.org/10.1007/978-3-031-25088-0_8

revive this art by incorporating computer vision techniques with advanced geometry [2]. The end results obtained have the potential to restore the enigmatic essence of the long lost Warli arts to some extent [3]. In this work, the primary focus was generating male and female figures that have basic differentiation, when seen from a viewer's perspective. This was a challenging yet exciting task. This was dealt by deploying fundamentals of geometry in the computer vision arena. It started with careful and precise generation of ratio of every joints of the figure body along with generation of upper and lower body torso in proper ratio. The ratios are obtained and used in accordance to basic human anatomy that distinguishes male and female body types.

The ultimate motive of the presented work is to generate a labelled dataset of Warli image figures. The motive behind this work is lack of availability of good datasets for this ancient arts. It is believed the dataset can mitigate this conundrum of lack of proper data and can act as a stepping stone for future researchers interested in digitally developing and reviving these ancient art forms.

2 Literature review

Creation of synthetic stick figures through generative adversarial neural networks (GAN) [4] in order to automate the random generation of figures from latent vector space using the proposed data set was quite robust and precise in creating out figures with desired male and female gender traits. Several research work have been done [5, 6] to revive the history and create an account of the Warli art in India. We have taken reference from these papers to understand about Warli more. [7] worked on fusion of modern art with Warli art. All these works have been done from a historical point of view. Our work is digital creation of synthetic Warli figures from scratch without the usage of any prior dataset. The algorithm we have used is novel and is primarily revolves around the convergence of computational geometry [8, 9] and computer vision [10].

We have used precise colour spaces [11, 12] and accurate anatomical features of male [13] and female [14] for generating the dataset. We have referred their works for better understanding of male and female anatomy and outline the visual differences between the two. Upon referring all the above mentioned works, we have designed our own methodology that generates male and female figures having varying poses and alignments.

Another novelty of the presented work is that it is completely based on spherical polar coordinates. Previous research have relied on using Fractal Geometry for pose estimation like [15]. But our work has bypassed the complexities of this approach and used a much simpler approach.

3 Approach

The aim of this work is to conserve Asian tribal art deploying artificial intelligence. The chapter aims at production of Warli art figures that can be further used by any neural model to generate dynamic human stick figures, rather than some rule based entities. In the chapter [4] the figures have been used to train a GAN model that could generate human stick figures from a given set of latent vector space.

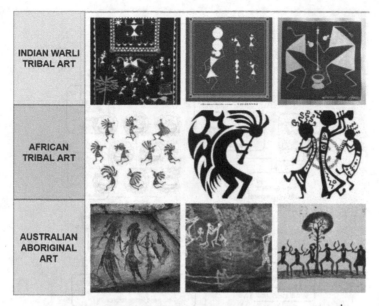

Fig. 1. Compilation of tribal art images from across the world[1]

3.1 Synopsis of the Working Methodology

The proposed methodology is a novel algorithm that that begins with distinct figure generation of male and female in a systematic sequential approach. The algorithm terminates after generating images in varied poses and body alignments which is controlled by a vector of angles represented by (θ). The domain in which (θ) varies is determined by precise computational geometry calculations, in accordance to human anatomy. The joints of the body are set in ratios that are inferred from principles of human anatomy. With these in mind, the upper and lower torso are generated. The body ratios of male and female are different along with variance in phenotypic traits. All these steps are properly summarised in Fig. 2.

3.2 Architecture of Creating the Stick Figures

The complete generation of synthetic images course through a sequence of stages. The first major step is generating the base image matrix[2]. We have pre-computed values of height and width of the matrix and created a matrix of 1 s or 0 s. This creates a complete black or white colour space that served as the base matrix.

Depending upon the dimensions of the base image matrix as well as the horizontal and vertical aperture of the concerned gender figure, a randomised function was initiated that provided the coordinates with which the initial head outline was created having a radius = r, that served as the basis of calculating all the body parts ratio of the entire figure. The limit of the head outline generating random function was such that the

---

[1] https://in.pinterest.com.
[2] https://aiartists.org/generative-art-design.

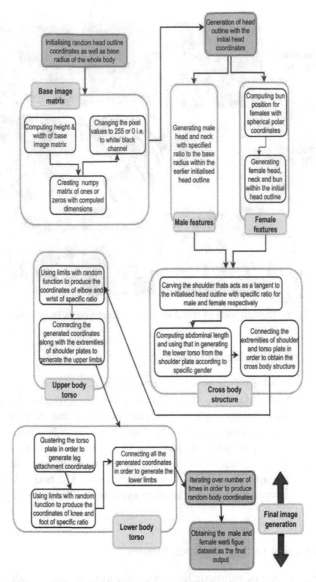

Fig. 2. Synopsis of the working architecture

total figure lies within the base image matrix. Within the created head outline the true head was created in such a way that the radius of both the outline head and real head coincides. The only difference is the radial length. Say the real head has a radius = R. So it can be inferred that r≥ R. The left over are inside the initial head outline provides the space for creating the neck for both male and female as well as the differentiating attribute of females i.e. the bun. Thus it can be inferred that the neck will be having a length= r − R.

In order to construct the phenotypic differentiating attribute in female figures i.e. the bun, a mathematical structural formula has been constructed in order to determine the bun position corresponding to the initial head outline and its radius(r).Depending upon the positive and negative values of trigonometrical ratios, the following formula was deduced in Eq. 1:

$$\theta_T = \lambda_1, \theta_2 \leq \lambda_1 \leq \theta_1$$
$$\lambda_2, \theta_3 \leq \lambda_2 \leq \theta_4 \tag{1}$$

Thus the coordinates are obtained as:

$$X_b = X_h + (k * r)\left(\cos\left(\theta^T\right)\right) \tag{2}$$

$$Y_b = Y_h + (k * r)\left(\sin\left(\theta^T\right)\right) \tag{3}$$

Here in Eq. 2 and Eq. 3, X_h and Y_h are the center of the initial head outline with radius=r and k is bun position-adjusting parameter. The parameter k was necessary to avoid the merging of bun into the head. The Fig. 3 depicts the deployment of the above formula in creating the differentiating trait.

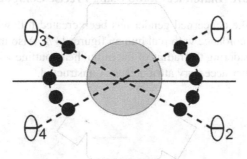

Fig. 3. Female differentiating attribute

The shoulder was constructed in a way that served as a tangent to the initial head outline. Thus we have the mid point coordinates of the shoulder as the abscissa same as that of head and the ordinate as the sum of initial head out-line ordinate and its radius. Now the length of the shoulder plate was decided following the normal human anatomical ratio. The extremities of the shoulder plate served two purposes, first it acted as the pivot for joining the upper limbs. Second, as the connecting pivot with the lower torso thus forming cross body structure.

This is one of the most fundamental and significant step of the algorithm. The lower torso was first generated and the extremities of the torso and shoulder plate were connected in order to obtain the cross body structure. The torso was generated at a particular distance from the shoulder plate. That specific distance is nothing but the sum of the lengths of upper and lower abdomen [16]. Thus the midpoint coordinates of the torso consists of abscissa equal to that of head outline and the ordinate is equal to the sum of ordinate of head outline, head outline radius and total abdominal length.

Finally it was the time to provide the figures with upper and lower limbs. Both the upper and lower limbs were created in two parts. First the generation of elbow and knee respectively and second, the generation of wrist or foot respectively. Both the upper and lower limbs were created through random functions with limits corresponding to normal human body ratio. The random function also allowed the figures to have different orientations of hands and legs, that contributed to the variation in the data set.

Once created the upper limbs are connected to the extremities of the shoulder plate depending on side orientation. The lower limbs are connected to the mid point of half of the torso depending upon left right orientation.

4   Viable Result Analysis

The above stated architecture has been put through various performance measuring techniques. Depending on the reports of various analysis the hyper parameters of the entire framework i.e the pixel values, figure height etc. are tuned in order to contribute towards the precision and robustness for the stated architecture.

4.1   Analysis of Figure Anatomical Ratio Using Precise Computational Geometry

The whole figure of the concerned gender has been created following some specified anatomical ratio in accordance with real human figures [17]. Also the whole figure has been constructed considering the radius of the initial head outline within which the real head and neck and other necessary attributes are constructed.

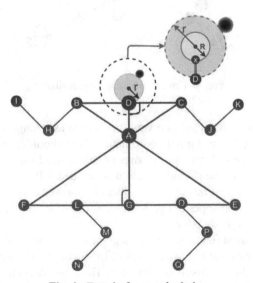

Fig. 4. Female figure calculation

Female figure anatomy ratio As mentioned earlier, all the ratio of body parts are determined in accordance with normal human figure. The female figures are generated using precise body measurements [18]. The parts whose exact ratios are not defined, those lengths have been calculated using the principles of geometry.

In the Fig. 4 let it be assumed that the initial head outline has a radius $= r$ and the final head has a radius $= R$. Let XD represent the neck of the figure that has been drawn inside the initial head outline. The special differentiating attribute for the female figure i.e. the bun is generated such that the center of head outline and that of bun is at a of "K" pixel units. In this case the value of "K" for the observed radius of head outline has been obtained as

$$k = 4 \text{ pixel units}$$

And the radius of the differentiating feature i.e. the bun has been initialised to 5 pixel units, so that the bun exactly touches the real head of the figure. In order to calculate the body dimensions [19, 20], trigonometric equations [21] and similarity of triangle are used. Basically comparing with real human body ratio, values of 7 parameter are obtained with respect to the initial head outline radius (Table 1).

Following the above ratios, the lower torso length has been calculated. Let

$$-AFG = \theta_1$$

and

$$-FAG = \theta_2$$

Table 1. Ratio of different body parts.

Body part	Notation	Ratio
Head	R	0.67 r
Neck	r − R	0.33 r
Ulna and radius	HI, JK	3 r
Humerus	HB, CJ	3 r
Shoulder	BC	6 r
Upper abdomen	AD	2 r
Lower abdomen	AG	4 r
Femur	LM, OP	3 r
Tibia and fibula	MN, QP	3r

In $\triangle AFG$ and $\triangle ADC$ we have:

$$-AFG = -ACD = \theta_1 \tag{4}$$

$$\Rightarrow \quad FAG = -CAD = \theta_2 \tag{5}$$

$$-AGF = -ADC = 90° [\text{Right angles}] \tag{6}$$

Therefore $\triangle AFG \sim \triangle ADC$ Thus we have the side angle ratio as

$$\frac{AG}{AD} = \frac{AF}{AC} = \frac{FG}{CD} \tag{7}$$

Again we have,

$$\tan\theta_1 = \frac{AG}{FG} \tag{8}$$

Also,

$$\tan\theta_1 = \frac{AD}{CD} \tag{9}$$

Thus from both trigonometry and similarity of triangles we have:

$$\frac{AG}{FG} = \frac{AD}{CD} \tag{10}$$

$$FG = \frac{AG * CD}{AD} \tag{11}$$

Putting the values of various dimensions we obtain $FG = 6r$
Thus we have

Body part	Notation	Ratio
Lower torso	FE	12 r

Male figure anatomy ratio The male figure body parts ratio are also calculated following the real human body anatomy. Thus the part lengths that change for the male figure is the shoulder length as well as the lower torso. Otherwise the dimensions of the two upper limbs as well as the two lower limbs remain the same as in female figure. Also the dimensions of neck and head do not undergo any further changes.

The Fig. 5 depicts the deviation of the figure from female ones. It can also be noticed that the differentiating feature of female i.e. the bun has been left out which is quite natural. Thus we have the following body dimensions of the male figure (Table 2).

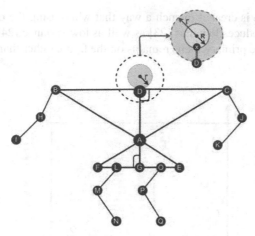

Fig. 5. Male figure calculation

Table 2. Ratio of different body parts.

Body part	Notation	Ratio
Head	R	0.67 r
Neck	r − R	0.33 r
Ulna and radius	HI, JK	3 r
Humerus	HB, CJ	3 r
Shoulder	BC	12 r
Upper abdomen	AD	4 r
Lower abdomen	AG	2 r
Femur	LM, OP	3 r
Tibia and fibula	MN, QP	3 r

Again following the above table of male figure dimensions the lower torso length has been calculated following the same trigonometrical and geometrical concepts as in female figure calculation. Thus we obtain,

Body part	Notation	Ratio
Lower torso	FE	6 r

Thus the main difference that can be observed in the generated male and female figure is the inversion of upper and lower triangle along a vertical segment separating lower and upper abdomen [22].

Dimension of Base Image matrix The base image matrix is the first generated image that acts as a background to the created figures. The dimension of the base image matrix, as shown in image 6 is created in such a way that while using the data set with some sort of models, it produces low bias [23] as well as low variance [24]. So its generated in such a way that the primary focus remains on the figure rather than the noise created by the background.

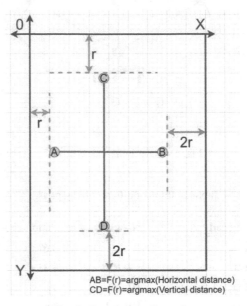

Fig. 6. Base image dimension

Thus from the Fig. 6 we have the following equations:

$$X \text{ axis} = \text{argmax}_i(\text{Horizontal aperture} + \lambda) + 3r \tag{12}$$

$$Y \text{ axis} = \text{argmax}_i(\text{Vertical apperture} + \lambda) + 3r \tag{13}$$

where λ serves as a regularization parameter. Thus depending upon the ratios of the concerned gender the following dimensions of the base image matrix have been obtained (Table 3).

Table 3. Dimensions of base image matrix

Gender	$\text{argmax}_i(X_{fig.})$	$\text{argmax}_i(Y_{fig.})$	X	Y
Female	18 r	14 r	21 r	17 r
Male	24 r	14 r	27 r	17 r

4.2 Selection of BGR Color Channels

Color channel selection was a major challenge in the entire data set creation. The color factor contributes significantly towards having a clear separating hyper plane [25] between the various targets. Thus it was determined through hyper parameter tuning with 3d plots of the data points. Out of various plots two types of plots were notable [26].

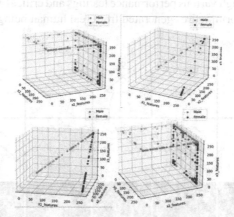

Fig. 7. 3d plot(1) with data points (Color figure online)

In the Fig. 7 which contains green male figure and blue female figure both with white background, it can be seen, though there can be a clear hyper plane separating the two targets, but there is some mixture of few data points. Al-though they can be separated with some sort of kernel trick, yet a call was taken to completely distinguish the targets so that even with a linear kernel one can have low variance. The Figs. 7 and 8 were plotted and visualised using plotting libraries of Python.

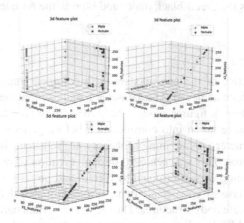

Fig. 8. 3d plot(2) with data points

Thus in the Fig. 8 which consists of green male figure with black background and blue female figure with white background, can have a clear separable linear hyper plane, without any mixture of data points unlike previous one, contributing towards very low variance during testing.

4.3 Final Image Data Set Generation

After undergoing through various performance testings and critical analysis, what finally obtained is the tribal form figures generated from real human beings.

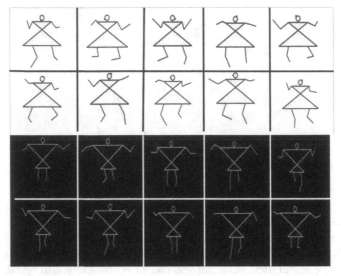

Fig. 9. Final female and male data set of figures (Color figure online)

The Fig. 9 depicts the green-black males and blue-white females.

5 Conclusion

Inline with the objective of the presented work, a complete generation of dataset of Warli art figures has been achieved. The dataset generated comprises of 30,000 spatially augmented male and female figures; ready to be used as dataset for deep learning models. Various parameters were taken into consideration before generating the figures. The most important parameter was defining a phenotypic trait that distinguishes between male and female figures. This was achieved through creation of bun in female figures, whose spatial positioning was determined by careful and precise selection of a domain of angles. Also, we have given special attention to anatomical details and differences between male and female body structures. The second important parameter was the color space in use. We used BGR color space because it gave outstanding results in terms of feature map-ping, as shown through the series of 3D plots that we discussed in Sect. 4.2.

Our generated dataset has already been tested with a real project. This dataset was fed into a Generative Adversarial Network (GAN) model [27] that, generated a noise matrix from the information extracted and used the generator [28] and discriminator trained and learned to build a complete different set of figures. These outcome was excellent and validated the working of our dataset. Ultimately, it can be inferred that the dataset generated has the potential to mitigate the issues relating to lack of available dataset in the field of tribal arts and can be used to train complex deep learning models.

References

1. Nair, R., Patil, O., Surve, N., Andheria, A., Linnell, J.D., Athreya, V.: Sharing spaces and entanglements with big cats: the Warli and their Waghoba in Maharashtra, India. Front. Conserv. Sci. (2021)
2. Whalley, A.: Dynamic Aesthetics and Advanced Geometries, pp. 63–82 (2019)
3. Neogi, D., Das, N., Deb, S.: A deep neural approach toward staining and tinting of monochrome images. In: Bianchini, M., Piuri, V., Das, S., Shaw, R.N. (eds.) Advanced Computing and Intelligent Technologies, vol. 218, pp. 25–36. Springer, Singapore (2022). https://doi.org/10.1007/978-981-16-2164-2_3
4. Das, N., Kundu, S., Deb, S.: Image synthesis of Warli tribal stick figures using generative adversarial networks. In: 2021 IEEE 6th International Conference on Computing, Communication and Automation (ICCCA), pp. 266–271 (2021)
5. Gawai, M.: Changing dimensions of Warli painting
6. Srivastava, M.: Warli art-a reflection of tribal culture of Maharashtra (2019)
7. Arya, N., Yadav, N., Sodhi, S.: Development of designs by adaptation of Warli art motifs. Int. J. Sci. Res. **5**, 6–3 (2016)
8. Saha, R.A., Ayub, A.F.M., Tarmizi, R.A.: The effects of geogebra on mathematics achievement: enlightening coordinate geometry learning. Procedia – Soc. Behav. Sci. **8**, 686–693 (2010). International Conference on Mathematics Education Research 2010 (ICMER 2010)
9. Ramalingam, S., Taguchi, Y., Marks, T., Tuzel, O.: P2: a minimal solution for registration of 3D points to 3D planes. In: Daniilidis, K., Maragos, P., Paragios, N. (eds.) Computer Vision, vol. 6315, pp. 436–449. Springer, Cham (2010). https://doi.org/10.1007/978-3-642-15555-0_32
10. Freeman, W.: Computer vision for interactive computer graphics. Comput. Graph. Appl. **18**, 42–53 (1998)
11. Lanier, L.: Manipulating Colors, Channels, and Spaces, pp. 14–35 (2018)
12. Li, T., Zhu, H.: Research on color algorithm of gray image based on a color channel, pp. 3747–3752 (2020)
13. Rovito, M., Maxson, R.: Male anatomy, pp. 39–52 (2020)
14. Zaidel, A.: Female anatomy and hysterical duality. Am. J. Psychoanal. **79**, 40–68 (2019). https://doi.org/10.1057/s11231-019-09180-8
15. Ning, G., Zhang, Z., He, Z.: Knowledge-guided deep fractal neural networks for human pose estimation (2017)
16. Eisenhart, L.: Coordinate geometry (2021)
17. Nelson, D.: Anatomical body planes. Science Trends (2019)
18. Jariyapunya, N., Musilová, B.: Analysis of female body measurements in comparison with international standard sizing systems (2014)
19. Mukhopadhyay, P.: Human Body Dimensions, pp. 17–28 (2019)
20. Cicchella, A.: Human body dimensions for biomechanical modelling: a review (2020)

21. Mutafchiev, D.Z., Savov, T.P.: On the solution of a trigonometric equation. Godshnik na Visshite Uchebni Zavedeniya. Prilozhna Matematika (2021)
22. Neogi, D., Das, N., Deb, S.: Fitnet: a deep neural network driven architecture for real time posture rectification. In: 2021 International Conference on Innovation and Intelligence for Informatics, Computing, and Technologies (3ICT), pp. 354–359 (2021)
23. Zor, C., Windeatt, T.: A unifying approach on bias and variance analysis for classification (2021)
24. Novello, P., Poëtte, G., Lugato, D., Congedo, P.: Variance based samples weighting for supervised deep learning (2021)
25. Diao, L., Gao, J., Deng, M.: Clustering by constructing hyper-planes (2020)
26. Khan, M.A., Dharejo, F., Deeba, F., Kim, J., Kim, H.: Toward developing tangling noise removal and blind in painting mechanism based on total variation in image processing (2021)
27. Goodfellow, I.J.: Generative adversarial networks (2014)
28. Yu, N., Li, K., Zhou, P., Malik, L., Davis, L., Fritz, M.: Inclusive GAN: improving data and minority coverage in generative models. In: Vedaldi, A., Bischof, H., Brox, T., Frahm, J.M. (eds.) Computer Vision, vol. 12367, pp. 377–393. Springer, Cham (2020). https://doi.org/10.1007/978-3-030-58542-6_23

Facial Emotion Recognition Based on Textural Pattern and Histogram of Oriented Gradient

Moutan Mukhopadhyay[1]([✉]), Aniruddha Dey[2], Ankush Ghosh[3], and Rabindra Nath Shaw[3]

[1] Department of Computer Science Engineering, MAKAUT, Kolkata, India
moutanbanerjee@gmail.com
[2] Department of Information Technology, MAKAUT, Kolkata, India
[3] School of Engineering and Applied Science, Neotia University, Kolkata, India

Abstract. In the past few years Emotion detection from images has become very popular due to its immense applications fields in day-to-day life. Various computer visions techniques are applied to detect facial emotions but it's a very challenging task in real time scenario. Most of real-life images are taken in the poor illumination condition and it fails to achieve good recognition accuracy. LBP and LTP both the textural feature descriptor come into the picture to overcome such condition. Histogram of Oriented Gradient (HOG) detects the edges and corners from the images very efficiently. Textural feature descriptor captures the local pattern. HOG and textural feature descriptor capture different types of information of the image. In the proposed method textural image and HOG image fusion is performed to increase the accuracy for recognizing the facial expression from images. The performance of proposed method is validated on CK+ dataset.

Keywords: Textural feature · Feature descriptor · Convolution neural network · Histogram oriented gradient · Emotion recognition

1 Introduction

Over the last decade facial expressions detection are gaining popularity for its numerous applications areas such as human computer interactions, interactive game development, virtual reality, surveillance, e-learning, health industry, law, safe driving and marketing sector etc. [1, 2].

According to Ekman, there are 7 basic emotional states such as fear, disgust surprise, anger, sadness and happiness and neutral. Human facial expressions can be detected by analysing facial features like eyelids, eyebrows and jawline, and mouth movements. Other than facial expressions there are several ways to detect human emotions such as text, speech, body gesture, heart beat etc. [3]. Of the several approaches facial expression and speech-based methods are prominent in human emotion detection. Facial expression-based approach is more efficient than speech-based approach in detecting the emotions such as happiness sadness, anger, and neutral [4]. Support Vector Machine (SVM), Multilayer Perceptron (MLP) [5] are some of the useful computer visions algorithms are

© The Author(s), under exclusive license to Springer Nature Switzerland AG 2023
R. N. Shaw et al. (Eds.): ICACIS 2022, CCIS 1749, pp. 111–119, 2023.
https://doi.org/10.1007/978-3-031-25088-0_9

used for detecting facial expressions. In the recent past deep learning-based algorithm Convolution neural network (CNN) has become very popular in the field of facial expression classification due to its automatic feature extraction method and better accuracy [6]. By fine tuning of CNN model good performance accuracy can be achieved in detecting seven basics emotions. CNN shows remarkable facial emotion recognition accuracy over different benchmark datasets such as CK+, FER 2013, JAFFE, KDEF, and RAF datasets [7].

The one of the major limitations of existing facial emotion recognition approach is, it performs very well under controlled environment such as good illumination condition. But in real life scenario facial images are often low-resolution images which are taken in poor lighting condition. So practically it is a quite challenging task to detect emotions from real life facial images. Textural feature descriptor Local binary pattern (LBP) is rotation and illumination invariant [8]. LBP is mostly used as feature extractor for textural classification and facial emotion recognition. LBP efficiently describes local information and requires low computation. As LBP is noise sensitive, so another textural feature descriptor Local Ternary Pattern (LTP) is proposed. In case noise handling LTP is more robust than LBP and it overcomes the problems of LBP [9].

LBP and LTP textural features images perform stably and robustly over low resolutions facial images. Over the facial expression dataset FER 2013 dataset LBP based CNN model achieves good recognition accuracy which is better than other feature extraction operators with CNN. LBP feature extraction technique achieves good accuracy in detecting facial expressions recognition [10]. Different LBP feature fusion-based approaches also performs well in facial emotion detection.

In the work a fusion technique of LBP and HOG feature vector are used in Deep stacked auto encoder to reduce the dimension and SVM is used as classifier [11]. Features extracted from different facial expression regions such as both the left and right eyes, mouth, nose, using a fusion of HOG and LBP feature vector. PCA reduce the dimensionality of new feature vector and SVM is used as classifier for detecting facial expression. The fusion approach was validated over the popular datasets. Such as JAFFE, CK +, RaFD [12]. HOG feature descriptor [13] scans the entire image and extracts the feature vector for each of the images of facial expression dataset. The newly produced feature vectors are passed through the SVM classifier for predicting facial emotions. In compared to other filters like Discrete Wavelet Transform (DWT) or Gabor filter HOG gives better recognition accuracy 85% [14]. HOG along with graph signal processing reduces the feature vector dimension and also decreases the training time of the KNN classifier.

In our approach benchmark datasets CK+ is converted into textural images such as HOG, LBP and LTP images. Then fusion of HOG and LBP or LTP images are performed. Then the deep learning model is trained with the fused images to detect the emotions from the fused textural images. Then recognition accuracy of HOG with LBP and HOG with LTP is compared.

The remaining part of the chapter is planned as follows. The proposed methodology is presented in Sect. 2, the experimental results discussion is presented in Sect. 3, and Sect. 4 draws the conclusion of the work.

2 Proposed Methodology

In this experiment, two textural facial image approaches LBP or LTP image is fused with HOG features images. As LBP and LTP textural images need low computational power and works well in low resolution images. HOG detects edges very efficiently. In our experiment a fusion of HOG and LBP and HOG and LTP have been performed. Proposed methodology is given in Fig. 1. In our proposed approach there are three steps:

i.   First step is conversion of images of facial expression dataset CK+ is into textural (LBP and LTP) images and also HOG images.
ii. Then in the second step fusion textural images (LBP or LTP) with HOG images are performed. Then all the class labelling has been done as original dataset.
iii. Training and testing of deep learning model CNN with newly created dataset which consists of fused images. Then finally emotion is predicted from the fused images.

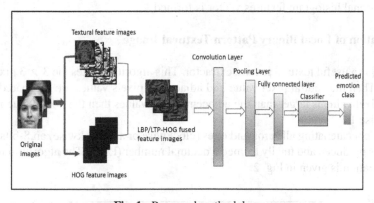

Fig. 1. Proposed methodology

A. Creation of HOG Features Image

HOG, is a popular global feature descriptor that useful for feature extraction and to detect the shape of the object. HOG is useful in detecting the edges and corners of the image. HOG only extracts the useful information and remove the unnecessary information from the image. HOG is illumination invariant textural feature descriptor. HOG simplifies the representations of images retaining only crucial information.HOG features of the selected image are obtained as [11]:

• The entire image is split into blocks and further into cells. The cell size is taken as 8 × 8 pixels or 16 × 16. Usually, a block is taken as 2 × 2 cells.
• The entire input images are divided into cells and blocks, where the default cell size is 8 × 8 pixels and 2 × 2 cells in a block.

- The gradient magnitude and orientations are calculated for each of the pixel in the cell within the block. The equations for calculating Gradient magnitude (Eq. 1) and orientations (Eq. 2) are given below:

$$\text{Gradient magnitude} = \sqrt{G_x^2 + G_y^2} \tag{1}$$

$$\text{Gradient orientation} = \tan^{-1}\left(\frac{G_y}{G_x}\right) \tag{2}$$

For each gradient magnitude, the corresponding bin (0–180^0) is assigned based on the histogram gradients. Total number of bins are 9. For the 64 pixels 9 features vectors are extracted. From each block a 36-point feature vector is extracted.

- Then the normalization is done for each block for reducing the effect of illumination condition variations.

Once histogram computation for all the blocks is over then finally after concatenation N dimensional histogram features vector is formed.

B. Creation of Local Binary Pattern Textural Image

LBP [15] is a useful textural feature extractor. This algorithm takes the 3×3 pixels sub images. Then the central pixel value and adjacent 8 pixels values are compared. If the central pixel value is larger than the adjacent pixels values then the pixel value is set to 0 otherwise 1.

After concatenating all zeros and ones (clockwise or anticlockwise) an 8-bits binary number is produced and finally formed a decimal number (LBP). The algorithm for LBP image creation is given in Fig. 2.

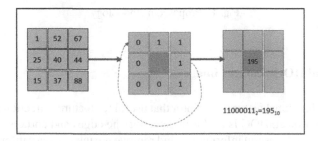

Fig. 2. LBP image creation

C. Creation of Local Ternary Pattern Image

Another textural feature descriptor LTP overcomes all the drawbacks of LBP as it is more robust to noise than LBP and illumination invariant [16]. LTP algorithm performs very well in case of low resolution and blurred images [17]. LTP is 3-valued codes such as −1, 0 and 1. The ternary code is partitioned into binary codes such as upper LBP and lower LBP to reduce the dimensionality. In the high LBP −1 is replaced with 0 and in the lower LBP with 1 is replaced with 0 and −1 is replaced with 1. Then the binary value of each pixel is produced and after concatenation a decimal number is formed. In this way by concatenating two binary patterns the final LTP image is produced. The algorithm for LBP image creation is given in Fig. 3.

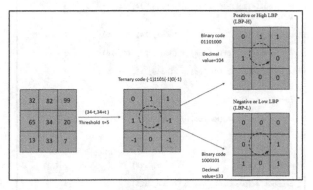

Fig. 3. LTP image creation

D. Fusion of HOG with Textural Images

From the CK+ dataset, at first all the images are transformed into HOG images LBP and LTP images. Using Open CV library in python the HOG image is blended or added with the LBP or LTP image. Equal weights are assigned to HOG and LBP or LTP images so that it gives a feeling of blending or fusion. Images are added as per the equation below:

$$G(x) = (1 - \alpha)F(x) + \alpha F1(x) \tag{3}$$

In Eq. (3) value of α varies between 0 to 1. Here two such as HOG and LBP or LTP images are taken to blend together. Here both the images are given equal weightage (α) such as of 0.5 and 0.5. Then the final fused image is formed by fusion of the HOG images and the LBP or LTP images. All the HOG and LBP or LTP images of CK+ images are transformed into fused images and corresponding emotions levels are added according to the original CK+ dataset. Finally new modified dataset of fused images is formed.

E. Facial Expression Classification from Fused Facial Images Using CNN

In our approach CNN architecture consists of three convolution layers and three max pooling layers followed by one fully connected layer. In the proposed architecture rectified linear activation function or ReLU is used in all the convolution layer and in the final output layer SoftMax activation function is used. The final layer produces a vector output which is the probability of each possible output classes such as happy, sad, contempt, fear, disgust, angry, surprise. For each layer both batch normalization and dropout have been performed. Thus, the CNN model predicts the final output as emotion class with highest probability score. The summary of proposed CNN architecture is given in the Fig. 4.

```
Layer (type)                  Output Shape            Param #
=================================================================
conv2d_12 (Conv2D)            (None, 48, 48, 6)        456

max_pooling2d_12 (MaxPoolin   (None, 24, 24, 6)        0
g2D)

conv2d_13 (Conv2D)            (None, 24, 24, 16)       2416

activation_4 (Activation)     (None, 24, 24, 16)       0

max_pooling2d_13 (MaxPoolin   (None, 12, 12, 16)       0
g2D)

conv2d_14 (Conv2D)            (None, 10, 10, 64)       9280

max_pooling2d_14 (MaxPoolin   (None, 5, 5, 64)         0
g2D)

flatten_4 (Flatten)           (None, 1600)             0

dense_8 (Dense)               (None, 128)              204928

dropout_4 (Dropout)           (None, 128)              0

dense_9 (Dense)               (None, 7)                903

=================================================================
Total params: 217,983
Trainable params: 217,983
Non-trainable params: 0
```

Fig. 4. Proposed CNN architecture summary

3   Results and Discussion

In the study, Extended Cohn-Kanade (CK+) facial expressions datasets [18] are converted into textural images using LBP and LTP and HOG operator. The Extended Cohn-Kanade (CK+) dataset [18] comprises sequences of 593 videos from 123 different people including male and female, and age of persons ranges between 18 to 50 years. Resolution of Image Frames are either 640 × 490 or 640 × 480 pixels. All the images of database are labelled with one of 7 basic emotion classes such as happiness, sadness, anger, neutral, disgust, fear, and surprise.

The image frames of the dataset are transformed into fused images of HOG and LBP or HOG and LTP. Then in the first approach, training and testing of the CNN model is performed on the dataset of HOG and LBP fused images.

In the second approach, the CNN model is trained on the dataset of LTP and HOG fused images. Then both the approaches were compared in terms of average emotion recognition accuracy.

Here we have compared two approaches. In the first method, the deep learning model is trained with the transformed dataset that consists of HOG and LBP fused images with labelled 7 basic emotions (same as original CK+ database). In the second method, the deep learning model is trained with the same transformed CK+ dataset that consists of HOG and LTP fused images with 7 basic emotions. For both the approaches the fused dataset is divided into two sets, training set and test set that consists of 80% sample images and 20% sample images respectively.

In the both the proposed approach fused (LBP + HOG or LTP + HOG) images are used as input to the model in the place of normal grey scale images.

Accuracy of CNN model over LBP and HOG fused images of CK+ database is compared with LTP and HOG fused images of CK+ database is compared. LBP-HOG fusion approach gives 97% accuracy while LTP-HOG fusion approach gives 96% facial emotion recognition accuracy. Training and validations accuracy graph of the LTP-HOG fusion and LBP-HOG fusion approach is given in the Fig. 5(a) and (b) respectively. Facial Expression Recognition accuracy (%) comparisons for different approaches are given in Table 1.

Table 1. The accuracy of the different methods

Methods	Accuracy
LBP + CNN [19]	79.56
CNN [20]	74%
Fine-tuned AlexNet CNN [5]	76.64
HOG-ESR [21]	88.3%
LBP + HOG + CNN	**97.2%**
LTP + HOG + CNN	**96%**

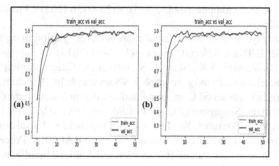

Fig. 5. Training and validation accuracy graph of facial emotion detection (a) LTP -HOG fused images (b) LBP-HOG fused images

4   Conclusion

This chapter proposes a novel fusion technique of Histogram oriented gradient (HOG) feature and LBP and LTP textural images in facial expression detection. The result section demonstrates the efficiency of the proposed method compared to other Facial Emotion Recognition approach. Both the textural image shows very good recognition accuracy while blending with HOG images. Textural images contain very low-level information and HOG contains only essential information of the edges and corners. Blending of HOG and textural images reduce the length of the feature vector. So, it is easier to train the CNN model with low level information and this method requires less computation time to train the classifier.

References

1. Ozdemir, M.A., Elagoz, B., Alaybeyoglu, A., Sadighzadeh, R., Akan, A.: Real time emotion recognition from facial expressions using CNN Architecture. In: 2019 Medical Technologies Congress (TIPTEKNO), Izmir, pp. 1–4 (2019). https://doi.org/10.1109/TIPTEKNO.2019. 8895215
2. Krithika, L.B., Lakshmi Priya, G.G.: Student Emotion Recognition System (SERS) for e-learning improvement based on learner concentration metric. In: International Conference on Computational Modeling and Security (CMS 2016), Bangalore (2016)
3. Ménard, M., Hamdi, H., Richard, P., Daucé, B.: Emotion recognition based on heart rate and skin conductance. In: 2nd International Conference on Physiological Computing Systems, Proceedings, pp. 26–32 (2015)
4. Nannapaneni, R.: Human Emotion Recognition Using Machine Learning. Dell Technologies Proven Professional Knowledge Sharing, pp. 1–24 (2019)
5. Kartali, A., Roglić, M., Barjaktarović, M., Đurić-Jovičić, M., Janković, M.: Real-time algorithms for facial emotion recognition: a comparison of different approaches. In: 14th Symposium on Neural Networks and Applications (NEUREL), Belgrade (2018)
6. Adholiya, A.: Facial expression recognition using CNN with keras. Biosci. Biotech. Res. Comm. Special Issue **14**(5), 47–50 (2021)
7. Mohan, K., Seal, A., Krejcar, O., Yazidi, A.: FER-net: facial expression recognition using deep neural net. Neural Comput. Appl. **33**(15), 9125–9136 (2021). https://doi.org/10.1007/ s00521-020-05676-y
8. Happy, S.L., Routray, A.: Automatic facial expression recognition using features of salient facial patches. IEEE Trans. Affect. Comput. **6**(1), 1–12 (2015)
9. Palimkar, P., Bajaj, V., Mal, A.K., Shaw, R.N., Ghosh, A.: Unique Action identifier by using magnetometer, accelerometer and gyroscope: KNN approach. In: Bianchini, M., Piuri, V., Das, S., Shaw, R.N. (eds.) Advanced Computing and Intelligent Technologies. LNNS, vol. 218, pp. 607–631. Springer, Singapore (2022). https://doi.org/10.1007/978-981-16-2164-2_48
10. Slimani, K., Kas, M., El Merabet, Y., Messoussi, R., Ruichek, Y.: Facial emotion recognition: a comparative analysis using 22 LBP variants. In: MedPRAI 2018: Proceedings of the 2nd Mediterranean Conference on Pattern Recognition and Artificial Intelligence, Rabat Morocco (2018)
11. Lakshmi, D., Ponnusamy, R.: Facial emotion recognition using modified HOG and LBP features with deep stacked autoencoders. Microprocess. Microsyst. **82**, 1–9 (2021)
12. Islam, B., Mahmud, F., Hossain, A.: High performance facial expression recognition system using facial region segmentation, fusion of HOG & LBP features and multiclass SVM. In: 10th International Conference on Electrical and Computer Engineering (ICECE), Dhaka, Bangladesh (2018)
13. Dalal, N., Triggs, B.: Histograms of oriented gradients for human detection. In: IEEE Computer Society Conference on Computer Vision and Pattern Recognition, San Diego, CA (2005)

14. Jain, C., Sawant, K., Rehman, M., Kumar, R.: Emotion detection and characterization using facial features. In: 3rd International Conference and Workshops on Recent Advances and Innovations in Engineering, Jaipur (2018)
15. Ojala, T., Ainen, M.P., Aenp, T.: Multiresolution gray-scale and rotation invariant texture classification with local binary patterns. IEEE Trans. Pattern Anal. Mach. Intell. **24**(7), 971–987 (2002)
16. Sinha, T., Chowdhury, T., Shaw, R.N., Ghosh, A.: Analysis and Prediction of COVID-19 confirmed cases using deep learning models: a comparative study. In: Bianchini, M., Piuri, V., Das, S., Shaw, R.N. (eds.) Advanced Computing and Intelligent Technologies. LNNS, vol. 218, pp. 207–218. Springer, Singapore (2022). https://doi.org/10.1007/978-981-16-2164-2_18
17. Ghosh, M., et.al.: Robustface recognition by fusing fuzzy type 2 induced multiple facial fused image. In: 2021 IEEE 4th International Conference on Computing, Power and Communication Technologies (GUCON), pp. 1–6 (2021). https://doi.org/10.1109/GUCON50781.2021.9573871
18. Lucey, P., Cohn, J.F., Kanade, T., Saragih, J., Ambadar, Z., Matthews, I.: The extended cohn-kanade dataset (CK+): a complete dataset for action unit and emotion-specified expression. In: IEEE Computer Society Conference on Computer Vision and Pattern Recognition – Workshops, pp. 94–101. IEEE, San Francisco (2010)
19. Mukhopadhyay, M., Dey, A., Shaw, R.N., Ghosh, A.: Facial emotion recognition based on textural pattern and convolutional neural network. In: IEEE 4th International Conference on Computing, Power and Communication Technologies (GUCON), Kuala Lumpur (2021)
20. Goyal, S.B., Bedi, P., Rajawat, A.S., Shaw, R.N., Ghosh, A.: Multi-objective fuzzy-swarm optimizer for data partitioning. In: Bianchini, M., Piuri, V., Das, S., Shaw, R.N. (eds.) Advanced Computing and Intelligent Technologies. LNNS, vol. 218, pp. 307–318. Springer, Singapore (2022). https://doi.org/10.1007/978-981-16-2164-2_25
21. Zhong, Y., Sun, L., Ge, C., Fan, H.: HOG-ESRs face emotion recognition algorithm based on HOG feature and ESRs method. Symmetry **13**(228), 1–18 (2021)

Fruit-Net: Fruits Recognition System Using Convolutional Neural Network

Olivia Saha Mandal[1], Aniruddha Dey[2(✉)], Subhrapratim Nath[2],
Rabindra Nath Shaw[3], and Ankush Ghosh[3]

[1] Department of Computer Science and Engineering, CIT, Kolkata, India
[2] Department of Computer Science and Engineering, MSIT, Kolkata, India
anidey007@gmail.com
[3] University Center for Research and Development (UCRD), Chandigarh University, Mohali, Punjab, India
{r.n.s,ankushghosh}@ieee.org

Abstract. For many industrial applications, classifying fruits is an essential process. A supermarket cashier can use a fruit classification system to distinguish between different types of fruit and their prices. Additionally, it can be used to determine whether a particular fruit species satisfies a person's nutritional needs. In this chapter, we propose a framework for fruit classification using deep learning techniques. More specifically, the framework is a comparison of two different deep learning architectures. The first is a 6-layer light model proposed for convolutional neural networks, and the second is a carefully tuned deep learning model for group-16 visual geometry. The proposed approach is tested using one publicly accessible color-image dataset. The images of fruit that were utilized for training came from our own photos, Google photos, and the data that ImageNet 2012 gave. This database contained 1.2 million images and 1,000 categories. The 1,200 fruit images that had been divided into six groups had been assessed and categorized. The average classification performance was 0.9688 out of a possible range of 0.8456 to 1.0 depending on the fruit, and each photo took about 0.25 s to classify. With only a few errors, the CNN algorithm was able to successfully classify the fruit photographs into the six categories. On the dataset, the CNN, VGG16, and Inception V3 models each achieved classification accuracy results of 96.88%, 72%, and 71.66% respectively.

Keywords: Fruit recognition · Convolutional neural network · Classification · VGG16 · Inception V3

1 Introduction

Fruits are an important part of a balanced diet and offer many health benefits. While some fruits are available throughout the year, some are exclusively during specific times of the year. India's economy continues to be significantly influenced by agriculture. In India, 70% of the land is used for agriculture. In terms of the top fruit growers worldwide,

India comes in third. Deep learning methods are therefore helpful for both marketers and consumers when used to categorize fruits. Currently, information technologies are playing a bigger role in the agriculture sector. We use deep learning-based techniques for fruit sorting to provide highest quality fruit to the customers.

Software for classifying and identifying fruits is crucial since it helps to raise the fruit's quality. It can be challenging to identify a fruit in a store. Manually classifying and valuing anything is difficult. The task of manually counting ripe fruits and assessing their quality is challenging. Rising labor costs, shortages of skilled workers, and rising storage costs are a few of the major problems with fruit production, marketing, storage and more. The soft computer vision system offers considerable information on the variety and quality of fruits by reducing costs, improving quality maintenance requirements, and delivering important information. Fruit classification and recognition is one of the most recent developments in computer vision. The set of features, the types of features, the features chosen from the extracted data, and the type of classifier used all have an impact on how accurate a fruit identification system is. Fruit images taken under poor conditions are of poor quality and hide recognizable features. In order to emphasize the nature and characteristics of fruit photographs, techniques for enhancing fruit images are needed.

In all facets of human living, including video surveillance, human-machine interfaces, and picture recovery, object detection [1–4] has received considerable attention. Face recognition in practical applications is extremely challenging due to the wide variations in illumination, posture, obstruction, and shoot point. A very significant and vibrant area of research is image classification. Face recognition, video analysis, image categorization, and other applications of image recognition are available. In the field of image recognition, deep learning (DL), a branch of machine learning (ML), has achieved great results [5]. Hierarchical structures are used to process image attributes by DL and greatly improve the effectiveness of image recognition [6]. In other words, the use of image recognition and DL in supply chain and logistics is starting to take hold as a concept. For example, picture recognition can improve logistics and shipping, as well as correct the faults that plague many fully automated transport vehicles as a result of widespread track identification issues [7].

Agro-related businesses such as food processing, marketing, packaging and fruit sorting have become an increasing focus of research in recent years. Because there are numerous types of the same fruit grown around the world (for example, over 7,100 different varieties of apple; see http://usapple.org), processing and sorting of special crop plants like banana, orange, cherry, apple, mango, and citrus require a lot of time and effort. Therefore, automation can reduce labor expenses and quickly boost production. In earlier studies, researchers proposed various approaches from CV to manually extract fruit traits and ML to classify the CV traits. Several DL approaches to quality assessment and robotic harvesting have been implemented for fruit detection and classification, but these algorithms have few classes and small datasets. In 2017, Liu et al. [8] presented literature analyses of novel fruit classification techniques. Fruit grading algorithms would need to quickly yield adequate accuracies given the development of deep learning [9, 10]. Modern computer vision techniques include real-time tracking of fruit and vegetable objects [13], nitrogen estimation in fruits and vegetables [12], automated fruit and vegetable sorting [11], and others. Most of the scientific fruit sorting methods, including pattern sorting, are sorted. When rating fruit quality, attention is given to both the overall visual changes and freshness. Despite deep learning's recent surge in popularity, deep learning methods were not used in more than half of the studies [14].

The motivation thorough examination of the available classification methods, the following flaws are looked into:

1. Poor categorization results are caused by the heterogeneous character of images, which is another significant hurdle.
2. Similarities in fruit species include similarities in shape, color, texture, and intensity.
3. High diversity within the variety, depending on the ripeness and maturity of the fruit.

This chapter introduces various CNN, VGG16, Inception V3 deep learning frameworks for fruit image classification to overcome the above shortcomings.

Create a fruit classification model using deep learning applications. In the proposed study, convolution layers are used to extract features from CNN, VGG16, and Inception V3 is employed to categorize the fruits. The main contributions of the chapter are:

- CNN, VGG16, Inception V3 deep learning programmers were used to classify the fruit photos.
- CNN, VGG16, Inception V3 were integrated to create a fruit recognition system that is frequently used for both recognition and classification. This study examines all of these methods for doing fruit recognition and classification.
- The experiment carried out utilizing the suggested method produced pretty effective and encouraging fruit classification findings.

The rest of the chapter is organized as follows. Section 2 defines proposed architectures for the CNN, VGG16, and InceptionV3 models. The investigational results on the fruit database Sect. 3. Finally, Sect. 4 summarises the concluding remarks.

2   Proposed Methods and CNN Structure

Convolutional neural networks, or CNN for short, are one type of deep learning model. Potential elements of such networks include loss layers, ReLU layers, fully-linked layers, convolution layers and average pooling layers. A Rectified Unit (ReLU) layer is then added to each CNN model, which is then followed by a Pooling layer or multiple convolutional layers, and one or more fully connected layers. This is how a CNN is typically built. A CNN considers the architecture of the photographs when analyzing photos, as opposed to a typical neural network, which disregards the structure of the data being processed. Note that traditional neural networks transform their input into a one-dimensional array before training a classifier. The learnt classifier will become more responsive to changes in location as a result.

Some of the finest solutions to problems from the MNIST dataset have been demonstrated using inter deep neural networks. The study claims that they employ numerous maps within each layer as well as many layers of pseudo neurons. Although the complexity of such nets makes training them more challenging, graphics processors and programming created expressly for them may help to get around this problem. Winner-take-all neurons with maximum pooling are used to build the network, and these neurons select the winner.

According to the results of yet another study, convolutional networks have been demonstrated to attain higher levels of accuracy in the field of computer vision. An all-convolutional network that performs at exceedingly high levels is described in full in the publication. The research chapter advises substituting equal-function convolutional layers for pooling and convolution layers. The problem can be resolved by employing shorter convolutional inside the network, which also functions as a form of regularization, however this may increase the amount of variables and add inter-feature correlations The explanations from each of the strata that make up the CNN network are given below.

2.1 Convolutional Layers

The name of these layers was inspired by the convolutional method. Condensation is a mathematical process that, when applied to two functions, produces a third function that is a single transformed (convolved) version of the original function. As a result of the total that only a portion of the original purpose is translated, the resulting function offers an integral of a point-wise multiplication of the two roles. The amount of translation of one of the main focuses affects this integral.

In a convolutional layer, clusters of neurons are joined together to form kernels. The kernels reliably maintain the same depth as the input, despite their very small size. Neurons in the kernel are connected only to a small area of input called the receptive field. This is because for high-dimensional inputs like images, connecting every cell to every early stop is very inefficient. The receptive field is the name given to this area of the input. For illustrative purposes, a picture that is 100 × 100 has 10,000 pixels, but if the first 100 neurons were present, there would be 1,000,000 parameters. Instead of storing weights across the dimensions of the input, each neuron stores weights for the dimensions of its core input. The kernels traverse the input space both horizontally and vertically, extracting high-level properties and resulting in a two-dimensional activation map. A value that specifies the speed at which the kernel is floating is called a parameter. Convolution layers are created by stacking the resulting activation maps, and these layers are then used to choose the inputs for the following layer.

A convolutional layer is added to 32 × 32 image to produce 28 × 28 activation map. The picture size is decreased when the number of convolutional layers is increased, which causes data loss and the disappearing gradient problem. We use padding to make this appropriate. The padding of input data with constants can make it larger. Since this constant is often zero, the method is known as zero padding. This means that the generated feature map will be padded to the same extent as the feature map. If add an odd number of additional columns, a second column is added to keep left and right padding consistent. According to this criterion, "valid" padding is equivalent to "no padding". This enables a kernel to ignore image pixels and not output them. The step affects the behavior of the convolution process when using larger images and more complex kernels, where the kernel shifts the input and the strides argument is used to determine the number of positions to skip. When a kernel slides the input, the strides argument is used to determine how many positions to skip. Rectified Linear Units-based activation function max is used in this layer. The nonlinear properties of the network are improved, not diminished.

2.2 Pooling Layers

Convolution is used to reduce the spatial dimension of the representation and the computational load of the network. Overfitting can also be avoided by pooling layers. The most typical filter size with a stride of two is 2×2. The input is consequently decreased by a factor of four.

2.3 Fully Connected Layers

Normal neural network layers are regarded as fully coupled layers. Each output from the layer below is linked to every neuron in a layer that has full connectivity. The calculations that are carried out in the background of a convolution layer are the same as those carried out in a fully linked layer. So it is possible to switch back and forth between the two (Fig. 1).

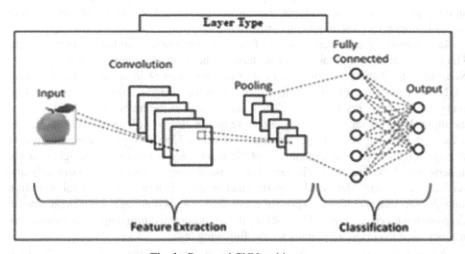

Fig. 1. Proposed CNN architecture

We employed a deep neural network to finish this challenge. The sorts of layers employed in this kind of network include convolution, pooling layers, rectified layers, convolution layer and loss layers, as was already established. Recurrent Unit (ReLU) layer, a Pooling layer, one or more convolutions, and finally one or even more fully connected layers are placed before each convolution. This is how a CNN is typically built.

Rectified Linear Unit (ReLU): A ReLU activation function executes a threshold operation to each input value, where any value negative is set as zero and for positive value output the input value [5]. ReLU function is defined as:

$$fr = ReLU(z) = max\{0, z\} \tag{1}$$

where fr is function RELU over input z and max() function takes values either 0 or input z.

Softmax: Softmax function that transforms a vector of numbers into a vector of probabilities [5]. Function is state as below:

$$\sigma(\vec{z})_i = \frac{e^{z_i}}{\sum_{j=1}^{K} e^{z_j}} \tag{2}$$

where σ is Softmax function, $\vec{z}$ input vector, e^{z_i} exponential function for input vector, K is number of classes, e^{z_j} is exponential function for output vector.

The CNN takes into account the shape of the images it is analyzing, unlike a typical neural network. One feature that sets the CNN apart from other neural networks is this one. A one-dimensional array is formed from an input before it is reassigned to a traditional neural network. The training classifier is less sensitive to changes in location as a result.

2.4 Architecture Based on VGG-16

A more complex CNN model is VGG-16. There are five convolutional operation blocks inside. A max-pooling layer connects adjacent blocks. Each block has a collection of 3×3 layers of convolutions. Within each block, the number of convolution kernels remains constant and increases from 64 in the first block to 512 in the last block [5, 7]. There are a total of 16 learnable layers.

2.5 Architecture Based on Inception V3

Convolutional neural networks are the foundation of the deep learning model known as Inception V3 that is used to classify images. The Inception V3 is a advanced version of the Inception V1, a foundational model that was first released as Google Net in 2014 [5, 7]. It was designed by a Google team, as the name suggests.

The data were over fit when numerous deep layers of convolutions were used in a model. The Inception V1 model employs the concept of having many filters of various sizes on the same level to prevent this from occurring. Thus, in the inception models, parallel layers are used in place of deep layers, making the model larger rather than deeper.

The first step is to identify the 200 kinds of objects within the image, also known as the local action of the item. The second is referred to as the separation of images and involves writing each image in one of the 1000 categories.

3   Empirical Results

Both the method used to create the data set and the information that is contained in it will be covered in this section. The apples were photographed while rotating it with a motor, and then selected frames from the video were used to produce the visuals. Fruits were seeded into a slow-speed motor (three revolutions per minute), rotor for a 20-s clip, which was then recorded. We placed a blank sheet of white chapter behind the fruit to serve as a backdrop. However, the backdrop was inconsistent due to the various ways the light was falling; therefore we had to provide an algorithm to distinguish the fruits from the background. Always start at the top of the image and mark all pixels there. The flood fill method is followed here. Then, if we find any pixels nearby that have a color range that is smaller than a certain value, we mark all of those pixels as well. Up until there are no more pixels to mark, we repeat the previous phase iteratively.

All of the defined pixels are taken into account as the background and are then filled with white. The pixel count after that is regarded as a segment of the item. A component of the algorithm used to create each movie is the maximum value that may be permitted for the distance between any two adjacent pixels. The fruit was reduced so that it would fit within a 300×300 image. Our aim to be able to handle considerably larger photos in the future, but this will require much prolonged training sessions. Table 1 describes number of fruit images for each fruit.

Table 1. Number of images for each fruit

Label	Training images	Test images
Freshapples	186	46
Freshbanana	190	43
Freshoranges	165	41
Rottenapples	263	65
Rottenbanana	245	61
Rottenoranges	178	44

Inception-v3 is introduced to get 72% accuracy whereas VGG16 used network model for image identification introduced to get 71.66% accuracy in the ImageNet database. The behavior of training and validation accuracy and loss versus epoch number during fine-tuning the VGG16 and Inception V3 is shown in Fig. 2 and Fig. 3, respectively (Fig. 4).

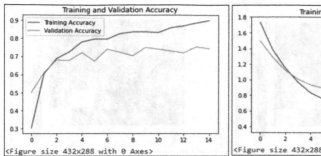
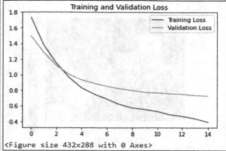

Fig. 2. Training and validation accuracy and loss of VGG16

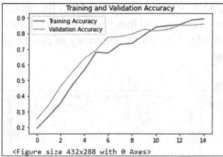
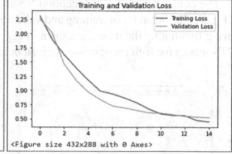

Fig. 3. Training and validation accuracy and loss of inception V3

Model Accuracy 0.72	precision	recall	f1-score	support
apple	0.81	0.68	0.74	50
banana	0.74	0.90	0.81	50
cantaloupe	0.63	0.58	0.60	50
grapefruit	0.72	0.42	0.53	50
grapes	0.73	0.90	0.80	50
kiwi	0.70	0.84	0.76	50
accuracy			0.72	300
macro avg	0.72	0.72	0.71	300
weighted avg	0.72	0.72	0.71	300

Model Accuracy 0.7166666666666667	precision	recall	f1-score	support
apple	0.58	0.72	0.64	50
banana	0.82	0.90	0.86	50
cantaloupe	0.71	0.48	0.57	50
grapefruit	0.59	0.40	0.48	50
grapes	0.72	0.94	0.82	50
kiwi	0.86	0.86	0.86	50
accuracy			0.72	300
macro avg	0.71	0.72	0.70	300
weighted avg	0.71	0.72	0.70	300

Fig. 4. Model accuracy of inception V3 and VGG16

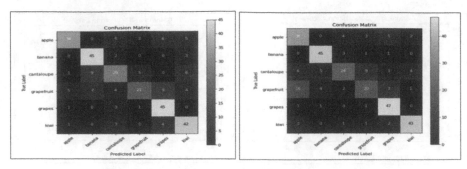

Fig. 5. Confusion matrix of inception V3 and VGG16

The confusion matrix of Inception V3 and VGG16 for the test dataset is illustrated in Fig. 5. The behavior of training and validation accuracy and loss versus epoch number during fine-tuning the model is shown in Fig. 6, Fig. 7 shows the summary of proposed CNN model for fruit recognition is given below:

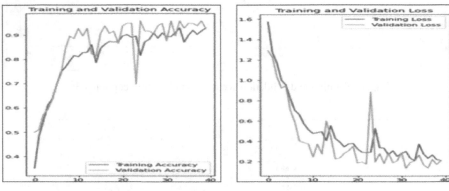

Fig. 6. Training and validation accuracy and loss of proposed CNN

```
Layer (type)                    Output Shape              Param #
================================================================
sequential (Sequential)         (32, 300, 300, 3)         0

conv2d (Conv2D)                 (32, 298, 298, 32)        896

max_pooling2d (MaxPooling2D)    (32, 149, 149, 32)        0

conv2d_1 (Conv2D)               (32, 147, 147, 64)        18496

max_pooling2d_1 (MaxPooling2     (32, 73, 73, 64)         0

conv2d_2 (Conv2D)               (32, 71, 71, 64)          36928

max_pooling2d_2 (MaxPooling2     (32, 35, 35, 64)         0

conv2d_3 (Conv2D)               (32, 33, 33, 64)          36928

max_pooling2d_3 (MaxPooling2     (32, 16, 16, 64)         0

conv2d_4 (Conv2D)               (32, 14, 14, 64)          36928

max_pooling2d_4 (MaxPooling2     (32, 7, 7, 64)           0

conv2d_5 (Conv2D)               (32, 5, 5, 64)            36928

max_pooling2d_5 (MaxPooling2     (32, 2, 2, 64)           0

flatten (Flatten)               (32, 256)                 0

dense (Dense)                   (32, 64)                  16448

dense_1 (Dense)                 (32, 6)                   390
================================================================
Epoch 1/40
31/31 [==============================] - 125s 3s/step - loss: 1.6974 - accuracy: 0.2853 - val_loss: 1.4010 - val_accuracy: 0.3750
Epoch 2/40
31/31 [==============================] - 101s 3s/step - loss: 1.4557 - accuracy: 0.3810 - val_loss: 1.3707 - val_accuracy: 0.3854
Epoch 3/40
31/31 [==============================] - 105s 3s/step - loss: 1.1688 - accuracy: 0.5333 - val_loss: 0.8481 - val_accuracy: 0.7188
Epoch 4/40
31/31 [==============================] - 112s 4s/step - loss: 1.0128 - accuracy: 0.6290 - val_loss: 0.9454 - val_accuracy: 0.6146
Epoch 5/40
31/31 [==============================] - 113s 4s/step - loss: 0.7981 - accuracy: 0.7127 - val_loss: 0.7851 - val_accuracy: 0.6979
Epoch 38/40
31/31 [==============================] - 120s 4s/step - loss: 0.2342 - accuracy: 0.9183 - val_loss: 0.2219 - val_accuracy: 0.8854
Epoch 39/40
31/31 [==============================] - 133s 4s/step - loss: 0.2922 - accuracy: 0.8871 - val_loss: 0.2789 - val_accuracy: 0.8958
Epoch 40/40
31/31 [==============================] - 123s 4s/step - loss: 0.2126 - accuracy: 0.9264 - val_loss: 0.2792 - val_accuracy: 0.8854
```

Fig. 7. Summary CNN model

Some of the correctly and incorrectly classified fruit images are shown in Fig. 8 and Fig. 9.

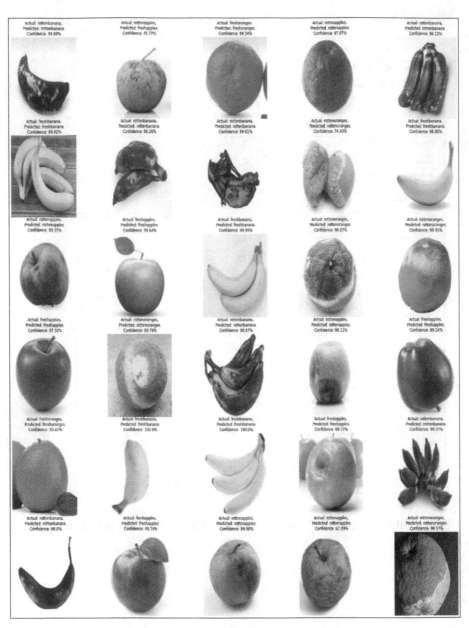

Fig. 8. Some of the fruit images that classified correctly

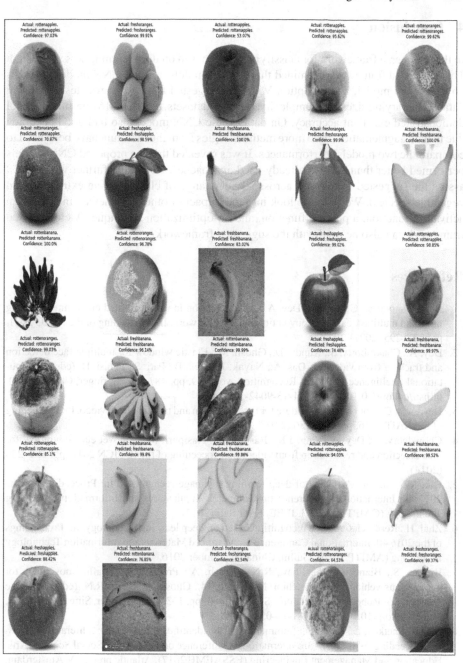

Fig. 9. Some of the fruit images that classified incorrectly

4 Conclusion

In this chapter, a framework for classifying fruits based on deep learning was suggested. The suggested framework examined three CNN models: a small CNN model, a VGG-16 fine-tuned model, and Inception V3. The suggested framework was tested on two datasets of varying sizes and complexity. On both datasets, the VGG-16 fine-tuned model demonstrated excellent accuracy. On dataset, the CNN model also had good accuracy due to data augmentation. Two more methodologies from the literature have been used to compare the two models' performances. It was revealed that the proposed CNN models performed better than the two already-used approaches. Regarding further work, we'll assess the suggested framework across a wider range of classes (using extra fruit and vegetable species). We will also look into the impact of other parameters, including an activation function, a pooling function, and an optimization technique. A cloud-based framework can also be used with the suggested framework.

References

1. Bhattacharya, S., Ghosh, M., Dey, A.: Face detection in unconstrained environments using modified multitask cascade convolutional neural network. In: Proceeding of the ICI2C 2021, pp. 287–295 (2021)
2. Dey, A., Chakraborty, S., Kundu, D., Ghosh, M.: Elastic window for multiple face detection and tracking from video. In: Das, A., Nayak, J., Naik, B., Pati, S., Pelusi, D. (eds.) Computational Intelligence in Pattern Recognition, vol. 999, pp. 487–496. Springer, Cham (2019). https://doi.org/10.1007/978-981-13-9042-5_41
3. Dey, A.: A Contour based procedure for face detection and tracking from video. In: Proceeding of the RAIT 2016, pp. 252–256 (2016)
4. Chowdhury, S., Dey, A., Sing, J.K., Basu, D.K., Nasipuri, M.: A novel elastic window for face detection and recognition from video. In: Proceeding of the ICCICN 2014, pp. 252–256 (2014)
5. Pak, M., Kim, S.: A review of deep learning in image recognition. In: Proceedings of the 2017 4th International Conference on Computer Applications and Information Processing Technology (CAIPT), pp. 1–3. IEEE, Kuta Bali (2017)
6. Zhai, H.: Research on image recognition based on deep learning technology. In: Proceedings of the 2016 4th International Conference on Advanced Materials and Information Technology Processing (AMITP 2016), Guilin, China, September 2016
7. Biswas, S., Bianchini, M., Shaw, R.N., Ghosh, A.: Prediction of traffic movement for autonomous vehicles. In: Bianchini, M., Simic, M., Ghosh, A., Shaw, R.N. (eds.) Machine Learning for Robotics Applications. SCI, vol. 960, pp. 153–168. Springer, Singapore (2021). https://doi.org/10.1007/978-981-16-0598-7_12
8. Liu, F., Snetkov, L., Lima, D.: Summary on fruit identification methods: a literature review. In: Proceedings of the 2017 3rd International Conference on Economics, Social Science, Arts, Education and Management Engineering (ESSAEME 2017), Atlantic press, AV Amsterdam, Netherlands, July 2017
9. Bhargava, A., Bansal, A.: Fruits and vegetables quality evaluation using computer vision: a review. J. King Saud Univ. Comput. Inf. Sci. **33**, 243–257 (2018)
10. Pandey, R., Naik, S., Marfatia, R.: Image processing and machine learning for automated fruit grading system: a technical review. Int. J. Comput. Appl. **81**(16), 29–39 (2013)

11. Cunha, J.B.: Application of image processing techniques in the characterization of plant leafs. In: IEEE International Symposium on Industrial Electronics, pp. 612–616 (2003)
12. Tewari, V.K., Arudra, A.K., Kumar, S.P., Pandey, V., Chandel, N.S.: Estimation of plant nitrogen content using digital image processing. Agric. Eng. Int. CIGR J. **15**(2), 78–86 (2013)
13. Mukhopadhyay, M., et al.: Facial emotion recognition based on textural pattern and convolutional neural network. In: 2021 IEEE 4th International Conference on Computing, Power and Communication Technologies (GUCON), pp. 1–6 (2021). https://doi.org/10.1109/GUCON50781.2021.9573860
14. Tripathi, M.K., Maktedar, D.D.: A role of computer vision in fruits and vegetables among various horticulture products of agriculture fields: a survey. Inf. Process. Agric. **7**, 183 (2019)

Prediction of Glaucoma Using Deep Learning Based Approaches

Tiyasha Dhara[1][(✉)], Arpan Adhikary[1], Koushik Majumder[1], Santanu Chatterjee[1], Rabindra Nath Shaw[2], and Ankush Ghosh[2]

[1] Department of Computer Science and Engineering, Maulana Abul Kalam Azad University of Technology, Kolkata, West Bengal, India
tiyashadhara98@gmail.com
[2] University Center for Research and Development (UCRD), Chandigarh University, Mohali, Punjab, India

Abstract. Glaucoma is an eye related condition, which mainly occurs due to the damage to the optic nerve, that connects the eye to our brain. Unfortunately, the damage due to glaucoma is irreversible and it is usually with high pressure in the eye. There are different types of glaucoma. Some are primary there is no other eye condition involved and it can be open-angle or closed-angle. Some are secondary glaucoma because of other eye conditions like inflammation in the eye or previous surgeries etc. But in general, most of the glaucoma patients have no symptoms. Glaucoma detection become a very popular field of study and research. Different approaches are being used by different researchers in Glaucoma classification and detection. In this chapter, we have taken a handwritten dataset from Kaggle which consists of the glaucomatous eye and healthy normal eye. We have applied VGG19, Xception which is a CNN architecture to achieve the model's performance in terms of sensitivity, specificity, accuracy and F1 score. This research outcome will help in the early diagnosis of Glaucoma disease in healthcare industry.

Keywords: Glaucoma · Convolutional Neural Network (CNN) · VGG16 · Xception · ResNet50 · DenseNet · MobileNet

1 Introduction

Glaucoma is basically an eye disease that occurs due to the damage of our optic nerve. This nerve transfers information from the eye to the brain and that is the main job role of the optic nerve. There has aqueous humor fluid in the front part of the eye and that fluid is drained out from the cornea through the channel. If any case channel gets blocked inside pressure on the eye increases [1, 2]. This natural pressure is called intraocular pressure (IOP). As this IOP increases optic nerve may become damaged. People who have a family history, high blood pressure, age over 60, or diabetes have a high chance to get affected. There exist five severe types of glaucoma. Chronic or open-angle glaucoma, acute or angle-closure glaucoma, secondary glaucoma, normal-tension glaucoma and congenital glaucoma. One of the most common type of glaucoma is open-angle glaucoma. [3, 4] In

R. N. Shaw et al. (Eds.): ICACIS 2022, CCIS 1749, pp. 134–145, 2023.
https://doi.org/10.1007/978-3-031-25088-0_11

our proposed work, we have analyzed glaucoma affected eye and healthy eye classifying using RESNET, which is a CNN architecture. Section 2 gives the detailed description about the related works in this area and Sect. 3 gives the detailed information about our collected dataset. In the rest sections, we have discussed the detailed about data preparation, proposed methodology, results and conclusion.

2 Related Works

In the recent past, ML and DL classifiers have been taken into consideration for many researches by the researchers. Using the ML and DL classifiers, models are made capable of classifying glaucoma more accurately within very less time period. In this section, some of the related works related to our chapter and their results are discussed.

Jinho Lee et al. [5] in their study built a progression-based ML model, which will predict normal-tension glaucoma. For this, visual field examination was taken for each of the users twice. This test was carried out within 3 months of intervals. Functional changes on VF tests were classified for each eye. RF and extra trees classifier were used for classification. Using extra-trees classifier, AUC of 0.811 was achieved. Whereas, using RF classifier, same AUC was achieved.

Serte et al. [6] built a observable deep learning model to detect glaucoma using transfer learning approaches i.e., Xception, GoogLeNet, ResNet-50and ResNet-152. Five popular datasets i.e., Drishti-GS1, HRF, sjchoi86-HRF, RIM-ONE, ACRIMA were used in their work. They compared their work with other papers and got the highest AUC 0.95 with HRF dataset by using ResNet-152.

Christopher et al. [7] evaluated ResNet50 and ResNet34 over the "Diagnostic Innovations in Glaucoma Study/African Descent and Glaucoma Evaluation Study" and "Matsue Red Cross Hospital" two independent dataset. Those two datasets were collected from United States and Japan. They got highest AUC 95% over the DIGS/ADAGES dataset.

Qaisar Abbas [8] proposed a "Glaucoma-Deep" system and calculated the accuracy 99%, sensitivity 84.50%, specificity 98.01%. The author had tested his system by using 1200 publicly and privately available retinal images. To extract the features from raw dataset CNN architecture were used. "DRIONS-DB", "sjchoi86-HRF", "HRF-dataset" and "PRV-Glaucoma" popular datasets were used in his work.

Chai et al. [9] composed a multi-branch neural network (MB-NN) model to extract features automatically from a collected dataset. They used AlexNet, VGG16, Inception_V3, CNN and MB-NN models in their work. They achieved accuracy 0.9151, sensitivity 0.9233 and specificity 0.9090 by using MB-NN model.

3 Data Collection

The dataset is acquired from Kaggle which contains both training and test data of glaucoma patient and healthy patient [10]. The dataset contains 50 training images along with 51 test images. There have two different folders one is images and another one is GT in each directory. In the image folder optic disk, cup masks are associated with the image (Figs. 1 and 2).

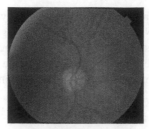

Fig. 1. Glaucomatous eye.

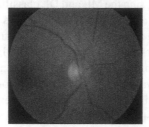

Fig. 2. Normal eye.

4   Data Preparation

The work was done on Jupyter notebook. Images inside the training and test folder loaded to the corresponding location in jupyter. We have separated the dataset into training and testing images in 8:2 ratio. Then the images were loaded in color mode and the target size is set to (224 × 224). In the next section, we give brief description of our used models.

5   Models Used in Our Work

VGG16 Model

Visual Geometry Group at Oxford has been created VGG which is a successor of Alexnet. VGG uses some knowledge from its predecessor and improve on them. VGG uses CNN to improve accuracy. In that paper we used VGG16 which is a variant of VGG model. VGG 16 is one of the CNN architectures which was proposed by Andrew Zisserman and Karen Simonyan. Main advantage of VGG 16 is that it contains the convolutional layers of 3 × 3 filter along with stride 1. Also it contains the maxpool layer of 2 × 2 filter of stride 2 [11]. It ends with 2 fully connected layers with softmax for output. It has 16 layers that have weights. It was trained over 14 milion images of 1000 classes.

Convolutional layer input for VGG16 is 244 × 244 RGB image is fixed. The filter size of the convolutional layer is 3 × 3 and all the given imagers are passes through the convolution layer.

Images are passed through the initial stacks of two convolutional layers, which are of size 3 × 3. Here the 'relu' activation function is used. Both of the layers contain 64 filters. Here the convolutional stride is fixed to 1 pixel. The output activation map remains same as the input image dimension. This activation maps are then passed through the spatial max-pooling over a 2 × 2 pixel window, where the stride is also set to 2 pixels. Thus, the activation at the end of the initial stack become of size 112 × 112 × 64. The activation flow through the next stack, which is similar as the first stack but contains 128 filters instead of 64 filters. So, the activation after 2nd layer become of size 56 × 56 × 128. The third layer contains three convolution layers followed by a max pool layer. Here 256 filters are applied and thus the size of the output stack become of 28 × 28 × 256. At the end of these stacks, the output become of size 7 × 7 × 512. The stack of these convolutional layers is followed by three fully connected layers, which contains fully connected layers in-between. Initial two layers have 4096 neurons each. The last connected layer servers as the output layer of the model. At the output layer, 'softmax' is used as the activation layer for categorical classification.

It is a pre-trained model, which is available in the 'keras' library. It is trained on 'imagenet' dataset which contains 1000 possible classes. In our work, we have used the transfer learning method to train our custom PD dataset. This model works well for it (Fig. 3).

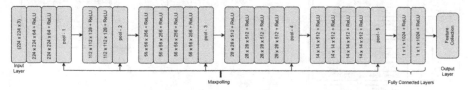

Fig. 3. VGG16 architecture.

Xception
Xception is a deep CNN architecture that has 71 layers. That also known as an extreme version of the inception module. It was introduced by Google in 2015. Xception is one of the extension of the Inception model architecture, which replaces the standard inception modules. ILSVRC dataset was tested for this architecture, which is consisted of 15 million labeled high-resolution images with 22,000 categories in it [12]. For input image inception has used 1 × 1 convolutional layer. From each input spaces, different types of filters were used on each of the depth spaces. Reverse step is done by xception model. Instead of compressing the input images, firstly, it applies the filters on each of the depth map. Finally compresses the input space by applying 1x1 convolutional across the depth.

Input data or input image first go through the entry level then reached to middle level that step repeated eight times. Finally, the input data reaches to exit level. BN (Batch Normalization) is done on each layer. Xception architecture overperformed over VGG-19 in most of the classical classification challenges.

Xception mainly relies on two main points one is Depth wise Separable Convolution another one is Point wise Separable Convolution. Where Depth wise convolution is the channel-wise (n × n) spatial convolution. If we have 10 channels, then we must have 10 (n × n) spatial convolution. Point wise convolution is 1 × 1 convolution which is used to change the dimension of the image, after depth wise separation is done.

It is an open-source module of Keras application. We have used this pre-defined model to our dataset and it has classified the subjects. The performance of Xception model was outstanding for our dataset (Fig. 4).

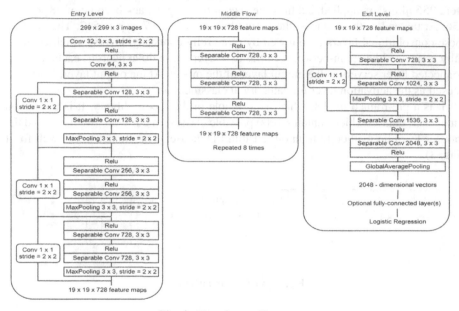

Fig. 4. Xception architecture.

ResNet50

Resnet50 model is 50 layers deep residual network. To solve the difficult problem (i.e. image recognition, face recognition, image classification) accurately deep convolution neural network has been introduced. In CNN there have added advantage to increase the number of layers to solve more difficult problem. Due to the extra added layers difficulty may arise on the time of training, here the Resnet introduced. It was first introduced in 2015 and won the first position in ILSVRC 2015 classification competition. With the help of one million image from imagenet database that model was trained. Resnet-50 architecture contains sequences of convolutional blocks with average pooling. Softmax was used at the final layer for classification. Conv1_x, conv2_x, conv3_x, conv4_x and conv5_x are the 5 convolution layers in that architecture. The given input image is passing through a convolutional layer, which has 64 filters followed by a maxpooling layer and kernel size of (7 × 7). The maxpooling layer has the stride length of 2 for both the cases. In conv2_x, the layers are grouped in pairs as the residual networks are connected together. This process continues till the 5th convolutional layer. After this layer, aver-agepooling is applied at the fully connected layer, followed by a softmax function for classification.

By using identity mapping it also settled down vanishing gradient problem by using alternative shortcut for the gradient. Resnet also resolve the overfitting problem. Skip connection is one of the major advantages of RasNet50. Due to those reasons ResNet performed well if the layers will increase. ResNet improves the efficiency of the neural network minimizing the percentage of error. This makes the model training easier and much deeper than the previous layers (Fig. 5).

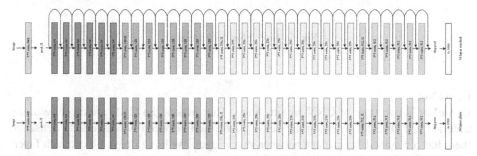

Fig. 5. ResNet50 architecture.

MobileNet

Mobilenet is a faster and smaller model convolution neural network architecture that is mainly used for mobile applications. Due to its small size, it uses in embedded and mobile applications hence it is named as MobileNet. That has 28 layers. The very first layer of mobilenet is the full convolution layer and other consecutive layers are BU (Batch Normalization) layer and ReLu activations. The last three layers are the pooling layers, which are followed by the fully connected layer and softmax activations. MobileNet is used for classification prediction. It uses a depthwise separable convolution layer which makes mobilenet faster. Depthwise separable convolution reduces the parameter as compared with the normal same depth net.

MobileNet is a depth wise separable convolution that helps to reduce the model size and complexity. Each depthwise separable convolution consists of a pointwise and depthwise convolution. For each of the output channel, depthwise convolution create the single filter. Combining the output of the depthwise convolution, pointwise convolution create 1×1 convolution. Depthwise convolution separates the output into two layers: one separate layer for filtering and another layer for combining.

A standard convolutional layer takes the input as ($DF \times DF \times M$) with the feature map F. It produces a ($DF \times DF \times N$) with feature map G. Here M is the number of input channels and N is the number of output channel. DF is the spatial height and width for the input feature map. The standard convolutional layer is parameterized of size ($DK \times DK \times M \times N$), where DK is the spatial dimension of the kernel, which is assumed to be square. Depthwise convolution is extremely efficient related to standard convolution. It only filters the input channels but does not combine them to create new features. MobileNet uses (3×3) depthwise separable convolutions, that takes 8–9 times less computation times than standard convolution (Fig. 6).

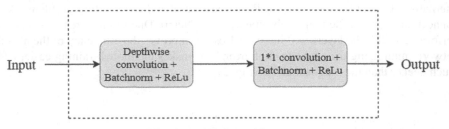

Fig. 6. MobileNet architecture.

DenseNet

DenseNet is one type of CNN architechture. That makes the CNN architecture more accurate and efficient by using the dense connection between two layers. In densenet there has a connectivity pattern between every layer. Within a dense block, each layer is connected. Every layer collects the feature map information from its previous layer which makes a model more compact and resolves the overfitting problem. Densenet is much deeper so training a model is easier. In case of ResNet previous layers are merged with the next layer where as DenseNet merge all the previous layer output to the next layer.

Each and every layer of DenseNet adds only a limited number of parameter and improve the gradient flow in the network. A dense block is the group of layers, that are connected to all the previous layers. A single dense layer is made of batch normalization, a (3×3) convolution and ReLU activation. Whereas, transition layer is made of batch normalization, (1×1) convolution and average pooling (Fig. 7).

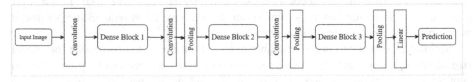

Fig. 7. DenseNet architecture.

6   Proposed Methodology

In this proposed methodology, we have used CNN architecture for glaucoma classification. CNN automatically preprocesses the input images for extracting the features. The VGG16 classifier contains 16 layers of neural networks for classification. It is used for large-scale image recognition. We have used the dataset for both training and testing purposes. It is then preprocessed for feature extraction. We have used 4 different CNN architectures i.e., VGG16, Exception, DenseNet, and MobileNet for glaucoma classification. Here we used these models on our dataset and compared their results. For the models we fixed the input size to (100 × 100), where the weights were set to 'imagine' on average pooling. For input layers, the activation function was 'relu' and for the dense layer 'softmax' was used as the activation function. As we have two output labels i.e., glaucoma and normal, so we have taken the loss function as 'categorical_crossentropy' for all the models. While training the model, 6 images were sent in a single batch. We have passed 26 iterations for the VGG16 model, whereas 3000 iterations were passed for the Xception model. For DenseNet, we passed 30 epochs. Whereas for MobileNet, the batch size was 8. All the models gave us decent accuracy. All these architectures are Keras applications and they can be called through tensorflow.keras module. We have used the 'adam' optimizer for all the cases. These all methods were done as a part of Transfer learning. All the methods are pretrained using 'imagenet' image set. We have used the pre-trained models in our dataset. As our dataset contains both glaucomatous and normal eye, so classification was easy using these pre-trained models.

7 Result and Discussion

The main contribution of this work was the proposal of the image data as input to the CNN for glaucoma detection. CNN includes convolution layers for feature learning and fully connected layers for glaucoma detection. The most effective result obtained for this work is 90%. Below, we have attached the snapshots of our obtained results. In our work, we have taken the transfer learning concept. We have taken VGG16, Xception, ResNet50, MobileNet and DenseNet for our work. These models are pre-trained with imagenet set. We have taken this advantage and used these pre-trained models to our dataset. Below, we have attached the snapshots of all the relevant results (Fig. 8).

	precision	recall	f1-score	support
0	0.67	1.00	0.80	4
1	1.00	0.67	0.80	6
accuracy			0.80	10
macro avg	0.83	0.83	0.80	10
weighted avg	0.87	0.80	0.80	10

Fig. 8. Accuracy measurement using VGG16.

We have also measured the accuracy comparison between training and validation data for Glaucoma eye. In this graph, X-axis denotes the no of epochs played. Whereas, Y-axis denots the accuracy measurement (Fig. 9).

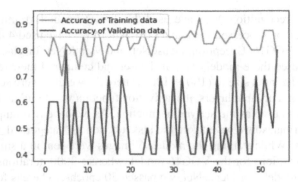

Fig. 9. Accuracy comparison between training and validation data using VGG16.

Xception model also showed the same accuracy as VGG16. We have also measured precision, recall and f1-score for the model (Fig. 10).

	precision	recall	f1-score	support
0	1.00	0.50	0.67	4
1	0.75	1.00	0.86	6
accuracy			0.80	10
macro avg	0.88	0.75	0.76	10
weighted avg	0.85	0.80	0.78	10

Fig. 10. Accuracy measurement using Xception.

The accuracy comparison is also done for Xception model. X-axis here denotes the number of epochs runs and y axis denotes the accuracy measurement (Fig. 11).

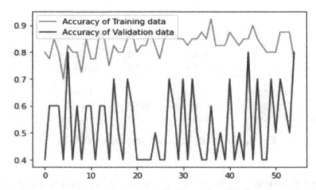

Fig. 11. Accuracy comparison between training and validation data using Xception.

MobileNet gave the same accuracy like the previous two models. For this model, the input images were flipped vertically. But horizontal flip was not done for this model (Fig. 12).

	precision	recall	f1-score	support
0	0.67	1.00	0.80	4
1	1.00	0.67	0.80	6
accuracy			0.80	10
macro avg	0.83	0.83	0.80	10
weighted avg	0.87	0.80	0.80	10

Fig. 12. Accuracy measurement using MobileNet.

The training accuracy was more for mobilenet than the validation accuracy. The number of epochs runs for this work is 100 (Fig. 13).

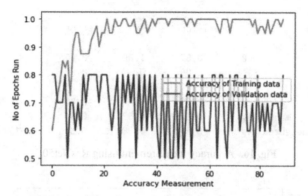

Fig. 13. Accuracy comparison between training and validation data using MobileNet.

DenseNet gave the highest accuracy for our work. We achieve 90% accuracy for our work. So, we can consider DenseNet as our benchmark model (Fig. 14).

	precision	recall	f1-score	support
0	0.80	1.00	0.89	4
1	1.00	0.83	0.91	6
accuracy			0.90	10
macro avg	0.90	0.92	0.90	10
weighted avg	0.92	0.90	0.90	10

Fig. 14. Accuracy measurement using DenseNet.

The accuracy measurement for this gives us better visual representation than the others. We can compare this accuracy with other models and find the difference between DenseNet and other models (Figs. 15, 16 and 17).

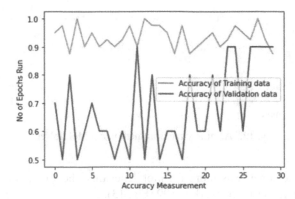

Fig. 15. Accuracy comparison between training and validation data using DenseNet.

	precision	recall	f1-score	support
0	0.67	1.00	0.80	6
1	1.00	0.67	0.80	9
accuracy			0.80	15
macro avg	0.83	0.83	0.80	15
weighted avg	0.87	0.80	0.80	15

Fig. 16. Accuracy measurement using ResNet50.

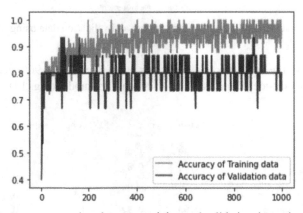

Fig. 17. Accuracy comparison between training and validation data using ResNet50.

8   Result and Discussion

Glaucoma is one of the eye nerve diseases that challenges the population globally. In our dataset, mainly two types of images i.e., Glaucoma and healthy were taken. After running the CNN models, we have achieved decent accuracy. The result showed that VGG16 gave 80% accuracy for glaucoma and healthy images. Whereas, using Xception model, we achieved 80% accuracy for glaucoma and healthy images. But as we have limited data to train, so, in future we can train the model with more images. More training images will enable the model to learn faster and be more accurate. VGG16 and Xception are already pretrained model. We have also use MobileNet, DenseNet, ResNet. Got better accuracy 90% in DenseNet architecture. So, our next task will be to use CNN with more layers. Keras also has different applications unlike VGG19 and Xception. Those applications can also be tested further to check the accuracy. The best model then can be used for glaucoma classification. Also, for this particular dataset, different models can take different times to run. The most suitable model, time wise and accuracy wise can be taken for further test.

References

1. Wang, P., et al.: Machine learning models for diagnosing glaucoma from retinal nerve fiber layer thickness maps. Ophthalmol. Glaucoma **2**(6), 422–428 (2019)
2. Son, J., Shin, J.Y., Kim, H.D., Jung, K.H., Park, K.H., Park, S.J.: Development and validation of deep learning models for screening multiple abnormal findings in retinal fundus images. Ophthalmology **127**(1), 85–94 (2020)
3. Thakur, N., Juneja, M.: Classification of glaucoma using hybrid features with machine learning approaches. Biomed. Sig. Process. Control **62**, 102137 (2020)
4. Asaoka, R., Murata, H., Iwase, A., Araie, M.: Detecting preperimetric glaucoma with standard automated perimetry using a deep learning classifier. Ophthalmology **123**(9), 1974–1980 (2016)
5. Lee, J., Kim, Y.K., Jeoung, J.W., Ha, A., Kim, Y.W., Park, K.H.: Machine learning classifiers-based prediction of normal-tension glaucoma progression in young myopic patients. Jpn. J. Ophthalmol. **64**(1), 68–76 (2019). https://doi.org/10.1007/s10384-019-00706-2
6. Serte, S., Serener, A.: A generalized deep learning model for glaucoma detection. In: 2019 3rd International Symposium on Multidisciplinary Studies and Innovative Technologies (ISMSIT), pp. 1–5. IEEE (2019)
7. Christopher, M., et al.: Effects of study population, labeling and training on glaucoma detection using deep learning algorithms. Transl. Vis. Sci. Technol. **9**(2), 27 (2020)
8. Abbas, Q.: Glaucoma-deep: detection of glaucoma eye disease on retinal fundus images using deep learning. Int. J. Adv. Comput. Sci. Appl. **8**(6), 41–45 (2017)
9. Chai, Y., Liu, H., Xu, J.: Glaucoma diagnosis based on both hidden features and domain knowledge through deep learning models. Knowl.-Based Syst. **161**, 147–156 (2018)
10. Dataset used for the paper. https://www.kaggle.com/datasets/lokeshsaipureddi/drishtigs-retina-dataset-for-onh-segmentation
11. Chakraborty, A., Chatterjee, S., Majumder, K., Shaw, R.N., Ghosh, A.: A comparative study of myocardial infarction detection from ECG data using machine learning. In: Bianchini, M., Piuri, V., Das, S., Shaw, R.N. (eds.) Advanced Computing and Intelligent Technologies. LNNS, vol. 218, pp. 257–267. Springer, Singapore (2022). https://doi.org/10.1007/978-981-16-2164-2_21
12. Ting, D.S.W., et al.: Development and validation of a deep learning system for diabetic retinopathy and related eye diseases using retinal images from multiethnic populations with diabetes. JAMA **318**(22), 2211–2223 (2017)

Detection of Parkinson's Disease Through Telemonitoring and Machine Learning Classifiers

Arpan Adhikary[1], Koushik Majumder[1(✉)], Santanu Chatterjee[1], Anurag Dasgupta[2], Rabindra Nath Shaw[3], and Ankush Ghosh[3]

[1] Department of Computer Science and Engineering, Maulana Abul Kalam Azad University of Technology, West Bengal, Kolkata, India
koushikwbutcse@gmail.com
[2] Valdosta State University, Valdosta, GA 31698, USA
[3] University Center for Research and Development (UCRD), Chandigarh University, Mohali, Punjab, India

Abstract. Parkinson's Disease (PD) is one of the incurable neurodegenerative disorders. This progressive nervous system disorder mainly occurs at the age of early 60 and become worst day by day. Till now we do not have any particular medicine or surgery for this disease. As PD cannot be fully curable, so it is important to detect PD at its early stage to prevent more harm. PD detection is also important at its early stage as by the time of manifestation of clinical symptoms occur, more than 60% dopaminergic neurons lost by the time. Parkinson's Disease detection has now become a popular field of study and research. In this chapter, we use the audio medical measurement of 42 people, who are distinguished with early-stage Parkinson's Disease. The subjects were hired for a six months trial of a remote-controlled disease to remotely diagnose between PD and healthy people. The data were automatically recorded in subjects' homes. We have applied Linear Regression, Polynomial Regression, Elastic-Net, Lasso, Decision Tree, k-Nearest Neighbour, Random Forest and Gradient Boosting Regression on the dataset, to achieve the model's performance in terms of accuracy. This research will be useful in early diagnosis of Parkinson's disease and to prevent its' harmful impact on the patients.

Keywords: Parkinson's Disease (PD) · Machine learning · Linear regression · Polynomial regression · Elastic-net · Lasso · Decision tree · k-Nearest neighbour · Random forest and gradient boosting regression

1 Introduction

Parkinson's Disease (PD) is a common brain and nerve disorder. Generally, it affects the people mainly above 60 but depending upon some external scenarios, it can affect people of different ages. It can be genetic. People, exposed to pesticides and medicine like phenothiazine, reserpine etc. for a long period of time can also be affected by this disease

[1, 2]. People with PD meet some well-known symptoms i.e., slowness of movement, tremoring, rigidity, speech disorder etc. Some patients go through a pre-motor stage of 5–20 years before the occurrence of PD symptoms [3]. In this stage, patients face sleep behavioral disorder, rapid eye movement, olfactory loss, decreased sense of smell etc. Though any proper treatment for this disease is not discovered, but regular medication, meditation, physiotherapy can improve the patients' health to some extent [4, 5]. As speech disorder is one of the major symptoms of PD. Since examining speech disorder is easier, reliable and can be extensively adopted in telemonitoring process, it is now becoming a core area of research in Parkinson's Disease detection and prediction. In our chapter, we have predicted the UPDRS indicators from the sound measurements. Section 2 gives the detailed description about the related works done in this area; Sect. 3 gives the detailed information about our dataset. In the rest sections, we have discussed the detailed about data preparation, proposed methodology, results and discussion.

2 Related Works

In the recent past, ML and DL classifiers were taken into consideration by many researchers to classify Parkinson's Disease. Different features i.e., Freezing of GAIT (FoG), speech disorder data, walking data, handwritten image etc. were taken. Some of the research chapters are discussed in this section.

Pedro Gómez-Vilda1 et al. [6] in their study detect Parkinson's Disease from speech articulation. They have co-related the kinetic behaviour of patients' jaw-tongue biomedical system. They took the dataset of sustained vowels, which were recorded with the PD patients. The similar work was done for the normal people. They achieved 99.45% accuracy for Male patients and 99.42% accuracy for female patients. The sensitivity measurement was 99% for male patients and 99.42% for female patients.

Imanne El Maachi et al. [7] took gait sample as input to classify PD from healthy people. 1-D convnet neural network was used to build a DNN model. They have separated their work in two separate parts. First part contains 18 parallel 1D convnet to corresponding system inputs. In the second part of their work, PD was classified using Unified Parkinson's Disease Rating Scale (UPDRS) scale. They achieved 98.7% accuracy for their work.

Shivangi et al. [8] used deep neural networks for Parkinson's Disease detection. They introduced VGFR Spectrogram detector and voice impairment classifiers to diagnose PD at its early stage. CNN was implemented on gait signals, which were converted to spectrogram image. Deep dense ANN was implemented on voice recording to predict this disease. Using VGFR, they achieved 88.1% accuracy, while using Voice Impairment Classifier, they achieved 89.15% accuracy.

Gabriel Solana-Lavalle et al. [9] used kNN, MLP, SVM and RF on a small set of vocal features to detect PD. The main aim of this work was to increase the accuracy for PD detection and reduce the number of features for PD detection. Firstly, the speech samples were recorded from different individuals and processed for feature extraction. In the next stage, they have standardized to set the mean at 0. They achieved 94.7% of accuracy, 98.4% of sensitivity, 92.68% of specificity and 097.22% of precision for their work.

Tao Zhang et al. [10] shows different characteristics of voice signals between PD patents and healthy people. They used energy direction features which are based on Empirical mode decomposition. The work was done on two different datasets and achieved 96.54% and 92.59% accuracy repeatedly for both of the works. For classification, SM and RF classifiers were used on the extracted features and the best accuracy was calculated.

3 Data Collection

This is an open-source dataset, which is collected from UCI Machine Learning Repository [11]. The dataset first was created by Athanasios Tsanas and Max Little. Both of them are from the University of Oxford. They have collaborated with 10 medical centers from US. The telemonitoring device, which was used for data collection, was developed by Intel Corporation. This device was used to record the speech signals. The main objective was to predict the clinical Parkinson's Disease (PD) based on the Unified Parkinson's Disease Rating Scale (UPDRS).

4 Dataset Information

The dataset we take for our work contains the biomedical voice measurements of 42 people, who were already affected with early-stage PD. A six months trial was done using the telemonitoring device at the patients' home. The columns include an index number of each patient. Other columns include the patients' age, gender, duration from the initial date of admission, two motor indicators: motor UPDRS and total UPDRS. 16 other medical sound measurements were taken in the next 16 columns.

5 Data Pre-processing

The subject column in our dataset basically identifies each subject uniquely. But it is unordered and make no sense. It can also be confused for the classifiers while training the model. So, we can convert this column using one-hot encoding or discard it. But using one-hot encoding will add too many features to the dataset, then it will be hectic task to manage the features. So, the safest way is to remove the subject column from the dataset.

Our dataset does not contain any null values. So, we have directly divided the table into input and output elements. We have split the data in 7:3 ratio. 'SelectKBest' method was used to select the feature according to the k highest score. It takes the first k features which have the highest scores. As, we have around 200 data for each subject, so we have selected the best features for further processing.

To find the relation between two variables, co-relation measurement is the commonly used term. The most common co-relation measuring formula is Pearson co-relation. It assumes that the random variables of the dataset are distributed with a Gaussian normal distribution and linearly dependent on another variable. Linear co-relation is measured in the range of $(-1,1)$, where 0 indicates no-relation between two variables and 1 indicates highly co-relation between two variables. We have two variables motor UPDRS and total UPDRS as the random variables, so we checked the co-relation of other features with respect to these two features one by one (Figs. 1 and 2).

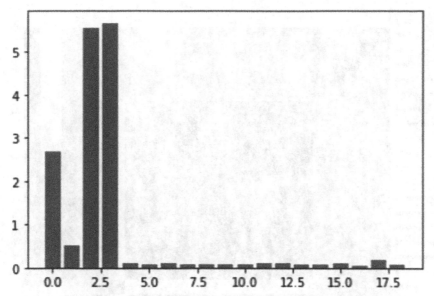

Fig. 1. Measured co-relation of the features to motor-UPDRS

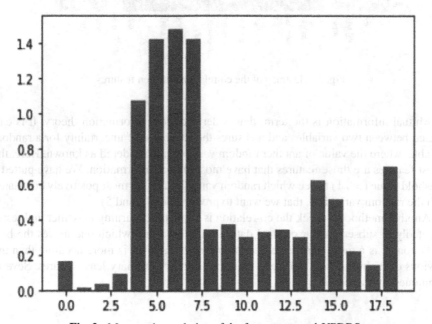

Fig. 2. Measured co-relation of the features to total-UPDRS

This heatmap shows the co-relation between the features. It is a graphical representation of the features, that shows the relation between the values. Here, we have co-related the initial features. Here, dark shades show high co-relation and white shows no co-relation between the columns (Fig. 3).

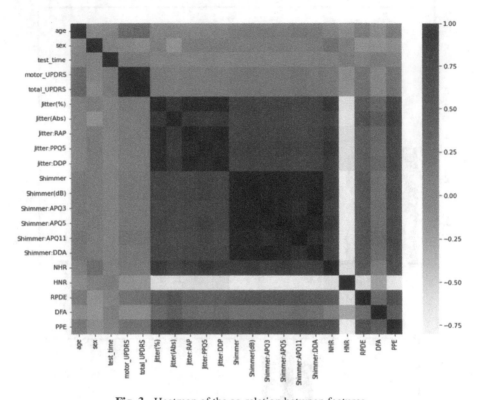

Fig. 3. Heatmap of the co-relation between features

Mutual information is the term, that is derived from information theory. It is calculated between two variables and measures the reduction of uncertainty for a random variable, where the value of another random variable is considered as known. Here, the k-best features are those features that have most mutual information. We have putted a threshold value (>0.1) to see which random variables are the most positively co-related with the random variable y, that we want to predict (Figs. 4 and 5).

Another method to check the co-relation is a machine learning classifier and test it repeatedly in subsets of our original data set, until we find which one makes the best prediction. It is a more expensive computing method, but it is more accurate than the previous ones. In this case, we have used the classifier ordinary least squares. Several techniques are there to do this,

```
age              0.273665
motor_UPDRS      1.000000
total_UPDRS      0.947231
Shimmer          0.102349
Shimmer(dB)      0.110076
Shimmer:APQ11    0.136560
HNR              0.157029
RPDE             0.128607
DFA              0.116242
PPE              0.162433
Name: motor_UPDRS, dtype: float64
```

Fig. 4. Measured most positive co-relation with motor-UPDRS

```
age              0.310290
motor_UPDRS      0.947231
total_UPDRS      1.000000
Shimmer:APQ11    0.120838
HNR              0.162117
RPDE             0.156897
DFA              0.113475
PPE              0.156195
Name: total_UPDRS, dtype: float64
```

Fig. 5. Measured most positive co-relation with total-UPDRS

o **Backward Elimination**

In backward elimination process, we started training the model with all the features and then started removing the features in every step. We have evaluated the performance of the algorithms through its matric p-value, which was set to 0.05. When the p-value is greater than 0.05, we removed the attribute, else we kept those.

o **Recursive Feature Elimination (RFE)**

In this process also we have removed the features until we reached to the best possible solution. But the main difference between backward elimination and RFE is, RFE uses the accuracy score. RFE takes the number of features as input and calculate the accuracy score. The output of RFE shows the ranking among the features.

6   Feature Selection and Model Training

After having all the previous work done, we have chosen a subset of most important features to work further. The subset of features was taken only based on the backward elimination.

Principal Component Analysis (PCA) is an unsupervised machine learning technique which is used to minimize the dimensionality of data. At the same time, it increases the interpretability, and minimizes the information loss. It also helps to capture the most relevant features in the dataset. PCA has three steps. In the first step, it standardizes the range of the continuous initial features. Due to this, all the initial variables contribute equally to the analysis. After standardization, covariance of matrix computation is done to check the relationship among the input features. In order to determine the principal components of the features, in the next step, the eigen vectors and eigen values are computed. We have used PCA to find the best possible features that were extracted from the voice samples.

After feature extraction, we have used Linear Regression, Polynomial Regression, Elastic-Net, Decision Tree, k-Neighbor, Random Forest, Least Absolute Shrinkage and Selection Operator (Lasso), and Gradient Boosting to train our model.

Linear Regression
Linear Regression is a supervised machine learning model that finds the best fitted linear relationship between the independent and dependent variables. Linear Regression is of two types, Simple Linear Regression and Multiple Linear Regression. In Simple Linear Regression, only one dependent variable is possible. Whereas, in Multiple Linear Regression, more than one independent variable is possible. As, in our dataset, two dependent variables are there: motor UPDRS and total UPDRS, so we have used Multiple Linear Regression.

Suppose y is the dependent variable and b_0 is the intercept. b_1, b_2, ..., b_n are the coefficients of the independent variables x_1, x_2, ..., x_n. Then the equation will be,

$$y = b_0 + b_1 x_1 + b_2 x_2 + \cdots + b_n x_n$$

The main motive of Linear Regression is to find the best fitted linear line and optimal values of the intercept and coefficients to minimize the error. Here, error is the difference between the actual and predicted value.

Polynomial Regression
In polynomial regression, the relationship between the dependent and independent variables are described as the nth degree polynomial of the independent variable. It describes a non-linear relationship between the value of independent variables and the conditional mean of the dependent variable.

Suppose y is the dependent variable and b_0 is the intercept. b_1, b_2, ..., b_n are the coefficients of the independent variable x. Then the equation will be,

$$y = b_0 + b_1 x_1^2 + b_2 x_1^3 + \cdots + b_n x_1^n$$

Sometimes it is also called as a special case of the Multiple Linear Regression (MLR) as it adds some polynomial terms to the MLR equation.

This method is used to train the model in a non-linear manner.

Lasso
Lasso is a regression model based on the linear regression technique. It refers to the shrinking of the extreme values of the data sample towards the central values. This process makes lasso regression better, stable and less erroneous than others. It is considered

as one of the most suitable models for the scenarios having multi co-linearity. Lasso makes the regression method simpler in terms of the number of features which are used for the work. Lasso performs L1-regularization and the penalty added is equivalent to the magnitude of co-efficient. Lasso uses a regularization method which automatically penalize the extra features taken i.e., the features which are less co-related to the target variable.

Elastic Net Regression

Elastic Net regression is a linear regression that uses the penalties from lasso technique for regression model regularization. Elastic Net method performs regularization and variable selection simultaneously. It is the most appropriate for the scenarios where the dimensional data is larger than the number of samples. Variable selection and grouping play a major key role for elastic net techniques. It does not eliminate the high collinearity co-efficient.

Decision Tree

Decision Tree (DT) is a supervised machine learning algorithm, which is used for both classification and regression problems. DT is one of the predictive modelling approaches, that is used in data mining, statistics and machine learning. This algorithm split the input data into the sub-spaces based on some certain functionalities. It helps to reach to a conclusion based on some conditional control statement. But it is mostly used for classification problems. It is a tree-structured based classifier, in which each internal nodes represents each feature of the dataset. The branches of the tree represent the decision rules. Whereas, each leaf node of the tree represents the outcome of the algorithm. Decision nodes makes the decision rules. The goal of DT is to create a model, that can predict the value of the target variable by using simple decision rules inferred from the data features.

K-Nearest Neighbors

kNN is one of the supervised learning algorithms, that can also be used for both classification and regression problems. But it is generally used for classification problems. Here K is an important parameter for kNN. This algorithm counterfeits the similarity of the available data with the new data. Based on the data points' similarity, it puts the new data to the most similar category of the available data. Based on similarity, the algorithm easily classifies the new data points. kNN algorithm is robust to the noisy training samples and it is effective when training dataset is large. It is a non-parametric algorithm, that does not make any assumptions on the underlying data. It is a slow learner algorithm, as it does not learn from the training samples immediately. It stores the dataset and at classification process, it performs the necessary actions on the dataset.

Random Forest

RF is an ensemble learning algorithm, which is used for both classification and regression. It builds decision trees based on different samples. The algorithm takes their majority vote for classification. To build a RF, we need some DT, which must not be co-related or have low co-relation. RF can handle the dataset of continuous variables for regression problems and categorical variables for classification problems. But this algorithm performs better for classification problems. RF combines multiple trees to predict a class of the dataset. So, it is possible that some of the DT predict the correct output. While the rest DT may not predict the correct output. But, together, they all can predict the correct output. So, there are two assumptions: the predictions of each tree must have very low co-relations and some actual values in the feature variable should be there, so that the classifier can predict accurate results. RF takes less training times and predict highly accurate output, even for large dataset.

Gradient Boosting Regression (GBR)
Gradient Boosting is one of the machine learning (ML) technique that is also used for both classification and regression problems. It produces a predictive machine learning model from an ensemble of weak predictive models. It is used to find the non-linear relationship between the dependent and the independent variables. This algorithm works better with missing values, outliers and high cardinality categorical values.

7   Result and Discussion

The main contribution of this work was the proposal of the subjects' voice signal data as input to the Machine Learning algorithm for PD detection. Employing public dataset, we evaluated the detection capability of PD from different machine learning classifiers. The most effective result we achieved using Decision Tree classifier. It gives us the accuracy of 100% on training dataset. Whereas, for control dataset, it gives us the accuracy of 97.05%. The algorithms used in our chapter represents a non-invasive and reliable methods for Parkinson's Disease detection. At first, we have taken the features to train our model, which are highly co-related with the dependent variables. Based on that we have created the dataframe for training and testing. Principle Component Analysis (PCA) was done for grid search with cross validation of the data. 'compute_metrics' function was used to calculate the matrices. Least square and mean square are also used to find the error on the training and control samples by the classifiers. 'GridSearchCV' is a technique, which searches through the best parameter values from the given grid of parameters. Grid search technique was used for lasso, elastic net, decision tree, gradient boosting and random forest to assemble the steps, which can be cross-validated together by setting different parameters. Below, we have compared between different classifiers used based on their accuracies on training and control set, errors in both of the samples and time taken to fit and predict the results (Table 1).

From the table, we can find, though Random Forest gave us better accuracy than the other algorithms, but it takes the most time to be fitted. Gradient Boosting also takes quite considerable time than others. As RF makes the decision based on different DTs, so for real-time prediction, it is slow.

In the below graph, we have compared between the training accuracy achieved by the classifiers that are used in our work. This barplot gives us a clear idea about the accuracy measurement. Figure 7. Shows the running time measurement of different algorithms. In this figure we can clearly see that RF and BGR took very high time than the other algorithms (Fig. 7).

Table 1. Comparing different classifiers based on the results.

Classifier name	Accuracy on training data set	Accuracy on control data set	Average square error in training samples	Mean square error in control samples	Time to fit and predict (seconds)
Linear regression	93.79%	93.95%	5.2793	5.4187	0.018
Polynomial regression	96.55%	92.12%	3.1680	3.5858	0.138
LASSO	92.57%	93.48%	5.4880	5.4530	1.863
Elastic net	93.79%	93.95%	5.2793	5.4187	14.745
Decision tree	100.00%	97.05%	0.0000	0.2189	0.231
k-Nearest neighbors	89.71%	79.10%	0.5586	1.7661	0.156
Random forest	99.73%	98.63%	0.0150	0.0973	12.527
Gradient boosting regressor	98.63%	97.74%	0.9905	1.0945	5.538

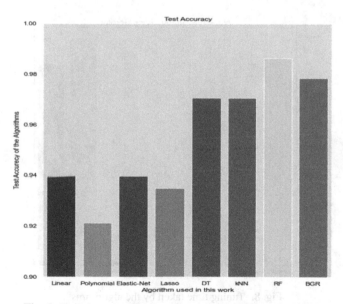

Fig. 6. Training accuracy measurement of different classifiers

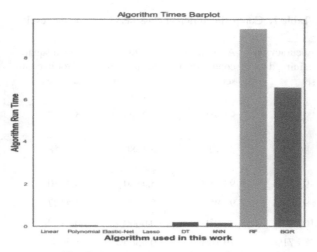

Fig. 7. Running times of the algorithms

Algorithm tuning time is an important parameter for model selection. It is used to check, how much time the algorithms take to be trained using the dataset. Different classifiers take different times based on the features added to the dataset. Here in this bar plot, we showed the comparison of the classifiers that are used in this work (Fig. 8).

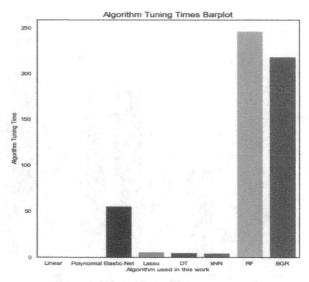

Fig. 8. Tuning time taken by the algorithms

R^2 is a statistical measure of fit which indicates the portion of dependent variable which is explained by the independent variable in a regression model. We have taken R^2 measure for our work (Fig. 9).

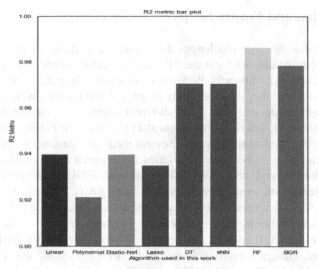

Fig. 9. R^2 metrics measure for the algorithms

Mean Square method is another technique, that is used to measure the regression models' performance. It takes the distance between the data points and the regression line to squares them removing negative sign. It gives more weightage to the larger difference. Smaller MSE shows the best fitted line (Fig. 10).

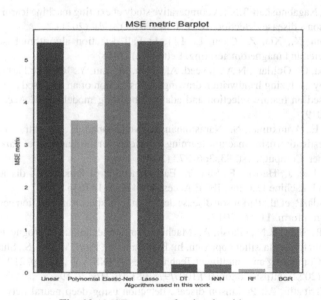

Fig. 10. MSE measure for the algorithms

8 Conclusion and Future Scope

PD is a nerve disorder, that challenges the population globally as it is uncertain in prediction. In our dataset, we have used the audio measurements of 42 peoples, who were already classified with early Parkinson's Disease. The patients were sent for a six-months trial where they were remotely diagnosed and the data were automatically recorded through the device. Total 5,875 different sounds were measured for the test. UPDRS is a rating tool, that is used to gauge and progression of PD in the patients. This scale has been modified over the years. Several medical organizations have modified UPDRS and continues to be one of the bases for research and treatment for PD. In this work, we have taken both motor UPDRS and total UPDRS score for PD detection. Using Linear Regression, we achieve 93.79% for training data. Whereas, for control data, we achieve 93.95% of accuracy. Polynomial Regression gives us 96.55% and 92.12% of accuracy for both training and control data. The best accuracy we achieved using Decision Tree classifier. It gives us the accuracy of 100% and 97.05% for both training and control data. Though we have achieved better accuracies using the classifier used, but the tuning time for Elastic-Net, RF and BGR was bit longer. So, in future, it can be tested further with the other algorithms. Also, the best fitted algorithm: both time wise and complexity wise can be taken for further process. After UPDRS score, we will classify PD patients from normal people and progression of PD.

References

1. Pahuja, G., Nagabhushan, T.N.: A comparative study of existing machine learning approaches for Parkinson's disease detection. IETE J. Res. **67**(1), 4–14 (2021)
2. Shi, T., Sun, X., Xia, Z., Chen, L., Liu, J.: Fall detection algorithm based on triaxial accelerometer and magnetometer. Eng. Lett. **24**(2) (2016)
3. Ali, L., Zhu, C., Golilarz, N.A., Javeed, A., Zhou, M., Liu, Y.: Reliable Parkinson's disease detection by analyzing handwritten drawings: construction of an unbiased cascaded learning system based on feature selection and adaptive boosting model. IEEE Access **7**, 116480–116489 (2019)
4. Abdulhay, E., Arunkumar, N., Narasimhan, K., Vellaiappan, E., Venkatraman, V.: Gait and tremor investigation using machine learning techniques for the diagnosis of Parkinson disease. Future Gener. Comput. Syst. **83**, 366–373 (2018)
5. Wang, W., Lee, J., Harrou, F., Sun, Y.: Early detection of Parkinson's disease using deep learning and machine learning. IEEE Access **8**, 147635–147646 (2020)
6. Gómez-Vilda, P., et al.: Parkinson disease detection from speech articulation neuromechanics. Front. Neuroinform. **11**, 56 (2017)
7. Palimkar, P., Shaw, R.N., Ghosh, A.: Machine learning technique to prognosis diabetes disease: random forest classifier approach. In: Bianchini, M., Piuri, V., Das, S., Shaw, R.N. (eds.) Advanced Computing and Intelligent Technologies. LNNS, vol. 218, pp. 219–244. Springer, Singapore (2022). https://doi.org/10.1007/978-981-16-2164-2_19
8. Johri, A., Tripathi, A.: Parkinson disease detection using deep neural networks. In: 2019 Twelfth International Conference on Contemporary Computing (IC3), pp. 1–4. IEEE (2019)

9. Mridha, K., et.al.: Plant disease detection using web application by neural network. In: 2021 IEEE 6th International Conference on Computing, Communication and Automation (ICCCA), pp. 130–136 (2021). https://doi.org/10.1109/ICCCA52192.2021.9666354

10. Zhang, T., Zhang, Y., Sun, H., Shan, H.: Parkinson disease detection using energy direction features based on EMD from voice signal. Biocybern. Biomed. Eng. **41**(1), 127–141 (2021)

11. Dataset used for this work. https://archive.ics.uci.edu/ml/datasets/parkinsons+telemonitoring

Implementation of Smart Contract Using Ethereum Blockchain

Asmita Patel[✉] and Buddha Singh

School of Computer and Systems Sciences, Jawaharlal Nehru University, New Delhi, India
patel.asmita30@gmail.com

Abstract. Blockchain technology has greatest impact in the last few decades. The blockchain has distributed ledger of all transactions across a peer-to-peer network. In the existing traditional seller-buyer system, the seller provides an interface to the user for ordering goods. This system provides a facility to the customer for payments of their orders through a trusted third party which is a bank. In case the centralized system is failed then the functioning of the entire system is affected along with the loss of data integrity. For the solution to this problem Smart contract provides distributed peer-to-peer communication. In this proposed work, the transaction among the nodes is coordinated by the smart contract. This smart contract-based seller-buyer exchange model provides peer-to-peer transactions in which no data is dependent on a central authority. In this proposed model, the seller and buyer communicate directly by a set of protocols that executes automatically when conditions are met. Further, this method maintains data consistency, transparency, and integrity because all the transactions among the nodes execute in a distributed way. The consensus mechanism among the nodes validates and authenticates the peer-to-peer transaction in the blockchain.

Keywords: Smart contract · Ethereum blockchain · Consensus mechanism · MyEtherWallet · Ganache · Remix IDE

1 Introduction

Blockchain technology is best recognized for cryptocurrencies and their applications in the financial sector, the Internet of Things (IoT), supply chain, and secure sharing of data [2]. Types of blockchains that are used today have different architectures for blockchain frameworks. The first well-known application of Blockchain technology (BT) is Bitcoin. The Bitcoin ecosystem work on the basic principle of blockchain technology which includes a digital signature, timestamp, hashed public key, mining of blocks, and consensus mechanism [1]. Some pitfall of the system is it requires computationally expensive mining and the reason is the existence of malicious agents in the network could hamper the data integrity. And the data integrity cannot be compromised with the computational cost.

R. N. Shaw et al. (Eds.): ICACIS 2022, CCIS 1749, pp. 160–169, 2023.
https://doi.org/10.1007/978-3-031-25088-0_13

A permission blockchain does not necessarily require a mining mechanism for data integrity. The basic idea behind any kind of system where we want to keep our data safe and maintain the consistency and integrity of data there is a distributed algorithm Byzantine fault tolerance (BFT) [2]. So, they are directly implemented in permission blockchain whereas in cryptocurrency systems they are implemented indirectly through mining mechanisms. Private blockchains are useful such as in medical data systems, land record registration, and various kinds of logging systems [4]. Some private blockchains are Hyperledger and Corda. According to the need of the application, a developer can choose any public or private blockchain [7, 8].

The public blockchain such as Bitcoin, Ethereum, and Iota, anyone can join the network and participate in its transactions. The public blockchain is transparent i.e., everyone in the network can see all transactions, therefore applications of a public blockchain network are for mass consumption.

1.1 Research Problem

Blockchain is one of the fast-growing technologies and is widely applicable in the field of supply chain, commercial applications, and market structures. Blockchain technology mostly deals with and is widely accepted in both financial and non-financial areas. One of the challenging issues computational costs of mining [3]. The validity of the new block is checked by the consensus mechanism used in the blockchain platform. If a continuously new block is added to the chain, then computational cost also increases.

Alternative approaches to the execution of smart contracts based on centralized systems were being explored even before Satoshi Nakamoto's landmark work that introduced Bitcoin. The use of these platforms to create smart contracts, however, has a significant drawback because of its centralized nature, which resulted in limitations such as relying on trusted third parties and having a single point of failure in the central server. In this work, we use the Ethereum platform which is suitable for a variety of applications. Unfortunately, little research has been done on using hybrid architectures to construct smart contracts.

2 Background and Related Work

The technologies involved in blockchains such as cryptographically certified blocks and Merkle trees were developed in the early 1990s. In 2008, a pseudonymous person(s) named "Satoshi Nakamoto" published a white paper on Bitcoin, which introduces the concept of blockchain technology [1]. Since the early days, people are trusted the centralized bank system to keep safe our money. However, the global financial crisis in 2008, breach the trust of customers in their banks. Then people require a peer-to-peer electronic cash system for payment without involving any third party. It would happen by digital signature but to prevent the problem of double-spending, still requires an authorized third party. Satoshi proposes a solution for the problem of double spending [5]. The network timestamps work by inserting them into a continuous series of hash-based Proof-of-Work (PoW) and creating an unchangeable record.

Blockchain technology uses cryptocurrency for the transaction. Bitcoin (BTC) first released as open-source software in 2009, is the first decentralized cryptocurrency. The basic technology behind Bitcoin is called Blockchain. It has the power to completely transform the digital world through a distributed ledger, where each work is verified and recorded only after reaching an agreement between all parties. The distributed network provides additional privacy and security as it is very difficult to compromise information verified by all participants. Ever since blockchain technology came into existence, it has been the center of attraction for researchers [6]. The journey of Blockchain technology so far is as follows (Fig. 1).

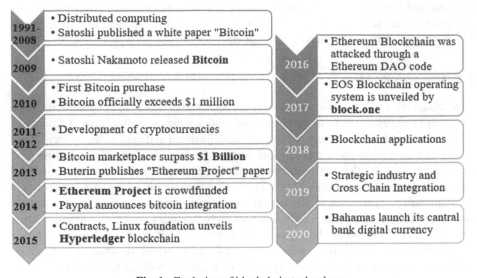

Fig. 1. Evolution of blockchain technology

3   System Model

The smart contract is a set of protocols, that executes automatically with the fulfillment of an agreement between two or more parties when conditions are met. Smart contracts are run on Ethereum virtual machines (EVM) [6]. It is a blockchain-based program similar to real-world contracts but it works digitally (Fig. 2(a)).

In this proposed model, until a specific objective is achieved, the smart contract keeps all of the money that has been received. The smart contract now allows an application's users to transfer funds. The contract will automatically transfer the necessary quantity of ether created on the seller's side of an application to the seller's wallet if the buyer makes the transfer. If the transaction is not completely executed, the money automatically goes back to the buyer's wallet (Fig. 2(b)).

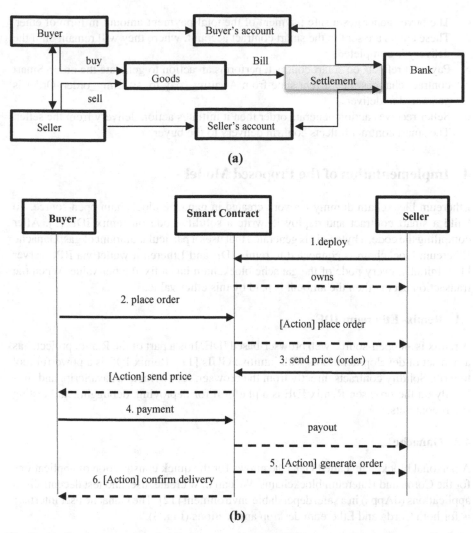

Fig. 2. (a) Current scenario of seller-buyer agreement (b) Event sequence diagram of smart contract for seller-buyer exchange

The sequence of actions performed between the buyer, seller, and smart contract.

1. Seller deploys the smart contract for the buyer's account that provides a client-side application. This interactive application performs various financial transactions and facilitates to purchase of various goods.
2. The buyer places order of item (I) with quantity (X), and that order is received by the seller. The smart contract of a seller processes the order and performs an action.
3. Seller provides the best-selling price on the smart contract. The buyer receives the price through the action sent price.

4. The buyer generates a safe payment of the total payment amount in form of ether. These ethers are sent to the smart contract account, where they will remain until the delivery is completed.
5. Payment reflects on smart contract, performs an action to generate the order. Smart contract changes the current state from Awaiting_pay to Awaiting_order. Order is generated to deliver.
6. Seller receives action generate order then it initiates action delivery from the seller. The smart contract reflects confirm delivery to the buyer.

4   Implementation of the Proposed Model

Ethereum blockchain dummy network created in ganache blockchain open-source. To build a smart contract and deploy it, write a solidity code on remix IDE [9]. After compiling the code, a bytecode is generated that uses a particular amount of gas. Ganache Ethereum blockchain is connected to remix IDE and Ethereum wallet via RPC server [10]. Initially, every node of the ganache blockchain has a fixed ether value. When the transaction occurs then the amount is paid by this ether value.

4.1   Remix- Ethereum IDE

A remix is an open-source web browser-based IDE. It is a part of the Remix project, has a rich set of development tools with intuitive GUIs [11]. Remix IDE is a powerful tool to write Solidity contracts directly from the browser. It is written in JavaScript and runs locally on the browser. Remix IDE is a platform for deploying, debugging and testing smart contracts.

4.2   Ganache

A personal blockchain called Ganache allows for the quick construction of applications for the Corda and Ethereum blockchains. We can now create, use, and test decentralised applications (dApps) in a safe, dependable environment [12]. The Ganache user interface is for both Corda and Ethereum desktop applications (Fig. 3).

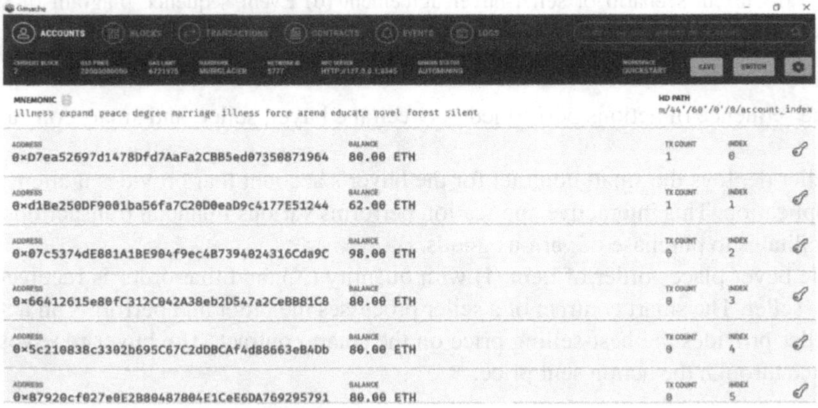

Fig. 3. Ganache Ethereum blockchain

Ganache ethereum blockchain contains a total of 10 nodes index from 0 to 9 here, it may be increased up to 100 nodes. Initially, every node has 80 ETH, performs transactions between the node of index 1 to the node of index 2. After performing the transaction node 1 has 62 ETH and node 2 has 98 ETH and one transaction count is added on node 1 (Fig. 4).

TX 0×1e1a05f457a164a7deedb7d0c3d42a877ee3b815e05bee4f27f6d0c7d597cea3

SENDER ADDRESS		TO CONTRACT ADDRESS		CONTRACT CALL
0×d1Be250DF9001ba56fa7C20D0eaD9c4177E51244		0×07c5374dE881A1BE904f9ec4B7394024316Cda9C		
VALUE	GAS USED	GAS PRICE	GAS LIMIT	MINED IN BLOCK
18.00 ETH	21000	41000000000	21000	1
TX DATA				
0x				

Fig. 4. Transaction

A new block is created for a transaction that contains Gas used, Gas limit, mined time, block hash, and transaction hash (Fig. 5).

BLOCK 1

GAS USED	GAS LIMIT	MINED ON	BLOCK HASH
21000	6721975	2021-08-27 17:20:30	0×b76d94848a3bf3dc7fe88b9908213235b48f91973b4709cfcb22589a529e35b4

TX HASH
0×1e1a05f457a164a7deedb7d0c3d42a877ee3b815e05bee4f27f6d0c7d597cea3

FROM ADDRESS	TO CONTRACT ADDRESS	GAS USED	VALUE
0×d1Be250DF9001ba56fa7C20D0eaD9c4177E51244	0×07c5374dE881A1BE904f9ec4B7394024316Cda9C	21000	18000000000000000000

Fig. 5. Mined block

4.3 Deploy the Contract

If we are using JavaScript VM (virtual machine) environment, it deploys the contract instantly [11]. If we are using Injected Web3 environment, then we have to need to approve the transaction. It requires the Gas amount to be mined transaction. The smart contract and the Injected web3 link directly to the wallet, making the transaction. Selecting the contract that needs to be deployed and then **deploying** it. The smart contract is successfully deployed and recorded in the blockchain (Fig. 6).

Fig. 6. Deploy of smart contract

Create an account on MyEtherWallet, which provides a client-side interface to the blockchain. Connect this ether wallet to the ganache Ethereum blockchain by adding a custom network to the wallet. Set the value of the ganache server to the custom network that is the host and port number. Now the Ethereum blockchain is ready to deploy the contract. Deploy of contract uses bytecode of smart contract. Bytecode and ABI (application binary interface) are generated after the compilation of the smart contract.

The gas limit is calculated automatically. After deploy the bytecode Raw Transaction is generated. To interact with smart contracts, use contract address and ABI (Fig. 7).

Fig. 7. Interact with smart contract

After deploying the contract, a block is created and a transaction is added to the chain. The updated ledger adds a new mined block in the blockchain of our transaction.

5 Performance Analysis

The term "smart contract performance" describes a system's capacity to deliver in a timely manner and maintain performance as the number of active contracts rises [11]. Table 1 presents the execution cost of a smart contract on remix IDE.

Table 1. Smart contract execution cost.

Status	True transaction mined and execution succeed
Transaction hash	0x28a013ace239005124452d00649c64c57bc5cd7c6f26d6c2975bf142202fd6a7
From	0x5B38Da6a701c568545dCfcB03FcB875f56beddC4
To	Payment.(constructor)
Gas	454574 gas
Transaction cost	395281 gas
Execution cost	395281 gas

5.1 Gas Cost

Each computational step requires a cost of 1 gas for execution. But more complex steps can take a higher amount of gas. Every byte takes 5 gas amounts in the transactional data [14].

A sender X sends 10000 gas to Y for execution. Each gas price is 0.001 ether. That means $10000 \times 0.001 = 10$ ether is deducted from the account of X to use the services. Y consumes 5000 gas before sending a message to Z. And Z consumes 3000 gas in the internal execution. Z returns the calculated ether amount i.e., $2000 \times 0.001 = 2$ ether to Y. After that either Y consumes this amount or returns to X.

5.2 Average Execution Time

The ganache was built to replicate the rate at which Ethereum blocks are mined in order to test the contract's typical execution time. In real life, a private blockchain with numerous connected nodes would be used to achieve this approach. According to Etherscan32, Ethereum blocks typically take between 10 and 30 s to complete, with most blocks taking between 10 and 20 s. In order to test the solutions' average execution times, we ran the tests at a rate of 10 s for each block to get an understanding of the best-case solution execution time. A preset sequence of events needed to be derived for each solution to see how each solution responds to the requests in order to ensure that the tests were fair for each system. A mixture of complete sequences of actions that can be carried out on the blockchain is made up of the series of occurrences that were selected.

There is increased latency for accepting transactions because the testing was carried out using a web browser built with MetaMask to confirm each transaction (Fig. 8).

Fig. 8. Rinkeby test network with Metamask wallet

When we deploy the transaction on Injected Web3 environment, the linked metamask account will directly be open. The fee of deploying the contract "shopping" requires 0.000157 Gas. The gas price is 1.000000008 GWEI i.e., gegawei or 10^9 wei (Wei is the smallest unit of ether).

6 Conclusion

This chapter presents smart contract deployment on the Ethereum blockchain network. In a centralized system, a central authority or third party ensures the reliability of transactions [13]. But in a peer-to-peer system, it is difficult to establish trust among each participant for every transaction. Ethereum blockchain uses a protocol to commit a transaction is called a smart contract. The development of smart contracts for distributed applications (dApp) provides secure and reliable transactions. A distributed application of the proposed seller-buyer interchange model based on blockchain will use this smart contract for payment settlement between seller and buyer. After purchasing the good's buyer can directly pay from his ether wallet to the seller's ether wallet without the need of a third party. Blockchain ensures secure, valid, and reliable payment.

6.1 Future Work

The Ethereum blockchain platform is better to implement a distributed application. It provides a solution for efficient, safe, and reliable seller-buyer online exchange. There are still various issues that will need to be discussed and researched for future study.

1) The development of the distributed application will provide a faster and easier way to purchase goods for a buyer.
2) The extension of such an application can be integrated with other manufacturing companies in a chain. It's possible that the cost of intermediaries will drop even further.
3) Experiments must be carried out in the context of realistic settings. Different components and nodes are deployed in various locations in a real-world application situation. They don't communicate with each other because they live on opposite sides of the world. The delay indicated by the internet connection can have a significant impact on the findings of the research.
4) In a blockchain, data is immutable and consistent that can be used for market analysis. The recommender system can also use the ledger of blockchain because it is more reliable.

References

1. Nakamoto, S.: Bitcoin: a peer-to-peer electronic cash system (2009). https://bitcoin.org/bit coin.pdf
2. Macdonald, M., Liu-Thorrold, L., Julien, R.: The blockchain: a comparison of platforms and their uses beyond bitcoin. In: COMS4507 – Advanced Computer and Network Security (2017). https://doi.org/10.13140/RG.2.2.23274.52164
3. Singh, S., Hosen, A.S., Yoon, B.: Blockchain security attacks, challenges, and solutions for the future distributed IoT network. Special section on Internet-of-Things Attacks and Defence. IEEE Access, 26 January 2021
4. Krishnapriya, S., Sarath, G.: Securing land registration using blockchain. In: Third International Conference on Computing and Network Communications (CoCoNet 2019), vol. 171, pp. 1708–1715 (2020)

5. Alam, K.M., Rahman, J.M.A., et al.: A blockchain-based land title management system for Bangladesh. J. King Saud Univ. Comput. Inf. Sci. (2020). https://doi.org/10.1016/j.jksuci.2020.10.011

6. Rawat, D.B., Chaudhary, V., Doku, R.: Blockchain technology: emerging applications and use cases for secure and trustworthy smart systems. J. Cybersecur. Priv. **1**, 4–18 (2020)

7. Idrees, S.M., Nowostawski, M., et al.: Security aspects of blockchain technology intended for industrial applications. MDPI J. Electron. **10**, 951 (2021)

8. Kibet, A.K., Bayyou, D.G., Esquivel, R.A.: Blockchain: it's structure, principles, applications and foreseen issues. J. Emerg. Technol. Innov. Res. **6**(4) (2019). ISSN: 2349-5162

9. Saraf, C., Sabadra, S.: Blockchain platforms: a compendium. In: IEEE International Conference on Innovation Research and Development, Bangkok, May 2018

10. Malsa, N., Vyas, V., Gautam, J., Shaw, R.N., Ghosh, A.: Framework and smart contract for blockchain enabled certificate verification system using robotics. In: Bianchini, M., Simic, M., Ghosh, A., Shaw, R.N. (eds.) Machine Learning for Robotics Applications, vol. 960, pp. 125–138. Springer, Singapore (2021). https://doi.org/10.1007/978-981-16-0598-7_10

11. Ethereum: What is Ether (2015). https://www.ethereum.org/ether

12. Aggarwal, S., Kumar, N., Chelliah, P.R.: Cryptographic consensus mechanisms. In: Advance in Computers, vol. 121, pp. 211–226, 8 November 2020. Elsevier (2020). https://doi.org/10.1016/bs.adcom.2020.08.011

13. Savchenko, N.: Decentralized applications architecture: back end, security and design patterns, Blog 2 April 2019. https://www.freecodecamp.org/news/how-to-design-a-secure-backend-for-your-decentralized-application-9541b5d8bddb/

14. Ethereum whitepaper. https://ethereum.org/en/whitepaper/#ethereum-accounts

Prediction of Compressive Strength of Geopolymer Concrete by Using Random Forest Algorithm

Manvendra Verma[1], Kamal Upreti[2(✉)], Mohammad Rafeek Khan[3], Mohammad Shabbir Alam[3], Soumi Ghosh[4], and Prashant Singh[5]

[1] Department of Civil Engineering, GLA University, Mathura, Uttar Pradesh, India
manvendra.verma@gla.ac.in
[2] Department of Computer Science and Engineering, Akhilesh Das Gupta Institute of Technology & Management, Delhi, India
kamalupreti1989@gmail.com
[3] Department of Computer Science, College of Computer Science and IT, Jazan University, Jizan, Saudi Arabia
mokhan@jazanu.edu.sa
[4] Department of Information Technology, Maharaja Agrasen Institute of Technology, Delhi, India
[5] Department of Computer Science and Engineering, Sunder Deep Engineering College, Ghaziabad, India

Abstract. Geopolymer concrete is a new invention of the concrete industry. It could be the future of all construction fields due to its performance against severe conditions, and strength. It is a perfect alternative to conventional concrete. It is more sustainable, ecological, durable, and economic than conventional concrete. In the present era, machine learning techniques are also the future of all research and development industries. These techniques predict the results based on their previous data. In the construction industry, the find the results or value are very difficult, time consumable, and laborious. These techniques make them very easier to predict the strength of mix design without making samples and destructive tests. The aim of this study is to predict the compressive strength of flyash-based geopolymer concrete by using deep learning and random forest algorithm and comparing them with different errors and coefficient correlation. After the simulation of data, it is proved that the random forest algorithm is the most suitable technique for the prediction of compressive strength. After the developing a model, the various errors were found for accuracy. The mean absolute error, root mean square error, relative absolute error, and root relative squared error are 1.63%, 2.68%, 30.28%, and 37.47%, respectively for the deep learning predicted compressive strength. The errors provide the proof of model accuracy to predict the compressive strength on the basis of ingredients proportions.

Keywords: Green concrete · Geopolymer concrete · Sustainable · Machine learning · Random forest algorithm

R. N. Shaw et al. (Eds.): ICACIS 2022, CCIS 1749, pp. 170–179, 2023.
https://doi.org/10.1007/978-3-031-25088-0_14

1 Introduction

In a new age, humanity has reached several developmental landmarks. Improvements to society's infrastructures are possible [1]. As a result, the building sector is essential to societal progress. When building anything, concrete is one of the first things that should be required. Geopolymer concrete is a green concrete that is entirely replace the cement by fly ash and GGBFS and alkaline solution and it is work as binding material, while the conventional concrete is regular and household usable concrete from last two three decades [2–6]. Concrete is the second most useful substance after water in the world [7]. Since cement serves as the major binding element in traditional concrete components, its manufacture results in the emission of around one tonne of carbon dioxide [8]. Fly ash and ground granulated blast furnace slag (GGBFS) are used in lieu of cement in geopolymer concrete [9]. The concrete uses a high emission ingredient, cement. As a result, Geopolymer concrete cuts down on carbon footprints by roughly 80% compared to regular concrete [10].

The release of carbon dioxide has a direct effect on the warming of the planet [11]. Because of this, sustainable development is crucial for the industry's long-term success. Comparatively, geopolymer is less expensive than traditional concrete [12]. It cuts the cost roughly 40% of its original [13]. Due to its superior strength and longevity, geopolymer concrete may replace traditional concrete [14]. To manufacture geopolymer concrete, an alkaline solution is used to activate the pozzolanic material (such as fly-ash, slag, or metakaolin) that substitutes the cement in traditional concrete [15]. Sodium or potassium hydroxides and silicates might be employed as an alkaline ingredient in geopolymer concrete [16]. The chemical reactions and chemical bonding of geopolymer concrete are unique in comparison to those of regular concrete [17]. As Prof. Davidovits initially shown, the term "geopolymer" comes from the bond formed in these processes. In comparison to traditional concrete, geopolymer concrete performed better in laboratory testing, suggesting it may be a viable option. It might be a future of the sustainable building sector [18].

Both external and internal elements contribute to the overall strength of geopolymer concrete [19]. Materials quality and varied compositions are examples of internal variables, whereas curing type, time, temperature, humidity, and air containment are examples of exterior influences [20]. The composition and particle size of the binding materials are crucial for starting the reaction and for achieving the desired strength once the reaction has taken place, but the ratio of these two parameters also plays a significant role in regulating the final strength [21]. Compressive strength of cured geopolymer concrete under ambient conditions is enhanced by addition of slag to the formulation [22]. The early strength of the concrete is being boosted by the faster reaction time of the finer particles of flyash and slag owing to their increased surface availability [23]. It's also difficult to obtain a strong reaction from the liquid to binder [24]. Because water is needed for and during geopolymer reaction initiation, but would release during hardening and is not required in geopolymer end reaction products, a minimum liquid content is required to react with all elements of geopolymer concrete [25]. The durability of geopolymer concrete is closely related to the composition liquid content that is optimal for the material [26]. Bond strength is greatly influenced by the choice and application of the superplasticiser in geopolymer concrete [27]. The SNF-based superplasticiser is most well-suited to the geopolymer concrete boding. Initiating the geopolymer reaction relies heavily on the purity and concentration of the alkaline solution [28]. The strength and performance of concrete are directly affected by the molarity of sodium or potassium hydroxide used in the process [29]. Oven-cured samples readily obtained strength than ambient-cured specimens, demonstrating the importance of curing temperature and circumstances in achieving the desired design strength. In addition to its strength, geopolymer concrete is very resistant to harsh climates [30, 31]. To that end, geopolymer concrete might be a game-changer for green building in the future. Geopolymer concrete has a wide variety of uses across the globe. Tunnel and platform building projects in Delhi, India's DMRC (Delhi Metro Rail Corporation) are now using geopolymer concrete.

2 Materials and Method

Fly ash, an alkaline solution (sodium hydroxide and sodium silicate), coarse particles, fine aggregates, superplasticizer, water, and water are the components of geopolymer concrete. Before beginning mass manufacturing of concrete, the quality of all raw ingredients is rigorously tested in labs to ensure consistency. In all cases, flyash is brought in from the closest thermal plant, while alkaline solution and superplasticizer are often acquired from the chemical sector. We use coarse and fine aggregates sourced from our immediate area. The water is utilised in accordance with the local requirements. It takes 20–24 h of mixing time before the alkaline solutions may be prepared. Since geopolymer concrete takes longer to mix in mixers than regular concrete, mixing it by hand is impractical. The use of M-sand in geopolymer concrete is encouraged. As a consequence of its finely divided grains, it performs better than regular sand [32–40].

It is crucial to design the ratio among alumina, silica, and sodium oxide content, thus an XRF test was performed on flyash and other pozzolanic materials to determine the mineral contents contained in the raw samples. In most cases, the chemical solutions' mineral content or minimum assay will be provided by the manufacturer when the chemicals are acquired. Laboratory tests were conducted on both coarse and fine aggregates to determine their particle sizes, fineness modulus, bulk density, moisture content, silt content, specific gravity, shape, size, elongation index, flakiness index, crushing value, impact value, and abrasion value, respectively. The mixed concrete design was chosen only after all these testing was completed.

Today, advanced machine learning methods are essential. They might potentially be used in any area of scientific inquiry or innovation. Mathematical instruments and models provide the basis for these methods. The need to foresee the future necessitates vastly different approaches from each of them. The random forest algorithm method is widely used since it is simple to compute and make predictions based on stored data.

A minimum of three layers are required for an MLP, including an input layer, a hidden layer, and an output layer. They have complete connectivity, with all nodes in one layer linked by weight to all nodes in the following layer. Deep neural networks, a kind of machine learning model, are known as "deep learning." This article's objective is to advise readers on how to best tailor the activation function and loss function of a neural network's last layer to achieve their desired commercial outcomes.

The neural network will contain a single neuron in its last layer, and this neuron will return a continuous numeric result. The genuine value, which is similarly continuous, is compared to the predicted value to get insight into the prediction's accuracy. The method relies fundamentally on the linear function. Function's value might range from 0 to infinity. This method uses the mean squared error mathematical model after the linear function analysis. The mean squared error between the model's prediction and reality is calculated in this way. Mean square error analysis between anticipated and actual values is shown in Fig. 2. The formula for calculating the mean squared error was (1).

$$MSE = \frac{1}{n} \sum\nolimits_{i=1}^{n} (y_i - \overline{y}_i)^2 \tag{1}$$

where $\overline{y}_i$ are the predicted value and y is true the value.

3 Results and Discussion

Here, we present the findings of the machine learning methods multilayer perception (also known as deep learning) and the random forest algorithm (RFA). To begin, we will import the laboratory results from testing geopolymer concrete mix designs into MATLAB, setting aside 70% of the data for model development and 30% for usage before training the model. The original dataset consisted of 61 records, all of which were numerical representations of the 11 components. The path that machines learning approaches follow is shown in Fig. 1. There is one universal process upon which all machine learning methods are built, although their implementations and parameter settings vary widely [41]. It demonstrates the initial features of basic data input to build modal, and then the approach to construct the model from the input data and the desired output data [42]. The projected data and the actual data can be comparable [41].

These machine learning methods follow a defined workflow to efficiently predict from a defined set of output data [43]. Figure 1 depicts the whole procedure used by the deep learning method to foretell the final outcomes. Input, output, and data training are the three main components of this task. Initially, 11 input parameters and a single output parameter are gathered. Following data gathering, it would begin training classifiers and data sets. Loading the input data and configuring the training classifier's input parameters are the first steps in the data set training procedure. The next step is to complete the data training using classifiers, after which you will get the results. The procedure employs a data-training method called 10-fold cross-validation in an effort to lower the margin of error between anticipated and actual outcomes. That's the whole procedure of deep learning to foretell outcomes using real-world data.

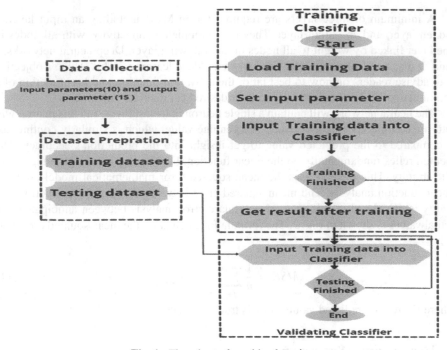

Fig. 1. Flowchart of machine learning

$$R^2 = \frac{\left(n \sum x_i y_i - \sum x_i \sum y_i\right)^2}{\left(n \sum x_i^2 - \left(\sum x_i\right)^2\right)\left(n \sum y_i^2 - \left(\sum y_i\right)^2\right)} \quad (2)$$

$$MAE = 1/n \sum_{i=1}^{n} |x_i - y_i| \quad (3)$$

$$RMSE = \sqrt{\left(\frac{1}{n}\right) \sum_{i=1}^{n} |x_i - y_i|^2} \quad (4)$$

$$RAE = \frac{\sum_{i=1}^{n} |x_i - y_i|}{\sum_{i=1}^{n} |x_i - (1/n) \sum_{i=1}^{n} x_i|} \quad (5)$$

$$RRSE = \sqrt{\frac{\sum_{i=1}^{n} (x_i - y_i)^2}{\sum_{i=1}^{n} \left(x_i - (1/n) \sum_{i=1}^{n} x_i\right)^2}} \quad (6)$$

The real findings of compressive strength of geopolymer concrete samples are remarkably comparable to the results discovered by the methods of machine learning. Table 1 presents a comparison of the results of compressive strength measurements taken using real, and random forest methodologies. There are sixty rows of data showing the

Table 1. Compressive strength of specimen's actual values and predicted value

Actual compressive strength (Mpa)	Predicted compressive strength (Mpa)
21.5	21.5
24.4	24.4
22.9	22.9
21.7	21.7
16.2	16.2
21.3	21.3
23.6	23.6
24.1	24.1
24	24
23.4	23.4
25.4	25.4
29.1	29.1
26.4	26.4
25.1	25.1
18.1	18.1
23.8	23.8
27.6	27.6
28.9	28.9
28.4	28.4
27.6	27.6

compressive strength of the material. Each row has three columns of real compressive strength, while the rows themselves are predicted via deep learning and random forest algorithms. The units used to describe the compressive strength are MPa. The majority of the values are averaged out to be between 25 and 45 MPa. The numerous equations are used in order to verify the error that exists between the actual compressive strength and the projected value. Errors were computed by using the following mathematical formulae to get the R2, MAE, RMSE, RAE, and RRSE. These calculations are presented in the form of Eqs. 2–6. The different error values that were determined using the equations are shown in Table 2. It takes into account the neighbouring correlation coefficient, as well as the mean absolute error, the root mean square error, the relative absolute error, and the root relative squared error.

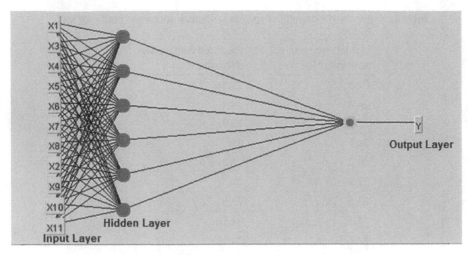

Fig. 2. Neural network

Table 2. Different errors between actual and predicted values

	Random forest
Correlation coefficient (R^2)	0.9321
MAE	1.6276
RMSE	2.6814
RAE	30.2785
RRSE	37.4683%

4   Conclusion

The experimental investigation in laboratories, to provide the compressive strength of the specimens for different ingredients proportions. Then, random forest algorithm machine learning techniques is used predict the future compressive strength for different ingredients proportions by developing a model. After the developing a model, the various errors were found for accuracy. The mean absolute error, root mean square error, relative absolute error, and root relative squared error are 1.63%, 2.68%, 30.28%, and 37.47%, respectively for the deep learning predicted compressive strength. The errors provide the proof of model accuracy to predict the compressive strength on the basis of ingredients proportions.

References

1. Verma, M., Dev, N.: Geopolymer concrete: a way of sustainable construction. Int. J. Recent Res. Asp. **5**, 201–205 (2018)

2. Davidovits, J., Quentin, S.: Geopolymers inorganic polymeric new materials. J. Therm. Anal. **37**, 1633–1656 (1991)
3. Davidovits, J.: Geopolymers and geopolymeric materials. J. Therm. Anal. **35**, 429–441 (1989)
4. Davidovits, J.: Geopolymer Chemistry and Applications, 5th edn. (2020)
5. Davidovits, J.: 30 years of successes and failures in geopolymer applications. Market trends and potential breakthroughs. In: Geopolymer 2002 Conference, Melbourne, Australia, 28–29 October 2002, pp. 1–16 (2002)
6. Davidovits, J.: Geopolymer Chemistry & Applications (2015)
7. Upreti, K., Verma, M.: Prediction of compressive strength of high-volume fly ash concrete using artificial neural network. J. Eng. Res. Appl. **1**, 24–32 (2022). https://doi.org/10.55953/JERA.2022.2104
8. Syed, M.H., Upreti, K., Nasir, M.S., Alam, M.S., Kumar Sharma, A.: Addressing image and Poisson noise deconvolution problem using deep learning approaches. Computat. Intell., 1–15 (2022). https://doi.org/10.1111/coin.12510
9. Verma, M., Dev, N.: Geopolymer concrete: a sustainable and economic concrete via experimental analysis (2021). https://doi.org/10.21203/rs.3.rs-185150/v1
10. Verma, M., Dev, N.: Effect of ground granulated blast furnace slag and fly ash ratio and the curing conditions on the mechanical properties of geopolymer concrete. Struct. Concr. **23**, 2015–2029 (2022). https://doi.org/10.1002/suco.202000536
11. Verma, M.: Experimental investigation on the properties of Geopolymer concrete after replacement of river sand with the M-sand. In: International e-Conference on Sustainable Development and Recent Trends in Civil Engineering, pp. 46–54 (2022)
12. Verma, M., Nigam, M.: Mechanical behaviour of self compacting and self curing concrete. Int. J. Innov. Res. Sci. Eng. Technol. **6**, 14361–14366 (2017). https://doi.org/10.15680/IJIRSET.2017.0607245
13. Verma, M., Dev, N.: Effect of liquid to binder ratio and curing temperature on the engineering properties of the geopolymer concrete. Silicon **14**, 1743–1757 (2021). https://doi.org/10.1007/s12633-021-00985-w
14. Verma, M., Dev, N., Rahman, I., Nigam, M., Ahmed, M., Mallick, J.: Geopolymer concrete: a material for sustainable development in Indian construction industries. Curr. Comput. Aided Drug Des. **12**, 514 (2022). https://doi.org/10.3390/cryst12040514
15. Verma, M., et al.: Experimental analysis of geopolymer concrete: a sustainable and economic concrete using the cost estimation model. Adv. Mater. Sci. Eng. **2022**, 1–16 (2022). https://doi.org/10.1155/2022/7488254
16. Upreti, K., Vargis, B.K., Jain, R., Upadhyaya, M.: Analytical study on performance of cloud computing with respect to data security. In: 2021 5th International Conference on Intelligent Computing and Control Systems (ICICCS), pp. 96–101 (2021). https://doi.org/10.1109/ICICCS51141.2021.9432268
17. Garg, C., Namdeo, A., Singhal, A., Singh, P., Shaw, R.N., Ghosh, A.: Adaptive fuzzy logic models for the prediction of compressive strength of sustainable concrete. In: Bianchini, M., Piuri, V., Das, S., Shaw, R.N. (eds.) Advanced Computing and Intelligent Technologies. LNNS, vol. 218, pp. 593–605. Springer, Singapore (2022). https://doi.org/10.1007/978-981-16-2164-2_47
18. Chouksey, A., Verma, M., Dev, N., Rahman, I., Upreti, K.: An investigation on the effect of curing conditions on the mechanical and microstructural properties of the geopolymer concrete. Mater. Res. Express. **9**, 055003 (2022). https://doi.org/10.1088/2053-1591/ac6be0
19. Palimkar, P., Bajaj, V., Mal, A.K., Shaw, R.N., Ghosh, A.: Unique action identifier by using magnetometer, accelerometer and gyroscope: KNN approach. In: Bianchini, M., Piuri, V., Das, S., Shaw, R.N. (eds.) Advanced Computing and Intelligent Technologies. LNNS, vol. 218, pp. 607–631. Springer, Singapore (2022). https://doi.org/10.1007/978-981-16-2164-2_48

20. Verma, M., Dev, N.: Review on the effect of different parameters on behavior of Geopolymer Concrete. Int. J. Innov. Res. Sci. Eng. Technol. **6**, 11276–11281 (2017). https://doi.org/10.15680/IJIRSET.2017.0606210

21. Kumar, R., Verma, M., Dev, N.: Investigation of fresh, mechanical, and impact resistance properties of rubberized concrete. In: International e-Conference on Sustainable Development and Recent Trends in Civil Engineering, pp. 88–94 (2022)

22. Verma, M., Dev, N.: Effect of superplasticiser on physical, chemical and mechanical properties of the geopolymer concrete. In: Challenges of Resilient and Sustainable Infrastructure Development in Emerging Economies, Kolkata, India, pp. 1185–1191 (2020)

23. Verma, M., Dev, N.: Sodium hydroxide effect on the mechanical properties of flyash-slag based geopolymer concrete. Struct. Concr. **22**, E368–E379 (2021). https://doi.org/10.1002/suco.202000068

24. Verma, M., Juneja, A., Saini, D.: Effect of waste tyre rubber in the concrete. In: International e-Conference on Sustainable Development and Recent Trends in Civil Engineering, 4–5 January 2022, pp. 99–103 (2022)

25. Kumar, R., Verma, M., Dev, N., Lamba, N.: Influence of chloride and sulfate solution on the long-term durability of modified rubberized concrete. J. Appl. Polym. Sci., 1–15 (2022). https://doi.org/10.1002/app.52880

26. Gupta, A., Gupta, N., Saxena, K.K., Goyal, S.K.: Investigation of the mechanical strength of stone dust and ceramic waste based composite. Mater. Today Proc. **44**, 29–33 (2021). https://doi.org/10.1016/j.matpr.2020.06.011

27. Gupta, A.: Investigation of the strength of ground granulated blast furnace slag based geopolymer composite with silica fume. Mater. Today Proc. **44**, 23–28 (2021). https://doi.org/10.1016/j.matpr.2020.06.010

28. Gupta, A., Gupta, N., Saxena, K.K.: Experimental study of the mechanical and durability properties of Slag and Calcined Clay based geopolymer composite. Adv. Mater. Process. Technol. **00**, 1–15 (2021). https://doi.org/10.1080/2374068X.2021.1948709

29. Parashar, A.K., Gupta, A.: Investigation of the effect of bagasse ash, hooked steel fibers and glass fibers on the mechanical properties of concrete. Mater. Today Proc. **44**, 801–807 (2021). https://doi.org/10.1016/j.matpr.2020.10.711

30. Goyal, S.B., Bedi, P., Rajawat, A.S., Shaw, R.N., Ghosh, A.: Multi-objective fuzzy-swarm optimizer for data partitioning. In: Bianchini, M., Piuri, V., Das, S., Shaw, R.N. (eds.) Advanced Computing and Intelligent Technologies. LNNS, vol. 218, pp. 307–318. Springer, Singapore (2022). https://doi.org/10.1007/978-981-16-2164-2_25

31. Gupta, A., Gupta, N., Saxena, K.K.: Mechanical and durability characteristics assessment of geopolymer composite (GPC) at varying silica fume content. J. Compos. Sci. **5** (2021). https://doi.org/10.3390/JCS5090237

32. IS 383 1970: Specification for coarse and fine aggregates from natural sources for concrete. Bureau of Indian Standards, pp. 1–20 (1997)

33. IS 2386 (Part II): Methods of test for aggregates for concrete Part II Estimation of deleterious materials and organic impurities. Bureau of Indian Standards 2386 (1998)

34. IS 2386 (Part VIII): Methods of test for aggregates for concrete Part VIII Petrographic examination. Methods of test for aggregates for concrete Part II Estimation of deleterious materials and organic impurities. Bureau of Indian Standards 2386 (1997)

35. IS 2386 (Part V): Methods of test for aggregates for concrete Part V Soundness. Bureau of Indian Standards (1997)

36. IS 2386 (Part I): Methods of test for aggregates for concrete Part I Particle size and shape. Bureau of Indian Standards 2386 (1997)

37. IS 2386 (Part III): Methods of test for aggregates for concrete Part III Specific gravity, density, voids, absorption and bulking. Bureau of Indian Standards 2386 (1997)

38. IS 2386 (Part VII): Methods of test for aggregates for concrete Part VII Alkali aggregate reactivity. Bureau of Indian Standards (1997)
39. IS 2386 (Part IV): Methods of test for aggregates for concrete Part IV Mechanical Properties. Bureau of Indian Standards 2386 (1997)
40. IS 2386 (Part VI): Methods of test for aggregates for concrete Part VI Measuring mortar making properties of fine aggregate. Bureau of Indian Standards 2386 (1997)
41. Ananthi, J., Sengottaiyan, N., Anbukaruppusamy, S., Upreti, K., Dubey, A.K.: Forest fire prediction using IoT and deep learning. Int. J. Adv. Technol. Eng. Explor. 9, 246–256 (2022). https://doi.org/10.19101/IJATEE.2021.87464
42. Palanikkumar, D., Upreti, K., Venkatraman, S., Roselin Suganthi, J., Kannan, S., Srinivasan, S.: Fuzzy logic for underground mining method selection. Intell. Autom. Soft Comput. 32, 1843–1854 (2022). https://doi.org/10.32604/IASC.2022.023350
43. Juneja, N., Upreti, K.: An introduction to few soft computing techniques to predict software quality. In: 2nd International Conference on Telecommunication Networks, TEL-NET 2017, January 2018, pp. 1–6 (2018). https://doi.org/10.1109/TEL-NET.2017.8343581

Cardiovascular Disease Prognosis and Analysis Using Machine Learning Techniques

Anmol Kapoor[1], Shreya Kapoor[2], Kamal Upreti[2(✉)], Prashant Singh[3], Seema Kapoor[4], Mohammad Shabbir Alam[5], and Mohammad Shahnawaz Nasir[5]

[1] Department of Computer Science and Engineering, Maharaja Surajmal Institute of Technology, Delhi, India
[2] Department of Computer Science and Engineering, Akhilesh Das Gupta Institute of Technology and Management, Delhi, India
kamalupreti1989@gmail.com
[3] Department of Computer Science and Engineering, Sunder Deep Engineering College, Ghaziabad, India
[4] Department of Science, Mira Model School, Delhi, India
[5] Department of Computer Science, College of Computer Science and IT, Jazan University, Jizan, Saudi Arabia
mnasir@jazanu.edu.sa

Abstract. Cardiovascular disease (CVD), includes a number of conditions that affect the heart and, in recent decades, has been the leading cause of death worldwide. Heart disease is linked to a variety of dangers, making it urgently necessary to find precise, reliable, and reasonable ways to make an early diagnosis and start treating the condition. Early diagnosis of cardiovascular illnesses can assist high-risk individuals in deciding on lifestyle changes that will minimise issues, which can be a big medical advancement. Since it takes more intelligence, time and expertise to provide 24-h medical consultations for patients, it is not always possible to accurately monitor patients every day. While an incorrect diagnosis of CVD can be catastrophic, an accurate diagnosis can lower the chance of major health issues. In order to compare the findings and analysis, various machine learning methods and deep learning are used.

Data analysis is a frequently used technique for analysing enormous amounts of data in the healthcare industry. In order to help healthcare professionals forecast heart illness, researchers analyse enormous volumes of complex health records utilising various statistical and machine learning (ML) techniques.

The main objective is to identify an appropriate method for heart disease prediction that is effective and precise. In this chapter, we conducted research on heart disease from the perspective of data analytics. To identify and anticipate the patterns of diseases, we applied different data analytical techniques on data sets of various sizes. We determined which algorithms were the most pertinent and also examined the accuracy, sensitivity, specificity and precision rate of various algorithms.

Keywords: Artificial intelligence · Cardiovascular medicine · Machine learning · Support Vector Machine

R. N. Shaw et al. (Eds.): ICACIS 2022, CCIS 1749, pp. 180–194, 2023.
https://doi.org/10.1007/978-3-031-25088-0_15

1 Introduction

Over the past few years, artificial intelligence (AI) has drastically transformed the nature of healthcare by offering fresh perspectives and chances to enhance care [1]. While Machine Learning (ML) is extending healthcare paths and creating new horizons in cardiovascular fitness, AI is progressing in other facets of human life, such as automated voice recognition systems and self-driving cars [2].

An all-encompassing term, AI, refers to the employment of algorithms and software that exhibits human-like cognition while evaluating, perceiving, and comprehending complex medical and health data [3]. AI can be applied to any machine that exhibits qualities of intelligence, such as understanding, rational and logical thinking. Machine learning (ML), a component of AI, is a term used to describe computers that can retrieve information from data, enhance their functionality, or anticipate future developments [6]. An algorithm is only a series of steps that must be taken to arrive at a solution. In order to learn how to process information, algorithms must be trained. Learning from data sets and generalising to novel, previously undiscovered circumstances are the fundamental objectives of these techniques. Clinicians are now interested in AI's recent resurgence and how it is being used in a range of commercial and academic domains. The application of AI, particularly the subfield of ML algorithms in preventive, diagnostics, vulnerability analysis, treatment and choice of medication has been accelerated by the convergence of unprecedented computer power and data storage capacity [4].

Finding hidden patterns and estimating the presence value on a scale are the objectives of applying data mining techniques to the dataset. The amount of data needed to forecast cardiac disease is enormous and too difficult to collect and analyse using traditional methods. Although there is a knowledge gap, the healthcare sector is an information-rich area. Cardiologists base their judgments regarding patient treatment on statistics, and they typically possess direct exposure to more comprehensive statistical data on patients. Healthcare systems have a lot of data online, but there is a shortage of efficient analysis tools to find hidden patterns in the data [5].

In the present environment, a majority of people express concerns about the different diagnostic tests performed by physicians, which cost them effort and resources. In some instances, a patient's effective therapy may not begin until an appropriate diagnosis has been made. When lethal infections are involved, it may have severe effects. For this, several clinics utilize decision-making tools for straightforward questions like the patient's age, which gender is much more likely to have the ailment, whether younger or older people are more likely to have it, etc. If we make use of the information that is concealed in such a database, we can solve a variety of additional issues that arise in the healthcare sector when it comes to the treatments offered to people.

Through the numerous cardiac characteristics of the patient, we investigated models for heart disease prediction, and we used machine learning techniques to identify imminent heart illness. It is clear that using AI-derived methodologies is the finest method for making fact-based decisions. To find the most pertinent data, AI requires tight cooperation between computer scientists, clinical investigators, clinicians, other healthcare professionals, and regulatory agencies [7].

2   Literature Review

Medicine is getting more complex, there is difficulty in understanding all the data correctly and facing the workload of modern medicine. This trend is prevalent in cardiology as well. One of the most serious health conditions, cardiovascular disease (CVD) has a high morbidity and mortality rate and a growing prevalence [8].

A branch of computer science called artificial intelligence (AI) tries to imitate human reasoning, learning, and knowledge storage [9]. Artificial general intelligence (AGI) refers to a holistic purpose system with the ability to reason and think critically and with a broad knowledge base that enables dynamic intelligence in a wide range of subjects and applications that mirror or even surpass the human psyche. Without a set of guiding principles to direct its actions, AI can intelligently complete a task and adapt to a variety of scenarios. Though using separate constructs—general and applied AI—it instead analyses and learns from the patterns in the data that it gathers [10].

AI and ML are set to affect almost all facets of human experience. Recent advances in cardiovascular (CV) treatment have sparked a plethora of interest in AI, ML techniques. AI and digitized medical records provide the potential to advance medical awareness of problems and introduce a tailored strategy for CV care in the era of contemporary medicine. AI methods have been applied to cardiovascular medicine to improve clinical care, enable affordability, find genotypic and phenotypic characteristics in well-established ailments, and lower recurrence and fatality rates [9].

AI can help perform well defined tasks that physicians perform such as Test interpretation, prognosis and diagnosis. It also helps support underserved communities for example remote cardiology screening. It also helps to integrate multiple modalities and develop novel tools which includes combining electronic medical record notes with images to improve risk prediction.

In order to create algorithms that mimic people's perception, judgement, and feature identification, AI, a swiftly developing cross-disciplinary field, incorporates various fields of science, engineering and medicine. Three main objectives of AI in CVD are to enhance patient assistance, increase effectiveness, and enhance therapeutic results. Cardiology is well-positioned to profit particularly from AI due to the expansion of possible sources of new patient data and improvements in research and treatments [12].

The most prevalent type of AI is ML, in which specialized statistical algorithms 'learn' by inferring trends from records. Unsupervised ML is a type of learning where algorithm discovers statistical correlations in unlabelled data, while supervised machine learning employs huge amounts of classified information to build an algorithm to reliably anticipate the result.

To maximise value and get beyond the diversity, intricacy, and inherent noise associated while applying AI algorithms to outer patient populations, vast quantities of precisely annotated data sets are necessary [17].

When a model has trouble adjusting to new, slightly altered data, it is said to be over fit. The majority of current studies have only been trained and evaluated in research settings, which is a substantial hurdle for cardiological research. Another difficulty is the inclusion of biases while selecting data sets for AI. In particular, adversarial approaches, where input data for algorithms are given which appear "normal" but lead to model distortion resulting from slight discrepancies, before and after training, are vulnerable to Deep neural network (DNNs). Fortunately, scientists have created a regularisation technique that lessens the effect of adversarial noise on a DNN model's output [12]. Beyond such remedies, consistent constructive criticism from doctors as well as prospective users is crucial in the creation of a programme.

Applications of AI include improving system-wide logistical procedures as well as supporting decision-making for the care of specific patients and new pathophysiologic discoveries. Furthermore, challenges and impediments discovered in present CVD experiments are looked at. Long term potential for predicting CVD risk and evaluation are suggested using inclusive multi-modal big data techniques [13].

We focus on cardiology-specific predictive modelling concepts and speculate on how AI and ML might be used in cardiovascular medicine in the future. This chapter examines typical supervised learning techniques and reviews a few applications in cardiology.

3   Methodology

The model is developed using scientific data, and it is tested on updated results before being used to draw conclusions. Utilizing a fraction of the available scientific data, the trained ML model's performance is assessed (which is absent while training). Typically, it is termed as evaluation procedure. The correctness of the ML model is one performance metric that is assessed during this procedure. The ratio of properly estimated characteristics to all characteristics available for prediction characterises the accuracy of a ML model's performance over unseen data.

3.1   Categories of Machine Learning

According to classical statistics, ML is more concerned with creating computerized medical decisions that aid practitioners in making more precise estimates than it is with developing simple approximated value models. Supervised, unsupervised, and reinforcement learning are the three subtypes of ML. The table below (Table 1) provides an explanation of how these models are used in cardiology.

Table 1. Machine learning techniques

Learning	Description	Example application	Drawback
Supervised	It happens in the presence of a supervisor. In this, the output is already known. The machine is fed with lots of input data. The model is built to predict the outcome. It involves a labelled dataset. It's a fast learning mechanism with very high accuracy. It includes regression and classification problem	1. A prediction model for acute myocardial infarction can be built utilising regularised regression and genomic measures as well as prognostic features 2. Decision trees are used for the diagnosis of cardiovascular events risk 3. Plasma metabolites are utilised to predict in-stent restenosis using support vector machines [14]	small datasets can result in low accuracy
Unsupervised	It is an independent learning process and can take place without the help of a supervisor. There is no output mapping with the input. It involves an unlabelled dataset. It is used to identify genotypic or phenotypic characteristics from concealed formations and novel disease mechanism present in the information without user intervention that is the hidden patterns can be detected	1. Deep learning algorithms are used for development of patient prognosis using electronic health data in an unsupervised manner 2. The technique of tensor factorization is utilised to subtype congestive heart failure with maintained ejection fraction 3. Type 2 diabetes mellitus is subtyped using the topological data analysis technique using digital health data [15]	Initial cluster patterns are difficult to identify which might lead to inaccurate results

(*continued*)

Table 1. *(continued)*

Learning	Description	Example application	Drawback
Reinforcement	It's a hybrid of supervised and unsupervised technique and is a long term iterative process. In this, learning takes place from feedback and past experiences. More the feedback, higher is the accuracy of the algorithm so self-learning takes place by trial and error. It is also called as Markov Decision Process(MDP)	Using templates like "No pneumothorax or pleural effusion" and "Lungs are clear," the template database is built from previously existing knowledge based on human medical reports. REINFORCE is used to train the retrieval and generation modules together, with sentence-level and word-level incentives, respectively [16]	Based on feedback and past experiences, it's a trial and error method

3.2 Working Model

The entire collection of data is randomly split into a training set (generally 80%) and a testing set (generally 20%). The training dataset is the content that the machine uses to develop its information processing skills. The training data set is first used to build a trained model with certain hyper parameters. Next, the effectiveness of this trained model is assessed on an unidentified test set. Testing dataset is a group of unobserved data used solely to evaluate the effectiveness of a classifier that has been completely stated. The aim is to find the most effective model using pre-processed data (supervised, unsupervised or reinforced learning). The built model uses any one of the algorithms such as Support Vector Machine (SVM), Naïve Bayes (NB), K-Nearest Neighbour (KNN), Genetic Algorithm (GA), Random Forest (RF), Artificial Neural Networks (ANN) or Gradient Boosting (GB). Then, this model is trained. The trained model is used to test unknown data. After this, a confusion matrix is prepared which predicts us the success of our model.

The flowchart for the suggested methodology is shown in Fig. 1.

3.3 Data Tools

There are numerous ML models available right now, each with their own unique features, applications, and restrictions. The algorithms function by being given a starting set of information and as they gain precision over period, more information is added to the previous set. The machine becomes more efficient as a result of this practise of periodically subjecting the algorithms to fresh information Categorization, prescriptive analytics, and data management operations all require the use of ML algorithms. The primary ML tools are briefly described and categorised in Table 2.

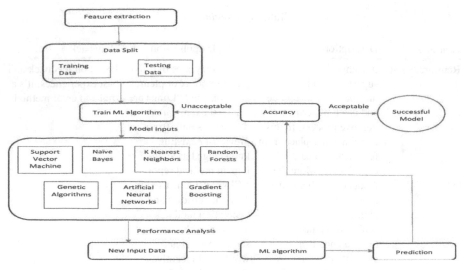

Fig. 1. Working model

Table 2. Brief overview and categorization of the primary Machine Learning tools

Algorithm	Learning	Overview
SVM	Supervised	The goal is to identify a function known as a hyperplane from the resolution of a linear system constructed from multiple training subset instructions. The test sub-set lessons are grouped into two distinct groups using this hyperplane [17]
KNN	Supervised	A vector norm is a mathematical function that links a vector with a value $>= 0$ and satisfies certain requirements. The distance between two vectors is the norm of their difference. The KNN determines the separation between each vector (lesson) that makes up the database using a norm. The k vectors that are closest to each vector in the database are then identified
ANN	Supervised	A structure known as a graph, which is made up of a combination of edges and nodes is employed. Nodes in a graph are stacked with weighted edges connecting them, that stand for the value that has been given to a particular link. The notion is that these values are applied to create an output from a set of inputs [18]
NB	Supervised	Bayes' conditional probability investigations are used to determine which group an individual lesson belongs to (out of a total of n possible categories) [19]
GB	Supervised	It is a tree-based method that creates sequential decision trees that can be linked to improve the prediction by using gradient vectors pertaining to a mathematical function's direction of highest growth [31]

(continued)

Table 2. (*continued*)

Algorithm	Learning	Overview
RF	Supervised	In a random forest, each tree's behaviour is predicted using values from a random vector that was randomly collected for each tree in the forest and had the same distribution [30]
GA		This method mimics natural selection, in which the most competent organisms are chosen to reproduce in so as to give rise to the subsequent generation of offspring's

3.4 Evaluation

Confusion matrix, accuracy score, sensitivity are all utilized in the evaluation process.

A confusion matrix is a structure that resembles a table and contains target value in addition to true positive and true negative values. There are four elements to its definition:

1. True positive (TP) - items are labelled as true and are also true in reality.
2. False positive (FP) - where the values are accurate, yet they're misidentified.
3. False negative (FN) - occurs when a true result is mistakenly deemed to be unfavourable.
4. True negative (TN) - genuinely and unmistakably had a negative number.

Predicted Value

	+ve	-ve
Predicted Values	True-Positive	False-Negative
	False-Positive	True-Negative

Accuracy: It is calculated as the difference between values obtained and a standard value. Accuracy is the percentage of accurately anticipated observations to all observations. It is a fantastic indicator, only when the numbers of false positives and false negatives are almost equal in the dataset. To assess the effectiveness of a model, we must consider additional factors.

$$Accuracy = \frac{TP + TN}{TP + TN + FP + FN}$$

Precision: Precision is determined by dividing the overall number of positively identified data sets by the proportion of accurately categorized positive cases (True Positive) (either correct or incorrect)

$$Precision = TP/(TP + FP)$$

Specificity: measures how successfully a model is able to identify negative situations by calculating the percentage of actual instances that were classified as negative. It is also known as the "real negative rate." The equation is:

$$Specificity = TN/(TN + FP)$$

Sensitivity: the percentage of cases that were actually positive were accurately forecasted as positive or TP. Another name for sensitivity is recall. In other words, a person who was unhealthy was projected to be unhealthy [11]. The equation is:

$$Sensitivity = TP/(TP + FN)$$

4 Result

Data pre-processing is a critical period in the ML process since the calibre of how successfully our model learns directly depends on the data and the knowledge that can be derived from it. It is essential that we pre-process the dataset before supplying it to the model for this reason.

To apply ML techniques and optimize sensitivity and specificity, we only select those attributes that are significantly reliant on one another. Modern cardiovascular medicine studies using machine learning technologies are mentioned in Table 3.

Table 3. Studies in contemporary cardiology using machine learning techniques

Algorithm	Authors	Purpose of data collection/data collected	No. of samples/datasets	Result
Support Vector Machine (SVM)	Berikol et al. [20]	Clinical, ECG, laboratory (troponin I and CK-MB levels) data are used to establish whether or not an acute coronary syndrome is present	228	Accuracy: 99.13% Sensitivity: 98.22% Specificity: 100% Precision: 100%

(continued)

Table 3. (*continued*)

Algorithm	Authors	Purpose of data collection/data collected	No. of samples/datasets	Result
Random Forests (RF)	Pal Madhumita et al. [21]	The goal is to foresee a patient's development of heart disease	303	Accuracy: 86.9% Sensitivity: 90.6% Specificity: 82.7%
	P. Sujatha et al. [22]	Techniques used to diagnose cardiovascular disease in its early stages	91	Precision: 88.9%
K-nearest neighbors (KNN)	Al-Mallah et al. [23]	Electrocardiographic and clinical data for ten different time periods to evaluate survival	34212	Sensitivity: 87.4% Specificity: 97.2%
	P. Sujatha et al. [22]	Techniques used to diagnose cardiovascular disease in its early stages	91	Accuracy: 72.53% Precision: 75.51
Artificial Neural Networks (ANN)	Muhammad Saqib et al. [24]	The heart disease dataset from the UCI Machine Repository is used for this project, which aims to provide an accurate diagnosis of heart illness	–	Accuracy: 95.31% Sensitivity: 95.35% Specificity: 95.28%
Gradient Boosting (GB)	Muhammad et al. [25]	Patients with coronary artery disease diagnostic data were taken into consideration	506	Accuracy: 90.90% Sensitivity: 87.20% Specificity: 91.12%
	P. Ghosh et al. [26]	To create a reliable system for properly forecasting heart illness	–	Precision: 84%

(*continued*)

Table 3. (*continued*)

Algorithm	Authors	Purpose of data collection/data collected	No. of samples/datasets	Result
Genetic algorithms (GA)	Stuckey et al. [27]	For predicting cardiovascular disease in patients	606	Sensitivity: 92%, Specificity: 62% Predictive value for coronary disease: 96%
	S. Kanwal et al. [28]	To find an efficient method for treating and detecting cardiovascular diseases	–	Accuracy: 92% Precision: 96%
Naive Bayes (NB)	Vincy Cherian et al. [29]	13 attributes were chosen for predicting coronary artery disease	50	Accuracy: 86% Sensitivity: 75% Specificity: 96.1% Precision: 94.7%

This comparative data analysis work's main goal is to provide a means of heart attack prediction. There is a chance to discover previously unrecognized sickness details utilising historical cardiac records. To help in the prognosis of heart problems and to provide a novel viewpoint on hidden patterns in the data, the CVD prediction system will apply data mining strategies to medical records.

In our comparison of performance, we found that SVM algorithm has 99.13% accuracy (Fig. 2), 98.22% sensitivity (Fig. 3), specificity: 100% (Fig. 4) and 100% precision (Fig. 5). So it is a better algorithm compared to other ML algorithms (Fig. 6) in predicting cardiovascular diseases.

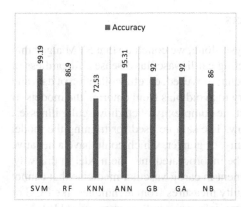

Fig. 2. Accuracy evaluation of current models

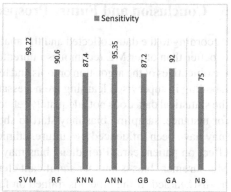

Fig. 3. Sensitivity evaluation of current models

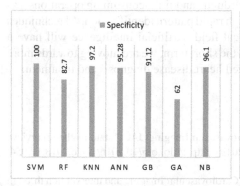

Fig. 4. Specificity evaluation of current models

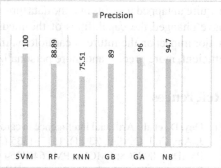

Fig. 5. Precision rate evaluation of current models

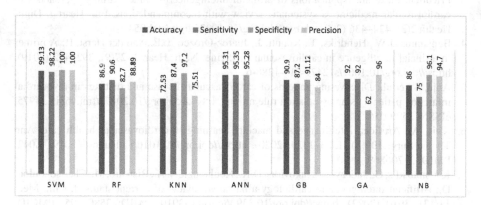

Fig. 6. Overall comparison of existing models

5   Conclusion and Future Prospects

According to the data collected and the analysis done, we conclude that SVM algorithm is better than other ML techniques in predicting cardiovascular diseases. Regardless of the objectives of the algorithm or tools and techniques used, careful collection of data and labelling in supervised learning are necessary to avoid bias from entering the models. If the statistical data does not adequately reflect the complexity of cardiovascular illnesses, for instance, sampling bias may start to show. The sample used for training the model may have been influenced by culture, ethnicity, or gender, which could have a negative effect on patient care. Prejudicial bias may be incorporated into the model in this way. Measurement bias is another significant element in cardiovascular medicine that cannot be disregarded. If the model is trained on faulty measures from techniques like ECG or cardiac MRI, or on incorrect and noisy picture data, error will be introduced [16].

AI will automate a lot of tasks physicians perform (diagnosis, treatment, prescription) in the next decade and will also enable new algorithms that were previously impossible. By enabling humans to automate formerly arduous and time-consuming operations and acquire untapped insights into the data through rapid pattern identification, AI techniques have changed the capabilities of the medical field. Artificial intelligence will have a major impact on the future of cardiology. In the short term, we are moving towards more efficient, more precise and more personalized heart disease diagnosis and treatment.

References

1. Dey, D., et al.: Artificial intelligence in cardiovascular Imaging: JACC state-of-the-art review. J. Am. Coll. Cardiol. **73**(11), 1317–1335 (2019). https://doi.org/10.1016/j.jacc.2018.12.054. PMID: 30898208; PMCID: PMC6474254
2. Seetharam, K., Shrestha, S., Sengupta, P.P.: Cardiovascular imaging and intervention through the lens of artificial intelligence. Interv. Cardiol. **16**, e31 (2021). https://doi.org/10.15420/icr. 2020.04. PMID: 34754333; PMCID: PMC8559149
3. Friedrich, S., et al.: Applications of artificial intelligence/machine learning approaches in cardiovascular medicine: a systematic review with recommendations. Eur. Heart J. Digit. Health **2**(3), 424–436 (2021). https://doi.org/10.1093/ehjdh/ztab054
4. Benjamins, J.W., Hendriks, T., Knuuti, J., Juarez-Orozco, L.E., van der Harst, P.: A primer in artificial intelligence in cardiovascular medicine. Neth. Hear. J. **27**(9), 392–402 (2019). https://doi.org/10.1007/s12471-019-1286-6
5. Anju, S., et al.: Discovering patterns of cardiovascular disease and diabetes in myocardial infarction patients using association rule mining. https://doi.org/10.20473/fmi.v58i3.34975. eISSN: 2599-056x
6. Kilic, A.: Artificial intelligence and machine learning in cardiovascular health care. Ann Thorac Surg. **109**(5), 1323–1329 (2020). https://doi.org/10.1016/j.athoracsur.2019.09.042. PMID: 31706869
7. Koulaouzidis, G., Jadczyk, T., Iakovidis, D.K., Koulaouzidis, A., Bisnaire, M., Charisopoulou, D.: Artificial intelligence in cardiology-a narrative review of current status. J. Clin. Med. **11**(13), 3910 (2022). https://doi.org/10.3390/jcm11133910. PMID: 35807195; PMCID: PMC9267740
8. Alam, M.S., Jalil, S.Z.A., Upreti, K.: Analyzing recognition of EEG based human attention and emotion using machine learning. Mater. Today Proc. **56**, Part 6, 3349–3354 (2022). https://doi.org/10.1016/j.matpr.2021.10.190. ISSN 2214-7853

9. Krittanawong, C., Zhang, H., Wang, Z., Aydar, M., Kitai, T.: Artificial intelligence in precision cardiovascular medicine. J. Am. Coll. Cardiol. **69**(21), 2657–2664 (2017). https://doi.org/10.1016/j.jacc.2017.03.571. PMID: 28545640

10. Seetharam, K., Shrestha, S., Sengupta, P.P.: Artificial intelligence in cardiovascular medicine. Curr. Treat. Options Cardiovasc. Med. **21**(5), 1–14 (2019). https://doi.org/10.1007/s11936-019-0728-1

11. Upreti, K., Singh, U.K., Jain, R., Kaur, K., Sharma, A.K.: Fuzzy logic based support vector regression (SVR) model for software cost estimation using machine learning. In: Tuba, M., Akashe, S., Joshi, A. (eds.) ICT Systems and Sustainability. LNNS, vol. 321, pp. 917–927. Springer, Singapore (2022). https://doi.org/10.1007/978-981-16-5987-4_90

12. Haq, I.U., Chhatwal, K., Sanaka, K., Xu, B.: Artificial intelligence in cardiovascular medicine: current insights and future prospects. Vasc Health Risk Manag. **12**(18), 517–528 (2022). https://doi.org/10.2147/VHRM.S279337. PMID: 35855754; PMCID: PMC9288176

13. Faizal, A.S.M., Malathi Thevarajah, T., Khor, S.M., Chang, S.-W.: A review of risk prediction models in cardiovascular disease: conventional approach vs. artificial intelligent approach. Comput. Methods Program. Biomed. **207**, 106190 (2021). https://doi.org/10.1016/j.cmpb.2021.106190. ISSN: 0169-2607

14. Johnson, K.W., et al.: Artificial intelligence in cardiology. J. Am. Coll. Cardiol. **71**(23), 2668–2679 (2018). https://doi.org/10.1016/j.jacc.2018.03.521. PMID: 29880128

15. Abdolmanafi, A., Duong, L., Dahdah, N., Cheriet, F.: Deep feature learning for automatic tissue classification of coronary artery using optical coherence tomography. Biomed Opt Express. **8**(2), 1203–1220 (2017). https://doi.org/10.1364/BOE.8.001203. PMID: 28271012; PMCID: PMC5330543

16. Li, Y.: Reinforcement learning applications, 19 August 2019. https://arxiv.org/abs/1908.06973

17. Haider, M., Upreti, K., Nasir, M., Alam, M., Sharma, A.K.: Addressing image and Poisson noise deconvolution problem using deep learning approaches. Comput. Intell. (2022). https://doi.org/10.1111/coin.12510

18. Dilsizian, M.E., Siegel, E.L.: Machine meets biology: a primer on artificial intelligence in cardiology and cardiac imaging. Curr. Cardiol. Rep. **20**(12), 1–7 (2018). https://doi.org/10.1007/s11886-018-1074-8

19. Webb, G., Boughton, J., Wang, Z.: Not so Naive Bayes: aggregating one-dependence estimators. Mach. Learn. **58**, 5–24 (2005). https://doi.org/10.1007/s10994-005-4258-6

20. Berikol, G.B., Yildiz, O., Özcan, İT.: Diagnosis of acute coronary syndrome with a support vector machine. J. Med. Syst. **40**(4), 1–8 (2016). https://doi.org/10.1007/s10916-016-0432-6

21. Palm, M., Parija, S.: Prediction of heart diseases using random forest. J. Phys. Conf. Ser. **1817**, 012009 (2021)

22. Chakraborty, A., Chatterjee, S., Majumder, K., Shaw, R.N., Ghosh, A.: A comparative study of myocardial infarction detection from ECG data using machine learning. In: Bianchini, M., Piuri, V., Das, S., Shaw, R.N. (eds.) Advanced Computing and Intelligent Technologies. LNNS, vol. 218, pp. 257–267. Springer, Singapore (2022). https://doi.org/10.1007/978-981-16-2164-2_21

23. Al-Mallah, M.H., et al.: Using machine learning to define the association between cardiorespiratory fitness and all-cause mortality (from the henry ford exercise testing project). Am. J. Cardiol. **120**(11), 2078–2084 (2017). https://doi.org/10.1016/j.amjcard.2017.08.029. PMID: 28951020

24. Saqib Nawaz, M., Shoaib, B., Ashraf, M.A.: Intelligent cardiovascular disease prediction empowered with gradient descent optimization, Heliyon **7**(5), e06948 (2021). https://doi.org/10.1016/j.heliyon.2021.e06948. ISSN: 2405–8440

25. Muhammad, L.J., Al-Shourbaji, I., Haruna, A.A., Mohammed, I.A., Ahmad, A., Jibrin, M.B.: Machine learning predictive models for coronary artery disease. SN Comput. Sci. **2**(5), 1–11 (2021). https://doi.org/10.1007/s42979-021-00731-4
26. Ghosh, P., et al.: Efficient prediction of cardiovascular disease using machine learning algorithms with relief and LASSO feature selection techniques. IEEE Access **9**, 19304–19326 (2021). https://doi.org/10.1109/ACCESS.2021.3053759
27. Stuckey, T.D., et al.: Cardiac Phase Space Tomography: a novel method of assessing coronary artery disease utilizing machine learning. PLoS ONE **13**(8), e0198603 (2018). https://doi.org/10.1371/journal.pone.0198603. PMID: 30089110; PMCID: PMC6082503
28. Kanwal, S., Rashid, J., Nisar, M.W., Kim, J., Hussain, A.: An effective classification algorithm for heart disease prediction with genetic algorithm for feature selection. In: 2021 Mohammad Ali Jinnah University International Conference on Computing (MAJICC), pp. 1–6 (2021). https://doi.org/10.1109/MAJICC53071.2021.9526242
29. Cherian, V., Bindu, M.S.: Heart disease prediction using naïve Bayes algorithm and Laplace smoothing technique. Int. J. Comput. Sci. Trends Technol. (IJCST) **5**(2), 68–73 (2017)
30. Upreti, K., et al.: Prediction of mechanical strength by using an artificial neural network and random forest algorithm. J. Nanomater. **2022** (2022). https://doi.org/10.1155/2022/7791582
31. Souza Filho, E.M., et al.: Artificial intelligence in cardiology: concepts, tools and challenges - "The Horse is the One Who Runs, You Must Be the Jockey". Arq Bras Cardiol. **114**(4), 718–725 (2020). https://doi.org/10.36660/abc.20180431. English, Portuguese. PMID: 32491009

Cardiac Disease Detection Using IoT-Enabled ECG Sensors and Deep Learning Approach

Pranali P. Lokhande[1,2]([envelope]) and Kotadi Chinnaiah[1]

[1] Computer Science and Engineering, Raisoni Centre of Research and Innovation,
G H Raisoni University, Amravati, India
pranali.lokhande@gmail.com, pplokhande@mitaoe.ac.in,
kotadi.chinnaiah@raisoni.net
[2] School of Computer Engineering, MIT Academy of Engineering,
Alandi(D), Pune, India

Abstract. These days, heart disease is a fatal disease. People from different age ranges are suffering from this disease. They sometimes are unaware of the spread of this disease and its overall impact on their health. To handle this concern, it is important to be known about the details of heart disease and the regular follow-up of the same in this era. Though the transience rate can be radically regulated when the disease is detected in the initial phases and some precautionary actions are adopted as soon as possible. We have proposed the detection of heart disease for protecting the patient's life by combining Deep Learning methods along with the Internet of Things. In order to perform proper sorting of available information, the ANOVA-F test is used as a novel feature selection algorithm. Through the proposed system, the severity level of the disease will be identified. For that purpose, it is essential to provide accurate input data using ECG sensors and IoT devices. For that purpose, it is required to categorize patient data as per kind of heart disease and its severity. Convolutional Neural Network Model will be used for the classification process. We will notify the concerned doctors about patients' health on a timely basis by referring to available data.

Keywords: Heart disease detection · ANOVA-F test · Feature selection · Convolutional Neural Network · ECG sensors · Internet of Things

1 Introduction

Nowadays, heart disease is a disease impacting several lives. Individuals are unaware of the severity and the type of heart disease they are suffering from. It is essential to be conscious of the type of heart disease and to take intensive care of disease in this fast-moving life. The diagnosis of heart disease is a difficult job as it needs expertise along with advanced information. In view of gathering the sensor values for heart disease detection, the Internet of Things (IoT) is applied in the clinical field. For performing the prediction of cardiac disease, several investigators are working in this area. In hospitals, there is an important development in intensive care units in healthcare sectors. Nowadays

© The Author(s), under exclusive license to Springer Nature Switzerland AG 2023
R. N. Shaw et al. (Eds.): ICACIS 2022, CCIS 1749, pp. 195–204, 2023.
https://doi.org/10.1007/978-3-031-25088-0_16

movable healthcare nursing systems with rising skills need time. The use of Internet of Things techniques can help in the growth of the medical field and transfer control from direct consulting to the online consultation. Deep learning helps produce smart computerized applications that will assist specialists to identify the disease by making use of the Internet of Things.

2 Literature Review

The exhaustive literature survey has been carried out through various sources. A comprehensive review of the literature is presented below.

D. Komalavalli, R. Sangeethapriya, R. Indhu, N. Kanimozhi and G. Kasthuri [1] have considered a system in which ML techniques are applied to create a simple Tensor-Flow model. It detects major features helpful in increasing accuracy for cardiovascular disease prediction. Various sets of features and classification algorithms are used in the prediction.

Sandhiya S, Palani U [2] have implemented a Heart disease monitoring system using the Deep Learning techniques and the Internet of Things by keeping the patient information as records. In this system, the algorithm for choosing the appropriate features is applied for sorting using a deep learning algorithm. Then the system screens the illness level as per inputs composed via IoT devices. Also, it categorizes the patient's particulars as per kinds of heart disease and the severity.

Bing Zhang et al. [3] proposed a BP prediction system using the CART model using biological attributes. Using the method of cross-validation, the optimum model parameters were calculated. Here, the comparison of the CART model with other standard methods is done. For choosing the most correlated variables, the Pearson correlation coefficient was also used.

Mohammad Ayoub Khan [4] has proposed a heart disease prediction system that uses wearable IoT devices along with an MDCNN classifier. Wearable technologies are used efficiently in the healthcare industry, mainly in chronic heart disease. Many patient's life who are located in remote places where medical facilities are unavailable can be saved by using these monitoring and prediction systems. Here, heart disease is predicted using pre-processing, feature selection, and classification.

Md. Milon Islam et al. [5] have applied smart healthcare to display the vital features of patients. Hospital staff can collect the patient's test report for the 4 cases where they have done tests outside the hospital. This system can help doctors and nurses in emergencies where rough information is available to them.

Shawni Dutta et al. [6] has proposed and implemented a system using deep learning methods and a stacked GRU layer-based model. Relevant features influencing heart disease are considered while designing the model with essential constraint tuning.

Irfan Javid et al. [7] have considered a grouping of Deep Learning and Machine Learning models for implementing their proposed system. It is considered for detection of the cardiac disease. This method may be highly beneficial to support the clinicians to examine the patient cases concerning their treatment.

Yuanyuan Pan et al. [8] here, the usage of a Convolutional Neural Network model is proposed and implemented for the prediction of cardiac disease. Prediction as well as.

classification done in the system, have focussed on reducing the wrong diagnosis.

Asma Baccouche et al. [9] have done categorization of four sorts of heart disease in their proposed system. The proposed system illustrated a method of taking mean and arbitrary under matching of the records, to similarly create a relational dataset for preparing classification models.

Qingyun He et al. [10] In their system, IoT technology is joined with the hospital data to provide online interaction of remote placed patients with doctors and to detect and monitor heart disease patients remotely. So, here it is tried to find the finest way to detect and control heart disease using sensor data.

P. Ramprakash et al. [11] have proposed a self-acting analysis model for heart disease detection by making use of a deep neural network. Analysis of patients' data will be done for detecting the disease.

Jian Ping Li et al. [12] have implemented heart disease diagnosis based on machine learning. Classification is done by machine learning classifiers. Feature selection is done by feature selection algorithms.

M. Ganesan et al. [13] have developed a combination of the Internet of Things and a Cloud-based heart disease detection model. Here, sensors are used to forecast people having heart disease. The patient information is classified.

Bo Jin et al. [14] have implemented an analytical model outline for heart failure verdict via LSTM methods. In the trial data examination and pre-processing, patient diagnostic actions were displayed.

Vineet Sharma et al. [15] have done classification using machine learning classification methods. The neural networks perform the classification to detect heart disease. Here, the use of SVM classifier is done for the classification. It will reduce the odds of misdiagnosis.

Abdullah Alharbi et al. [16] have proposed a heart rate prediction system to notice the initial danger of less heart rate. In the proposed system, various neural networks are used for training and testing purposes.

Armin Yazdani et al. [17] have used important features in WARM for heart disease prediction to get the maximum confidence score.

Karim Bayoumy et al. [18] have emphasized the elementary engineering values of regular wearable sensors, and wherever they can be likely to the errors. Nowadays, trials such as device correctness, scientific legitimacy, the absence of consistent supervisory rules, and worries for ill person's secrecy are still clogging the extensive acceptance of modern wearable techniques in scientific exercise.

K. Butchi Raju et al. [19] have proposed a computerized health care model using the method of cloud, fog, and edge computing. It has collected data from various hardware devices.

Edward Choi et al. [20] have anticipated an analytical model outline for HF judgment using Gated Recurrent Unit Networks.

REMARKS OF LITERATURE REVIEW

- The strategy of using a combination of IoT and Deep Learning techniques has the potential to predict heart disease.

- No researcher has addressed the issue of reducing the energy consumption and extended time monitoring of sensor devices.
- From the social point of view by increasing the accuracy of heart disease prediction lives of many patients can be saved effectively.
- Using Neural Networks, the HR prediction system works well to notify the initial danger of low HR.

3   Motivation and Contribution to Society

3.1   Key Parameters to Consider

- To discover an efficient mechanism to continually observe the ECG signal of patients using IoT sensor devices to achieve suitable prediction accuracy.
- To have an improved vision for differentiating between the behavior of various heart disease detection methods.
- To improve the capability of the system to handle a large amount of information obtained from the Internet of Things sensor devices for the whole day continuously.
- The Execution time of the system and the use of a large amount of energy are the factors that need to be reduced.

3.2   Role of the Proposed System

- The proposed system has the potential to increase the feature selection and classification techniques precision needed for Heart Disease Prediction.
- The proposed system will reduce medical errors and will contribute to saving many lives by early detection and controlling the disease effectively.
- Use of IoT and Deep Learning Techniques will be done in the proposed Heart Disease Prediction System by considering Medical Field.
- This proposed system has the potential of enhancement to the existing system because the combination of medical decision support with patients' Electronic Health Records will decrease mistakes, enhance the privacy of the patient and reduce undesirable changes in the treatment.
- Automation of systems predicting diseases will help doctors as well as patients in terms of treatment and wellness of health.
- Heart Disease is a fatal disease and it has affected many peoples throughout the world.
- We can control the mortality rate of individuals suffering from this disease using an accurate and efficient prediction system.
- The proposed system will help doctors a better way to deal with it promptly and will heal patients more precisely.
- Also, it will be profitable in accordance with the equipment, analysis and detection.

4   Proposed System Architecture

See Fig. 1.

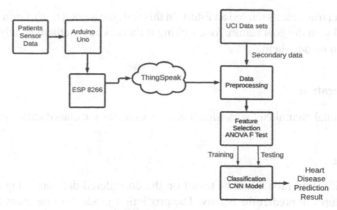

Fig. 1. Block diagram of proposed system

5 Proposed System Methodology

5.1 Requirement Analysis

- The First step of the proposed system will be to gather the patient's information using the digital standard 12-lead electrocardiograms [21] and IoT Sensor devices like ECG Sensors [22].
- Also, it is required to collect information from UCI Data Sets and consider them as secondary input.

5.2 Data Preprocessing

- Missing and noisy information will be removed from the data set through data pre-processing.
- Different pre-processing techniques used can be: Mean normalization, standardization and whitening.

5.3 Feature Selection

- By choosing appropriate features, the accuracy of heart disease prediction can be improved. The process of Feature selection begins by picking a small subset of the utmost applicable features from huge group of unique features, that affect the result most. The benefits of feature selection involve upgrading of data quality, a reduced amount of evaluation time by the prediction model, analytical performance development and an effective data gathering procedure.
- A feature selection method called the ANOVA-F test [23] will be used to choose the utmost significant features from the datasets.
- A group of parametric numerical models and their approximation measures that regulate the average of many trials of data sourced from a similar supply is termed Analysis of Variance (ANOVA). A group of numerical examinations that utilizes a few arithmetic techniques to find the proportion of the variance values such as the modification

of 2 distinct trials etc. is termed an F-test. In this test, the association of every feature is performed with the goal feature for checking if there is any mathematically important association among them.

5.4 Classification

- Convolutional Neural Network Model will be used for the classification process [4].

5.5 Testing

- The classification model will be tested on the considered datasets using the chosen set of features to predict the results. The prediction model will be trained on whole data with 80% training and 20% testing subsets.
- It will provide accurate results after passing through multiple phases of evaluation.

6 Datasets

6.1 Heart Disease Dataset

It includes four databases as Cleveland, Hungary, Switzerland, Long Beach V [26]. Few attributes from the data set are as follows:

1. Age
2. Sex
3. Chest pain type (4 values)
4. Resting blood sugar
5. Resting blood pressure
6. Serum cholesterol in mg/dl
7. Fasting blood sugar > 120 mg/dl
8. Resting electrocardiographic results (values 0, 1, 2)

6.2 Heart Failure Prediction Dataset [27]

Few attributes from the data set are as follows:

1. Resting BP
2. Cholesterol
3. Fasting BS
4. Resting ECG
5. Max HR
6. Exercise Angina

6.3 Cardiovascular Disease Dataset [28]

Few attributes from the data set are as follows:

1. Systolic blood pressure
2. Diastolic blood pressure
3. Weight
4. Gender
5. Age
6. Height
7. Cholesterol

6.4 PTB-XL Dataset [29]

Few attributes from the data set are as follows:

1. ecg_id
2. patient_id
3. device
4. recording_date
5. report
6. scp_codes

7 Evaluation Parameters

Performance of the proposed system will be obtained based on the standard metrics [2] as follows:

The result of the person infected with the disease and recognized properly is measured as the True Positive (TP). The result of the person not infected with the disease and recognized as infected is measured as the False Positive (FP). The result of the person not infected with the disease and recognized as not infected is measured as the True Negative (TN). The result of the person infected with the disease and recognized as not infected is measured as the False Negative (FN). All of the above-mentioned measures are applied to find specificity, sensitivity and prediction accuracy. The potential to find out individuals affected by a particular disease accurately is termed Sensitivity.

The potential to find out individuals not affected by a particular disease accurately is termed Sensitivity. To calculate accuracy of the classification, we have to use sensitivity and specificity.

They are represented mathematically as follows:

$$ST = [TP/(TP + FN)] \times 100$$
$$SP = [TN/(TN + FP)] \times 100$$
$$AY = [(TP + TN)/(TP + TN + FP + FN)] \times 100$$

where ST stands for sensitivity, SP stands for specificity and AY stands for accuracy. All these estimation parameters are applied for checking the performance of the proposed disease monitoring system.

8   The Choice of Method for ECG Signal Reading

Various options are available for the ECG Signal reading based on sampling techniques. Table 1 illustrates the variation based on its performance [24].

Table 1. Sampling Techniques for ECG Reading

Unique ECG signal			
Name of segment	Duration (seconds)	Count of samples	Sampling rate
SQ	0.850	200	175.23
PQRST	0.480	85	210.15
QRS	0.05	20	190.05
RR	0.7	150	180.21
Uniform sampling technique			
Name of segment	Duration (seconds)	Count of samples	Sampling rate
SQ	0.890	153	185.23
PQRST	0.390	75	180.15
QRS	0.06	15	255.05
RR	0.90	160	195.21
Adaptive sampling technique			
Name of segment	Duration (seconds)	Count of samples	Sampling rate
SQ	0.775	115	130.26
PQRST	0.400	55	155.25
QRS	0.150	25	118.09
RR	0.85	125	125.21

Our proposed system has utilized the adaptive sampling for the purpose of ECG readings. The decision for the same is dependent on the research study done by Yuan et al. [25] which specifies that for the reduction in the energy consumption it is efficient to make the selection of adaptive sampling.

9   Conclusion

Nowadays heart disease is considered as one of the deadliest diseases having a high impact on mortality and turning into one of the reasons for demise everywhere in the world. The harm produced by this illness can be minimized highly if suitable measures of clinical care are taken at the initial steps.

As we are making the combination of ECG Sensor data using IoT and considering the UCI data set like CVD, Framingham and ECG Data sets as Secondary data, it will help in getting more variation in the data used in the analysis as compared to existing systems. Also, the proposed system will select the significant features using ANOVA F TEST which provides a good impact on the performance of the model. The use of the Convolutional Neural Network model for the classification technique will give us accurate heart disease prediction results for the large data set.

Acknowledgment. I would like to thank my Research Project Guide, Dr. Kotadi Chinnaiah for providing his valuable suggestions and guidance towards the selection of the proposed system and completion of this chapter.

References

1. Komalavalli, D., Sangeethapriya, R., Indhu, R., Kanimozhi, N., Kasthuri, G.: An effective heart disease prediction using machine learning technique. ICTACT J. Soft Comput. **11**(03), 2323–2327 (2021)
2. Sandhiya, S., Palani, U.: An IoT enabled heart disease monitoring system using grey wolf optimization and deep belief network. Research Square, January 2022
3. Zhang, B., Wei, Z., Ren, J., Cheng, Y., Zheng, Z.: An empirical study on predicting blood pressure using classification and regression trees. IEEE. Access **6**, 21758–21768 (2018). IEEE Special Section on Human-Centred Smart Systems and Technologies
4. Khan, M.A.: An IoT framework for heart disease prediction based on MDCNN classifier. IEEE Access **8**, 34717–34727 (2020)
5. Islam, M.M., Rahaman, A., Islam, M.R.: Development of smart healthcare monitoring system in IoT environment. SN Comput. Sci. **1**(3), 1–11 (2020). https://doi.org/10.1007/s42979-020-00195-y
6. Dutta, S., Bandyopadhyay, S.K.: Early detection of heart disease using gated recurrent neural network. Asian J. Cardiol. Res. **3**(1), 8–15 (2020). Article no. AJCR.57729
7. Javid, I., Alsaedi, A.K.Z., Ghazali, R.: Enhanced accuracy of heart disease prediction using machine learning and recurrent neural networks ensemble majority voting method. Int. J. Adv. Comput. Sci. Appl. **11**(3), 540–551 (2020)
8. Pan, Y., Fu, M., Cheng, B., Tao, X., Guo, J.: Enhanced deep learning assisted convolutional neural network for heart disease prediction on the internet of medical things platform. IEEE Access **8**, 189503–189512 (2020). Special Section on Deep Learning Algorithms for Internet of Medical Things
9. Baccouche, A., Garcia-Zapirain, B., Olea, C.C., Elmaghraby, A.: Ensemble deep learning models for heart disease classification: a case study from Mexico. Information **11**(4), 207 (2020)
10. He, Q., Maag, A., Elchouemi, A.: Heart disease monitoring and predicting by using machine learning based on IoT technology. In: 5th International Conference on Innovative Technologies in Intelligent Systems and Industrial Applications (CITISIA). IEEE (2020)
11. Ramprakash, P., Sarumathi, R., Mowriya, R., Nithyavishnupriya, S.: Heart disease prediction using deep neural network. In: Proceedings of the Fifth International Conference on Inventive Computation Technologies (ICICT). IEEE Explore (2020)
12. Li, J.P., Haq, A.U., Din, S.U., Khan, J., Khan, A., Saboor, A.: Heart disease identification method using machine learning classification in e-healthcare. IEEE Access **8**, 107562–107582 (2020)
13. Ganesan, M., Sivakumar, N.: IoT based heart disease prediction and diagnosis model for healthcare using machine learning models. In: Proceeding of International Conference on Systems Computation Automation and Networking. IEEE (2019)

14. Jin, B., Che, C., Liu, Z., Zhang, S., Yin, X., Wei, X.: Predicting the risk of heart failure with EHR sequential data modelling. IEEE Access **6**, 9256–9261 (2018). Special Section on Recent Computational Methods in Knowledge Engineering and Intelligence Computation

15. Sharma, V., Rasool, A., Hajela, G.: Prediction of heart disease using DNN. In: Proceedings of the Second International Conference on Inventive Research in Computing Applications (ICIRCA). IEEE Xplore (2020)

16. Alharbi, A., Alosaimi, W., Sahal, R., Saleh, H.: Real-time system prediction for heart rate using deep learning and stream processing platforms. Complexity **2021** (2021). https://doi.org/10.1155/2021/5535734

17. Yazdani, A., Varathan, K.D., Chiam, Y.K., Malik, A.W., Ahmad, W.A.W.: A novel approach for heart disease prediction using strength scores with significant predictors. BMC Med. Inform. Decis. Mak. **21**, 194 (2021). https://doi.org/10.1186/s12911-021-01527-5

18. Huneria, H.K., Yadav, P., Shaw, R.N., Saravanan, D., Ghosh, A.: AI and IOT-based model for photovoltaic power generation. In: Mekhilef, S., Favorskaya, M., Pandey, R.K., Shaw, R.N. (eds.) Innovations in Electrical and Electronic Engineering. LNEE, vol. 756, pp. 697–706. Springer, Singapore (2021). https://doi.org/10.1007/978-981-16-0749-3_55

19. Raju, K.B., Dara, S., Vidyarthi, A., Gupta, V.M., Khan, B.: Smart heart disease prediction system with IoT and fog computing sectors enabled by cascaded deep learning model. Comput. Intell. Neurosci. **2022** (2022). https://doi.org/10.1155/2022/1070697

20. Choi, E., Schuetz, A., Stewart, W.F., Sun, J.: Using recurrent neural network models for early detection of heart failure onset. J. Am. Med. Inform. Assoc. **24**(2), 361–370 (2017)

21. Gliner, V., Keidar, N., Makarov, V., Avetisyan, A.I., Schuster, A., Yaniv, Y.: Automatic classification of healthy and disease conditions from images or digital standard 12-lead electrocardiograms. Sci. Rep. **10**, 1–12 (2020)

22. Ramasamy, S., Balan, A.: Wearable sensors for ECG measurement: a review. Sens. Rev. **38**, 412–419 (2018)

23. Rajawat, A.S., Bedi, P., Goyal, S.B., Shaw, R.N., Ghosh, A.: Reliability analysis in cyber-physical system using deep learning for smart cities industrial IoT network node. In: Piuri, V., Shaw, R.N., Ghosh, A., Islam, R. (eds.) AI and IoT for Smart City Applications. SCI, vol. 1002, pp. 157–169. Springer, Singapore (2022). https://doi.org/10.1007/978-981-16-7498-3_10

24. Ghifari, A.F., Perdana, R.S.: Minimum system design of the IoT-based ECG monitoring. IEEE (2020)

25. Yuan, Z., Kim, J.H., Cho, J.D.: Adaptive sampling for ECG detection based on compression dictionary. J. Semicond. Technol. Sci. **13**, 608–616 (2013)

26. https://www.kaggle.com/datasets/johnsmith88/heart-disease-dataset

27. https://www.kaggle.com/datasets/fedesoriano/heart-failure-prediction

28. https://www.kaggle.com/datasets/sulianova/cardiovascular-disease-dataset

29. Wagner, P., Strodthoff, N., Bousseljot, R.-D., Samek, W., Schaeffter, T.: PTB-XL, a large publicly available electrocardiography dataset (version 1.0.1). PhysioNet (2020). https://doi.org/10.13026/x4td-x982

Critical Evaluation of SIMON and SPECK BLOCK Cipher for Different Modes of Operation

Monika Jangra[1], Swechchha Gupta[2(✉)], and Buddha Singh[2]

[1] Shri Vishwakarma Skill University, Palwal 121102, Haryana, India
[2] SC & SS, Jawaharlal Nehru University, New Delhi 110067, India
swechchhagupta18@gmail.com

Abstract. A secure, lightweight block cipher provides a comprehensive security solution for applications that run on resource-constrained devices. The Simon and Speck are lightweight block ciphers developed especially for restricted hardware to offer data security. Raspberry Pi is a resource-constraint device employed in various projects, including the creation of gadgets, games, monitoring and surveillance technologies, basic automated machines, robotics, etc. This chapter examines the performance of SIMON and SPECK families on a Raspberry Pi device to see how efficient and fast these algorithms work for different modes of operation. As the objective of designing SIMON and SPECK was to ensure security on very restricted devices, the security strength of SIMON and SPECK families are also explored in different modes of operation. The simulated results of the Raspberry Pi device demonstrate that SPECK performed faster in encryption time and provides a high level of throughput and efficiency compared to SIMON families in all modes of operation. On the other hand, SIMON families performed better in terms of security strength than SPECK families. Therefore, this study can be applied to determine the appropriate performance and security trade-off in contexts with limited resources.

Keywords: Light-weight cryptography · Block ciphers · Modes of operation

1 Introduction

The limited-resource devices are currently widely employed in a variety of applications, including RFID tags, contactless smartcards, WSN, medical equipment, and IoT [15]. Restricted devices typically has limited compute capabilities, incredibly modest storage capacities, and limited power usage. Cryptographic protection for resource-constraint devices is needed as confidential information is transmitted and changed more frequently. It is challenging to achieve the performance of devices with minimal resources while maintaining appropriate security [10].

SIMON and SPECK was developed to make security feasible on highly re stricted devices [12]. Simon and Speck offer a wide variety of block sizes and key sizes [1]. It is

© The Author(s), under exclusive license to Springer Nature Switzerland AG 2023
R. N. Shaw et al. (Eds.): ICACIS 2022, CCIS 1749, pp. 205–213, 2023.
https://doi.org/10.1007/978-3-031-25088-0_17

crucial to examine the security and performance of SIMON and SPECK in every aspect. Therefore, different modes of operation are considered here.

In cryptography, deterministic and probabilistic modes of operation are used. However, determinism, gives rise to encryption attacks. Therefore, probabilistic encryption is used. SIMON and SPECK families are implemented for probabilistic mode of operations. The modes that have been selected here for performance analysis are the CBC, PCBC, OFB, CFB and CTR. The security, effectiveness, and performance of these operation modes are examined and compared [5].

Our objective is to examine the trade-off between performance and security strength of both SIMON and SPECK families in the context of resource-constrained networks. Encryption time and throughput metrics are considered here and avalanche effect is considered to evaluate the security strength [14]. The contribution of this research are given as follows:

- We analyzed and compared the performance of several versions of SIMON and SPECK of lightweight block cipher on a Raspberry Pi device for five different modes of operation.
- The security strengths of both families are examined by the avalanche effect metric in five different modes of operation.
- It has been expected that this article can be used as a beneficial reference for the trade-off between security strength and performance in restricted devices contexts for future implementation.

In this chapter, after a brief introduction, a short overview of SIMON and SPECK families and modes of operation are described in Sect. 2. The experiment results analysis of security strength and performance of resource-constrained devices is conducted in Sect. 3. Finally, we sum up the article with the conclusion in Sect. 4.

2 Background

2.1 SIMON and SPECK

The goal of developing Simon and Speck was to make security possible on resource-constrained devices. Here, we briefly explain the Simon and Speck algorithms. For detailed information, the reader is referred to [2].

SIMON and SPECK block ciphers offered a variety of block sizes and key sizes. The SIMON and SPECK families are made up for word sizes like 16, 24, 32, 48 and 64 bits. For complete explanation, referred to [4].

SIMON and SPECK block ciphers are based on Feistel structure [7]. Feistel structure has its round function [8]. The round function for SIMON is represented in Eq. 1:

$$R(x, y) = (y \oplus f(x) \oplus k, x) \tag{1}$$

where $f(x) = \left(sh \ \& \ sh^8\right) \oplus sh^2$ and k is n-bit round key generated by a key schedule mechanism. x and y are n-bit input quantities. Also, sh^j is left circular shift and sh^{-j} is right circular shift.

Equation (2) represents the round function of SPECK:

$$R(x, y) = f(x, y, \alpha, k), f(x, y, \alpha, k), \oplus sh^\beta y \qquad (2)$$

$f(x, y, \alpha, k) = (sh^{-\alpha}x + y) \oplus k$. For $\alpha = 7, n = 16, \beta = 2 = 16$.

Other-wise, we use $\alpha = 8$ and $\beta = 3$.

As shown in Table 1, the round function is formed several times, with the number of repetitions depending on the block and key sizes.

Table 1. SIMON and SPECK parameters.

Block size	Key size	SIMON rounds	SPECK rounds
32	64	32	22
48	72	36	22
	96	36	23
64	96	42	26
	128	44	27
96	96	52	28
	144	54	29
128	128	68	32
	192	69	33
	256	72	34

Each algorithm needs a key schedule algorithm to generate a sequence of round keys for every round. For complete details, refer the readers to [3].

The SIMON key schedules produce a series of key words $(k_0, k_1 \ldots \ldots, k(m\ 1))$, where, $m\ \varepsilon\ 2, 3, 4$.

SPECK key schedules based on the round function. The two sequences k_i and l_i are generated in chapter [11].

2.2 Modes of Encryption

A data block is encrypted to produce ciphertext using a key; numerous data blocks are encrypted sequentially. However, the length of the data block getting encrypted is extremely short. Therefore, Mode of operation is used to encrypt bigger amounts of data by combining the block cipher with some operations and feedback mechanism. There are different modes for block ciphers that are commonly used in cryptography. These modes are classified as deterministic or probabilistic. In deterministic encryption methods, a specific plaintext is mapped to a fixed cipher if the key does not modify [5]. Electronic Code book (ECB) mode comes under deterministic encryption method. Probabilistic encryption techniques employ randomness to generate a non-deterministic cipher. Cipher Block Chaining (CBC) mode, Propagating Cipher Block Chaining (PCBC), Output Feedback

(OFB) mode, Cipher Feedback (CFB) mode, and Counter (CTR) mode comes under this method. Probabilistic encryption methods are discussed in this article. Deterministic encryption is susceptible to attacks because identical plaintext blocks yield identical ciphertext blocks. Therefore, ECB mode is not an effective method of encryption. Therefore, Probabilistic modes of operation are examined and compared with respect of its security, efficiency, and performance.

In order to generate a probabilistic encryption, the CBC mode uses an initialization vector (IV), which creates randomness. The decryption operation is inverse, and it consists of decrypting the current block of ciphertext and appending the previously encrypted block to the outcome. An Initialization Vector is applied to encrypt the initial block, and that result is divided into two halves. The final ciphertext is generated by XORing the first part with the plaintext. The ciphertext is put into the shift register and XORed with the next block of plaintext. The plaintext block influences the encryption of subsequent blocks in CBC mode.

PCBC encryption technique is similar to CBC but has an additional requirement. The current ciphertext must be XORed with the current plaintext before being XORed to succeeding plaintext.

In OFB mode, it is possible for the feedback mechanism to operate offline in this mode, which is one of the merits of using this mode.

The CFB mode and the OFB mode are very similar. The ciphertext is given back to the block cipher rather than the previous key stream to construct the next stream.

The Counter (CTR) mode is closely related to the Output Feedback (OFB) and Cipher Feedback (CFB) modes [9]. As its stream generator, it employs a block cipher, with a counter value as its input. Whenever a newly added key stream is produced, the value of the counter should update. Nowadays, the CTR mode is frequently utilised and recommended.

3   Experiment Results and Analysis

The simulation results of SIMON and SPECK families for different modes of operation is presented here. We examined the security strength and performance of SIMON and SPECK under different modes in situations of resource-constrained environments which can assist in making the appropriate decision. The following section provides a detailed presentation of the comparisons, security strength, and performance analysis of both families.

3.1   SIMON and SPECK Performance Analysis

Both are specially developed for resource-constrained devices. Such devices must have low power consumption, fast processing speed, small circuit sizes, and low encryption time. High throughput is proportional to fast processing. The restricted devices that transmit a lot of data, such as cameras or vibration sensors, need high throughput [13]. Constrained devices consume less power if throughput is high [6]. The block cipher's efficiency is evaluated with the help of the throughput metric. Therefore, we have analyzed and compared SIMON and SPECK performance and provided the results in terms of throughput and low encryption time. Additionally, performance in various modes of operation is examined. The modes of operation are discussed here CBC, PCBC, OFB, CFB and CTR mode. The implementation is conducted using PYTHON and the Raspberry Pi device is used for performance evaluation. The device configuration are presented in below Table 2.

Table 2. Device configuration

Model	Pi3 B+
Processor	Cortex-A53(ARMv8) 64-bit SoC@1.4 GHz
RAM	1 GB LPDDR2 SDRAM
Operating system	Raspbian OS (32-bit)

Table 3, 4, 5, 6, and 7 illustrates the outcomes of SIMON and SPECK simulated on the raspberry device for CBC, PCBC, OFB, CFB and CTR modes of operation. The simulated results on the raspberry device show that SPECK outperforms SIMON in terms of throughput and encryption time. Ten variants of SIMON and SPECK are examined for performance efficiency. SPECK has nearly double the throughput of SIMON Ciphers. SPECK outperforms SIMON because it uses addition modulo, a more efficient choice for software implementation than the bitwise AND operation used by SIMON.

Table 3. Performance metrics of CBC mode

CBC size	Encryption time (ms)		Throughput (kbps)	
	SIMON	SPECK	SIMON	SPECK
32/64	57.60	34.02	0.43	0.73
48/72	39.34	22.90	0.63	1.09
48/96	39.49	23.46	0.63	1.06
64/96	34.81	19.75	0.71	1.26
64/128	35.94	20.27	0.69	1.23
96/96	28.70	14.31	0.87	1.74
96/144	30.78	15.00	0.81	1.66
128/128	27.97	12.18	0.89	2.05
128/192	28.23	12.49	0.85	2.00
128/256	29.58	13.00	0.84	1.92

Table 4. Performance metrics of CTR mode

CTR size	Encryption time (ms)		Throughput (kbps)	
	SIMON	SPECK	SIMON	SPECK
32/64	53.78	34.14	0.46	0.73
48/72	39.18	22.78	0.63	1.09
48/96	39.22	23.50	0.63	1.06
64/96	34.84	19.82	0.71	1.26
64/128	35.84	20.53	0.69	1.21
96/96	28.63	14.47	0.87	1.72
96/144	29.41	14.82	0.85	1.68
128/128	28.33	12.18	0.88	2.05
128/192	28.17	12.47	0.88	2.00
128/256	29.39	13.70	0.85	1.82

Table 5. Performance metric of OFB mode

OFB size	Encryption time (ms)		Throughput (kbps)	
	SIMON	SPECK	SIMON	SPECK
32/64	54.24	34.34	0.46	0.72
48/72	39.50	23.08	0.63	1.08
48/96	39.56	23.91	0.63	1.04
64/96	34.54	20.08	0.72	1.24
64/128	36.03	20.49	0.69	1.21
96/96	28.73	14.47	0.87	1.72
96/144	29.36	14.85	0.85	1.68
128/128	27.72	12.26	0.90	2.03
128/192	28.43	12.57	0.87	1.98
128/256	29.54	13.15	0.84	1.90

Table 6. Performance metrics of CFB

CFB size	Encryption time (ms)		Throughput (kbps)	
	SIMON	SPECK	SIMON	SPECK
32/64	55.75	34.22	0.44	0.73
48/72	39.92	22.97	0.62	1.08
48/96	40.12	23.60	0.62	1.05
64/96	34.50	20.07	0.72	1.24
64/128	35.89	20.36	0.69	1.22
96/96	28.77	14.54	0.86	1.71
96/144	29.40	14.85	0.85	1.68
128/128	27.65	12.23	0.90	2.04
128/192	28.07	12.58	0.89	1.98
128/256	29.49	13.03	0.84	1.91

Table 7. Performance Metric of PCBC

PCBC size	Encryption time (ms)		Throughput (kbps)	
	SIMON	SPECK	SIMON	SPECK
32/64	59.59	34.35	0.41	0.72
48/72	39.50	23.10	0.63	1.08
48/96	39.53	23.67	0.63	1.05
64/96	34.50	20.43	0.72	1.22
64/128	36.08	20.39	0.69	1.22
96/96	28.78	15.57	0.86	1.60
96/144	29.39	14.97	0.85	1.66
128/128	28.10	12.28	0.88	2.03
128/192	28.20	12.56	0.88	1.99
128/256	29.51	13.13	0.84	1.90

3.2 SIMON and SPECK Security Analysis

The security of an encryption algorithm can be evaluated based on the avalanche effect metric. Cryptography techniques list the avalanche phenomenon as a desirable attribute. The avalanche metric measures the proportion of the cipher-text bits that change when the plain text is modified by a single bit. Here, this metric has been considered to assess the security efficiency of SIMON and SPECK families for five modes of operation namely CBC, CTR, PCBC, CFG and OFB. As, ECB mode is insecure and should not be used generally. Therefore, ECB mode is not discussed here. The avalanche effect is examined for each of the ten variants of SIMON and SPECK for various modes of operation. Figure 1, illustrates the outcomes of the simulation results.

The Avalanche Effect demands a diffusion strength metric of at least 50% for optimal results. It is clear from Fig. 1 that all encryption modes of SIMON and SPECK fulfill the 50% threshold. As the size of a block increases, it becomes secure because the changes are spread out over a greater number of bits. The Key size also affects security. From Fig. 1, it is observed that SIMON offers a stronger avalanche effect for block sizes 128/128, 128/192, and 128/256 in all modes.

S-box is used for differential property in the majority of lightweight block ciphers. SIMON and SPECK, on the other hand, do not employ the S-box functionality. Nevertheless, SIMON and SPECK are capable of maintaining a respectable differential strength using the avalanche effect metric. Comparing data from various SIMON and SPECK versions, we can conclude that, on average, SIMON provides superior security over SPECK.

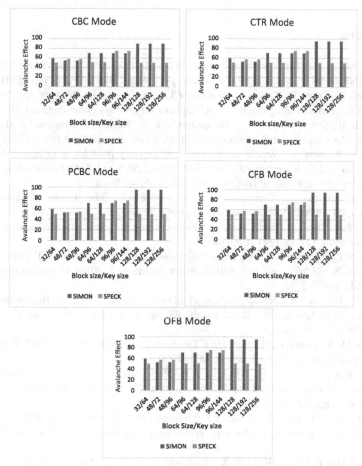

Fig. 1. Security comparison of SIMON and SPECK block ciphers family for different modes of encryption

4 Conclusion

The research examines performance of SIMON and SPECK in resource-constrained situations. The comparative Analysis of performance efficiency is carried out in all modes of operation. SIMON and SPECK are simulated on Raspberry Pi model3 B for comparative study. For security strength, the avalanche effect metric is considered. For each mode of operation, the avalanche effect is computed. The simulation results demonstrate that SIMON provides enough security but at a high expense in terms of resources. SIMON is, on average, more secure than SPECK in modes. However, its throughput is only half that of SPECK. Regarding resource usage, SPECK outperforms SIMON. SPECK reduces the power consumption of resource-constrained devices. Therefore, this research analysis can be utilized to evaluate the acceptable trade-off between security strength and resource performance in environments with restricted resources.

References

1. Appel, M., et al.: Block ciphers for the IoT—SIMON, SPECK, KATAN, LED, TEA, PRESENT, and SEA compared. In: Proceedings of Appel Block CF, pp. 1–37 (2016)
2. Beaulieu, R., Shors, D., Smith, J., Treatman-Clark, S., Weeks, B., Wingers, L.: The SIMON and SPECK families of lightweight block ciphers. Cryptology eprint archive (2013)
3. Beaulieu, R., Shors, D., Smith, J., Treatman-Clark, S., Weeks, B., Wingers, L.: SIMON and SPECK: block ciphers for the Internet of Things. Cryptology ePrint Archive (2015)
4. Biryukov, A., Roy, A., Velichkov, V.: Differential analysis of block ciphers SIMON and SPECK. In: Cid, C., Rechberger, C. (eds.) FSE 2014. LNCS, vol. 8540, pp. 546–570. Springer, Heidelberg (2015). https://doi.org/10.1007/978-3-662-46706-0_28
5. Bujari, D., Aribas, E.: Comparative analysis of block cipher modes of operation. In: International Advanced Researches and Engineering Congress, pp. 1–4 (2017)
6. Dhanda, S.S., Singh, B., Jindal, P.: Lightweight cryptography: a solution to secure IoT. Wirel. Pers. Commun. **112**(3), 1947–1980 (2020)
7. Hoang, V.T., Rogaway, P.: On generalized Feistel networks. In: Rabin, T. (ed.) CRYPTO 2010. LNCS, vol. 6223, pp. 613–630. Springer, Heidelberg (2010). https://doi.org/10.1007/978-3-642-14623-7_33
8. Kölbl, S., Roy, A.: A brief comparison of SIMON and SIMECK. In: Bogdanov, A. (ed.) LightSec 2016. LNCS, vol. 10098, pp. 69–88. Springer, Cham (2017). https://doi.org/10.1007/978-3-319-55714-4_6
9. Lipmaa, H., Rogaway, P., Wagner, D.: CTR-mode encryption. In: First NIST Workshop on Modes of Operation, vol. 39. Citeseer. MD (2000)
10. Lustro, R.A.F., Sison, A.M., Medina, R.P.: Performance analysis of enhanced SPECK algorithm. In: Proceedings of the 4th International Conference on Industrial and Business Engineering, pp. 256–264 (2018)
11. Park, T., Seo, H., Kim, H.: Parallel implementations of SIMON and SPECK. In: 2016 International Conference on Platform Technology and Service (PlatCon), pp. 1–6. IEEE (2016)
12. Pei, C., Xiao, Y., Liang, W., Han, X.: Trade-off of security and performance of lightweight block ciphers in industrial wireless sensor networks. EURASIP J. Wirel. Commun. Netw. **2018**(1), 1–18 (2018)
13. Rivero, J., Huynh, T.N.B., Smith-Evans, A., Thao, O., Cheng, Y.: Analyzing the efficiency of lightweight symmetric ciphers on IoT devices (2021)

14. Singh, S., Sharma, P.K., Moon, S.Y., Park, J.H.: Advanced lightweight encryption algorithms for IoT devices: survey, challenges and solutions. J. Ambient Intell. Human. Comput., 1–18 (2017). https://doi.org/10.1007/s12652-017-0494-4
15. Thakor, V.A., Razzaque, M.A., Khandaker, M.R.: Lightweight cryptography algorithms for resource-constrained IoT devices: a review, comparison and research opportunities. IEEE Access **9**, 28177–28193 (2021)

An Analysis on the Methods for Water Quality Prediction from Satellite Images and Camera Images

Mayank Singh, Subhadeep Chatterjee, Gautam Bhandari, Safeer Ahmad, Rendla Sai Advaith, Dhiraj Kumar Singh, and Jeba Shiney O[✉]

Kalpana Chawla Centre for Research in Space, Science and Technology, ECE, Chandigarh University, Gharuan, Punjab, India
jebashiney@gmail.com

Abstract. Water pollution is one of the critical issues in today's scenario as its severe effects can be seen in environment, wildlife, industries, agriculture, and most importantly human health. Safe water availability is the line wire of a healthy economy, but inadequately prioritized, globally these days. The most effective way for water quality monitoring on a large scale is remote sensing since its temporal and spatial range of data available from satellite images. This chapter presents an approach to cater to this issue using abundance of satellite data that can be used for extracting the optically active water quality parameters and water indexes NDTI, NDWI, NDCI, CDOM, Chlorophyll-a, TDS, TSS, SPM, SI, and SWI which in turn can be used for water quality prediction. Other challenges that have been addressed are cloud cover correction, impact of reflectance angle, satellite data resolution, and retrieval of parameters with respect to the domains of spatial and temporal changes in satellite data. Also, the changing watercolor is a direct indicator of changing water quality and can be used as a marker to determine the suitability of usage. Therefore, the RGB and hue values from camera images are also utilized to extract water quality parameters thus providing information on the usability of the surface water.

Keywords: Water quality · Remote sensing · Satellite images

1 Introduction

Water is most crucial to sustain the life of living organisms and humans. Contaminated water is the main reason behind various water borne diseases. Living organisms need water of sufficient quality to sustain life. Contamination levels should be maintained to certain tolerable limits to support existence of aquatic organisms. Out of 70% of total water on earth only 3% is fresh water. About 80% of water pollution comes from domestic wastewater, and 70% of industrial waste is thrown into water bodies. More than 6 billion pounds of garbage, mostly plastic, enters the ocean each year. Drinking contaminated water kills 2,97,000 children under the age of five each year. Waterborne diseases pose an economic burden close to USD 600 million a year in India. According to a survey Asia has the highest number of contaminated rivers in which The Ganges River in India is considered the second most polluted river in the world.

Traditional water quality monitoring comprises manual sampling at limited sampling points, followed by water quality analysis in the laboratory. However, this monitoring method is not comprehensive enough to monitor the overall water quality of a water body, nor can it accurately reflect the water quality at each location of the lake. In contrast, remote sensing technology is timesaving, enables a wide monitoring range and fast data acquisition, and renders data that can be intuitively interpreted [1]. The spectral reflectance (SR) data obtained from satellite images is utilized by a number of researchers as a reliable indicator in approximating the variations in water quality. Moreover, with the ample availability of remote sensed data and the introduction of technologies and computational power, these techniques are proving to be vital in decision-making, especially during disasters and pandemic [2].

The method proposed here for water quality detection is by using band values from satellite images and RGB values for clicked images. Sentinel-2 images are used because of its advantages of high spatial and temporal resolution and a wide width of 290°. The "color" of water is closely the best approximation related to the quality of the water. Therefore, water can be considered as "pure" when it has no blue-absorbing and blue-scattering components. However, the presence of phytoplankton pigments, such as chlorophyll-a (Chl-a), suspended solids (SP) and colored dissolved organic matter (DOM), gives green, yellow and brown color's [3]. The change in watercolor is mainly due to changes in these optically active ingredients (OACs). Therefore, the color of the water is also used indirectly to indicate water quality.

2 Existing Work

The impact of covid-19 lockdown on the water quality of lake Hussain Sagar is reported in. The analysis is based on the qualitative relationships with optically active parameters through spectral radiance and FUI. [4] presents estimation of water quality based on the correlation between different bands specially the red edge bands and the results have been validated with physical laboratory tests. [5] reports the changes in water quality parameters along ganga river at Varanasi, Mirzapur and Ghazipur during pre-lockdown, lockdown and post-lockdown using sentinel-2 and landsat-8 images. Major parameters considered are PH, Dissolved oxygen, Total Suspended solid, Normalized difference water index and Normalized difference turbidity index. A comparative analysis between sentinel-2 and Landsat-8 images is done on the basis of hue and FUI from remote sensing reflectance and water leaving radiance. It also reports the use of hue in classification of water from its color by its relationship with CDOM and Chlorophyll alpha for natural waters. Water anomaly is recognized on the basis of hue angle calculated from satellite images and it is compared with the on-site tested values [6]. A mobile application called "Hydro Color" is presented in [7]. This app uses water leaving radiance and reflectance from digital camera images to calculate water quality parameters. The relation between FUI scale and different parameters like turbidity, secchi disk depth and how these are implemented in citclops app is discussed in [8].

3   Approach

The proposed work is based on two types of image data, (i) satellite images and (ii) clicked images (photographs). The process flow diagram to extract useful information from both type of data is given in Fig. 1 and Fig. 2.

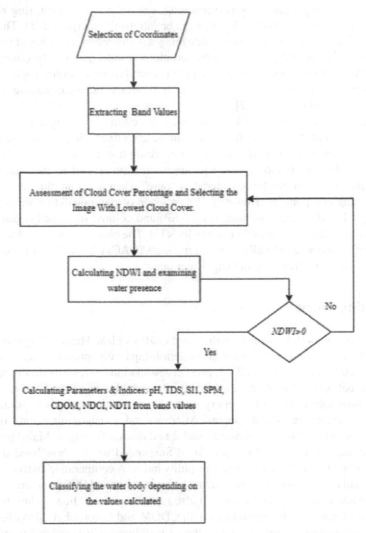

Fig. 1. Process workflow for water quality prediction from satellite images.

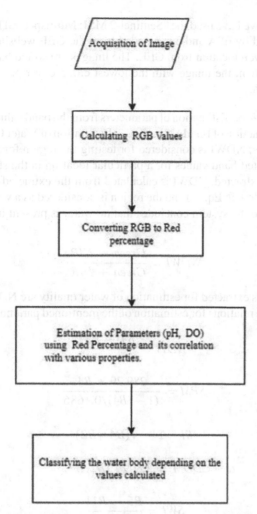

Fig. 2. Process workflow for water quality prediction from clicked images.

Section 4 details the process of image acquisition, extraction of parameters from the different band values and predicting the water quality.

4 Methodology

4.1 Satellite Images

Acquisition and Pre-preprocessing of Data. The work proposed here uses Sentinel-2 images as it offers universal coverage and open sourced optical-remote-sensing data. Sentinel-2 images are characterized by higher spatial resolution, richer spectral bands, shorter revisit cycles, and larger width [1–3].

In this research, we have used the "Sentinel-2 MSI: Multispectral Instrument, Level-1C" dataset provided by ESA and downloaded from the GEE website. After extracting the images of the given location from GEE. The images are sorted based on their cloud cover percentage. Then, the image with the lowest cloud cover percentage is selected for feature extraction.

Parameter Estimation. Estimation of parameters from the band values involves the following steps: 1. Extraction of Band Values and 2. Estimation of Water Quality parameters from the band values. NDWI is considered for testing the region for presence of water. Initially, pre-calculated band values for a particular location in the study area from the selected image are extracted. NDWI is calculated from the extracted band values using the relation given below in Eq. (1) and the region is considered as a water body if NDWI is greater than 0, else the system concludes that no water is present in the selected area of interest.

$$NDWI = \frac{Green - NIR}{Green + NIR} \tag{1}$$

The other parameters extracted for estimation of water quality are NDTI, SPM, CDOM, SWI and NDCI. The relations for estimation of the mentioned parameters are as follows.

$$NDTI = \frac{B4 - B3}{B4 + B3} \tag{2}$$

$$SPM = \frac{289.29 * B4}{(1 - B4)/0.1686} \tag{3}$$

$$SI - 1 = \sqrt{(B4 * B2)} \tag{4}$$

$$\alpha - CDOM = 2.809 * (B2/B4)^{-2.341} \tag{5}$$

$$SWI = \frac{B5 - B11}{B5 + B11} \tag{6}$$

$$NDCI = \frac{B5 - B4}{B5 + B4} \tag{7}$$

4.2 Clicked Images

The proposed work focusses on the digital camera image input for estimating water quality parameters, as an alternative low-cost technique which can serve as a crucial aid in case of disastrous situations. The camera sensor used to sense the water image is calibrated using a clinometer to adjust the required water image area for the further process and calculation of the image parameters namely Forel-Ule(FUI) scale and pH.

Extracting RGB Data Values. Digital cameras have sensors that create bitmap from the pixel for the calculation of RGB values from an image. Firstly, the image captured by the camera is converted into YUV Image format. The YUV format can be used to convert RGB to YUV and vice versa [5]. The YUV image format is compressed into JPEG based format according to the parameters given by the preview of image given by camera sensor and then converted into Byte array. This Byte array is decoded to Bitmap. For RGB values bitwise shifting is used on each pixel of the bitmap. The bitmap size used is 600×600 pixels. From the bitmap mean of the RGB values are calculated and used for further computations.

FUI Scale. The FUI scale is a watercolor estimation technique which provides a graphical estimate of the color of a body of water. The scale consists of 21 Values. The method is prominently used because it designates a number to a class of water and offers a better physical meaning to watercolor by relating it to many important water parameters like Turbidity, CDOM, SDD etc. [8]. Equations below give the relationship between FUI, Hue and the expressions to extract pH from R,G and B values.

$$FUI = \frac{HUE - 213.3682}{11.07361} \tag{8}$$

$$ph = 0.0956(R\%) + 4.2722 \tag{9}$$

$$R\% = \frac{R}{R + G + B} \times 100 \tag{10}$$

$$H = \begin{cases} \frac{\left(\frac{G-B}{max-min}+0\right)}{6}; & if\ max = R \\ \frac{\left(\frac{B-R}{max-min}+2\right)}{6}; & if\ max = G \\ \frac{\left(\frac{R-G}{max-min}+4\right)}{6}; & if\ max = B \end{cases} \tag{11}$$

Classification of Waterbody: Waterbodies can be categorized for serving different utilities based on the purity level estimated from the different parameters mentioned above. The classification model applied in the work reported here is based on the Designated use of water and its depending parameters which is given by the Central Pollution Control Board (CPCB), according to which five designated best uses as their associated values under each parameter have been identified (http://117.252.14.242/rbis/india_inf ormation/water%20quality%20standards.html).

This classification helps in planning and managing water quality targets and aid in designing suitable restoration programs for various water bodies.

5   Results and Discussion

For testing and validation, the study region selected is the Sutlej river. Sentinel-2 satellite images are used. Five images are clicked at different locations of the river and the values are calculated. The results are validated by physical testing of the collected samples from the river in the labs. Most of the researchers so far mostly use Landsat data for satellite images but this research uses Sentinel-2 data which provides 10 m spatial resolution and temporal refresh rate of dataset is every 5 days. This becomes one of the reasons for better results from mostly used Landsat data which has comparably less spatial resolution and larger temporal refresh rate. From the results formulated, it is concluded that water quality can be estimated using satellite image data and the clicked image data. The results of the three testing mechanisms are tabulated below (Fig. 3, Tables 1, 2 and 3).

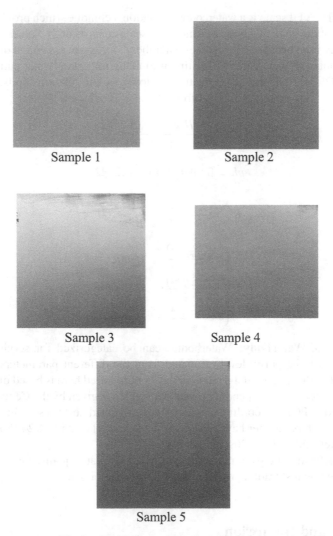

Fig. 3. Clicked image samples of Sutlej river

Table 1. Estimated parameters for clicked images of Sutlej river

Sample no.	pH	Dissolved oxygen	HUE	FUI
1.	7.44	5.17	251	3.00
2.	7.75	6.52	29	16
3.	7.52	5.52	348	12
4.	7.54	5.61	330	10
5.	7.53	5.54	24	17

Table 2. Estimated parameters for satellite images of Sutlej river

S. no.	NDTI	SPM (mg/l)	SI1	a-CDOM	SWI	NDCI
1.	−0.0195	53.26	0.5546	2.1156	0.1743	−0.0252
2.	−0.0226	58.28	0.5774	2.1325	0.1688	−0.0174
3.	−0.0247	64.23	0.6033	2.1247	0.1771	−0.0179
4.	−0.0055	57.72	0.5595	2.4203	0.1631	−0.0182
5.	−0.0250	48.46	0.5213	2.2767	0.1803	−0.0278

Table 3. Laboratory results for physically tested samples from Sutlej river

S. no.	pH calculated from camera image	pH calculated using physical samples in laboratory
1.	7.44	7.18
2.	7.75	7.06
3.	7.52	6.4–7.08
4.	7.53	7.69

6 Future Scope

From the results obtained it can be observed that the proposed system frame work can be efficiently utilized with certain upgradations to develop an application to determine the water quality around the globe from remote sensed images and also it can serve to develop a mobile application that aids a common man to assess the quality of water available during certain unprecedented situations like floods, war and pandemics when normal availability of potable water cannot be guaranteed.

References

1. Zhao, Y., Wang, S., Zhang, F., Shen, Q., Li, J., Yang, F.: Remote sensing-based analysis of spatial and temporal water colour variations in Baiyangdian lake after the establishment of the Xiong'an new area. Remote Sens. **13**(9), 1729 (2021)
2. Wagh, P., Sojan, J.M., Babu, S.J., Valsala, R., Bhatia, S., Srivastav, R.: Indicative lake water quality assessment using remote sensing images-effect of COVID-19 lockdown. Water **13**(1), 73 (2021)
3. Zhao, Y., et al.: Recognition of water colour anomaly by using hue angle and Sentinel 2 image. Remote Sens. **12**(4), 716 (2020)
4. Yigit Avdan, Z., Kaplan, G., Goncu, S., Avdan, U.: Monitoring the water quality of small water bodies using high-resolution remote sensing data. ISPRS Int. J. Geo Inf. **8**(12), 553 (2019)
5. Das, N., Bhattacharjee, R., Choubey, A., Agnihotri, A.K., Ohri, A., Gaur, S.: Analysing the change in water quality parameters along river Ganga at Varanasi, Mirzapur and Ghazipur using Sentinel-2 and Landsat-8 satellite data during pre-lockdown, lockdown and post-lockdown associated with COVID-19. J. Earth Syst. Sci. **131**(2), 1–28 (2022)
6. Van der Woerd, H.J., Wernand, M.R.: Hue-angle product for low to medium spatial resolution optical satellite sensors. Remote Sens. **10**(2), 180 (2018)
7. Leeuw, T., Boss, E.: The HydroColor app: above water measurements of remote sensing reflectance and turbidity using a smartphone camera. Sensors **18**(1), 256 (2018)
8. Garaba, S.P., Friedrichs, A., Voß, D., Zielinski, O.: Classifying natural waters with the Forel-Ule colour index system: results, applications, correlations and crowdsourcing. Int. J. Environ. Res. Public Health **12**(12), 16096–16109 (2015)

Energy Efficient Routing in Wirelss Sensor Network for Moving Nodes Using Moth Flame Algorithm Compared with Vector Based Routing

Ramisetty Lakshmi Pavan Kumar and Vijayalakshmi[✉]

Department of Electronics and Communication Engineering, Saveetha School of Engineering,
Saveetha Institute of Medical and Technical Sciences, Saveetha University,
Chennai 602105, Tamil Nadu, India
`vijayalakshmik.sse@saveetha.com`

Abstract. Aim: In this chapter energy efficient routing in wireless sensor networks for moving nodes using the Novel Moth Flame Algorithm compared with vector-based routing. This comparative analysis of energy-efficient routing with Novel Mouth Flame method and the Vector based routing protocol is carried out in NS 2 software with ten samples for each technique. The results show that efficient routing in a wireless sensor network for moving nodes, the novel Mouth flame algorithm achieves better energy consumption, delay, and packet delivery ratio when compared to the Vector based routing protocol. Statistical analysis also adds the value to the obtained results with significant value of 0.028 which is P < 0.05. The novel Mouth flame algorithm performs algorithm identifies a set of routes that can satisfy the delay constraints and proves that is better than the Vector based Routing Protocol for energy efficient routing in a wireless sensor network for moving nodes.

Keywords: Novel moth flame algorithm · Vector based routing · Wireless sensor network · Energy consumption · Packet delivery ratio · Delay

1 Introduction

When both the sensor node and the base station are regarded as mobile, the Wireless Sensor Network (WSN) becomes more difficult. The sensor nodes have limited power, chip memory, processing power, communication bandwidth, etc. because they serve as the power source for the system [1]. In addition to a few hundred or even thousands of sensor nodes, a WSN may have one or more BSs. Combining the use of so many nodes makes it possible to simultaneously collect data on the ambient conditions over a wide range of interest areas. Because of this, WSNs are perfect for a wide range of tasks, including fire detection, energy management, biomedical applications, environmental and habitat monitoring, surveillance and reconnaissance, home automation, object tracking, traffic control, inventory control, agriculture, machine failure diagnosis, and a variety of military applications [2]. However, despite the multiple advantages that WSNs provide,

R. N. Shaw et al. (Eds.): ICACIS 2022, CCIS 1749, pp. 223–232, 2023.
https://doi.org/10.1007/978-3-031-25088-0_19

there are significant issues that prevent them from functioning properly, such as congestion, link loss, weak security, poor QoS, and insufficient coverage [3]. The extremely short lifetime of WSNs' sensor nodes, caused by their stringent energy restrictions, is generally acknowledged to be by far the most significant drawback of these networks. Many different applications have been used with the mobile wireless sensor network. It is utilised in a variety of applications, including security-based applications, health monitoring systems, radiation, chemical plants, agriculture, and surveillance. Since the sensor node's capacity is so constrained, there are numerous design issues [4].

In recent past, around 1256 articles published in Google Scholar, and 345 articles published in Science Direct [5] related to energy efficient routing wireless sensor network. It has been suggested that the greatest shortcoming of WSNs is the very constrained lifetime of their sensor nodes as a result of their stringent energy limits. The reason for this is because sensor nodes are frequently positioned in challenging-to-reach locations, it is typically impractical to either replace or recharge the batteries that typically give the energy to the sensor nodes. The article [6] introduced that the main reason why sensor nodes' operations end and the overall lifetime of WSNs gradually decreases is due to their limited energy capacity. In paper [7] suggested data-centric routing protocol frequently chooses less-than-optimal routes to extend network lifetime. It employs a probability function based on the energy requirements of each path to select one of them. In this strategy, the only metric attribute considered is network lifespan. To increase network lifetime, it employs numerous paths, each with a specific probability, rather than the minimum energy way. The [8] purpose of the energy-saving routing protocols used in WSNs is to maintain the sensor nodes' functionality for as long as feasible, extend the network lifetime, and maintain network connectivity.

The limited energy supply of sensors caused by a clustered WSN's high energy consumption is one of the main issues that WSNs encounter. This work, proposes an energy efficient model to solve the high energy consumption problem in a clustered WSN. The aim of the chapter is to find a statistical analysis of Moth flame optimization algorithms compared to Vector based Routing protocols to perform better in wireless sensor networks.

2   Materials and Methods

Basically, it is considered with two groups, namely Moth Flame Algorithm and vector-based Routing. Group 1 is the Moth Flame Algorithm with the sample size of 10 and the vector based Routing algorithm is group 2 with the sample size of 10 and it was compared for delay, energy consumption and packet delivery ratio. Sample size has been calculated and it is identified as standard deviation for Moth Flame Algorithm is 0.9365 and vector based Routing is 0.9077.

2.1   Moth Flame Algorithm

A natural-inspired programme called the Moth algorithm seeks out the ideal answers to a certain problem. A technique known as transverse orientation for navigation allows moths to fly during the night. A moth can fly in a straight line over a great distance because it follows a constant angle in relation to the moon. Indeed, moths frequently fly in a spiral around artificial lights. Because they are not as far away as the moon, artificial lights produce this. The moths will retain their spiral flight pattern while attempting to maintain the same angle with the lights. MFO algorithm has been suggested and is based on the motion model of moths.

2.2 Vector Based Routing

A way vector steering convention is an organization directing convention which keeps up with the way data gets refreshed powerfully [9]. Updates that have circled through the organization and gotten back to a similar hub are handily distinguished and disposed.

3 Statistical Analysis

Using IBM SPSS version 21 [10], the analysis was carried out. It is a piece of statistical software that is used to analyse data. 10 iterations with a maximum of 10 samples were carried out for both the proposed and current algorithms, and for each iteration, the value obtained from the iterations of the Independent Sample T-test was carried out. The dependent variables are the packet delivery ratio, the energy, and the latency. In order to assess how well proposed and existing algorithms perform on dependent variables using independent two-tailed tests, the independent variables are the number of particles and population size.

4 Results

The simulation results for the comparison of the unique moth flame optimization algorithm and vector-based routing protocol were assessed in terms of delay, energy consumption, and packet delivery ratio. An NS2 simulator was used to test the algorithm, and the vector-based routing protocol's performance was compared. According to the simulation results, the new algorithm has less delay, uses less energy, and delivers more packets.

Figure 1 depicts the delay, which is the time required to send a data packet from one location to another. The Novel moth flame optimization algorithm is superior because it searches for the shortest path between source and destination nodes. Figure 2 shows the variation in energy consumption for different algorithms. It is defined as the total amount of energy consumed by all nodes in the network during the simulation. Energy consumption decreases as node mobility improves. The results clearly show that the proposed algorithm uses less energy than other vector based routing protocols. The ratio of total packets successfully delivered during data transmission to total packets sent is shown in Fig. 3 as the packet delivery ratio. When compared to a vector-based routing system, the Novel Moth Flame Optimization Algorithm has a greater Packet Delivery Ratio.

Figure 4 compares the mean delay ($\pm$1SD) for groups 1 (moth flame optimization algorithm) and 2 (control algorithm) (vector-based routing protocol). The moth flame optimization algorithm provides less delay than the vector based routing protocol. Figure 5 compares the mean packet delivery ratio ($\pm$1SD) for group 1 (moth flame optimization algorithm) and 2 (vector-based routing protocol). The vector based routing provides the highest packet delivery ratio than the moth flame optimization algorithm. Figure 6 compares the mean energy consumption ($\pm$1SD) for group 1 (moth flame optimization) and 2 (vector-based routing protocol). The moth flame optimization algorithm provides less energy consumption than vector based routing protocols.

Table 1 shows a statistical comparison of the mean values of the dependent variables. Table 2 shows the association between the dependent output variables with a 0.05 level of significance. The statistical report and the descriptive analysis both showed that the vector-based routing protocol is outperformed by the moth flame optimization technique.

Table 1. Represents descriptive statistical comparison of three parameters with respect to number of packets for Moth flame algorithm and Vector based routing algorithm. The mean of the delay is 5.20. The mean of the energy consumption is 2.50. The mean of the packet delivery ratio is 4.70.

Groups	Parameter	N	Mean	Std. deviation
Moth flame algorithm	Delay	1	5.20	3.393
	Energy consumption		2.50	3.028
	Packet delivery ratio		4.70	2.751
Vector based routing	Delay	10	15.10	4.677
	Energy consumption		9.70	2.058
	Packet delivery ratio		5.00	3.333

Table 2. Independent Sample Test for significance and standard error determination for all the three parameters. P value is 0.256($<$0.001) considered to be statistically significant and 95% confidence interval was considered.

Levene's test for equality of variables		F	Sig	T-test for equality of mean							
				t	df	Sig. (2-tailed)	Mean diff	Std error	95% confidence Interval of the difference		
									Lower	Upper	
Delay	Equal variances assumed	0.023	0.224	−3.827	18	0 .00	−9.900	1.827	−13.73	−6.061	
	Equal variances not assumed			−3.827	16.417	0.00	−9.900	1.827	−13.76	−6.034	

(continued)

Table 2. (*continued*)

Levene's test for equality of variables		F	Sig	T-test for equality of mean						
				t	df	Sig. (2-tailed)	Mean diff	Std error	95% confidence Interval of the difference	
									Lower	Upper
Packet delivery ratio	Equal variances assumed	0.021	.444	−.220	18	0.00	−.300	1.367	−3.171	2.171
			.444	−.2206	17.374	0.00	−.300	1.367	−3.171	2.579
	Equal variances not assumed									
Energy consumption	Equal variances assumed	0.02	.177	−6.20	18	0.00	−7.200	1.158	−9.632	−4.768
				−5.20	15.851	0.00	−7.200	1.158	−9.656	−4.744
	Equal variances not assumed									

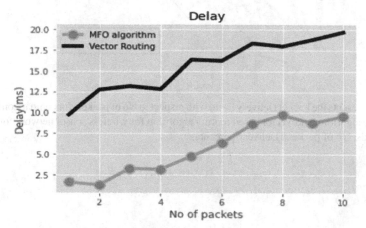

Fig. 1. Shows the comparison between Moth flame algorithm and Vector based routing algorithm for delay with respect to No of Packets in wireless sensor network for moving nodes. X axis: No of Packets, Y axis: Delay

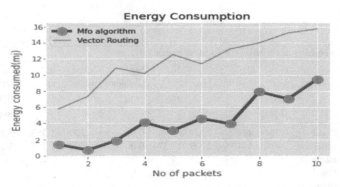

Fig. 2. Represents the comparison between Moth flame algorithm and Vector routing algorithm for Energy Consumption with respect to Energy consumption in wireless sensor networks for moving nodes. X axis: No of Packets, Y axis: Energy Consumption.

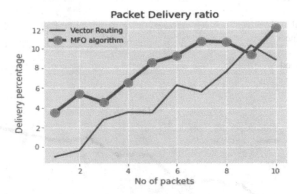

Fig. 3. Represents the Packet Delivery Ratio with respect to No of packets for comparison between Moth flame algorithm and Vector based routing algorithm for wireless sensor network for moving nodes. X axis: No of packets, Delivery percentage.

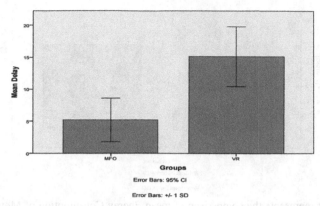

Fig. 4. Barchart represents the comparison of mean Delay of Moth flame algorithm and Vector based routing algorithm. X axis: Moth flame algorithm vs Vector based routing algorithm, Y axis: Mean Delay ± 1 SD.

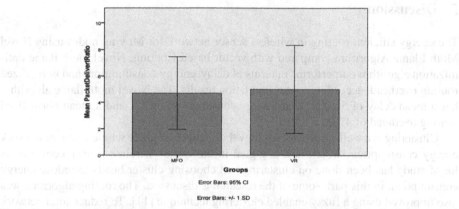

Fig. 5. Barchart represents the comparison of mean packet Delivery Ratio of Moth flame algorithm and Vector based routing algorithm..X axis: Regression Algorithm vs DSR Algorithm, Y axis: Mean Delay ± 1 SD

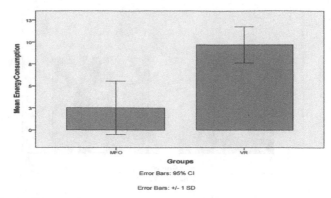

Fig. 6. Barchart represents the comparison of mean Energy Consumption of Moth flame algorithm and Vector based routing algorithm.X axis: Moth flame algorithm vs Vector based routing algorithm, Y axis: Mean Delay ± 1 SD.

5 Discussion

The energy efficient routing in wireless sensor network for Moving nodes using Novel Moth Flame Algorithm compared with vector based Routing. Novel moth flame optimization algorithm outperforms in terms of delay, energy consumption, and normalized routing overhead, according to the simulation results. The Novel moth flame algorithm has a mean delay of 5.20, a mean energy consumption of 2.5, and a mean normalized routing overhead of 4.70.

Clustering is a well-known technology that is used to reduce wireless sensor network energy consumption, which is a key goal in the use of wireless sensor networks. A lot of study has been done on clustering and choosing cluster heads to reduce energy consumption. In this part, some of the research is discussed. The routing algorithm was also improved using a fuzzy enabled clustering technique [11]. To reduce total network energy and efficiently extend the network lifetime, a decentralized fuzzy c-means energy-efficient routing protocol has been designed. However, this procedure does not employ optimization methods; instead, the election of CHs is carried out locally within each cluster. A clustering architecture based on discrete PSO and genetic algorithms (GA) for medium scale wireless sensor networks to increase network lifetime [12] was presented. A PSO-based energy efficient cluster head selection (PSOECHS) [13] that considers the distances to the base station (BS) and adds this condition to the fitness function was offered as a solution to the issue. By adjusting the CHs selection process and allowing for the change of the member node count for each cluster, PSOECHS prolongs the network's life [14]. For computing and choosing CHs, each node uses a lot of energy. (Heinzelman, Chandrakasan, and Balakrishnan 2002), [9] the suggested Low-Energy Adaptive Clustering Hierarchy (LEACH) algorithm permits efficient energy use, it ignores node information when choosing the CH nodes, such as residual energy, communication energy consumption, and the number of neighbor nodes.

The limitations of wireless sensor networks are dynamic changing topology with high energy consumption. The research will also create an analytical framework to calculate how cooperative diversity and overhearing communications affect WSN throughput, latency, dependability, and energy consumption.

6 Conclusion

The energy efficient routing in wireless sensor network for Moving nodes using a novel moth flame optimization technique was implemented. Further the comparison of vector-based routing protocol and novel moth flame optimization algorithm was performed. The obtained result shows that a delay of 6 ms, energy consumption of 12 mj and packet delivery ratio is 80% at node 10 by novel moth flame optimization algorithm which is better that vector-based routing protocal.

References

1. Sandhya, R., Sai, R.: Sai Sandhya, Sri Padmavati Mahila Visvavidyalayam, School of Engineering and Technology, Padmavati Nagar, Tirupati, Andhra Pradesh, and INDIA. Trusted and Energy Efficient Routing Protocol for Heterogeneous Wireless Sensor Networks. Int. J. Eng. Comput. Sci. (2016). https://doi.org/10.18535/ijecs/v5i10.64
2. Kandris, D., Nakas, C., Vomvas, D., Koulouras, G.: Applications of wireless sensor networks: an up-to-date survey. Appl. Syst. Innov. (2020). https://doi.org/10.3390/asi3010014
3. Bhanu Teja, N., Devarajan, Y., Mishra, R., Sivasaravanan, S., Thanikaivel Murugan, D.: Detailed analysis on sterculia foetida kernel oil as renewable fuel in compression ignition engine. Biomass Convers. Biorefinery (2021). https://doi.org/10.1007/s13399-021-01328-w
4. Wahid, A., Lee, S., Kim, D.: A reliable and energy-efficient routing protocol for underwater wireless sensor networks. Int. J. Commun. Syst. (2014). https://doi.org/10.1002/dac.2455
5. Preethi, K., Auxzilia, K.A., Preethi, G.L., Sekar, D.: Antagomir technology in the treatment of different types of cancer. Epigenomics (2021). https://doi.org/10.2217/epi-2020-0439
6. Zhu, C., Zheng, C., Shu, L., Han, G.: A survey on coverage and connectivity issues in wireless sensor networks. J. Netw. Comput. Appl. (2012). https://doi.org/10.1016/j.jnca.2011.11.016
7. Kong, L., Zhu, Y., Wu, M.-Y., Shu, W.: Mobile barrier coverage for dynamic objects in wireless sensor networks. In: 2012 IEEE 9th International Conference on Mobile Ad-Hoc and Sensor Systems (MASS 2012) (2012). https://doi.org/10.1109/mass.2012.6502499
8. Banerjee, A., et al.: Building of efficient communication system in smart city using wireless sensor network through hybrid optimization technique. In: Piuri, V., Shaw, R.N., Ghosh, A., Islam, R. (eds.) AI and IoT for Smart City Applications. SCI, vol. 1002, pp. 15–30. Springer, Singapore (2022). https://doi.org/10.1007/978-981-16-7498-3_2
9. Karthigadevi, G., et al.: Chemico-nanotreatment methods for the removal of persistent organic pollutants and xenobiotics in water - a review. Biores. Technol. 324, 124678 (2021)
10. Banerjee, A., et al.: Construction of effective wireless sensor network for smart communication using modified ant colony optimization technique. In: Bianchini, M., Piuri, V., Das, S., Shaw, R.N. (eds.) Advanced Computing and Intelligent Technologies. LNNS, vol. 218, pp. 269–278. Springer, Singapore (2022). https://doi.org/10.1007/978-981-16-2164-2_22
11. Rajawat, A.S., Barhanpurkar, K., Shaw, R.N., Ghosh, A.: Risk detection in wireless body sensor networks for health monitoring using hybrid deep learning. In: Mekhilef, S., Favorskaya, M., Pandey, R.K., Shaw, R.N. (eds.) Innovations in Electrical and Electronic Engineering. LNEE, vol. 756, pp. 683–696. Springer, Singapore (2021). https://doi.org/10.1007/978-981-16-0749-3_54

12. Paul, A., Sinha, S., Shaw, R.N., Ghosh, A.: A neuro-fuzzy based IDS for internet-integrated WSN. In: Bansal, J.C., Paprzycki, M., Bianchini, M., Das, S. (eds.) Computationally Intelligent Systems and their Applications. SCI, vol. 950, pp. 71–86. Springer, Singapore (2021). https://doi.org/10.1007/978-981-16-0407-2_6
13. Rao, P.C.S., Jana, P.K., Banka, H.: A particle swarm optimization based energy efficient cluster head selection algorithm for wireless sensor networks. Wireless Netw. 23(7), 2005–2020 (2016). https://doi.org/10.1007/s11276-016-1270-7
14. Shanmugam, V., et al.: Circular economy in biocomposite development: state-of-the-art, challenges and emerging trends. Compos. Part C Open Access 5, 100138 (2021)

Augmented Reality Using Gesture and Speech Accelerates User Interaction

Ajune Wanis Ismail[✉], Mohd Yahya Fekri Aladin, Nur Ameerah Abdul Halim, and Muhamd Shukri Abdul Manaf

Mixed and Virtual Reality Research Lab, ViCubeLab, School of Computing, Universiti Teknologi Malaysia, 81310 Johor Bahru, Johor, Malaysia
ajune@utm.my, shukrimanaf95@graduate.utm.my

Abstract. A user interaction technique is needed to manipulate the Augmented Reality (AR) content to make AR deliver realism. However, these problems persist, especially when they involve natural user interaction such as real hands and speech. Speech might be the most crucial part, especially in detecting the user's voice. The user's voice usually contains noises that come from the surroundings and every people produces different kinds of voice vibrations. Different genders also produce different voice vibrations. Robust real hand gestures are required to ensure the AR can accelerate the natural user interface. By providing users with more than one way to interact with AR, it tends to produce an efficient way of interaction. This chapter discusses the approach involves three main phases. In the first phase, study the interaction metaphor using gesture and speech in AR. After that, the second phase is carried out to perform a test application for the gesture and speech interaction. This chapter presents an appropriate interaction method that accelerates user interaction, it describes the implementation of gesture and speech interaction to the next level to see how AR could accelerate user interaction.

Keywords: Real-time gesture tracking · Speech inputs · Augmented Reality

1 Introduction

Extended Reality (XR) technologies consists of Mixed reality (MR), Augmented reality (AR) and virtual reality (VR) are two technologies recently have been useful improvised or enhanced the interface with understanding in complex data systems [1]. XR to compare with MR, we can see VR and AR as a subset to the MR. However, for XR, it was considering as an umbrella to cover these three environments [2]. The user will have an immersive experience in MR. People debated their confusing between MR and AR. MR has the capability to understand the real-world where not just only superimposes the object but it also can interact and understand the real world. However, AR content can overlay on the top of real world without to understand their physical surroundings [3].

People intends to develop AR and MR applications is to produce an information-enhanced environment. Also due to its promising trends and increment as the advanced

R. N. Shaw et al. (Eds.): ICACIS 2022, CCIS 1749, pp. 233–244, 2023.
https://doi.org/10.1007/978-3-031-25088-0_20

interaction methods can potentially applied. We knew without interaction AR becomes only browsing like a virtual object dancing on the pop-up book [4]. Gesture interaction in AR has been explored since two decades ago such as on desktop-based, using data glove and conventional marker-based. According to Lui [5], the interaction for an emerging technology focuses on human natural interaction (NUI) such as touch, vision, voice, motion and expression. NLU a language understanding, where we can apply to text and audio and for several reasons speech input has been commonly used in AR for interaction. Gesture interaction where user can use their hand gestures, and body movements to interact, in AR hand gesture interaction have found interesting instead of using apparatus and mobile, a touch screen metaphor, User can free their hand with hardware restriction and computer can simply track their bare hands. The problems have faced by developers are almost the same issues that arose during the early days of the development of the GUI [6]. With the adoption of wearable devices, VR & AR displays, affective computing, and voice user interface, [7] agreed that it necessary to review our understanding and definition of NUI. NUI seeks to harness the power of a much wider breadth of communication modalities that leverage skills people gain through traditional physical interaction. This chapter describes the implementation of gesture and speech interaction to the next level to see how AR could accelerate NUI.

2   Gesture and Speech Interactions

Hand and fingertip vision-tracking methods are widely used by prominent researchers to provide an easy way to interact with virtual objects in AR [8]. A marker-less AR system using a bare hand with a single optical camera to modify the system naturally, but the approach may be different compared with the ways in the real world. In common approach to implement tracking for human hands as a real object, the reference point to represent a finger needs to collide with AR objects. The challenging is when the interaction occurred in AR scene, the virtual object needs to visible on the marker or features in their real-time tracking. A human bare hand can hit the virtual object that appeared on the AR marker but at the same time can invite occlusion issue, where human hand covered the marker and the virtual object will disappear. Besides gesture, people has explored speech input to work or compliment gesture [9]. This issue has been improved by using a high precision free-hand gesture device such as Leap motion, and to implement gesture with speech input is possible [10]. The use of speech and gesture recognitions in AR have been studied to enhance the naturalness in AR system. The combination of gesture recognition and speech have been proven effective data manipulation for virtual environments as claimed by [11].

Gesture and speech also have been explored for multimodal AR interfaces. Multimodal interaction is considering an advanced interaction method that combine speech and hand gesture input in AR. Based on the current researches, this combination has delivered an intuitive way to interact. However, unimodal and multimodal concepts are required two different approaches, where in multimodal, a gesture must work along with the speech, it cannot be a separate command. This is how multimodal interaction could perform a direct manipulation and it should enhance the limitations in the unimodal interaction. For example, in G-SIAR (Gesture-Speech Interface for Augmented Reality) [10], they have used speech and gesture became the complementary attributes, and proof that it has improved the traditional GUI interfaces. G-SIAR has also recommended a proper guideline and very useful for this research. Therefore, the free-hand gesture in AR with a speech to accelerate user interaction has been explored in this chapter. Designing a user interaction techniques based on existing research guidelines for single object relocation, multiple object relocation, and uniform scaling. [12] has designed gestures and speech for multimodal and working on virtual heritage data. Then the extended version of [12] comes to work on a handheld device in [13]. Advanced interaction multimodal using gesture and speech has been explored in MR interface [14]. As for XR, its increased popularity has led to research opportunities for new and interactive ways of utilizing natural interaction such as gaze and eye tracking [15]. This recent new term XR system rises and provides unique design and implementation considerations, audio and gesture in XR also has proven to be important in creating an immersive experience.

3 Methodology

The research methodology is divided into several phases. Based on Fig. 1, this phase design and construct the interaction metaphor using gesture and speech for AR. The interaction between AR and 3D objects, gesture with 3D objects and speech with 3D objects is developed along with the AR interface. This methodology as a guideline to show the workflow and experiments that have been carried out for this research.

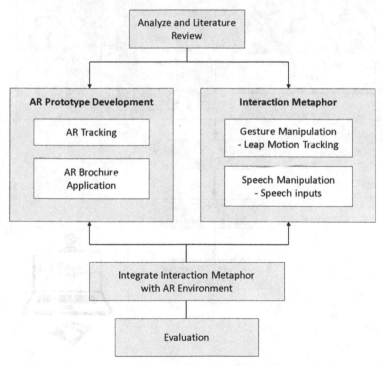

Fig. 1. Methodology

In the first box, AR tracking has been defined. Next is AR brochure application where features-based tracking using Vuforia to track the physical printed brochure to bring AR content. The tracking engine has been explained in AR framework as in Fig. 2. Second box has defined the interaction metaphor where gesture and speech input have been implemented for object manipulation. Leap motion tracking device has been used to track human bare hand, the gesture data runs in real-time to capture the gesture inputs. This chapter does not explain the evaluation phase, it limits to explain the gesture and speech in AR application only.

The AR user interface also is being designed for this study. It uses the feature-based tracking technique for AR. Based on Fig. 2, we can see it starts with getting input and identifying the marker pattern. The camera starts to do searching and the camera frame

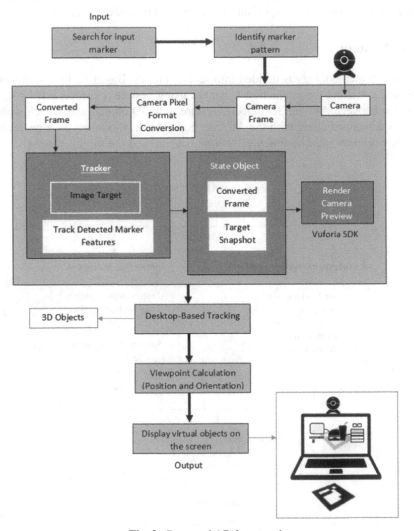

Fig. 2. Proposed AR framework

keeps retrieving the inputs in real-time. Tracker has been defined as an image target that has been converted into features-based using Vuforia SDK and this process has been called the AR tracking process. The next process is desktop-based tracking. When 3D objects have been loaded into a scene, when AR tracking is called, the viewpoint calculation process will produce position and orientation values.

Next is to invoke two interactions into AR. In this study, the hand gesture has been tracked using a device that attached to the computer. The gestures have been recognized in the pose detection when the device, a Leap Motion, sends the signal, the signal to start the skeleton calibration and eventually leads to the free hand gesture tracking. In this skeleton-based tracking, it works different compared to vision-based tracking. The Leap Motion tracks all the hand hierarchies of the user, as shown in Fig. 3. Using the hand gesture inputs, interactions such as Pinch, Grab and Release can be defined.

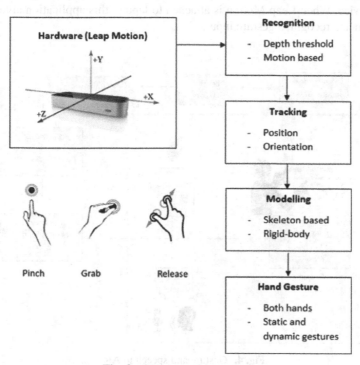

Fig. 3. Gesture tracking process

As for speech interaction, we have restricted it to only three-syllable. In order to recognize the speech, an input microphone is required in this process. When the speech input is recognized by the windows speech system, the application will respond to do the predefined actions. The grammars are stored in the speech recognition system and are retrieved to trigger the actions. Figure 4 shows in AR interface manager consists of gesture and speech inputs. As in gesture tracking process, every dynamic gestures required rigid body to enable the collision detection between hand with virtual objects in AR, the human's hand captured by Leap Motion has produced smooth gesture inputs.

There are nine commands that are declared and used in this research, which are "change to red", "change to yellow", "change to blue", "wear this watch", "remove watch", "zoom in", "zoom out", "add to cart" and "sm123" (as customer identification). The "change to color" command is just another option to change the color of 3D object with basic color. Besides that, "zoom in" and "zoom out" to enable mode of scaling that recognize the pinch gesture. If "zoom in" does not said by user, the pinch gesture does nothing. "Wear this watch" is the command to attach the 3D hand watch to virtual left hand whereas "remove watch" is to wear out and bring back the watch back to its starting position. "Add to cart" command is used to order the watch and "sm123" is for verification of customer identification before proceed with the payment.

While in Fig. 5, it can be seen the workspace setup where the Leap Motion was placed on the tabletop. There was a microphone, camera and computer that all devices and hardware have been properly set up. AR marker was set to stay along with the Leap Motion device. When Leap Motion is attached to laptop, this application able to track user's hand and recognize gesture inputs.

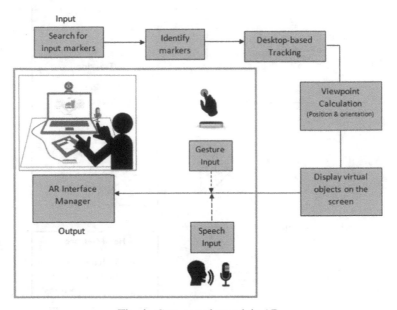

Fig. 4. Gesture and speech in AR

User interaction happens when a ray hits the collider that bounds the object; if the collider does not hit the object, the system will return to search for the ray-cast coordinates based on the controller movement. Once the object is hit, the interaction can be performed. Table 1 shows the proposed tasks and actions. Interaction is typical with the select and the release function. The release will end the interaction; the select function will trigger the selected object. Figure 6 demonstrates the gesture actions which has been defined in Table 1.

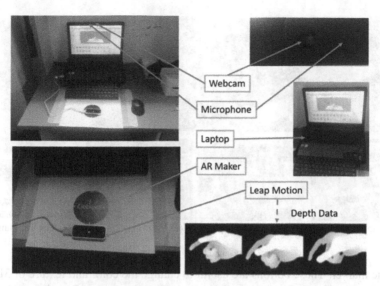

Fig. 5. A workspace setup

Table 1. Summary of related work for 3D reconstruction with the depth sensor device

	Tasks and cues	Gesture action
Manipulation: translation	Move hand towards the object and close hand to grab and move the object	Close hand, Grab (as in Fig. 6 (a))
Scaling	Put together thumbs and index fingers of both hands to resize	Pinch, Spread (as in Fig. 6 (b))
Selection: UI selection	Point the index finger and touch to select from UI	Pointing, Touch (as in Fig. 6(c))
Custom gesture: show extra menu	Flip left hand and show a palm to activate the extra menu	Flip hand (as in Fig. 6 (d))

4 Test Application

AR application is the application to prove the concept of interaction metaphor using gesture and speech in AR. Gesture manipulation and speech manipulation are not considered multimodal. This application has been developed to present a menu interaction consisting of 3D object manipulation and UI interaction. The concept being brought is a virtual hand watch store where users can alter the 3D hand watch with different materials consisting of color and texture, resizing it and even try it to get the first experience, as in Fig. 7.

User are able to initiate the gesture and interact with 3D buttons. Using palm up gesture, the gesture activates the 3D buttons that act as menu attached to left hand. This is called as palm UI. The first 3D button is an option to change the color and texture of 3D hand watch's strap whereas the second one is an option to change the design for 3D hand watch's case. When user touch the first 3D button, other 3D buttons will appear on

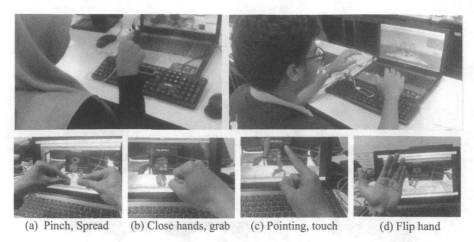

(a) Pinch, Spread   (b) Close hands, grab   (c) Pointing, touch   (d) Flip hand

Fig. 6. List of gestures

top of the marker. These buttons are useful to change the color and texture of 3D hand watch's strap and user can make a choice using touch gesture. Somehow, when user touch the second 3D button from palm UI, three 3D buttons will appear. These are the options of 3D hand watch's case design. User can make selection using touch gesture as well. User also can have experience wear the customized 3D hand watch on their left hand wrist with a speech command "wear this watch". In order to disband the 3D hand watch from hand, user have to say "remove watch". This will bring back the 3D hand watch to its starting position on top of the marker. If user finds the hand watch is too big for the hand, the scaling mode can be invoked using speech command "zoom in". When the command is recognized, user have ability to rescale the 3D hand watch using pinch gesture. This gesture requires both hands to works. If user is done with customization, they also are able to experience making order using speech command. The "add to cart" command will pop up the message to enter customer ID for verification before proceed with the payment.

Figure 7 (a) shows the application, and a virtual watch is presented in the middle. We can see the entire scene set on an AR marker. As for interactions, the application is able to track the user's hand and recognize gesture inputs. Users are able to initiate the gesture and interact with 3D buttons. By using a palm up gesture, the gesture activates the 3D buttons that act as a menu attached to the left hand (as in Fig. 7 (b)). This is called palm UI. The first 3D button is an option to change the color and texture of the 3D hand watch's strap, whereas the second one is an option to change the design for the 3D hand watch's case. When the user touches the first 3D button, other 3D buttons will appear on top of the marker. These buttons are useful to change the color and texture of the 3D hand watch's strap, and the user can make a choice using touch gestures (as in Fig. 7 (c)).

Figure 8 shows the texture changes by user has touched the virtual button. The watch turns yellow after the yellow box has been hit. While in Fig. 9, it shows that a user also can have experienced wearing the customized 3D hand watch on their left hand wrist with a speech command "wear this watch". In order to disband the 3D hand watch from hand, the user has to say "remove watch". This will bring back the 3D hand watch to

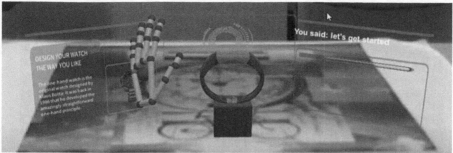

(a)   Gesture appears on AR scene

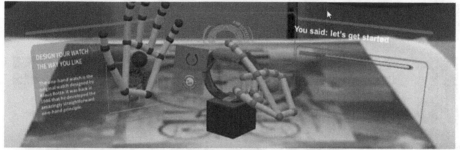

(b)   Gesture touches the Menu

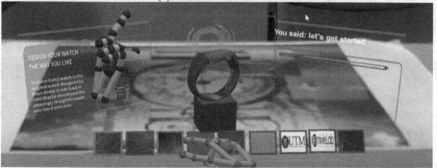

(c)   Gesture hits first menu to present a list of materials

Fig. 7. AR application with gesture

its starting position on top of the marker. If the user finds the hand watch is too big for the hand, the scaling mode can be invoked using the speech command "zoom in". When the command is recognized, the user has the ability to rescale the 3D hand watch using a pinch gesture. This gesture requires both hands to works.

This chapter presents a new method for naturally and intuitively manipulating AR objects through hand gesture and speech interactions. For the object selection and natural hand gestures for the object manipulation, the user can easily manipulate AR objects for simultaneous translation and rotation tasks. This application allows users to perform 6 DOF manipulation. How AR can accelerate the natural interaction when using gesture and speech it appears faster than need to find UI to click the buttons or hit the buttons using other methods. UI more easy to learn and the interface not complicated. This

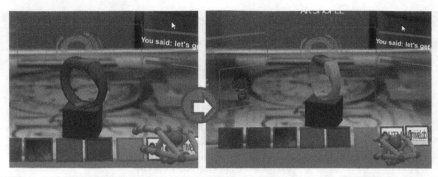

Fig. 8. Before and after results, the virtual watch in red color turns into yellow color after gesture touch the menu (Color figure online)

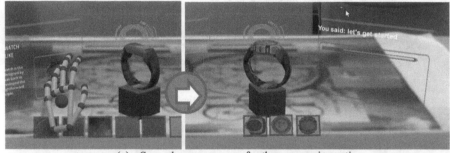

(a)   Second menu appears for the accessories option

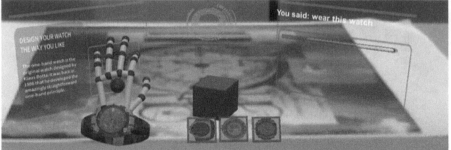

(b)   "Wear this watch" speech input with gesture, the virtual watch appears to user's left hand wrist

Fig. 9. Speech input with the gesture, the right panel to indicate speech input "wear this watch."

application shows the four types of gestures have been implemented and at least three words for speech input (Fig. 10).

Fig. 10. Speech input (a) "change to red", (b) "change to blue", and (c) "change to yellow", and "wear this watch" (Color figure online)

5 Conclusion

Interaction metaphor provides the user the intuitive way to interact with the virtual objects using their bare hands and speech inputs. Hence, interaction techniques in AR need to be as intuitive as possible. Therefore, this chapter aims to present AR interaction metaphor that combines gesture and speech in an intuitive manner. This chapter has described the methodology. The hand gesture recognition process using Leap Motion has been discussed and we have explored the different types of gesture inputs. The appropriate commands input for speech recognition to complement gesture interaction has been found in this chapter. The phase we have integrated the speech input to compliment the gesture in AR test application. The proposed method has proven the 6DOF objects manipulations with the real-time gesture interaction, supported by commands using speech. Based on the results, gesture with speech is able to accelerate user interaction at the appropriate UI design, it could produce intuitive interaction. The advanced interaction using gesture and speech has significantly influent the user experience with AR.

Acknowledgement. We appreciate ViCubeLab at Universiti Teknologi Malaysia (UTM) for the equipment and technical assistance. This work has been funded by the Ministry of Higher Education under FRGS, Registration Proposal No: FRGS/1/2020/ICT10/UTM/02/1.

References

1. Farahani, N., et al.: Exploring virtual reality technology and the Oculus Rift for the examination of digital pathology slides. J. Pathol. Inform. **7**, 22 (2016)
2. Ratcliffe, J., Soave, F., Bryan-Kinns, N., Tokarchuk, L., Farkhatdinov, I.: Extended Reality (XR) remote research: a survey of drawbacks and opportunities. In: Proceedings of the 2021 CHI Conference on Human Factors in Computing Systems, pp. 1–13, May 2021
3. Tepper, O.M., et al.: Mixed reality with HoloLens: where virtual reality meets augmented reality in the operating room. Plast. Reconstr. Surg. **140**(5), 1066–1070 (2017)
4. Nor'a, M.N.A., Ismail, A.W., Aladin, M.Y.F.: Interactive augmented reality pop-up book with natural gesture interaction for handheld. In: Lee, N. (eds.) Encyclopedia of Computer Graphics and Games, pp. 1–10. Springer, Cham (2019). https://doi.org/10.1007/978-3-319-08234-9_365-1
5. Liu, W.: Natural user interface-next mainstream product user interface. In: 2010 IEEE 11th International Conference on Computer-Aided Industrial Design & Conceptual Design 1, vol. 1, pp. 203–205. IEEE, November 2010

6. Norman, D.A.: Natural user interfaces are not natural. Interactions **17**(3), 6–10 (2010)
7. Fu, L.P., Landay, J., Nebeling, M., Xu, Y., Zhao, C.: Redefining natural user interface. In: Extended Abstracts of the 2018 CHI Conference on Human Factors in Computing Systems, pp. 1–3, April 2018
8. Chun, J., Lee, S.: A vision-based 3D hand interaction for marker-based AR. Int. J. Multimedia Ubiquitous Eng. **7**(3), 51–58 (2012)
9. Quek, F., et al.: Multimodal human discourse: gesture and speech. ACM Trans. Comput. Hum. Interact. **9**(3), 171–193 (2002)
10. Piumsomboon, T., Altimira, D., Kim, H., Clark, A., Lee, G., Billinghurst, M.: Grasp-Shell vs gesture-speech: a comparison of direct and indirect natural interaction techniques in augmented reality. In: ISMAR 2014 - IEEE International Symposium on Mixed and Augmented Reality - Science and Technology 2014, Proceedings, pp. 73–82 (2014)
11. Malkawi, A.M., Srinivasan, R.S.: Multimodal human-computer interaction for immersive visualization: integrating speech-gesture recognitions and augmented reality for indoor environments multimodal HCI-based visualization model immersive (2004)
12. Ismail, A.W., Billinghurst, M., Sunar, M.S., Yusof, C.S.: Designing an augmented reality multimodal interface for 6DOF manipulation techniques. In: Arai, K., Kapoor, S., Bhatia, R. (eds.) IntelliSys 2018. AISC, vol. 868, pp. 309–322. Springer, Cham (2019). https://doi.org/10.1007/978-3-030-01054-6_22
13. Nor'a, M.N.A., et al.: Fingertips interaction method in handheld augmented reality for 3D manipulation. In: 2020 IEEE 5th International Conference on Computing Communication and Automation (ICCCA), pp. 161–166. IEEE, October 2020
14. Aladin, M.Y.F., Ismail, A.W., Ismail, N.A., Rahim, M.S.M.: Object selection and scaling using multimodal interaction in mixed reality. In: IOP Conference Series: Materials Science and Engineering, vol. 979, no. 1, p. 012004. IOP Publishing, November 2020
15. Plopski, A., Hirzle, T., Norouzi, N., Qian, L., Bruder, G., Langlotz, T.: The eye in extended reality: a survey on gaze interaction and eye tracking in head-worn extended reality. ACM Comput. Surv. (CSUR) **55**(3), 1–39 (2022)

Survey and Performance Evaluation of Clustering and Cooperative Medium Access Protocols for Vehicular Networks

Poonam Verma(✉) ⓘ, Taru Garg ⓘ, and Anushka Shukla ⓘ

Department of Electronics and Communication Engineering, Thapar Institute of Engineering and Technology, Patiala, Punjab, India
poonam.verma@thapar.edu

Abstract. Vehicular Ad hoc Network (VANETs) are a type of adhoc networks wherein moving vehicles (the nodes) communicate among each other and Road Side Units (RSUs) over a wireless network. Considering the fast topology changes which happen in these networks it becomes necessary to have MAC protocols that can ensure reliable communications. In this chapter, the authors have discussed various MAC protocols that have been developed over years to reduce latency and improve QoS. The chapter provides an overview of the various cluster-based and cooperative MAC protocols that have been developed to support communication in VANETs. Further, this chapter also provides a comparative view of the various MAC protocols. The performance of various MAC protocols is analyzed using MATLAB and it is concluded that cooperative MAC protocols provide a better QoS than cluster-based protocols.

Keywords: Cooperative MAC protocols · Cluster-based MAC protocols · Cluster head · Throughput · QoS · IEEE 802.11p WAVE

1 Introduction

Wireless technology has had an unprecedented impact on our lives. The vast majority of applications and advantages it offers have made it even more relevant over the years. In the last decade, there has been a significant improvement in the same, which has further boosted the areas where it can be employed to improve the quality of life. One of such areas is travel and transport, where many accidents and thus loss of life can be avoided by leveraging this technology. This led to the evolution of a new branch of networking called Vehicular Ad hoc Networks (VANETs). Seeing the amount of potential VANET has in saving lives and reducing the number of accidents, thus making roads safer, it has become a prominent area for research and development. Much research has been done, and several standards have been put in place to ensure the QoS of these networks. Even various governments have started their own programs and put in place some regulations. Like, a spectrum of 75 MHz has been allocated by the US FCC which spans over 5.850 GHz to 5.925 GHz, which translates seven channels (one control and six service channel) of 10 MHz each along with a guard band of 5 MHz [1].

© The Author(s), under exclusive license to Springer Nature Switzerland AG 2023
R. N. Shaw et al. (Eds.): ICACIS 2022, CCIS 1749, pp. 245–257, 2023.
https://doi.org/10.1007/978-3-031-25088-0_21

The two basic components to a VANET are Vehicles and RSUs i.e., Road Side Units, which interact amongst themselves and with each other to enabling the functioning of VANETS. Thus, the communication in these networks can be divided into two categories, namely Vehicle-to-Vehicle (V2V) and Vehicle-to-Infrastructure (V2I) [3]. Just like the popularly known OSI Model for computer networks, VANETs have a similar architecture. Each layer in the architecture has its own functions. The Medium Access Control (MAC) sublayer sits just above the PHY layer and is responsible for a variety of tasks some of which are error checking, channel allocation, and frame formatting [4]. Figure 1 represents the different layers in the layered architecture of a VANET.

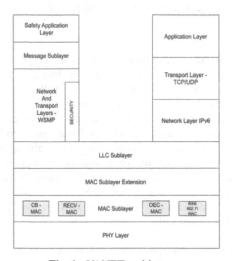

Fig. 1. VANET architecture

Over the years, a new IEEE standard IEEE 802.11p has been developed, which actually is a variant of IEEE 802.11a, but it stretches the definition and takes into consideration the following key points, these features form the basis of any form of communication, say it V2V or V2I [2]:

1. Highly mobile and dynamic environment
2. Message dissemination in adhoc manner
3. Less delay
4. Limited available resources like operating in reserved frequency band

The IEEE 802.11p amendment was introduced to increase the efficiency of communication and reduce the overhead in the IEEE 802.11 protocol. The MAC layer described by the IEEE 802.11p follows the concept of Distributed Coordination Function (DCF) which is based on a Carrier Sensing Multiple Access with Collision Avoidance (CSMA/CA) technique [3]. In this technique, a device first listens for the transmissions on the channel before initiating its own transmission, and in case the channel is occupied, i.e., some other device is transmitting at the time, it delays its transmission by the backoff number. While this technique is highly efficient for some networks, it has some significant drawbacks too. This protocol doesn't address the overhead due to collision, which is one major reason for latency. Hence, it's not effective during network congestion.

Further the layout of the chapter is as follows: Sect. 2 discusses the different MAC protocols proposed over the years for improving the Quality of Service (QoS) and reliability of communication amongst the vehicles. Section 3 then presents a comparative view of the various protocols, and lastly, Sect. 4 concludes the survey and performance analysis.

2   MAC Protocols for VANETs

This section discusses different parameters that are used to analyze the performance and establish the practicality of a MAC protocol and then proceeds on to discuss the various cooperative and cluster-based MAC protocols.

2.1   Performance Metrics for Evaluation of MAC Protocols

There are various performance metrics that help us in the classification and determination of how good a MAC protocol is. Though the performance of a protocol is greatly affected depending on what type of environment the protocol has been designed, a protocol might outperform another protocol in some specific environment but underperform in some other conditions. Still, a minimum basic QoS must always be ensured by a protocol to ensure its reliability and practicality. Some measures that can be used to effectively determine how good a MAC layer protocol are as follows [5]. Though there are various other parameters but for this chapter the discussion is only limited to the ones following:

1. Throughput is the measure of the average number of packets reaching their destination successfully in a given time slot [5]. The higher the throughput the better the network and thus the communication over that channel.
2. End-to-End Delay is described as the time taken by the packet to propagate to its destination after being transmitted from the source [5]. The end-to-end delay includes various components like transmission delay, propagation delay, etc. A higher delay leads to a poor QoS in the network.
3. Packet Loss is the measure of the amount/number of packets failing to reach their destination [5]. A high packet loss suggests a poor QoS. Various factors affect data packet loss in a network for e.g., issues in the poor signal strength, noise, network congestion, etc. [4]
4. Packet delivery ratio is defined as the ratio of the number of packets successfully received at the destination end to the total number of data packets transmitted at the source [5].

2.2   Discussion on Various MAC Protocols

This sub-section discusses the various MAC layer protocols that have been developed over the years to solve the issues faced in the use of WAVE (IEEE 802.11p). The chapter focuses on cooperative and Cluster-based MAC protocols for vehicular networks. Cooperative MAC protocols aim at improving the packet delivery rate by relaying the original message using other nodes (helpers). While cluster-based MAC protocols also focus on the same principle of improving the QoS, it takes a different route. These MAC protocols aim at reducing the number of link breakages, delay, and high relative mobility, thus providing for better and reliable communication. Figure 2. Summarizes the various MAC protocols studied in the chapter. The protocols have been divided into three broad categories, namely, cooperative, cluster-based, and hybrid MAC protocols that utilize both cooperation and clustering to achieve their functionality. To provide a baseline for comparison, WAVE (IEEE 802.11p) is used that is neither based on clustering nor cooperation. Further, a division has been done on whether a cluster-based or a cooperative MAC protocol uses a TDMA scheme or not.

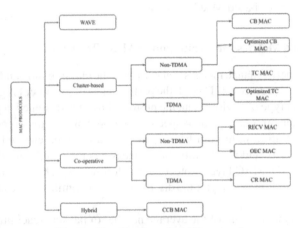

Fig. 2. Classification of MAC protocols

Cooperative Protocols. Cooperative MAC protocols are protocols that exploit the broadcast feature of the wireless channel [6]. The general idea behind all Cooperative MAC protocols is to disseminate a data packet to a vehicle (node) that could not directly receive the packet during the original transmission due to poor channel condition through a helper, whose Signal to Interference and Noise Ratio (SINR) is better than the original sender. Three MAC protocols CR MAC [7], RECV MAC [8], and OEC MAC [9] have been discussed in this chapter.

CR-MAC. This protocol [7] is a cooperative MAC protocol that focuses on reducing wireless channel impairments and hence improving transmission. In cooperative communication, relay nodes are responsible for sending data from source to destination if there is no reliable channel between them. The paper [7] has proposed three different data transmissions modes, namely, Cooperative Relaying (CR), Direct Transmission (DT), and Multi-Hop Relaying (MHR). Since the IEEE 802.11 standard supports direct transmission only, the control packets of IEEE 802.11 were modified in addition to new control packets, which are: RRTS, OR, RACK, RRR and RCR [7].

For the DT mode, it follows the IEEE 802.11 rules of direct transmission over RTS/CTS. In the CR mode, the protocol assumes that all the neighboring nodes are aware of the SNR (Signal-to-Noise Ratio) of both transmitting and receiving nodes.

In MHR mode, source and destination nodes are in different network coverage i.e., the destination node is unable to receive the RTS sent by the source node. For communication, the neighboring nodes can listen to the RTS as they will be in the network coverage of both the nodes. Finally, after the selection of optimal relay or optimal relay group, the RRR transmits to both the source and destination nodes.

Upon receiving RCR after the SIFS interval, the source node starts transmitting to the optimal relay as it recognizes that the destination node has sent the CTS and then the optimal relay or group of relays transfer message to the destination node. When the data is received, acknowledgement is sent to the relay node by the destination node, which in turn is sent to the source in the form of RACK, to indicate that the transmission was successful.

RECV MAC. The mentioned protocol [8] focuses on improving the reliability of communication, providing high throughput and low delay in transmission of messages with the help of cooperation among various nodes (vehicles), and provides support for both non-safety and safety messages. The co-operating nodes overhear the communications and can relay the data, given that they have better channel conditions than the actual sender. RECV MAC introduced some new packets to support the proposed protocol, which are as follows: KTH (Keen to Help), NACK (Negative Acknowledgment), SHM (Selected Helper Message), WTI (Willing to Involve), and CWSA (Cooperative WAVE Service Advertisement).

In RECV MAC protocol, once a vehicle has broadcasted a safety message, it will wait for a timeout period to see if any nodes send a NACK. If no NACK is received, the transmission is considered successful; else, if the sender receives a NACK, it would indicate that at least one of the nodes has failed to receive the transmitted message successfully. Each node waits for SIFS time after overhearing a transmission before transmitting a NACK. NACK contains all the necessary details to uniquely identify the packet and the node transmitting and receiving the message. Upon hearing this NACK, other nodes will transmit a KTH packet if they have a better SINR. After receiving these KTH, the original transmitter will select an optimal helper based on the SINR for each of the helpers and cooperate with the node to relay the message to the node that transmitted the NACK. If no other node has transmitted a KTH message or SIFS, then the transmitter will assume no co-operation is possible and will continue as normal.

For non-safety messages, WTI, SHM, and CWSA packets are used. A WAVE provider issues a WSA packet and initializes a BSS. Other nodes can participate in this communication by then transmitting a WTI packet. Other nodes overhearing this transmission having a better SINR than the one transmitting the WTI packet will transmit a CWSA packet and will offer to become a helper. The original WAVE provider which transmitted the WSA packet will select an optimal helper and send an SHM packet which will result in all other nodes suspending their cooperation for this WTI and the selected helper joining the BSS. Subsequently, the data will be relayed through this helper. In case no helper is present, data is directly transmitted to the receiver.

Further, the protocol takes into consideration whether or not sending the message through cooperation is beneficial as sometimes the overhead caused due to relaying might be large enough, resulting in no benefits. Only if it is beneficial, the transmitter will proceed to achieve cooperation with a helper. The protocol's baselines for communicating with other nodes are as follows: it will send a safety message through direct transmission if both the nodes are in the same network. On the other hand, it will use cooperation if the nodes are in different networks since it improves the maximum range of transmission. Only if a NACK is received cooperation will be achieved. Similarly, for non-safety messages, only if a CWSA packet is received cooperation will be achieved.

OEC MAC. OEC MAC protocol focuses on improving the QoS and lesser delay due to vehicles' mobility by introducing cooperative communication [9]. For this purpose, new control messages are proposed, and the existing ones are updated to support cooperation. The protocol uses OFDMA, which is used to group the subchannels separately, hence reducing the delay. For the efficient working of the protocol, new control messages are as follows: Optimal Relay Message (ORM), Cooperative Service Wave Advertisement (CWSA), Cooperation Request Message (CRM), Acknowledgement (ACK), and Cooperation Acceptance Message (CAM). ACK, CAM, and CRM are initiated for safety messages, while CWSA is mainly used for non-safety messages.

For the successful dissemination of safety or beacon messages, the source should know whether or not the previous transmission was successful. For this particular reason, ACK is taken into consideration. In OEC MAC, after transmission, the source will wait for the acknowledgment, i.e., ACK or timeout. If the source vehicle gets the ACK, the transmission is successful; otherwise, for unsuccessful transmission, the source broadcasts CRM to all the neighboring nodes in search of optimal relays. Then, a node with better condition of channel, SINR, and transmission rate, transmits CAM to the source. There can be two cases; if the source vehicle does not receive any CAM, then cooperation is not possible, and hence, a successful transmission is not possible. Second, the source chooses the optimal relay nodes between those who sent the CAM. The source will then send ORM to the optimal relay nodes and the other nodes after listening to ORM, stop transmitting CAM. The packet is then transmitted to the destination using the optimal relay.

Nodes that want to transmit non-safety messages are known as providers, which can either be a RSU or a vehicle. For the non-safety message transmission, the source establishes a BSS. The source will then choose the optimal relay by transmitting ORM, which signals other nodes to stop sending CWSA. The destination node will then join the BSS, and the data is transmitted to it using the optimal relay. Otherwise, the data is directly transmitted to the destination node, if no ORM is identified.

Cluster-Based Protocols. Cluster-based MAC protocols take into consideration the dynamic nature of VANETs and try to achieve reliable communication by forming small clusters with each cluster having its own Cluster Head (CH) acting as the coordinator. The clustering helps in the reduction of relative mobility and thus ensures a much more robust communication link. The various cluster-based protocols discussed in this chapter are as follows: TC MAC [11], Modified TC MAC [13], CB MAC [14], and Optimized CB MAC [15].

TC MAC. TC MAC [11] is a TDMA, cluster-based MAC protocol designed for both safety and non-safety applications in VANETs, which aims at providing collision-free intra-cluster communications.

An important part of TC MAC is its slot reservation protocol. TC MAC assumes k slotted Service Channel (SCH), and one Control Channel (CCH). Further, each SCH has frames that are divided into a total of $\lfloor \frac{N}{k} \rfloor + 1$ slots of the same size, where N is the total number of vehicles in the cluster. For any vehicle with local ID i in the network, it owns the $i\%k(th)$ channel during the $\lfloor i\%k(th) \rfloor$ slot. While all vehicles know about frames and slot boundaries, CH is responsible for announcing if any new node has joined.

Each participating and active vehicle is assigned its own mini slot which it uses to transmit periodic beacon updates and other status information messages (specifically the first byte is reserved for the status information). When CH needs to transmit a safety message, it will abandon any non-safety communication and set the status of its mini slot so as to make other nodes aware that this node (CH) will be using its next slot for data transmission. The message will then be transmitted on the next slot and is further repeated on other available slots. This ensures that the message is transmitted throughout the network reliably. Since sometimes messages might only be useful to some specific nodes, CH uses an N bit vector where, N is the number of vehicles, the nodes for which the bit is not set will ignore this transmission. Apart from the normal SM transmission, this method is also used for cluster governance. For non-safety unicast communications, CMs do not require the intervention of CH and will set up a connection by themselves using the appropriate channels and time slots. However, for non-safety multicast communications, the node might take help from CH. This relies on the number of vehicles that the message that needs to be sent. In case the number of vehicles is small, CM will themselves set up a connection. However, if the number of vehicles is large, the transmitting CM will take help from CH by sending it an appropriate request consisting of an N bit vector consisting of the nodes to which the data needs to be transmitted along with other fields like its ID, etc. Once the message is received by the CH, it will transmit the message using the N bit vector as mentioned above.

Considering the fact that a stable clustering algorithm reduces the re-clustering overhead and that fewer changes in CH leads to the same (stable cluster), [11] has used an algorithm suggested in [12] that uses traffic flow for the purpose of CH selection as it provides much better CH lifetimes. Though the scheme offers various advantages over the WAVE standard, it only discusses intra-cluster communications and also does not support multi-hop clusters.

Modified TC MAC. Modified TC MAC [13], as the name suggests, is an improved version of the original TC MAC and addresses some of the issues faced in TC MAC. The major issue faced in TC MAC was that it assumed and provided support for only communication in a single hop manner. This, however, has been taken into consideration by Modified TC MAC and is tackled with an appropriate implementation to accommodate for communication in a multi-hop manner. The CH selection and the slot reservation protocols remain the same; however, for the modification to work, the number of vehicles within the cluster must be less than a maximum cluster size value.

In Modified TC MAC, for unicast communication, wherein, say, a vehicle i wanting to disseminate a message to vehicle j which is outside its transmission range, i will take help from a proxy node p which is in range of j & i and is willing to relay messages for this communication. The process of selection of the proxy node starts with i sending an appropriate request on CCH in its own mini slot. As a result, potential helpers will reply to i in i's time slot on the SCH. Once the proxy has been determined, all messages are relayed through this node thus allowing for communication in a multi-hop manner. However even Modified TC MAC is unable to support inter-cluster communications.

CB MAC. CB MAC [14] is a cluster-based MAC protocol developed for both safety and non-safety message which uses the Global Positioning System (GPS) installed in the vehicle(s) to find the location and the direction of travel which then helps in the formation of clusters of vehicles located closely and moving in the same direction, making it a direction-aware protocol. Further, it introduces some new control packets like RTCF, ReTCI and RCIM [14], for the ease of formation and management of communication in this cluster-based system. A Cluster Head (CH) to which all the other vehicles (Cluster Members) can communicate freely acts as the coordinator for all the broadcast messages and for interacting with other messages.

The process starts with an isolated vehicle broadcasting a RTCF packet (RTCF is transmitted when there is a safety message that needs to be sent). If there is a CH that is able to detect the packet, it will revert with a ReCTI packet. In case of multiple CH sending ReCTI packet, the vehicle will join the cluster from which the first ReTCI packet was received to ensure the least delay. In case no CH responds, the vehicle will form a cluster of its own, making itself the CH. The protocol also elaborates on the leaving (exit from the cluster) process, which doesn't require the vehicle to transmit any special message, rather is done automatically and periodically by the CH based on the CTS packets and ACKs it receives. In case the CH itself wishes to leave the cluster, it can also do so and the CM will become aware of the same with a similar process. However, a new cluster will be formed or joined by the vehicles if and when they want to transmit messages. Further, in case two CHs are in close proximity, and it is desirable to have a joint cluster, the same can be done through the transmission of the RCIM packet, and the CH with most CM's becomes the CH for this merged cluster.

CM's transmit message to CH using RTS/CTS mechanism to ensure reliable transfer and mitigate the hidden node problem. Once the message is with CH, it will broadcast the message. Since using RTS/CTS mechanism for a broadcast would lead to collisions among the CTS packets no such mechanism is used for CH's transmission. Once CH has transmitted the messages, it will wait for ACK from the nodes in the cluster and transmit the message again to those nodes that weren't able to receive it.

Although the performance of CB MAC outperforms WAVE (IEEE 802.11p), its performance is greatly affected by the number of clusters, size of clusters and a simple static approach for determining the number of clusters causes the performance of CB MAC to deteriorate.

Optimized CB MAC. Optimized CB MAC [15] is not a new MAC protocol; rather it proposes a few improvements to the already introduced CB MAC protocol. Optimized

CB MAC majorly focuses on being able to enhance the performance of the MAC protocol in terms of delay, throughput, etc. As CB MAC doesn't propose a method for finding the optimal size of clusters for a given number of vehicles, its performance depends largely on the size of clusters. Having very large clusters or very small clusters leads to a significant decrease in performance due to increased packet collisions and poor resource utilization respectively. The optimization works by finding an optimal transmission probability for a given cluster size, and since transmission probability is directly proportional to throughput, it optimizes the throughput.

Though the one caveat to this optimization, the current literature only presents the effects the optimization has when all the vehicles always have packets for transmission i.e., saturated conditions are considered.

Hybrid Protocols. Hybrid MAC protocols are those protocols that use both cooperation and clustering to achieve their functionality. In this chapter, the authors have discussed CCB MAC [16].

CCB MAC. CCB MAC [16] is a direction-aware hybrid MAC protocol that uses both cooperation and clustering to achieve the transmission of messages and improve the transmission reliability of the messages. The SCH used for intra-cluster communication is divided into frames of equal length, each with an upstream and a downstream broadcast period. Each CM is assigned one slot from a fixed number of slots in the upstream period.

Every CH broadcast an invitation message every T_j period on the CCH; any vehicle that wants to join a cluster will listen to broadcasts on this channel for the T_j period. If the CM successfully detects the broadcast and ensures that the signal strength is greater than a threshold value, it sends back to the CH a request to join the cluster to which the CH sends an acknowledgment and other necessary data for the purpose of clustering. If the vehicle is unable to receive any transmission on the CCH within the T_j period indicating no other CH is in the transmission range, it will elect itself a CH and form a new cluster. Once in a cluster, the vehicle will start to receive the transmission from the CH and will also be able to send any SM to the CH. Although if the vehicle doesn't receive any messages for R+1 frames, it will assume that it has lost the connection to the CH, thus leaving the cluster and starting with the process again.

CCB MAC expects every CM to transmit a packet in its assigned slot no matter if it has no data. This is done so that the CH knows the existence of different members and the available free slots. The CH transmits consolidated safety messages during the downstream broadcast period. If some nodes fail to receive this transmission, i.e., no ACK is present in the packet broadcasted by the node for that packet, cooperation will be achieved to ensure the delivery. Since the other nodes can overhear the communications, they check if a packet lacks an ACK field for the previous broadcast and maintain a list for all such nodes given the transmission it received had a signal strength more than a predefined value. If this potential helper takes a decision to perform cooperation, it will send a request of cooperation message to the CH in the packet header. The CH will decide a maximum of two helpers from all the potential helpers who have sent the RoC message based on cooperation gain (for a given node, the number of nodes that will receive data packets that were not able to receive it earlier) to relay the earlier broadcasts in the idle slots. Once CH selects the helpers, it will transmit an AoC message to intimate the nodes about the selected helpers, slots for retransmission, etc., thus making the ones not selected for cooperation suspend their operation. This further ensures that no two potential helpers transmit in the same time slot, thus causing collision and delay.

The protocol has been designed and tested for the delivery of safety messages and might need modifications for the purpose of delivery of non-safety messages. However [16] indicates that relative mobility has not yet been considered for further analysis. The protocol suffers from a hidden node terminal, thus causing an increase in delay and degradation in the throughput offered by the scheme [14].

3   Performance Analysis of Various MAC Protocols

Table 1 summarizes the various MAC protocols and their characteristics as found during this research. For this chapter, the authors have only confined to safety messages as they form the most backbone for vehicular communication [17,18]. Moreover, only the more recent protocols have been analyzed as they offer much better results. Further, a comparative view in terms of their performance is also presented.

Table 1. Comparison of MAC protocols

Protocol	CR MAC	RECV MAC	OEC MAC	TC MAC	M. TC MAC	CB MAC	Optimized CB MAC	CCB MAC
References	[7]	[8]	[9]	[11]	[13]	[14]	[15]	[16]
Published	2010	2019	2020	2012	2013	2019	2020	2014
Cooperative	Y	Y	Y	–	–	–	–	Y
Clustering	–	–	–	Y	Y	Y	Y	Y
TDMA	Y	–	–	Y	Y	–	–	Y
Simulator	NS-2	MATLAB	MATLAB	NS-3	NS-3	MATLAB	MATLAB + SUMO	MATLAB

The optimization for both CB MAC and TC MAC i.e., Optimized CB MAC and Modified TC MAC offers better results, as expected. However, when comparing the two protocols, CB MAC seems to outperform the TDMA based schemes since they cannot utilize all the available time slots, which causes a decrease in the performance, further since TC MAC and Modified TC MAC both use local IDs which need to be broadcasted every time a new node joins the overhead caused is huge which causes the performance to degrade.

To analyze the performance of various cooperative MAC protocols, the vehicular environment is created and simulated in MATLAB. The parameter setting for developing the environment is listed in Table 2.

Both RECV MAC and OEC MAC outperform CR MAC in terms of end-to-end delay and throughput. Figure 3 shows that RECV MAC and OEC MAC both offer

Table 2. Network environment for simulation

Parameter	Value
Number of channel	1 (Control channel)
Vehicle arrival pattern	Deterministic
Broadcast of safety message	10 messages/sec
Vicinity of network	500 m
Vehicular population	10–100 veh/km

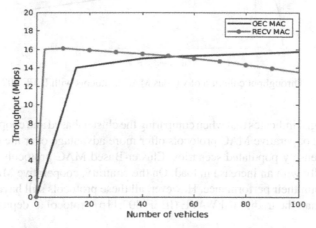

Fig. 3. Throughput Comparison of RECV and OEC MAC

similar throughput for a sparsely populated (vehicular nodes) environment while for densely populated environments OEC MAC is able to provide much better throughput and delay, thus offering a much better QoS in such environments.

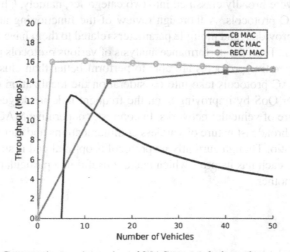

Fig. 4. Cooperative vs cluster-based MAC protocol: throughout comparison

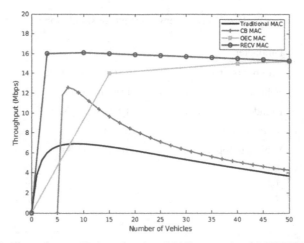

Fig. 5. Throughput collation of various MAC protocols with IEEE 802.11p

Further, Fig. 4 indicates that when comparing the cluster-based and cooperative MAC protocols, the cooperative MAC protocols offer more advantage over the cluster-based protocols in densely populated scenarios. Cluster-Based MAC protocols performance degrades rapidly with an increase in load. On the contrary, cooperative MAC protocols can still maintain their performance. However, all these protocols still have much better performance than the traditional WAVE (IEEE 802.11p) protocol as depicted in Fig. 5.

4   Conclusions

This chapter discusses and presents an overview of various cluster-based and cooperative MAC protocols developed for vehicular networks over the years. The various research articles studied were broadly classified into two categories, namely, Cluster-Based and Cooperative MAC protocols. A thorough review of the functioning and operation of each protocol is provided, and multiple parameters related to them have been discussed. It is clearly evident from the performance analysis of various protocols presented in the chapter that cooperative protocols are able to perform better than cluster-based ones. Cluster-based MAC protocols take into consideration the localization of vehicles and can achieve better QoS by improving upon the frequent link breakages caused due to the dynamic nature of vehicular networks. In contrast, cooperative MAC protocols take advantage of the broadcast nature of wireless communications and can achieve a better packet delivery ratio. Though currently no protocol is optimal and is suitable for use in any environment, each has its pros, which make it useful in a particular scenario while not so much in another.

References

1. Tan, I., Bahai, A.: Physical layer considerations for vehicular communications. Veh. Appl. Inter-Netw. Technol., 157–217 (2009)

2. Mittag, J., Schmidt-Eisenlohr, F., Killat, M., Torrent-Moreno, M., Hartenstein, H.: MAC layer and scalability aspects of vehicular communication networks. VANET: Veh. Appl. Inter-Netw. Technol., 219–269 (2010)
3. Jiang, D., Delgrossi, L.: IEEE 802.11p: towards an international standard for wireless access in vehicular environments. In: VTC Spring 2008 - IEEE Vehicular Technology Conference, pp. 2036–2040 (2008)
4. Silva, C.A.G.D., Pedroso, C.M.: MAC-layer packet loss models for Wi-Fi networks: a survey. IEEE Access 7, 180512–180531 (2019)
5. Belamri, F., Boulfekhar, S., Aissani, D.: A survey on QoS routing protocols in vehicular Ad Hoc network (VANET). Telecommun. Syst. 78(1), 117–153 (2021). https://doi.org/10.1007/s11235-021-00797-8
6. Korakis, T., Tao, Z., Slutskiy, Y., Panwar, S.: A cooperative MAC protocol for Ad Hoc wireless networks. In: Fifth Annual IEEE International Conference on Pervasive Computing and Communications Workshops (PerComW 2007), pp. 532–536 (2007)
7. Kamruzzaman, S.M.: CR-MAC: a multichannel MAC protocol for cognitive radio Ad Hoc networks. Int. J. Comput. Netw. Commun., 1–14 (2010)
8. Shah, A.S., Ilhan, H., Tureli, U.: RECV-MAC: a novel reliable and efficient cooperative MAC protocol for VANETs. IET Commun. 13, 2541–2549 (2019)
9. Karabulut, M.A., Shah, A.F.M.S., Ilhan, H.: OEC-MAC: a novel OFDMA based efficient cooperative MAC protocol for VANETS. IEEE Access 8, 94665–94677 (2020)
10. Ma, M., Liu, K., Luo, X., Zhang, T., Liu, F.: Review of MAC protocols for vehicular Ad Hoc networks. Sensors 20, 6709 (2020)
11. Almalag, M.S., Olariu, S., Weigle, M.C.: TDMA cluster-based MAC for VANETs (TC-MAC). In: 2012 IEEE International Symposium on a World of Wireless, Mobile and Multimedia Networks (WoWMoM), pp. 1–6 (2012)
12. Mohammad, S.A., Michele, C.W.: Using traffic flow for cluster formation in vehicular ad-hoc networks. In: IEEE Local Computer Network Conference, pp. 631–636 (2010)
13. Almalag, M.S., El-Tawab, S., Olariu, S., Weigle, M.C.: A modified TC-MAC protocol for multi-hop cluster communications in VANETs. In: 2013 International Conference on Connected Vehicles and Expo (ICCVE), pp. 832–837 (2013)
14. Shah, A.S., Ilhan, H., Tureli, U.: CB-MAC: a novel cluster-based MAC protocol for VANETs. IET Intell. Transp. Syst. 13, 587–595 (2019)
15. Shah, A.F.M.S., Karabulut, M.A., Ilhan, H., Tureli, U.: Performance optimization of cluster-based MAC protocol for VANETs. IEEE Access 8, 167731–167738 (2020)
16. Yang, F., Tang, Y.: Cooperative clustering-based medium access control for broadcasting in vehicular ad-hoc networks. IET Commun. 8, 3136–3144 (2014)
17. Verma, P., Singh, N., Sharma, M.: Modelling a vehicle-ID-based IEEE 802.11 OCB MAC scheme for periodic broadcast in vehicular networks. IET Commun. 12(19), 2401–2407 (2018)
18. Verma, P., Singh, N., Sharma, M.: Modeling and performance analysis of VI-CRA: a congestion control algorithm for vehicular networks. Int. J. Commun Syst 31(14), e3736 (2018)

Improve CNN Model Agro-Crop Leaf Disease Identification Based on Transfer Learning

Md Shamiul Islam[1], Ummya Habiba[2], Md Abu Baten[3], Nazrul Amin[3],
Imrus Salehin[4(✉)] (iD), and Tasmia Tahmida Jidney[5]

[1] Bangladesh University of Business and Technology, Dhaka, Bangladesh
[2] Bangladesh Agricultural University, Mymensingh, Bangladesh
[3] Northern University Bangladesh, Dhaka, Bangladesh
[4] Dongseo University, Busan 47011, South Korea
deeplab43@gmail.com
[5] Ahsanullah University of Science and Technology, Dhaka, Bangladesh

Abstract. Transfer learning is an optimization that assumes faster development and superior performance when modeling a second task. In this study, we have constructed an integrated model based on improved VGG16 and ResNet-50 network. For the improvement of CNN architecture, VGG16 full connected layer drops then it is connected with the next full collected layer due to reduce the computing complexity. ResNet-50 has been updated with its input image size layer. For the agro-crop leaf disease identification, BAU-agro data has been trained with this particular Improved CNN architecture model. Resulting in the trained model representing 95.89% accuracy in integrated algorithm model architecture. In our study, we have proposed fewer parameters and consumed less time for the absolute experiment and identification. The high-dimensional substance image characteristic data outcome by the developed VGG16 and Resnet-50 has initialized input into the Convolution Neural Network (CNN). For the training stage, it has been evaluated the expression types with high accuracy performed.

Keywords: VGG-16 · Resnet-50 · Image identification · Agriculture · CNN

1 Introduction

At the present time, food safety is first priority all over the world. The quality and amount of Agro-production can be impactful if food development cannot turn into automated and advanced [1]. But, it can be more dangerous if we do have not enough development in disease control. In the crop disease identification field primitive or manual calculation is still used. With the fast reformation of Machine learning (ML) and Artificial Intelligence (AI) application, the precision and accuracy of Crop leaf disease identification processing developed on Deep learning (DL) in substantive agricultural scenes have overcome that of consecutive agricultural specialists.

However, for the limited data set and the impact of the network's structure, the complex network structure has an overfitting issue, so with the lower accuracy of image

© The Author(s), under exclusive license to Springer Nature Switzerland AG 2023
R. N. Shaw et al. (Eds.): ICACIS 2022, CCIS 1749, pp. 258–265, 2023.
https://doi.org/10.1007/978-3-031-25088-0_22

recognition, which cannot correspond to the need for efficient analysis of authentic agricultural work scenes.

In our study main novelty is as follows:

- We have reduced our parameter from the existing CNN model to our improved model. Due to reducing the parameter, our model performed well as well as reduced the time complexity.
- Advanced identification system than the previous classification model according to CNN.

To overcome the problem, in our study we have proposed a developed transfer learning network [2]. Moreover, the proposal for the image experiment methods has been made with the ResNet-50 and VGG16 neural network models. At the same time the fine turn improves the image analysis model. Both algorithms have been developed to reduce the overfitting problem.

2 Related Work

High-amount agro production is a large issue all over the world. So, this is essential to ensure quality and security. However, crop disease has an impact on crop production. The improvement of big data and AI provides renewed ideas for crop-pest analysis and experiment [3, 4]. D. Xiao et al., in their research chapter, introduced a potato insect identification method based on FR-CNN (F = faster) and it remaining the CNN (Convolution Neural Network) [5]. The mobileNetv2-YOLOv3 lightweight network model has proposed the normalization and segment theory for pest image identity [6]. This deep neural network formation has been conducted over fitting prevent during architecture model training and testing. As a result of the collapse of image data accuracy calculation. Moreover, the image fact of diseases and insect is difficult and the present methods cannot be supported by dependable and full datasets. In this chapter authors compared six different CNN Architectures VGG16, InceptionV3, Xception, Resnet50, MobileNet, and DenseNet121 but they got best accuracy 95.48% on test data by using DenseNet121. They take the dataset from Plant Village dataset, and use 15 different plants 10 classes potato and tomato plants,8984 images for training,1176 images for validation and 1173 images for testing [7]. Using Xception and DenseNet (CNN Architectures) authors build a multi-plant disease diagnosis method. They collect their dataset from various online sources (tomato, potato, rice, corn, grape, apple) which contain total 28 diseases of 6 plants [8].

To reduce the prior problems, this experiment has proposed a leaf disease image analysis experiment establish by the update Transfer Learning network.

3 Crop Diseases Detection Technique and Recognition Model

From the idea of Transfer Learning, we have proposed the flowchart model. In this model, Crop Disease data passing through the pre-trained convolutional network with fine-tuning for the output generation.

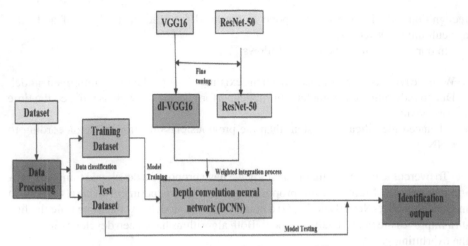

Fig. 1. Diagram of leaf diseases identification on a multilayer network model

Figure 1 shows, obtained the VGG16 and ResNet-50 based identification system which is using pre-training and fine-tuning. Initial network design is acquired by using ResNet-50 trained by dataset. Enhanced confirmation sets were used to fine-tune the pre-training pattern. After that, some number of iterations to optimize the network convergence of the corresponding convolution neural network sequence disease detection models dl-VGG16 and ResNet-50 are obtained.

4 Data Processing

4.1 Dataset

In this experiment, we have used an Image dataset from the Bangladesh Agricultural University Agro-disease database.

Fig. 2. Data sample BAU-Agro disease

For the analysis, the data set contain a total of 14 class and 13,024 different images. BAU-Agro Disease takes on a large quantity of image arrangement crop leaves such as Corn, Rice, Potato and Wheat. In this experiment, a total of 10,000 images have used for training and identification. Besides this, another 3024 images have been used for testing. The resolution size of each individual sample image is 224 × 224 × 3. Moreover, some samples image and categories name has been shown in Fig. 2.

4.2 Dataset Processing

The number of leaf diseases image provided on the BAU-Agro dataset is unsmooth. Therefore, the dataset has to optimize and divided for testing and training [9].

Furthermore, we are aware that in order to train deep learning models, larger datasets or a considerable amount of data are required. As a consequence of this, the process of augmenting images can be utilized to achieve the objective of increasing the size of the dataset. After the stage of image augmentation, the picture dataset goes through another pre-processing step which is known as size normalization. In this stage, you will resize each of the photos so that they can be contained within a single image that has been standardized. For the sake of this specific research, the dimensions of each image were altered to be 224 by 224 pixels. After that, the photographs are divided up into groups and given the appropriate processing for each of those groups. The batch size that we employ is 32, which is the default value for this accuracy-controlling parameter. This parameter is used to control how accurate the model is. Training the model: The suggested model is trained with the deep neural architectures ResNet50 and VGG16, and those weights are utilized to initialize the weights of the learned model once it has been trained. The neural network is able to learn from the features that were retrieved by repeatedly carrying out the process of back propagation.

This process involves modifying the weights in order to reduce error, which allows the neural network to learn from the features that were retrieved. "Fine-tuning" refers to the process of making minute adjustments to the weights, while "dl-VGG16" is the name given to the improved version of the formula.

5 Transfer Learning Network

5.1 VGG-16 Architecture

In this research, the VGG16 architecture network has been selected as a pre-train model of transfer learning. In the VGG16 model [10] architecture, we have eliminated the FC layer 1 drop and by a direct route have linked it with the FC layer 2. Secondly, the sample of individual neurons that have been remaining two FC layers is preventing. FC have denoted as a fully connected layer. While decrement of the amounts of parameters could be perform the features adopted by the last convolution layer more peculiar that is beneficial to enhance the unification outcome. Minimizing the depth of all structural neural networks in in several processes to reduce the number of parameters (dl-VGG16) is beneficial to counteract overfitting to a particular limitation in Fig. 3.

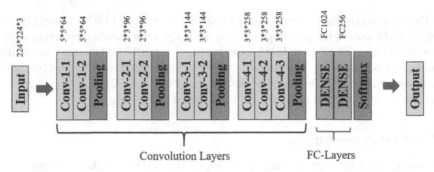

Convolution Layers   FC-Layers

Fig. 3. VGG-16 improve architecture

5.2 ResNet-50

Resnet-50 is a pertained model for image classification in Convocation Neural network (CNN, or ConvNet) which is applied to solve exploding gradient and degradation problem that faced while training a deep neural network model. Resnet-50 has 50 layers and it trained on a million images of 1000 categories from imageNet. ResNet-50 contain of 48 ConV layers, 1 average pool layer and 1 max pool layer and it consists of 3.8 $\times 10^9$ floating point operations. The symbol images are fed to the model and various parameters are configured like batch size is equal to 32, number of epoch is equal to 50 and learning rate is 3×10^2. The workflow of ResNet-50 is shown in Fig. 4.

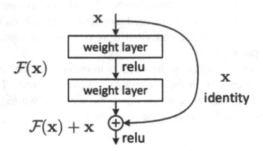

Fig. 4. Workflow of ResNet-50 architecture.

In CNN every layer learns low or high level features while being trained for the task at hand. It instead of trying to learn features, model and tries to learn some of residual. Here we can see, The output function Y is define in Eq. (1), when input and output both are of the same dimensions.

$$y = F(x, \{W_j\}) + x \tag{1}$$

where, X is the input to the residual block $F(x, \{W_j\})$ and W_j represents the weight layers. If take different dimensional input and output, the shortcut performs identity mapping by padding the extra zero entries with the dimension that is increased and then matched by using the projection shortcut as in Eq. (2).

$$y = F(x, \{W_j\}) + W_s x \tag{2}$$

6 Experiment and Analysis

The data presented in Figure illustrates that the dl-VGG16 obtains a higher level of training accuracy during the training process at a faster pace, which is proof that the suggested network has a quicker fitting time, in Fig. 5. Taking a look at the outcomes of the training makes this very clear. When compared to the VGG16 network, the accuracy achieved by the dl-VGG16 network is significantly higher.

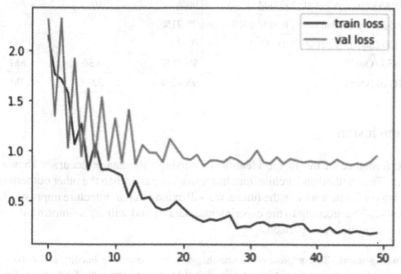

Fig. 5. Accuracy loss graphical view

If we use the test set as an illustration, the improved VGG16 network has a recognition accuracy of over 90%, which suggests that its fitting effect is also significantly improved [11]. The goal of the proposed method is to further improve the recognition accuracy by combining the feature extraction advantages supplied by the dl-VGG16 network with the classification characteristics offered by the network. This will allow for a more robust combination of both sets of benefits. Enhance CNN's ability to identify diseases that affect agro-crop leaves (Table 1).

Table 1. Experimental analysis and baseline comparison

Model name	Model accuracy	Model loss	Parameter
I VGG16 (Wu, S, 2021) [12]	90.51	9.49	1.3M
VGG-16-transfer (Yong Wu, et al. 2018) [13]	83.53%	16.47	1M
VGG-19-transfer (YongWu, et al. 2018) [13]	84.71%	15.29	–
PretrainedVGG16 (Tammina, S 2019) [14]	86.50%	13.5	–
VGG19 (Sahili, Z.A., et al. 2022) [15]	90%	10	–
ResNet50 (A. Sai Bharadwaj Reddy 2019)	95.91%	–	–
ResNet50 (Sagar, A., et al. 2021) [16]	0.98	–	–
ResNet50 (Our)	**99.50%**	**0.50**	1.8M
dl-VGG16 (Our)	**96.02%**	**3.9**	1.7M

7 Conclusion

The performance of the image identification using this dataset accuracy shown well perform. This method and architecture framework is easier than the other outperforming algorithms or frameworks. In the future, we will extend our architecture improve VGG16 and ResNet-50 according to the experimental dataset and will try to improve the model with some baseline comparison.

Acknowledgement. To complete our research, work our honorable Faculty and Advisor help us. We use a Machine learning/Deep Learning lab at Dongseo University, South Korea for better results and experiments. But to complete our research we have no special funding.

References

1. Paymode, A.S., Malode, V.B.: Transfer learning for multi-crop leaf disease image classification using convolutional neural network VGG. Artif. Intell. Agric. **6**, 23–33 (2022)
2. Thenmozhi, K., Srinivasulu Reddy, U.: Crop pest classification based on deep convolutional neural network and transfer learning. Comput. Electron. Agric. **164**, 104906 (2019)
3. Parraga-Alava, J., Alcivar-Cevallos, R., Morales Carrillo, J., et al.: LeLePhid: an image dataset for aphid detection and infestation severity on lemon leaves. Data **6**(5), 1–7 (2021)
4. Zhu, J., Wu, A., Wang, X., Zhang, H.: Identification of grape diseases using image analysis and BP neural networks. Multimedia Tools Appl. **79**(21–22), 14539–14551 (2019). https://doi.org/10.1007/s11042-018-7092-0
5. Xiao, D., Feng, J.Z., Feng, J., Lin, T., Pang, C., Ye, Y.: Classification and recognition scheme for vegetable pests based on the BOF-SVM model. Int. J. Agric. Biol. Eng. **11**(3), 190–196 (2018)
6. Liu, J., Wang, X.: Early recognition of tomato gray leaf spot disease based on MobileNetv2-YOLOv3 model. Plant Methods **16**(1), 1–16 (2020)
7. Sumalatha, G., Krishna Rao, D., Singothu, D.: Transfer learning-based plant disease detection. Comput. Biol. J. (2021)

8. Kabir, M.M., Ohi, A.Q., Mridha, M.F.: A multi-plant disease diagnosis method using convolutional neural network. In: Uddin, M.S., Bansal, J.C. (eds. Computer Vision and Machine Learning in Agriculture. AIS, pp. 99–111. Springer, Singapore (2021). https://doi.org/10. 1007/978-981-33-6424-0_7

9. Jepkoech, J., Mugo, D.M., Kenduiywo, B.K., Too, E.C.: Arabica coffee leaf images dataset for coffee leaf disease detection and classification. Data Brief **36**(1), Chapter ID 107142 (2021)

10. Liu, Y., Zhang, X., Gao, Y., Qu, T., Shi, Y.: Improved CNN method for crop pest identification based on transfer learning. Comput. Intell. Neurosci., Chapter ID 9709648, 8 p. (2022)

11. Salehin, I., Talha, I.M., Saifuzzaman, M., Moon, N.N., Nur, F.N.: An advanced method of treating agricultural crops using image processing algorithms and image data processing systems. In: 2020 IEEE 5th International Conference on Computing Communication and Automation (ICCCA), pp. 720–724 (2020). https://doi.org/10.1109/ICCCA49541.2020.925 0839

12. Mridha, K., et al.: Plant disease detection using web application by neural network. In: 2021 IEEE 6th International Conference on Computing, Communication and Automation (ICCCA), pp. 130–136 (2021). https://doi.org/10.1109/ICCCA52192.2021.9666354

13. Wu, Y., Qin, X., Pan, Y., Yuan, C.: Convolution neural network based transfer learning for classification of flowers. In: 2018 IEEE 3rd International Conference on Signal and Image Processing (ICSIP), pp. 562–566. IEEE, July 2018

14. Tammina, S.: Transfer learning using vgg-16 with deep convolutional neural network for classifying images. Int. J. Sci. Res. Publ. (IJSRP) **9**(10), 143–150 (2019)

15. Sahili, Z.A., Awad, M.: The power of transfer learning in agricultural applications: AgriNet. arXiv preprint 2207.03881 (2022)

16. Sagar, A., Jacob, D.: On using transfer learning for plant disease detection. BioRxiv, pp. 2020–05 (2021)

Per User Based Multi Threshold Scheduling for BER Improvement Compared to Priority Scheduling in MU-MIMO Networks

T. Pavan Kalyan and K. Chanthirasekaran[✉]

Department of Electronics and Communication Engineering, Saveetha School of Engineering,
Saveetha Institutes of Medical and Technical Sciences, Saveetha University,
Chennai, Tamil Nadu, India
{thirumalasettypk18,chanthirasekarank.sse}@saveetha.com

Abstract. This work aims to improve Bit Error Rate by Novel Per User based Multi Threshold scheduling (PUMTS) compared to Priority scheduling (PS) for MU-MIMO Wireless Networks. In this work there are two groups, in each group 20 samples were collected with pre-test power of 80% (G-power). Group 1 is taken as PUMTS and group 2 is taken as Priority scheduling (PS). Through simulation, the novel PUMTS has achieved the Bit Error Rate of 0.175×10^{-4} and PS has achieved the Bit Error Rate of 0.885×10^{-4} with significance of $p = 0.000$ (2 tailed). This study shows that the PUMTS is significantly better than PS in the improvement of Bit Error Rate.

Keywords: Bit error rate · Novel per user based multi threshold scheduling · MU-MIMO networks · Priority scheduling · Efficiency · Wireless networks

1 Introduction

The research is about the improvement of packet delivery ratio and getting better performance to the users. MU-MIMO (Clerckx and Oestges 2013) is an era wherein basically agencies collectively antennas on the higher throughput and higher spectrum efficiency. MIMO structures have ended up mainstays of wi-fi networks due to their spectral efficiencies and variety gains. The MU-MIMO networks are applied in virtual homes (Holland 2018), mobile networks (Vahid et al. 2015) and LTE (Elnashar 2014) structures etc.

In the past 7 years 47 articles have been published based on the Bit Error Rate improvement of MU-MIMO Networks. Among all previous chapters they discussed fair scheduling, Priority scheduling and threshold based fair scheduling. We proposed here a novel per user based multi threshold scheduling for BER improvement to get the better performance. Closed-form in (Altamirano et al. 2019) has been proposed for average BER improvement for time-invariant-channel. The closed-form expressions for BER in (Kibona et al. 2020) were proposed under imperfect-CSI for wireless networks. BER Analysis with Maximum MR linear precoding in (Kibona et al. 2019) were proposed and extended for massive MU-MIMO networks under Time Division Duplex (TDD).

© The Author(s), under exclusive license to Springer Nature Switzerland AG 2023
R. N. Shaw et al. (Eds.): ICACIS 2022, CCIS 1749, pp. 266–273, 2023.
https://doi.org/10.1007/978-3-031-25088-0_23

Antenna selection in (Gangwar and Chandra 2013) were proposed and it is a promising low-complexity solution that solves the pressing problem of the increased hardware and signal processing complexity of MU-MIMO networks and they analyze the spectral efficiency. Inter-symbol interference (ISI) in (Gupta and Saini 2012) were proposed multipath fading with different equalization algorithms and they analyze the characteristics and efficiency of scheduling scheme. The PAPR-guaranteed BER minimization in (Peng et al. 2018) has been proposed and through precoding in uplink massive MIMO networks the problem is solved. A Precoded algorithm with enhanced BER performance based on the Symmetric Accelerated Over Relaxation (SAOR) method in (Hu et al. 2019) was proposed for wireless networks to analyze the characteristics and efficiency of scheduling scheme. New precoding techniques to mitigate the inter-user-interference (IUI) in (Jedda et al. 2016) were proposed.

All the above studies have obtained a high bit error rate. To improve the bit error rate, a novel scheduler is needed. The main purpose of the novel Per user based multi threshold scheduling is to improve the performance by decreasing the bit error rate compared to the previous networking threshold schedulers through that the users will satisfy the service.

2 Materials and Methods

The research was conducted in the Department of Electronics and Communication Engineering at Saveetha School of Engineering, SIMATS, Tamil Nadu, India. Two groups each of sample size 20 has been taken for both threshold schedulers. Group 1 is considered for the novel Per user based Multi Threshold scheduling scheduler and group 2 is considered for the Priority Scheduling Scheduler (Zhao and Zeng 2017). The statistical tool with G power of 80%.

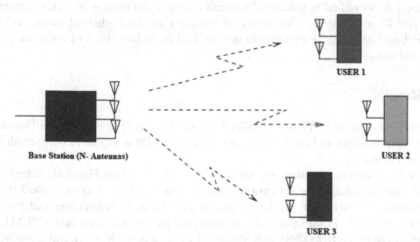

Fig. 1. Downlink of a multiuser MIMO network: A BS communicates simultaneously with several multiple antenna terminals. The base station (N antennas) is communicated to multiple users for multiple input and multiple output networks.

Figure 1 shows the Downlink of a MU-MIMO network: A BS communicates simultaneously with several multiple antenna terminals. The base station (N antennas) is communicated to multiple users for multiple input and multiple output networks. The Scheduling algorithm 1 novel Per User based Multi Threshold Scheduling and the Scheduling algorithm 2 Priority scheduling (Jayakody et al. 2019) is used for scheduling the 25 active users with 11 resources.

3 Novel Per User Based Multi Threshold Scheduling Algorithm

1) Random user generators are Uk and the number of resources declared is denoted by 'R'.
2) Random threshold schedulers are T1&T2 for each user respectively.
3) Compare each user strength with each user threshold value T1 and generate a scheduled user list 'k1'.
4) Compare each user strength with each user threshold value T2 and generate a scheduled user list 'k2'.
5) Find the length of k1 and k2 are denoted x1 and x2 respectively.
6) If $x2 > R$ then final scheduled user ks = k2 else if $x2 > x1$ then final schedule user ks = k1.
7) Send this scheduled user ks into MIMO Network for packet delivery ratio estimation.
8) Calculate average packet delivery ratio for different resources [R].

The testing setup was done using MATLAB R2018a Software. The tests are carried out on a device with a core i3 processor and 4 GB of RAM. The obtained results of PUMTS and PS were validated with statistical Software in terms of Bit Error Rate.

The statistical analysis is carried out using the SPSS tool (McCormick and Salcedo 2017). The significance is calculated using the Independent t-test. The Independent variables are identified as number of transmit antennas and number of receive antennas in a AWGN-noise signal. The dependent variables are the L-channel matrix and Bit Error Rate. Using the SPSS software the standard deviation, standard error and mean were calculated.

4 Results

Simulation is done in MATLAB 2018Ra Software. The Per User based Multi Threshold Scheduling and Priority Scheduling were simulated and Bit error rate of both schedulers has been obtained.

Table 1 shows the simulation results of Per User based Multi Threshold Scheduling and Priority Scheduling for Bit error rate for different numbers of users. Table 2 shows the Statistical Analysis of Per User based Multi Threshold Scheduling and Priority Scheduling models. From Table 2, it is observed that the mean bit error rate of PUMTS is 0.0000175 and PS is 0.0000885 with Standard Deviation of 0.00000716 and 0.00004082 respectively. Table 3 shows the Independent sample T-test is performed for the two groups for significance and standard error determination. The T-test showed the standard error difference is 0.00000927 with significance of 0.006.

Table 1. Simulation results are obtained through MATLAB 2018Ra of Per User based Multi Threshold Scheduling and Priority Scheduling for Bit Error Rate for MU-MIMO Networks.

Sl. no	Bit error rate	
	PS $\times 10^{-4}$	PUMTS $\times 10^{-4}$
1	2.0	0.1
2	2.0	0.1
3	1.0	0.1
4	0.9	0.2
5	0.8	0.2
6	0.8	0.1
7	0.7	0.1
8	0.7	0.2
9	0.7	0.2
10	0.6	0.1
11	0.6	0.1
12	0.5	0.1
13	0.6	0.2
14	0.6	0.2
15	0.7	0.2
16	0.8	0.2
17	0.8	0.2
18	0.9	0.3
19	1.0	0.3
20	1.0	0.3

Figure 2 shows the comparison of the bit error rate of Per User based Multi Threshold Scheduling and Priority Scheduling. While the number of users reaches 15 the Per User based Multi Threshold Scheduling will be obtained as 0.2×10^{-4} and the Priority Scheduling will be obtained as 0.7×10^{-4}.

At the number of Users is 25 the Per User based Multi Threshold Scheduling will be obtained as 0.3×10^{-4} and the Priority Scheduling will be obtained as 2×10^{-4}. Figure 3 shows the barchart mean BER performance graph of Per User based Multi Threshold scheduling (PUMTS) and Priority Scheduling (PS) with error bars.

Table 2. SPSS Statistical Analysis of Per User based Multi Threshold Scheduling and Priority Scheduling for Bit Error Rate. The Mean, Standard Deviation and Standard Error Mean are obtained for 20 iterations. This performance represents better outcomes for PUMTS than PS.

Group statistics					
	Group	N	Mean	Std. deviation	Std. error mean
Bit error rate (BER)	Priority scheduling (PS)	20	0.0000885	0.00004082	0.00000913
	Per user based multi threshold scheduling (PUMTS)	20	0.0000175	0.00000716	0.00000160

Table 3. Independent sample T-test is performed for the two groups for significance and standard error difference. Levene's Test for equality of variances showed a significance of 0.006 for Bit Error Rate.

Levene's test for equality of variances				T-test for equality of means					95% confidence interval of the difference	
F		Sig	t	df	Sig (2-tailed)	Mean difference	Std. error difference	Lower	Upper
Bit error rate (BER)	Equal variances assumed	8.330	0.006	7.662	38	0.000	0.00007100	0.00000927	0.00005224	0.00008976
	Equal variance not assumed			7.662	20.169	0.000	0.00007100	0.00000927	0.00005168	0.00009032

5 Discussion

Per User based Multi Threshold Scheduling is simulated with 25 numbers of active users and 11 resources in base stations. Through the simulation it is found that the Per User based Multi Threshold Scheduling BER performance is significantly better than Priority Scheduling BER performance.

Joint power Allocation and scheduling techniques for Bit Error Rate minimization in (Ko et al. 2021) was proposed for the MU-MIMO framework and analyzed the characteristics and performance of scheduling scheme. The estimated bit error rate is 0.46×10^{-4} in (Altamirano et al. 2019) for time-invariant-channel and they analyzed the spectral efficiency. The obtained bit error rate is 0.49×10^{-4}. The closed-form expressions for BER in (Kibona et al. 2020) is 0.39×10^{-4} and they analyze the characteristics and efficiency of scheduling scheme. in The estimated bit error rate is 0.43×10^{-4} in (Kibona et al. 2019) for massive MU-MIMO networks under Time Division Duplex mode of operation in the downlink transmission for wireless networks. An analytical method in (Kageyama and Muta 2019) was proposed to evaluate achievable BER performance of downlink OFDM with the peak cancellation in massive MIMO systems using arbitrary

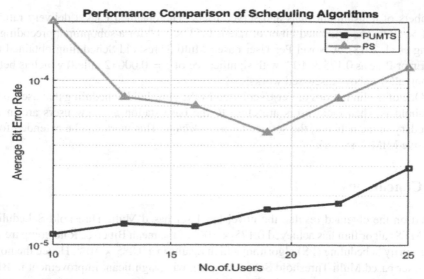

Fig. 2. Bit Error Rate performance comparison of Per User based Multi Threshold Scheduling and Priority Scheduling. X Axis: No. of. Users and Y Axis: Average Bit Error Rate.

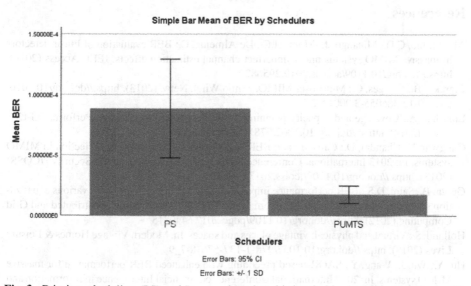

Fig. 3. Priority scheduling (PS) and Per user based multi threshold scheduling classifiers with Bit Error Rate has been depicted in the form of a bar chart. X Axis: PS vs PUMTS algorithms Y Axis: Median value of BER of detection. (±1 SD)

numbers of transmit antennas and served users. The obtained Packet delivery ratio is 0.74×10^{-4}. The estimated bit error rate is 0.53×10^{-4} for a suboptimal precoding in (Peng et al. 2018). A Novel Per User based Multi Threshold Scheduling obtained the Bit Error Rate as 0.175×10^{-4} with significance of $p = 0.000$ (2 tailed) which is better among all the above discussed works.

One of the limitations of Per User based Multi Threshold Scheduling that uses multi threshold is when more users are close to the base station and few users are in the boundary of the network, the service fairness decays. This work can be extended for a massive MIMO network.

6 Conclusion

Based on the obtained results, the novel Per User based Multi Threshold Scheduling (PUMTS) algorithm has achieved 0.175×10^{-4} of the mean Bit error Rate compared to the Priority Scheduling (PS) algorithm which results in a 0.885×10^{-4}. Hence the novel Per User based Multi Threshold Scheduling is having significant improvement in BER performance compared to Priority Scheduling.

References

Altamirano, C.D., Minango, J., Mora, H.C., De Almeida, C.: BER evaluation of linear detectors in massive MIMO systems under imperfect channel estimation effects. IEEE Access (2019). https://doi.org/10.1109/access.2019.2956828

Clerckx, B., Oestges, C.: Multi-user MIMO. Mimo Wirel. Netw. (2013). https://doi.org/10.1016/b978-0-12-385055-3.00012-2

Elnashar, A.: Coverage and capacity planning of 4G networks. Des. Deploy. Perform. 4G-LTE Netw. (2014). https://doi.org/10.1002/9781118703434.ch6

Gangwar, V., Chandra, D.: Capacity and BER improvement through antenna selection in MIMO systems. In: 2013 International Conference on Optical Imaging Sensor and Security (ICOSS) (2013). https://doi.org/10.1109/icoiss.2013.6678401

Gupta, B., Saini. D.S.: BER performance improvement in MIMO systems using various equalization techniques. In: 2012 2nd IEEE International Conference on Parallel, Distributed and Grid Computing (2012). https://doi.org/10.1109/pdgc.2012.6449815

Holland, S.: Virtual and physical: vintage places and spaces. In: Modern Vintage Homes & Leisure Lives (2018). https://doi.org/10.1057/978-1-137-57618-7_9

Hu, Y., Wu, J., Wang, Y.: SAOR-based precoding with enhanced BER performance for massive MIMO systems. In: 2019 International Conference on Artificial Intelligence in Information and Communication (ICAIIC) 2019. https://doi.org/10.1109/icaiic.2019.8668984

Jayakody, D.N.K., Srinivasan, K., Sharma, V.: 5G Enabled Secure Wireless Networks. Springer, Cham (2019). https://doi.org/10.1007/978-3-030-03508-2

Jedda, H., Nossek, J.A., Mezghani, A.: Minimum BER precoding in 1-bit massive MIMO systems. In: 2016 IEEE Sensor Array and Multichannel Signal Processing Workshop (SAM) (2016). https://doi.org/10.1109/sam.2016.7569655

Kageyama, T., Muta, O.: Bit error rate analysis of MRC precoded massive MIMO-OFDM systems with peak cancellation. In: 2019 IEEE 90th Vehicular Technology Conference (VTC2019-Fall) (2019). https://doi.org/10.1109/vtcfall.2019.8891444

Kibona, L., Jian, L., Yingzhuang, L.: BER analysis using zero-forcing linear precoding scheme for massive MIMO under imperfect channel state information. Int. J. Electron. (2020). https://doi.org/10.1080/00207217.2019.1692248

Kibona, L., Liu, J., Liu, Y.: BER analysis using MRT linear precoding technique for massive MIMO under imperfect channel state information. In: 2019 Photonics & Electromagnetics Research Symposium - Fall (PIERS - Fall) (2019). https://doi.org/10.1109/piers-fall48861.2019.9021414

Ko, K., Byun, I., Lee, J., Shin, W.: Joint power allocation and scheduling techniques for BER minimization in multiuser MIMO systems. IEEE Access (2021). https://doi.org/10.1109/access.2021.3074980

Rajawat, A.S., Rawat, R., Shaw, R.N., Ghosh, A.: Cyber physical system fraud analysis by mobile robot. In: Bianchini, M., Simic, M., Ghosh, A., Shaw, R.N. (eds.) Machine Learning for Robotics Applications. SCI, vol. 960, pp. 47–61. Springer, Singapore (2021). https://doi.org/10.1007/978-981-16-0598-7_4

Peng, W., Zheng, L., Chen, D., Ni, C., Jiang, T.: Distributed precoding for BER minimization with PAPR constraint in uplink massive MIMO systems. IEEE Access (2018). https://doi.org/10.1109/access.2017.2707396

Vahid, S., Tafazolli, R., Filo, M.: Small cells for 5G mobile networks. In: Fundamentals of 5G Mobile Networks (2015). https://doi.org/10.1002/9781118867464.ch3

Zhao, Y., Zeng, H.: The virtual deadline based optimization algorithm for priority assignment in fixed-priority scheduling. In: 2017 IEEE Real-Time Systems Symposium (RTSS) (2017). https://doi.org/10.1109/rtss.2017.00018

Cervical Cancerous Cell Detection Using Enhanced Classification and Embedded Deep Learning Method

Jannatul Ferdous Shanu and Ayesha Aziz Prova[✉]

Central Women's University, Dhaka, Bangladesh
ayeshaaziz.csejnu@gmail.com

Abstract. The health of women is seriously threatened by cervical cancer, which is the second most common gynecological malignancy. More than 85% of fatalities from cervical cancer among women globally occur in underdeveloped nations, making it one of the top causes of early death among women. The rate of cervical cancer in Bangladesh is mostly 70%. Several imaging tests, such as a Pap smear, cervicography, and colposcopy, are used to check for this prevalent cancer. These tests are used to make judgments, but the structural intricacies of cervical cells may make the process more difficult. This study proposed an Improved Naive Bayes (INB) algorithm. This classification method INB provides better results in compared to support vector machine (SVM), random forest tree (RFT), and Naïve Bayes for cervical cancer. The accuracy of the proposed method becomes 95% which is in general 7% greater than all the previous algorithms used.

Keywords: RCNNs · RKM · MRI · CT · INV · SVM · RFT · Biomedical imaging tools · Pap smear · Cervicography

1 Introduction

1.1 Overview

Tumors or cancer cells are a collection of irregular cells that form when cells in the human body grow and split beyond normal levels, resulting in a mass. Tumors can be classed as being malignant at the most basic level (cancerous). The abnormal growth of cells in the human body indicates that the mass (tumor) is cancerous. In fact, globally it accounts for the second most deaths. 4,280 women will die from invasive cervical cancer, which will see an estimated 14,100 additional cases identified globally. With an average diagnostic age of 50, cervical cancer is most frequently discovered in women between the ages of 35 and 44. Only ladies under the age of 20 experience it. Many older women are unaware that cervical cancer risk does not diminish with age (Fig. 1).

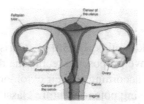

Fig. 1. Pictorial view of Cervical Cancer cell

Taking cells from the cervix and studying them under a microscope is the process of a Pap smear test. A Pap smear's main objective is to find abnormal cells that, if left untreated, can develop into cancer. With a Pap smear, non-cancerous conditions including infection and inflammation can also be found. The benefits of a pap smear include early detection of cancers of the cervix, endometrium, fallopian tubes, and perhaps the ovary, as well as follow-up care after radiation, chemotherapy, and surgery. Research on a classification model for cervical cancer has been conducted using statistical and data mining techniques, such as Multivariate Adaptive Anatomic Pathology, using the cervical dataset provided by the Chung Shan Medical University Hospital Tumor Registry and 12 predictor variables such as age, cell type, tumor grade, tumor size, pT, pStage, surgical margin involvement, lymph node metastases (LNM), the number of other RT fractions, and RT target. Using data from Pap smear tests, Rianantika [16] exploited analogies between the Jaccard coefficient and Cosine coefficient to assist in the diagnosis of cervical cancer. As a result, the objective of this work is to investigate the

2   Basic Concept of Machine Learning Methods

Branch of computer science of artificial intelligence in which a computer learns from the past (input data) and makes predictions about the future. Performance of the system should be at least human-level.

2.1   Cervical Cancer

The working procedures are:

✓ **Evaluation on sipakmed**
✓ **Cell Characteristics**
✓ **Support Vector Machine**
✓ **Multi-layer Perceptron**
✓ **Image Feature**

- *Convolutional Neural Network*
- *Deep Features*

3   Literature Review

Marina E. Plissiti, P. Dimitrakopoulos, G. Sfikas, Christophoros Nikou, O. Krikoni, A. Charchanti (2018). They have proposed a technique that divides Pap smear picture classifications into five groups according to their cytomorphological characteristics. To serve as a benchmark for assessing potential future classification methods, they explain the evaluated approaches based on support vector machines and deep neural networks and demonstrate each classifier's performance.

Yulia Ery Kurniawati, Adhistya Erna Permanasari, and Silmi Fauziati (2021) used data that were obtained from the medical records of the Pap smear test results. There are seven classifications and 38 symptoms. To assess the classifier's performance, Naive Bayes, Support Vector Machines (SVM), and Random Forest Tree were utilized.

4   Methodology

Below is the given pictorial view of how the mechanism will be working throughout. Change in the naïve bayes algorithm has been done and named as Improved naïve bayes (INB) (Fig. 2).

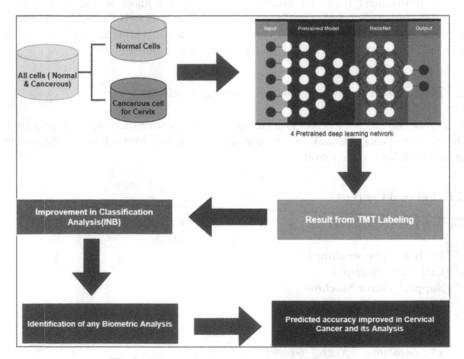

Fig. 2. Experimental workflow for Cervical Cancer

4.1 Sipakmed Dataset

The most recent open cervical imaging dataset is the SIPaKMeD dataset. It stands for Superficial/Intermediate, P for Parabasal, K for Koilocytotic, M for Metaplastic, and D for Dyskeratotic, and its name is derived from the initial letters of the cell type names in the dataset. It was given to help with the early identification of cervical cancer in 2021. Plissiti (Plissiti et al. 2021) used Pap smear slides to crop 4059 single cell images from 980 cervical tissue images (Table 1).

Table 1. Distribution of Sipakmed dataset

Category	Amount of images	Quantity of cells
Superficial/intermediate	134	807
Parabasal	97	767
Koilocytotic	250	835
Metaplastic	279	800
Dyskeratotic	303	798
Total	**966**	**4049**

Normal Cells

These are cell layers cells, and their kind is determined by where they are located on the epithelium layers and how mature they are. Types are:

- *Superficial-Intermediate cells*
- *Parabasal cells*

Abnormal Cells

Abnormal cells have morphological alterations in their appearance. They are structural components that indicate the presence of abnormal situations. Almost the majority of instances are caused by the human papillomavirus (HPV). Types are:

- *Koilocytotic cells*
- *Dyskeratotic cells*

Benign Cells

These cells indicate the transformation zone, which is where the majority of precancerous and cancerous problems in the cervical region arise.

Metaplastic Cells

Essentially, metaplastic cells are tiny or large parabasal-type cells with distinct cellular borders, peculiar nuclei, and occasionally a sizable intracellular vacuole. In contrast to the staining on the borders, the

5 Results and Discussions

The performance of a classifier is most frequently evaluated using the accuracy metric. This study used a different metric to assess performance since accuracy suffers from unbalanced data [9]. The usual methods for assessing classifiers on classes with imbalances are precision and recall. How frequently a positive class occurrence in the dataset was correctly predicted by the classifier is measured by the classifier's recall [9]. The frequency with which an event predicted to be positive actually turns out to be positive is a quantity known as precision [9]. A given False Positive Rate may be used to calculate the percentage of cases that will be properly identified using ROC curve (FPR)) (Table 2 and Figs. 3, 4).

Table 2. Accuracy comparison among all (measurements are taken in %)

Name	Accuracy	Precision	Recall	Roc	F1 score
Naïve Bayes	78.93	69.43	78.95	91.22	--------
SVM	78.67	66.67			
Random forest	80.18	75.96	80.18	93.39	--------
Proposed Method (INB)	**92.73**	**75**	**90**	--------	**81.18**

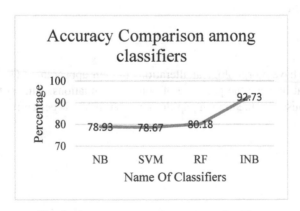

Fig. 3. Accuracy comparison among classifiers

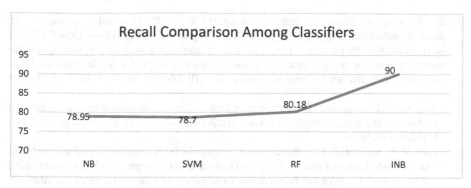

Fig. 4. Recall comparison among classifiers

6 Conclusion

One of the most dangerous cancers is cervical cancer. This research aims to increase the accuracy in the detection of this. The previous Naïve Bayes algorithm had an accuracy of 88% and also seems not to be working on many important features whereas in Improved naïve Bayes the accuracy is 95% and also worked on many important features. For the proposed method F1 score is also calculated which validates the results even more. When compared to previous algorithms INB seems to have the highest accuracy and recall. It also seems that the precision of INB is similar to the precision of the Random forest algorithm. This research presents a cervical cancer screening approach based on deep learning. The benefits of transfer learning were taken advantage of, and several pre-trained networks were compared.

References

1. Plissiti, M.E., Dimitrakopoulos, P., Sfikas, G., Nikou, C., Krikoni, O., Charchanti, A.: SIPAKMED: a new dataset for feature and image-based classification of normal and pathological cervical cells in Pap smear images. In: 2018 25th IEEE International Conference on Image Processing (ICIP), pp. 3144–3148 (2018). https://doi.org/10.1109/ICIP.2018.8451588
2. Jia, A.D., Li, B.Z., Zhang, C.C.: Detection of cervical cancer cells based on strong feature CNN-SVM network. Neurocomputing **411**, 112–127 (2020)
3. Plissiti, M.E., Dimitrakopoulos, P., Sfikas, G., Nikou, C., Krikoni, O., Charchanti, A.: SIPAKMED: a new dataset for feature and image-based classification of normal and pathological cervical cells in Pap smear images. In: 2018 25th IEEE International Conference on Image Processing (ICIP), pp. 3144–3148. IEEE, October 2018
4. Plissiti, M.E., Dimitrakopoulos, P., Sfikas, G., Nikou, C., Krikoni, O., Charchanti, A.: SIPAKMED: a new dataset for feature and image based classification of normal and pathological cervical cells in Pap smear images. In: 2018 25th IEEE International Conference on Image Processing (ICIP), pp. 3144–3148. IEEE (2018)
5. Taha, B., Dias, J., Werghi, N.: Classification of cervical-cancer using Pap-smear images: a convolutional neural network approach. In: Valdés Hernández, M., González-Castro, V. (eds.) MIUA 2017. CCIS, vol. 723, pp. 261–272. Springer, Cham (2017). https://doi.org/10.1007/978-3-319-60964-5_23

6. Shi, J., Wang, R., Zheng, Y., Jiang, Z., Zhang, H., Yu, L.: Cervical cell classification with graph convolutional network. Comput. Methods Programs Biomed. 1(198), 105807 (2021)
7. Kurniawati, Y.E., Permanasari, A.E., Fauziati, S.: Comparative study on data mining classification methods for cervical cancer prediction using Pap smear results. In: 2016 1st International Conference on Biomedical Engineering (IBIOMED), pp. 1–5. IEEE, 5 October 2016
8. Jahan, S., et al.: Automated invasive cervical cancer disease detection at early stage through suitable machine learning model. SN Appl. Sci. 3(10), 1–17 (2021). https://doi.org/10.1007/s42452-021-04786-z
9. Latief, M.A., Siswantining, T., Bustamam, A., Sarwinda, D.: A comparative performance evaluation of random forest feature selection on classification of hepatocellular carcinoma gene expression data. In: 2019 3rd International Conference on Informatics and Computational Sciences (ICICoS), pp. 1–6. IEEE (2019)
10. Sinha, T., Chowdhury, T., Shaw, R.N., Ghosh, A.: Analysis and prediction of COVID-19 confirmed cases using deep learning models: a comparative study. In: Bianchini, M., Piuri, V., Das, S., Shaw, R.N. (eds.) Advanced Computing and Intelligent Technologies. LNNS, vol. 218, pp. 207–218. Springer, Singapore (2022). https://doi.org/10.1007/978-981-16-2164-2_18
11. Sagala, N.T.: A comparative study of data mining methods to diagnose cervical cancer. J. Phys.: Conf. Ser. 1255(1), 012022 (2019)
12. Dewi, Y.N., Riana, D., Mantoro, T.: Improving Naïve Bayes performance in single image Pap smear using weighted principal component analysis (WPCA). In: 2017 International Conference on Computing, Engineering, and Design (ICCED), pp. 1–5. IEEE (2017)

Hybridization of AES and RSA Algorithm in File Encryption Using Parallel Computing

Sakshi Parikh[1][✉], Raghav Jhanwar[1], and Apoorv Singh[2]

[1] School of Information Technology and Engineering, VIT, Vellore, India
sjparikh78@gmail.com
[2] School of Electronic Science and Engineering, VIT, Vellore, India

Abstract. As technology advances there is an increase in the amount of data transmitted over the network. One of the biggest challenges facing is safety. Cryptography is the study of computational methods related to information security, including privacy, integrity of data, business validation, and source verification, which provides security. In this chapter, we propose a hybrid cryptographic solution using the AES and RSA algorithm as well as the OpenMP shared memory method for memory. The proposed hybrid algorithms aim at better security and efficiency of data.

Keywords: Encryption · AES · RSA · Hybrid · OpenMP API

1 Introduction

Cryptography is a science for keeping messages secure. The way, when we hide a message in such a way that its content becomes an encrypted message, which is the cipher text. The process of converting a cipher text into a blank text is to remove encryption. Asymmetric cryptography, also known as public key cryptography, refers to each cryptographic method that employs pairs of keys. The owner's private secret keys are used to encrypt any public keys that are no longer being circulated [1, 2]. Symmetric cryptography is a cryptographic system that uses a single key to encrypt and decrypt [3]. This project is a combination of both symmetric and asymmetric encryption systems that provide a system that can overcome the same obstacles of both methods and enable secure data transactions to reduce efficiency.

Another crucial aspect of cryptographic algorithms is the speed of the cipher, which is just as significant as the level of security. Under this chapter, we provide a software strategy that relies on the translation of C source code that represents the consecutive AES encryption.

This chapter is arranged as follows; The AES and RSA algorithm are briefly reviewed, given a brief description of the matching tools used, then comes a short description of compliance, methods of AES. Finally these test outputs regarding the effectiveness of the compatible techniques were shown.

© The Author(s), under exclusive license to Springer Nature Switzerland AG 2023
R. N. Shaw et al. (Eds.): ICACIS 2022, CCIS 1749, pp. 281–291, 2023.
https://doi.org/10.1007/978-3-031-25088-0_25

2 Literature Review

AES and RSA algorithms are selected for encryption for this method. A technique for data transfer in Bluetooth technology was put forth in one of the studies of such nature. It was grounded on AES DOI and RSA. The 128-bit key will be encrypted by RSA throughout the encryption procedure. The sender's message will then be encrypted using the AES algorithm [4].

Another such solution incorporates two cryptosystems into a security protocol to offer a significantly more secure communication process. It makes use of the RSA algorithm. In addition, it utilizes the Rijndael S-box of AES, which is thought to be the quickest method for the critical route from plaintext to cypher text [5].

Three new hybrid cryptographic systems—Twofish+RSA, AES+RSA, and AES+ElGamal—were created. Among the new hybrid models presented, AES+RSA benefits from both symmetric and asymmetric approaches, making it substantially more secure, although the Twofish+RSA hybrid cryptographic system is quicker [6].

Similar work proposes the use of RSA and AES hybrid algorithms to electronic mail communication, and uses the Java language to set the eclipse platform [7].

In software, the three well-known encryption methods ECC, RSA, and AES are used to encrypt images. The three well-known encryption methods have been discussed, and their performance has been assessed. The three well-known encryption methods have been discussed, and their performance has been assessed. This resulted with ECC algorithm encryption as the most secure algorithm. When compared to AES and RSA algorithms, ECC has the highest throughput [8].

An electronic learning system design that uses digital signatures and encryption as security was suggested in a related piece of work. AES 128-bit is used in encryption. Authentication, nonrepudiation, and integrity are provided through digital signatures and hash functions, which are accomplished by using RSA 2048 and SHA 256. Functional testing demonstrates that the encryption procedure renders the file unreadable in both storage and transport. In conclusion, the application may provide confidentiality services [9].

3 Methodology

3.1 RSA Algorithm

Messages are encrypted and decrypted using the RSA algorithm in modern systems. RSA algorithm is an asymmetric cryptography technique. Asymmetric refers to the use of both the public key and the secret key as shown in Fig. 1. Thus, the private key is kept secret while the public key is accessible to everyone. No one other than the browser can encrypt data even if an external company has a public browser key [2].

Two numbers make up the public key, one of which is the product of the other two major numbers multiplied together. The secret keys are also found in the same two main numbers [3]. Thus, if a user cannot make a big number, this secret key is threatened. Therefore, the size of the key is the only factor affecting encryption, and doubling or tripling the key size increases encryption power dramatically. RSA keys can typically be 1024 or 2048 bits in length, however experts think that keys with 1024 bits may soon be broken. So far, it appears to be impossible [10].

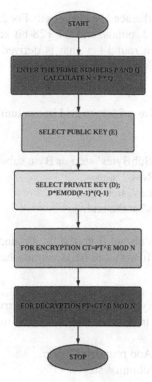

Fig. 1. Algorithm RSA flowchart

3.2 Advanced Encryption Standard (AES) Algorithm

AES is a more well-known and commonly used symmetric encryption technique. The features of AES are as follows –

- Use of Block encryption
- Group encryption of 128-bit with key lengths of 128, 192, and 256 bits
- Single encryption and decryption key for a symmetric algorithm
- Powerful and quicker than Triple-DES
- Gives all the details and specification of the design.

AES includes series of connected functions, some of which involve inserting inputs with a certain output (changed) and others involving pushing bits around (permissions) [11].

Interestingly, the AES does all its calculations in bits instead of bits. 128 bits of plain text are therefore treated as 16 bytes by AES. In order to process the 16 bytes as a matrix, they are arranged in 4 rows and columns [12].

AES cycles vary and are influenced by key length. For 256-bit keys, the AES employs 14 rounds, for 192-bit keys, 12 rounds, and for 128-bit keys, 10 rounds. These rounds each employ a distinct 128-bit round key that is derived from the initial AES key.as shown in Fig. 2 [13].

Encryption Process

Every block is treated by AES as a 16-byte grid in a column-major configuration. Every round has four steps:

- The first step is called the 'SubBytes' step or Byte substitution step.
- It is followed by the 'ShiftRows' step.
- Then comes the 'MixColumns' step.
- Finally we 'Add Round Key' at the end.

The MixColumns round is absent from the final round. In the algorithm, SubBytes handle substitution, while ShiftRows and MixColumns handle permutation.

Decryption Process

The AES encryption and decryption procedures are carried out in the opposite order. The four steps are carried out in reverse order for every round –

- The first step is called the 'Add round key' step.
- It is followed by the 'Mix columns' step.
- Then comes the 'Shift Rows' step.
- Finally we do 'Byte substitution' or 'SubBytes' at the end.

3.3   OpenMP API

Development for multi-platform shared-memory multiprocessing is supported through the programming interface known as OpenMP. The rules extend the programming language sequence by allowing for the production of Single-Program Multi-Structured Data, task-sharing structures, synchronizing building, and the ability to interact with both open and private data. A single function known as a master thread is the first function in the OpenMP program. A big series forms a string team when it encounters a comparable circuit. Every series with in the group is used in association with a statement from the associated location. These group threads are aligned at the conclusion of the respective region. However, just the main thread keeps running until the subsequent circuit is reached [14].

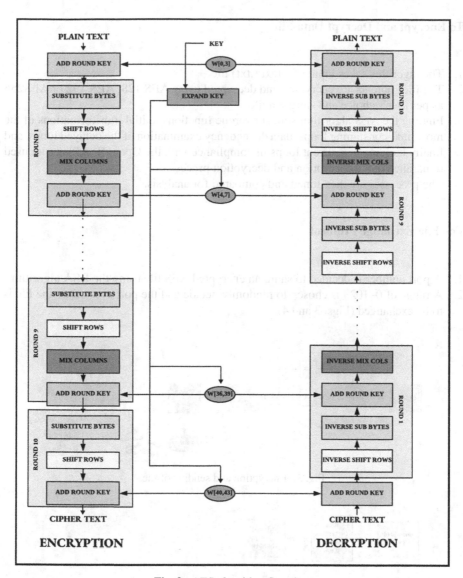

Fig. 2. AES algorithm flowchart

3.4 Proposed Method

In the proposed algorithm (Hybrid AES-RSA) the goal was achieved by integration of two algorithms called RSA and AES in the form of shared memory using OpenMP API.

To Encrypt and Decrypt Data File

1. The algorithm takes input of a text (.txt) file
2. The file contents are encrypted and decrypted using AES 128, AES 192 or AES256 as per user's choice and stored in file.
3. Finding the AES algorithm's most overdue functions, initial transformations of the most time-consuming loops, data dependency examination of the delayed loops, and finally building concurrent loops in compliance with the OpenMP API are all used to parallelize the encryption and decryption process.
4. The processes are then timed and compared for analysis.

For File Exchange Protocol

1. A port number is decided to share an encrypted AES file using the RSA algorithm.
2. A range of 0–1023 is chosen to randomly decide and the port every time the file is to be exchanged (Figs. 3 and 4).

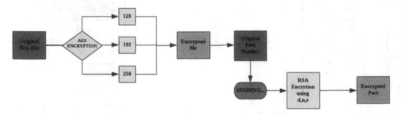

Fig. 3. Encryption and sending of file

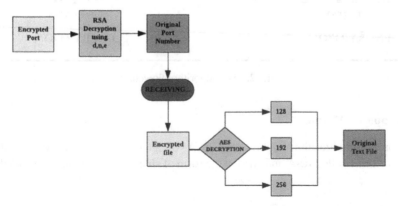

Fig. 4. Receiving and decryption of file

4   Output

(See Figs. 5 and 6).

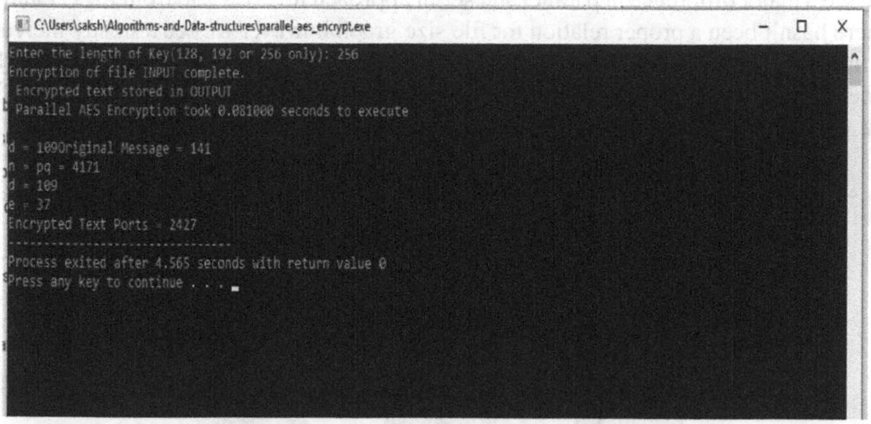

Fig. 5. The process of encryption

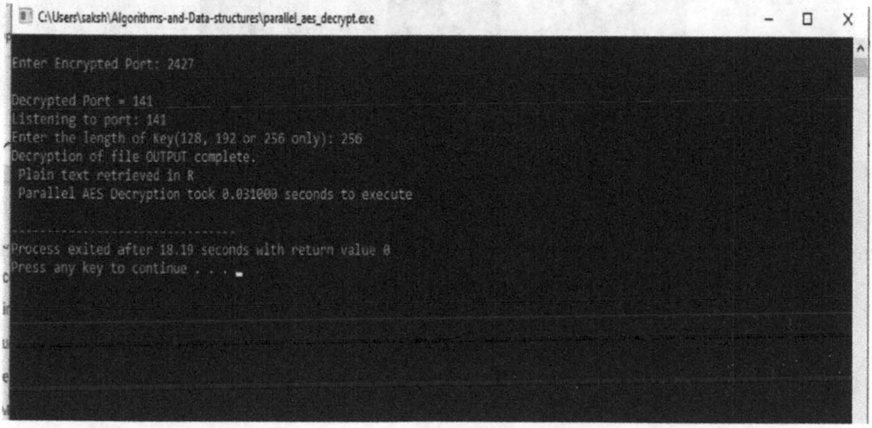

Fig. 6. The process of decryption

5   Results and Discussion

From the given graphs we see a clear distinction between the parallel and serial approach. In all the graphs parallel AES algorithms have taken less time in comparison to the serial. We see a major difference in parallel and serial approach for AES 256 from Figs. 7 and 8. There hasn't been a proper relation for file size graph however we see a steady increase in time for parallel graph with respect to the file size. Moreover we also deduce that the time of execution for the decryption process was more than the encryption process for the algorithm (Figs. 9 and 10).

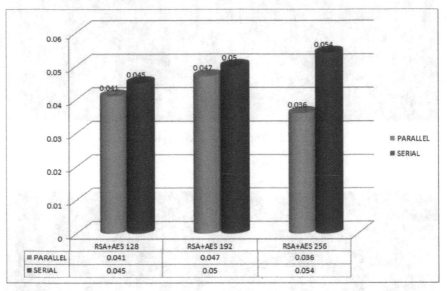

Fig. 7. Time of execution (in sec) comparison between parallel and serial for hybrid RSA+AES 128, RSA+AES 192, RSA+AES 256 Encryption

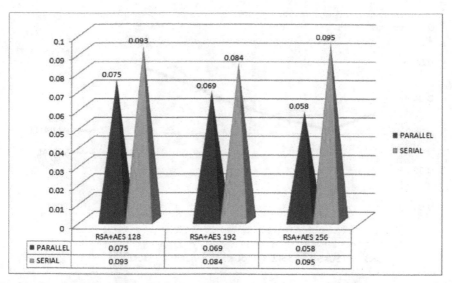

Fig. 8. Time of execution comparison between parallel and serial for RSA+AES 128, RSA+AES 192, RSA+AES 256 Decryption

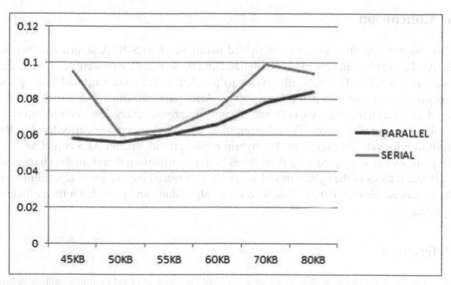

Fig. 9. Time of execution comparison between parallel and serial for different file size and RSA+AES 256 Decryption

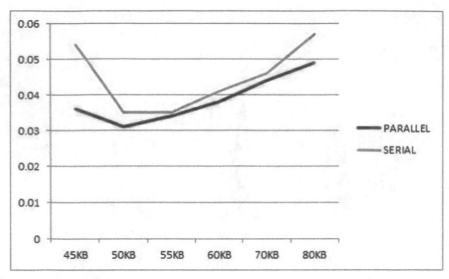

Fig. 10. Time of execution comparison between parallel and serial for different file size and RSA+AES 256 Encryption

6 Conclusion

This chapter describes an enhanced hybrid parallelized AES-RSA algorithm. Parts of the AES algorithm that could be parallelized and those that cannot were separated. The usage of OpenMP directives allowed us to parallelize the code while addressing the synchronization and data dependency issues. After parallelization, execution times for serial and parallelized codes both significantly improved. AES 256 showed effective results after parallelization. The addition of RSA added an extra security level to the algorithm for safe file exchange. The hybrid model provides better AES compliance on the plain and as integrated with RSA it has better distribution; therefore the chances of algebraic attacks in the hybrid model are reduced. Overall the proposed algorithm used the beneficial characteristics of the two know algorithms and provided a time efficient solution.

References

1. Mahalle, V.S., Shahade, A.K.: Enhancing the data security in cloud by implementing hybrid (RSA & AES) encryption algorithm. In: 2014 International Conference on Power, Automation and Communication (INPAC), pp. 146–149. IEEE, October 2014
2. Kumar, B., Boaddh, J., Mahawar, L.: A hybrid security approach based on AES and RSA for cloud data. Int. J. Adv. Technol. Eng. Explor. **3**(17), 43 (2016)
3. Liu, Y., Gong, W., Fan, W.: Application of AES and RSA hybrid algorithm in E-mail. In: 2018 IEEE/ACIS 17th International Conference on Computer and Information Science (ICIS), pp. 701–703. IEEE, June 2018
4. Albahar, M.A., Olawumi, O., Haataja, K., Toivanen, P.: Novel hybrid encryption algorithm based on AES, RSA, and Twofish for Bluetooth encryption (2018)

5. Alegro, J.K.P., Arboleda, E.R., Pereña, M.R., Dellosa, R.M.: Hybrid Schnorr, RSA, and AES cryptosystem (2019)
6. Jintcharadze, E., Iavich, M.: Hybrid implementation of Twofish, AES, ElGamal and RSA cryptosystems (2020)
7. Chaouch, A., Bouallegue, B., Bouraoui, O.: Software application for simulation-based AES, RSA and elliptic-curve algorithms (2016)
8. Baihaqi, A., Briliyant, O.C.: Implementation of RSA 2048-bit and AES 128-bit for secure E-learning web-based application (2017)
9. Rawat, R., Rajawat, A.S., Mahor, V., Shaw, R.N., Ghosh, A.: Dark web—Onion hidden service discovery and crawling for profiling morphing, unstructured crime and vulnerabilities prediction. In: Mekhilef, S., Favorskaya, M., Pandey, R.K., Shaw, R.N. (eds.) Innovations in Electrical and Electronic Engineering. LNEE, vol. 756, pp. 717–734. Springer, Singapore (2021). https://doi.org/10.1007/978-981-16-0749-3_57
10. Patil, P., Narayankar, P., Narayan, D.G., Meena, S.M.: A comprehensive evaluation of cryptographic algorithms: DES, 3DES, AES, RSA and Blowfish. Proc. Comput. Sci. **78**, 617–624 (2016)
11. Alegro, J.K.P., Arboleda, E.R., Pereña, M.R., Dellosa, R.M.: Hybrid Schnorr, RSA, and AES cryptosystem. Int. J. Sci. Technol. Res. **8**(10), 1777–1781 (2019)
12. Al Hasib, A., Haque, A.A.M.M.: A comparative study of the performance and security issues of AES and RSA cryptography. In: 2008 Third International Conference on Convergence and Hybrid Information Technology, vol. 2, pp. 505–510. IEEE, November 2008
13. Chandu, Y., Kumar, K.R., Prabhukhanolkar, N.V., Anish, A.N., Rawal, S.: Design and implementation of hybrid encryption for security of IOT data. In: 2017 International Conference on Smart Technologies for Smart Nation (SmartTechCon), pp. 1228–1231. IEEE, August 2017
14. Gabriel, E., et al.: Open MPI: goals, concept, and design of a next generation MPI implementation. In: Kranzlmüller, D., Kacsuk, P., Dongarra, J. (eds.) EuroPVM/MPI 2004. LNCS, vol. 3241, pp. 97–104. Springer, Heidelberg (2004). https://doi.org/10.1007/978-3-540-30218-6_19

Lightweight Trust Aware Hybrid Key Management Scheme for WSN to Reduce the Energy Consumption in Comparison with TERP and LTB-AODV

Gorrolla Bhanu Prakash and C. Tamizhselvan[✉]

Department of Electronics and Communication Engineering, SIMATS School of Engineering, Saveetha Institute of Medical and Technical Sciences, Chennai, Tamilnadu, India
{gorrollabp18,tamizhselvanc.sse}@saveetha.com

Abstract. The aim of the work is to propose a Lightweight Trust-aware Hybrid key Management (LTHM) scheme for WSN to reduce the energy consumption in comparison with TERP. Materials and Methods: The performance analysis of energy consumption value for WSN network using Trust-aware Hybrid key management (N = 10 samples) was compared with TERP (N = 10 samples) and LTB-AODV (N = 10 samples) algorithms where G-power is 0.8 with alpha and beta values are 0.05 and 0.2 with a confidence interval of 95%. Results: The analysis shows that the Trust-aware Hybrid key management has a low and high energy consumption of 3.01 J and 12.46 J in comparison with TERP algorithm whose energy values are 4.12 J and 14.92 J and for LTB - AODV algorithm, the energy values are 5.23 J and 16.48 J. The results obtained were considered to be error-free since the significance value is 0.0268 (p < 0.05) with pre-test power of 80% in SPSS statistical analysis. Conclusion: A novel Trust-aware Hybrid key management scheme provides significantly better outcome value of Energy Consumption (12.46 J) when compared with TERP and LTB - AODV.

Keywords: Wireless Sensor Network · TERP · Novel Trust validation · Hybrid key management LTHM · Energy

1 Introduction

Security is a term which comprises integrity, data confidentiality, availability and authentication. For the secure transfer of information, cryptography is used. Cryptography is the process of converting a message or information into a code that cannot be understood by an unauthorized third party [1]. The purpose of the research is to precise the accuracy of Intrusion Detection Systems (IDS) [2] in Lightweight Trust aware Hybrid Key Management scheme for WSN to reduce the energy consumption in comparison with TERP. Remote sensor organizations (WSN) are overall arising at speeding up the speed in [3]. A few sorts of exploration on WSN innovation and guidelines are distributed yearly, both licensed and open norms. As of late, botnet assaults, joined with the Internet

© The Author(s), under exclusive license to Springer Nature Switzerland AG 2023
R. N. Shaw et al. (Eds.): ICACIS 2022, CCIS 1749, pp. 292–299, 2023.
https://doi.org/10.1007/978-3-031-25088-0_26

of Things (IoT), have affected numerous web name servers and web specialist co-ops. Numerous IoT gadget designers, call-backs all the IoT gadgets which are affected by botnet assaults. Subsequently, in the present situation, security and dependability are seen as a need in WSN and IoT [4].

A remote sensor network portrayed an assortment of arbitrarily sent little sensors that are helping out one another. The attributes of the sensor network are consolidated situation, arbitrary sending, variation geography, restricted data transmission, portable or stilled sensors, self-configurable sensor hubs [5]. In the present situation, the world uses this information gathered by sensors from distant conditions [6]. This information doesn't really contain mistakes and doesn't change during transmission. WSN has different freedoms for adversaries to compromise the organization [7] because of the transmission nature and versatility, it generally draws in numerous dangers towards the network. The limitations in the Wireless Sensor Network is consumption of energy [8]. To overcome the above limitations, Lightweight Trust aware Hybrid key Management scheme is proposed to reduce the energy consumption in WSN and it is compared with LTHM and TERP.

2 Materials and Methods

In this chapter, the research work was done in the Wireless Security Lab, Department of Electronics and communication Engineering, Saveetha School of Engineering, SIMATS. The three algorithms are considered with three groups, each group having 10 samples. Samples were calculated by using previous study results, in clinical.com [16]. G power calculation is used to analyze the samples with the minimum power of 0.8 (fixed) and the maximum accepted error is 0.05 (fixed) and beta is 0.2.

Group 1 is the LTHM algorithm have 10 samples and the TERP algorithm is considered as group 2 has 10 samples and group 3 is LTB-AODV with sample size of 10. Novel trust validation can help to retain the network stability and improves the communication of nodes and also reduced the power consumption of the nodes while transmitting the data with each others.

Applying the novel trust validation concept to the proposed algorithm is used improve the security level of the network by avoiding untrusted actions and nodes. The basic system configuration for MATLAB software [13] is i3 processor and 5th generation with 4 GB RAM and 32-bit processor, 8 MB cache up to 1.60 GHz.

2.1 Statistical Analysis

In this work, the independent sample T- test is used to analyze the samples. The analysis was done using IBM SPSS version 21 [9]. Both LTHM and TERP algorithms have 10 sample nodes and for each iteration they are predicted by reducing the energy consumption. In this work, key size, lifetime and sensitivity are considered as the independent variables where the energy is considered as a dependent variables.

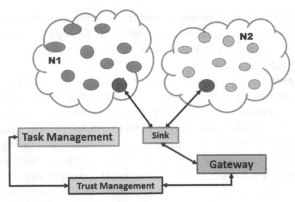

Fig. 1. The proposed model shows two networks and each network having a sample of 10 nodes. Each network has a sink node which is used to connect with servers for trust management and task management. The results are obtained by comparing the energy consumption of TERP, LTB-AODV and proposed LTHM.

Table 1. Shows the group statistics table of T-Test analysis for LTHM, TERP and LTB-AODV are compared with respect to mean values of 6.6360, 8.1350 and 8.9520.

	Group	N	Mean	Standard deviation	Std. error mean
Energy	LTHM	10	6.6360	3.05969	0.96756
	TERP	10	8.1350	3.46965	1.09720
	LTB-AODV	10	8.9520	3.79716	1.20077

Table 2. The statistical calculations for independent samples test between LTHM, TERP and LTB-AODV. The significance value is 0.0268. Independent samples t-test is applied for comparison of LTHM, TERP and LTB-AODV with the confidence interval as 95%.

	FF	Sig.	t	df	Sig.(2-tailed)	Mean Difference	Standard error difference	95% confidence interval (lower)	95% confidence Interval (upper)
Equal variances assumed	0.48	0.0268	− 1.025	18	0.001	−1.49900	1.46288	−4.57240	1.57440
Equal variances not assumed			− 1.025	17.723	0.001	−1.49900	1.46288	−4.57585	1.57785

3   Results

This project observes that the Wireless Sensor Network consumes less energy consumption by using LTHM. By using different samples and different algorithms like TERP (14.48 J) and LTB-AODV (16.48 J) which says that LTHM (12.46 J) is most suitable for wireless sensor networks.

Table 1 shows the statistical analysis of wireless sensor networks using LTHM as group 1, TERP as group 2 and LTB-AODV as group 3. LTHM has a mean value of 6.6360, Standard deviation (EV) is 3.06 and Standard-Error Value (SEV) is 0.96. TERP has a mean value of 8.1350, Standard Deviation (SD) is 3.47 and SEV is 1.09. LTB-AODV has a mean value of 8.9520, SD is 3.80 and SEV is 1.20.

Table 2 shows the independent sample test using T-test the significance value 0.0268 shows, there is significance between LTHM, TERP and LTB-AODV. Figure 1 shows the proposed work architecture having sensor networks, gateway, trust management and task management.

In Fig. 2 shows the energy consumption of wireless sensor networks by using LTHM (3.01 J) and TERP (4.12 J). Figure 3 shows the energy consumption level between LTHM (3.01 J) and LTB-AODV (5.23 J). Figure 4 shows the overall comparison of energy level between LTHM, LTB-AODV and TERP where the x-axis is number of nodes and y-axis is energy consumption. From Fig. 4, it is inferred that the energy consumption of LTHM is less when compared with TERP and LTB-AODV. Figure 5 shows the graphical plot of an independent sample T-test. It is a comparison of mean. X-axis: Groups of LTHM, TERP, and LTB-AODV and Y-axis is the feature with error bars ± 1SD.

Novel Trust validation is a significant factor that influences the security in WSN. Trust has, without a doubt, played an essential job in security over all in all at some time in the past, systems using WSN Hybrid key management scheme compared over TERP Hybrid key management scheme with better energy.

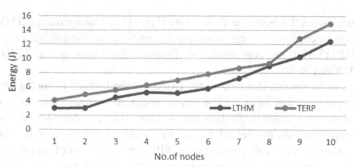

Fig. 2. The proposed LTHM achieved the energy consumption of 3.01 J and 12.46 J and TERP achieved the energy consumption of 4.12 J and 14.92 J.

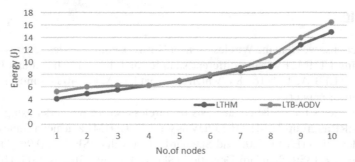

Fig. 3. The proposed LTHM achieved the energy consumption of 3.01 J and 12.46 J and LTB-AODV achieved the energy consumption of 5.23 J and 16.48 J.

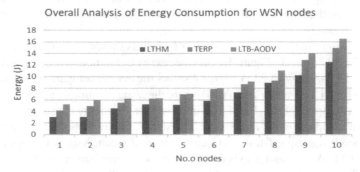

Fig. 4. Comparison of energy consumption level between LTHM (12.46 J), TERP (14.92 J) and LTB-AODV (16.48 J) routing protocols with a high trust level

4   Discussion

In this research work, Lightweight Trust aware Hybrid key Management (LTHM) scheme was proposed to minimize energy consumption in Wireless Sensor Network where by using LTHM (12.46 J) and compared with different algorithms such as TERP (14.92 J) and LTB-AODV (16.48 J).

The master key is the idea behind the LEAP method which is erased after the distribution of pairwise key between the sensor nodes. It increases the resilience of the network but reduces scalability when new sensor nodes are deployed in the network [21]. Security Protocols for Sensor Networks termed as SPINs. In this method, each sensor node shares a key with a base station. SPIN provides better toughness but it have poor scalability and creates more congestion in the network because the base station needs to send the pairwise keys for every sensor node in the network to form secure communication.

A novel location based key establishment scheme for WSNs [26] which is a combination of hexagonal grid-based deployment model and a 25-polynomial based key establishment scheme to establish a link layer key for neighboring sensor nodes. A polynomial pool-based scheme using a grid based key establishment provides all the advantages of the polynomial based pool pre-distribution and promises that any two

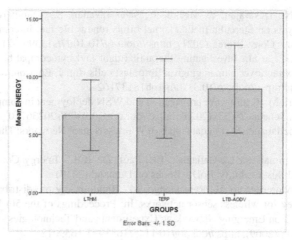

Fig. 5. The Simple Bar graph for LTHM and LTB-AODV is compared with TERP accuracy. The accuracy of TERP is 6.6360 higher value than the LTHM 8.1350. The main difference between a novel Trust validation and TERP is $p < 0.05$ (Independent sample test). X-axis: novel Trust Validation accuracy vs TERP accuracy Y-axis: Mean of accuracy, for identification.

nodes can establish a pair-wise key. Efficient cluster-based power saving scheme, the cluster heads are elected based on location and the average residual energy of sensor nodes. It is a centralized algorithm and requires the information of location of each node [28] Heuristic based clustering methods have been used by many researchers to increase the lifetime of a network by minimizing the energy resource of the network. It provides a better distribution of the CHs and cluster size.

Lightweight Trust Aware Hybrid Key Management scheme for WSN is proposed to reduce the energy consumption in comparison with TERP and LTB-AODV. The limitations of the proposed work were prediction of intrusion and Trust Validation. In future, it will be improved by finding intruders and increasing the validation certificate in terms of time.

5   Conclusion

The Lightweight trust aware Hybrid key Management scheme for WSN is proposed to reduce the energy consumption in comparison with TERP and LTB-AODV. The current study focused on WSN over TERP for higher classification in detecting intrusion. It can be slightly improved based on the TERP data sets analysis in future. The outcome of the WSN shows LTHM have (12.46 J) less than TERP (14.92 J) and LTB-AODV (16.48J).

References

1. Baskar, M., Renuka Devi, R., Ramkumar, J., Kalyanasundaram, P., Suchithra, M., Amutha, B.: Region centric minutiae propagation measure orient forgery detection with finger print analysis in health care systems. Neural Process. Lett. (2021). https://doi.org/10.1007/s11063-020-10407-4

298   G. B. Prakash and C. Tamizhselvan

2. Bhanu Teja, N., Devarajan, Y., Mishra, R., Sivasaravanan, S., Thanikaivel Murugan, D.: Detailed analysis on Sterculia foetida kernel oil as renewable fuel in compression ignition engine. Biomass Conv. Bioref. (2021). https://doi.org/10.1007/s13399-021-01328-w
3. Bhavikatti, S.K., et al.: Investigating the antioxidant and cytocompatibility of Mimusops Elengi Linn extract over human gingival fibroblast cells. Int. J. Environ. Res. Public Health 18(13) (2021). https://doi.org/10.3390/ijerph18137162
4. Celaya-Echarri, M.: Radio wave propagation and WSN deployment in complex utility tunnel environments. Sensors 20(23) (2020). https://doi.org/10.3390/s20236710
5. Dargie, W., Poellabauer, C.: Fundamentals of Wireless Sensor Networks: Theory and Practice. Wiley (2010)
6. Fagas, G., Gammaitoni, L., Gallagher, J.P., Paul, D.: ICT - Energy Concepts for Energy Efficiency and Sustainability. BoD – Books on Demand (2017)
7. Gandino, F., Montrucchio, B., Rebaudengo, M.: Random key pre-distribution with transitory master key for wireless sensor networks. In: Proceedings of the 5th International Student Workshop on Emerging Networking Experiments and Technologies - Co-Next Student Workshop 2009 (2009). https://doi.org/10.1145/1658997.1659012
8. International Electrotechnical Commission: Internet of Things: Wireless Sensor Networks (2014)
9. Jagannathan, P., Gurumoorthy, S., Stateczny, A., Divakarachar, P.B., Sengupta, J.: Collision-aware routing using multi-objective seagull optimization algorithm for WSN-based IoT. Sensors 21(24) (2021). https://doi.org/10.3390/s21248496
10. Paul, A., Sinha, S., Shaw, R.N., Ghosh, A.: A neuro-fuzzy based IDS for internet-integrated WSN. In: Bansal, J.C., Paprzycki, M., Bianchini, M., Das, S. (eds.) Computationally Intelligent Systems and their Applications. SCI, vol. 950, pp. 71–86. Springer, Singapore (2021). https://doi.org/10.1007/978-981-16-0407-2_6
11. Karthigadevi, G., et al.: Chemico-nanotreatment methods for the removal of persistent organic pollutants and xenobiotics in water - a review. Biores. Technol. 324(March), 124678 (2021)
12. LaPlante, F., Belacel, N., Kardouchi, M.: A heuristic automatic clustering method based on hierarchical clustering. In: Duval, B., van den Herik, J., Loiseau, S., Filipe, J. (eds.) ICAART 2014. LNCS (LNAI), vol. 8946, pp. 312–328. Springer, Cham (2015). https://doi.org/10.1007/978-3-319-25210-0_19
13. Ali, Q.I.: Simulation Framework of Wireless Sensor Network (WSN) Using MATLAB (2012)
14. Lin, I.-C., Huang, S.-Y.: A polynomial based key establishment scheme for heterogeneous sensor networks. In: 2009 Fifth International Conference on Information Assurance and Security (2009). https://doi.org/10.1109/ias.2009.264
15. Maleh, Y., Sahid, A., Ezzati, A., Belaissaoui, M.: Key management protocols for smart sensor networks. Secur. Priv. Smart Sens. Netw. (2018). https://doi.org/10.4018/978-1-5225-5736-4.ch001
16. McCormick, K., Salcedo, J., Peck, J., Wheeler, A.: SPSS Statistics for Data Analysis and Visualization. Wiley (2017)
17. Meng, B.: A secure internet voting protocol based on non-interactive deniable authentication protocol and proof protocol that two ciphertexts are encryption of the same plaintext. J. Netw. (2009). https://doi.org/10.4304/jnw.4.5.370-377
18. Mukherjee, P., Pattnaik, P.K., Panda, S.K.: IoT and WSN Applications for Modern Agricultural Advancements: Emerging Research and Opportunities: Emerging Research and Opportunities. IGI Global (2019)
19. Banerjee, A., et al.: Building of efficient communication system in smart city using wireless sensor network through hybrid optimization technique. In: Piuri, V., Shaw, R.N., Ghosh, A., Islam, R. (eds.) AI and IoT for Smart City Applications. SCI, vol. 1002, pp. 15–30. Springer, Singapore (2022). https://doi.org/10.1007/978-981-16-7498-3_2

20. Pandey, M., Verma, S.: Energy consumption patterns for different mobility conditions in WSN. Wirel. Sens. Netw. (2011). https://doi.org/10.4236/wsn.2011.312044
21. Preethi, K., Auxzilia, K.A., Preethi, G.L., Sekar, D.: Antagomir technology in the treatment of different types of cancer. Epigenomics (2021). https://doi.org/10.2217/epi-2020-0439
22. Sawant, K., et al.: Dentinal microcracks after root canal instrumentation using instruments manufactured with different NiTi alloys and the SAF system: a systematic review. NATO Adv. Sci. Inst. Ser. E Appl. Sci. **11**(11), 4984 (2021)
23. Shanmugam, V., et al.: Circular economy in biocomposite development: state-of-the-art, challenges and emerging trends. Compos. Part C: Open Access **5**(July), 100138 (2021)
24. Tamizhselvan, C., Vijayalakshmi, V.: Distributed time-dependent key management scheme for internet of things. Recent Adv. Comput. Sci. Commun. (2022). https://doi.org/10.2174/2666255813999200928220535
25. Banerjee, A., et al.: Construction of effective wireless sensor network for smart communication using modified ant colony optimization technique. In: Bianchini, M., Piuri, V., Das, S., Shaw, R.N. (eds.) Advanced Computing and Intelligent Technologies. LNNS, vol. 218, pp. 269–278. Springer, Singapore (2022). https://doi.org/10.1007/978-981-16-2164-2_22
26. Touati, Y., Daachi, B., Arab, A.C.: Energy Management in Wireless Sensor Networks. Elsevier (2017)
27. Ullah, F., Zahid Khan, M., Mehmood, G., Qureshi, M.S., Fayaz, M.: Energy efficiency and reliability considerations in wireless body area networks: a survey. Comput. Math. Methods Med. **2022**(January), 1090131 (2022)
28. Veerasimman, A., et al.: Thermal properties of natural fiber sisal based hybrid composites – a brief review. J. Nat. Fibers 1–11 (2021)
29. Wang, X., Yang, Z., Feng, Z., Zhao, J.: A WSN Layer-cluster key management scheme based on quadratic polynomial and Lagrange interpolation polynomial. Sensors **20**(16) (2020). https://doi.org/10.3390/s20164388
30. Yang, J.: Energy Efficient Data Aggregation in Wireless Sensor Networks (2015)
31. Zhou, J.: Efficient and secure routing protocol based on encryption and authentication for wireless sensor networks. In: 2010 International Conference on Artificial Intelligence and Education (ICAIE) (2010). https://doi.org/10.1109/icaie.2010.5641155

A Comparative Analysis of SIW Bandpass Filters Loaded with Different Shapes of DGS-DMS for Satellite Communication

A. Banu Priya[1(✉)], H. Umma Habiba[1], and Masood Hajamohideen[2]

[1] Bharath Institute of Higher Education, Chennai, India
banuannadurai@gmail.com
[2] MIT, Chennai, India

Abstract. The performance of SIW bandpass filters with various DGS (Defected Ground Structure) shapes is compared in this Chapter, and the bandpass filter properties of DMS (Defected Microstrip Structure) are also discussed. The same SIW layout is utilized to create several SIW bandpass filters for satellite communications using various DGS and DMS structure forms. In order to assess the filter characteristics in terms of return loss, insertion loss, and bandstop characteristics, the filter structures are optimized. ADS software is used to construct and simulate each filter structure for comparative analysis.

Keywords: Bandpass filter · Substrate integrated waveguide (SIW) · Defected Ground Structure (DGS) · Satellite communication · Advanced Design Software (ADS)

1 Introduction

Because of their small size, low price, and dependability, bandpass filters are frequently employed in RF and microwave subsystems. Metal rectangular waveguides are utilized to get around the low selectivity, high parasitic radiation loss, and high insertion loss of microstrip line filters. A revolutionary planar circuit known as the Substrate Integrated Waveguide (SIW) is conceived and developed [1, 2], despite the fact that it has a large size and poor integration with planar circuits. Due to the substrate integrated waveguide's (SIW) superior performance, low cost of manufacturing, size, and power handling capacity, it has been widely used in wireless communication systems. In comparison to previous substrate integrated waveguide filters, hybrid cavity substrate integrated waveguide filters, which combine circular and rectangular cavities, exhibit improved frequency selectivity and quality factors [3–5]. The upper stopband sharp rejection can be improved by using the quarter mode substrate integrated waveguide (QMSIW) with source load coupling structure in [6]. Using triple mode stub resonators allows for the creation of a microstrip narrow bandpass filter with broad stopband rejection and high selectivity, since the degenerate mode's resonant frequency can be changed to fit the filter's bandwidth [7–9]. Frequency responsiveness, out of band rejection, and skirt selectivity are all provided by a triple mode filter loaded with CSRR in a SIW cavity [10]. Another method, known as Defected Ground Structure (DGS) [11–13], uses faults or slots integrated on the ground plane of microwave planar circuits to increase selectivity and improve upper stopband performance. Using the resonant characteristics of the CSRR and two dumbbell DGS, it is possible to create two passbands with transmission zero in the center [7, 14–16]. Defected microstrip structure (DMS), a different approach, is presented and examined; it has the advantages of simple design, performance control, and small size [18–20]. Unwanted harmonic response is suppressed using stopband characteristics in a DMS-DGS [19] based filter structure.

This research examines the effects of DGS and DMS on the bandpass properties of various SIW configurations. To achieve the filter performance, a slot is etched on the bottom and top planes of the SIW cavity. For different DGS and DMS geometries for satellite communication, several SIW topologies are compared, simulated, and examined.

2 Basic Structure of SIW

Traditional SIW BPF is created by connecting upper and lower metal plates of a dielectric substrate using an array of metalized via holes, as shown in the Fig. 1. The diameter d, through hole spacing p, microstrip transmission line length Lm, microstrip transmission line width Wm, effective length of the SIW Leff, and effective width of the SIW Weff are the geometrical parameters of the filter. The SIW structure is made up of a microstrip feeding line, a microstrip tapered transition, and a SIW cavity. The structure is built using a Rogers substrate with a relative permittivity of 3.5 and a thickness of 0.5 mm. Tapered via transition allows for the simple transformation of microstrip energy. For optimal impedance matching and low reflection losses, the microstrip to SIW transition is used. A provided formula can be used to relate the SIW structures' effective width and length.

$$W_{eff} = W_{SIW} - \frac{d^2}{0.95p} \tag{1}$$

$$L_{eff} = L_{SIW} - \frac{d^2}{0.95p} \tag{2}$$

The desired passband's resonance frequency can be specified as

$$f_0 = \frac{c_0}{\epsilon_r}\sqrt{(\frac{1}{W_{eff}})^2 + (\frac{1}{L_{eff}})^2} \tag{3}$$

In order to reduce radiation losses and leakage losses between the via holes, the diameter between the via holes and the filter should be kept to a minimum. The filter should also meet the following requirements. d/WSIW0.4, d/p > 0.5 The SIW BPF is intended to attain quality factor, and using the provided formula,

$$Q_e = \frac{f_0}{BW} \tag{4}$$

where f_0 and BW stand for the filter's resonant frequency and bandwidth, respectively.

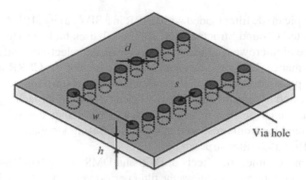

Fig. 1. Basic SIW structure

3 Design of SIW Bandpass Filter Structures

3.1 SIW Filter I

Figure 2 depicts the proposed SIW BPF with circular dumbbell DGS. The SIW structure is produced by etching a circular head DGS in the ground plane of the SIW cavity. The SIW cavity's ground plane's etched gap serves as the electric field's focus point. In addition to enhance the out of band rejection, a transmission zero is made using the DGS. By adding rows of vias with a diameter of 0.4 mm, both horizontally and vertically, optimization can be accomplished. The suggested filter has a 0.5 mm thickness and was created on a Rogers substrate with a dielectric constant of 3.5. The filter is modelled using EM simulation software like Advanced Design System to obtain S-parameters (ADS). For fine-tuning the resonance frequency to accomplish the filter performance, circular dumbbell DGS is introduced.

$L_{eff} = 5$ mm, $W_{eff} = 5.2$ mm, $W_T = 1.5$ mm, $W_M = 0.8$ m, $L_T = 1.2$ mm, $d = 0.4$ mm, $P = 0.75$ mm, $W = 1.3$ mm, $r = .0.3$ mm are the filter dimensions.

Figure 3 displays the simulated SIW BPF s-parameters for various through diameters with a center frequency of 29.7 GHz and very little insertion loss. When the via's width is enlarged, the resonance shifts to the lower frequency side with minimal return loss. The simulated results, using a central frequency of 29.7 GHz, show insertion loss of 1.7 dB, return loss of > 20 dB, 3-dB bandwidth of 3.3%, and stopband attenuation of more than 30 dB/decade. The filter is suitable for fixed satellite services and has a center frequency of 29.7 GHz (FSS).

3.2 SIW Filter II

The suggested SIW bandpass filter with two U-slot DGS is laid out in Fig. 4. To reduce leakage losses and provide good impedance matching to the structure, the filter structure is tapered via transition between the microstrip line and SIW structure. The SIW cavity can be optimized by adding two rows, one each horizontally and vertically, of 0.8 mm metallic vias. To enhance the upper stopband performance, a double equilateral U-slot was etched onto the bottom ground plane of the filter. The effective inductance and capacitance will change as the DGS is added to the ground plane of the SIW structure,

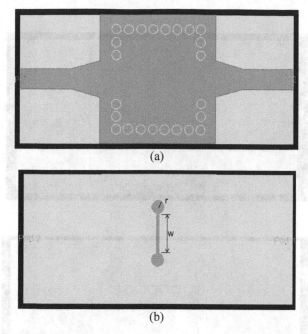

Fig. 2. Proposed SIW BPF (a) Top view (b) Bottom view

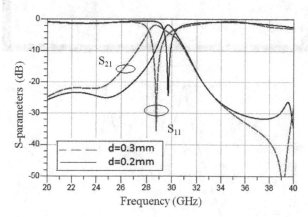

Fig. 3. SIW BPF response in simulation for various through diameters

which will alter the resonant frequency of the filter. The characteristic impedance of the line will also vary as a result of the addition of DGS.

The dimensions of the filter are $L_{eff} = 13.4$ mm, $W_{eff} = 9.7$ mm, $W_{d=1}$ mm, $L_d = 6$ m, $d = 0.8$ mm, $P = 0.75$ mm, $W_T = 6$ mm, $L_T = 5$ mm, $W_M = 0.9$ mm, $L_M = 2.5$ mm.

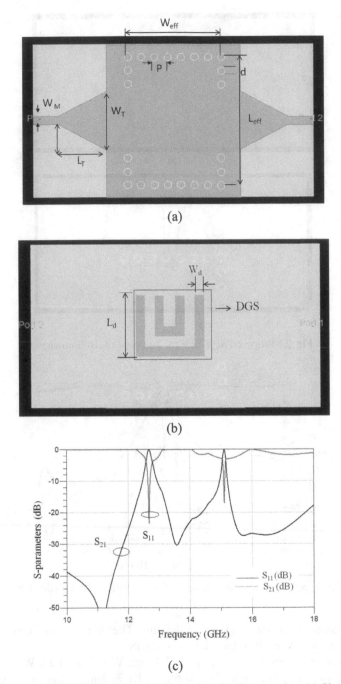

Fig. 4. The proposed SIW BPF's layout (a). T op view (b). Bottom view (c) Simulation of the proposed SIW BPF's frequency response

To prevent slot mode propagation, the DGS slots must be isolated from other slots. The suggested filter is built on a Rogers substrate with a 3.5 dielectric constant and 0.5 mm thickness.

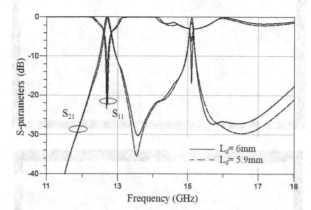

Fig. 5. The proposed filter's frequency response as a function of the DGS slot's length

The simulated S-parameters of the filter for various DGS slot lengths are shown in Fig. 5. The upper stopband attenuation moves downward, the upper stopband attenuation changes somewhat in the first band of the filter, and the return loss is reduced for both bands. The two equilateral U-slot DGS's dimensions are altered to enable filter operation at dual bands of 12.68 GHz and 15.10 GHz with return loss ≥ 17 dB, extremely low insertion loss of 0 dB, upper stopband attenuation ≥ 25 dB, and application for fixed and broadcast satellite services.

3.3 SIW Filter III

The DGS, which was very recently introduced, essentially comprises of slots or SIW structure ground plane flaws. The SIW's configuration is depicted in Fig. 6 with DGS etched into the bottom substrate. Analyze the DGS loaded SIW immediately. To increase out of band rejection, the DGS, which is made up of square slots joined by a narrow slit at the edge, is etched on the bottom layer of the substrate. The DGS slots' dimensions are chosen so that the passbands fall within the filter's stopband. EM simulations are used to establish the proposed filter' scattering parameters.

With the aid of an electromagnetic simulation called ADS, which has a central frequency of 13.85 GHz, the settings of the filters are changed.

Figure 7 depicts the transmission response of the suggested filter, which at the center frequency of 13.85 GHz has an insertion loss of 0.002 dB and a return loss of > 26 dB. The DGS dimensions have an impact on the SIW BPF's bandwidth and center frequency during the simulation process. Figure 8 displays the filter's simulated outcomes for various DGS widths. As can be seen, by adjusting the DGS width, the lower attenuation and resonant frequency move to the higher frequency side of the spectrum without affecting the attenuation of the upper stopband. The filter's advantages include its small

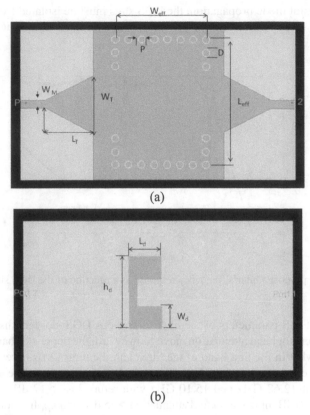

(a)

(b)

Fig. 6. The proposed SIW BPF's structure (a). Top view (b). Bottom view

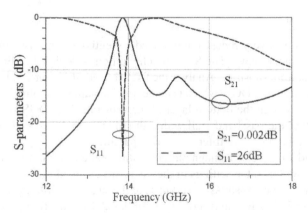

Fig. 7. Frequency response of the proposed filter

size, low insertion loss, and center frequency of 13.85 GHz, which is suitable for satellite services. Return loss is also better than 26 dB.

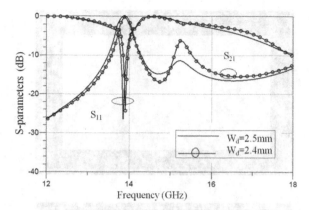

Fig. 8. SIW BPF simulation results for various DGS widths

3.4 SIW Filter IV

The geometrical parameters of the filter are L_{eff} = 15.9 mm, W_{eff} = 14.1 mm, W_d = 1.2 mm, W_M = 0.86 mm, L_d = 1.8 mm, d = 0.8 mm, P = 1.5 mm, L_m = 3.7 mm.

Figure 9 shows the proposed SIW BPF filter with DGS and DMS. The cross slot DGS of the SIW cavity is etched from the ground plane. Along the etched portion of the structure, the current is distributed. The cross-slot DGS with length Ld and slot width Wd measurements. The upper stopband attenuation is increased by optimizing the DGS's size.

Figure 10 displays the simulated results of the proposed SIW BPF filter when the length of the DGS is changed. As the length of the DGS is reduced, the filter's resonant frequency somewhat shifts towards its lower frequency side with reduced return loss. Figure 11 depicts the filter's frequency response for various through diameters. By reducing the via diameter, the filter's lower attenuation moves to the higher frequency side, and the resonant frequency moves to the lower frequency side as well. Filter with fractional bandwidth of 0.15%, 9.4 GHz center frequency, 22.7 dB of return loss, and 0.45 dB of insertion loss. The rejection of the out of band is > 20 dB. Military and meteorological FSS satellites can use the intended SIW filter.

3.5 SIW Filter V

The geometrical parameters of the filter are L_{eff} = 14 mm, W_{eff} = 16 mm, W_T=6.1 mm, W_M = 0.9 m, L_T = 5.01 m, d = 0.8 mm, P = 1.4 mm, W_m = 0.64 mm, L_m = 2.8 mm, L_d = 2.8 mm, W_d = 2.2 mm, W_l = 0.73 mm.

The SIW bandpass filter is designed using a non-uniform DGS unit based on the suggested DGS architecture. Two square heads joined by a U-slot DGS in the ground plane of the SIW cavity make up the DGS configuration suggested in this filter (see Fig. 12), which will further enhance stopband performance. The SIW structure's etched gap is where the electric field distribution is more concentrated, which eventually changes the inductance and capacitance of transmission lines. To suppress the erroneous passband

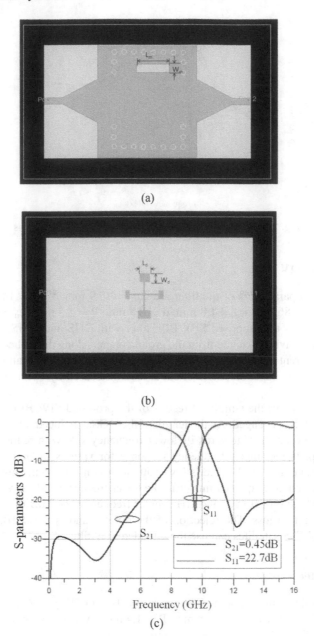

Fig. 9. Design of the suggested SIW filter (a) Top view (b) Bottom View (c). Results of the proposed filter in simulation

and assign transmission zeros to out-of-band signals, DGS are researched and used. Passband ripple has significantly improved with the use of DGS.

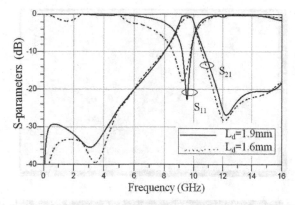

Fig. 10. Results of the proposed filter in simulations for various DGS lengths

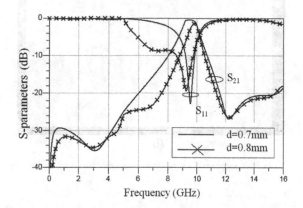

Fig. 11. Filter frequency response with various through diameters

A defective microstrip structure (DMS) method is formed by etching two horizontal rectangular gaps in the centre of the conducting strips. This method offers slow wave properties and gets rid of unwanted response in the right frequency range. Similar to DGS, DMS lengthens the microstrip line electrically and messes with its current distribution, both of which tend to raise the line's inductance and capacitance. The DMS dimensions are selected to produce the best possible filter response.

Figure 13 depicts the simulated response of the filter when the DGS unit's length is changed. It demonstrates that by shortening the DGS, the condition of under coupling with reduced insertion loss arises, allowing the DGS length to be adjusted to an ideal value to prevent under coupling in the filter response. SIW can be used with defective ground structure (DGS) to improve out of band suppression. The DMS can be used to create a finite passband and obtain stopband attenuation up to −38 dB in order to further enhance the stopband performance. The simulated response of the suggested filter for various DMS lengths is shown in Fig. 14. This suggests that when the lower stopband attenuation decreases, the filter's lower passband moves closer to its higher resonant frequency.

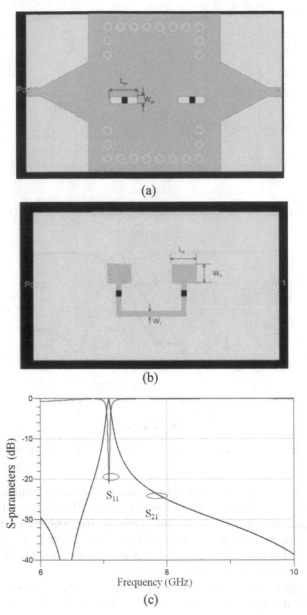

Fig. 12. The proposed filter's design (a). Top view (b). Bottom view (c) Response of the proposed filter to frequency

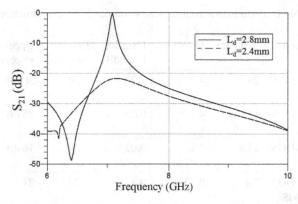

Fig. 13. Simulated S_{21} of the filter for varying length of DGS

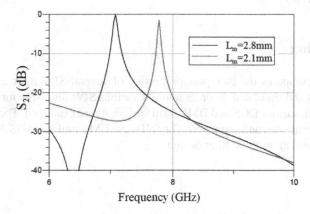

Fig. 14. Simulated S_{21} of the filter for varying length of DMS

The filter is 26 mm × 16 mm overall, including the input and output tapered microstrip lines. The filter design produces a narrow bandwidth thanks to the employment of 50 microstrip lines coupled on either side of the SIW cavity. The simulation results with a centre frequency of 7 GHz, insertion loss of 0.02 dB, return loss of > 20 dB, 3-dB bandwidth of 2.8%, and stopband attenuation of above 35 dB/decade are used to verify the results. The benefit of the suggested filter is enhanced out of band rejection, good return loss, and lower insertion loss.

Table 1 compares the performance of various SIW filter structures using different shapes of DGS and DMS.

Table 1. Performance comparison on various SIW filter structures

Filter	Structure	f_0 (GHz)	FBW (%)	Insertion loss (dB)	Return loss (dB)	Upper stopband	Size(mm)
SIW filter I	SIW-DGS	29.7	4.31	1.7	>20	30 dB	10 × 6
SIW filter II	SIW-DGS	12.6 & 15.10	4.7	0.05	>17	25 dB	26 × 16.5
SIW filter III	SIW-DGS	13.8	5	0.02	>26	16 dB	27 × 16
SIW filter IV	SIW-DGS & DMS	9.4	0.15	0.4	>20	21	28 × 17
SIW filter V	SIW-DGS & DMS	7	2.8	0.02	20	35	26 × 16

4 Conclusion

This Chapter compares the bandpass properties of several SIW filter topologies that have been built and simulated. In order to build various SIW filter structures for satellite communication, various DGS and DMS form variations are examined. The effectiveness of the filters is evaluated and compared. The full wave EM simulator ADS 2011.11 allows for the implementation of the filter design.

References

1. Chen, X.-P., Wu, K.: Substrate integrated waveguide filters. IEEE Microw. Mag. 1527-3342/14 (2014)
2. Panda, C.S., Nayak, R., Behera, S.K.: Design and analysis of a compact substrate integrated waveguide bandpass filter for Ku band applications. IEEE (2016). 978-1-5090-4556-3/16
3. Gopinath, A., Lal, P.R.: Substrate Integrated waveguide based hybrid cavity filter for Ku-band applications. In: International Conference on Communication and Signal Processing. IEEE (2017). 978-1-5090-3800-8/17
4. Moitra, S., Mondal, B., Kundu, J., Mukhopadhyay, A.K., Bhattacharjee, A.K.: Substrate integrated waveguide (SIW) filter using stepped-inductive posts for Ku-band applications. IET (2013)
5. Shen, W., Yin, W.-Y., Sun, X.-W., Wu, L.-S.: Substrate-Integrated Waveguide Bandpass Filters with Planar Resonators for System-on-Package. IEEE Trans. Compon. Packag. Manuf. Technol. **3**(2) (2013)
6. Deng, F., Wong, S.-W., Chen, R.-S., Feng, S.-F., Chu, Q.-X.: An improved compact substrate intergrated waveguide (SIW) bandpass filter with sharp rejection and wide upper stopband. IEEE (2015). 978-1-4799-8767-2/15
7. Huang, Y.M., Shao, Z., You, C.J., et al.: Size-reduced bandpass filters using quarter-mode substrate integrated waveguide loaded with different defected ground structure patterns. IEEE (2015). 978-1-4799-8275-2/15

8. Jiang, H., Wang, Y., Wang, L.: Compact microstrip narrow bandpass filter with good selectivity and wide stopband rejection for Ku-band applications. Progr. Electromagn. Res. Lett. **57**, 55–59 (2015)

9. Liu, Z., Xiao, G., Zhu, L.: Triple mode bandpass filteron CSRR loaded substrate integrated waveguide cavities. IEEE Trans. Compon. Packag. Manuf. Technol. **6**(7), 1101–1107 (2016)

10. Khandelwal, M.K., Kanaujia, B.K., Kumar, S.: Defected ground structure: fundamentals, analysis, and applications in modern wireless trends. Hindawi Int. J. Antennas Propag. **2017**, 22 (2017). Article ID 2018527

11. Singh, P., Tomar, R.: The use of defected ground structures in designing microstrip filters with enhanced performance characteristics. In: Conference on Electronics, Telecommunications and Computers (2013)

12. Kumar, A., Karthikeyan, M.V.: Design and realization of microstrip filters with defected ground structures (DGS). Int. J. Eng. Sci. Technol. 679–686 (2016)

13. Li, W., Tang, Z., Cao, X.: Design of a SIW bandpass filter using defected ground structure with CSRRs. Hindawi Active Passive Electron. Components **2017**, 6 (2017). Article ID 1606341

14. Chu, H., Shi, X.Q.: Compact ultra wide band bandpass filter based on SIW and DGS technology with a notch band. J. Electromagn. Waves Appl. **25**, 589–596 (2012)

15. Wang, Z.-D., Wei, F., Shi, X.W.: Design of dual band bandpass filter with DGS. In: International Conferences on Microwave and Millimeter Wave Technology (2012)

16. Suhas, D., Lakshmi, C.R., Srinivasa Rao, Z., Kannadasan, D.: A systematic implementation of elliptic low-pass filter using defected ground structure. J. Electromagn. Waves Appl. 1–13 (2015)

17. Habiba, H.U., Priya, A.B., Shaw, R.N., Ghosh, A.: Design of low dimensional SIW bandpass filter based on DGS and DMS technologies for radar and satellite communications. In: Mekhilef, S., Shaw, R.N., Siano, P. (eds.) ICEEE 2022. LNEE, vol. 894, pp. 702–706. Springer, Singapore (2022). https://doi.org/10.1007/978-981-19-1677-9_63

18. Laya, N., et al.: Design of half mode substrate integrated waveguide (HMSIW) filter with series defective microstrip structure (DMS) for Ku band operation. IEEE (2017). 978-1-5386-1703-8/17

19. Zhang, H., Kang, W., Wu, W.: Dual-band substrate integrated waveguide bandpass filter utilizing complementary split-ring resonators. Electron. Lett. **54**(2), 85–87 (2018)

20. Boutejdar, A., Omar, A., Al Sharkawy, M., Darwish, A.: A simple transformation of improved WLAN band pass to low pass filter using defected ground structure (DGS), defected microstrip structure (DMS) and multilayer-technique. J. Microw. Optoelectron. Electromagn. Appl. **12**(1), 111–129 (2013)

21. Hong, J.-S., Lancaster, M.J.: Microstrip Filters for RF/Microwave Applications. Wiley (2001)

22. Watkins, J.: Circular resonant structures in microstrip. IET Electron. Lett. **5**(21), 524–525 (1969)

23. Webster, J.: Defected Microstrip Structure. Wiley (2013)

24. Pozar, D.M.: Microwave Engineering, pp. 1–4. Addison-Wesley, Reading (1990)

25. Hunter, I.C.: Theory and Design of Microwave Filters. Institution of Electrical Engineers, London (2001)

Efficient Energy Consumption Model
for Clusters in Wireless Sensor Network

Swechchha Gupta[(✉)] and Buddha Singh

SC&SS, Jawaharlal Nehru University, New Delhi 110067, India
swechchhagupta18@gmail.com

Abstract. Wireless sensor network has magnetized in modern year on account of its extensive scope of benefits in a forthcoming era of automation and remote monitoring. Currently, wireless sensor network has numerous challenging issues. One of the major concerns is energy consumption of nodes. The performance and extension of network lifespan of sensor node is a crucial issue that has not been appropriately resolved yet. In this research work, energy consumption model for clusters in sensor network is proposed. The homogeneous sensors are uniformly dispersed in monitoring region and sink is positioned in the center. In this energy consumption model, the wireless sensor network is partitioned into many clusters, each with its own cluster head. The member nodes in clusters are further partitioned into annuli based on the average hop progress. The energy consumption of nodes varies according to the relaying load on the nodes and the distance of nodes from cluster head. The proposed model minimizes the energy consumed by the nodes and maintaining the adequate network coverage. Simulations compare our proposed model to the classic LEACH scheme. The outcomes show that our proposed model significantly increases network lifetime, and outperform the LEACH method.

Keywords: WSN · Clusters · Energy consumption · Annuli

1 Introduction

Sensor network is set of sensor devices which transfer information collected from a monitored field over wireless links. The sensor nodes deployed for monitoring purpose in a geographic area. The deployment of the nodes are deterministic or random fashion. The deploy territory is administrable or unmanageable or dangerous environment because human interfere is not possible in the deploy region [1]. All sensors are connected and communicate to each other by radio signals. Sensors obtain the physical information by sensing that zone, unite information from every node, compute it and forwarded it to the base station or sink through network and finally accessed by the users through internet. Sink serves as an interface between the network and the end users. The sensor nodes in WSN are small scale and inexpensive devices. They have limited bandwidth, mathematical, storage and communication capacity. The prime challenge is the design of energy of sensor devices [4]. Due to continuous data transmission, sensors need

© The Author(s), under exclusive license to Springer Nature Switzerland AG 2023
R. N. Shaw et al. (Eds.): ICACIS 2022, CCIS 1749, pp. 314–323, 2023.
https://doi.org/10.1007/978-3-031-25088-0_28

long lifetime. Nodes have limited battery power and for surveillance also it wants long battery backup. This is due to the fact that sensor device activities such as Sensing, Processing, aggregating and Communication contribute to WSN energy consumption and lifetime decreases [3]. Various energy consumption model have been developed. Still the performance and extension of network lifetime of sensor node is an important issue that has not been appropriately resolved yet. The clustering protocol [7] such as LEACH [8] suffer from load balancing and no priority given to the residual energy. Sensor nodes distribution is not based upon the annulus in the network in earlier work. Therefore, a better energy consumption model for each cluster is considered in this research work.

The remaining of this chapter is structured as follows. Section 2, summarizes existing methods. Section 3 provides a description of the network model and proposed energy consumption model. The simulation results shown in Sect. 4 demonstrate the efficiency of our proposed model. Section 5 concludes the chapter with several ideas for future research.

2 Related Work

Many energy consumption techniques have been introduced to reduce the energy consumption in WSN in literature. The preceding work on extending network lifetime in WSN is discussed in this section, along with its limitations and drawbacks. In conventional randomized sleep scheduling technique, cluster head randomly selects the nodes from a cluster in sensor network and put into a sleep state. In RS technique, the energy consumption is calculated at cluster level for sensor networks [2]. The authors investigated energy-efficient linear distance sleep scheduling (LDS). In the LDS [5] scheme, the overall energy consumption of sensor nodes is determined based on the distance from cluster head. The sensor nodes which ae far away from cluster head, consumes more energy. Therefore, overall network lifetime decreased. Balanced energy sleep scheduling is another sleep scheduling in sensor networks which reduces the power consumption. The BS method distributes the sensing and communication power demand evenly among all sensor nodes. It distributes the power load of the communication activities among all sensor nodes in the clusters [6]. LDS and RS schemes are also investigated in terms of their energy consumption coefficient of variation. This provides inefficient results. In optimal scheduling [10]. Researchers considered only a single node and then concentrated on the trade-offs between energy usage and packet latency. Obviously, this causes additional packet latency. Another method, dynamic sleep scheduling (DSS) [9] method is dramatically reduced the delay and increased the average energy per packet. Overhearing can be reduced if nodes can figure out when to send and receive packets. It reconfigures the network on a regular basis and distributes the energy consumption load to the sensor nodes more equally. Also, Various (MAC) protocol is used for reducing the energy consumption by the sensors to prolong lifespan of sensor devices. A MAC protocol checks the channel access in a network to transmit the data of sensors.

3   Proposed Energy-Consumption Model

The energy consumption model for clusters in WSN is proposed based on certain network parameters. In this model, the wireless sensor network is partitioned into many clusters, each with its own cluster head. The member nodes in the cluster are further partitioned into n annuli based on the average hop progress. Then nodes from different annuli will send the environment data to the CH. The CH will transmit the quality information to the base station. The nodes which are far distant from the CH dissipate very little energy in relaying the load. The majority of the energy used by these nodes is for transmission. There are several assumptions related to the proposed energy consumption.

3.1   Network Model

The basic assumptions are given as below

- Sensor nodes are randomly dispersed in a deployment region with redundant in numbers. Therefore, extraneous number of sensors can be put into sleep state and some of them in active mode without compromising the network coverage of the sensor network.
- The sensors that have been deployed are all same i.e., homogeneous with the same functionalities for detecting events.
- All sensors can transmit with sufficient energy to change the amount of transmit power to reach sink. Therefore, it uses minimum transmission power which require for transmission with its cluster head.
- All sensor nodes transmit equal size of packets in sensor network.
- All nodes have same sensing range.
- Monitoring area divided into many clusters.
- A cluster further divided into many annuluses.
- Every annulus has same width in a cluster.

The energy consumption of nodes is computed based on the annulus, to which the nodes belong in a cluster. Afterwards, expected energy consumption of a cluster is computed by aggregating the energy consumption of all the annulus in the cluster. Therefore, overall expected energy consumption in sensor network is calculated by multiplying the estimated energy consumed by one cluster by the total number of clusters in the network.

Let N number of sensor nodes are uniformly deployed in a $M \times M$ region. The density of network is $\lambda = \frac{N}{M^2}$ and the deployment region partitioned into k clusters. The average number of nodes in a cluster is (N/k) and the optimal number of clusters computed in the chapter [8] is given in Eq. 1:

$$k_{opt} = \frac{\sqrt{N}}{\sqrt{2\pi}} \sqrt{\frac{\epsilon_{fs}}{\epsilon_{mp}}} \frac{M}{d_{toBS}^2} \tag{1}$$

where d_{toBS}^2 is the distance from cluster head to base station.

The radius of cluster is R and area of a cluster is πR^2. The region is $M \times M$ and this is partitioned into k number of clusters and the radius of cluster can be expressed as:

$$M \times M = k.(\pi R^2) \Rightarrow M^2 = k.\pi R^2$$

$$R = \frac{M}{\sqrt{\pi k}}$$

The cluster is further partitioned into n annuli based on the average hop progress (r) and the value of r computed in the paper [11] is given in Eq. 2.

$$r = \sqrt{3}\lambda \int_0^{r_c} x^2 e^{\frac{\pi \lambda (x^2 - r_c^2)}{3}} dx \qquad (2)$$

The width of annuli considered equivalent to average hop progress. Therefore, the number of annuli (n_a) in a cluster are computed in Eq. 3.

Number of annuli in a cluster $n_a = \left\lceil \dfrac{R}{r} \right\rceil$, where $[n_a = 1, 2, 3 \ldots, i, i+1, n]$

The electronic energy is the energy consume in processing of one bit data and it is represented by E_{elec} in Eq. 3. It depends upon many factors like modulation, filtering, digital coding and distance. The amplifier energy depends upon the distance from sender to the receiver. The energy consumption computed either by free space model or multipath fading model. In proposed model, for energy consumption computation free space model is considered. Because transmission of information will always be carried out hop by hop, therefore, the power will be lost by the factor of r^2 always.

The energy consumed by i annular sensors to transmit k bit of data in each round is given in Eq. 3:

$$E_{trans}^i = k * E_{elec} + k * \left(\varepsilon_{fs} r^2 \right)$$

$$E_{trans}^i = k \left[E_{elec} + \left(\varepsilon_{fs} r^2 \right) \right] \qquad (3)$$

The Energy consumed by i annular sensors to receive the k bit of data is defined in Eq. 4:

$$E_{rec}^i = k * E_{elec} \qquad (4)$$

The area of ith annular (A_a^i) in a cluster can be calculated by subtracting the area of ith hop with the area of $(i-1)^{th}$ hop in Eq. 5:

$$A_a^i = \pi (ir)^2 - \pi ((i-1)r)^2$$

$$A_a^i = \pi \left[(ir)^2 - ((i-1)r)^2 \right]$$

$$A_a^i = \pi \left[i^2 - (i-1)^2 \right] r^2$$

$$A_a^i = \pi [2i - 1] r^2 \qquad (5)$$

The average number of sensor nodes in i^{th} annular can be computed by multiplying the area of ith annular with density in Eq. 6:

$$n_a^i = \lambda.A_a^i$$

$$n_a^i = \frac{N}{M^2}.\pi[2i-1]r^2 \tag{6}$$

The energy consumed by all nodes of ith annular is computed by multiplying the number of nodes at i^{th} annular with the energy used in transmit and/or to receive the data packet by a sensor node is given in Eq. 7:

$$E\left(n_a^i\right) = n_a^i * \left[E_{trans}^i + E_{rec}^i\right] \tag{7}$$

Equation (7) representing the energy consumption by all nodes of ith annular. Similarly, we can compute the energy consumption of $(i+1)^{th}$ annular and n^{th} annular in a cluster

$$E\left(n_a^{(i+1)}\right) = n_a^{(i+1)} * \left[E_{trans}^{(i+1)} + E_{rec}^{(i+1)}\right]$$
$$E\left(n_a^{(i+2)}\right) = n_a^{(i+2)} * \left[E_{trans}^{(i+2)} + E_{rec}^{(i+2)}\right]$$

$$\ldots\ldots\ldots\ldots$$

$$\ldots\ldots\ldots\ldots$$

$$\ldots\ldots\ldots\ldots$$

$$E(n_a^n) = n_a^n * \left[E_{trans}^n + E_{rec}^n\right]$$

The total relay energy consumed by the nodes at i^{th} annular is computed by the summation of energy consumed by the nodes from n^{th} annular to $(i+1)^{th}$ annular. The relay energy $\left(E_{rel}^i\right)$ is computed in Eq. 8:

$$E_{rel}^i = E\left(n_a^{i+1}\right) + E\left(n_a^{i+2}\right) + \ldots + E(n_a^n)$$

$$E_{rel}^i = \sum_{(i+1)}^n E\left(n_a^{i+1}\right) \tag{8}$$

The average energy consumed by any sensor node in i^{th} annular for relaying the data between n^{th} annular to i^{th} annular can be calculated by dividing the E_{rel}^i to the number of nodes at i^{th} annular.

$$E_{rel}^{i^{avg}} = E_{rel}^i / n_a^i$$

$$E_{rel}^{i^{avg}} = \frac{\sum_{(i+1)}^n E_{rel}(n_a^{i+1})}{n_a^i} \tag{9}$$

The expected energy consumed by any sensor node at i^{th} annular will include its transmission energy and relaying energy. Therefore, the expected energy consumption by any sensor in i^{th} annular is calculated in Eq. 10

$$E_{total}^i = E_{trans}^i + E_{rel}^{i^{avg}}$$

$$E_{total}^i = k\left[E_{elec} + \left(\varepsilon_{fs}r^2\right)\right] + \frac{\sum_{(i+1)}^n E_{rel}\left(n_a^{i+1}\right)}{n_a^i} \tag{10}$$

Thus, the expected energy consumed by any sensor node in i^{th} annular in a cluster is obtained. Clearly, we can see that the amount of energy consumed by nodes is determined by the annular in which nodes are placed. Therefore, total energy consumed by a cluster can be computed by multiplying the E_{total}^i with total number of nodes in a cluster. This can be expressed in Eq. 11:

$$E_{cluster} = (N/k) * E_{total}^i$$

$$E_{cluster} = (N/k) * \left\{k\left[E_{elec} + \left(\varepsilon_{fs}r^2\right)\right] + \frac{\sum_{(i+1)}^n E_{rel}\left(n_a^{i+1}\right)}{n_a^i}\right\} \tag{11}$$

The total energy consumed by nodes in the network ($E_{network}$) is calculated by multiplying with energy of one cluster ($E_{cluster}$) to the number of clusters in the deployment region. $E_{network}$ is expressed in Eq. 12:

$$E_{network} = k * E_{cluster}$$

$$E_{network} = k * (N/k) * \left\{k\left[E_{elec} + \left(\varepsilon_{fs}r^2\right)\right] + \frac{\sum_{(i+1)}^n E_{rel}\left(n_a^{i+1}\right)}{n_a^i}\right\}$$

$$E_{network} = N * \left\{k\left[E_{elec} + \left(\varepsilon_{fs}r^2\right)\right] + \frac{\sum_{(i+1)}^n E_{rel}\left(n_a^{i+1}\right)}{n_a^i}\right\} \tag{12}$$

This proposed energy consumption model is applied in classic LEACH technique to further decrease the consumption of energy and increases network lifetime.

4 Simulation Parameters and Result Analysis

4.1 Simulation Parameters

The performance of proposed model is evaluated in terms of number of network lifetime and average residual energy of every node in each round. The network lifespan is computed using the number of alive sensor nodes. The Python version 3.9.5 is used for the simulations results. The simulation results are the average of 50 rounds. The 100 sensor nodes are deployed in 100×100 m^2 monitoring region. The parameters are considered for the implementation of proposed algorithm given as follows (Table 1):

Table 1. Simulation parameters

Parameters	Values
Number of sensors	100
Number of rounds	50
Area of network	1000 m^2
Energy for transmitting one bit (E_{trans})	1.0000e−07
Energy for receiving one bit (E_{rec})	1.0000e−07
E_{fs}	0.3400e−9
Initial energy of sensor node	2 J
Data aggregation energy	1.0000e−08

4.2   Result Analysis

The result of proposed model for 100 sensor nodes shown in Fig. 1 and Fig. 2. The simulation is run for the 50 round and the number of nodes alive are shown. The alive sensor after 43 rounds clearly visual in simulation results. The sensor network has a lifespan of 43 rounds.

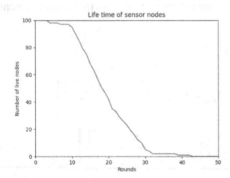

Fig. 1. Network Lifetime of proposed algorithm for 100 nodes

Fig. 2. Average residual energy of proposed algorithm for 100 nodes

The residual energy of sensor nodes is computed for each round and the result analysis of residual energy is obtained. The graph is plotted for residual energy of every sensor node in each round. Every sensor node has 2 J initial energy. Therefore, 200 J energy will be generated for 100 nodes. The simulation result shown in Fig. 2.

Furthermore, for testing the scalability of the proposed model, the number of nodes are increased from 100 to 200. The remaining parameters are the same as in the first case. We examine the outcome of this scenario and obtain the simulation result shown in Fig. 3 and Fig. 4. The average of 50 round of simulation result have been taken. In Fig. 3, it is clear that all sensor nodes expired on round 26. The sensor network has a lifespan of 26 rounds, which is a better network lifetime.

The average residual energy of sensor nodes are computed. The Fig. 4, indicates the result of average residual energy consumption for each round.

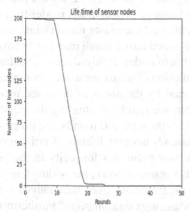

Fig. 3. Network Lifetime of proposed algorithm for 200 nodes

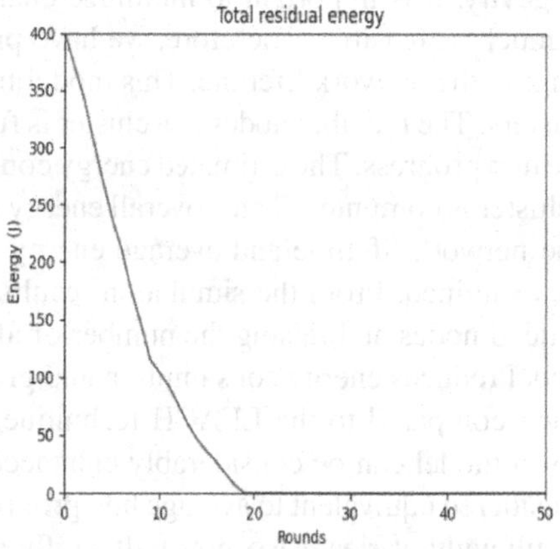

Fig. 4. Average residual energy of proposed algorithm for 200 nodes

When the proposed energy consumption model is applied in classic LEACH technique, the consumption of energy is reduced further compare to classic LEACH. The simulation result are obtained in terms of alive nodes for proposed model. Simulation results shows that by applying proposed energy consumption model on LEACH gives better performance than the classic LEACH. The comparison between proposed model and LEACH is shown in Fig. 5.

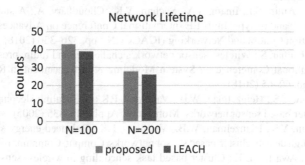

Fig. 5. Comparative result of proposed and LEACH

Therefore, the simulation results of proposed model decreases the energy consumption significantly and increases the network lifetime as compared to the existing LEACH protocol.

5 Conclusion

The energy efficiency of sensors in wireless sensor network is critical to the network's longevity. It is important to minimize energy usage and extend the network's lifespan as much as feasible. Therefore, we have proposed energy consumption model for prolonging the network lifetime. This model first partitioned the sensor network into many clusters. The member nodes in a cluster is further divided into n annuli based on the average hop progress. The estimated energy consumption of nodes deployed at any annular in a cluster is computed. Thus, overall energy consumption of sensor network is computed. The network lifetime and average energy consumed by the nodes of proposed model are examined. From the simulation results, we can see that by decreasing the number of dead nodes and raising the number of alive nodes through 100 rounds, the proposed model reduces energy consumption and greatly extends network lifetime. Furthermore, when compared to the LEACH technique, the sensor network's longevity in the proposed model can be considerably enhanced. In this research work, the width of annuli considered equivalent to average hop progress. In the future, we study the changes as the annuli width varies. Also, how will it influence node energy consumption? Furthermore, we can observe how the network lifetime can be increased.

References

1. Sharma, V., Patel, R.B., Bhadauria, H.S., Prasad, D.: Deployment scheme in wireless sensor network to achieve blanket coverage in large scale open area: a review. Proc. Egypt. Inf. J. 45–56 (2016)
2. Hu, J., Ma, Z., Sun, Z.: Energy-efficient MAC protocol designed for wireless sensor network for IoT. In: IEEE International Conference on Computational Intelligence and Security, pp. 721–725 (2010)
3. Singh, M.K., Amin, S.I., Imam, S.A., Sachan, V.K., Choudhary, A.: A survey of wireless sensor network and its type. In: IEEE International Conference on Advances in Computing, Communication Control and Networking (ICACCCN), pp. 326–330 (2018)
4. Patel, N.R., Kumar, S.: Wireless sensor network's challenges and future prospects. In: IEEE 2018 International Conference on System Modeling & Advancement in Research Trends (SMART), pp. 60–65 (2018)
5. Deng, J., Han, Y.S., Heinzelman, W.B., Varshney, P.K.: Scheduling sleeping nodes in high density cluster based sensor networks. Mob. Netw. Appl. 825–835 (2005)
6. Deng, J., Han, Y.S., Heinzelman, W.B., Varshney, P.K.: Balanced-energy sleep scheduling scheme for high density cluster-based sensor networks. Comput. Commun. 1631–1642 (2005)
7. Chauhan, S., Awasthi, L.K.: Cluster based task scheduling in wireless sensor network. Int. Comput. Appl. (2011)
8. Heinzelman, W.B., Chandrakasan, A.P., Balakrishnan, H.: An application-specific protocol architecture for wireless microsensor networks. IEEE Trans. Wirel. Commun. 660–670 (2002)
9. Nazir, B., Hasbullah, H: Dynamic sleep scheduling for minimizing delay in wireless sensor network. In: IEEE in Saudi International Electronics, Communications, Photonics Conference (SIECPC), pp. 1–5 (2011)
10. Sheu, J., Lai, C., Chao, C.: Power-aware routing for energy conserving and balance in ad hoc networks. In: Proceedings of the 2004 IEEE Conference on Networking, Sensing, and Control, Taipei, Taiwan, pp. 468–473, March 2004

11. Wang, Y., Wang, X., Agrawal, D.P., Minai, A.A.: Impact of heterogeneity on coverage and broadcast reachability in wireless sensor networks. In: The Fifteenth International Conference on Computer Communications and Networks (ICCCN), October 2006 (2006)

Emotion Identification from Tamil Song Lyrics Using Machine Learning Algorithms

M. Rajasekar$^{(\boxtimes)}$ and Angelina Geetha

Hindustan Institute of Technology and Science, Chennai, India
sekarca07@gmail.com

Abstract. In Indian cinema the songs are playing a vital role to make the movie as Hit. These songs are having such kind of emotions to attract the viewers. Emotions are the powerful expression of human thoughts. In Indian culture the emotions are described in various human situations. The Indian traditional dance Bharatha Natyam, the emotions are described as face and gesture actions. People experience nine different emotions in nine different situations. In this Chapter a novel machine learning approach to identify emotions from the song lyrics is introduced. The novel emotion detection approach is proposed using machine learning methods and implemented with Tamil song lyrics composed by Isai Gnani Ilayaraja which are collected from various sources. The corpus size was 2248 lyrics. The emotional labels were identified using keywords assigned for each labels. Three machine learning methods are used to check the identify emotion labels. They are Naïve Bayes, Support Vector Machine, and K-Nearest Neighbor models. The final result concludes that the naïve bayes model performs good (82.3% of accuracy). The F1-Score values for Naïve bayes model are 0.89.

Keywords: Emotion detection · Emotion identification · Tamil song lyrics · Naïve Bayes · SVM · K-NN

1 Introduction

Emotions are the powerful expression of human thoughts. In spite of variety of cultures and human languages, the emotions are expressed in different forms. Prediction of emotion is a developing field in Natural Language Processing. There are numerous emotion detection research approaches to recognize emotion from text, speech, gesture and action [1]. This work presents a novel approach to detect the emotions from song lyrics. We have developed a song lyrics corpus in Tamil language.

In Indian culture the emotions are described in various human situations. The Indian traditional dance Bharatha Natyam, the emotions are described as face and gesture actions. People experience nine different emotions in nine different situations. Everyone possesses both positive and negative demonic or heavenly feelings [2]. But if we want to lead a calm life, we must learn to control all of our emotions. Rasa is the emotional state of mind, and the nine emotions collectively are referred to as

R. N. Shaw et al. (Eds.): ICACIS 2022, CCIS 1749, pp. 324–338, 2023.
https://doi.org/10.1007/978-3-031-25088-0_29

Navarasa. Shringara (love/beauty), Hasya (laughing), Karuna (sorrow), Raudra (anger), Veera (heroics/courage), Bhayanaka (terror/fear), Bibhatsa (disgust), Adbutha (surprise/wonder), and Shantha (peace) are the nine different emotions (peace or tranquility) [2]. This Navarasa (nine rasas) are the important elements of Indian arts and cultures such are music, dance, musical instruments, cinema and literatures.

The nine emotions that make up our emotional spectrum serve as evidence of who we are, and those of us with greater emotional quotients have a propensity for impulsive and strong reactions [3]. In India the emotions are used in dance, drama, cinema, and songs. One can show these nine types of emotions in his action with or without dialog he/she can be a fantastic actor/actress. So these emotions are playing a vital role in Indian culture. Especially in songs there is variety of songs classified by emotions. In the songs one who can show or sing with variety of emotions that song will be very popular. Usually when an audience can listen the songs with its lyrics and music then they can understand about the song emotions whether the song is joy, love, romantic, anger, sad, or heroism. Manually they can understand the emotion of a song. This work explains the proposed novel system to predict the emotion of a song by evaluating its lyrics. Using machine learning algorithms, automatic emotion detection system is designed.

2 Related Works

There are numerous methods for extracting emotions from text that use a probabilistic approach. Deep learning assisted semantic text analysis [4] (DLSTA) has been proposed for big data human emotion identification. Concepts from natural language processing can be utilised to identify emotions in text. Word embeddings are frequently utilised in numerous NLP applications, such as question-answering, sentiment analysis, and machine translation. NLP approaches help learning-based systems perform better by fusing the text's semantic and syntactic properties. The numerical results demonstrate that the suggested method, when combined with other cutting-edge methodologies, yields a 98.02% classification accuracy rate and a 97.22% expressively higher quality of human emotion detection rate.

Examining Machine Learning Techniques for Text-based Emotion Recognition on Social Media [5] is proposed to investigate numerous well-liked machine learning techniques to identify emotions in social media conversations. This research includes a variety of algorithms, including both conventional machine learning and deep learning methods. The AffectiveTweets dataset utilised in this study has a baseline F1Score of 0.71 with word N-grams and SentiStrength. The research makes considerable contributions to the exploration of various machine learning techniques, leading to the examination of 2302 features sets, each of which has 100–1000 features collected from the text. The findings show that the Generalized Linear Model offers the best F1 score (0.901), Accuracy score (0.92), Recall score (0.902), and Precision score (0.902) with an accuracy standard deviation of 1.2%.

Emotion Recognition from Poems by Maximum Posterior Probability [6] is proposed for emotion recognition from Poems. Nine emotions are categorised from the poems based on the Navarasa under the Rasa Theory that is stated in the Natyashastra penned by "Bharatha Muni." The nine fundamental emotions, often known as the "Navarasa," include love, sadness, anger, hatred, fear, surprise, courage, joy, and peace. As far as we know, there isn't a corpus of texts with poems based on the nine emotions. From English poetry, we manually labelled a corpus with emotions. An extensive collection of poetry by Indian poets from the years 1850 to 1950 made up the corpus that was established. The poems were taken from the internet, and we used tenfold Naive Bayes classifiers to identify the emotion of each poem with a high degree of probability.

PERC-An Emotion Recognition Corpus for Cognitive Poems [1] is based on the Natya Shastra's description of the Navarasa (nine emotions), which is annotated by specialists. The Fleiss kappa measurement and central-limit theorem analyses of experimental data show that the PERC is truly a benchmark corpus with outstanding inter-annotator reliability. This unique corpus is accessible to the general public for computational poetry study.

Kāvi: An Annotated Corpus of Punjabi Poetry with Emotion Detection Based on 'Navrasa' [7] is created to predict the emotions from Punjabi poems. The primary goal of this work is to identify emotions in Punjabi poetry using a variety of traits seen in Punjabi poetry. This is a ground-breaking method of emotion recognition from Punjabi poetry. The Indian idea of "Navrasa" was used to manually annotate the "Kvi" Punjabi poetry corpus. The 948 poems in this corpus were divided into the nine emotion states listed in "Navrasa": "karuna," "shringar," "hasya," "raudra," "veer," "bhayanak," "vibhata," "adbhut," and "shaanti." The Kappa Fleiss index was developed for inter-annotator agreement on this manually annotated corpus. The classifier was built using the many features (linguistic, poetic, and statistical), and the two machine learning methods Naive Bayes (NB) and Support Vector Machine (SVM) were tested with these features. It was discovered that using SVM increased overall accuracy of the emotion classification test to 70.02%. Furthermore, it was discovered that poetic qualities performed better at detecting emotions than linguistic features.

3   Emotions for Tamil Song Lyrics

This proposed research work contributes in the emotion annotated Tamil corpus development of the song lyrics in Tamil language composed by Music director Ilayaraja. The content of proposed corpus is 2248 song lyrics composed by Ilayaraja are collected from 402 movies from 1976 to 2020. The song lyrics corpus contains the fields as lyric Id, lyric text, start lyric, movie name, writer of the lyric, music director, singer(s) of the song and year of movie released. This lyrics corpus tagged with nine emotions as explained in 'Navarasa' theory. Proposed system, based on the words in lyric the emotions are predicted. The list of words to describe the emotions is explained here. Most of the emotion detection approaches used to label nine emotions like Love, Joy, Surprise, Peace, Anger, Courage, Sad, Hate, and Fear. These emotions are appearing as many different forms in Tamil song lyrics. The emotion labels for Tamil song lyrics are showed in Table 1.

Table 1. Proposed emotion labels

Navarasa emotion labels	English emotion labels	Proposed tamil song lyrics emotion labels
Shringara	Love	Love
		Romance
Hasya	Joy	Happy
Adbhutha	Surprise	Nature
		Beauty
Shantha	Peace	Sleep mode
		Melody
Roudhra	Anger	Women angry
		God angry
Veera	Courage	Victory
		Self motivation
Karuna	Sad	Love failure
		Death
Bhibatsa	Hate	Hate love
Bhayanakam	Fear	Ghost
		God

4   Emotion Extraction Model

The Emotion extraction process is described in the Fig. 1. The song lyrics are collected from various sources. Then the corpus is cleaned and processed for future annotation process. Then the list of keywords identified for each emotions. Then the corpus is annotated manually with its related emotion. The annotated song lyric corpus is used to detect emotions from song lyrics. In this proposed method we have used three machine learning models to detect the emotions from song lyrics dynamically.

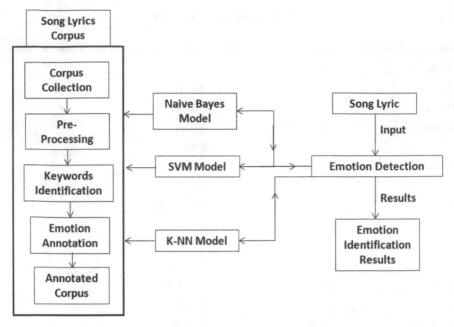

Fig. 1. Emotion detection overall architecture

4.1 Naive Bayes Classification

Naive Bayes Classifier is a probabilistic way of guessing the possibility of output label. It accepts conditional independence between the input attribute values given the class labels. Naive Bayes classification follows the Bayes theorem:

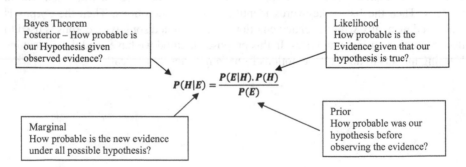

In the Bayes theorem such terms as Posterior probability, Likelihood probability, Marginal probability and prior probability are mentioned.

Bayes rule is a way to go from P (X|Y) to find P (Y|X).

$$P(X|Y) = \frac{P(X \cap Y)}{P(Y)} \qquad\qquad P(Y|X) = \frac{P(X \cap Y)}{P(X)}$$

P (Evidence | Outcome)   P (Outcome | Evidence)
(Known from training data)   (to be predicted to test data)

In this model, the input data are known from trained data that is called evidence. For output the outcomes are to be predicted to test data.

In Naive Bayes classification, prediction is classified as two types: Single feature prediction and multi feature prediction.

$$P(Y = k|X) = \frac{P(X|Y = k) \times P(Y = k)}{P(X)} \tag{1}$$

Single feature prediction

$$P(Y = k|X_1 \ldots X_n) = \frac{P(X_1|Y = k) * P(X_2|Y = k) * \ldots * P(X_n|Y = k)P(Y = k)}{P(X_1) \times P(X_2) \ldots P(X_n)}$$

Multi feature prediction

$$\tag{2}$$

This model has been proved as fruitful in text classification challenges. Naive Bayes classifier works in Bayes theorem is given in the Eq. 1.

$$P(A|B) = \frac{P(B|A) \times P(A)}{P(B)} \tag{3}$$

The output(m) of given class label (C) can be calculated using the Eq. 2.

$$\hat{m} = k \in \{1, \ldots\ldots, k\} argmax(C_k \prod_{i=1}^{n} p(x_i|C_k) \tag{4}$$

ALGORITHM FOR NAIVE BAYES CLASSIFICATION:

TRAINMULTINOMIAL NB (C, D)
1 V ← EXTRACT NAMED ENTITIES (D)
1   N ← COUNT DOCS(C)
2 for each c ∈ C
3   do N_c ← COUNT DOCS in CATEGORY (D, c)
4   prior[c] ← $\frac{N_c}{N}$
5     $text_c$ ← CONCODANATE TEXT OF ALL DOCS IN CATEGORY (D, c)
6   for each t ∈ V
7   do T_{ct} ← COUNT TOKENS OF SAME TERMS ($text_c$, t)
8   for each t ∈ V
9   do condprob [t][c] ← $\frac{T_{ct}+1}{\sum_{t'} (T_{ct'}+1)}$
10   return V, prior, condprob

TESTMULTINOMIAL NB (C, V, prior, condprob, d)
1 W ← EXTRACT TOKEN FROM DOC (V, d)

2 *for each* $c \in C$
3   *do* $score[c] \leftarrow \log prior\ [c]$
4   *for each* $t \in W$
5   *do* $score\ [c] \leftarrow \log condprob[t][c]$
6 *return* $\arg max_{c \in C}\ Score[c]$

The workflow of Naive Bayes classification is described in the Fig. 2.

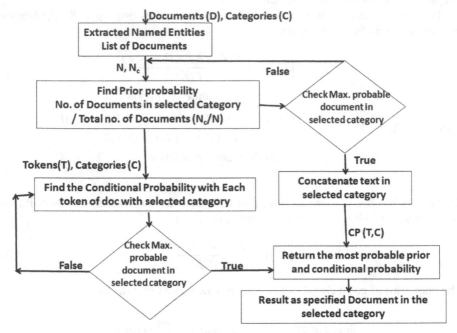

Fig. 2. Workflow of Naive Bayes classifier

4.2 Support Vector Machine

The Support Vector Machine (SVM) is the most well-known Supervised Learning model, and it's used to solve problems like classification and regression. It is mostly used in Machine Learning to solve classification problems. The goal of the SVM algorithm is to find the optimum line or decision limit for isolating n-dimensional space into classes so that fresh data may be readily placed in the correct classification later. Text classification, image classification, face detection, and object identification are all done using the SVM model.

Linear and non-linear SVM classification models are the two types of SVM classification models.

In linear SVM classification model the classification is done within the two axes values. This model can create classification line based on the values. But in the non-linear SVM model kernel trick is used to perform the classification.

The derivation of SVM in linear model.

$$Y = mX + c \tag{5}$$

$$X_2 = mX_1 + c \tag{6}$$

$$mX_1 - X_2 + c = 0 \tag{7}$$

Change the notation of gradient m into weight $m = w_1/w_2$ and $b = c/w_2$ $w_1X_1 + w_2X_2 + b = 0$ (for 2 dimension).

$w_1X_1 + w_2X_2 + w_3X_3 + b = 0$ (for 3 dimension)
$w_1X_1 + w_2X_2 + w_3X_3 \ldots\ldots\ldots\ldots + w_hX_h + b = 0$ (for h dimension)

To write in vector form

$$W^TX + b = 0 \tag{8}$$

$$y_i(wTxi + b) >= 1 \; for \; \forall I \tag{9}$$

But for non-linear model the following formula is used to perform the classification.

$$K(\vec{x}, \vec{l^i}) = e^{-\frac{\left\| \vec{x}\vec{l^i} \right\|^2}{2\sigma^2}} \tag{10}$$

ALGORITHM FOR SUPPORT VECTOR MACHINES CLASSIFICATION
MULTINOMIAL SVM (C, D, Train_X, Train_Y)
1 V ← EXTRACT NAMED ENTITIES (D)
2 E ← LabelEncoder(C)
3 for each c ∈ C
4 do Train$_Y$ ← Encoder_Fit_Transform(Train_Y)
5 do Train$_Y$ ← Encoder_Fit_Transform(Test_Y)
6 for each c ∈ C
7   do TF(c) ← TF(Text in C)
8   do IDF(c) ← IDF(Tokens in selected category Documents)
9 SVM ← svm classifier(c ← 1.0, kernal ← linear, degree ← 3, gamma ← auto)
10 for each c ∈ SVM
11 do SVM. Fit (Train_Tfidf, Train_Y)
11 do prediction_svm ← SVM. Predict(Test_X_TFIDF)
12 return (predictions_SVM, Text_Y)

The above algorithm explains the logic of SVM classifier. The workflow of SVM classifier is given in Fig. 3.

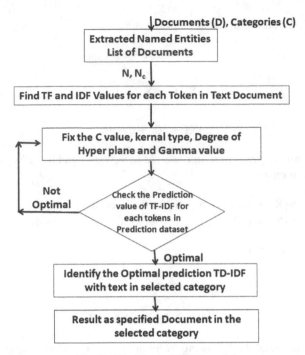

Fig. 3. Workflow of SVM model

4.3 K-Nearest Neighbor Classifier

The K-NN classifier is supervised machine learning algorithm for text categorization. Given a text document, the K-NN algorithm finds the K nearest neighbor element among the whole training documents. It uses the categories of K-NN to calculate the weight of neighbor candidate. The similarity score of each document with the selected word is to be calculated and the minimum value of neighbor weight is to be found. The resulting weighted sum is used as neighbor score. It is to be obtained for the test document. Based on the weighted value the word is to be categorized.

The KNN classification is done to draw a classification distance line based on the parameters. The distance learning formula is,

$$Euclidean\ distance(d) = \sqrt{\sqrt{(x_2 x_1)^2 + (y_2 y_1)^2}} \tag{11}$$

Steps in implementation of KNN

1: Choose the number K of neighbors
2: Take the K nearest neighbors of the new data point, according to the Euclidean distance
3: Among these K neighbors, count eh number of data points in each category.
4: Assign the new data point to the category where you counted the most neighbors
   Workflow of KNN is given in Fig. 4.

Based on the Euclidean distance evaluation, the distance learning line can be drawn between the actual attributes to predicting attributes.

ALGORITHM FOR KNN CLASSIFICATION

Algorithm KNN (C, D)

1 $c \leftarrow$ *EXTRACT NAMED ENTITIES (D)*

2 *for each $c \in C$*

3   **do** $N_c \leftarrow$ *K Nearest Neigbour (D)*

4   **do** $i \leftarrow$ *COUNT DOCS(N_c)*

5   **do** $prob[c][d] \leftarrow \frac{i}{k}$

6   **do** $C \leftarrow argmax_c \times prob\ [c][d]$

7   $text_c \leftarrow$ *CONCODANATE TEXT OF ALL DOCS IN CATEGORY (D, c)*

8   **return** $C, text_c$

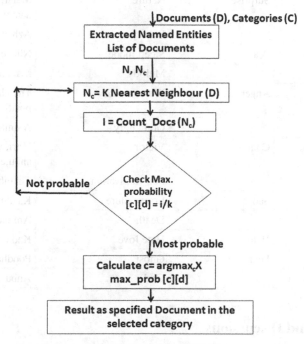

Fig. 4. Workflow of KNN

The above three machine learning models were used to do the classification task to classify the documents according to the categories. The performances of all the three models were compared.

4.4 Emotional Keywords

See (Table 2).

Table 2. Sample keywords for proposed Tamil lyric emotional labels

Navarasa emotion labels	English emotion labels	Proposed Tamil Song lyrics Emotion Labels	Sample Keywords
Shringara	Love	Love	Kadhal, Mayile, Kuyile,Maane, Theane, unakku, unnai, kalyanam, anbu
		Romance	Kadhal, malar, thamarai
Hasya	Joy	Happy	Vetri, raja, mudhalali
Adbhutha	Surprise	Nature	Malar, malai, punjai, nanjai
		Beauty	Azhagu, penmai
Shantha	Peace	Sleep mode	Nilave
		Melody	Maalai, nilave
Roudhra	Anger	Women angry	Thendral, puyal, poatti
		God angry	Amman, kaali, sivan
Veera	Courage	Victory	Vetri, velvadhu, anpu,ethiri
		Self motivation	Thambi
Karuna	Sad	Love failure	Kaadhal, kalyanam
		Death	Amma, thaayin
Bhibatsa	Hate	Hate love	Kadhal
Bhayanakam	Fear	Ghost	Poodham, pei, pisasu
		God	Anbu, kadavul

5   Results and Discussions

By implementing these machine learning methods, the lyric corpus has been classified as the following number of emotions (Table 3).

Table 3. Emotion identification results

Tamil song emotional labels	Total number of lyrics	Identified by Naïve Bayes model	Identified by SVM model	Identified by K-NN model
Love	532	478	467	437
Romance	453	421	417	434
Happy	290	243	245	213
Nature	148	90	121	116
Beauty	185	156	113	121
Sleep mode	74	43	32	44
Melody	186	146	107	142
Women angry	18	12	16	15
God angry	15	11	11	12
Victory	12	6	6	5
Self motivation	8	4	5	5
Love failure	48	32	27	30
Death	27	18	15	20
Hate love	68	53	47	42
Ghost	24	19	15	13
God	47	26	32	28
Total	**2135**	**1758**	**1676**	**1677**

6 Metrics for Evaluation

The accuracy of the models is calculated using the formula as given in Eq. 12.

$$Accuracy = \frac{n}{N} \tag{12}$$

where, n – number of correctly predicted documents.

N – Number of documents in the corpus.

In any machine learning methods the evaluation criteria is shown as following confusion matrix. The confusion matrix is a summary of prediction results on a classification problem (Table 4).

Table 4. Confusion matrix of classification problem

	Event	No-event
Event	True positive	False positive
No-event	False negative	True negative

The values of confusion matrix are,

- True positive – For correctly predicted event values
- False positive – For incorrectly predicted event values
- True negative – For correctly predicted no-event values
- False negative – For incorrectly predicted no-event values

Based on the confusion matrix the evaluation values are calculated as,

$$Precision = \frac{true\ positives}{true\ positives + false\ positives} \tag{13}$$

$$Recall = \frac{true\ positives}{true\ negatives + false\ negatives} \tag{14}$$

$$F1 = 2 \times \frac{Precision \times Recall}{Precision + Recall} \tag{15}$$

By calculating the evaluation metrics using formula 12, 13, 14, and 15 the following details are captured (Fig. 5 and Fig. 6, Table 5 and Table 6).

Table 5. Accuracy metrics

Tamil song emotional labels	Total number of lyrics	Identified by Naïve Bayes model	Identified by SVM model	Identified by K-NN model
Total	2135	1758	1676	1677
Accuracy		82.3	78.5	78.5

To verify these evaluation metric values from confusion matrix, we concluded that Naive Bayes model performed to identify the emotion labels for given Tamil song lyrics when compared with other models.

Accuracy for Emotion Detection

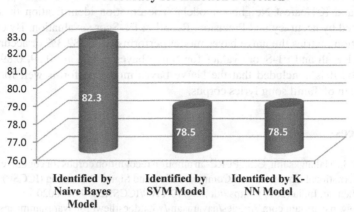

Fig. 5. Accuracy comparison

Table 6. Evaluation metrics

Machine learning models	Precision	Recall	F1 score
Naive Bayes model	0.898	0.89	0.894
Support vector machine model	0.898	0.804	0.848
K-nearest neighbor model	0.935	0.823	0.875

Evaluation Metrics for Emotion Detection by Machine Learning Methods

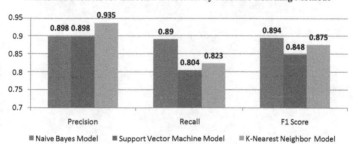

Fig. 6. Evaluation metrics comparison

7 Conclusion

The novel emotion detection approach is proposed using machine learning methods and implemented with Tamil song lyrics composed by Isai Gnani Ilayaraja which are collected from various sources. The corpus size was 2248 lyrics. When these corpus lyrics are pre-processed the corpus size is reduced as 2135 lyrics. The emotional labels were identified using keywords assigned for each labels. Three machine learning methods are used to check the identify emotion labels. They are Naive Bayes, Support Vector Machine, and K-Nearest Neighbor models. The emotion identification these models are evaluated by accuracy and Precision, Recall & F1-Score evaluation. By comparing the evaluation metrics the naïve bayes model performs good (82.3% of accuracy). The Precision, Recall and F1-Score values for Naïve bayes model are 0.89, 0.89 and 0.89 respectively. It is concluded that the Naïve bayes model performs well for Emotion Identification of Tamil song lyrics corpus.

References

1. Sreeja, P.S., Mahalakshmi, G.S.: PERC-an emotion recognition corpus for cognitive poems. In: 2019 International Conference on Communication and Signal Processing (ICCSP), pp. 0200–0207. Chennai, India (2019). https://doi.org/10.1109/ICCSP.2019.8698020
2. http://www.navarasam.com/Articles/navarasam/whatdoesthewordnavarasammeans
3. https://timesofindia.indiatimes.com/blogs/tea-with-life/navratri-is-the-festival-to-control-nine-emotions/
4. Guo, J.: Deep learning approach to text analysis for human emotion detection from big data. J. Intell. Syst. **31**(1), 113–126 (2022). https://doi.org/10.1515/jisys-2022-0001
5. Mukhopadhyay, M., Dey, A., Shaw, R.N., Ghosh, A.: Facial emotion recognition based on textural pattern and convolutional neural network. In: 2021 IEEE 4th International Conference on Computing, Power and Communication Technologies (GUCON), pp. 1–6. Kuala Lumpur, Malaysia (2021). https://doi.org/10.1109/GUCON50781.2021.9573860
6. Sreeja, P.S., Mahalakshmi, G.S.: Emotion recognition from poems by maximum posterior probability. Int. J. Comput. Sci. Inform. Secur. **14**, 36–43 (2016)
7. Saini, J.R., Kaur, J.: Kāvi: an annotated corpus of Punjabi poetry with emotion detection based on 'Navrasa.' Procedia Comput. Sci. **167**, 1220–1229 (2020). https://doi.org/10.1016/j.procs.2020.03.436

AI Based Interactive System-HOMIE

Ishika Aggarwal[1], Subrata Sahana[1(✉)] (iD), Sanjoy Das[2], and Indrani Das[3] (iD)

[1] Department of Computer Science and Engineering, Sharda University, Greater Noida, India
`2020549602.ishika@pg.sharda.ac.in`, `subrata.sahana@sharda.ac.in`
[2] Department of Computer Science, Indira Gandhi National Tribal University-RCM,
Manipur, India
[3] Department of Computer Science, Assam University, Silchar, India

Abstract. The main purpose of this chapter is to propose an AI Interactive system. In today's Fast Working world, hard work and time management holds a key feature. While in that time management one doesn't get enough time to explore himself, his/her emotions and enough time to interact with Friends and Family. This busy schedule leads one apart from socialization, and it's the key to mental wellbeing.

The term loneliness is often misunderstood. It is not an objective condition, but rather a subjective one. Loneliness is different for everyone and there are many factors that contribute to it, including the feelings of isolation, anxiety, mental health and depression.

Machine learning has been used for many purposes and it can also be used to help people with loneliness, anxiety, and depression. Machine learning is helping people who are lonely and struggling with anxiety and depression. The technology is being used to create virtual assistants that provide support and guidance. By using machine learning, these assistants can learn about the user's specific needs and provide targeted assistance.

Keywords: Depression · Anxiety · Loneliness · AI technology · Machine learning and Stress

1 Introduction

The motive of this chapter is to implement an idea, by which we can reduce the mental stress on people's mind by implanting a simple idea which includes the basics of two highly advanced technologies, i.e. AI and machine learning? The idea is to make a digital roommate for those who live alone, which can be made more responsive by syncing with cloud (which is feature of AI interactive System like Google home).

The plan is to make a pair of machines which includes a Smart Band, and an AI Interacting System. As soon as one enters home with the band on their wrist, the AI will automatically detect it, and will eventually recognize their mental state/ mood, and will start a conversation. So that it can alter your mind state and give you a more pleasant mind-set. So that one can work with a better mood and achieve his/her peak working state.

R. N. Shaw et al. (Eds.): ICACIS 2022, CCIS 1749, pp. 339–347, 2023.
https://doi.org/10.1007/978-3-031-25088-0_30

Machine learning is commonly used for analysing and predicting outcomes however; machine learning can be used on a more personal level which is used for people with anxiety and depression. It's trying to find people who are lonely and connect them with the resources they need [1].

Machine learning has been used to try and address the problem of loneliness. The idea behind this technology is that if we can understand what causes loneliness in general then we can better understand how to solve it for individuals. In order to use AI as a solution for loneliness, we need to first understand it. The three primary causes of loneliness are: Lack of social support Lack of connection to the broader community feeling disconnected from one's own identity [2]. These factors can be explored through predictive models that take these three types of information into account and predict how an individual may be feeling, based on their life situation.

Machine learning has been used for many purposes and it can also be used to help people with loneliness, anxiety, and depression. It is a new technology, and it is used to study and predict the behaviour of people. It is used to find out how people are feeling and to help them in their daily lives. It can help people to understand their mental state and provide them with the necessary help. Machine learning has been used for many purposes, and it can also be used to help people with loneliness.

Studies have shown that machine learning can help people who are struggling with anxiety and depression. The machine learning algorithms can be used to predict a person's risk of developing anxiety or depression, and they can also be used to recommend treatments. The advantage of machine learning is that the computer is not biased and it can detect patterns that a human may not see [3].

One way is that machine learning can help to identify different types of loneliness. Machine learning can also track a person's mood and activities to help identify when they are feeling lonely. It is effective in reducing loneliness and it has worked for people with anxiety and depression. The algorithms are being used to predict who is at risk for loneliness and to provide support for people who are already lonely.

This technology can help people who are struggling with loneliness and anxiety or depression. By using machine learning, these people can get the help they need to connect with others and feel less alone. Machine learning helps lonely people to reduce their anxiety and depression levels.

The machine-learning algorithm works by providing people with feedback about their social media interactions. This can help people to feel more connected to others and to reduce their loneliness [5].

2 Literature Review

Distressing emotions toolkit: it is a literature content which contains the information of how to calm you down [16] Table 1.

    Watson Tone analyzer: It analyzes the mental state of any person based on his/her tone of conversation [17].

    Feel: it is a smart band which analyzes the emotional state and is also connected to an application [18].

Table 1. Other products for better emotional state

Product available	Company	Year	Cost	Features
Distressing emotions toolkit	Healthy mind concepts	2018	$50.00	The toolkit consists of information, text, images and other contents. This Toolkit is useful for you to learn how to handle your distressing emotions or feelings
Watson tone analyzer	IBM	2015	Standard: $325-$6500	Using Tone analyzer can detect each caller's mood, whether happy, angry or disgusted
Feel	Sentio-Solution Inc.	2016	$149	Feel wristband monitors a variety of physiological signals throughout the day to recognize changes in your emotions Science
Healthy office	Toshiba Research Europe Ltd.	2016		He Healthy Office framework for learning mood recognition models and aggregating results in a privacy – preserving manner

Healthy office: Similar to feel mentioned above, this device also analyzes and alerts about the emotional state, while its use was within an organization, for employees of that organization.

3 Components of HOMIE

Though the device includes a Smart Band and an AI Interacting System but there are various other unmentioned technologies used:

1. Body Temperature and Blood Pressure

   - By Smart Band we could analyze the body factors,

2. AI responsive Server

   - AI interactive device will be connected to the server which will give responses according to mood.

3. Applets as per requirements.

  • Applets will be activated depending on the emotional state of individual.

4. Wi-Fi, Bluetooth

  • Interconnection between Smart Band, AI interactive device and servers.
  • Smart Band(s) (Fig. 1)
  • AI responsive devices (Fig. 2)

Fig. 1. Smart bands

Fig. 2. AI responsive device

4   Working of HOMIE

The most important part of this device would be that AI Interactive system would detect the Band, as soon as wearer enters the home/vicinity of AI device's detection. The band will send the ECG, PPG, body Temperature reports to AI device which further sends the data to the server, where server would apply a predefined algorithm to detect one's Emotion Arousal, and give a command to AI System such that it would start a conversation.

The conversion will be according to the person's mind state detected by the server using the algorithm. The conversation will be such that it leads to better mental state. It can also use the body factors to analyze the physical state also (Fig. 3).

A. *Block Diagram*

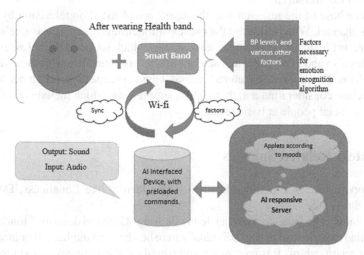

Fig. 3. Proposed architecture

B. *Effect*

- As everybody know that a speech or simple talk can change a person's mood from anger, sadness into a confident and happy person. Like when a person is in anger or sadness it will start a conversation by simple sarcasm.
- While on the other hand for people who are suffering from mental problems related to depression, anxiety, alienation. One will never know easily whether he/she is suffering any of the mental disease until it's too late, most of the people don't even consider it as a disease while it's deadly one.
- But our device can detect it at a small level, which can be treated easily and not even require heavy medicine dosage. One never feels alone as long as one is having conversation.

C. *Extra Features*

- Emergency alert: The Ai will detect emergency situations by using same emotional arousal algorithm. It will notify the nearest hospital which helps to evacuate deadly conditions.
- Calling feature: There will be absolute chances when one will not like to interact with a recorded voice and he/ she will like to have a real time conversation with

their friends. Hence, the user can request a conversation to any person from their contact list.

- Alert features: The device will notify one about his/her important events, and also alerting them about various small things (drinking water to prevent dehydration, BP levels etc.) which lead to better and healthy lifestyle.

D. **Base of the Research**

The base of the research was the report broadcasted on television by a certain news channel. Which featured the causes of loneliness and it affects one's lifestyle. The report featured various other case studies which included the below-mentioned studies also and how adults and senior citizens are found to suffer more from these problems. The report also featured various ways to escape these problems. Which are taken into consideration and though of a simple way, which included rehabilitation of less social people at basic levels.

5 Context Related Surveys

This report features the report related to major factors like Loneliness, Depression, Anxiety, Stress etc.

Loneliness: The Dutch researcher Jenny de Jong- Gierveld described loneliness as a state of mind experienced by the individual where he/she feels unpleasant or inadmissible quality of relationships. It is a complex and usually unpleasant emotional response for isolation.

It includes anxious feelings about lack of communication or connection with other people/ beings.

Loneliness doesn't depend on number of friends you have or how much time you spend alone or your social standings, rather it can be defined by a longing for a greater social interaction.

A. **Why is Loneliness bad for us**

The health consequences of loneliness have become the focus of talks in recent years. Media also warns us of loneliness epidemic. There are complex links between loneliness and its physical and mental consequences.

One of the reasons that loneliness is so bad for us is because it makes it harder for us to control our daily habit and behavior. It also affects our perseverance and willpower and makes it harder to regulate our behavior: which lead middle aged adults to drink alcohol, have unhealthy diets. Drug abuse is also observed to be linked to loneliness.

B. **October 2014 – Loneliness and social isolation – Results**

More than 2500 people responded to relationships Australia's online survey in October, 2014. Almost 80% of survey respondents identified as female. 90% of survey respondents were in age group of 20–59 years (Fig. 4 and Fig. 5).

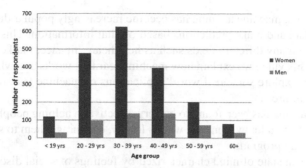

Fig. 4. Loneliness and social support demographics (Men & Women with age groups in the survey)

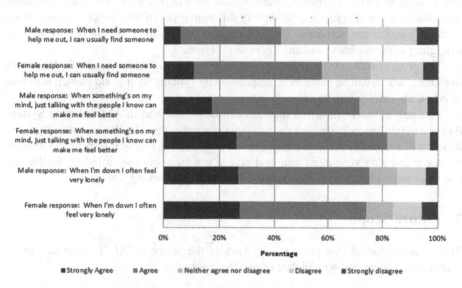

Fig. 5. Loneliness and social support survey output graphic

C. *October 2014 – Loneliness and social isolation – Results*

The first feature missing here is Cost effectiveness of the final products. Homie also include interactive system which helps one relieve themselves. Other products will only act as a wearable device or readable context but Homie helps one to overcome the feeling of loneliness. As well as there are many other additional features mentioned above.

6   Conclusions

Machine learning has been used for many purposes and it can also be used to help people with loneliness. There are some companies that have developed chatbots that can interact with people and provide them with emotional support.

In recent years, machine learning has become increasingly popular due to its ability to learn from data and make predictions based on that information. This technology is being applied to many different fields such as healthcare, finance, marketing, and even agriculture. In this video we explain how machine learning works and what problems it solves. We then explore some real world applications of machine learning in our lives now and in the future.

Machine learning has been found to be very effective in helping people with anxiety and depression. If you know someone who is lonely, encourage them to seek help from a machine learning program.

Loneliness is a state of mind characterized by feelings of social disconnection and lack of companionship. Many studies have shown that loneliness is associated with poor health outcomes, including higher mortality rates and increased risk of chronic diseases. There are many different types of loneliness, and each person experiences it in a different way. Machine learning can help to identify different types of loneliness, as well as track a person's mood and activities. This information can be used to help people who are struggling with loneliness and anxiety or depression.

The product will help those lonely people to have a digital roommate for those who live alone, which can be made more responsive by syncing with cloud (which is feature of AI interactive System like Google home).

This pair of machines which includes a Smart Band, and an AI Interacting System. As soon as one enters home with the band on their wrist, the AI will automatically detect it, and will eventually recognize their mental state/ mood, and will start a conversation. So that it can alter your mind state and give you a more pleasant mindset. So that one can work with a better mood and achieve his/her peak working state.

7 Future Scope

The future scope of this project is as vast as the scope of AI. The device can be continuously upgraded with update of used technologies.

1. The device can be continuously upgraded in term of software and hardware with development of technology.
2. The AI interactive session can be updated to latest queries, methods to stimulation of mood, according to research growth.
3. The speed of interaction automatically increases with increase in data transfer speed in future data services.
4. On the other hand, the hardware can be made more durable.
5. The processers can be upgraded to latest technology, by simple alteration in language of source code

References

1. Miller, R.E., LaValle, L.: Writing for Wikipedia: Applying Disciplinary Knowledge to the Biggest Encyclopedia. ACRL (2022)

2. Smith, D., Leonis, T., Anandavalli, S.: Belonging and loneliness in cyberspace: impacts of social media on adolescents' well-being. Aust. J. Psychol. **73**(1), 12–23 (2021)
3. Nikolova, G.: Determination of the stress intensity factor of polymer composites with recycled materials. Eng. Sci. **LIX**, 24–33 (2022)
4. Weber, R.: The lonely society-philip slater: the pursuit of loneliness: american culture at the breaking point (Boston: Beacon Press, 1970. Pp. xiii, 154. $7.50). The Rev. Politics **33**(3), 425–427 (1971)
5. Ménard, M., Richard, P., Hamdi, H., Daucé, B., Yamaguchi, T.: Emotion Recognition based on Heart Rate and Skin Conductance. In: PhyCS, pp. 26–32. (2015)
6. Das, S., Das, I., Nath Shaw, R., Ghosh, A.: Advance machine learning and artificial intelligence applications in service robot. In: Nath Shaw, R., Ghosh, A., Balas, V.E., Bianchini, M. (eds.) Artificial Intelligence for Future Generation Robotics, pp. 83–91. Elsevier (2021). https://doi.org/10.1016/B978-0-323-85498-6.00002-2
7. Fischer, C.: Incentives can't buy me knowledge: the missing effects of appreciation and aligned performance appraisals on knowledge sharing of public employees. Rev. Public Pers. Adm. **42**(2), 368–389 (2022)
8. Samanci, H., Thulin, M.: Act like a human, think like a bot: a study on the capabilities required to implement a social bot on a social media platform (2022)
9. Guillemette, A., et al.: Impact and appreciation of two methods aiming at reducing hazardous drug environmental contamination: the centralization of the priming of IV tubing in the pharmacy and use of a closed-system transfer device. J. Oncol. Pharm. Pract. **20**(6), 426–432 (2014)
10. Haas, E.J.: The role of supervisory support on workers' health and safety performance. Health Commun. **35**(3), 364–374 (2020)
11. Robert, A., Suelves, J.M., Armayones, M., Ashley, S.: Internet use and suicidal behaviors: internet as a threat or opportunity? Telemedicine e-Health **21**(4), 306–311 (2015)
12. Drum, D.J., Denmark, A.B.: Campus suicide prevention: bridging paradigms and forging partnerships. Harvard Rev. Psychiatry **20**(4), 209–221 (2012)
13. Henry, A., Wright, K., Moran, A.: Online activism and redress for institutional child abuse: function and rhetoric in survivor advocacy group tweets. Int. Groups Adv. **11**(4), 493–516 (2022). https://doi.org/10.1057/s41309-022-00165-0
14. Gründer, G.: How we live together. In: How Do We Want to Live?, pp. 129–137. Springer, Heidelberg (2022). https://doi.org/10.1007/978-3-662-64225-2_10
15. Wallace, S.G.: Kids Out of the House-Lonely But (Almost) Never Alone (2019)
16. Mascarenhas, S., et al.: A virtual agent toolkit for serious games developers. In: 2018 IEEE Conference on Computational Intelligence and Games (CIG), pp. 1–7. IEEE (2018)
17. Norman, K.P., et al.: Natural language processing tools for assessing progress and outcome of two veteran populations: cohort study from a novel online intervention for posttraumatic growth. JMIR Formative Res. **4**(9), e17424 (2020)
18. Söderberg, E.: An evaluation of the usage of affective computing in healthcare. In: USCCS 2022, pp. 69–78 (2022)
19. Zenonos, A., Khan, A., Kalogridis, G., Vatsikas, S., Lewis, T., Sooriyabandara, M.: Healthy-Office: Mood recognition at work using smartphones and wearable sensors. In: 2016 IEEE International Conference on Pervasive Computing and Communication Workshops (PerCom Workshops), pp. 1–6. IEEE (2016)
20. Khurana, Y., Jindal, S., Gunwant, H., Gupta, D.: Mental health prognosis using machine learning. SSRN 4060009 (2022)

Factors Influencing Security Issues in Cloud Computing

Vanshika Maheshwari[1], Subrata Sahana[1]([✉]) [iD], Sanjoy Das[2], Indrani Das[3] [iD], and Ankush Ghosh[4]

[1] Department of Computer Science and Engineering, Sharda University, Greater Noida, India
`2020572155.vanshika@pg.sharda.ac.in, subrata.sahana@sharda.ac.in`
[2] Department of Computer Science, Indira Gandhi National Tribal University-RCM, Manipur, India
[3] Department of Computer Science, Assam University, Silchar, India
[4] Center for Research & Development, Chandigarh University, Sahibzada Ajit Singh Nagar, India

Abstract. Computing is a new computing paradigm that enables firms to do this without making a huge initial investment. Despite the potential advantages of cloud technology, modeling security remains a worry, limiting cloud model adoption. Additional factors such as prototype model, multi-tenancy, adaptability, and the tiered dependency stacking have been introduced to the problem scope beneath the cloud model, increasing the complexity of the security threat. In this work, we examine the cloud security challenge in depth. We investigated the issue from the standpoint of a cloud system, cloud service delivery models, computing stakeholders, and cloud stakeholders.

Keywords: Cloud computing · Cloud management · Cloud security · SaaS · PaaS · IaaS · Cloud computing STACK

1 Introduction

Web-based, highly scalable cloud-based systems that deliver computing capacity "as a service" are known as Cloud Computing. The National Institute of Standards and Technology (NIST) came up with the most widely acknowledged definition of computer platform (NIST) [1]. The cloud model has two fundamental characteristics: multi-tenancy and elasticity. Elasticity allows a service's resources to be scaled up and down in response to current service demands. Multi-tenancy allows multiple tenants to share the same service instance. Both qualities are aimed at maximizing resource use, lowering costs, and increasing service availability.

Researchers and practitioners have accepted cloud computing as a means of supporting a wide range of applications, especially physically demanding applications to inexpensive services. According to a Gartner survey [2], the cloud industry was worth USD 58.6 billion during 2009, $ 68 billion by 2010, and $ 148 billions in 2014. Cloud

R. N. Shaw et al. (Eds.): ICACIS 2022, CCIS 1749, pp. 348–358, 2023.
https://doi.org/10.1007/978-3-031-25088-0_31

computing appears to be a promising platform based on these findings. On the other hand, it draws the attention of attackers to any design flaws that may exist.

Despite the many benefits and profit that cloud computing could provide, there are a number of unsolved issues that are affecting this model's credibility at this point and pervasiveness. The open research difficulties with the cloud computing idea include locks, multi-tenancy, and isolation, information management, support, flexibility motors, SLA management staff, and cloud security, to name a few.

From the standpoint of cloud users, the main barrier to adoption of the cloud computing system is security. [3] even though:

- Businesses outsource system security to a third-party hosting provider (loss of control).
- The existence of resources belonging to different tenants in the same area using same system edition and being unaware of the security controls.
- The SLAs between cloud consumers and cloud providers do not include any security guarantees.
- The risk of an attack grows when this combination of valuable assets is hosted on publicly accessible infrastructure.

Security requires a considerable expenditure, a considerable lot of resources, but is a difficult topic to master from the perspective of cloud providers. However, as recently said, removing security from cloud services model's future revenue stream will result in a drop in revenue. As a result, cloud providers must comprehend their customers' worries and research innovative privacy solutions to satisfy them.

The existing issues and challenges concerning cloud computing security are analysed in this chapter. Concerns about service delivery models, architecture, cloud stakeholders, and cloud characteristics are classified into four categories. Our goal is to figure out where the cloud model has flaws. A thorough investigation is conducted to determine the fundamental causes of each issue. This will help caps and security suppliers grasp the situation better. It also aids researchers in determining the proportions and gaps in the current problem.

2 Literature Survey

Several studies have highlighted the difficulties and issues surrounding cloud computing security. The Cloud Services Use Case group [3] examines the many uses case – and their corresponding needs – that can be found on the cloud storage. Users, programmers, and domain experts are all involved in the use case analysis. ENISA [4] looked at the many security flaws associated with cloud computing adoption, as well as the commodity at risk, as well as the likelihood, repercussions, and cloud storage concerns that could result to such dangers. In "Key Risks to Cloud Computing", the CSA [5] analyzes similar activities. Balachandra and data localization, separation, and recovery aims. Data protection, price, and secret information privacy are among the high-level security concerns raised by Kresimir et al. [7] in cloud computing platforms. ITIL, ISO/IEC 27001, and the Standard Virtual machines Format were among the several security management standards Kresimir mentioned (OVF). XML-attacks, Browser-related assaults, and getting flooded attacks are among the technological security concerns that have emerged because of cloud computing adoption, according to Meiko et al. [8]. Bernd and associates [9] highlight the cloud service's security issues. The potential vulnerabilities were grouped into three areas by the authors: technology-related, cloud-related, or security regulations. The security issues of cloud – based deployment methods are highlighted by Subashini et al. [10], who focus on the SaaS paradigm. The Cloud Computing Essential Regions (CSA) [5] outlines fundamental characteristics of cloud computing. In each area, they offer a set of standards for cloud service providers, clients, and business assets to adhere to. On many of these topics, the CSA released a series of extensive publications.

To discover the core causes and important contributing aspects in the security problems identified in earlier research, we investigated the cloud in depth. This will help with an improved understanding of the issue and delivery of solutions.

3   Architecture of Cloud Computing and Its Implications for Security

Three customer service mechanism and three basic deployment options are available inside the Cloud Computing platform. [1]. The following are the models for deployment: (1) A private cloud is really a dedicated platform for a single organization. (2) The term public cloud refers to a cloud platform that enables anyone to sign up and use the infrastructure. (3) A hybrid cloud is a private cloud with public cloud services. Because clients can use public clouds to host their services, including criminal users, They're the most vulnerable type of deployment. [6] go over the criteria of the security SLA.

Figure 1 depicts the various. Delivery models: (.IaaS) Infrastructure_as_a_service: As internet-based services, cloud providers supply cloud servers, storage, and networking. This service model is supported by virtualization technologies. Amazon EC2 was a very well IaaS provider.

(.PaaS) Platform as a service (PaaS) is a model in which cloud providers supply platform, resources, as well as other services that allow clients to build, install, and they can administer their own programmed without having to download anything and installing most of these gadgets or other services from their own computers. The PaaS paradigm can be built up on the surface of cloud environments or on top about an IaaS architecture. Most well PaaS solutions are Google App engine and Microsoft Azure.

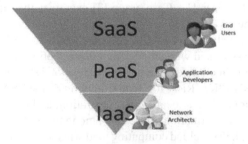

Fig. 1. Model for delivering cloud services [18]

SaaS: When cloud providers offer end users programmers housed on cloud infras-tructure as an internet-based service, they are referred to as software as a service. This strategy can be used to PaaS, Lass, or cloud platform. Salesforce is a fantastic example of a software-as-a-service (SaaS) application.

As shown in Fig. 1, each delivery model offers a variety of possible implementa-tions, complicating the establishment of a security related architecture for every service delivery model. Furthermore, different service methodologies may coexist in a single cloud platform, complicating the system security process even further.

4 Charactersistics of Cloud Computing and Security Implications

Multi-tenancy means that tenants share computing resources, storage, services, and applications. Figure 2 depicts the many techniques to multi-tenancy realization. Tenants in method 4 are routed to a load balancer, which routes requests to the most appropriate instance based on the load on the current instance. The most dangerous approaches are 3 and 4, because tenants are coexisting in memory and hardware on the same process. Secure multi-tenancy is essential because resource sharing jeopardizes the integrity of tenants' IT assets. In ability to implement secure multi-tenancy, there will be data separa-tion and regional accountability, In preventing data breaches, where renters have limited information or control over the actual position of their resource (may have the most power over file storage), like as country and the people or territorial level). a series of coordinated attacks aimed at co-locating with target assets [11]. In IaaS, isolation should be taken into account VM storage, CPU, storage, memory in databases, and networks. Isolating between operational services and API calls should be a part of PaaS isolation. Isolation should be utilised in SaaS to separate transactions and tenant data carried out by various tenant on the same instance.

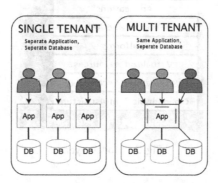

Fig. 2. Multi-tenancy approach [12]

The ability to modify the pool of options given to a system based on the market is referred to as flexibility. Other tenants can use a tenant's system places resources thanks to the flexibility to adjust up or down a tenant's resources it's possible that it'll raise privacy worries. Tenant A, for example, downsized to free up space, which are now allocated to renter B, who utilizes them to determine tenant A's earlier contents. Elasticity also contains a service allocation mechanism that keeps track of the provider's pool of available services. This is the list that is used to assign resources to services. Those deployment algorithms should take into account cloud customers' security and regulatory concerns, such as not putting competing services on same server and keeping data within tenants' country borders. In order to fulfil demand and maximize resource utilization, A migration technique for which services are migrated by one host system to another and then by one cloud to another may be included in placement engines. The same security restrictions should be considered in this migration method. In addition, Users' security preferences should be sent together with the programmer services and initiates a mechanism for enforcing security requirements on unknown settings as described by cloud users, as well as modifying the current cloud security architecture.

5 Deep Dependencies of Cloud Computing Stack

The cloud-based approach is built on a high stack of interconnected object layers, each of which is dependent on the lower layers for functionality and security. The IaaS Cloud infrastructural layer (storage, networks, and servers), This paradigm encompasses the virtualization layer (hypervisors) as well as the virtualized resource layer (VMs, virtual storage, virtual networks). PaaS is a model that includes the platform layer (Servers for apps and websites, as well as IDEs and other tools), as well as the APIs and Services layers. This layer is reliant on IaaS-provided resource virtualization. As demonstrated in Fig. 3, The SaaS model refers to software and services that are made available to end customers as a service. When offering services to multi-tenant, it relies on the layer of platform to serve the service and a layer of hypervisor to improve resource consumption.

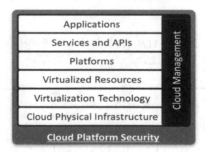

Fig. 3. Model layers

Because the security of one object/layer is reliant on the safety of the others, the extensive dependence stacking among clouds entities worsens the cloud security dilemma. Any compromise of any cloud item has ramifications for the entire cloud platform's security. Each layer/object in the cloud has its list of expectations and risks, therefore delivering a secure service necessitate a set of security controls. As a result, there are a large range of security controls to handle. Furthermore, coordinating such disparate security measures to meet security requirements is a difficult undertaking, especially when requirements and security protocols at every tier conflict. This could cause a security model inconsistency. As a result, there is a need for a uniform security control management module. Based on security requirements, this component must coordinate and integrate the security controls of the various layers.

6 Stakeholders in Cloud Computing and Security Consequences

In a cloud computing environment, there are three parties involved: the cloud provider, the service provider, as well as the service client.

Each partner has its own security protocols, as well as requests and abilities from other stakeholders. As a result, there really are [13]:

- A collection of security criteria that several tenants have placed on a resource that could be in conflict.
- A set of protection requirements imposed on a source by a group of renters, some of whom may be at odds. To combat new risks, each service's security setting should be regulated and enforced at the domain level of resources and during performance, considering the possibility of shifting needs whenever user demands change.
- The implemented security features must be negotiated and agreed upon by providers and consumers. However, there are no common security specification notations that cloud stakeholders may use to represent and explain on their decided to offer security attributes.
- All stakeholders all have their own privacy management systems in place to describe their resources, anticipated risks and their consequences, as well as how to mitigate those risks.

Because cloud providers are unfamiliar with the architectures of managed services, they are unable to develop effective and reliable security controls. In addition, cloud servers must comply with a flood of new security standards while also maintaining a broad collection of security measures that must be modified. This makes the duties of security administrators much more complex. There is transparency among cloud producers and users about what safety measures are in place, what risks are present, and what kind of data breaches occur on software systems and hosted services. This one is called "innocent until proven guilty" [14], and it asserts that cloud clients must have faith in service providers, but that cloud providers should provide tools to assist users in validating their trustworthiness and monitoring security compliance.

7 Models for Delivery of Cloud Computing Services and Their Security Implications

Each service delivery model's significant security concerns are summarized. A few of these issues fall under the purview of cloud vendors, whereas others fall under the purview of cloud users. Each service delivery model's serious security concerns are summarized. A few of these issues fall under the purview of cloud services, whereas others fall under the purview of cloud users.

A. *IaaS Problems:*

VM privacy and security– Protect virtual machines and apps from common attacks that affect traditional data centers, using traditional or cloud-based security technologies to combat malware and viruses Cloud users are responsible for virtual machine security. Every cloud user can implement their unique security measures consumer's needs, risk tolerance, and security management methodology.

Securing the VM image source – with exception of real servers, virtual machines are vulnerable even when they are turned down. VM images can be hacked by inserting harmful code or stealing the VM file itself. The security of the VM image library is the responsibility of cloud providers. Another disadvantage of VM architecture is that they can keep the original owner's data, which could be helpful to a new client.

Security of virtual networks – By exploiting Dns, Ip vulnerability, or the vSwitch software to share broadband networks among numerous renters on the same host (using vSwitch) or on networks, network-based VM assaults become possible.

Securing Vmware virtual bounds – Unlike physical servers, virtual machines have virtual bounds. Virtual machines that share a same CPU, memory, and I/O are known as shared virtual machines, network interface card, and other resources on the same physical server. The cloud provider is in charge of VM security. Virtual bounds – Unlike physical servers, virtual machines have virtual bounds. Virtual machines sharing the same CPU, memory, I/O, network interface card, and other resources on the same physical server. The cloud provider is in charge of VM security.

Security of hypervisors – A hypervisor acts as a "virtualized," converting physical resources into virtual machines and vice versa. It controls virtual computers' access to physical server resources. Because all VM operations are unencrypted and traceable, any breach of the hypervisor jeopardizes the VMs' privacy. Hypervisor security falls within the purview of cloud and service providers. In this situation, the hypervisor software supplier, such as Vsphere or Xen, is known as the SP.

B. *PaaS_ Security Problems:*

SOA security issues - the PaaS system is based on the SOA model. As a result, any security flaws uncovered in the SOA domains are inherited, including DOS, Man-in-the-middle, Config file, Replay, Database, Injector, and input recognition assaults are all examples of person attacks [8, 15]. For cloud-based systems to be secure, authentication protocols, the use of permission and WS-Security standards is critical. This security problem affects cloud service providers, providers, and users alike.

API Security – APIs for administration functions such as business operations, security measures, and application management could be provided via PaaS, among others. OAuth, for example, is a set of security measures and standards [16], should be used to establish a standardized authentication process for queries to such APIs. There is also a requirement for API separation in memory. The cloud providers are responsible for this problem.

C. *SaaS Security Issues:*

Implementing and ensuring security in the SaaS model is a joint duty between cloud services and suppliers (software vendors). The security issues mentioned in the previous models are carried over to the SaaS model, including data security management, because it is built on top of them. Vulnerability detection for web apps – online apps that will be published on a public cloud must be checked and checked for vulnerabilities [17]. Using the Nationwide Security Database (NVD) and the National Weakness Assessment, such scans should be updated to reflect newly discovered vulnerabilities and attack paths (UWA). To minimize any current or newly discovered vulnerabilities, firewalls must be in place. Vulnerability detection for web apps – online apps which will be distributed on a cloud service must be checked and scanned for weaknesses [17]. Using the Nacional Exposure Database (NVD) and the National Weakness Assessment, such scans should be kept up with newly identified vulnerabilities and attack routes (UWA). To minimize any current or newly discovered vulnerabilities, firewall should be in place.

Misconfiguration and breaking of web application security – Web application security misconfiguration and vulnerabilities in application-specific security mechanisms are a big problem in SaaS. Security misconfiguration is even more critical in multi-tenancy situations, as each renter has their own set of rules that may conflict with one another, resulting in security issues. Cloud service security policies are commonly recommended for implementing privacy in a continuous, dynamic, and resilient manner.

D. *Security Concerns in Cloud Management*

The Cloud Management Layer (CML) serves as a "kernel" that may be expanded to include and coordinate various components. SLA organization, service quality in terms, invoicing, flexibility, Infrastructure as a service, PaaS, SaaS applications registration, and cloud security management are all CML components. This layer provides a set of APIs and capabilities that client applications can utilize to connect to the cloud platform. As a result, the CML layer shares the same security problems as the PaaS model. Security Concerns with Cloud Access Methods These resources are accessible by (1) for online apps—SaaS web browsers (HTTP/HTTPS); (2) Protocols for internet providers and Apis – PaaS and CML APIs include internet providers' File format, HTTP, and RPC ports, as well as PaaS and CML APIs and (3) For virtual servers and disc services – IaaS – remote connection, VPN, and FTP are used. In order to safeguard data exchanged between both the cloud service and its users, security policies should address security risks associated with these protocols.

8   Security Enablers for Cloud Computing

A. *IAM and Federation (Identity and Access Management) (IAM)*

Any security-conscious system relies on identity. Individuals, programs, platforms, clouds, and other items can be recognized by the development team and other parties. An identity is a collection of data linked to a certain entity. This knowledge is useful due of the context. Users' "private" information should not be revealed through identity. A systematic and comprehensive Identity and access management solution should be provided by or supported by cloud platforms. All cloud products and cloud users should be able to access identity context information using this system. It should have the following information: identity Identity information, single

sign-on providing and de-provisioning, authentications, security, identification linking, identification map, identification confederation, and federal state identification
characteristics.

B.   *Key Management*

One of the main goals for cloud computing security is to maintain confidentiality
(CIA triad). The most prevalent method of keeping data, process, and communications private is encryption. There are encryption algorithms that use asymmetric or
symmetric keys. Both encrypted systems have a serious issue with secure key management, or generating, storing, accessing, and exchanging secret keys in a secure
manner. When using PaaS, app keys are also needed for any API and service calls
made by other applications. The app's key, as well as every other data required by
the programme to use these APIs, should be kept safe.

C.   *Security Management*

Cloud – based security management is becoming a more difficult research challenge due to the huge number of cloud participants, deeper dependence stacking, and
a big range of security products to suit security needs. Security management should
comprise security requirements and rules, security control parameters party policies,
and input on the environments and Among security system and cloud stakeholders,
there are security controls. CML should have a security management plug-in.

D.   *Lifecycle of Secure Software Development*

The safe software development process includes gathering requirements, threat
modeling, and incorporating security requirements into system modeling and generated code. Cloud-based apps will change the lifecycles and processes used to create
safe systems. Developers can use the PaaS to create secure cloud-based apps by
using a set of generic security enablement components. Security engineering for
cloud-based software should also develop to meet new security requirements. To
address a wide variety of client security requirements, adaptive safety should be
enabled in apps. To makes utilization strong security and application security management, adaptable app security relies on cloud-based security management and
cloud security services.

E.   *Optimisation of the security-performance tradeoff*

In the cloud computing model, service level agreements (SLAs) are utilized to
provide services. Efficiency, durability, and security goals should all be included in
SLAs. SLAs also detail the penalties that will be imposed if the SLA is breached. One
of the SLA objectives, providing a high level of security, involves a large increase in
resource usage, which has an impact on the performance goal. When using utility for
performance and security, cloud management should analyse the exchange between
performance and security. We should also concentrate on providing adaptable safety,
in which security boundaries are set in accordance with existing and projected threat
level, as well as other factors.

F.   *Security federation across many clouds*

When a client utilises apps that make advantage of many clouds' services, he
must ensure that his security requirements are met on both the cloud and in the
middle. When many clouds collaborate to deliver a greater amount of production or
integration, All cloud platforms' security criteria should be federated and enforced.

9 Conclusions

Cloud computing is one of the most appealing computing models for telecom operators, cloud service providers, and other businesses and cloud clients alike. However, we must close the existing security flaws in need to go get the most out of model. In light of the above data, the cloud security issue can be summarized as follows:

- Virtualization and SOA, for example, have security vulnerabilities that are carried down from of the technology used.
- Multi-tenancy and isolating are important parts of the clouds security threat, requiring a top to bottom approach from of the SaaS layer through infrastructure facilities.
- Security management is necessary to govern and manage such a vast number of needs and restrictions.
- A thorough safety shell should be included in a cloud, as seen in Fig. 3, so any access to a cloud software object first must pass through security features.

10 Future Work

We're working into the issue of cloud-based security management. The system security operations of cloud clients have generated a security gap and As a result of the cloud paradigm's application, cloud providers have risen. To address this issue, users must: (1) obtain security standards from a variety of stakeholders at various stages of processing; (2) Compare and contrast security standards with cloud architecture, patterns of safety, and implementation of those laws in terms of security; and (3) provide cloud manufacturers and users with updated security status information. To overcome the difficulties of cloud security management, we propose using an adaptive model-based technique. Models will aid in issue abstraction and the capture of various stakeholders' security requirements at different levels of detail. Adaptability will aid in the delivery of an unified, flexible, and cloud security paradigm that is enforced. The feedback loop will monitor security conditions in order to improve current cloud-based security paradigms and bring users up to speed on their assets' security.

References

1. Mell, P., Grance, T.: The NIST definition of cloud computing. National Institute of Standards and Technology. Information Technology Laboratory, Version, 15(10.07) (2009)
2. Gens, F., Mahowald, R.P., Richard, L.: Villars. 2009. IDC Cloud Computing 2010 (2010)
3. Almorsy, M., Grundy, J., Müller, I.: An analysis of the cloud computing security problem. arXiv preprint arXiv:1609.01107 (2016)
4. Enisa, C.C.: Benefits, risks and recommendations for information security. Eur. Netw. Inform. Secur. **23**, 1–6 (2009)
5. Stavinoha, K.E.: What is Cloud Computing and Why Do We Need It (2010). Retrieved 18 Sep 2015
6. Kandukuri, B.R., Rakshit, A.: Cloud security issues. In: 2009 IEEE International Conference on Services Computing, pp. 517–520. IEEE (2009)

7. Popović, K., Hocenski, Ž.: Cloud computing security issues and challenges. In: The 33rd International Convention Mipro, pp. 344–349. IEEE (2010)
8. Jensen, M., Schwenk, J., Gruschka, N., Iacono, L.L.: On technical security issues in cloud computing. In: 2009 IEEE International Conference on Cloud Computing, pp. 109–116. IEEE (2009)
9. Grobauer, B., Walloschek, T., Stocker, E.: Understanding cloud computing vulnerabilities. IEEE Secur. Priv. **9**(2), 50–57 (2010)
10. Subashini, S., Kavitha, V.: A survey on security issues in service delivery models of cloud computing. J. Netw. Comput. Appl. **34**(1), 1–11 (2011)
11. Ristenpart, T., Tromer, E., Shacham, H., Savage, S.: Hey, you, get off of my cloud: exploring information leakage in third-party compute clouds. In: Proceedings of the 16th ACM conference on Computer and communications security, pp. 199–212 (2009)
12. Zhang, W., et al.: A comprehensive study of co-residence threat in multi-tenant public PaaS clouds. In: Lam, K.-Y., Chi, C.-H., Qing, S. (eds.) ICICS 2016. LNCS, vol. 9977, pp. 361–375. Springer, Cham (2016). https://doi.org/10.1007/978-3-319-50011-9_28
13. Tajadod, G., Batten, L., Govinda, K.: Microsoft and Amazon: a comparison of approaches to cloud security. In: 4th IEEE International Conference on Cloud Computing Technology and Science Proceedings, pp. 539–544. IEEE (2012)
14. Holstein, D.K., Stouffer, K.: Trust but verify critical infrastructure cyber security solutions. In: 2010 43rd Hawaii International Conference on System Sciences, pp. 1–8. IEEE (2010)
15. Zhang, W.: Integrated security framework for secure web services. In: 2010 Third International Symposium on Intelligent Information Technology and Security Informatics, pp. 178–183. IEEE (2010)
16. Bin, W., Yuan, H.H., Xi, L.X., Min, X.J.: Open identity management framework for SaaS ecosystem. In: 2009 IEEE International Conference on e-Business Engineering, pp. 512–517. IEEE (2009)
17. Fong, E., Okun, V.: Web application scanners: definitions and functions. In: 2007 40th Annual Hawaii International Conference on System Sciences (HICSS'07), pp. 280b–280b. IEEE (2007)
18. Vaibhav, A., Shukla, D., Das, S., Sahana, S., Johri, P.: Security challenges, authentication, application and trust models for vehicular ad hoc network-a survey. IJ Wireless Microw. Technol. **3**, 36–48 (2017)

Code-Based Cryptography: A Comparative Study of Key Sizes

Manoj Kumar Singh[(✉)]

SC&SS, Jawaharlal Nehru University, New Delhi 110067, India
mkniranjan.ittech@gmail.com

Abstract. In today's era, cryptography is used in our daily life such as health, finance, armed forces and entertainment, etc. Cryptography secured data and communications by applying mathematical transformations. Cryptography provides confidentiality, integrity, and availability (CIA triad). Codes have the capacity to encrypt and transmit data, which inspires the idea of code-based cryptography. The combination of characteristics of codes and traditional cryptography provides security against quantum attacks. In this chapter, we have reviewed the state of the art of code-based cryptography and the usefulness of rank-metric codes in the reduction of key size. We have also reviewed different code-based cryptosystems based on different types of codes, which help in reducing the key size without degrading the security level.

Keywords: Code-based cryptography · Symmetric key cryptography · Asymmetric key cryptography · Rank-metric codes

1 Introduction

Cryptography plays a crucial role in the world. It is a science and art, which has been in existence since Roman times. Cryptography is a technique that converts a message from a readable form into an unreadable form. For example, Julius Caesar invented the Caesar cipher technique by shifting the alphabet and it was used during World War II. The message which is in its original form is called plain text and the unreadable format of the message is known as the cipher text. The sender and intended recipient of the message can interpret the contents. This process of converting plain text into unintelligible text and vice-versa is called cryptography [1]. The process which converts the original message into an unreadable format (cipher text) is known as encryption. The process that converts the cipher text into the original format is known as decryption. Cryptography is classified into two categories, first is symmetric key cryptography and second is asymmetric key cryptography. Asymmetric key cryptography is popularly known as public key cryptography. Only one key is used in symmetric key cryptography for encryption and decryption. Unlike symmetric key cryptography, two keys are used in public key cryptography. One key is known as the public key and another key is known as the private key. The encryption is done by the public key and decryption is done by the private key or vice-versa [2]. The basic model of the public key cryptosystem is represented in Fig. 1.

There are mainly five security goals of cryptography which protects the stored information as well as the transmitted data. The cryptographic goals are:

- **Confidentiality:** It keeps the communication private. It does not disclose information with unauthorized user. Data is encrypted for keeping confidential so that the third party will not be able to read data easily. In this, only authorized users are allowed to access the data.

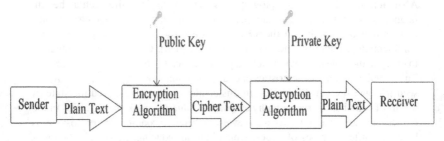

Fig. 1. The basic model of the public key cryptosystem

- **Integrity:** The completeness and accuracy of the data must be protected. Data must not be changed or erased during transmission and storage. Integrity shows that data is not altered by an unauthorized user during the transmission. It deals with the detection of unauthorized changes in data.
- **Authentication:** Authentication confirms the sender's identity. It measures the validity of transmission, data, and source, or verifies the user's identity for receiving the particular information. Authentication confirms the user's identity before allowing access to resources. This includes user ID, password, fingerprint and others.
- **Availability:** It provides easy and timely access to authorized users. This includes protection against hackers, malicious code and other threats that can block access to information.
- **Non-repudiation:** It ensures that the sender has proof of delivery and the recipient has proof of identity of the sender. Therefore, no party can refuse to send, receive or access data.

The public key techniques basically depend on three hard mathematical problems as prime factorization, discrete logarithm or the elliptic curve discrete logarithm problems [3]. The Rivest-Shamir-Adleman (RSA) algorithm is based on prime factorization and discrete logarithm problems. Diffie-Hellman (DH) key exchange, Digital Signature Algorithm (DSA) and Elliptic Curve Digital Signature Algorithm (ECDSA) are based on the discrete logarithm problem or elliptic curve discrete problem [4]. In 1994, Peter Shor discussed and reported that the prime factorization and discrete log problem can be solved using matter's physical properties in quantum computers. Shor's algorithm can lead to breaking public key encryption schemes. This algorithm runs on a quantum computer. Current quantum computers are using only a few numbers of qubits (quantum bits) [5].

There is a need to update our current cryptographic primitives. The new cryptographic schemes will resist the threat of quantum computers. However, quantum computers are able to run the algorithms for decoding keys. Quantum computers will compromise the current network and data security [6].

There are mainly five categories of post-quantum cryptography based on the different concepts as represented in Fig. 2. Lattice-based cryptography is based on the concept of linear algebra, while multivariate cryptography is related to multivariate equations. Code-based cryptography is based on coding theory. Hash-based cryptography is done by using hash functions [7].

Fig. 2. Classification of post-quantum cryptography

2 Related Work

Coding theory was introduced in 1940 and became an integral part of engineering, from that time. It plays an important role in mathematics and particularly in computer science. In 1948 Claude Shannon gave a theorem, which states that the maximum transmission over a noisy communication channel is possible and this result is the base of the coding theory [8].

The model of coding theory for sending or receiving a message is represented in Fig. 3. The purpose of this model is to improve the study of error correction techniques. These techniques allow the receiver to retrieve the channel error message without communicating with the sender. The idea may sound simple, but the methods for error correction can be complicated [8].

Let F be a finite field. $\mathbb{N}$ represents the set of natural numbers. n and N are natural numbers. Suppose $\mathbb{F} = \mathbb{F}_q$ is the field having q elements, $N = q^m$ and m is chosen such that $m < n$. Then the field $\mathbb{F}_{q^m}$ has the elements $1, 2, \cdots, q^m - 1$.

Channel is a communication link via code word that is transmitted before it is seen by the receiver. Errors may occur when a communication takes place. For a code $\mathcal{C} \in \mathbb{F}^n$, the decoder gets the message $c \oplus e$, where e is the arbitrary element of $\mathbb{F}^n$ or e is the error vector what we are adding. The map i is defined in such a way that the receiver can find which code words had been sent. Code words are the elements of code.

Let the element $x \in \mathbb{F}^n$ and x_i is the ith coordinate of x.

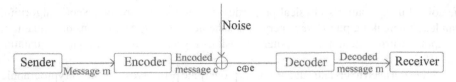

Fig. 3. Coding theory working model

Definition 2.1. Let $x, y \in \mathbb{F}^n$. Define a metric space $d_H : \mathbb{F}^n \times \mathbb{F}^n \to \{0, 1, ..., n\}$ by

$$d_H(x, y) := |\{x_i \neq y_i \text{ for } 1 \leq i \leq n\}|$$

i.e. number of different coordinates of x, y. It is known as Hamming metric.

Definition 2.2. Suppose $\mathcal{C}$ is a code in $\mathbb{F}^n$. Then the minimum distance of a code $\mathcal{C}$ is defined as

$$d_H^{min}(\mathcal{C}) = \min\{d_H(x, y)|x, y \in \mathcal{C}, x \neq y\}$$

Definition 2.3. Let $x \in \mathbb{F}^n$, then Hamming weight of x is

$$Wt_H(x) = d_H(x, 0)$$

This implies the number of non-zero coordinates of x is known as the Hamming Weight.

2.1 Cryptosystems

In 1978, McEliece introduced a public key cryptographic system known as the McEliece cryptosystem, based on coding theory. This system encrypts and decrypts in an efficient way, but it was not possible to use for practical applications at the time of its development due to its large key size. So it was a theoretical concern. As pointed out above, the problem with the McEliece cryptosystem is that it requires a large public key size in comparison to the other cryptosystems with the same security level.

- **McEliece Cryptosystem**

    It is the first cryptosystem which was introduced on coding theory. McEliece cryptosystem uses generator matrix for encryption and it operates on the field $\mathbb{F}_2$.

    The McEliece cryptosystem uses linear codes. There are various techniques to generate binary linear codes such as Goppa codes, Hamming codes, Reed Solomon codes, Hadamard codes etc. McEliece cryptosystem provides more security with Goppa codes in comparison to the other binary linear codes. Binary Goppa codes are a kind of error-correcting codes which is generated by a polynomial $f(x)$ of degree k over a Galois field $GF(2^m)$. This polynomial $f(x)$ has distinct roots.

Key Generation:

- Since there is a need of three matrices to generate public-key.
- Let $[n, k]$ be a binary linear code which corrects up to t errors.
- Consider the generator matrix G of order $k \times n$.
- Select an arbitrary $k \times k$ invertible matrix S over $\mathbb{F}_2$.
- Choose a random $n \times n$ Permutation matrix P.
- Now compute a matrix of order $k \times n$

$$G_{Pub} = SGP$$

- So, now the public key is (G_{Pub}, t) and the private key is (S, G, P).

Encryption:

- Suppose x is message for transmission and (G_{Pub}, t) is the public-key.
- Encode the message x as a n-length binary string and weight up to t.
- Encryption as follows:

$$y = xG_{Pub} + e \pmod 2$$

where, e is the possible error vector.

Decryption:

- Calculate $y' = yP^{-1}$.
- With the help of check matrix H and y', compute Hy'^T.
- To find an equivalent syndrome, find error vector e which has smallest weight i.e. minimum distance between zero vector and error vector such that $Hy'^T = He^T$.
- Compute $x' = y' + e$.
- Find a matrix x_0 such that $x_0 G = x'$.
- Compute $x = x_0 S^{-1}$.

- **Niederreiter Cryptosystem**

  In 1986, Herald Niederreiter modified McEliece cryptosystem which uses a parity check matrix in place of the generator matrix. It has the same security level as McEliece cryptosystem has. Niederreiter cryptosystem encrypts much faster than the McEliece cryptosystem. It is also used to generate the digital signature. This system is much more secure when it uses binary Goppa codes.

Key Generation:

- Since there is a need of three matrices to generate public-key.
- Let $[n, k]$ be a binary linear code which corrects up to t errors.
- Consider the parity check matrix H of order $(n - k) \times n$.
- Select an arbitrary $k \times k$ invertible matrix S over $\mathbb{F}_2$.
- Choose a random $n \times n$ Permutation matrix P.

- Now compute a $(n - k) \times n$ matrix

$$H_{Pub} = SHP$$

- So, now the public key is (H_{Pub}, t) and the private key is (S, H, P).

Encryption:

- Suppose x is message for transmission and (H_{Pub}, t) is the public-key.
- Encode the message x as a n-length binary string and weight up to t.
- Encryption as follows:

$$y = H_{Pub}x^T$$

Decryption:

- Now we have cipher text $y = H_{Pub}x^T$ and (S, H, P) is the private-key. To decode y, follow the given steps.
- First compute, $y_1 = S^{-1}y$, we get $S^{-1}y = HPx^T$
- Apply syndrome decoding algorithm for code to retrieve Px^T.
- Get the message x, by using

$$x^T = P^{-1}Px^T$$

2.2 Attacks

There are mainly two kinds of attacks done on code-based cryptosystems which are structural and decoding attacks [9]. These attacks are given below.

Structural Attacks: Structural attacks used special classes of codes in code-based cryptography. The attackers took advantage of the code structure for breaking those cryptosystems in which special classes of codes were used [10]. Overbeck's attack is used for rank metric codes cryptosystems and the cryptanalysis of Niederreiter cryptosystem has done by the Sidelnikov-Shestakov attack.

Researchers practice with the extremely structural code which can be collected efficiently. In current time, a substantial amount of research has been done on structural attacks.

Otmani et al. performed a cryptanalysis of the McEliece cryptosystem using Quasi Cyclic Low Density Parity Check codes. The attack is done on Quasi cyclic structure to get reduce version of the private key and it reconstructs the private key by using Stern's algorithm [11].

Faugere et al. discussed an algebraic attack for McEliece cryptosystem and for those cryptosystems in which non-binary Quasi Cyclic and Quasi-Density codes are used. The attacker establishes systems of equations and finds the solution. The solution of that system will work as a decoder for the respective code [12].

Decoding Attacks: In code based cryptography, there are basically two kinds of decoding attacks. First one is information set decoding and second one is the birthday algorithm. The generalization of birthday algorithm was given by Wagner in 2002. This increases the algorithm efficiency [13].

Bernstein et al. represented different techniques for enhancing the Information Set Decoding attacks. The researchers showed the comparison of various decoding algorithms. They studied the behaviour, minimum and the maximum cost of these algorithms. Bernstein et al. presented a better version of Information Set Decoding algorithm.

Code-based cryptography is a secure and resistant method against the quantum attacks, but still there is a need for modification in the parameters. The traditional knowledge is that Shor's algorithm needs a double key size of these cryptosystem. Grover's algorithm gives a square root speed up on key searching over symmetric key algorithms and searching for pre images and collisions by a cube factor on hashes functions with the help of this algorithm [14].

2.3 Preliminaries

Let q be a prime. Suppose that $\mathbb{F}_q$ is a field having q elements and $\mathbb{F}_{q^m}$ is field extension over $\mathbb{F}_q$ of order q^m. Let $\{y_1, \ldots \ldots y_m\}$ be an independent set of $\mathbb{F}_{q^m}$. This forms the $\mathbb{F}_q$-basis for $\mathbb{F}_{q^m}$, then every element $x \in \mathbb{F}_{q^m}$ is uniquely represented as

$$x = \sum_{i=1}^{m} x_i y_i$$

for $x_i \in \mathbb{F}_q$. Thus the vector x can be represented in the form of column vector $[x_1, x_2, \ldots \ldots x_m] \in \mathbb{F}_q^{m \times 1}$, for an element $\in \mathbb{F}_{q^m}$, so it can be represented as a matrix $A[a] \in \mathbb{F}_q^{m \times n}$, so each subset $CC\mathbb{F}_{q^m}^n$ can be seen as a subset of $\mathbb{F}_q^{m \times n}$, $\mathcal{C} \subseteq \mathbb{F}_{q^m}^n$ is linear over the field $\mathbb{F}_{q^m}$ ($\mathbb{F}_{q^m} - linear$) when code words can be seen in the form of vectors, then these type of codes are called as linear rank metric codes.

Rank $q(A)$ and rank $q^m(A)$ denote the rank of the matrix A over the field $\mathbb{F}_q$ and $\mathbb{F}_{q^m}$ respectively. Consider the field extension $\mathbb{F}_{q^{mu}}$ with $u > 1$. Then $\mathbb{F}_q \subseteq \mathbb{F}_{q^m} \subseteq \mathbb{F}_{q^{mu}}$ by using vector space property, we can write $\mathbb{F}_{q^{mu}} \approx \mathbb{F}_{q^m}^u$.

Definition 2.3.1. Let $a, b \in \mathbb{F}_{q^m}^n$. The rank distance between a & b is given by

$$d_r(a, b) = rank\ q(a - b) = rank\ q(A - B)$$

Lemma 2.3.2. The map $d_r : \mathbb{F}_{q^m}^n \times \mathbb{F}_{q^m}^n \to \{0, 1, \ldots \ldots m\}$ in >Definition 2.3.1 defines a metric space.

2.4 Rank Metric Code

Delsarte proposed rank metric codes and further these codes was improved by Gabidulin. The rank metric codes are considered over a field extension. Suppose that L is a field extension of K of degree n, i.e. $K \subseteq L$ *and* $[L : K] = n$. Now consider the finite fields $K = \mathbb{F}_q$ *and* $L = \mathbb{F}_{q^n}$ for prime q.

Rank metric codes which meet singleton bound condition are known as maximum rank distance codes (MRD codes). This type of codes was generated with the help of generalized polynomials and further they were generalized in [23]. Sheeky created a new family of codes which is associated with Gabidulin code, and later they were generalized in the form of twisted Gabidulin code. In general, the codes which are emerging from the Sheeky construction are non-linear over field extension, but in some cases it also consists of the associated linear MRD codes. Apart from this, other known codes are not performing the singleton bound, which are linear. There exist some linear or non-linear constructions over a subfield of $\mathbb{F}_{q^n}$.

3   Comparison of the Code-Based Cryptosystems

Now, we take different code-based cryptosystems, which depend on the different types of codes. Distinct codes are used to reduce the key size and these cryptosystems also resist the attack by quantum computers. Some of them are based on binary linear codes and some of them are on non-binary linear codes as shown in Table 1.

Table 1. Different code-based cryptosystems based on codes

Sr. no.	Encryption techniques	Basic codes
1.	McEliece Cryptosystem	Binary Goppa code
2.	Niederreiter Cryptosystem	Binary Goppa code
3.	Bike	Quasi Cyclic-Moderate density parity check code
4.	McNie	Rank- metric code
5.	LEDApke	Quasi Cyclic-Moderate density parity check code
6.	HQC	Quasi Cyclic-Moderate density parity check code
7.	Big Quake	Quasi Cyclic-Goppa code
8.	RQC	Rank-metric code
9.	FL Cryptosystem	Rank-metric code
10.	LAKE	Rank-metric code
11.	QC-MDPC KEM	QC-MDPC
12.	GPT Cryptosystem	Rank-metric code
13.	CGPT Cryptosystem	Rank-metric code
14.	LEDAkem	QC-Moderate density parity check code

The Table 2 shows that how many size of memory is required for each code-based cryptosystems. We can conclude that initially McEliece cryptosystem has very large key size, and large key size is the main drawack of code-based cryptography. There has been done a lot of work to reduce the key size of the code-based cryptosystems.

Table 2. Comparison of key sizes of some code-based cryptosystems

Cryptosystems	Size of public-key (in bytes)	Size of private key (in bytes)	Size of cipher text (in bytes)
Classic McEliece	1357824	14120	240
HQC	7245	40	14469
LEDAcrypt	4424	2232	4464
BIKE	5122	580	5154
RQC	4090	40	8164

4 Conclusion

Code-based cryptography made a particular place in post-quantum cryptography since its development. After the development of McEliece cryptosystem, it is the secure public-key encryption scheme which provides security against quantum attacks. The main problem is the large public-key size of this cryptosystem. Various types of binary linear codes such as moderate density parity check codes, quasi cyclic low density parity check codes and rank metric codes such as Gabidulin codes, twisted Gabidulin codes play an important role in key size reduction. As we have analyzed different code-based cryptosystem which are mainly based on the Hamming metric and rank-metric. Rank-metric codes reduce the key size and enhance the security level. Rank-metric codes encrypt more efficiently.

References

1. Stinson, D.R.: Cryptography: Theory and Practice, 63rd edn. Chapman and Hall/CRC (2005)
2. Menezes, A.J., Van Oorschot, P.C., Vanstone, S.A.: Applied Cryptography, p. 17. CRC, Boca Raton (1996)
3. Kessler, G.C.: An Overview of Cryptography (2003)
4. Kocher, P.C.: Timing attacks on implementations of Diffie-Hellman, RSA, DSS, and other systems. In: Koblitz, N. (ed.) CRYPTO 1996. LNCS, vol. 1109, pp. 104–113. Springer, Heidelberg (1996). https://doi.org/10.1007/3-540-68697-5_9
5. Shor, P.W.: Polynomial-time algorithms for prime factorization and discrete logarithms on a quantum computer. SIAM J. Comput. **26**, 1484–1509 (1997)
6. Preskill, J.: Quantum computing in the NISQ era and beyond. Quantum **2**, 79 (2018)
7. Chen, L., et al.: Report on post-quantum cryptography, vol. 12. US Department of Commerce, National Institute of Standards and Technology, USA (2016)
8. Malsa, N., Vyas, V., Gautam, J., Shaw, R.N., Ghosh, A.: Framework and smart contract for blockchain enabled certificate verification system using robotics. In: Bianchini, M., Simic, M., Ghosh, A., Shaw, R.N. (eds.) Machine Learning for Robotics Applications. SCI, vol. 960, pp. 125–138. Springer, Singapore (2021). https://doi.org/10.1007/978-981-16-0598-7_10
9. Bernstein, D.J., Lange, T., Peters, C.: Attacking and defending the McEliece cryptosystem. In: Buchmann, J., Ding, J. (eds.) PQCrypto 2008. LNCS, vol. 5299, pp. 31–46. Springer, Heidelberg (2008). https://doi.org/10.1007/978-3-540-88403-3_3

10. Berger, T.P., Loidreau, P.: How to mask the structure of codes for a cryptographic use. Des. Codes Crypt. **35**, 63–79 (2005). https://doi.org/10.1007/s10623-003-6151-2
11. Otmani, A., Tillich, J.-P., Dallot, L.: Cryptanalysis of two McEliece cryptosystems based on quasi-cyclic codes. Math. Comput. Sci. **3**(2), 129–240 (2010)
12. Faugère, J.-C., Otmani, A., Perret, L., De Portzamparc, F., Tillich, J.-P.: Structural cryptanalysis of McEliece schemes with compact keys. Des., Codes Crypt. **79**(1), 87–112 (2015)
13. Horlemann, A.L., Puchinger, S., Renner, J., Schamberger, T., Wachter-Zeh, A.: Information-Set Decoding with Hints. In: Wachter-Zeh, A., Bartz, H., Liva, G. (eds.) Code-Based Cryptography. CBCrypto 2021. Lecture Notes in Computer Science, vol. 13150. Springer, Cham (2022). https://doi.org/10.1007/978-3-030-98365-9_4
14. Niederhagen, R., Waidner, M.: Practical post-quantum cryptography. Fraunhofer SIT (2017)

Advance Collision Prevention System

Namrata Singh[1]([⊠]), Meenakshi Srivastava[2], Sumit Mohan[1], Ashif Ali[1],
Varun Kumar Singh[1], and Prashant Singh[1]

[1] Department of Computer Science and Engineering, Sunder Deep Engineering College,
Ghaziabad, India
nam2817120@gmail.com

[2] Department of Information Technology, Amity Institute of Information Technology,
Amity University, Lucknow, India
msrivastava@lko.amity.edu

Abstract. This chapter presents the efficient working model of the Advance Collision Prevention System (ACP System) using computer vision and machine learning (ML). The facial expression detection technique is widely used in the recognition of facial expression to understand human intention. In this chapter, we capture the driver's face in real-time and process every frame to detect the drowsy and yawn expression to determine whether the driver is feeling sleepy or not using computer vision. Simultaneously we apply a machine-learning algorithm to detect if the driver is using a cell phone while driving. The proposed algorithm works in day and night both and makes the system (ACP System) more advance and highly efficient to prevent any such collisions which may occur due to human error like lack of concentration while driving.

Keywords: Drowsiness detection · Yawn detection · Object detection · Computer vision · Machine learning · Collision prevention · R-CNN · TensorFlow

1 Introduction

Mobile phones are the major cause of road accidents, about 2,138 people were killed and 4,746 were injured in 2016 only because of using a cell phone while driving.

Other statistics say that annually 150 thousand people die in India due to 'drowsy or sleep-driving' and it's cause for the 40% highway accidents. And with time these numbers are increasing year-by-year. It is not possible to make people aware when they are already aware of anything, almost everyone knows that one should take good sleep before driving and not to use a cell phone while driving, and we also know that most accidents occur due to human errors.

© The Author(s), under exclusive license to Springer Nature Switzerland AG 2023
R. N. Shaw et al. (Eds.): ICACIS 2022, CCIS 1749, pp. 369–383, 2023.
https://doi.org/10.1007/978-3-031-25088-0_33

This hurdle can be overcome by making the automobiles/vehicles intelligent enough to easily identify and alert the driver when he/she is about to make any mistake which may cost their life. Now, this is a challenging task to make a vehicle(car) capable to detect human errors accurately and most important is in real-time. So, in this chapter, we are presenting the working model of the Advance Collision Prevention System (ACP System) which is an intelligent model based on machine learning and computer vision.

The ACP System is capable of detecting the drowsiness and yawning of the driver along with this it can also detect and alert if the driver is using a cell phone while driving. We performed tests of our system in both day and night time as it is obvious that the chances of drowsiness and yawning are more during the night because human beings are habitual for sleeping at night. Through computer vision, we detect the driver's face and then the dlib face detector and face shape predictor along with some mathematical calculation make the system strong enough to prevent any such possible collision which may likely happen if the driver is feeling sleepy. The distraction due to the cell phone is overcome by implementing the machine learning algorithm i.e. R-CNN model for detecting cell phone.

The unique combination of drowsy, yawn, and cell phone detection make the system capable of preventing major road accidents which are caused by distraction or lack of focus while driving. The system is also cost-efficient as it is developed by using only open-source software technologies. And it also reduces the injury treatment cost and vehicle repairing costs. Road accident reports analysis says that road accidents cost India about 5% of GDP every year.

2   Literature Survey

As explained in [1], Haar Cascade classifier is used for face detection and then eye center tracking is performed after that Adaptive Gaussian Binary Thresholding is applied for monitoring eye state and finally the application of dynamic double thresholding method results in drowsiness detection.

A SMS based notification system for the current location using GPS navigation, and warning alarm for the driver if drowsiness is detected is implemented in [2], here the author used cloud-based IoT system for analyzing eye conditions. PERCLOS (PERcentage of eyelid CLOSure) is one of the most used techniques for the drowsiness detection system [3, 4, 10] according to a study by Walter Wierwille. Yawn detection is also performed in [3] by calculating the number of times the driver has yawned.

In the drowsiness detection model presented by D. Selvathi [5], LBP based and MAX pooling-based feature extraction with SVM classification is performed using Deep learning which detects the drowsy state of the driver by analyzing the eyes, open or closed for a long duration.

Sanghyuk Park, et al. [6], the used Deep network on NTHU-drowsy driver detection benchmark dataset for drowsiness detection. Two processes i.e. learning feature representation and ensemble detection uses networks: AlexNet, VGG-FaceNet and FlowImageNet and architectures: Independently-averaged architecture (IAA) and Feature-fused architecture (FFA) respectively.

The idea of implementing the combination of EEG and ANN is represented by Tiberiu Vesselenyi, et al. [7], Electroencephalography (EEG) by the help of electrodes mounted on driver's cap and Artificial Neural Network (ANN) and Eye Aspect Ratio (EAR) method for eye state analysis using a camera is used for driver drowsiness detection. Fuzzy inference system is used for multi-criterial decision.

The concept of using Circular Hough Transform (CHT) for Micro-sleeps extraction and yawning frequency calculation is presented in research work by N. Alioua et al. [8]. In their approach, the counter gets incremented with each frame if the mouth and the eye-opening condition is satisfied until the threshold is reached, then an alarming system is used to alert the driver.

Pixel filtering approach is used by F. Hashemzadeh, et al. [9]. In the proposed model for drowsiness detection based on ARM microcontroller, first face detection is performed over black and white image frame to find the vertical and horizontal region of the face using column and row indices respectively. Further image filtering using a 5 x 5-pixel filter is used for pupil detection. This process is performed over the detected face region only but not over the complete image frame. Finally, drowsiness is detected by analyzing the brightness between the eyebrows and pupils.

In the work of Shiyuan Zhang, et al. [11], a smartwatch is used for monitoring driver's hand on/off steering along with a heart rate sensor. When the driver is about to enter in drowsy state the heart rate fluctuation will decrease and the driver will tend to leave the steering wheel. An SVM classifier is also used for hand movement data which is collected when the hand is on the steering wheel.

The concept of Electrooculography (EOG) with Artificial Neural Network (ANN) is proposed by Keith Marlon R. Tabal, et al. [12]. Electrodes were placed on the driver's face by the help of a cap and signals were collected, then those collected signals were converted to digital form by using analog-to-digital converter (ADC) which further feeds into the ANN for training using the back-propagation algorithm (BPA). Finally, the ANN was uploaded into the microcontroller for drowsiness detection.

Viola-Jones algorithm is widely used for object detection. Vidyagouri B. Hemadri and Umakant P. Kulkarni [13] used the Viola-Jones algorithm for face detection and further lips and eye detection is performed by the Canny edge detector and Harr classifier respectively. The driver's drowsiness is determined by the criteria of calculating the number of frames for which eyes are closed or mouth is open.

Vivek Nair and Nadir Charniya in their work [14] used Haar cascade classifier for face and eye detection and yawn detection is performed by template matching using normalized correlation coefficient method. An MQ-3 alcohol sensor is also implemented for drunk state detection. If the driver is found drunk or in a drowsy state, the alarm system will activate and the driver's seat will vibrate and emergency lights will turn 'ON'.

3 Methodology

3.1 Algorithm

1. Vehicle active.
2. Camera active: Capture driver's face in real-time.
3. Extract information from video frames using Computer vision.
4. Face detection using Dlib face detector.

5a. Extracting eyes and lips shape using Dlib face predictor.

    a. Calculating Eye Aspect Ratio (EAR).

$$EAR = \frac{\| p2 - p6 \| + \|p3 - p5\|}{2\| p1 - p4 \|}$$

    b. Calculating distance between upper and lower lips.

$$upper\_mean = \frac{\| p1 + p2 + p3 + p4 + p5 + p6\|}{6}$$

$$lower\_mean = \frac{\| p7 + p8 + p9 + p10 + p11 + p12\|}{6}$$

$$distance = \| upper\_mean - lower\_mean \|$$

    c. If calculated EAR is less than the threshold value: Increment counter.

Else: go to step e.

    d. If the counter is greater than the consecutive frame threshold: Drowsiness Alert.

Else: go to step e.

    e. If calculated lips distance is more than the threshold value: Yawn Alert.

Else: go to step 6

5b. Cell phone detection using Region-Convolutional Neural Network (R-CNN) on TensorFlow.

    a. If Cell phone detected: Cell phone Alert.

Else: go to step 6

6. If vehicle active: go to step 3

Else: go to step 7

7. Stop camera feed/ release camera.

3.2 Flow Chart

(Fig. 1).

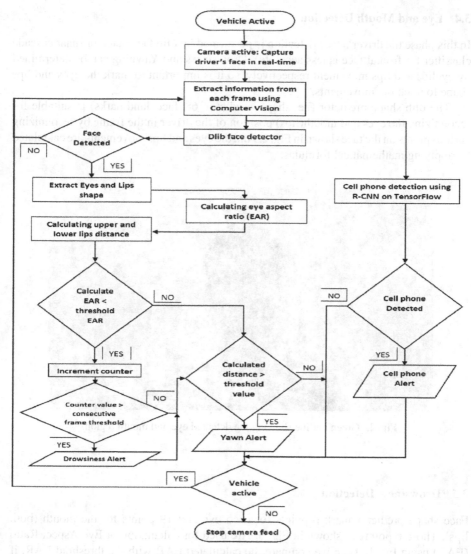

Fig. 1. Flow chart of proposed algorithm.

3.3 Live Video Capture

An ordinary digital camera is used to capture the driver's face in real-time. And for extracting information from each frame, the live video feed is processed through OpenCV, an open-source library for computer vision.

3.4 Eye and Mouth Detection

In this phase the driver's face detection is performed by dlib face detector (haar cascade classifier for frontal face is less accurate). Drowsiness and Yawning can be determined by eyelids and lips movement respectively, so it is important to mark the eyes and lips shape to track the movements.

The dlib shape predictor (i.e. shape_predictor_68_face_landmarks) is suitable for recognizing the eyes and mouth(lips) position of the driver in the frame by recognizing various points on the face shown in Fig. 2. And the eyes and lips movements are calculated by applying mathematical formulas.

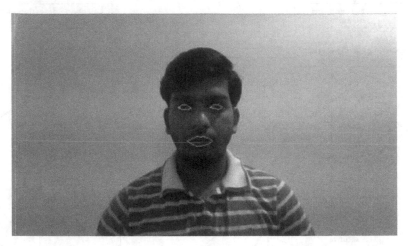

Fig. 2. Green outline showing the detected eye and mouth region.

3.5 Drowsiness Detection

Face shape predictor mark 6 points for each eye and 19 points for the mouth (both lips). Those 6 points as shown in Fig. 3. Are used for calculation of Eye Aspect Ratio (EAR) using Eq. 1. Then we compare the calculated EAR with the threshold EAR, if the calculated EAR is less than the threshold value then an alarm will be raised for drowsiness detection. A comparison between different levels of calculated EAR values is shown in Fig. 4 with the help of a graph.

$$EAR = \frac{||p2 - p6|| + ||p3 - p5||}{2||p1 - p4||} \tag{1}$$

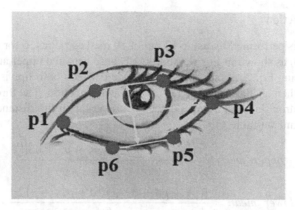

Fig. 3. Marked points on eye for calculation EAR.

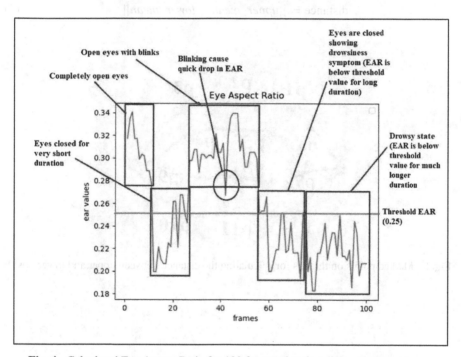

Fig. 4. Calculated Eye Aspect Ratio for 100 frames showing different states of eyes.

In the above figure blue line represents the calculated EAR value and green line represents the Threshold EAR value (0.25).

3.6 Yawn Detection

Yawn detection is performed by using 12 out of 19 marked points, 6 for each lip (upper lip and lower lip) as shown in Fig. 5. And the distance between upper and lower lips is calculated by using Eq. 2, 3 and 4. If the distance between both lips is more than the threshold value then an alarm will be raised for yawn detection. The threshold value in both the cases (drowsiness and yawn detection) depends on the distance between the driver and the camera (Table 1).

$$upper\_mean = \frac{\|p1 + p2 + p3 + p4 + p5 + p6\|}{6} \tag{2}$$

$$lower\_mean = \frac{\|p7 + p8 + p9 + p10 + p11 + p12\|}{6} \tag{3}$$

$$distance = \|upper\_mean - lower\_mean\| \tag{4}$$

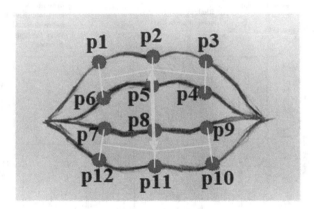

Fig. 5. Marked points on the lips for calculating the distance between upper and lower lips.

3.7 EAR and Yawn Frequency Analysis

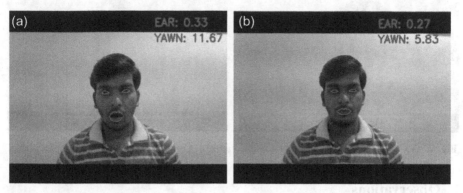

Fig. 6. (a) Partially open eyes with a close mouth. (b) Open eyes with a partially open mouth.

Table 1. EAR and Yawn frequency analysis performed over the different eye and mouth conditions.

Eye and mouth condition	EAR frequency	Yawn frequency
Partially open eyes with close mouth	0.27	5.83
Open eyes with partially open mouth	0.33	11.67

3.8 Cell Phone Detection

Machine learning is one of the best ways to detect the cell phone by applying object detection algorithm. Here, we input the video frames through OpenCV to the machine-learning R-CNN model (i.e. faster_rcnn_rcsnet101_coco) using TensorFlow which works fast with high accuracy and detects the cell phone shown in Fig. 7 (a) and Fig. 6 (b). An alarm will be raised to alert the driver if the cell phone is detected (Tables 2 and 3).

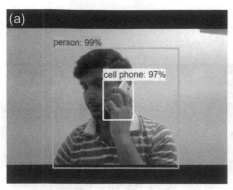 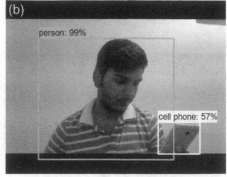

Fig. 7. A Cell phone detected during a phone call. (**b**). Cell phone detected during messaging.

4 Observations

Table 2. Observations based on the literature survey.

Author	Publication Year	Drowsy Detection	Yawn Detection	Cell phone Detection	Methodology	Other Algorithm/ Technique	Result
Fuzail Khan, Sandeep Sharma	2020	Available	n/a	n/a	Eye center tracking and Adaptive Gaussian Binary Thresholding for monitoring eye state and dynamic double thresholding method for drowsiness detection	Haar cascade classifier for face detection	Alarm system
Auni Syahirah Abu Bakar, Goh Khai Shan, Gan Lai Ta and Rohana Abdul Karim	2019	Available	n/a	n/a	Cloud-based IoT system analyses the eye condition and sleep state	Notification of current location using GPS navigation through SMS to relatives	Alarm system
Eddie E. Galarza, Fabricio D. Egas, Franklin M. Silva, Paola M. Velasco, and Eddie D. Galarza	2018	Available	Available	n/a	Percentage of eyelid closure (PERCLOS) and yawn frequency	HCI (Human-Computer Interface) implementation using smartphones	Alert
Anirban Dasgupta, Anjith George, S. L. Happy, Aurobinda Routray, and Tara Shanker	2013	Available	n/a	n/a	Percentage of eyelid closure (PERCLOS)		Alarm system

(continued)

Table 2. (*continued*)

Author	Publication Year	Drowsy Detection	Yawn Detection	Cell phone Detection	Methodology	Other Algorithm/ Technique	Result
D. Selvathi	2020	Available	n/a	n/a	SVM Classification	LBP and MAX Pooling based feature extraction using Deep Learning	Alert
Sanghyuk Park, Fei Pan, Sunghun Kang, and Chang D. Yoo	2017	Available	n/a	n/a	Implementation of Deep network on NTHU-drowsy driver detection benchmark dataset	AlexNet, VGG-FaceNet and FlowImageNet Networks for learning feature representation and IAA and FFA architecture respectively for ensemble detection	Alert
Tiberiu Vesselenyi, Alexandru Rus, Tudor Mitran, Sorin Moca, and Csokmai Lehel	2020	Available	n/a	n/a	EEG signals along with Artificial Neural Network (ANN) and Eye Aspect Ratio (EAR) for eye state analysis		Alert system
Nawal Alioua, Aouatif Amine, Mohammed Rziza, and Driss Aboutajdine	2011	Available	Available	n/a	Micro-sleeps extraction and yawning frequency calculation based on Circular Hough Transform (CHT)		Alarm system
F. Hashemzadeh, M. J. Ostadi, and B. Mohammadi-ivatloo	2017	Available	n/a	n/a	Pupil detection using pixel filter and analyzing brightness between eyebrows and pupils		Alarm system
Salvatore Vitabile, Alessandra De Paola, and Filippo Sorbello	2011	Available	n/a	n/a	Percentage of eyelid closure (PERCLOS)		Alarm system
Shiyuan Zhang, Hui He, Zhi Wang, Mingze Gao, and Jinsong Mao	2018	Available	n/a	n/a	The motion of hands-on/off steering wheel and heart rate analysis		Alert system
Keith Marlon R. Tabal, Felicito S. Caluyo, and Joseph Bryan G. Ibarra	2016	Available	n/a	n/a	Electrooculography (EOG) and Artificial Neural Network (ANN)		Alarm system

(*continued*)

Table 2. (*continued*)

Author	Publication Year	Drowsy Detection	Yawn Detection	Cell phone Detection	Methodology	Other Algorithm/ Technique	Result
Vidyagouri B. Hemadri and Umakant P. Kulkarni	2013	Available	Available	n/a	Viola-Jones algorithm for face detection, the canny edge detector is used for lips edge detection and Harr classifier for eye detection		Alert system
Vivek Nair and Nadir Charniya	2019	Available	Available	n/a	Haar cascade classifier is used for face and eye detection, and template matching is used for yawn detection	Drunk state detection is performed by using MQ-3 alcohol sensor	Alarm system

Table 3. Observations based on algorithm implementation.

Drowsy Detection	Yawn Detection	Cell phone Detection	Methodology	Other Algorithm/ Technique
Available	Available	Available	Eye aspect ratio (EAR) for drowsiness detection and distance between upper and lower lips used for Yawn detection	Cell phone is detected by machine learning R-CNN model using TensorFlow

5   Results

We performed various tests for drowsiness, yawn, and cell phone detection in day and night time shown in Fig. 8. It is observed that drowsiness and yawning are detected well in both day and night time.

In daytime, sunlight is enough while in night time street light or moonlight will be quite helpful.

Cell phone in day time is detected easily while in night time it required some light which is in few cases fulfilled by cell phone light itself. For better detection of the cell phone at night, an extra camera can be used for the side view angle (Table 4).

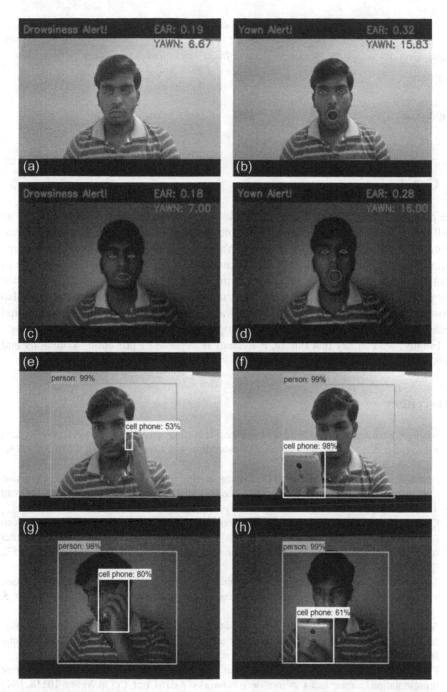

Fig. 8. (a) Drowsiness detected in the daytime. (b). Yawning detected in the daytime. (c). Drowsiness detected in the night time. (d). Yawning detected in the night time. (e). Cell phone detected during a phone call in daytime. (f). Cell phone detected during message typing in daytime. (g). Cell phone detected during a phone call in the night time. (h). Cell phone detected during message typing in the night time.

Table 4. Observation based on algorithm testing.

Lighting condition	EAR frequency	Yawn frequency	Drowsiness alert	Yawn alert
Day time	0.19	6.67	Yes	
	0.32	15.83		Yes
Night time	0.18	7.00	Yes	
	0.28	16.00		Yes

6 Conclusion

The proposed vision-based Advance Collision Prevention System (ACP System) is an intelligent system with the power of machine learning. The result of the unique combination of the system which is Drowsy, Yawn, and Cell phone detection, the three major factors for distraction and lack of focus while driving, is accurate and precise in real-time as for prevention of collision it is important to act with-in time. Performance tests performed during both day and night time produced impressive outputs. It is also a cost-efficient model as no expensive hardware is required but only an ordinary digital camera is used for live video capturing and open-source software technologies.

Finally, we can say that our ACP System is capable of preventing collisions and saving lives.

References

1. Khan, F., Sharma, S.: Development of low-cost real-time driver drowsiness detection system using eye centre tracking and dynamic thresholding. Int. Conf. Intell. Sys. Desi. Appl. **940**, 262–271 (2020)
2. Abu Bakar, A.S., Shan, G.K., Ta, G.L., Abdul Karim, R.: IOT—Eye Drowsiness Detection System by Using Intel Edison with GPS Navigation. In: Proceedings of the 10th National Technical Seminar on Underwater System Technology, vol 538, pp. 485–493 (2019)
3. Galarza, E.E., Egas, F.D., Silva, F.M., Velasco, P.M., Galarza, E.D.: Real time driver drowsiness detection based on driver's face image behavior using a system of human computer interaction implemented in a smartphone. Proc. Int. Conf. Info. Technol. Sys. **721**, 563–572 (2018)
4. Dasgupta, A., George, A., Happy, S.L., Aurobinda, R., Shanker, T.: An on-board vision-based system for drowsiness detection in automotive drivers. Int. J. Adv. Eng. Sci. Appl. Math. **5**, 94–103 (2013)
5. Selvathi, D.: FPGA based human fatigue and drowsiness detection system using deep neural network for vehicle drivers in road accident avoidance system. Hum. Behavi. Analy. Using Intell. Sys. **6**, 69–91 (2020)
6. Park, S., Pan, F., Kang, S., Yoo, C.D.: Driver drowsiness detection system based on feature representation learning using various deep networks. Asian Conf. Comp. Vision **10118**, 154–164 (2017)
7. Vesselenyi, T., Rus, A., Mitran, T., Moca, S., Lehel, C.: Fuzzy Decision Algorithm for Driver Drowsiness Detection. In: Dumitru, I., Covaciu, D., Racila, L., Rosca, A. (eds.) SMAT 2019, pp. 458–467. Springer, Cham (2020). https://doi.org/10.1007/978-3-030-32564-0_53

8. Alioua, N., Amine, A., Rziza, M., Aboutajdine, D.: Driver's fatigue and drowsiness detection to reduce traffic accidents on road. Int. Conf. Comp. Analy. Imag. Patter. **6855**, 397–404 (2011)

9. Hashemzadeh, F., Ostadi, M.J., Mohammadi-ivatloo, B.: A fast and simple drowsiness detection system based on ARM microcontrollers. Intell. Indus. Sys. **3**(1), 23–28 (2017). https://doi.org/10.1007/s40903-017-0069-x

10. Biswas, S., Bianchini, M., Shaw, R.N., Ghosh, A.: Prediction of Traffic Movement for Autonomous Vehicles. In: Bianchini, M., Simic, M., Ghosh, A., Shaw, R.N. (eds.) Machine Learning for Robotics Applications. SCI, vol. 960, pp. 153–168. Springer, Singapore (2021). https://doi.org/10.1007/978-981-16-0598-7_12

11. Zhang, S., He, H., Wang, Z., Gao, M., Mao, J.: Low-power listen based driver drowsiness detection system using smartwatch. Int. Conf. Cloud Comput. Secu. **11067**, 453–464 (2018)

12. Garg, C., Namdeo, A., Singhal, A., Singh, P., Shaw, R.N., Ghosh, A.: Adaptive Fuzzy Logic Models for the Prediction of Compressive Strength of Sustainable Concrete. In: Bianchini, M., Piuri, V., Das, S., Shaw, R.N. (eds.) Advanced Computing and Intelligent Technologies. LNNS, vol. 218, pp. 593–605. Springer, Singapore (2022). https://doi.org/10.1007/978-981-16-2164-2_47

13. Hemadri, V.B., Kulkarni, U.P.: Detection of drowsiness using fusion of yawning and eyelid movements. Int. Conf. Adva. Comp. Commu. Cont. **361**, 583–594 (2013)

14. Nair, V., Charniya, N.: Drunk driving and drowsiness detection alert system. Int. Conf. ISMAC in Computat. Visi. Bio-Eng. **3**, 1191–1207 (2019)

Energy Efficient Routing in Underwater Acoustic Sensor Network Using Crow Optimization Algorithm Over Aodv

Y. Yashwanth Reddy and Vijayalakshmi[✉]

Department of Electronics and Communication Engineering, Saveetha School of Engineering,
Saveetha Institute of Medical and Technical Sciences, Saveetha University, Chennai 602105,
Tamil Nadu, India
vijayalakshmi.sse@saveetha.com

Abstract. The proposed work aims to provide an Energy Optimization routing protocol to enhance Underwater Acoustic Sensor Networks (UWASNenergy)'s efficiency, packet delivery ratio, and normalised routing overhead using the Novel CROW Optimization algorithm in comparison to the AODV Optimization algorithm. The number of samples taken for the two groups is 20. Each group containing a pre-test power of 80% led to the collection of 10 samples. A novel CROW optimization technique is used in group 1, while an AODV algorithm is used in group 2. The NS 2 simulator carries out simulation and measures network performance using the metrics of average energy consumption, delay, and normalised routing overhead. Using SPSS Software, a statistical analysis was performed. A novel CROW optimization algorithm achieves 15% of energy consumption, 25% of delay and 2% of Normalized routing overhead when compared to AODV algorithm. A statistical analysis reveals that the significant value that was achieved is ($P < 0.05$). The simulation results show that novel CROW optimization algorithm performs significantly better energy efficiency than AODV algorithm.

Keywords: Underwater Acoustic Sensor Networks (UWASN) · Novel Crow Optimization Algorithm (COA) · AODV · Delay · Energy consumption · Normalized routing overhead

1 Introduction

UASNs are composed of a number of underwater acoustic sensor nodes that perform operations like navigation, surveillance, resource exploitation, intrusion detection, and data collection while being deployed in underwater observation zones [1]. Energy efficiency is a serious challenge due to the underwater sensor nodes' tiny size, low energy capacity, and difficulty in replacement. Data transfer efficiency from underwater sensor nodes to a sink node (SN) faces significant hurdles due to the complex underwater environment [2]. In UWASN, the optimization process is used to enhance the range and range-free localization of node locations. Underwater sensor network node positioning is carried out via the sequential greedy optimization approach using iteration and decision variables [3]. However, the WSN routing optimization techniques increase the efficiency of high throughput routing and prolong battery life [4]. Numerous studies have demonstrated the utilisation of the clustering topology to transfer data between clusters results in energy savings, collision avoidance, and load balancing.

In the past five years, a number of research publications on extending the lifespan of underwater acoustic sensor networks (UWASN) have been published, including 132 in IEEE Xplore and 245 in Google Scholar. The issue of energy consumption in underwater acoustics wireless sensor networks is what this research aims to address [5] based on an enhanced crow optimization (COA) method, suggests an energy-efficient clustered routing strategy. In UWASN, many algorithms, including joint energyaware routing, and opportunistic routing, are used to conduct efficient routing from source to destination nodes [3]. To carry out the optimization process to minimize delay and packet drop while increasing throughput and network lifetime [6]. The geographical and temporal variability, Doppler and GS, and geographical however, are the difficult issues in UWASN. In under water acoustic sensornetwork [7] concentrate only on changes in salinity and temperature. Utilizing the Lion Optimization Algorithm for channel selection in LOCAN fixes the problems caused by water column concentrate only on changes in salinity and temperature. Utilizing the Lion Optimization Algorithm for channel selection in LOCAN fixes the problems caused by water column fluctuation and improves throughput, battery life, and network lifetime. And improves throughput, battery life, and lifetime of the network.

Underwater acoustic networks have issues with spatial and temporal fluctuation, propagation delays, and water level variations that cause early node failure, higher energy costs, and longer delays. By employing the noval Crow optimization technique and comparing it to the AODV algorithm, the suggested algorithm aims to reduce energy consumption, delay, and normalised routing overhead in Underwater Acoustic Sensor Networks (UWASN).

2 Materials and Methods

The study was carried out at SIMATS's Saveetha School of Engineering, Department of Electronics and Communication Engineering, in Chennai. For the pretest analysis, two groups (datasets) with 10 samples each are gathered for the Crow optimization algorithm and the AODV algorithm, with pre-test power of 80%, error of 0.5, threshold of 0.05, and confidence level of 95%.

Using aqua-sim in NS2, sample preparation for group 1 analyses energy, latency, and normalised routing overhead of the AODV algorithm by randomly altering depth for various time intervals. Network coding is developed in NS2 in order to emulate routing performance.The programme analyses routing metrics for each node with a millisecond interval using an energy model for acoustic propagation. The NS2 software is used for the testing setup.

When preparing samples for Group 2, the Novel Crow optimization algorithm's energy, latency, and normalised routing overhead are examined by arbitrarily changing the depth for various time slots while utilising Aqua-Sim in NS2. Network coding is developed in NS2 in order to emulate routing performance.For acoustic propagation, the algorithm employs an energy model, and routing metrics are examined for each node at intervals of one millisecond.To improve the total network efficiency, Group 1 has a revolutionary Crow optimization algorithm. Fast convergence and periodic convergence based on dynamic topology are features of the novel crow optimization technique.

This section outlines the step-by-step process for implementing the COA.

Step 1: initialize the issue and change the parameters

Step 2: Set the birds' starting position and memory

Step 3: Examine fitness (objective) performance

Step 4: Create new position

Step 5: Examine whether new positions are feasible

Step 6: Examine fitness function of new positions

Step 7: revise memory

Step 8: Verify the termination standard.

Steps To obtain itermax, continue steps 4 through 7. When the termination requirement is satisfied, the optimal memory position relative to the value of the objective function is provided as the optimization problem's solution.

2.1 Statistical Analysis

For statistical comparison of variables including latency, energy consumption, and normalised routing overhead, IBM SPSS 27.0.1 [8] was used. The significance value of the independent t-test was $p < 0.05$ which was done in SPSS Software. The statistical analysis for novel Crow optimization algorithm and AODV algorithm was done. The calculation is done with G-power 0.8 and confidence interval of 95%. Normalized routing overhead, latency, and energy are the dependent variables. Using independent two-tailed tests, particle count and population size are the independent variables.

3 Results

The simulation results are presented for the effectiveness of the new Crow optimization algorithm (COA) is assessed in terms of its energy usage, delay, Normalized Routing Overhead for efficient data transfer, and methods for hole identification and repair. The performance of the novel crow optimization algorithm was compared to that of the AODV algorithm on an NS2 simulator.

Figure 1 depicts the Delay, which represents the time needed to send a data packet from source to destination. Novel Crow Optimization Algorithm (COA)-based strategy that has been suggested is superior since it searches for the path between source and destination nodes while focusing on minimising node-to-node delays. Figure 2 displays the variances in energy consumption for several algorithms. It can be described as the overall energy used by all network nodes within a specific simulation time. The energy usage grows along with the node's movement. Results unmistakably demonstrate that the suggested method consumes less energy than alternative approaches. Figure 3 depicts the normalised routing overhead fluctuation. a measure of how many bytes the target has successfully received. As node mobility grew, routing methods experienced a reduction in normalised routing overhead.

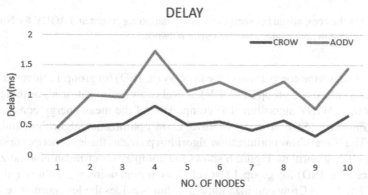

Fig. 1. Shows the comparison between CROW optimization algorithm and AODV for delay in underwater acoustic sensor network.

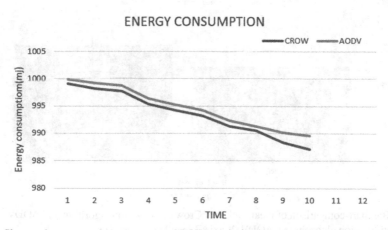

Fig. 2. Shows the comparison between CROW optimization algorithm AODV for Energy Consumption in underwater acoustic sensor network.

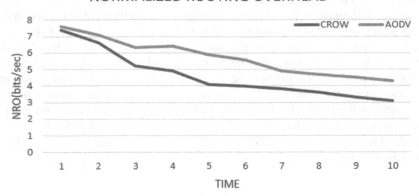

Fig. 3. Shows the comparison between Crow optimization algorithm and AODV for Normalized Routing Overhead in underwater acoustic sensor network.

Figure 4 shows the comparison of mean delay (± 1SD) for group 1 (Novel Crow optimization algorithm) and group 2 (AODV). Novel Crow optimization algorithm provides less delay than AODV algorithm. The comparison of the mean energy consumption is shown in Fig. 5 (± 1SD) for group 1 (Novel Crow optimization algorithm) and group 2 (AODV). The Novel Crow optimization algorithm provides the less energy consumption than the AODV algorithm. Figure 6 shows the comparison of mean Normalized routing overhead (± 1SD) for group 1 (Novel Crow optimization algorithm) and group 2 (AODV). The Novel Crow optimization algorithm provides the less normalized routing overhead than the AODV algorithm.

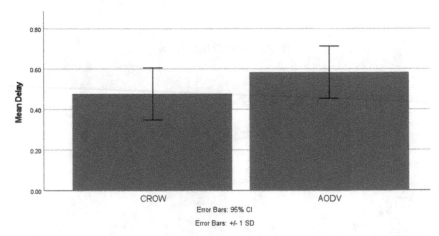

Fig. 4. Barchart-comparison of mean Delay of Crow optimization algorithm and AODV. X axis: Crow optimization algorithm vs AODV, Y axis: Mean Delay ± 1 SD

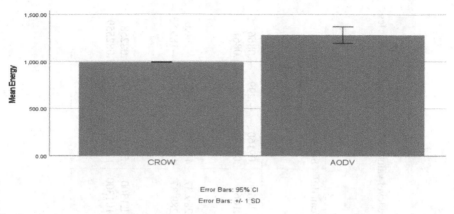

Fig. 5. Barchart-comparison of mean Energy consumption of Crow optimization algorithm and AODV algorithm. Axis: Crow optimization algorithm vs AODV, Y axis: Mean Energy consumption $\pm$ 1 SD.

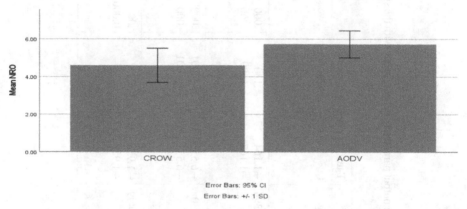

Fig. 6. Barchart-comparison of mean Normalized Routing Overhead of Crow optimization algorithm and AODV. X axis: Crow optimization vs AODV, Y axis: Mean NRO $\pm$ 1 SD.

Table 1. Represents deriptive statistical comparison of three parameters with respect to time for Crow optimization algorithm and AODV.

Groups	Parameter	N	Mean	Std. deviation
CROW Algorithm	Delay	10	48.76	.20377
	Energy consumption		992.91	5.157
	Normalized Routing Overhead		4.600	1.432
AODV Algorithm	Delay	10	59.33	.19427
	Energy consumption		1282.2	139.55
	Normalized Routing Overhead		5.730	1.1304

The mean values of the dependent variables are compared statistically in Table 1 utilising a 0.05 significance threshold for analysis. Table 2 shows correlation between the output variables that are dependent. It was demonstrated through statistical analysis

Table 2. The table shows the variances between the three output parameters in accordance with the significance level values. The significance level is less than 0.05 for two tails which is good.

Levene's test for equality of variances				T-test for equality of means							
		F	sig	t	dif	Oneside p	Two side p	Mean diff	Std error	95% confidence interval of the difference Lower upper	
Delay	Equal variances assumed	.005	.0394	−1.164	17	.130	.000	−.1066	.09160	−.299	.0866
	Equal variances not assumed			−1.167	16.93	.1309	.000	−.1066	.09136	−.299	.0861
Energy consumption	Equal variances assumed	63.536	.030	−6.553	18	< .001	.000	−289.37	44.160	−382.15	−196.6
	Equal variances not assumed			−6.553	9.025	< .001	.000	−289.37	44.160	−389.22	−189.53
Normalized Routing overhead	Equal variances assumed	.476	.0499	−1.958	18	.033	.000	−1.1300	.5771	−2.342	.08258
	Equal variances not assumed			−1.958	17.052	.033	0.000	−101300	17.056	−2.347	.082559

and descriptive analysis that the Crow optimization method perform better than the AODV optimization algorithm.

4   Discussion

This study addressed the issue of energy consumption in underwater acoustic sensor networks by introducing an energy-efficient clustered routing strategy based on the novel Crow optimization technique.In underwater acoustic networks, the innovative Crow Optimization Algorithm (COA) outperforms the currently used AODV algorithm.

When developing clustered routing algorithms, many researchers have used ACO algorithms in UWSNs. Designing a routing method that uses as little energy as possible while still maximising network longevity is of utmost importance.Therefore, this [9] provides an enhanced ACO-based clustering routing technique for UWSNs. [10] focus the clustering routing algorithm exploits the clustering topology and a multi-hop approach for inter-cluster data transfer, which allows it to conserve energy, prevent collisions. [11] developed a multilevel underwater clustering strategy, where the logical level and the cluster are generated depending on the amount of energy that remains in the nodes rather than their location. [12] a fuzzy-based clustering routing protocol has been developed for UWSNs, where the residual energy, the distance, the node density, the load, and the connection quality are taken into consideration as fuzzy logic's inputs to select CHNs and determine the cluster size.

Energy efficiency is a serious challenge due to the underwater sensor nodes' tiny size, low energy capacity, and difficulty in replacement. Additionally, UWSNs have drawbacks such a high error rate, low bandwidth, and long propagation delay. Therefore, it will be crucial for UWSNs in the future to create an energy-efficient routing technique for data transfer in a complex undersea environment.

5   Conclusion

This research work introduced an energy efficient clustering routing method based on the cutting-edge crow optimization technique, the problem of energy consumption in underwater sensor networks is addressed. It outperforms the AODV method in terms of energy consumption, delay, and normalised routing overhead.The simulation results shows that novel Crow optimization algorithm (COA) performs significantly better energy efficiency than AODV algorithm.

References

1. Yahya, et al.: Cooperative routing for energy efficient underwater wireless sensor networks. IEEE Access 7, 141888–141899 (2019). https://doi.org/10.1109/access.2019.2941422
2. Zhou, Q., Zheng, Y.: Long link wireless sensor routing optimization based on improved adaptive ant colony algorithm. Int. J. Wireless Inf. Networks 27(2), 241–252 (2019). https://doi.org/10.1007/s10776-019-00452-9

3. Shi, Q., He, C., Chen, H., Jiang, L.: Distributed wireless sensor network localization via sequential greedy optimization algorithm. IEEE Trans. Signal Process. **58**(6), 3328–3340 (2010). https://doi.org/10.1109/tsp.2010.2045416

4. Ahmed, G., Zhao, X., Fareed, M.M.S., Fareed, M.Z.: An energy-efficient redundant transmission control clustering approach for underwater acoustic networks. Sensors **19**(19), 4241 (2019). https://doi.org/10.3390/s19194241

5. Sun, Y., Dong, W., Chen, Y.: An improved routing algorithm based on ant colony optimization in wireless sensor networks. IEEE Commun. Lett. **21**(6), 1317–1320 (2017). https://doi.org/10.1109/lcomm.2017.2672959

6. Banerjee, A., et al.: Construction of Effective Wireless Sensor Network for Smart Communication Using Modified Ant Colony Optimization Technique. In: Bianchini, M., Piuri, V., Das, S., Shaw, R.N. (eds.) Advanced Computing and Intelligent Technologies. LNNS, vol. 218, pp. 269–278. Springer, Singapore (2022). https://doi.org/10.1007/978-981-16-2164-2_22

7. Ghoreyshi, S.M., Shahrabi, A., Boutaleb, T.: An opportunistic void avoidance routing protocol for underwater sensor networks. In: 2016 IEEE 30th International Conference on Advanced Information Networking and Applications (AINA) (2016). https://doi.org/10.1109/aina.2016.96

8. Sathiyaraj, R., Bharathi, A.: An efficient intelligent traffic light control and deviation system for traffic congestion avoidance using multi-agent system. Transport **35**(3), 327–335 (2019). https://doi.org/10.3846/transport.2019.11115

9. Banerjee, A., et al.: Building of Efficient Communication System in Smart City Using Wireless Sensor Network Through Hybrid Optimization Technique. In: Piuri, V., Shaw, R.N., Ghosh, A., Islam, R. (eds.) AI and IoT for Smart City Applications. SCI, vol. 1002, pp. 15–30. Springer, Singapore (2022). https://doi.org/10.1007/978-981-16-7498-3_2

10. Wang, M., Chen, Y., Sun, X., Xiao, F., Xu, X.: Node energy consumption balanced multi-hop transmission for underwater acoustic sensor networks based on clustering algorithm. IEEE Access **8**, 191231–191241 (2020). https://doi.org/10.1109/access.2020.3032019

11. Bansal, R., Maheshwari, S., Awwal, P.: Energy-efficient multilevel clustering protocol for underwater wireless sensor networks. In: 2019 9th International Conference on Cloud Computing, Data Science & Engineering (Confluence) (2019). https://doi.org/10.1109/confluence.2019.8776984

12. Goyal, N., Dave, M., Verma, A.K.: Fuzzy based clustering and aggregation technique for under water wireless sensor networks. In: 2014 International Conference on Electronics and Communication Systems (ICECS) (2014). https://doi.org/10.1109/ecs.2014.6892804

Sign Language Recognizing Using Machine Learning

Yogendra Singh Rathore[1]($\boxtimes$), Dhyanendra Jain[2], Prashant Singh[3], Waseem Ahmed[2], and Amit Kumar Pandey[4]

[1] Department of Computer Science and Engineering, ShriRam College of Engineering and Management, Gwalior, India
yogendra.cse2006@gmail.com

[2] Department of CSE-AIML, ABES Engineering College, Ghaziabad, India
waseem.ahmed@abes.ac.in

[3] Department of Computer Science and Engineering, Sunder Deep Engineering College, Ghaziabad, India

[4] Department of CSE-DS, ABES Engineering College, Ghaziabad, India

Abstract. Sign language is a type of language that includes postures and body motions in addition to hand gestures. For ages, sign language was the only way to connect with each other. But in early times, without the knowledge of different varieties of language, it became hard to communicate. Now as the world is becoming more advanced and digitalised, deaf and blind people find the basic mode of communication more disrupting and uneasy. To resolve this issue, Sign language recognition/interpreter system becomes a necessity to help the people in need. This is possible because to Machine Learning and Human Computer Interaction (HCI).

Keywords: HCI · Machine learning · ASL translator · NLP

1 Introduction

"More than 75 million people worldwide have speech or hearing impairments. The deaf and the mute community makes sign languages to communicate, which include postures or the body movements, eye, brow, and hand gestures that are employed in various combinations to distinguish between lexical differentiation, grammar structure, etc. It is therefore clear that visual perception is crucial for understanding sign language. Our system's main goal is to convert hand signals to text. The framework makes it easier for people who have hearing or speech impairments to use sign language to interact with others. This will result in the mediator typically serves as a translator or translator's medium—being excluded. By translating a sign language input to speech or text output, this would provide the user with a user-friendly environment. The estrangement that is experienced by the deaf/mute community serves as further motivation for this goal. The deaf and mute population has increased rates of depression and loneliness, particularly when they are exposed to the hearing culture. The communication gap between

© The Author(s), under exclusive license to Springer Nature Switzerland AG 2023
R. N. Shaw et al. (Eds.): ICACIS 2022, CCIS 1749, pp. 393–400, 2023.
https://doi.org/10.1007/978-3-031-25088-0_35

both the deaf as well as the hearing causes significant obstacles that significantly lower living quality. Lack of access to knowledge, a lack of social relationships, and trouble integrating into society are a few examples [2].

American Sign Language is the fourth most useful language in North America and the most often utilised sublingually in the entire world. It is utilised not only in the United States but also in West Africa, Asia, Canada, and Mexico. ASL is used for community communication by more than 35 additional countries, including Jamaica, Panama, Thailand, and Malaysia, where English is the primary language of exchange. ASL is the main form of communication for about three million hearing-impaired people in the US and Canada [2].

""ASL is a broad and complex language that uses signs created by finger and hand movements along with body postures and facial expressions. ASL has many variations since it is regarded as a precise and authentic language, just like French and Spanish do. A large percentage of the population with speech impairments benefit greatly from ASL as a great way of communication. Its basis, state, future potential, and global effect are all pretty remarkable and eye-opening [3]. "ASL offers a collection of twenty six hand signs referred to as follows (Fig. 1).

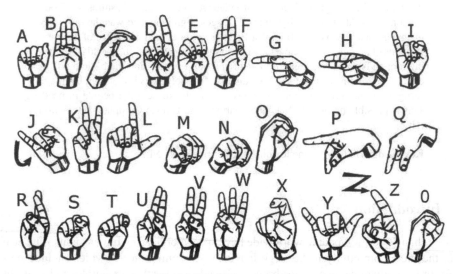

Fig. 1. Set of 26 gesture signs.

2 Literature Review

We have used American Sign Language(ASL) number of times in the past for development. According to the literature survey conducted, the previous techniques used were.

2.1 Support Vector Machine (SVM)

The SVM is a pattern recognition technique. It falls under the category of supervised learning. This technique is an instance of supervised learning and has been shown to be particularly effective at handling newly encountered data because it divides the feature space for each class. We have to input data into SVM and predicts which class will produce the output for each set. As well as SVM, parallel hidden Markov models were used to classify gestures in SASL [3]. That can be used to write out a large number of accessible English words. 26 American Manual Alphabetic characters are created using the 19 different hand shapes of American Sign Language. There is a set of ten numeric motions available in ASL to sign the digits "0" – "9". The group of 26 gestures for the English alphabet's letters (A to Z) is seen in the figure above.

2.2 Human Computer Interaction

The idea of HCI is to deals with how people and computers interact. The main goal of this emerging topic is to make the computer better understand humans. It has connections to a variety of subjects, including as computer science, media studies, and behavioral sciences. The term HCI is used in a variety of ways. Among them are MMI, CHI, HMI.

2.3 Virtual Reality Modelling Language

For the creation of 3-dimensional models and web-based models, VRML (virtual reality modelling language) was developed. It may be used to create an object's three-dimensional structure. Additionally, it resembles HTML. The capacity of this language to specify three-dimensional credentials, comparable to coordinates and geometric values, makes it the primary language used in sign language recognition systems.

2.4 Bag of the Features

(Bag of the features) is a type of pattern recognition algorithm that uses the visual vocabulary to identify a certain picture. Bag-of-features implements four main processes: feature extraction, learning the visual vocabulary, visual vocabulary quantization, and recognition of features. However, there is assured disadvantage to employing this approach, including issues with the camera's orientation, lighting, and internal characteristics.

2.5 Particle Swarm Optimization

"The area of computational science uses a computational technique called particle swarm optimization to resolve optimization issues. By using straightforward algebra, a number of potential solutions, or "particles," are iteratively moved throughout a search space.

3 Methodology

ASL–American sign language mostly used in America and its nearest countries, We have a large dataset to train a CNN Model without Overfitting on small dataset. All the alphabets are static in nature (Don't have to move) except 'J' and 'Z' They are Dynamic in nature. We have to move our hand in a certain way to recognize the alphabets.[5, 6].

It is a customised deep CNN model and not a pre-trained model. Because of its many convolution layers and pooling layers, CNN is one of the most efficient frameworks for object, face, and image identification [7, 8]. Our customised model has 5 Conv2D layers, with max pooling layers following each Conv2D layer. Convolutional layer is the building block of the CNNs. It is then followed by an Artificial Neural Network that is composed of two hidden layers and one output layer with a single neuron for classification. Our input image is applied as a vector of 3x3 convolutions in all the convolutional layers wherein each is followed by 2D max pooling. --Mohammad Badhruddouza Khan. The input image is delivered into the flattening layer after passing through the convolutional and pooling layers. This operations on the particles' velocities", positions, and other properties. This algorithm combines neural networks with other algorithms to produce better results than many other models as demonstrated by its high performance in various categories, including accuracy, precision and F-measure [1, 4]. Layer reduces the computational cost of the incoming image by flattening it into a column. This is subsequently fed into the dense layer/fully linked layer.Each layer in the fully connected layer extracts features, and the network generates a prediction based on thesefeatures [9, 10], known as forward propagation.

This proposed model uses two activation functions: ReLU and sigmoid activation functions. The rectified linear function (ReLU) is a nonlinear function that results in zero when the input is negative and one when it is positive. This sort of activation function is widely utilised in CNNs since it solves the problem of vanishing gradients and increases layer non-linearity. The final dense layer that collects all of the previous layers' output uses the sigmoid activation function because binary classification output was required. After this loss function (metric measuring how well a neural network model performs) The binary cross-entropy function is used to compute this. The Adam optimization technique is used in the model (Figs. 2, 3 and 4).

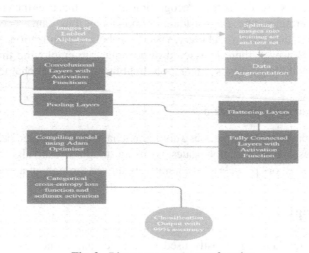

Fig. 2. Binary cross- entropy function.

4   Result

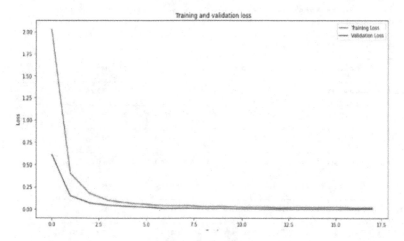

Fig. 3. Training and Validation Loss.

```
34/34 [==============================] - 51s 2s/step
              precision    recall  f1-score   support

           A       0.97      1.00      0.99       300
           B       1.00      1.00      1.00       300
           C       1.00      1.00      1.00       300
           D       1.00      1.00      1.00       300
           E       1.00      0.99      1.00       300
           F       1.00      0.99      0.99       300
           G       1.00      1.00      1.00       300
           H       1.00      1.00      1.00       300
           I       0.99      1.00      1.00       300
           J       1.00      1.00      1.00       300
           K       1.00      1.00      1.00       300
           L       1.00      1.00      1.00       300
           M       1.00      1.00      1.00       300
           N       0.99      1.00      1.00       300
           O       1.00      0.97      0.99       300
           P       1.00      1.00      1.00       300
           Q       1.00      1.00      1.00       300
           R       0.99      0.99      0.99       300
           S       1.00      1.00      1.00       300
           T       1.00      1.00      1.00       300
           U       0.98      1.00      0.99       300
           V       1.00      0.98      0.99       300
           W       1.00      1.00      1.00       300
           X       1.00      0.98      0.99       300
           Y       1.00      1.00      1.00       300
           Z       1.00      1.00      1.00       300
         del       0.99      1.00      1.00       300
     nothing       1.00      1.00      1.00       300
       space       1.00      1.00      1.00       300

    accuracy                           1.00      8700
   macro avg       1.00      1.00      1.00      8700
weighted avg       1.00      1.00      1.00      8700
```

```
Model: "sequential"
-------------------------------------------------------------------
Layer (type)              Output Shape             Param #
===================================================================
conv2d (Conv2D)           (None, 64, 64, 32)       2432
-------------------------------------------------------------------
max_pooling2d (MaxPooling2D) (None, 32, 32, 32)    0
-------------------------------------------------------------------
dropout (Dropout)         (None, 32, 32, 32)       0
-------------------------------------------------------------------
conv2d_1 (Conv2D)         (None, 32, 32, 64)       51264
-------------------------------------------------------------------
max_pooling2d_1 (MaxPooling2 (None, 16, 16, 64)    0
-------------------------------------------------------------------
dropout_1 (Dropout)       (None, 16, 16, 64)       0
-------------------------------------------------------------------
conv2d_2 (Conv2D)         (None, 16, 16, 64)       102464
-------------------------------------------------------------------
max_pooling2d_2 (MaxPooling2 (None, 8, 8, 64)      0
-------------------------------------------------------------------
dropout_2 (Dropout)       (None, 8, 8, 64)         0
-------------------------------------------------------------------
conv2d_3 (Conv2D)         (None, 8, 8, 128)        204928
-------------------------------------------------------------------
max_pooling2d_3 (MaxPooling2 (None, 4, 4, 128)     0
-------------------------------------------------------------------
flatten (Flatten)         (None, 2048)             0
-------------------------------------------------------------------
dense (Dense)             (None, 256)              524544
-------------------------------------------------------------------
activation (Activation)   (None, 256)              0
-------------------------------------------------------------------
dense_1 (Dense)           (None, 29)               7453
===================================================================
Total params: 893,085
Trainable params: 893,085
Non-trainable params: 0
-------------------------------------------------------------------
```

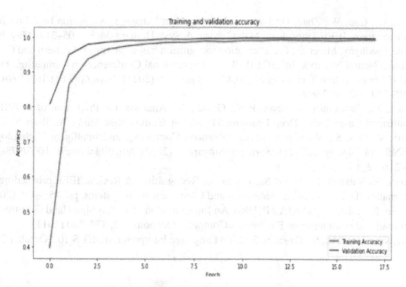

Fig. 4. Training and Validation Accuracy

5 Conclusion

Our system is fully capable of interpreting the ASL symbols. Our model operates in the way described below: In the subsequent step, gesture recognition is performed to compare the image acquired from the user with the images in the training database, allowing the displayed gesture to be deciphered. The camera operates and receives the user's input image. It goes through the detecting phase to see if it's a hand. For picture recognition, the Support-Vector Machine model is utilised. The outcome is displayed in the following phase, where the recognised symbol is changed to text. After completion of all the àbove steps successfully, ASL translation is completely done and thus we can move forward to check its accuracy and analyse its performance". We have managed to achieve an accuracy of 99% .

References

1. Wu, J., Sun, L., Jafari, R.: A wearable system for recognizing american sign language in RealTime using IMU and surface EMG sensors. IEEE J. Biomed. Heal. Informatics **20**(5), 1281–1290 (2016). https://doi.org/10.1109/JBHI.2016.2598302
2. Ding, L., Martinez, A.M.: Modelling and recognition of the linguistic components in American sign language, ‖ Image Vis. Comput. **27**(12), 1826–1844 (2009). Nov.
3. Kelly, D., Delannoy, R., Mc Donald, J., Markham, C.: A framework for continuous multimodal sign language recognition. In: Proc. Int. Conf. Multimodal Interfaces, Cambridge, MA, pp. 351–358 (2009)
4. Augustian Isaac, R., Sri Gayathri, S.: Sign Language Interpreter. IRJET **5**(10) (October 2018). p-ISSN – 2395-0072
5. for The Deaf and Dumb. Image Vis. Comput. **27**(12), 1826–1844 (Nov. 2009)

6. Fang, G., Gao, W., Zhao, D.: Large vocabulary sign language recognition based on fuzzy decision trees. IEEE Trans. Syst. Man Cybern. A Syst. Humans **34**(3), 305–314 (May 2004)

7. Mukhopadhyay, M., et al.: Facial emotion recognition based on Textural pattern and Convolutional Neural Network. In: 2021 IEEE 4th International Conference on Computing, Power and Communication Technologies (GUCON), pp. 1–6 (2021). https://doi.org/10.1109/GUCON50781.2021.9573860

8. Sinha, T., Chowdhury, T., Shaw, R.N., Ghosh, A.: Analysis and Prediction of COVID-19 Confirmed Cases Using Deep Learning Models: A Comparative Study. In: Bianchini, M., Piuri, V., Das, S., Shaw, R.N. (eds.) Advanced Computing and Intelligent Technologies. LNNS, vol. 218, pp. 207–218. Springer, Singapore (2022). https://doi.org/10.1007/978-981-16-2164-2_18

9. Purva, N., Vaishali, K.: Indian Sign language Recognition: A Review. IEEE proceedings on International Conference on Electronics and Communication Systems, pp. 452–456 (2014)

10. Pravin, F., Rajiv, D.: HASTA MUDRA An Interpretation of Indian Sign Hand Gestures. 3rd International conference on Electronics Computer technology **2**, 377–380 (2011)

11. Augustian Isaac, R., Sri Gayathri, S.: Sign Language Interpreter. IRJET **5**(10) (October 2018)

A Review of Clustering Techniques on Image Segmentation for Reconstruction of Buildings

Duraimoni Neguja[1]($\boxtimes$) and A. Senthil Rajan[2]

[1] Alagappa University, KaraiKudi, Tamil Nadu, India
neguja@gmail.com
[2] Computational Logistics, Alagappa University, KaraiKudi, Tamil Nadu, India

Abstract. The discovery of a new clustering technique on segmented images based on building structures is a challenging process for researchers. In this chapter, clustering techniques on image segmentation in buildings reform is a mingled process of segments of image. This chapter suggests review of vsrious clustering techniques and the improved strategy for the assembling of partitioned image segments of a representation into several areas according to a similarity trial value. In this chapter, various clustering techniques on distributed particles of image segments is studied as a more complicated procedure that results in computerized model but still common algorithm is not in function. Hence 41 years ago, finding a centralized algorithmic method in clustering separately with help of available data is changed by the lively growth of a broad variety of extremely fussy techniques. Most of the existing clustering techniques are greatly explicit to a definite kind of facts, and a little study is trail to widen common agenda that incorporates the clustering methods. Clustering can be a entirely habitual procedure, but it accomplishes its most excellent outcomes with partially regular techniques, that are directed by a individual machinist. This idea of partial automated procedure obviously engages a situation in which the creature hand will relate with the algorithms and the data in order to produce most favourable clustering methods. The simplest example of the use of a manual interference throughout the charge of clustering outputs on the concern of available procedures. Beyond the kind of input data, the machinist will have to warily choose the finest bespoke process, which major of the moment cannot be done in a routine forum. The prejudiced position of sight of the person is mandatory. Fuzzy C-means clustering, Parallel K-means clustering, Hierarchical density-based clustering and more clustering procedures are compared and studied.

Keywords: Clustering techniques · Parallel · K-means · Hierarchical · Density based · Fuzzy · C-means

1 Introduction

A formulation supported measure to guess the numerical inequality amid of a given couple of plotting points, and typify the idea in terms of that evaluates. This space can be figured by means of chronological Quadratic Equation [1]. A distributed component method activity following the construction blueprint is whole, gathering most uses of distributed building parts when defending the exceptional visualization and plan of the edifice. This purpose is accomplished by applying a partial under caring technology contingent on the grouping of entity areas and succeeding customer justification of the acquiring groups to spot pedestal units delegate of each point [2]. Huddle pattern ruins the mainly motivating feature of crams on gathering procedure [3]. Alike constructions shaped in poles apart instance eras, except distribution steady general skins [4]. A typical measure of Lexicalization as sequential parallel K-means algorithm is used [5]. This method can very much develop the huddles velocity with no omitting or still get hold of improved exactness, particularly for major set of information [6]. The clustering is performed on complicated predictions of data set [7]. The results focuses on inherent cluster values with differing characteristics [8]. The improper information on automobile and openly distributed parts of structures using the mentioned facts. The formula evaluated a lively diagrammatic method to set apart edifice and plants [9]. Un supervised algorithmic patterns are followed [10]. A preset technique has to be residential to categorize by introducing a pertinent and efficient proposal system. contrast place to take out alike silhouette constitutes to study that put of process entitle gathering. To reply this challenging, pre-orderly manner is used to mock-up the places, utilization contours and a multiple phenomenon sequential gathering method, utilizing the characteristics of pre-organized space, has been developed using a built in system [11]. Later giving out is needed to produce distinct grouping tagged by added schedule absorption. To tackle these matter, a measurable and argument less different points of gathering formula to straight yield the grouping brands by maxima fasten pixels, named as competent single-way different areas grouping with compromise points [12].

These topics let slip the confront of denoting of max out load fine by totaling of making required fashionable task and other ways of incorrectness such as information intake and restructuring techniques [13]. Acclimatizing preceding methods to eventually Single connected groupring by means of plot lessen guides to more incompetent answers while lone needs to calculate indensed concerned grouping orders. Basic, the solution is processed , that is foundation on an precise, so far extremely calculative requiring, selected areas concurrency service [14]. Bunch calculations of the gained systems can next be rapidly and precisely accredited to the contribution facts [15]. The maximization of group relation is utilized [16]. The out comes provide the researchers a new method [17]. The alternative parameters graphical chattels and the returns are defined. The raspy dissimilarity assess indicates the extent of design differences, which is used in the clustering method to get hold of the remoteness among figures position [18]. The restructuring is found tedious [19]. The nearly all significant technical hypothesis is that by the employ of bunch of replica of techniques, eventual pointer can be amplified, the choice of stuff and scientific pedestal of building manufacture can be enlarged, and the asset strength of the structure group can be shaped [20]. The position of improvement of process is projected [21]. The model can efficiently eliminate din and hold mark particulars of metaphors on diagram. It presents a new street for division of metaphors in lopsided fields [22]. The partitioning of image and forming the clusters is very complex procedure [23]. It is tricky to conclude the best numeral of grouping midpoints robotically without envision [24]. The ordinary come near wherever similar datasets into one cluster by considering a few prototype or intrinsic information likeness in a single cluster [25]. A characteristic eradicating code to modify unwanted skin to methodically decrease the surface belongings reason by unwanted factors [26]. The review of various methods is considered [27]. Rapidly finding the structures with disaster [28]. Multiple clustering is processed [29]. Clustering on huge data sets is effective in the process [30]. The uncorrected information in clustering is followed [30]. The projected work is tested with current data sets [31]. The projected work is compared with present process [32]. Numerous methods were projected performing profound grouping in the building area. Various functions are resulting unusual cavernous gathering system in this field [33]. The discovery of limits are pointed out in the clusters [34]. It is vital to classify an efficient cut piece process, so the document executes the examination of the collecting pedestal picture division methods used on the compelling quality picture of the person head to perceive the fair stuff agitated power element [35]. Each policy patterns to get a reduce depiction of its instructional catalog exploiting a few category of replica of similarity [36].

2 Performance Metrics of Clustering Techniques

2.1 Parallel K-means clustering technique

The parallel K-means clustering technique is the significant method of clustering nearest point of K-centralized midpoint on multiple views of the given image. The image 0 is captured by the digital camera and read by pixels. The nearest suitable pixel point is identified for clustering. Since multiple directions the clustering takes place, it is known as Parallel K-means clustering.

Procedure K-Parallel compare (k, v)
Input: Image, the Partitioned image, the sample pixel value
Output: <k', v'> set, where the k' is the sequence of the nearest midpoint and data' is a string consists of
1. Buid the test object from v;
2. miniDist = Double.MAX *VAL;
3. sequence = -1;
4. For j=0 to midpoint.length do
dist= CalcDist(object, midpoint[j]);
If dist < miniDist {
miniDist = dist;
sequence=End For
6. Take Sequence as k';
7. Build v' as a string consists of the data of various directions;
8. result < k' , v' > set
9.End

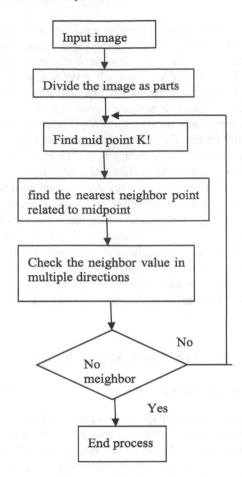

In some experiments selecting the midpoints arbitrarily cannot give exact outputs. There are various views of the data, the outcomes obtained are also discrete. The distance of length of the segment can differently depends on the facts. It grants the private optimum of the mean square defect procedure.

2.2 Hierarchical Clustering Technique

The algorithm assembles identical instances of data items into groups called cluster objects. The ending point is a set of connected data values or groups, where each data point is unique from each other cluster data, and the data values inside each group are widely related to each other.

This hierarchical clustering technique is divided into two types, those are Agglomerative Hierarchical Clustering and Divisive Hierarchical Clustering. Agglomerative hierarchical clustering groups the data points according to similarity.

Procedure: Agglomerative clustering.

1. Make each data value a single-valued group → forms N clusters.
2. Take the two nearest cluster points and make them one point → forms N-1 clusters.
3. Take the two nearest points and make them into one group → Forms N-2 clusters.
4. Repeat step-3 until you are given single group point.

Procedure: Divisive clustering.
Assign all of the evaluations to one group and then divide the group to two least alike groups. At last, pass through recursively on each data until there is one group for each reading. So this clustering technique is correctly conflicting to Agglomerative clustering. The various instances and their parameters are availed by hierarchical grouping.

2.3 Fuzzy C-means Clustering Technique

Fuzzy sense standard can be worn to collect multiple aspect of facts, conveying apiece spot a relationship in every group midpoint as of 0 toward 100 suggestions. This can be extremely influential to match up to usual complex-dataset grouping wherever each position is allocated a brittle, accurate tag. This technique acts by passing on relationship to every information dot resultant to apiece bunch inside on the origin of reserve amid the group hub and the records slot.

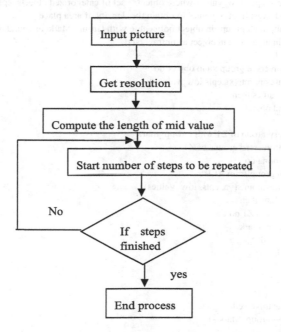

Added value is next to the huddle midpoint further is its relationship near to the marked gather midvalue. Noticeably, summing up of connection of every facts ought to be identical to solitary.

It is an unconfirmed gathering method which allows to make a fluffy divider of facts. The strategy relies on a constraint m that, which follows to the level of ambiguity of the result. Huge data of fuzzy logic will shape the modules and all essentials apt to feel right to all groups. The outputs of the maximization crisis based upon the value m. That is, unlike choices of Fuzzy data will classically guide to various divisions.

Procedure FCM.

Step1: Let F represent the occurrences of each instance in Dataset.

Step2: generate directpoint I = small(Dataset): large(Dataset).

Step3:Choose arbitrary midvalue at nearest 2.

Step4:calculate association environment:

2.4 Density Based Clustering Technique

Density-Based Clustering is conversed to lone of the finely identified unproven facts and knowledge, old in mock-up edifice and gathering methods. The details locates in the area set apart by two groups of low down peak thickness are deliberate as sound. The environs by a line measure of a agreed entity are recognized as the nearest point. If the nearest point includes the smallest value, Minimum points of happenings, then it is called a center point.

Procedure Density Clustering
INPUT: objects, epts, low_values where object = set of categorized objects, epts=areafill, low_values = lowest digit of values to obtain the density of area place.
OUTPUT: Output all groups in object noticeable with Group_Mark or sound object
Process obtain all groups in object as untraversed
Group_Mark 1
for every untraversed group xa in object do
Z1←FindNearestpoints(xa,epts,low_values)
if |Z|1 < low_values then
set xa as sound object
else.
set xa and every group of Z1 with Group_mark
AList←all untraversed groups of Z1
until AList is none do
ya←remove a group from AList
Z1←FindNearestpoints(ya, epts, low_values)
If |Z1| low_values then
for each group d in Z1 do
set d with Group_mark
if d is untraversed
AList←d AList
end for
set ya as visited
end until
end if set xa as traversed
group_Mark← group_Mark -1
end for
end process.

3 Problems of Clustering Methods

3.1 Parallel K-means clustering

Parallel k-means has difficulty in grouping data points anywhere similar data are of different sizes and thickness. To collect such facts, it is need to simplify Parallel k-means as portrays in the reward part. Grouping outer points. Midpoints can be moved by exclusive points, or the points might get possess huddle in its place of life form ignored.

Defining the number of groups to be allotted for clustering and finding the mid value are two major problems that occur in this type of clustering.

3.2 Hierarchical Clustering

Deficient in of a Global purpose role: agglomerative hierarchical clustering techniques perform clustering on a local level and as such there is no global objective function like in the K-Means Procedure. This is actually an advantage of this technique because the time and space complexity of global functions tends to be very expensive.

Limitations of Hierarchical Clustering: Sensitivity to noise and outliers. Faces Difficulty when handling with different sizes of clusters. It is breaking large clusters. In this technique, the order of the data has an impact on the final results.

Ability to Handle Different cluster Sizes: we have to decide how to treat clusters of various sizes that are merged together.

Merging Decisions Are Final: one downside of this technique is that once two clusters have been merged they cannot be split up at a later time for a more favorable union.

3.3 Problems Using Density Based Clustering

DBSCAN cannot gather data-sets with huge dissimilarity in concentration well, since then the min points mixture cannot be chosen properly for all clusters. Choosing a significant epoins value can be difficult if the data isn't well understood. DBSCAN is not entirely deterministic.

The main advantage of a clustered solution is automatic recovery from failure, that is, recovery without user intervention. Disadvantages of clustering are complexity and inability to recover from database corruption.

In a clustered setting, the cluster uses the same lecture to for Directory Server and Directory Server assistant, regardless of which cluster node is actually management of the service. That is, the address is transparent to the client process. In a replicated environment, If the clusters representing the entire population were formed under a biased opinion, the inferences about the entire population would be biased as well.

4 Performance Analysis of Clustering Techniques

Process	Storage value	Study1	Study2	Study 3
Parallel K means	$16z1 + 32k1(2d + 1) + 128$	4142	4612	8712
FCM	$16k(18n + 16d + 15) + 512$	192404	1537636	200468
Hierarchical	$4a^2 + 20m + 32$	32040028	32040028	32040028
Density	$2k(8m + 10d + 5) + 4d(n + d + 1) + 107$	96279	1218015	2388471

5 Conclusion

In this chapter the study of various clustering techniques is analyzed and reviewed. The Parallel K-Means technique regularly needs the fewest quantity of storage, which is dependent of the amount of trial,. The Parallel and Fuzzy C-Means Procedures are complete among the speedy Procedures, and they are particularly hasty while there are a great figure of groups other than in Parallel k-means the k should be recognized to earlier so that unlike first state produces changed outputs. Grouping Procedures should be selected depends on the natural world of the hitch to be resolved, features of the substances to be verified and the likely groups, and the amount of the setback and evaluation control on hand. Some troubles can be recovered by easy K-means gathering, when other situations may require more multifaceted Procedures with well-built storage required.

References

1. Xiong, W., Cheung, C.M., Sander, P.V., Joneja, A.: Rationalizing architectural surfaces based on clustering of joints. IEEE Trans. Visual. Comput. Graphics **28**, 4274–4288 (2022)
2. Feist, S., Sanhudo, L., Esteves, V.: Miguel pires and antónio aguiar costa "semi-supervised clustering for architectural modularisation." Buildings **12**, 303 (2022)
3. Jubair, A.M., et al.: Optimization of clustering in wireless sensor networks: techniques and protocols. Appl. Sci. **11**, 11448 (2021)
4. Araldi, A., Emsellem, D., Fusco, G., Tettamanzi, A., Overal, D.: Exploring building typologies through fast iterative Bayesian clustering. In: Communications SAGEO'2021 – La Rochelle, 5–7 May 2021
5. Cohen-Addad, V., Lattanzi, S., Norouzi-Fard, A., Sohler, C.: Parallel and efficient hierarchical k-median clustering. In: 35th Conference on Neural Information Processing Systems (NeurIPS 2021)
6. Weng, S., Gou, J., Fan, Z.: h-DBSCAN: A ssimple fast DBSCAN algorithm for big data. In: Proceedings of Machine Learning Research 157, 2021 ACML (2021)
7. Zhang, H., Davidson, I.: Deep descriptive clustering. In: Proceedings of the Thirtieth International Joint Conference on Artificial Intelligence (IJCAI-21) (2021)
8. Jain, M., AlSkaif, T., Dev, S.: Validating clustering frameworks for electric load demand profiles. IEEE Trans. Ind. Inf. **17**(12), 8057–8065 (2021). https://doi.org/10.1109/TII.2021.3061470

9. Gamal, A., et al.: Automatic LIDAR building segmentation based on DGCNN and euclidean clustering. J. Big data **7**, 102 (2020)
10. Talei, H., Benhaddou, D., Gamarra, C., Benbrahim, H., Essaaidi, M.: Smart building energy inefficiencies detection through time series analysis and unsupervised machine learning. Energies **14**(19), 6042 (2021). https://doi.org/10.3390/en14196042
11. Lévy, L.-N., Bosom, J., Guerard, G., Amor, S.B., Bui, M., Tran, H.: Application of pre-topological hierarchical clustering for buildings portfolio. In: SMARTGREENS 2021 – 10th International Conference on Smart Cities and Green ICT Systems, pp. 228–235 (2021)
12. Liu, S., et al.: Efficient one-pass multi-view subspace clustering with consensus anchors. In: Association for the Advancement of Artificial Intelligence. www.aaai.org (2021)
13. Eggimann, S., et al.: Spatiotemporal upscaling errors of building stock clustering for energy demand simulation. Energy Buildings **258**, 111844 (2022). https://doi.org/10.1016/j.enbuild.2022.111844
14. Rajawat, A.S., Rawat, R., Barhanpurkar, K., Shaw, R.N., Ghosh, A.: Vulnerability analysis at industrial internet of things platform on dark web network using computational intelligence. In: Bansal, J.C., Paprzycki, M., Bianchini, M., Das, S. (eds.) Computationally Intelligent Systems and their Applications. SCI, vol. 950, pp. 39–51. Springer, Singapore (2021). https://doi.org/10.1007/978-981-16-0407-2_4
15. Kauffmann, J., et al.: From clustering to cluster explanations via neural networks. IEEE Trans. Neural Netw. Learning Syst. 1–15. https://doi.org/10.1109/TNNLS.2022.3185901
16. Bedi, P., Goyal, S.B., Rajawat, A.S., Shaw, R.N., Ghosh, A.: A framework for personalizing atypical web search sessions with concept-based user profiles using selective machine learning techniques. In: Bianchini, M., Piuri, V., Das, S., Shaw, R.N. (eds.) Advanced Computing and Intelligent Technologies. LNNS, vol. 218, pp. 279–291. Springer, Singapore (2022). https://doi.org/10.1007/978-981-16-2164-2_23
17. Banerjee, A., et al.: Construction of effective wireless sensor network for smart communication using modified ant colony optimization technique. In: Bianchini, M., Piuri, V., Das, S., Shaw, R.N. (eds.) Advanced Computing and Intelligent Technologies. LNNS, vol. 218, pp. 269–278. Springer, Singapore (2022). https://doi.org/10.1007/978-981-16-2164-2_22
18. Xiao, R.: Comparing and clustering residential layouts using a novel measure of grating difference. Nexus Netw. J. **23**(1), 187–208 (2020). https://doi.org/10.1007/s00004-020-00530-z
19. Goyal, S.B., Bedi, P., Rajawat, A.S., Shaw, R.N., Ghosh, A.: Multi-objective fuzzy-swarm optimizer for data partitioning. In: Bianchini, M., Piuri, V., Das, S., Shaw, R.N. (eds.) Advanced Computing and Intelligent Technologies. LNNS, vol. 218, pp. 307–318. Springer, Singapore (2022). https://doi.org/10.1007/978-981-16-2164-2_25
20. Ischenko, A.V., Shishkunova, D.V., Guryanov, N.P.: Clustering and its key features' formation in construction. IOP Conf. Series: Mater. Sci. Eng. **1083**, 012103 (2021)
21. Munawar, H.S., Ullah, F., Qayyum, S., Shahzad, D.: Big data in construction: current applications and future opportunities. Big Data Cogn. Comput. **6**(1), 18 (2022). https://doi.org/10.3390/bdcc6010018
22. Wang, C., Pedrycz, W., Yang, J., Zhou, M.C., Li, Z.W.: Wavelet frame-based fuzzy c-means clustering for segmenting images on graphs. IEEE Trans. Cybern. **50**(9), 3938–3949 (2020). https://doi.org/10.1109/TCYB.2019.2921779
23. Jasim, W., Mohammed, R.: A survey on segmentation techniques for image processing. Iraqi J. Electr. Electron. Eng. **17**(2), 73–93 (2021). https://doi.org/10.37917/ijeee.17.2.10
24. Palimkar, P., Bajaj, V., Mal, A.K., Shaw, R.N., Ghosh, A.: Unique action identifier by using magnetometer, accelerometer and gyroscope: KNN approach. In: Bianchini, M., Piuri, V., Das, S., Shaw, R.N. (eds.) Advanced Computing and Intelligent Technologies. LNNS, vol. 218, pp. 607–631. Springer, Singapore (2022). https://doi.org/10.1007/978-981-16-2164-2_48

25. Singha, S., Srivastava, S.: Review of clustering techniques in control system. Procedia Comput. Sci. **173**, 272–280 (2020)
26. Kumar, A., Das, S., Tyagi, V., Shaw, R.N., Ghosh, A.: Analysis of classifier algorithms to detect anti-money laundering. In: Bansal, J.C., Paprzycki, M., Bianchini, M., Das, S. (eds.) Computationally Intelligent Systems and their Applications. SCI, vol. 950, pp. 143–152. Springer, Singapore (2021). https://doi.org/10.1007/978-981-16-0407-2_11
27. Mittal, H.: A comprehensive survey of image segmentation: clustering methods, performance parameters, and benchmark datasets. Multimedia Tools Appl. **81**, 35001–35026 (2022)
28. Han, Q., Yin, Q., Zheng, X., Chen, Z.: Remote sensing image building detection method based on Mask R-CNN. Complex Intell. Syst. **8**(3), 1847–1855 (2022). https://doi.org/10.1007/s40747-021-00322-z
29. Liu, W., et al.: Renyi's entropy based multilevel thresholding using a novel meta-heuristics algorithm. Appl. Sci. **10**, 3225 (2020). https://doi.org/10.3390/app10093225
30. Herman, E., Zsido, K.-E., Fenyves, V.: Cluster analysis with K-mean versus K-medoid in financial performance evaluation. Appl. Sci. **12**, 7985 (2022)
31. Akhtar, M.N., et al.: Implementation of parallel k-means algorithm to estimate adhesion failure in warm mix asphalt. Adv. Civil Eng. **2020**, 1–26 (2020). https://doi.org/10.1155/2020/8848945
32. Sinha, T., Chowdhury, T., Shaw, R.N., Ghosh, A.: Analysis and prediction of COVID-19 confirmed cases using deep learning models: a comparative study. In: Bianchini, M., Piuri, V., Das, S., Shaw, R.N. (eds.) Advanced Computing and Intelligent Technologies. LNNS, vol. 218, pp. 207–218. Springer, Singapore (2022). https://doi.org/10.1007/978-981-16-2164-2_18
33. Prashanthi, B., Sowjanya, G.: Clustering techniques in medical analysis using deep representations. Int. J. Adv. Sci. Technol. **29**(12s), 2184–2189 (2020)
34. Mukhopadhyay, M., et.al.,: Facial emotion recognition based on textural pattern and convolutional neural network. In: 2021 IEEE 4th International Conference on Computing, Power and Communication Technologies (GUCON), pp. 1–6 (2021). https://doi.org/10.1109/GUCON50781.2021.9573860
35. Manoharan, S.: Performance analysis of clustering based image segmentation techniques. J. Innovative Image Process. (JIIP) **02**(01), 14–24 (2020)
36. Dubey, S.K., Vijay, S., Pratibha: A review of image segmentation using clustering methods. Int. J. Appl. Eng. Res. **13**(5), 2484–2489 (2018)

Deep Neural Networks for Wild Fire Detection and Monitoring with UAV

Vishal Gewali[✉] and Sanjeeb Prasad Panday

Institute of Engineering, Tribhuwan University, Pulchowk Campus, Lalitpur, Nepal
074msice020.vishal@pcampus.edu.np, sanjeeb@ioe.edu.np

Abstract. Unmanned Aerial Vehicles (UAVs) which are equipped with camera sensors are easy means for making observations in remote, inconvenient and inaccessible areas and assist to apprehend the situation for many emergencies and disaster management applications. With the increase in the frequency and the severeness of the forest fire in the recent times, UAVs become the cost-effective means to provide high resolution images in wildfire detection in comparison to other techniques such as satellite and CCTV Cameras. This chapter is focused in the use of two different variations of CNN architectures models of VGG (VGG16, VGG19) and GoogleNet (InceptionV3, Xception) in developing models to correctly classify the forest fire and evaluating their performance. The models are analyzed in different UAV video footages using the Grad-CAM algorithm over the heat-maps to determine how well the model is working in the differentiating the given sample. Using the Adaboost optimizer, all models have shown the accuracy of over 96% and InceptionV3 model is found to have the better performance in comparison to the other VGG models, and also has shown slightly better outcomes against its latter version, Xception.

Keywords: Forest fire monitoring · VGG Architectures · GoogleNet architectures · GradCam

1 Introduction

Climate change, global warming and several other human activities has led to a significant increase of meteorological disasters all around the world. According to the Ecological Threat Register 2020, there has been the witness of a ten-fold increase in the number of natural disasters since the 1960s and this rate is expected to rise in future. Nasa Earth Observatory has observed that the heat-waves hit Europe, North Africa, the Middle East and Asia from June to July 2022, breaking many long-standing records as temperatures topped 40 °C across the globe. The heat wave has caused raging fires in parts of Portugal, Spain and France, devastating much of the country [26]. The quantity and intensity of forest wildfire disasters are also increasing every year and are getting more dangerous to bring under control. Australian bushfires in September 2019 consumed more

© The Author(s), under exclusive license to Springer Nature Switzerland AG 2023
R. N. Shaw et al. (Eds.): ICACIS 2022, CCIS 1749, pp. 411–423, 2023.
https://doi.org/10.1007/978-3-031-25088-0_37

than 11 million hectares of land, claimed the lives of 33 people, burned more than 2000 houses, and forced thousands of others to flee their homes [27]. A recent study has showed that wildfires kills 3.39 million worldwide every year [1]. Fast Detection and Monitoring of such possible disasters are critical for minimizing their effects on the environment and to the humans.

Traditional methods of forest fire detection using high point towers and human observation involved extensive labor and threaten the safety of personnel. The observation using the satellites, air-crafts and remote cameras can provide information services during disaster. However, these techniques do have significant number of limitations regarding cost, risk of life, and resolution of the images. New technological advances like advanced camera sensors have paved the way toward the opportunity for Unmanned Aerial Vehicle technology to be potential to rise above the traditional information services by conquering those limitations with the capture of efficient bird eye view aerial images in real-time. In addition to various benefits of a UAV such as miniature size, low operation cost, exposure to hazardous surroundings and a high likelihood of the successful operation without the risk of losing aircrew personnel, UAVs can be deployed as fast as possible in the site and provide a distinctive means for the swift evaluation of the site situation for its risk reduction.

Deep learning algorithms have been accepted as a eminent approach for various computer vision applications including image comprehension, recognition and classification delivering exceptional outcomes across numerous applications. The use of such deep learning techniques in disaster management and emergency response applications [24] provide prominent benefits to fetch out the critical information and ensure better preparedness and response in critical scenarios and assist for taking some quick and decisive action. Additionally, such deep learning algorithms need to be made more explainable, find areas of weakness and bias, and improvise the algorithms [2]. It is obvious that we need to develop models that are transparent and can justify their predictions in order to increase confidence in proper functioning of the intelligent systems and advance towards their meaningful implementation into our daily lives. As in the traditional forest fire monitoring procedures, firefighters must reach the scene with little understanding of how and where the fire is spreading, placing their lives at risk. These factors highlight the need for more efficient fire detection monitoring mechanism.

The difficult terrain of Nepal poses the problem to access the different part of the country. It takes several days and week to reach various remote places. This has imposed several difficulties to control the forest wildfire in different part of country. Disasters do occur in various places at random time. Any delay in the response to such disaster affected area can lead to great loss of life and property. Fast detection, alert and immediate response are important aspects for dealing effectively with them. The deployment of Unmanned Aerial Vehicle (UAV) can perform the surveillance of the site and notify about the perspective wildfires for its immediate control. The early detection and analysis of the fire can assist in monitoring of the fire spread and the prevention of huge loss of lives and property. The successful monitoring of the imagery from the UAVs and timely alerts for any possible risks or risky calamitous scenarios leads to the prompt emergency response by corresponding authority. Such rapid responses lead to the protection of the live of humans, livestock as well as the properties and prevent great losses.

2 Related Works

Different approaches have been applied in the field of forest fire. The most popular methods in the past for distinguishing fire from the backdrop and detecting its pixel were color characteristics. Many color spaces, including hue, saturation, and intensity were used to depict fire pixels for this purpose [3]. However, these systems were unable to effectively detect fire due to their sensitivity to changes in light and the difficulty of adjusting the precise range of fire pixel color. In vision-based approach, the threshold of the images were taken to detect the fire [4], where the picture is converted to binarized image to distinguish fires from background and other non-fire entities which have the similar color as fire, thus detecting the location and motion of the forest fire. The outcomes demonstrated that the color characteristic by itself is not entirely sufficient for this goal.

In recent period, new technology mechanisms are being applied for improving the performance [8]. The machine learning approaches have been applied for the early detection of fire using the sensor at different sensitive location of the forest [10]. Use of CCTV and application of image processing techniques such as the haar cascade classifier algorithm have been used for fire detection in forest [23]. CCTV Surveillance camera were used and tuned to fire detection with the significant amount of accuracy [15]. But deployment of CCTV camera in large area is very clumsy and is not fully practical, as CCTV camera wires could be damaged by fires itself. Unmanned Aerial Vehicles are tested for the emergency response application using deep learning approach. Among various deep learning algorithms, a study shows that CNN method seem to be more accurate among the others [14]. VGG16 and VGG19 have been deployed to detect the damages caused by the cyclone [9]. Different CNN models such as VGG16, MobileNet, ResNet50 were tested using transfer learning in the emergency response applications and VGG16 showed the better performance among the others with the accuracy of 91.9% [24]. Likewise, fire detection technique applied using optical sensor to discriminate between fire and non-fire images [16] was found to accomplish 81–88% accuracy. The indoor fire detection was tested in Indonesia using InceptionV3 model with the accuracy of 97% [5]. These works are mostly found to be done using the transfer learning technique. Transfer learned models was found to perform way better than fully trained models when trained on same dataset [6]. A model created for forest fire detection in real time in VGG16 architecture using transfer learning obtained 94.5% accuracy [7].

Different deep learning architecture such as TransUNet, MedT, U-Net were tested with Corsican fire database containing 500 images and the classified RGB fire image evaluated using masks to understand the fidelity of results [12]. The models developed for classification of disaster event showed the better performance in VGG16 as 91.9%, while the others Resnet and MobileNet had the accuracy of 90.2% and 88.8% [24]. The binary classification of frames snapped from the fire videos captured from the UAV is computed using the Xception model and it showed 76% classification accuracy [13]. Different CNN Configurations such as AlexNet, GoogleNet, VGG13 were examined in wildfire detection in aerial still photographs [1]. For only given 289 images, the accuracy of GoogleNet configuration was found to be better and also had the less training time in comparison to the others. Five pretrained models of Resnet-50, DenseNet-201, EfficientNet-B3, VGG16, VGG19 were used in creating a model using the data of Hurricane Harvey and VGG19 showed the better results with accuracy of 77.53% [11]. So, the choice of the appropriate CNN configuration in the deep learning approach becomes the essential task.

There has been a number of works that visualize the internal representation learned by CNNs in an attempt to better understand their properties [17]. Grad-Cam Algorithm is used in the automatic classification of disaster event to generate the heatmap showing the region that mostly affected the classification for the cross-validation [9] [24]. Although earlier CNN models performed admirably in classification tasks, it is unclear why they perform so well or how can they be enhanced to perform more accurately. Forest fire has been the critical issue in the matter of lives and property and such fire models seek high level of accuracy with sufficient test samples. In addition, deep learning network being a black box, it is not possible to know how it is working in the classification process. To design a better model in detection of wildfires, we need to analyze the performance of the CNN configurations from inside. To be reliable that the model is interpreting well as it should be, the class-specific discriminative region of the particular fire class can be employed to understand its operation and refine the model to minimize the false detection of wildfires.

3   Methodology

This chapter involves the use of an efficient convolutional neural network suitable for classifying aerial images of fire and non-fire from a UAV for emergency response and disaster management applications.

3.1   Model

The system as shown in Fig. 1 comprises of two separate deep neural network architecture viz. VGG model and GoogleNet model and each of these architecture with two different variations i.e. VGG16/VGG19 and Inception V3/Xception are applied to the given set of datasets to deduce the different models. The models are re-operated several times in a closed loop to re-tune the hyper-parameters for better performance output.

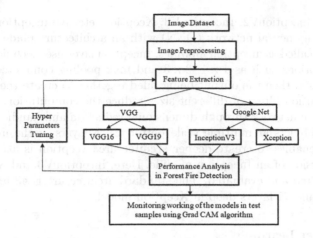

Fig. 1. Workflow diagram

3.2 Network Architecture

There exist different types of CNN network models that work over the convolution layers. The goal of convolutional layers is to identify and extract features from the image. CNN starts with the raw pixel data from the image, trains the model, and then automatically extracts the features for improved categorization. Here, the identification of wildfire is done with the two model types of the CNN which will perform classification on aerial data.

VGG Architecture. VGG (Visual Geometry Group) is one of the excellent CNN model architectures used in ILSVRC challenge. It was first put forward in the research "Very deep convolutional networks for large-scale image recognition" [18]. VGG is made up of blocks, which are made up of layers for 2D Convolution and Max Pooling. It comes in different models such as VGG16 and VGG19 and their standard architecture possess 16 and 19 layers respectively. As the number of layers rises, the CNN need to fit more and more complicated functions. Rather than having a lot of hyper-parameters, VGG is focused on using an architecture with very small convolution layers of 3 × 3 filter and max-pool layer of 2 × 2 filter. Convolution and max pool layers are arranged in the same manner throughout the whole design. At the very end, it has dense layers followed by a Soft-Max for computing output. Here, VGG16 and VGG19 models are tested and evaluated.

GoogleNet Architecture. GoogleNet is also is one of the excellent CNN model architectures used in ILSVRC challenge. It was first put forward in the research "Going Deeper with Convolutions" [19]. The large networks are susceptible to over-fitting and the GoogLeNet architecture solved exploding or vanishing gradient problem in such network through the utilisation of Inception module. Different versions of inception model have been developed till date such as

InceptionV1, InceptionV2, InceptionV3, Xception, etc. An inception network is basically a deep neural network (DNN) with an architecture made up of recurring modules called as inception modules. Inception layer uses techniques of small block convolutions such as 1×1, 3×3 and max pooling conducted in parallel in the input and then the output being piled together to create the final result. These convolution filters of different sizes reduce the computational expense of training a large network through dimensional reduction and handles the feature detection of objects at multiple scale better. Such layers in the middle of the architecture enables to create deeper architecture. Xception is also referred as "extreme" version of an Inception module. Here, InceptionV3 and Xception [25] model are tested and evaluated. The standard architecture is 48 layers deep in InceptionV3 and 71 layers deep in Xception model.

3.3 Transfer Learning

The concept of transfer learning is to get past the isolated way of learning and use the knowledge that is already acquired in one problem for solving other related problems. When we try to study new things or topics, it is not needed required to learn anything from scratch, but we can harness our knowledge from prior learning, exploiting the knowledge to improve generalization in another context. In the majority of convolutional networks, a layer becomes more specialized when it goes higher up in hierarchy. The first few layers learn extremely basic and universal characteristics that apply to practically all sorts of pictures. However, as we move up into deeper layers, the characteristics get more specific to the particular dataset on which the model was trained. In addition, in absence of the larger dataset for the deep neural network, the transfer learning can adjust to the unique characteristic to work with the new dataset, instead of learning generically from the base. Transfer learning is accomplished by instantiating the pre-trained model and adding the necessary number of fully-connected layers on top. The inner layers of pre-trained model is frozen and only the weights of the top layers are modified during training. Instead of training the CNN models from the scratch in deep neural Network, transfer learning technique is applied using the pre-trained models of VGG16, VGG19, InceptionV3 and Xception. Training with large amount of labeled data sets is not always possible such as in the current scenario of forest fire. So, the concept of transfer learning is chosen so as to conduct the training with low amount of data and it has improved the performance by reducing the training time.

3.4 DataSet

The vast majority of research projects on wildfire are found to rely on privately maintained databases or Internet-collected photos [22]. The image dataset for this research is taken by compiling different small groups of datasets of fire and non-fire scenes from the internet. Training data consists of 5226 images (3089 fire, 2137 non-fire). It is divided in train and validation in 90:10 ratio. The test data of 1900 (950 fire, 950 non-fire) images [21] is used in fire prediction.

Image augmentation technique of generating fresh training examples from the existing ones by making some slight variations to extend the count and amount of data which were available in smaller quantity thus helping in avoiding over-fitting. The various data augmentation techniques such as rotations, shearing, translations, mirroring and zooming are applied to increase the logical number of images in the dataset, i.e. each image probabilistically goes under a number of augmentations before being added to the batch for training purpose.

To work within the Nepalese Context, models are applied to the video footage of the fire and non-fire video footages compiled by flying the DJI Phantom 4 Pro and DJI Mavic Pro model drones and some internet collected video footage. These videos are used evaluate the performance of the different variations of VGG and GoogleNet.

3.5   Performance Evaluation

The Performance of developed models can be evaluated using confusion matrix and GradCam algorithm over Heatmaps. A confusion matrix is a table indicating how well a classification model is working on a set of test data for which the real values are known. It consist of True Positive (TP), False Positive (FP), True Negative (TN) and False Negative (FN) parameters and summarizes the performance of a model's categorization technique using Accuracy, Recall, Precision and F1-score. Grad-CAM or the Gradient-weighted Class Activation Mapping is a method for analyzing, what a neural network model is seeing in the given piece of image data. It is a class-specific technique and produces a separate visualization for each input class image. It generates a coarse localization map highlighting the key areas for class prediction in the image using the gradients of the target (e.g.,'fire' in a classification network) in the final convolutional layer [2]. The outputs can be viewed as the collections of colors that distribute the color as according to the values in the color-map. As a result, the visualization of the target localization helps in proper understanding of the model. Such mechanism makes deep learning algorithms more explainable, finds areas of weakness and bias, and improves our algorithms.

4   Implementations

The small fire dataset are collected from various internet sources and are compiled together. These training data are passed through the resizing the images to 224 * 224 for preprocessing. The fire images are encoded as 0 and non-fire images are encoded as 1 for easier processing. The architectures are developed using the Adabound optimizer. AdaBound is supposed to be not very sensitive to its hyper-parameters and behaves like Adam at the beginning of training, and gradually transforms to SGD at the end, i.e. trains as fast as Adam and as good as SGD, for developing deep learning models [20]. In VGG Architecture, the confusion matrix obtained and the data that it illustrates is as;

$$VGG16 \quad \begin{bmatrix} 911 & 39 \\ 25 & 925 \end{bmatrix} \qquad VGG19 \quad \begin{bmatrix} 929 & 21 \\ 47 & 903 \end{bmatrix}$$

Table 1. Performance comparison table of different architecture

Parameters	VGG16	VGG19	Inception V3	Xception
Accuracy	0.9663	0.9642	0.9868	0.9815
Precision	0.9733	0.9518	0.9843	0.9882
Recall	0.9589	0.9779	0.9894	0.9747
F1-score	0.9660	0.9647	0.9868	0.9814

Similarly, In GoogleNet Architecture, the confusion matrix obtained and the data that it illustrates is as;

$$InceptionV3 \quad \begin{bmatrix} 940 & 10 \\ 15 & 935 \end{bmatrix} \quad Xception \quad \begin{bmatrix} 926 & 24 \\ 11 & 939 \end{bmatrix}$$

The Table 1 shows the performance comparison of the different models in test dataset. The results depict that all the models do work perfectly with the accuracy greater than 96%. However, the GoogleNet Architectures (InceptionV3 and Xception) has the slight better values than the VGG16 Architectures counterparts in aspect of Accuracy, Precision, Recall and F1-score. The overall performance of InceptionV3 is found to be better among the all other evaluated ones. VGG16 has slight better performance in Accuracy, Precision and F1-score in comparison to VGG19. Similarly, InceptionV3 has slight better performance in Accuracy, Recall and F1 Score in comparison to Xception model. Taking the no-top layers and adding 4 layers on the top in the given pre-existed architectures, the number of layers in VGG16 become 17 while it becomes 20 in VGG19. Similarly, The number of layers in InceptionV3 becomes 51 and it becomes 74 in Xception. We can see that in the same type of architecture (in VGG16 and VGG19 or in InceptionV3 and Xception), the performance is declining with the increase in the number of layers. It shows that a model with large capacity than the optimum layer get more adapted to the training dataset only and it gets overfit or gets stuck or lost during the optimization process.

The performance of the Model Accuracy and Model Loss of both VGG16 and InceptionV3 architectures can be viewed from the graph of Fig. 2 and Fig. 3. The Model Accuracy Graphs shows the rise of the model accuracy with the number of epoch from 1 to 10 and getting saturated towards the end, showing almost the maximum accuracy that can be achieved. Similarly, the Model loss Graphs show the regular decline of the loss with the increase in epochs and getting toward the saturation at the end.

The CNN models act like a black box and predict the object as according to the different weights assigned in its layers. To understand what the model is seeing, is it really the thing to identify the class, the performance of the models is monitored using the Grad-Cam visualization over the heat-map to be ensured of the proper functioning of the model in the evaluation of the detection of the forest fire, and further enhance the performance evaluation of the model, if any. The developed models of VGG and GoogleNet architectures are applied

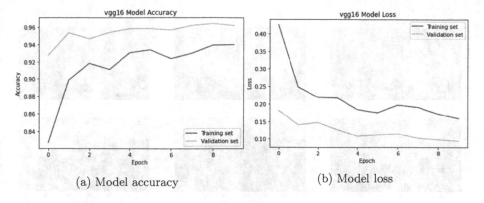

(a) Model accuracy

(b) Model loss

Fig. 2. VGG16 model accuracy and loss with respect to epochs processed

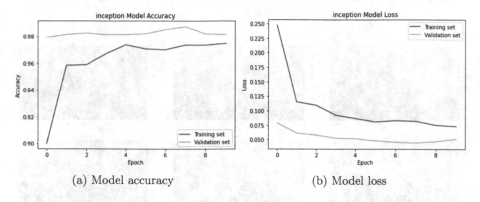

(a) Model accuracy

(b) Model loss

Fig. 3. InceptionV3 model accuracy and loss with respect to epochs processed

to the different forest fire/non fire videos to further evaluate their real field performance at random. The images are snapped from the video at first and the model analyzes the snapped picture if there is fire or not.

Figure 4 shows how the VGG16 model is identifying the image as a fire image. The red spot show the main identifier point that has concluded to decide the image as the fire. The red spot indeed is the fire spot on the video image. This show that this model is performing well in this video image as it should be. Similarly, Fig. 5 shows how the InceptionV3 model has concluded to classify the image. It also shows the fire region in the red spot signifying the proper functioning of the model in this video image. Similarly, Fig. 6 and Fig. 7 shows identification of fire the image by VGG19 and Xception Model. These models do work properly to distinguish the images as fire as confirmed by the visual representation.

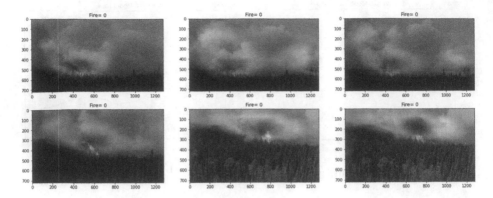

Fig. 4. Use of Grad-CAM algorithm to VGG16 model (Color figure online)

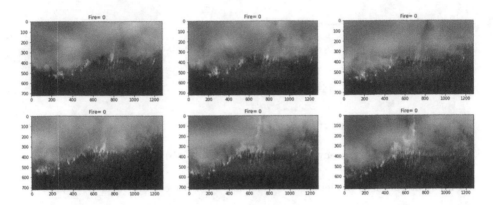

Fig. 5. Use of Grad-CAM algorithm to InceptionV3 model (Color figure online)

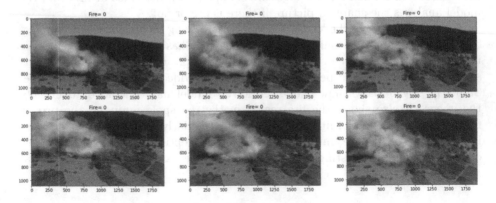

Fig. 6. Use of Grad-CAM algorithm to VGG19 model

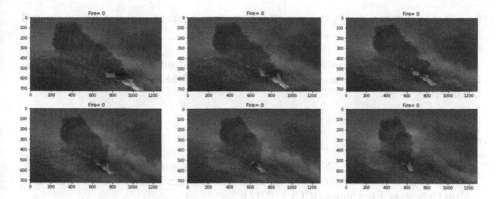

Fig. 7. Use of Grad-CAM algorithm to Xception model

5   Conclusion

The detection of wildfire and its monitoring has successfully been implemented in different deep neural Network Architecture of VGG and GoogleNet. The different versions of these architectures, i.e, VGG16, VGG19, InceptionV3, Xception are have been tested in various multimedia image captured from UAV and compared to achieve the model with better and enhanced performance. VGG16 architecture has obtained the accuracy of 96.63%, while VGG19 architecture approach has obtained the accuracy of 96.42%. Similarly, InceptionV3 architecture has shown the accuracy of 98.68%, while Xception architecture approach has shown the accuracy of 98.15%. It shows that as the number of layers increases, the complexity of the model increase and performance of a type of architecture begin to degrade, after reaching the optimum level. The obtained model are also tested on the heat-map using Grad-Cam for the performance monitoring and evaluation. The various models are found to trace the area of fire for its actual detection. Among the other different approaches of VGG16, VGG19 and Xception architectures, InceptionV3 has shown the proper classification of fire among the various UAV video footage and seems more appropriate method for the scenario of forest fire.

This research is performed under the limitation that the classification of fire is conducted only under the binary class of fire and non-fire and does not participate in the detection of smoke, fog and other similar entity. The observation of the site is conducted using the Quad-copter UAVs and as the legal limit of flying UAV (weight 4 pounds) in Nepal is 200 feet [28], the observation flights during this research experiment were performed within these limits for clear field of view of the ground.

In future, this work can be enhancement by using the GPS capability feature of the UAV to track and monitor the position of the given aircraft in the mid air region, thus preparing the 3D terrain structure. Similarly, the binary classification of fire and non-fire can be extended to further classes as smoke, fog, fire, no fire, etc. In similarly way, these multi class classification can also be conducted by implementing them on newer architectures.

Acknowledgements. This research work is performed under the supervision of the Department of Electronics and Computer Engineering, Pulchowk Campus, Institute of Engineering, Nepal.

References

1. Lee, W., Kim, S., Lee, Y., Lee, H. Choi, M.: Deep neural networks for wild fire detection with unmanned aerial vehicle. In: 2017 IEEE International Conference on Consumer Electronics (ICCE) (2017)
2. Selvaraju, R., Cogswell, M., Das, A., Vedantam, R., Parikh, D., Batra, D.: Grad-CAM: visual explanations from deep networks via gradient-based localization. In: Proceedings of the IEEE International Conference On Computer Vision, pp. 618–626 (2017)
3. Horng, W., Peng, J., Chen, C.: A new image-based real-time flame detection method using color analysis. In: Proceedings of the 2005 IEEE Networking, Sensing and Control, pp. 100–105 (2005)
4. Yuan, C., Liu, Z., Zhang, Y.: Vision-based forest fire detection in aerial images for firefighting using UAVs. In: 2016 International Conference on Unmanned Aircraft Systems (ICUAS), pp. 1200–1205 (2016)
5. Iqbal, M., Setianingsih, C., Irawan, B.: Deep learning algorithm for fire detection. In: 2020 10th Electrical Power, Electronics, Communications, Controls and Informatics Seminar (EECCIS), pp. 237–242 (2020)
6. Bari, A., Saini, T., Kumar, A.: Fire detection using deep transfer learning on surveillance videos. In: 2021 Third International Conference on Intelligent Communication Technologies and Virtual Mobile Networks (ICICV), pp. 1061–1067 (2021)
7. Yar, H., Hussain, T., Khan, Z., Koundal, D., Lee, M., Baik, S.: Vision sensor-based real-time fire detection in resource-constrained IoT environments. Comput. Intell. Neurosci. **2021**, 1–15 (2021)
8. Abid, F.: A survey of machine learning algorithms based forest fires prediction and detection systems. Fire Technol. **57**, 559–590 (2021)
9. Banerjee, S., Ghosh, A., Sorkhel, K., Roy, T.: Post cyclone damage assessment using CNN based transfer learning and Grad-CAM. In: 2021 IEEE Pune Section International Conference (PuneCon), pp. 1–7 (2021)
10. Dampage, U., Bandaranayake, L., Wanasinghe, R., Kottahachchi, K., Jayasanka, B.: Forest fire detection system using wireless sensor networks and machine learning. Sci. Rep. **12**, 1–11 (2022)
11. Khattar, A., Quadri, S.: Multi-source domain adaptation of social media data for disaster management. Multimed. Tools Appl., 1–29 (2022). https://doi.org/10.1007/s11042-022-13456-0
12. Ghali, R., Akhloufi, M., Jmal, M., Souidene Mseddi, W., Attia, R.: Wildfire segmentation using deep vision transformers. Remote Sens. **13**, 3527 (2021)
13. Shamsoshoara, A., Afghah, F., Razi, A., Zheng, L., Fulé, P., Blasch, E.: Aerial imagery pile burn detection using deep learning: the FLAME dataset. Comput. Netw. **193**, 108001 (2021)

14. Kukuk, S., Kilimci, Z.: Comprehensive analysis of forest fire detection using deep learning models and conventional machine learning algorithms. Int. J. Exp. Sci. Eng. **7**, 84–94 (2021)
15. Muhammad, K., Ahmad, J., Baik, S.: Early fire detection using convolutional neural networks during surveillance for effective disaster management. Neurocomputing **288**, 30–42 (2018)
16. Kim, S., Lee, W., Park, Y., Lee, H., Lee, Y.: Forest fire monitoring system based on aerial image. In: 2016 3rd International Conference on Information and Communication Technologies for Disaster Management (ICT-DM), pp. 1–6 (2016)
17. Zeiler, M.D., Fergus, R.: Visualizing and understanding convolutional networks. In: Fleet, D., Pajdla, T., Schiele, B., Tuytelaars, T. (eds.) ECCV 2014. LNCS, vol. 8689, pp. 818–833. Springer, Cham (2014). https://doi.org/10.1007/978-3-319-10590-1_53
18. Simonyan, K., Zisserman, A.: Very deep convolutional networks for large-scale image recognition. arXiv Preprint arXiv:1409.1556 (2014)
19. Szegedy, C., et al.: Going deeper with convolutions. In: Proceedings of the IEEE Conference on Computer Vision and Pattern Recognition, pp. 1–9 (2015)
20. Luo, L., Xiong, Y., Liu, Y., Sun, X.: Adaptive gradient methods with dynamic bound of learning rate. arXiv Preprint arXiv:1902.09843 (2019)
21. Khan, A., Hassan, B.: Dataset for forest fire detection (2020). https://doi.org/10.17632/gjmr63rz2r.1
22. Toulouse, T., Rossi, L., Campana, A., Celik, T., Akhloufi, M.: Computer vision for wildfire research: an evolving image dataset for processing and analysis. Fire Saf. J. **92**, 188–194 (2017)
23. Pranamurti, H., Murti, A., Setianingsih, C.: Fire detection use CCTV with image processing based Raspberry Pi. J. Phys. Conf. Ser. **1201**, 012015 (2019)
24. Kyrkou, C., Theocharides, T.: Deep-learning-based aerial image classification for emergency response applications using unmanned aerial vehicles. In: CVPR Workshops, pp. 517–525 (2019)
25. Chollet, F.: Xception: deep learning with depthwise separable convolutions. In: Proceedings of the IEEE Conference on Computer Vision and Pattern Recognition, pp. 1251–1258 (2017)
26. Nasa Earth Observatory: Heatwaves and Fires Scorch. https://earthobservatory.nasa.gov/images/
27. Future Earth, Global Fires. https://futureearth.org/publications/issue-briefs-2/global-fires/, 150083/heatwaves-and-fires-scorch-europe-africa-and-asia. Accessed 8 Sept 2022
28. Nepal (CAAN): Nepal Drone Regulations (2020). https://drone-laws.com/drone-laws-in-nepal/. Accessed 1 Sept 2022

PDR Improvements Using Per User Based Multi Threshold Scheduling Compared to Priority Scheduling for MU-MIMO Networks

T. Pavan Kalyan[1] and K. Chanthirasekaran[2(✉)]

[1] Research Scholar, Institute of ECE, Saveetha School of Engineering, Saveetha Institute of Medical and Technical Sciences, Saveetha University, Chennai, India
thirumalasettypk18@saveetha.com

[2] Institute of ECE, Saveetha Institutes of Medical and Technical Sciences, Saveetha School of Engineering, Saveetha University, Chennai, India
chanthirasekarank.sse@saveetha.com

Abstract. The aim of this work is to improve packet delivery ratio by Per User based Multi Threshold scheduling (PUMTS) compared to Priority scheduling (PS) for MU-MIMO Wireless Networks. There are two-groups; 20 samples in every group were tested with the pre-test power of 80% (G-power). Group 1 is taken as PUMTS and group 2 is taken as Priority scheduling (PS). Through simulation, the novel PUMTS has achieved the PDR of 0.9835 and PS has achieved the PDR of 0.9645 with significance of p = 0.000 (2-tailed). This study has shown that the PUMTS is having significant improvement than PS in the PDR.

Keywords: Packet delivery ratio · Novel per user based multi threshold scheduling · MU-MIMO networks · Priority scheduling · Bit error rate · Wireless networks

1 Introduction

The research is about the improvement of packet delivery ratio and getting better performance to the users. MU-MIMO [12] is a technology which essentially groups together antennas at a better throughput and better spectrum efficiency. MU-MIMO Networks is a known network for wider resource utilization and its diversity performance. The MU-MIMO networks are utilized in digital homes [1], cellular wireless networks [13] and LTE systems [6] etc.

In the past 7 years 63 articles have been published based on the packet delivery ratio improvement of MU-MIMO Networks. Among all previous works they discussed fair scheduling, Priority scheduling and threshold based fair scheduling. Novel Per user based multi threshold scheduling is proposed for PDR improvement to get the better performance [2]. Node-network conflict-free scheduling-Algorithm (N-N-S) in [7] was proposed for more slot utilizations to transfer more packets. A Probabilistic graphical model in [3] was proposed for the path delivering a packet based on threshold. Two

R. N. Shaw et al. (Eds.): ICACIS 2022, CCIS 1749, pp. 424–430, 2023.
https://doi.org/10.1007/978-3-031-25088-0_38

scheduling models in [5] have been used for bit-error-rate (B-E-R) improvement. The one-cell MU-M-I-M-O network [10] has been proposed with an N antenna. Two different systems of multihop cooperation in [11] were proposed for multi-hop diversity to measure B-E-R. Wireless environment user-selection method [9] has been proposed for different channel users. A joint-pilot and data-power allocation-scheme [14] were proposed for down-link and up-link transmission.

All the above studies have obtained a low packet delivery ratio. To improve the packet delivery ratio, a novel scheduler is needed. The main purpose of novel Per- user based multi threshold-scheduling is to improve the performance by increasing the packets delivery ratio compared to the previous networking threshold schedulers through that the users will satisfy the service.

2 Materials and Methods

ADC lab was used to carry out this research in SIMATS, Tamil Nadu, India. Two groups each of sample size 20 has been taken for both threshold schedulers. Group 1 is considered for the novel Per user based Multi Threshold scheduling scheduler and group 2 is considered for the Priority Scheduling Scheduler [15]. The statistical tool with G power of 80%.

Figure 1 shows the Downlink MU-M-I-M-O network. The base station (N antennas) is communicated to multiple users for multiple input and multiple output wireless networks. The Scheduling algorithm 1 novel Per User based Multi Threshold Scheduling and the Scheduling algorithm 2 Priority scheduling [15] is used for scheduling the 25 active users with 11 resources.

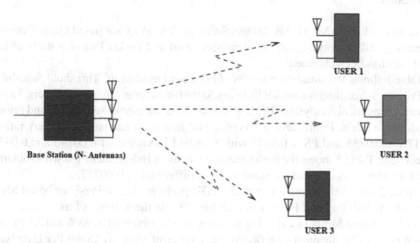

Fig. 1. Down-link M-I-M-O network: The base station (N antennas) is communicated to multiple users for multiple input and multiple output wireless networks.

3   Novel Per User Based Multi Threshold Scheduling Algorithm

1) Random user generators are Uk and the number of resources declared is denoted by 'R'.
2) Random threshold schedulers are T1&T2 for each user respectively.
3) Compare each user strength with each user threshold value T1 and generate a scheduled user list 'k1'.
4) Compare each user strength with each user threshold value T2 and generate a scheduled user list 'k2'.
5) Find the length of k1 and k2 are denoted x1 and x2 respectively.
6) If x2 > R then final scheduled user ks = k2 else if x2 > x1 then final schedule user ks = k1.
7) Send this scheduled user ks into MIMO Network for packet delivery ratio estimation.
8) Calculate average packet delivery ratio for different resources [R].

The testing setup was done using MATLAB R2018a Software. The tests are carried out on a device with a core i3 processor and 4GB of RAM. The obtained results of PUMTS and PS were validated with statistical Software in terms of Packet Delivery Ratio.

SPSS [8] is used for validation and the significance, mean values are also calculated. The Independent variables are identified as transmitting antennas numbers and receiving antennas numbers in a AWGN-noise signal. The dependent variables are the L-channel matrix and packet delivery ratio.

4   Results

Simulation is done in MATLAB 2018Ra Software. The Per User based Multi Threshold Scheduling and Priority Scheduling were simulated and Packet Delivery Ratio of both schedulers has been obtained.

Table 1 shows the simulation results of Per User based Multi Threshold Scheduling and Priority Scheduling for Packet Delivery Ratio for different numbers of users. Table 2 shows the Statistical Analysis of Per User based Multi Threshold Scheduling and Priority Scheduling models. From Table 2 it is observed that the mean packet delivery ratio of PUMTS is 0.9835 and PS is 0.9645 with Standard Deviation of 0.00745 and 0.03300 respectively. Table 3 shows the performance analysis of Independent T-test and obtained means are shown as 016 and the standard error difference is 0.00757.

Figure 2 shows the comparison of the PDR performance of Per-User based Multi-Threshold Scheduling and Priority Scheduling. While the number of users reaches 15 the Per User based Multi Threshold Scheduling will be obtained as 93% and the Priority Scheduling will be obtained as 86%. At the number of Users is 25 the Per User based Multi Threshold Scheduling will be obtained as 97% and the Priority Scheduling will be obtained as 98%. Figure 3 shows the barchart mean PDR performance graph of Per User based Multi Threshold scheduling (PUMTS) and Priority Scheduling (PS) with error bars.

Table 1. Simulation results are obtained through MATLAB 2018Ra of per user based Multi Threshold Scheduling and Priority Scheduling for packet delivery ratio for MU-MIMO networks.

Sl. No	Packet delivery ratio	
	PS	PUMTS
1	0.89	0.99
2	0.91	0.99
3	0.91	0.99
4	0.93	0.98
5	0.94	0.98
6	0.95	0.99
7	0.96	0.99
8	0.96	0.98
9	0.97	0.98
10	0.97	0.98
11	0.98	0.99
12	0.98	0.99
13	0.99	0.99
14	0.98	0.99
15	0.99	0.98
16	0.99	0.97
17	0.99	0.97
18	1.00	0.97
19	1.00	0.98
20	1.00	0.99

Table 2. SPSS statistical analysis of per user based Multi Threshold Scheduling and Priority Scheduling for packet delivery ratio. The mean value and other values are obtained for 20 iterations.

Group statistics					
	Group	N	Mean	Std. deviation	Std. error mean
Packet delivery ratio (PDR)	Priority scheduling (PS)	20	0.9645	0.03300	0.00738
	Per user based multi threshold scheduling (PUMTS)	20	0.9835	0.00745	0.00167

Table 3. Independent T-test performance of PUMTS to show the significance and obtained the 0.000 significance for Packet Delivery Ratio.

Levene's test for equality of variances			T-test for equality of means					95% Confidence interval of the difference	
F		Sig	t	df	Sig (2-tailed)	Mean difference	Std. Error difference	Lower	Upper
Packet delivery ratio (PDR)	Equal variances assumed	22.731	0.000	−2.511	38	0.016	−0.19000	0.00757	−0.03432	−0.00368
	Equal variance not assumed			−2.511	20.932	0.020	−0.01900	0.00757	−0.03474	−0.00326

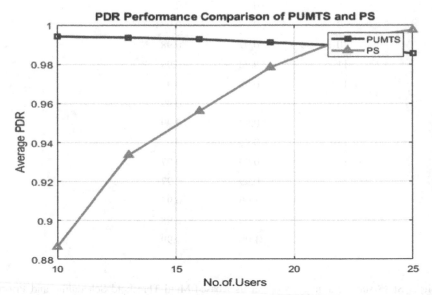

Fig. 2. Packet delivery ratio of PUMTS Multi Threshold Scheduling and Priority Scheduling. No. of Users VS Average Packet Delivery Ratio

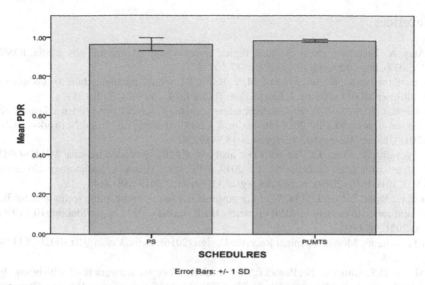

Fig. 3. Priority scheduling (PS) and Per user based multi threshold scheduling classifiers with Packet delivery ratio has been depicted in the form of a bar chart. X Axis: PS vs PUMTS algorithms Y Axis: Median value of PDR of detection. (± 1 SD)

5 Discussion

Per User based Multi Threshold Scheduling is simulated with 25 numbers of active users and 11 resources in base stations. Through the simulation it is found that the Per User based Multi Threshold Scheduling PDR performance is significantly better than Priority Scheduling PDR performance.

Algorithm proposed in [7] has obtained a packet delivery ratio of 83%. A Probabilistic graphical model in [3] was able to achieve the PDR of 87%. Two novel scheduling in [4] have obtained a packet delivery ratio of 85%. The single-cell MU-M I M O networks in [10] with K no. of single-antenna user-equipment (UE) and the obtained packet delivery ratio is 86%. Multi-user selection method in [9] with full-rank and rank-deficient methods was proposed and the Packet delivery ratio is 82%. An analytical method in [4] was proposed and obtained Packet delivery ratio is 89%. A Novel Per User based Multi Threshold Scheduling obtained the Packet Delivery Ratio as 97.9% which is better among all the above discussed works.

One of the limitations of Per User based Multi Threshold Scheduling uses multi threshold. When more users are close to the base station and few users are in the boundary of the network, the service fairness decays. This work can be extended for a massive MIMO network.

6 Conclusion

The Per User based Multi Threshold Scheduling (PUMTS) algorithm has achieved 98.35% of the mean packet delivery ratio compared to the Priority Scheduling algorithm which results in a 96.45%. Hence the Per User based Multi Threshold Scheduling is having significant improvement in PDR performance compared to Priority Scheduling.

References

1. Atay, A.: Theorizing diasporic queer digital homes: identity, home and new media. JOMEC J. (2017). https://doi.org/10.18573/j.2017.10139
2. Chanthirasekaran, K., Bhagyaveni, M.A., Rama, P.L.: Multi-parameter based scheduling for multi-user MIMO systems. J. Electr. Eng. Technol. **10**, 2406–2412 (2015)
3. Florencio, H., Neto, A.D.: Probabilistic inference of the packet delivery ratio in industrial wireless sensor networks. In: 2018 International Joint Conference on Neural Networks (IJCNN) (2018). https://doi.org/10.1109/ijcnn.2018.8489258
4. Kageyama, T., Muta, O.: Bit error rate analysis of MRC precoded massive MIMO-OFDM systems with peak cancellation. In: 2019 IEEE 90th Vehicular Technology Conference (VTC2019-Fall) (2019). https://doi.org/10.1109/vtcfall.2019.8891444
5. Ko, K., Byun, I., Lee, J, Shin, W.: Joint power allocation and scheduling techniques for BER minimization in multiuser MIMO systems. IEEE Access (2021). https://doi.org/10.1109/access.2021.3074980.
6. LTE Systems: Mobile Terminal Receiver Design (2016). https://doi.org/10.1002/9781119107422.ch3
7. Mantri, D.S., Kulkarni, N., Pawar, P.M., Prasad, R.: Node and network level scheduling algorithm for wireless sensor network. In: 2018 IEEE Global Conference on Wireless Computing and Networking (GCWCN) (2018). https://doi.org/10.1109/gcwcn.2018.8668585
8. McCormick, K., Salcedo, J.: SPSS Statistics for Data Analysis and Visualization. John Wiley and Sons (2017)
9. Pan, S., Chen, D., Yan, Y., Chen, Y.: Spatial resource squeezing and its usage in user selection for multi-user multiple-input multiple-output systems. IEEE Trans. Veh. Technol. (2017). https://doi.org/10.1109/tvt.2017.2774248
10. Sanguinetti, L., Moustakas, A.L., Bjornson, E., Debbah, M.: Large system analysis of the energy consumption distribution in multi-user MIMO systems with mobility. IEEE Trans. Wireless Commun. (2015). https://doi.org/10.1109/twc.2014.2372761
11. Som, P., Chockalingam, A.: Performance analysis of space-shift keying in decode-and-forward multihop MIMO networks. IEEE Trans. Veh. Technol. (2015). https://doi.org/10.1109/tvt.2014.2318437
12. Wong, W., Chan, S.-H.G.: Distributed joint AP grouping and user association for MU-MIMO networks. In: IEEE INFOCOM 2018 - IEEE Conference on Computer Communications (2018). https://doi.org/10.1109/infocom.2018.8486284
13. Banerjee, A., et al.: Building of efficient communication system in smart city using wireless sensor network through hybrid optimization technique. In: Piuri, V., Shaw, R.N., Ghosh, A., Islam, R. (eds.) AI and IoT for Smart City Applications. SCI, vol. 1002, pp. 15–30. Springer, Singapore (2022). https://doi.org/10.1007/978-981-16-7498-3_2
14. Rajawat, A.S., Bedi, P., Goyal, S.B., Shaw, R.N., Ghosh, A.: Reliability analysis in cyber-physical system using deep learning for smart cities industrial IoT network node. In: Piuri, V., Shaw, R.N., Ghosh, A., Islam, R. (eds.) AI and IoT for Smart City Applications. SCI, vol. 1002, pp. 157–169. Springer, Singapore (2022). https://doi.org/10.1007/978-981-16-7498-3_10
15. Zhao, Y., Zeng, H.: The virtual deadline based optimization algorithm for priority assignment in fixed-priority scheduling. In: 2017 IEEE Real-Time Systems Symposium (RTSS) (2017). https://doi.org/10.1109/rtss.2017.00018.Author. F.: Article title. Journal **2**(5), 99–110 (2016)

Framework for Land Registry System Using Ethereum Blockchain

Utkarsh Sahni[1], Suraj Garg[1], Tushar Srivastava[1], Tushar Sharma[1], Nitima Malsa[1(✉)],
Ankush Ghosh[2], Rabindra Nath Shaw[2], and Vimal Gupta[1]

[1] JSS Academy of Technical Education, Noida, India
nitima.malsa@gmail.com
[2] University Center for Research and Development, Chandigarh University,
Ajitgarh, Punjab, India

Abstract. Some governance system that holds records of land possession must include the land registration system as one of its key components. The current system has a number of problems and gaps that lead to corruption and disagreements. In order to resolve these challenges, a sizeable portion of precious government resources is needed from the judiciary and law enforcement organizations. Blockchain technology offers the ability to close these gaps and address problems with the land registry system, such as record tampering and selling the same plot of land to several buyers. In this chapter, a secure and trustworthy foundation for a blockchain-based land register system is suggested. The suggested architecture provides an algorithm for pre-agreement and incorporates the idea of smart contracts at various land registry phases. We first provide a description of the traditional system of registry land and examine its problems. Then, we presented a framework and discussed the possible advantages of integrating Blockchain technology into the land registry system. A selection of case studies is then given.

Keywords: Blockchain · Ethereum · Ganache · Land registry · Metamask · Remix IDE · Smart contract · Solidity · Truffle · Web3jss

1 Introduction

A means to transfer land ownership that protects stakeholder rights and increases public confidence is the land register system. Due to insufficient cooperation between multiple departments, the certification of land title requires a personal visit, which makes it time-consuming and usually attracts bribery. About 60–70% of world's population lacks access to the formal land registration system, where bribery is common; it is believed that about $700 million is paid in bribes at the Indian land registration office. Furthermore, according to a 2007 World Bank research, property title issues pertaining to land constitute the subject of 65% of court cases in the nation. Apart from land registry blockchain technology has various applications in different domains such as certification, identity verification, cryptocurrency and healthcare etc. [14, 17, 18].

The chapter-based land registry system has a number of drawbacks, such as high transaction costs, centralised control, the requirement to physically visit the property

R. N. Shaw et al. (Eds.): ICACIS 2022, CCIS 1749, pp. 431–440, 2023.
https://doi.org/10.1007/978-3-031-25088-0_39

site for verification, human error vulnerability, corrupt practices, deception, lack of transparency, third-party participation, decreased reliability, inefficiency, and ownership issues. Distributed ledger technology (DLT), which is gaining popularity, has emerged as a paradigm-shifting breakthrough in the context of transaction and record management. A number of properties, such as immutability, security, integrity, authenticity, and traceability, must be offered by any land registration system. According to various academics researching the land register system, employing blockchain technology might enhance the effectiveness of the present land registration system [5]. This would improve safety and openness. Without a middleman, it will also speed up and reduce the cost of the land acquisition. The benefits of using blockchain technology in the land registry system can be summed up as greater transparency, greater trust, increased predictive ability, durability, better control, cost savings, reduced energy consumption, consistency, ease of access, privacy, fighting corruption, and process optimization [7, 9, 10].

In 2016, Christopher Allen identified four stages of the digital identification paradigm: centralised identities, federated identification, user-centric identity, and self-sovereign identity (SSI) model. Any identity system must ensure that user data is secure from theft, illegal access, and data breaches. Following a comparison of the various identity models, the best identification model, especially for the use case of land register applications, is sought. This chapter analyses these components and validates the recommended changes based on 5three research topic (RQs). All other identity models, with the exception of SSI, are handled by entities rather than users. Users may handle their personal data individually and with the least amount of disclosure possible thanks to the self-sovereign identity model, which conforms with the identity principles.

1.1 Land Registry System

The four essential components of a land register system are as follows:

The primary goal of the land register system is to identify the legitimate owner of the property before submitting the necessary chapterwork for registration.

- *Unique identity*: The user identification procedure is not currently widely accessible or standardized. The user's identity does not need to be revealed thanks to the current blockchain technology.
- *The initial transition procedure:* All land-related transitions may be verified and stored using the blockchain technology. Additionally, it has the potential to transfer land ownership data. Before using blockchain technology for the transfer of land, the current land title documents must be recorded in the "genesis block" of the blockchain. Before continuing, it must be approved by all persons involved in the system.
- *Consent Principle:* In order to complete the land transfer, the true owner's consent, as indicated by the land record, is required. During this process, the following key problems were found:

1. Establishing the owner's legitimacy.
2. Accessible digital signatures for all users and owners.

3. The system or intermediary to confirm the coercion or transfer made under duress and without consent. Although the blockchain is designed to cut out all middlemen, coercion cannot be monitored in this situation.

- *Publication of record and /ownership databases:* The major goal is to make records trusted and easily accessible. These records may be made available for public inspection or by any reliable third party that can meet the demands of a potential buyer.

1.2 Limitations of Current Land Registry System

Due to limitations in the current system of land registration, the land registrar must proceed on the assumption that all outstanding debts are satisfied. The registration office can only record land transactions that are based on the payment proofs provided by the seller and the buyer; it is unable to independently verify the payment's authenticity or the amount paid. Due to the current corrupt system, it is difficult and expensive to update records, which prevents poor farmers from registering their ownership of the land. As a result, they are unable to take advantage of various government programs like low-interest loans, loan forgiveness, and support for agriculture. In the absence of a valid land title for money lending, the informal moneylenders are ensnaring the poor farmers. These farmers pay extremely high interest rates on the loan amount and, in the majority of cases, are unable to repay the loan amount.

Land registration is a time-consuming and labour-intensive procedure that requires a lot of chapter verification, in-person visits, inspections, and bribery at each level, all of which contribute to the delay and cost money and time. Because the land register process usually includes a change in owners and is unable to provide real-time information for any verification, the availability of records is another key issue. These records need to be examined, which involves time, several trips, bribes, and the risk of records being out of sync. Cost of implementation can also be reduced by reducing GAS cost [12].

Since the impoverished farmers lack a valid land title to use as collateral for loans, the informal hard money lenders are trapping them. The majority of the time, these farmers are unable to repay the loan and end up paying astronomically high interest rates. The land register system processes and verifies data using governmental institutions. Since not all land registration databases are linked to the land register system, the system's effectiveness and equity are degraded. The chapter-based land register system has a number of drawbacks, which have been discussed in this section. Because it is not computerised, the land registration method is flexible. Another difficulty with the land register system is land encroachment, as vacant land and ancient homes are frequently targets of encroachment in most nations. Furthermore, land invasion is most likely to affect elderly and NRI populations. Online registration is sometimes used to resolve some of these concerns, although the server problem is a major worry. Another concern is the middle man, who in the system of land registration levies a hefty fee to speed up the land registration procedure. The bogus middleman may occasionally use forged chapterwork to sell the property. Due to all of these factors, a sizable portion of assets stay unregistered and underutilized, which has an impact on economic growth. The losses to the national exchequer of financial benefits such as income tax, property tax, and other revenues. Due to all of these problems, the land register system exhibits a trust gap, which has cost money to land investors.

In addition, purchasing land has a higher transition cost than other types of investments, and after the land has been registered, there is a chance that local criminals would make threats against you.

1.3 Blockchain in Land Registry System

For the land registry system to facilitate the exchange of land titles, a sizable quantity of registration documents must be stored on centralised databases. Hand records are preserved in order to deal with the system's vulnerability to various sorts of alteration and changes. The registration office has dishonest employees who can assist you change these documents, but doing so takes a lot of effort and money. In order to increase transparency and openness, the land registry authorities have taken initiatives to profit from ICT technology. By copying and replicating data, transferring data from a single database to a distributed database safeguards the central store. The accuracy of records is still debatable, and it is still vulnerable to fraud and manipulation. A distributed ledger with features like preserving all transaction records, the owner of the land for a specific amount of time, and the time of the transaction can be described as the Blockchain in relation to the land registry system. It also provides options to follow up on data from earlier transactions.

Blockchain offers decentralized record management and storage, which has the ability to boost confidence and foster collaborative systems. Utilizing blockchain will improve the land register system's efficiency, improve synchronization, and help to address information availability and security challenges brought on by man-made disasters. Blockchain technology consists of peer-to-peer networks linked by dispersed networks, each of which has a copy of every transaction that was approved by the network's peers through consensus. The audit trail on the ledger is the result of attempts to modify outdated entries or interfering with real land registry transitions. The peer-to-peer specified chains, peer-based validation, consensus procedure for storing the records, and medium to ensure system security are all made possible by blockchain technology.

A distributed ledger is used to keep the records of the transitions, protecting the system from errors, insulation, and deliberate spontaneous record modification. Proof of existence is used to secure every record in the blockchain. Every stage of the land registration is written on the blockchain, which boosts record stability and security by notarizing the whole document. By making every step publicly available on the blockchain, "Proof of procedure" is established, protecting the records and establishing accountability. The transfer of ownership of land title by system can only be done if they have owner's private and upload the transaction. The owner has the choice to have a alternative mechanism to use their private key in the event of a device failure in those circumstances.

2   Literature Survey

Application	Author	Technology	Year
Land transaction system	[1] Yadav, A. S., Agrawal, S., and Kushwaha, D. S	Distributed Ledger Technology and trusted nodes consensus mechanism	2022
Smart land management: land acquisition and the associated challenges	[2] Ameyaw, P. D., and de Vries, W. T	Blockchain Technology	2021
Smart contract for decentralized water management system	[11] S. Tiwari, J. Gautam, V. Gupta, and N. Malsa	Blockchain Technology	2020
Improving the authenticity of real estate land transaction data	[4] Mohammed Shuaib, Shadab AlamSalwani Mohd Daud	Blockchain-Based Security Scheme	
Smart contract for academic certificate verification	[15] Pathak, S., Gupta, V., Malsa, N., Ghosh, A., Shaw, R.N	Using Ethereum Blockchain Technology	2022
Identity model for blockchain-based land registry system: a comparison. Wireless communications and mobile computing	[6] Shuaib, M., Hafizah Hassan, N., Usman, S., Alam, S., Bhatia, S., Koundal, D., and Belay, A	Blockchain Technology and Mobile Computing,	2022
Adoption framework for authentic land registry system in Malaysia	[3] Aborujilah, A., Yatim, M. N. B. M., and Al-Othmani, A	Blockchain Technology and Telecommunication Computing Electronics and Control	2021
Blockchain platforms and interpreting the effects of bitcoin pricing on cryptocurrencies	[13] Malsa, N., Vyas, V., Gautam, J	Blockchain Technology	2022
Framework and smart contract for blockchain enabled certificate verification	[16] Malsa, N., Vyas, V., Gautam, J., Shaw, R.N., Ghosh, A	Framework and Smart Contract for Blockchain using robotics	2021
Immutability and auditability: the critical elements in property rights registries," Annual World Bank conference on land and property	[8] A. Dobhal, M. Regan	Smart contract using blockchain technology	2016

3 Implementation of Blockchain in Land Registry

The buyer and the seller must first sign a pre-agreement contract, also referred to as a "smart contact," and after that submit a transfer request to the registration office in order to exchange land. Before utilising a surveyor and departmental records to establish the ownership of the land, the registry office verifies the identity of the buyer and seller. After the authentication and verification processes are complete, the financial transaction record is verified, and the required cash in the form of transfer fees and taxes are acquired, the transfer request will then be processed. After all of these steps have been accomplished, ownership is transferred, the ownership certificate is issued to the buyer, and the updated record is given to all interested departments. After all of these steps have been accomplished, transfer of ownership is done, the ownership certificate is issued to the buyer, and the updated record is given to all interested departments.

3.1 New Transaction Block

It is required to update these records at all agencies (including the Registration office, surveyor, revenue office, and banks) that store and verify these records when the transaction process is finished and ownership documents have been created. For that specific attribute, these parties or nodes use distributed ledger (DLT) to create a distinct distributed ledger that records both these transactions and all past records of transactions. The specific office can review and validate the transaction based on ownership data that were previously maintained in its distributed ledger. After being validated by the validating node, newly produced transaction blocks are broadcast to all other nodes in the DLT network. Before the new block is formally inserted into the blockchain, the other verifying nodes will confirm and concur on the created node using a consensus procedure.

3.2 Land Title Smart Contract

The information mentioned below is required for the pre-agreement contract process between the buyer and seller. Below is a detailed explanation of the internal contents;

- *Identity:* It keeps track of all users' information (ID, name, and sign) as well as the KYC feature for confirming their legitimacy.
- *Title:* It maintains and monitors information about the Title, including Id, Status, Address and the owner, on the blockchain.
- *Deed:* Maintains and stores information on deeds, such as buyer ID, seller ID, and payment status.
- *Agreements:* Keep records of various contracts, including purchase agreements, surveyor inspection reports, and agreements that are digital signature for deed transfers.
- *Digital Signature:* This feature preserves all system participants' digital signatures and enables you to save numerous signatories who are acting in various roles for the same document. Validates a digital signature's underlying structure.

4   Land Registry Model

Land registry and verification are the two modules of this suggested system.
Land Registry Module
See Fig. 1

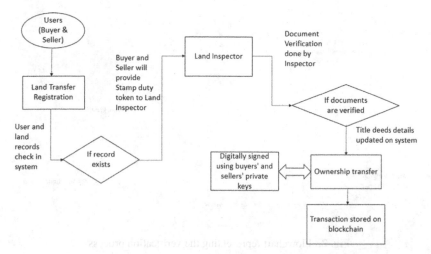

Fig. 1. Flowchart representing land registry system process

Three steps are carried out in this module 9:

- *User Login:* Users register on the system by submitting their contact information, email address, name, and Aadhar number, and the details are validated using the system's integration with Digi locker. If the user information is properly confirmed, the system will next produce the user's private and public keys using the AWS Key Management Store.

- *Buyer/Seller*: Prior to executing the conveyance deed, buyers and sellers must each present a token to the land inspector for document verification. Once the documents have been verified by the land inspector, the seller will provide the buyer's contact information, including their Aadhar number and email address. The buyer will then receive a notification via email regarding the land transfer process and may choose to accept or reject it. When the request is approved, the buyer enters their information, which is compared to the seller's information. If the information matches, a notification is issued to both the buyer and the seller about signing the conveyance deed.

- *Conveyance deed:* After the buyer and seller have agreed to the notification, the matching private keys are retrieved from the AWS key management store, a digital signature is created, stored on blockchain, and the digital file is emailed to the buyer. Events would be set off after the land transfer procedure was finished, and a smart contract would contact the land ownership function to update the land owner and create a blockchain transaction.

Verification Module:
Different third parties will check the owner and land details throughout the verification process by uploading the digital file to the system, matching the digital file with the records held on the blockchain, and then sending the data of the owner and land details to the third party via email (Fig. 2).

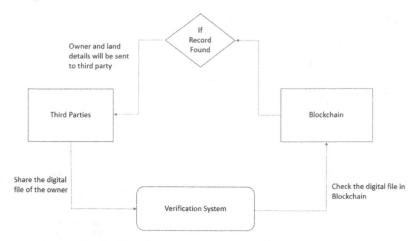

Fig. 2. Flowchart representing the verification process

Third-party can be a financial institution where the owner can apply for a loan, the institution will ask for proof of land property, the owner can provide them with a digital file generated through the system and the institute will make a request for details and send notification via email to the system, provided digital file will be matched with the system blockchain records, if digital file found out, then the owner and land details will be sent to the bank via email. Blockchain is crucial in ensuring transparency throughout the process by digitally signing and certifying the land records without the use of any middlemen and safely recording the ownership transfer history of the land records on the blockchain.

The list of tools utilized during the process is as follows:

- *Smart Contracts:* When writing smart contracts, various functionalities and data structures are used, such as structures, arrays, contracts, modifiers, functions, and constructors. Different smart contracts are created for buyers, sellers, land inspectors, and events are generated in smart contracts for web applications.
- *Solidity*: Bin and abi files are produced using the Solidity compiler and the Solidity programming language, respectively. When interacting with the blockchain, the bin file is used, while the abi file is used to access the smart contract features.
- *Web3js:* Web3js is a javascript package that is used to link a web application to a blockchain via a rpc port. It creates web3 objects and uses their various functionalities to communicate with the ganache and truffle consoles.

- *Ganache*: Ganache is a testing environment for smart contracts, offering 10 pre-funded accounts for testing smart contracts and transactions.
- *Truffle:* truffle is a framework for deploying contracts that automatically generates the folders for migrations between the mainnet and TestNet as well as the structure for storing contracts.
- *Metamask*: It is a well-known cryptocurrency wallet that is praised for its simplicity of use, compatibility with desktop and mobile platforms, ability to buy, transmit, and receive cryptocurrencies directly from the wallet, and capacity to gather non-fungible tokens (NFTs) across two blockchains.

5   Conclusion

The traditional land registry system was examined in this research along with its current practices and problems. The conventional approach uses a lot of chapter resources, necessitates significant record keeping, and raises questions about record security, all of which indirectly increase costs. It is also susceptible to various types of tampering at every stage. The method is time-consuming and requires a lot of time for the updating and verification processes, which promotes corruption and increases the risk of duplicate spending (selling the same parcel of land to multiple buyers at the same time). People are wary of investing in land trading since it removes a sizable sum of money from the normal economic cycle, which slows down the development of any nation.

The government's ability to collect taxes and other forms of revenue is also impacted by these problems, and the amount of unaccounted money is rising. All of these problems could potentially be solved by blockchain technology. The main issues of tampering, repeated spending, and near real-time updating of land records are addressed in this chapter's design for a secure and reliable land registration system. The suggested solution is very cost-effective because it uses a lot fewer human resources and is more dependable. In addition, a pre-agreement contract algorithm between the buyer and seller was suggested in this study. At various interconnection nodes (offices), the processes for creating ownership records and updating those data have been thoroughly discussed. The suggested framework and algorithm will eventually be used in the actual setting.

References

1. Yadav, A.S., Agrawal, S., Kushwaha, D.S.: Distributed ledger technology-based land transaction system with trusted nodes consensus mechanism. J. King Saud Univ-Comput. Inf. Sci. **34**(8), 6414–6424 (2022)
2. Ameyaw, P.D., de Vries, W.T.: Toward smart land management: land acquisition and the associated challenges in ghana. A look into a blockchain digital land registry for prospects. Land **10**(3), 239 (2021)
3. Aborujilah, A., Yatim, M.N.B.M., Al-Othmani, A.: Blockchain-based adoption framework for authentic land registry system in Malaysia. TELKOMNIKA Telecommun. Comput. Electr. Control **19**(6), 2038–2049 (2021)
4. Shuaib, M., Alam, S., Daud, S.A.: Improving the authenticity of real estate land transaction data using blockchain-based security scheme

5. Athawale, S.V.: Decentralized application using blockchain for land registration. Appl. Bionics Biomech. **2022**, 3859629 (2022)
6. Shuaib, M., et al.: Identity model for blockchain-based land registry system: a comparison. Wireless Commun. Mobile Comput. **2022**(5670714) (2022)
7. Swan, M., et al.: Anticipating the economic benefits of blockchain. Technol. Innov. Manag. Rev. **7**(10), 6–13 (2017)
8. Dobhal, A., Regan, M.: Immutability and auditability: the critical elements in property rights registries. In: Annual World Bank Conference on Land and Property: Annual World Bank Conference on Land and Property (2016)
9. Domeher, D., et al.: Access to credit in the developing world: does land registration matter? J. Third World Quart. **33**(1), 161–175 (2012)
10. Vos, J.: Blockchain-based land registry: panacea illusion or something in between? IPRA/CINDER Congress, Dubai (2016)
11. Tiwari, S., Gautam, J., Gupta, V., Malsa, N.: Smart contract for decentralized water management system using blockchain technology. Int. J. Innov. Technol. Explor. Eng. **9**(5), 2046–2050 (2020). https://doi.org/10.35940/ijitee.e3202.039520
12. Masla, N., Vyas, V., Gautam, J., Shaw, R.N., Ghosh, A.: Reduction in gas cost for blockchain enabled smart contract. In: 2021 IEEE 4th International Conference on Computing, Power and Communication Technologies (GUCON), pp. 1–6 (2021). https://doi.org/10.1109/GUCON50781.2021.9573701
13. Malsa, N., Vyas, V., Gautam, J.: Blockchain platforms and interpreting the effects of bitcoin pricing on cryptocurrencies. In: Sharma, T.K., Ahn, C.W., Verma, O.P., Panigrahi, B.K. (eds) Soft Computing: Theories and Applications. Advances in Intelligent Systems and Computing, vol. 1380. Springer, Singapore (2022). https://doi.org/10.1007/978-981-16-1740-9_13
14. Pathak, S., Gupta, V., Malsa, N., Ghosh, A., Shaw, R.N.: Blockchain-Based Academic Certificate Verification System—A Review. In: Shaw, R.N., Das, S., Piuri, V., Bianchini, M. (eds) Advanced Computing and Intelligent Technologies. Lecture Notes in Electrical Engineering, vol. 914. Springer, Singapore (2022). https://doi.org/10.1007/978-981-19-2980-9_42
15. Pathak, S., Gupta, V., Malsa, N., Ghosh, A., Shaw, R.N.: Smart contract for academic certificate verification using ethereum. In: Shaw, R.N., Das, S., Piuri, V., Bianchini, M. (eds.) Advanced Computing and Intelligent Technologies. Lecture Notes in Electrical Engineering, vol. 914. Springer, Singapore (2022). https://doi.org/10.1007/978-981-19-2980-9_29
16. Malsa, N., Vyas, V., Gautam, J., Shaw, R.N., Ghosh, A.: Framework and smart contract for blockchain enabled certificate verification system using robotics. In: Bianchini, M., Simic, M., Ghosh, A., Shaw, R.N. (eds.) Machine Learning for Robotics Applications. SCI, vol. 960, pp. 125–138. Springer, Singapore (2021). https://doi.org/10.1007/978-981-16-0598-7_10
17. Malsa, N., Vyas, V., Gautam, J., Ghosh, A., Shaw, R.N.: CERTbchain: A step by step approach towards building a blockchain based distributed application for certificate verification system. In: 2021 IEEE 6th International Conference on Computing, Communication and Automation (ICCCA), pp. 800–806 (2021). https://doi.org/10.1109/ICCCA52192.2021.9666311
18. Malsa, N., Vyas, V., Gautam, J.: RMSE calculation of LSTM models for predicting prices of different cryptocurrencies. Int. J. Syst. Assur. Eng. Manag. (2021). https://doi.org/10.1007/s13198-021-01431-1

A Comprehensive Study of Plant Disease Detection Using Deep Learning Methods

Kashan Haider[1], Prasandeep[1], Maaz Ahmed[1], Ankit Pal[1], Sur Singh Rawat[2(✉)],
Vimal Gupta[2], Rabindra Nath Shaw[3], and Ankush Ghosh[3]

[1] Student Department of Computer Science and Engineering, JSS Academy of Technical
Education, Noida 201301, India
[2] Faculty, Department of Computer Science and Engineering, JSS Academy of Technical
Education, Noida 201301, India
{sur.rawat,vimalgupta}@jssaten.ac.in
[3] University Center for Research and Development, Chandigarh University, Punjab, India

Abstract. Growing crops for human consumption and financial benefit is known as agriculture. It is the capability of using cutting-edge methods to cultivate crops and raise animals. As a result, the quality of the crop production is crucial to the development of the economy. In the agriculture industry, plant diseases and pests pose the biggest threat to crop production. Thus, it is essential to develop a method for accurately recognizing these illnesses so that the appropriate steps can be taken to treat them, increasing crop quality and quantity. A reliable disease detection system can be created by combining tools for classifying and extracting information with computer vision or image processing techniques employing deep learning. Different researchers have offered different approaches for identifying plant diseases. This study analyses these techniques.

Keywords: Artificial neural network (ANN) · Deep learning · Plant disease

1 Introduction

With the surge in population the food requirement is also increasing rapidly. In these circumstances, plant diseases are important factors that cause a severe drop in crop quality and quantity and can have devastating effects on farmers. As the world's population grows, so does its demand for food. Food security may be achieved by using machine learning to identify damaged plants early. The plant's pictures can be used to detect illnesses.

Plant disease is frequently employed in research and teaching farmers correct agriculture in India. The diagnosis, or the identification of symptoms, signs, and other indicators, calls for both hunches and methodical methods. 70% of India's workforce works in agriculture, either directly or indirectly.

As a result, agriculture is the foundation of the Indian economy. Naturally, plant disease is a major factor in the destruction of plants, which lowers the quantity and quality of agricultural products. Plant diseases caused by bacteria, viruses, and fungi

R. N. Shaw et al. (Eds.): ICACIS 2022, CCIS 1749, pp. 441–458, 2023.
https://doi.org/10.1007/978-3-031-25088-0_40

can destroy crops in addition to restricting plant growth [3]. According to Grape Leaf Disease Identification using Machine Learning Techniques [46] the different groups are Black Rot, Esca, and Leaf Blight. These are seen in Fig. 1.

Black Rot   **Esca**   **Leaf Blight**   **Healthy**

Fig. 1. (a) Black rot affected (b) Esca (C) Leaf Blight (d) Healthy grape leaves

Plant diseases are a topic of study that includes examining a plant's physically observable features, tracking the illness, and investigating potential treatments. For the majority of the monitoring, diagnosing, and assessing manual treatment of leaf and plant diseases, experts in these fields were formerly required. They therefore required a lot of work, a lengthy processing time, and a significant financial investment. In fact, timely identification and classification of leaf diseases can aid in agricultural risk reduction and prevention. Since various diseases affect various plant leaves, various methods must be utilised to identify specific plant leaf ailments. For instance, image processing techniques could be used to identify plant leaf diseases.

Numerous techniques for identifying leaf diseases have been covered in this research report. A review of the literature is presented in Sect. 2 (Literature Review), followed by a description of research methodology in Sect. 3 (Methodology), an accumulation of challenges in Sect. 4 (Challenges), and a conclusion in Sect. 5 (Conclusion).

2 Literature Review

Saleem et al. published a study on deep learning models for diagnosing different plant diseases [1]. The following research gaps exist: With the use of efficient DL architectures, hyperspectral/multispectral pictures can be used for early identification of plant diseases. The disease classification and detection (DL) models need to be improved. A comprehensive empirical research, encompassing data classes and sizes, learning rate, and illumination, among other things, is needed to detect plant illnesses.

Four CNN models were combined by X. Guan [2]. To create a method for identifying plant illnesses, these models included Inception, Resnet, Inception Resnet, and Densenet. There were 4540 frames in the validation set and 31718 overall for the training set. With this approach, 87% accuracy was attained.

Kawasaki et al. [3] introduced a unique CNN-based plant disease detection system. In total, 800 images were used in the training. Our model successfully distinguished between illness and non-disease classes with a 94.9 percent accuracy rate using a four-fold cross validation technique.

There are problems and difficulties with the present plant disease detection technology, claim Arsenovic et al. [4]. They released a fresh dataset of 79265 pictures of leaves in natural settings. Researchers used two different neural network designs to classify plant diseases with 93.67 percent accuracy.

Convolutional neural networks were used by Jasim and Tuwaijari [5] to detect and classify plant leaf diseases with accuracy of 98.29% and 98.029% for testing and training of all datasets. The Plant Village dataset, which includes 20636 plant photos and 15 different leaf diseases, was utilised to concentrate on certain plant species including tomatoes, peppers, and potatoes.

Deep learning methods have been utilised by Nagaraju and Chawla [6] to automatically detect illnesses in hyperspectral images. The researchers claim that applying modern computer vision technologies is insufficient for automatic disease identification. The input data collection environment may have an effect on the analysis of sickness classification. It is challenging to distinguish between the healthy and sick parts since sickness symptoms are not well defined. The visual similarity of disease symptoms means that current methods must rely on differences to distinguish.

Amara et al. [7] presented the sigatoka and speckle types of banana leaf diseases, which are diagnosed using a deep learning approach, using the LeNet architecture of the Convolutional Neural Network. In terms of lighting, intricate backgrounds, and various resolutions, sizes, and orientations of real photographs, the outcome was successful.

A deep learning-based approach for detecting plant diseases has been proposed by Guo et al. [8] that increases training cost, flexibility, and accuracy. The Chan-Vese (CV) method was used to extract characteristics from the region proposal network. With the transfer learning approach, the final disease detection accuracy was 83.57%.

Hruska et al. [9] provided methods for hyperspectral image processing in agricultural applications using machine learning categorization. Now that unmanned aerial vehicles have access to hyperspectral sensors, it is possible to generate vast amounts of data while also getting accurate results.

Bai et al. [10] introduced and enhanced the Fuzzy C means technique for identifying cucumber leaf spots. This method overcomes FCM's underutilization of image pixel spatial information by using grey scale information from neighbours to enhance noise filtering.

The absence of clearly defined symptom borders, complex backdrops that are challenging to distinguish, and uncontrolled recording conditions that may exhibit challenging picture analysis characteristics are only a few of the major issues that Barbedo [11] addressed. Additionally, the author suggested some potential fixes for a few issues.

A sizable collection of 14828 images of sick tomato leaves was used by Brahimi et al. [12]. With 99.18 percent accuracy, the learning algorithm characteristics were automatically derived from CNN using raw pictures. Here, GoogleNet and AlexNet, two deep learning models, were contrasted with shallow models.

Cruz et al. [13] suggested a method for accurately 98.6% detecting OQDS on Olea Europaea L leaves infected with Xylella fastidiosa. The new method relied on Transfer learning, a deep learning application that uses the dataset to deal with a dearth of suitable training examples, whereas their earlier work used networks that were developed well before GoogLeNet and AlexNet and GoogLeNet networks.

On maize plants, DeChant et al. [14] developed a 96.7 percent accurate method for identifying northern leaf blight lesions. This method made use of the convolutional neural networks' computational framework.

Durmus et al. [15] used deep learning algorithms to identify disease on tomato plant leaves. By employing close-up photos of leaves, algorithm-coded robots or built-in sensors performed the operation in real time in a greenhouse. In this study, the accuracy of the SqueezeNet and AlexNet designs were assessed, scoring 94.3% and 95.65%, respectively. It was also found that the SqueezeNet model's size was 80 times less than the AlexNet model.

Ferentinos [16] built models of convolutional neural networks disease detection in plants using simple leaf pictures of well and sick plants. A dataset with 87,848 pictures, 58 classes, and 25 plants of [plant, disease] pairs was used to train the model. After training several model designs, a 99.53 percent success rate was attained.

Fuentes et al. [17] provided a deep learning detection for pests and disease in tomatoes using images captured from a camera at various resolutions. Faster Region-based Single Shot Multibox Detector (SSD), Convolutional Neural Network, and Region-based Fully Convolutional Network are three families of detectors that were used to identify nine classes. Utilising Residual Network (ResNet) extractors and VGG nets, they merged deep features. By employing class annotation and data augmentation, they showed how to improve accuracy and decrease the number of mistakes made during training.

Anyone can utilise the deep learning technique described by Mindhe et al. [18] for swiftly identifying plant ailments. This NN model was developed to identify 26 distinct diseases as well as 14 different crop kinds. The accuracy was 96.21 percent and the neural network ResNet 34 was used.

A technique using deep CNN- for disease detection in rice plant leaves and stems was proposed by Lu et al. [19]. (CNNs). Using 500 photographs of healthy and damaged rice plants, CNN was taught to identify 10 prevalent rice diseases. This model outperformed the Convnet trained model in accuracy, achieving 95.48 percent using 10-fold cross-validation.

CNN network was used by Ferreira et al. [20] to find weeds in soybean fields. Weeds are undesirable plants that restrict the growth of soybean plants, so they must be eliminated. 15000 images of soil, broad leaf soybeans, and grass weeds were initially captured. The CaffeNet architecture was used to train the neural network. Results of ConvNets, support vector machines, AdaBoost, and Random Forest were compared using shape, colour, and texture feature extraction methods.ConvNets were 98 percent accurate in identifying broadleaf and grass.

A deep CNN algorithm was proposed by Oppenheim and Shani [21] for the categorization of potato illnesses. After training, the system separates the tubers into five groups, including four categories for damaged tubers. Depending on how the Train-Test set is divided, the precision changes. The 10 percent train - 90% test model had the lowest accuracy (83.21 percent), while the 90 percent train - 10% test model had the highest accuracy (96.85%).

For tomato, corn, and potato, Arshad et al. [22] used ResNet50 with Transfer Learning to demonstrate plant disease identification. There are a total of 16 classes of various plant diseases. Here, ResNet50 was used to obtain 98.7% performance.

Chellapandi et al. [23] examined deep learning and transfer learning models for 38 different types of damaged plant leaves. The models employed were VGG19, InceptionV3, ResNet50, Vgg16, InceptionResnetV2, DenseNet, and MobileNet. With regard to these models, DenseNet obtained 99% accuracy.

EfficientNet and DenseNet models of Deep CNN were employed by Srinidhi et al. [24] to identify illness in Apple plant leaves. The photos of apple plant leaves were divided into four categories: healthy, scabbed, rusted, and various diseases. With the aid of Canny Edge Detection, Flipping, and Blurring, the dataset for the apple leaf disease is updated (data augmentation and picture annotation techniques).. Using EfficientNetB7 and DenseNet, the obtained accuracy was 99.8% and 99.75%, respectively.

CNN models like DenseNet, ResNet, and VGG were employed by Akshai et al. [25] to categorise the various plant diseases. Because employing DenseNet had a high success rate of 98.27%, they used CNN image-based categorization.

A CNN-based approach for disease identification in infected plant leaves is proposed by Ashok et al.[26] employing hierarchical feature extraction, an image processing technique that maps the input image's pixel intensities. 98% accuracy was attained.

A model for early diagnosis and detection of 32 plant diseases using CNN was proposed by Militante et al. [27]. This technology is able to identify and find numerous plant diseases, particularly those that affect sugarcane, potato, corn, grapes, potato, apple, and grapes. The accuracy achieved was 96.5%.

Authors Prasanna Mohanty and colleagues described a method for detecting plant disease by training a convolutional neural network in the chapter "Deep learning for Image-Based Plant detection" [28]. Plant health and illness are classified differently by the CNN model. On test data, the model has a 99.35% accuracy rate. A more varied set of training data can improve the accuracy of the suggested model, which obtains a 31.4% accuracy when used to classify photos obtained from internet sources.

The four basic steps in the disease diagnosis method are described in the chapter "Detection of the unhealthy zone of plant leaves and categorization of plant leaf disease using textural traits" [29] by S. Arivazhagan. The RGB input image is first given a colour transformation, the green pixels are then found and determined to be uninvolved, segmentation is then performed, and finally a classifier is employed for the features to categorise the diseases.

According to Kulkarni et al. in their research "Applying image processing approach to identify plant diseases" [30], plant illness is recognised utilising artificial neural network (ANN) and other image processing techniques. The suggested approach yields superior results with recognition rates of up to 91% and uses an ANN classifier and a Gabor filter to extract features.

The use of Generative Adversarial Networks to identify plant illness has been suggested in the study "Plant disease detection using CNN and GAN" [31] by Emanuel Cortes. The extraction of features makes use of background segmentation. The use of Gans appears to have potential for classifying plant diseases, however background-based segmentation did not increase accuracy.

In their study, "Convolutional Neural Network based Inception v3 Model for Animal categorization," Jyotsna Bankar et al. recommended utilising the Inception v3 model to categorise animals of various species [32]. The ability of Inception v3 to identify objects makes it useful in a number of image classifiers.

In their research titled "Intelligent diagnosis of Northern Corn Leaf Blight using Deep Learning Model," PAN Shuai-qun et al. Based on numerous DCNN models, [33] recommended using a Deep Convolutional Network (DCNN) to identify Northern Corn Leaf Blight (NCLB) in the maize crop. Using data augmentation techniques like picture segmentation, image scaling, image cropping, and image manipulation, a database with 985 leaf images of healthy and sick maize is created. Then, different CNNs were employed to detect illnesses, including AlexNet, GoogleNet, VGG16, and VGG19. is to isolate the affected area, which has been demonstrated to have a 99.94% accuracy rate using a pre-trained GoogleNet architecture using the SoftMax loss function.

In their study "Blackleg Detection in Potato Plants" [34], Manya Afonso, et al. recommend using convolutional neural networks to identify potato plants that have the blackleg disease. Two deep convolutional neural networks were trained on RGB images of healthy and diseased plants. One of these networks, ResNet18, yielded data with a 95% accuracy rate for the sick class.

M. Nandhini et al. in their study "Deep Learning model of sequential image classifier for crop disease detection in plantain tree cultivation" [35] offer a new sequential image classification model, the Gated-Recurrent Convolutional Neural Network, to detect the diseases by fusing RNN and CNN (G-RecConNN). This strategy aims to accomplish a number of advantages, such as less data pre-processing, straightforward online performance evaluation, advancements with accurate data, etc.

Identification of the Oryza sativa disease in rice plants was the aim of a study by Vimal K. Shrivastava et al., "Rice Plant disease Classification utilising transfer learning of deep convolutional neural networks [36]. Pictures of the diseased stems and leaves have been taken from a rice field. Pre-trained deep convolutional neural networks (DCNN) and support vector machines (SVM) are used as a feature extractor and classifier.

Convolutional neural network models with the Inception V3 model, Inception resnetV2, VGG19 (Visual Geometric Group 19), and Adam Optimizer were used by Mrs. M. Geetha Yadav 1, Rajasekhar Nennuri, et al. in the study "Identification of Plant Leaf Diseases Using Machine Learning Algorithms" [37] to identify and categorise fungal diseases in rice plants, such as bacterial leaf.

In the study of Faye Mohameth and Chen Bingcai titled "Plant Disease Detection using Deep Learning and Feature Extraction Using Plant Village" [38], Kane Amath Sada. To identify plant illnesses, they applied Deep feature extraction and Deep learning algorithms to the plant village data set. VGG16, Google Net, and ResNet 50 were three of the three deep learning models that were tested. Using state-of-the-art networks, they first retrieved features in this chapter using SVM and KNN, and then they performed transfer learning using fine-tuning. The accuracy % and execution time of the results were compared. Extracting features is more effective than transfer learning, according to modes' behaviour.

In their chapter "Deep Learning Model for Plant Disease Detection" [39], D. Raghunath Kumar Babu et al. offer a CNN model. Using the CNN method, they achieved an accuracy of more than 93% for 12 different plant species. Compared to other algorithms like SVM and random forests, their calculations were more accurate. CNN is therefore the better algorithm, giving more accuracy, according to this study.

Convolutional neural networks (CNNs) are used to identify plant illnesses, as described in the study "Convolutional Neural Networks in Detection of Plant Leaf Diseases: A Review" [40] by Tugrul et al. They have found a solution to the issue with conventional item detection and classification techniques.

According to Madhu Bala and Vineet Mehan's "Identification of Rice Plant Diseases Using Image Processing, Machine Learning, and Deep Learning: A Review" [41]. They have tested various segmentation approaches and concluded that the most crucial stage in using rice plants to detect diseases from the leaf image. The best accuracy for detecting disease in the rice crop was found to be better than 97% after a comparison of various approaches.

In their research "Plant Diseases Classification using Machine Learning," Tan Soo Xian and Ruzelita Ngadiran used Extreme Learning Machine (ELM), a machine learning classification system utilising a single-layer feed-forward neural network. They observed that this method has a higher accuracy of 84.94% than other models like the Support Vector Machine and Decision Tree.

According to the research "Deep Learning Utilisation in Agriculture: Detection of Rice Plant Diseases Using an Improved CNN Model" [43] by Ghazanfar Latif et al., they investigated tools like GoogleNet, VGG16, VGG19, DenseNet201, and AlexNet and employed CNN models for the non-normalized dataset. They discovered an overall 83% accuracy for both the non-normalized dataset and the normalised data set using these methodologies and tools.

The purpose of the chapter "Plant Disease Detection using Machine Learning" [44] by Ramesh, et al. was to identify crop illnesses using a Deep Learning technique, specifically a Convolutional Neural network. Additionally, they created a model with the help of the TensorFlow and Keras frameworks, and they also implemented this model in Android apps. As a result, the overall findings demonstrate that the Mobile Net model performs better than previous models and offers greater accuracy in identifying diseases. Other applications of machine learning algorithms are described in the studies [56–58].

Convolutional neural networks (CNN) based on deep learning were utilised by Chowdhury Rafeed Rahman et al. in their study "Identification and Recognition of Rice Diseases and Pests Using Convolutional Neural Networks" [45] to detect the diseases by the success of CNNs in picture classification. Using this deep learning model, the suggested architecture obtained the necessary accuracy of 93.3%.

According to S.M.'s study "Grape Leaf Disease Identification using Machine Learning Techniques" [46], P. and Jaisakthi SVM, random forest, and Adaboost algorithms were used by Mirunalini et al. for classification. 93.035% accuracy was attained on Grapes Leaves utilising global thresholding and SVM. Various methods[47–52] presents image processing techniques using the patch based image model for detecting object of interest in the image.Table 1 reports the study of these chapters over Dataset, Approaches used and Results obtained by the Researchers.

Table 1. List of research achievements using various models of deep learning for detecting diseases in plant leaves.

S.No	Researchers	Dataset	Approach	Result
1	Muhammad Hammad Saleem [1]	The 54,306 photos in the PlantVillage dataset, which depict 14 different crops with 26 distinct plant diseases, have been used	Hyperspectral/multispectral images can be exploited for early disease detection of plants using effective DL architectures	To identify illness symptoms, a number of mappings and visualisation techniques were assembled
2	Xulang Guan [2]	Total 36258 leaf images divided into 10 plant categories	Inception, Resnet CNN-style networks Resnet, Densenet, and Inception were integrated	Accuracy of 87%
3	Kawasaki et. al [3]	total 800 Cucumber leaves	Used Caffe framework of CNN model	Accuracy of 94.9%
4	Arsenovic et. al [4]	PlantVillage dataset of 79265 images	Used traditional augmentation methods and generative adversarial networks	Accuracy of 93.67%
5	M. A. Jasim and J. M. Al-Tuwaijari [5]	20636 images of tomato, pepper and potatoes from PlantVillage dataset	ConvNets variation of CNN model	Accuracy of 98.029%
6	Amara et. al [7]	3700 images from PlantVillage of bananas categorised into healthy, black sigatoka and black speckles	LeNet variation of CNN model	Found accuracies for different combinations of training and testing
7	Guo et al. [8]	Dataset of 1000 leaves using Plant Photo Bank of China	Using the transfer learning model of deep learning	83.57% accuracy
8	Bai et. al [10]	129 images of cucumber disease in the diseased database of vegetables	Updated Fuzzy C-means algorithm	88% accuracy of segmentation

(continued)

Table 1. (*continued*)

S.No	Researchers	Dataset	Approach	Result
9	Brahimi et. al [12]	14,828 tomatoes leave images of nine diseases	GoogleNet, AlexNet and shallow models based on handcrafted features	99.18% accuracy
10	Cruz et. al [13]	Olive tree leaves from the PlantVillage dataset: 100 healthy leaves, 99 X. fastidiosa-positive leaves, and 100 X. fastidiosa-negative leaves	CNN trained with stochastic gradient descent approach	Olive Quick Decline Syndrome (OQDS) detection accuracy is 98.60 ± 1.47% in testing
11	DeChant et. al [14]	Self-shot 1796 leaf photos of maize plants	Convolutional neural network computing pipeline	96.75 accuracy for identifying NLB lesions
12	Durmus et. al [15]	Tomato leaves images from PlantVillage dataset	AlexNet and SqueezeNet versions of CNN	Testing accuracy of 95.65% and 94.3% through AlexNet and SqueezeNet respectively
13	K. P. Ferentinos [16]	87,848 images of an open database which contains 25 plant varieties of 58 distinct classes	VGG and AlexNetOWTBn architecture of CNN model	Classification accuracy is 99.53% using the VGG model
14	Fuentes et. al [17]	5000 images of tomato from PlantVillage dataset under different environment conditions	Region-based Convolutional Neural Network, faster Single Shot Multibox Detector, and Region-based Convolutional Neural Network	NA
15	Mindhe et. al [18]	54,444 images from PlantVillage dataset	ResNet 34 version of CNN	96.21%
16	Lu et. al [19]	500 healthy and diseased images of rice	Multistage CNN model	95.48% accuracy for 10 rice disease identification

(*continued*)

Table 1. (*continued*)

S.No	Researchers	Dataset	Approach	Result
17	Ferreira et. al [20]	15000 photographs of dirt, soybeans, broadleaf, and grass weeds	For training CaffeNet and for detection ConvNets architectures are used here	Accuracy of 98%
18	Oppenheim & Shani [21]	There are 2465 photos of potatoes	VGG version of CNN model	Categorization accuracy ranges from 83.21% to 96.85%
19	Arshad et. al [22]	PlantVillage dataset of tomato, potato and corn	ResNet50 with transfer learning	98.7% accuracy was achieved using ResNet50
20	Chellapandi et. al [23]	54,306 images of 14 types of plants from Git-Hub database of SP Mohanty	Compared eight pre trained models with one self made model	With DenseNet 99% accuracy was achieved
21	Srinidhi et al. [24]	3600 image dataset of apple leaf disease	EfficientNetB7 and DenseNet models of CNN	Both DenseNet and EfficientNetB7 achieved accuracy levels of 99.75% and 99.8%, respectively.
22	Akshai et. al [25]	55,000 images of 14 species of plants from PlantVillage dataset	Compared VGG, ResNet and DenseNet	Accuracy of 98.27% using DenseNet
23	Ashok et. al [26]	Tomato leaf dataset	Hierarchical feature extraction based CNN algorithm	98% accuracy
24	Militante et. al [27]	35,000 images of tomato, grape, corn, apple and sugarcane	CNN based model	96.5% accuracy

(*continued*)

Table 1. (*continued*)

S.No	Researchers	Dataset	Approach	Result
25	S. Arivazhagan[29]	To identify diseases like early scorch, yellow spots, brown spots, late scorch, bacterial and fungal diseases, 500 plant leaves of 30 different native plants were collected	SVM classifier is used	Accuracy of 94.74%
26	Kulkarni et al. [30]	Collected various plant leaves to identify diseases	Plant diseases are recognised utilising artificial neural networks (ANN) and a Gabor filter to extract features	Accuracy of 91%
27	Emanuel Cortes[31]	For the purpose of identifying 25 different plant species, 86,147 photos of healthy and unhealthy plants were collected	The use of Generative Adversarial Networks to identify plant illness	Accuracy of 80% and above in the training phase
28	Jyotsna Bankar et al. [32]	Approximately 2000 images collected and 400 per mammal to identify the behaviour of animals	Inception v3 model was used to categorise animals of various types	Accuracy of the trained model is 97.92%
29	Shuai-qun et al. [33]	A database comprising 985 leaf images of healthy and sick maize is produced using data augmentation technique	Deep Convolutional Network (DCNN) to diagnose Northern Corn Leaf Blight (NCLB) in the maize crop	Accuracy of 99.94%
30	Manya Afonso, et al. [34]	532 images of potato plants were selected across the six different dates	Identifying potato plants with blackleg disease using convolutional neural networks	Accuracy of 95%

(*continued*)

Table 1. (*continued*)

S.No	Researchers	Dataset	Approach	Result
31	M. Nandhini et al. [35]	4627 images of diseased and healthy plants selected to identify 4 banana diseases	RNN and CNN (G-RecConNN) were used to detect diseases	NA
32	Vimal K. Shrivastava et al. [36]	Sample images used in this chapter were collected from rice field of Indira Gandhi Agricultural University	Pre-trained deep convolutional neural networks (DCNN) and support vector machines (SVM) are used as a feature extractor and classifier	Accuracy of 91.37%
33	Rajasekhar Nennuri, et al. [37]	Several images of rice plants selected to identify fungal diseases like bacterial leaf blight, Browns pot and Leaf smut	Convolutional neural network models with the Inception V3 model, Inception resnetV2, VGG19 (Visual Geometric Group 19), and Adam Optimizer to classify rice plant fungal disease	Accuracy of 90%
34	Faye Mohameth [38]	The plant village data set is used	The three deep learning models that were examined were VGG16, Google Net, and ResNet 50	The accuracy % and execution time of the results were compared
35	D. Raghunath Kumar Babu et al. [39]	54,300 images, 25 diseases, 13 crop species	Compared CNN with other algorithms like SVM and random forest	Accuracy of 93% for 12 different plant species using CNN
36	Madhu Bala [41]	Selected various rice plant leaves to identify diseases	Testing of various segmentation approaches have been done	Accuracy of 97%
37	Tan Soo Xian [42]	The Plant Village dataset	A machine learning classification algorithm based Extreme Learning Machine (ELM)	Accuracy of 84.94%
38	Ghazanfar Latif et al. [43]	Used a dataset of 6330 images	For the non-normalized dataset, tools like GoogleNet, VGG16, VGG19, DenseNet201, and AlexNet used CNN models	Overall accuracy of 83%

(*continued*)

Table 1. (*continued*)

S.No	Researchers	Dataset	Approach	Result
39	Chowdhury Rafeed Rahman et al.[45]	From paddy fields, a total of 1426 photographs of sick rice leaves were obtained.	CNN is used	Accuracy of 93.3%
40	Mirunalini et al. [46]	5675 grape leaves from the plant village website	Algorithms like SVM, random forest, and Adaboost were used	Accuracy of 93.035%

3 Methodology

A block diagram represented in Fig. 2 shows Leaf Image Dataset, Image pre-processing, CNN model, Training, Testing and Disease detection of plant leaf.

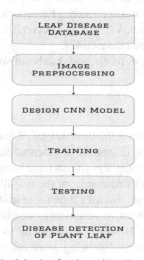

Fig. 2. Methodologies for detecting plant leaf disease

A. Image pre-processing: Preprocessing is done to enhance the image's quality so that we can analyse it more effectively. Pre-processing enables us to remove unwanted distortions and improve specific properties that are essential for the application we're developing. The properties may change depending on the use.

B. Design CNN model: Due to its exceptional performance and precision, CNN model is used in this chapter to identify plant disease.

C. Training: Training is the process used to carry out system learning. It utilises a portion of the dataset. The effectiveness of the model relies on this crucial component of the system.

D.   Testing; With the remaining dataset images, the model is tested. This model will be used for unknown photos if accuracy is attained with a low threshold.

E.   Disease detection of plant leaf: The finished CNN model can then be used for real-time data once the aforementioned processes, including image pre-processing, CNN model construction, training, and testing, have been completed.

4   Challenges and Future Scope

Various researchers have expressed different opinions on this specific subject. These are listed below:

- Disease of plant leaves detection using traditional augmentation methods and generative adversarial networks[4].
- CNN trained with a stochastic gradient descent approach[13].
- Compared eight pre-trained models with one self made model[23].
- Pre-trained deep convolutional neural networks (DCNN) and support vector machines (SVM) are used as a feature extractor and classifier[33].
- Testing of various segmentation approaches have been done[41].
- Tools like GoogleNet, VGG16, VGG19, DenseNet201, and AlexNet employed CNN models for the non-normalized dataset[43].
- Algorithms like SVM, random forest, and Adaboost were used [46].

5   Conclusion

Plant diseases are discovered using the three stages of feature extraction, classification, and segmentation. For accurate diagnosis, segmentation, and prediction, a variety of machine learning and deep learning algorithms have been widely used. They have been classified and utilised to extract features from them. Although these technologies performed better at diagnosing plant diseases than more traditional approaches like image processing, they also had disadvantages including computer complexity, protracted execution times, and higher costs. However, it is crucial to create a strategy that is more time- and resource-efficient while also being more effective in spotting plant diseases early on. As a result, more work will be required in the future to overcome current obstacles, improve current efforts, and provide reliable, efficient methods for early automatic identification.

References

1.   Saleem, M.H., Potgieter, J., Arif, K.M.: Plant disease detection and classification by deep learning. Plants 8(11), 468 (2021)

2.   Guan, X.: A novel method of plant leaf disease detection based on deep learning and convolutional neural network. In: 6th International Conference on Intelligent Computing and Signal Processing (ICSP), pp. 816–819 (2021). https://doi.org/10.1109/ICSP51882.2021.9408806

3. Kawasaki, Y., Uga, H., Kagiwada, S., Iyatomi, H.: Basic study of automated diagnosis of viral plant diseases using convolutional neural networks. International Symposium on Visual Computing, pp. 638–645 (2015). https://doi.org/10.1007/978-3-319-27863-6_59

4. Brahimi, M., Arsenovic, M., Laraba, S., Sladojevic, S., Boukhalfa, K., Moussaoui, A.: Deep learning for plant diseases: detection and saliency map visualisation. In: Human and machine learning, pp. 93–117 (2017). https://doi.org/10.1007/978-3-319-90403-0_6

5. Jasim, M.A., Al-Tuwaijari, J.M.: Plant leaf diseases detection and classification using image processing and deep learning techniques. In: International Conference on Computer Science and Software Engineering (CSASE), pp. 259–265 (2020)

6. Nagaraju, M., Chawla, P.: Systematic review of deep learning techniques in plant disease detection. In: Int. J. System Assurance Eng. Manage. **11**(3), 547–560 (2020)

7. Amara, J., Bouaziz, B., Algergawy, A.: A deep learning-based approach for banana leaf diseases classification. Datenbanksysteme für Business, Technologie und Web (2017)

8. Guo, Y., et al.: Plant disease identification based on deep learning algorithm in smart farming. Discrete Dynamics in Nature and Society (2020)

9. Hruška, J., et al.: Machine learning classification methods in hyperspectral data processing for agricultural applications. In: International Conference on Geoinformatics and Data Analysis pp. 137–141 (2018)

10. Bai, X., Li, X., Fu, Z., Lv, X., Zhang, L.: A fuzzy clustering segmentation method based on neighbourhood grayscale information for defining cucumber leaf spot disease images. Computers and Electronics in Agriculture **136**, 157–165 (2017). https://doi.org/10.1016/j.compag.2017.03.004

11. Barbedo, J.G.A.: A review on the main challenges in automatic plant disease identification based on visible range images. Biosystems Eng. **144**, 52–60 (2016)

12. Brahimi, M., Boukhalfa, K., Moussaoui, A.: Deep learning for tomato diseases: classification and symptoms visualisation. Applied Artificial Intelligence **31**(4), 299–315 (2017). https://doi.org/10.1080/08839514.2017.1315516

13. Cruz, A.C., Luvisi, A., De Bellis, L., Ampatzidis, Y.: X-FIDO: An effective application for detecting olive quick decline syndrome with deep learning and data fusion. Frontiers in Plant Science **8**, 1741 (2017). https://doi.org/10.3389/fpls.2017.01741

14. DeChant, C., et al.: Automated identification of northern leaf blight-infected maize plants from field imagery using deep learning. Phytopathology **107**(11), 1426–1432 (2017)

15. Durmuş, H., Güneş, E.O., Kırcı, M.: Disease detection on the leaves of the tomato plants by using deep learning. In: 6th International Conference on Agro-Geoinformatics, pp. 1–5 (2017)

16. Ferentinos, K.P.: Deep learning models for plant disease detection and diagnosis. Computers and Electronics in Agriculture **145**, 311–318 (2018)

17. Fuentes, A., Yoon, S., Kim, S.C, Park, D.S.: A robust deep-learning-based detector for real-time tomato plant diseases and pests recognition. Sensors **9**, 2022 (2017)

18. Mindhe, O., Kurkute, O., Naxikar, S., Raje, N.: Plant disease detection using deep learning. In: International Research Journal of Engineering and Technology, pp. 2497–2503 (2020)

19. Lu, Y., Yi, S., Zeng, N., Liu, Y., Zhang, Y.: Identification of rice diseases using deep convolutional neural networks. Neurocomputing **267**, 378–384 (2017)

20. Ferreira, A. dos Santos, Freitas, D.M., Silva, G.G. da, Pistori, H., Folhes, M.T.: Weed detection in soybean crops using ConvNets. Computers and Electronics in Agriculture **143**, 314–324 (2017)

21. Oppenheim, D., Shani, G.: Potato disease classification using convolutional neural network. Advances in Animal Biosciences, pp.244–249 (2017)

22. Arshad, M.S., Rehman, U.A., Fraz, M.M.: Plant disease identification using transfer learning. In: 2021 International Conference on Digital Futures and Transformative Technologies (ICoDT2), pp. 1–5 (2021). https://doi.org/10.1109/ICoDT252288.2021.9441512
23. Chellapandi, B., Vijayalakshmi, M., Chopra, S.: Comparison of pre-trained models using transfer learning for detecting plant disease. In: 2021 International Conference on Computing, Communication, and Intelligent Systems (ICCCIS), pp. 383–387 (2021). https://doi.org/10.1109/ICCCIS51004.2021.9397098
24. Srinidhi, V.V., Sahay, A., Deeba, K.: Plant pathology disease detection in apple leaves using deep convolutional neural networks : apple leaves disease detection using efficientnet and densenet. In: 2021 5th International Conference on Computing Methodologies and Communication (ICCMC), pp. 1119–1127 (2021). https://doi.org/10.1109/ICCMC51019.2021.9418268
25. Akshai, K.P.A., Anitha, J.: Plant disease classification using deep learning. In: 2021 3rd International Conference on Signal Processing and Communication (ICPSC), pp. 407–411 (2021). https://doi.org/10.1109/ICSPC51351.2021.9451696
26. Ashok, S., Kishore, G., Rajesh, V., Suchitra, S., Sophia, S.G.G., Pavithra, B.: Tomato leaf disease detection using deep learning techniques. In: 2020 5th International Conference on Communication and Electronics Systems (ICCES), pp. 979–983 (2020). https://doi.org/10.1109/ICCES48766.2020.9137986
27. Militante, S.V., Gerardo, B.D., Medina, R.P.: Sugarcane disease recognition using deep learning. In: 2019 IEEE Eurasia Conference on IOT, Communication and Engineering (ECICE), pp. 575–578 (2019). https://doi.org/10.1109/ECICE47484.2019.8942690
28. Mohanty, S.P., Hughes, D.P., Salathé, M.: Using deep learning for image-based plant disease detection. Front. Plant Sci. **7**, 1419 (2016)
29. Arivazhagan, S., Shebiah, R.N., Ananthi, S., Varthini, S.V.: Detection of unhealthy regions of plant leaves and classification of plant leaf diseases using texture features. Agric. Eng. Int. CIGR J. **15**(1), 211–217 (2013)
30. Kulkarni, A.H., Patil, A.: Applying image processing techniques to detect plant diseases. Int. J. Modern Eng. Res. **2**(5), 3661–3664 (2012)
31. Cortes, E.: Plant Disease Classification Using Convolutional Networks and Generative Adversarial Networks. Stanford University Reports, Stanford (2017)
32. Bankar, J., Gavai, N.R.: Convolutional neural network based inception V3 model for animal classification. Int. J. Advanced Research in Computer Communication Eng. **7**(5), 142–146 (2018)
33. Mridha, K., et al.: Plant disease detection using web application by neural network. In: 2021 IEEE 6th International Conference on Computing, Communication and Automation (ICCCA), pp. 130–136 (2021). https://doi.org/10.1109/ICCCA52192.2021.9666354
34. Afonso, M., Blok, P.M., Polder, G., Van der Wolf, J.M., Kamp, J.: Blackleg detection in potato plants using convolutional neural networks. IFAC-ChaptersOnLine **52**(30), 6–11 (2019)
35. Nandhini, M., Kala, K.U., Thangadarshini, M., Verma, S.M.: Deep Learning model of sequential image classifier for crop disease detection in plantain tree cultivation. Comput. Electron. Agric. **197**, 106915 (2022)
36. Shrivastava, V.K., Pradhan, M.K., Minz, S., Thakur, M.P.: Rice plant disease classification using transfer learning of deep convolutional neural networks. Int. Archives Photogrammetry, Remote Sensing & Spatial Information Sciences **3**(6), 631–635 (2019)
37. Yadav, M.M.G., Nennuri, R., Rajeshwari, D., Rishitha, V., Puneeth, T.: Identification of plant leaf diseases using machine learning algorithms. Annals of the Romanian Society for Cell Biology **25**(6), 6866–6875 (2021)

38. Mohameth, F., Bingcai, C., Sada, K.A.: Plant disease detection with deep learning and feature extraction using plant village. J. Computer and Communications **8**(6), 10–22 (2020)
39. Babu, D.R.K., Chaithanya, M., Sandhya, M., Shireesha, G.: Deep learning model for plant disease detection. In: International Journal of Recent Technology and Engineering (IJRTE), Vol. 9, Issue 1, pp. 750–754 (2020)
40. Gupta, V., Bibhu, V.: Deep residual network based brain tumor segmentation and detection with MRI using improved invasive bat algorithm. Multimedia Tools and Applications, pp.1–23 (2022)
41. Palimkar, P., Shaw, R.N., Ghosh, A.: Machine learning technique to prognosis diabetes disease: random forest classifier approach. In: Bianchini, M., Piuri, V., Das, S., Shaw, R.N. (eds.) Advanced Computing and Intelligent Technologies. LNNS, vol. 218, pp. 219–244. Springer, Singapore (2022). https://doi.org/10.1007/978-981-16-2164-2_19
42. Bala, M., Mehan, V.: Identification of Rice Plant Diseases Using Image Processing, Machine Learning & Deep Learning: A Review (2021)
43. Xian, T.S., Ngadiran, R.: Plant diseases classification using machine learning. In: Journal of Physics: Conference Series, Vol. 1962, No. 1, p. 012024. IOP Publishing (2021)
44. Latif, G., Abdelhamid, S.E., Mallouhy, R.E., Alghazo, J., Kazimi, Z.A.: Deep learning utilisation in agriculture: detection of rice plant diseases using an improved CNN model. Plants **11**(17), 2230 (2022)
45. Malsa, N., Singh, P., Gautam, J., Srivastava, A., Singh, S.P.: Source of treatment selection for different states of india and performance analysis using machine learning algorithms for classification. In: Soft Computing: Theories and Applications, pp. 235–245). Springer, Singapore (2020). https://doi.org/10.1007/978-981-15-4032-5_23
46. Gautam, J., Atrey, M., Malsa, N., Balyan, A., Shaw, R.N., Ghosh, A.: Twitter data sentiment analysis using naive bayes classifier and generation of heat map for analyzing intensity geographically. In Advances in Applications of Data-Driven Computing, pp. 129–139. Springer, Singapore (2021). https://doi.org/10.1007/978-981-33-6919-1_10
47. Ramesh, S., Hebbar, R., Niveditha, M., Pooja, R., Shashank, N., Vinod, P.V.: Plant disease detection using machine learning. In: 2018 International Conference on Design Innovations for 3Cs Compute Communication Control (ICDI3C), pp. 41–45 (2018). IEEE
48. Rahman, C.R., et al.: Identification and recognition of rice diseases and pests using convolutional neural networks. Biosys. Eng. **194**, 112–120 (2020)
49. Jaisakthi, S.M., Mirunalini, P., Thenmozhi, D.: Grape leaf disease identification using machine learning techniques. In: 2019 International Conference on Computational Intelligence in Data Science (ICCIDS), pp. 1–6 (2019). IEEE
50. Rawat, S.S., Verma, S.K., Kumar, Y.: Infrared small target detection based on non-convex triple tensor factorisation. IET Image Proc. **15**(2), 556–570 (2021)
51. Rawat, S.S., Verma, S.K., Kumar, Y.: Reweighted infrared patch image model for small target detection based on non-convex $\mathscr{L}$p-norm minimisation and TV regularisation. IET Image Proc. **14**(9), 1937–1947 (2020)
52. Rawat, S.S., Alghamdi, S., Kumar, G., Alotaibi, Y., Khalaf, O.I., Verma, L.P.: Infrared small target detection based on partial sum minimization and total variation. Mathematics **10**(4), 671 (2022)
53. Rawat, S.S., Singh, S., Alotaibi, Y., Alghamdi, S., Kumar, G.: Infrared target-background separation based on weighted nuclear norm minimization and robust principal component analysis. Mathematics **10**(16), 2829 (2022)
54. Singh, S., et al.: Hybrid Models for Breast Cancer Detection via Transfer Learning Technique
55. Singh, S., et al.: Deep Attention Network for Pneumonia Detection Using Chest X-Ray Images
56. Malsa, N., Vyas, V., Gautam, J.: RMSE calculation of LSTM models for predicting prices of different cryptocurrencies. Int. J. Syst. Assur. Eng. Manag., 19 (2021). https://doi.org/10.1007/s13198-021-01431-1

458   K. Haider et al.

57. Gupta, P., Malsa, N., Saxena, N., Agarwal, S., Singh, S.P.: Short-term load forecasting using parametric and non-parametric approaches. In: Pant, M., Sharma, T.K., Verma, O.P., Singla, R., Sikander, A. (eds.) Soft Computing: Theories and Applications. AISC, vol. 1053, pp. 747–755. Springer, Singapore (2020). https://doi.org/10.1007/978-981-15-0751-9_68
58. Gautam, J., Malsa, N., Gautam, S., Gaur, N.K., Adhikary, P., Pathak, S.: Selecting a family planning method for various age groups of different states in India. In: 2021 IEEE 4th International Conference on Computing, Power and Communication Technologies (GUCON), pp. 1–6 (2021). https://doi.org/10.1109/GUCON50781.2021.9573825

Application of a Novel Deep Learning Model to Recognize and Predict Kidney Disease in the Context of Image Processing

S. Sreeji[✉], B. Sathiyaprasad[✉], R. Asha, G. Kavitha, and K. Babu

Department of Computer Science and Engineering, Sathyabama Institute of Science and Technology, Jeppiaar Nagar, Rajiv Gandhi Salai, Chennai 600 119, India
sreeji.cse@gmail.com, sathiya.prasad@yahoo.com

Abstract. Chronic Kidney Disease (CKD) is a gradual decline of renal function that eventually results in kidney damage or failure. As the illness progresses, it becomes more challenging to diagnose. Evaluating various phases of CKD using routine doctor consultation data may help with early diagnosis and encourage beneficial intervention. Therefore, researchers offer a strategy for categorizing CKD that makes use of an optimization technique that is motivated by the learning procedure. Artificial intelligence is a concept that helps to make all such Things in this world seem impossible. As a risk-causing agent, some inventions are still surprised by their activity or ability. Even doctors are expecting some advancements to scan the patient's body and analyse the disease. In this scenario, advanced machine learning algorithms have been introduced that help to find the presence of kidney disease inside a human body. In this research, a novel deep learning model is designed to recognize and predict kidney disease. The model is designed as a hybrid of a Fuzzy Deep Neural Network (FDNN) and is compared with the traditional method. From the output, it shows that the proposed model has obtained an accuracy of 99.23%, which is better than the existing. Additionally, the accuracy of the presence of chronic disease in the human body can be confirmed without the doctor's acknowledgement as an extended work. While compared to existing information mining classifications, efficiency comparison shows how the proposed approach achieves improved accuracy of classification, precision, F-measure, and sensitivity metrics.

Keywords: Kidney disease · Image processing · Fuzzy logic · Deep neural network · Hybrid of fuzzy with deep neural network (FDNN)

1 Introduction

Computer vision techniques that are similar to video surveillance, segmentation of a particular image would come under the image saliency detection. Due to the issue of the low-resolution image, a method named Convolutional Neural Network (CNN) and the deep learning of CNN help to impress the quality of the image by its outlook and make it by clearing the identification [1]. In this paper [2], the author has explained the

R. N. Shaw et al. (Eds.): ICACIS 2022, CCIS 1749, pp. 459–474, 2023.
https://doi.org/10.1007/978-3-031-25088-0_41

issue-solving methods in three different aspects, which are faced, while using CNN. Facial expression recognition is a kind of progress, but it will not give the proper result through live detection. So when FER is connected with the CNN method, it gives a better and more understandable quality of content. Normally, the use of machine vision is to create a laser spot energy, which functions to work under a superposition area, where other than the testing programs, the models would involve a convolutional network with a Deep Learning concept (DL) [3]. If there could be any such possibility that helps in finding the presence of acute kidney disease in a human body, then it would be more helpful for doctors and patients to solve this query with the help of machine learning (ML) concepts. While checking the accuracy of the results, it shows non-renal SOFA prediction even if there is a presence of acute kidney disease (AKD) [4].

The term "health information categorization" refers to the fact of using a classifier model with data sets as well as enhancing the definition of healthcare. The organization of clinical records is being used to identify and predict objectives. This importance of health information has wide-ranging effects on how extraction outcomes are predicted [5]. These techniques aid medical professionals in reaching precise analytical conclusions during specific diagnoses. However, as tree topologies in classifications might well be easily coupled [6], the decision tree is still used in planning decisions with trees as a type of classification technique. To become more specific, information retrieval tools could be designed to find valid, beneficial, and logical frameworks, instances, themes, or decision-making elements hidden inside health information [7]. Either children or adults can suffer from chronic kidney disease (CKD), wherein the kidney's ability to operate consistently deteriorates [8].

CKD is widely researched as a result of something like a gathering of individuals who are known to be more at risk of developing renal problems, including those who have hypotension, obesity, or who have a biological parent who has been diagnosed with CKD [9]. Because the decline in renal function has to be noticeable over long periods, this varies from severe renal disease [10]. In light of the information gathered from previous patients, individuals with the same health illness can sometimes be combined, as well as excellent treatment options can indeed be provided. [11]. Regular occurrence identification techniques create single, essential features and functionality that describe the entirety of such a sample [12]. Constant kidney pollution is a major clinical emergency that is still being ignored today. A condition known as endless renal disease occurs when the kidneys become damaged and are unable to transport hazardous substances in the blood [13]. Some new works aim at identifying life-limiting illnesses including Renal Disease using sequence estimates including Naive Bayes & Artificial Neural Network (ANN) models such as C4.5 to forecast CKD occurrence times [14].

2   Literature Review

For both the concept of artificial intelligence and the machine learning concept, camera quality and the images that are captured by the camera should be understandable by the machines. In this paper [15], the authors have been introducing different technologies under remote airborne monitoring in which it starts with aerial imaging scenes. Finally, at the end of completion, the result has been recorded with 85% accuracy and 79%

recognition dark accuracy. Autism is one of the worst diseases, where the children get affected the most in that In this case, if the disease had been rectified earlier, then possibilities might have increased in level. Here, screening testing is flagged with the disease to identify its presence using the Deep Learning Model [16]. Using the Internet of Medical Things (IoMT), the captured images received from the cameras are auto-analyzed and identify the presence of disease in the human body, and this paper [17] explains the histopathological image recognized through its verified output by the value of 96.88%. While in the list of industrial revolutions, DL (Deep Learning) and ML (Machine Learning) acquire the fourth position, and, by its nature, DL is being formed under the neural network (artificial). The author describes how to extract features from medical data using a Bi-LSTM-based RNN architecture. The obtained data was then identified using a deep belief network with CNN (DBN-CNN) [18]. In this article [19], the author explains the comprehensive view of Deep Learning techniques by adding its taxonomy applications. Due to the large-scale consumption of data, data-parallel processing methods have been introduced in the processing system, and this rise has earned many benefits under the orchestration resources through allocating different computation sources. In this article [20], the author has introduced the Deep Learning interfacing model. Both the ML and DL concepts are working under the maintenance of their algorithm. This paper [21] makes us understand the actual method of using an algorithm under the machine learning concept, or in some cases, there would be a situation to detect the algorithm automatically if it's necessary. In recent times, web corruption has occurred here. The reason would be either the host or some hackers, Bi-LSTM (Bi-directory ling short term memory) is one of the web attack managers which is used to protect the web-based application based on the number of orders. The output checking is done with two different modes, by which the first mode has been passed under 93.1% and the second mode would reach 93.91% [22].

For example, when a person is affected by a kidney or any other disease, the possibilities for other disease-spreading increase. For example, when a man/woman gets affected by a kidney disease, there are many possibilities for it to get spread by cardiovascular or kidney failure, so there is an estimated time which should be found by such doctors or by the machines [23]. Even though our mobile phones are working under some machine learning algorithm, in some mobile phones the user would have the facility to unlock their phones using face identity. Face prediction is traditionally done through a separate mechanism under neural concepts, and in this paper [24], the author used electrocardiography to complete his testing process. At the same time, both the ML and DL concepts do not help only for healthcare management; they do help for classifying and analyzing some of the Indore identification that is similar to crime and robbery. Here the author has shown an accuracy rate of up to 75% by using the hotspot connection along with the city [25]. It is harder for a machine to differentiate the presentation of the image within the black and white surface but if there is some color differentiation between the images then it would be easier to make clear results as output, finally [26] there is a possibility to identify the presence of stones inside a human kidney by the machine analyzation.

It's expected that such alternative or comprehensive prescriptions emphasize therapies that claim to improve quality of life, prevent illness, and take care of diseases that

conventional medicine has already had limited treatment success with. The manufacturer had demonstrated a preference for using iridology to distinguish between different
forms of kidney from either the norm or the exception [27]. A total of 192 individuals
with chronic kidney illness as well as 169 people without renal disease were evaluated.
Utilizing wavelet transformation as well as the Flexible Neuro-Fuzzy Inference System,
a method of securing, processing, and characterization of iris images was designed to
reduce reliance on iridologists. The findings showed that for the two individuals having kidney problems as well as the normal ones, the findings individually showed a
right arrangement of 81 percent and 92 percent [28]. CNN was built up to recognize
10 major crop diseases using a database of 500 common photos with ill & healthy
grain stems and leaves collected in agricultural exploration fields. The suggested Convolution neural algorithm obtained an accuracy of 95.48 percent using the 10-cover
cross-endorsement architecture. Compared with a traditional classification model, this
reliability is massively greater [29].

3   Proposed System

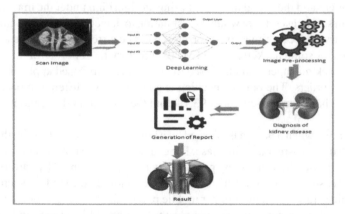

Fig. 1. Proposed model for kidney disease prediction

As recent research allows the direct observation or imaging of the entire vascular system,
so when it is an external body part then it would be an easier task only when the task is to
be done inside the internal parts of a human body does it take enough time to delay. While
checking over the large-scale retinal studies it has been stated that all such concepts could
relate to or combine Artificial Intelligence and Deep Learning methodology. Finally, the
actual thing to use Artificial Intelligence under the concepts of health caring the main
reason would be the data foundations. When there is high availability of medical type
data then it would be the main reason for making advancements. And the second optional
thing is due to the rise of complex algorithms which would be the backbone of AI and
ML. Images are the only hints for the machines and by understanding the errors and
comparison concepts the machines do function according to the questions that arise
from the user side. Using Fig. 1 let us imagine the method of the proposed system.

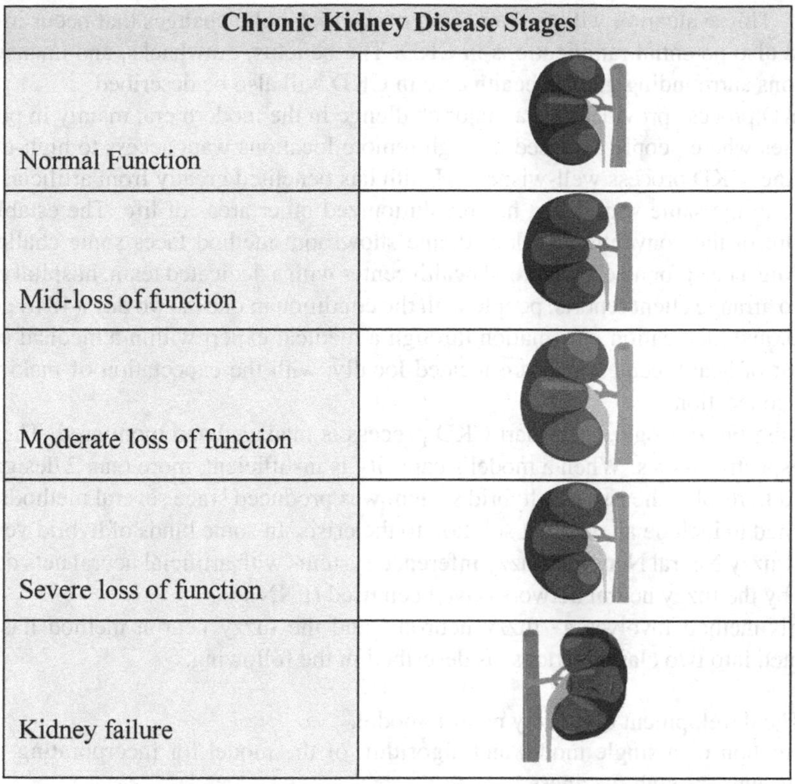

Chronic Kidney Disease Stages	
Normal Function	
Mid-loss of function	
Moderate loss of function	
Severe loss of function	
Kidney failure	

Fig. 2. Stages of renal kidney disease (https://www.miskawaanhealth.com/understanding-chr onic-kidney-disease/)

Figure 2 depicts the stages of chronic kidney disease in any human being. The stages start from Stage 1 to Stage 5, and it is common to both the right and left kidneys. In this research, the prediction and analysis of these five stages are considered; also, the numerical features are extracted from the kidney images to perform the prediction.

3.1 Proposed Work

Chronic kidney disease (CKD) frequently displays symptoms of illness and constipation, which are linked to a decline in life quality and also an increased risk of death. The inflammatory CKD process may have an influence on the development of illness, cachexia, and kidney osteodystrophy but rather increases stroke disease in people with CKD. Ghrelin seems to be a form of estrogen produced in the stomach. Ghrelin's biomedical effects have been mediated through the development of the hormone secretagogue receptor (GHSR). Ghrelin's potential benefits on food consumed but also meal appreciation suggest that it might be a successful therapy for anorexic CKD patients. Ghrelin was shown to have anti-inflammatory factors in comparison to its food cravings stimulating effects. This evaluation will go over some of the metabolic changes that occur in ghrelin and also potential ramifications in CKD. The benefits, drawbacks, and unanswered questions surrounding ghrelin health care in CKD will also be described.

CKD process providers are a major challenge in the modern era, mainly in popular countries where people accessed through remote locations want access to high-quality medicine, CKD process well-wishers. Health has benefited greatly from artificial intelligence in the same way that it has revolutionized other areas of life. The established structure of the conventional telemedicine showroom method faces some challenges, including a need for a neighborhood health center with a dedicated team, hospital equipment to arrange client reports, people with the condition in one or two days(48 h) getting treated, and medication information through a medical expert within a medical center, the cost of health centers that are located locally, with the expectation of making the Wi-Fi connection.

Using Fuzzy Logic, the Smart CKD process is managed and monitored. There are two respective issues: When a model's capacity is insufficient, more than 2 designs are merged to resolve the issue. A hybrid system was produced since several methods were combined to include an efficient solution to the crisis. In some kinds of hybrid versions of the Fuzzy Neural Network, fuzzy inference systems with artificial neural nets defined either by the fuzzy neural network have been used (FNN).

This method involves a "fuzzy neuron," and the fuzzy neuron method has been separated into two classifications, as described in the following.

(i)   The development of a fuzzy neuron model.
(ii) creation of a single model and algorithm of the model for incorporating neural systems through fuzziness.

The neural system discovers the $f[n, n+1]$ operation, which is a partition of the self-assurance earned through fuzzy inference. This should gain $f(n+1)$ utilizing the period denoted by k and the framework condition $k+1$. A stochastic modification module enhances the authorization with $f(k)$ the fluffy role and also the expected possibility regarding decisions, but also produces a finished product.

$$m'(k) = d(m(k), g[k, k+1]) \tag{1}$$

To evaluate the fuzzy guideline, the fuzzy rule unit $m'(k)$ is organized and evaluated with Eq. (1). The data device is a standard predecessor that gains a unit $d(m(k))$. The behavior control is communicated by unit $(g[k, k+1])$. The procedure is finished with a defused combination.

With input nodes, the signs and weight training are actual values. The data does not affect these signs. The yield is nearly identical to the data. The signal n_i may work with a truck full of materials s_i to build such items.

$$g = s_i n_i, i = 1, 2. \tag{2}$$

Here data input is taken as g which is gathered in the ability to implement such data is represented in Eq. (2).

$$FL = g_1 + g_2 = s_1 k_1 + s_2 k_2 \tag{3}$$

Cachexia disease is defined by muscle loss and anorexia, but also increased energy expense in affected patients and chronic disease (CKD). Cachexia is a significant predictor of mortality in CKD patients, which itself is 100- to 200-fold greater than in general populations. Cachexia is still one of the most inflammatory conditions, which differs from nutrition, which itself is said to be a shortage of nutrients.

To determine the FL's Fuzzy logic production (refer to Eq. (3)), the neuron employs its work transfer $f(y)$, which can be a sigmoid function result, $f(y) = (1 + e^{-y})^{-1}$, which is represented in Eq. (4).

$$y = f(FL) = f(s_1 k_1 + s_2 k_2) \tag{4}$$

An ordinary neural net is a basic network that employs Sigmoid function f, redundancy, and other inclusions.

For the decision support system used during AI-based electronic health records, a collection of fuzzy rules was defined. These laws are based on both factual and fuzzy data. The examples that follow relate to fuzzy rules.

- If the blood pressure is high, the temperature is high, and the pulse rate is low, judgment is high.
- If your blood pressure is high and your pulse rate is low, your judgment is likely to be impaired.
- If the temperature is normal, the pulse is rapid, and the blood pressure is moderate, then the judgment is low.
- If the temperature is low and the heart rate is high, then determine whether the blood pressure is low.
- If the temperature and pulse rate are both normal, then the judgment is high if the blood pressure is low.

Because once performing tasks, the mode command technology uses both the point of entry and the available spectrum for data transfer, but the web access transmits s_i^g is given in Eq. (5).

$$s_i^g = \alpha_i R log log \left(1 + \frac{|g_{i,n}|^2 Y_{i,n} g^{-n}}{\sigma^2} \right) \tag{5}$$

where i represents the percentage of access of internet bandwidth utilized by terminal update new tasks, $g_{i,n}$ represents the relation recession scaling factor among access point and terminal, and $Y_{i,n}$ represents terminal products and services, g^{-n} represents node facility distance, b represents news team loss, but also σ^2 represents interaction noise level.

Accordingly, the efficiency of g_i data link data transfer is elaborated as in Eq. (6).

$$d_i^k = \beta_i B log log \left(1 + \frac{|g_{n,i}|^2 X_n g^{-b}}{\sigma^2} \right) \tag{6}$$

In which β_i signifies the fraction of power transmission frequency bandwidth occupied by the terminal able to receive work-related jobs, $g_{n,i}$ signifies the link economic downturn relation between the entry point and terminal, and X_n signifies the foundation network's transmitting speed.

Muscle mass is going to waste through cachexia, but fats are also underutilized. Anorexia, described as a loss of appetite, is common in CKD patients. Disease in CKD patients can also be related to reducing the smell and taste of food, early satiation, neurohormonal filtration, acetylate cyclase instability, better cognitive tryptophan, but also increased inflammatory cytokines. Anorexia not only diminishes verbal energy but also protein intake, which makes a significant contribution to cachexia. Increased resting energy consumption was linked to increased mortality but also cardiovascular mortality in CKD patients, but it was also linked to the pervasiveness of cachexia in such patients. There seems to be no effective treatment for cachexia in CKD. Health and nutrition techniques like caloric diets supplemented with anabolic steroids have largely failed. As a result, there is a pressing need for the development of new drug agencies for such a possibly deadly CKD difficulty.

Job n (i) is however, evaluated here on gateways if it is not offloaded to edge networks. Equation (7) shows the time delay in completing various jobs geographically.

$$X_i^n = \frac{g_i}{g_i^k} \tag{7}$$

which g_i^k shows the capacity of the terminal g_i to process information and organize tasks regionally. As a consequence, the overall duration delay captured by g_i Research scholars on a local scale is illustrated in Eq. (8).

$$g_i^m = \sum_{m \in g}^{i} (1 - \alpha_i) g_i^m \tag{8}$$

In this case, if various activities such as a t-norm or the n_i–co-norm are used for connecting the reach information to such a neuron, the result is termed a hybrid artificial neuron and is shown in Eq. (9).

$$g_i^n = \frac{m_i}{g_i^n} \tag{9}$$

Discoveries about the pathophysiology of cachexia through CKD maintain innovative therapeutic approaches. Cachexia through CKD is caused by an increase in the frequency of inflammatory responses, which work on the CNS and create a flow between the release and function of a lot of key neuropeptides, influencing metabolic activity. Leptin but also center melanocortin structures have already been proposed as cytokine activity targets within the hypothalamus and is still one of the critical regulators of appetite and energy metabolism.

These changes result in fuzzy neural design that is reliant on fuzzy mathematics tasks. The bandwidth delay duration is relative to the amount of information obtained and the network throughput for data transfer, as explained by Eq. (10).

$$g_i^n = \frac{g_i}{b_i^k} \tag{10}$$

A set of fuzzy rules is described for the CKD process delivery system used in the AI-based CKD process. These rules have been supported by facts of fuzzy data, and the server's computing duration is comparable to the magnitude of stands and the server's computing capability, as given in Eq. (11).

$$b_i^f = \frac{f_i}{X_i} \tag{11}$$

The temperature controller is an integrated circuit that measures the temperature of the body in degrees Celsius. The voltage level for the temperature is shown. This sensor's make and model is LM35. This framework of the body temperature controller is thought to perform much better than a linear temperature controller. As a result, the duration spent on un-loading the assigned task s_i to the network edge is transmitted as in Eq. (12).

$$s_i^n = s_i^c + s_i^h + s_i^f \tag{12}$$

The following emergency requirements are monitored: respiratory arrest, heart condition, vagal convulsion, and pressure detector. As a result, the time frame related to the task of unloading s_i the edge device is conveyed as in Eq. (13).

$$X_i^n = \sum_{i=1}^{n} (\alpha_i d_i^n) \tag{13}$$

The pulse rate seems to be the primary indicator of critical medical behavior and health fitness. Within the patient outcomes and management field, the (PRS) is the most commonly managed and investigated sensor.

$$m_i^n = \sum_{i=1}^{n} \left(g_i^n + d_i^n \right) \tag{14}$$

As in the hypothalamus, two different identity documents of neurons regulate food intake. Each neuronal subset produces neurotrophic factor Y (NPY), which enhances food intake, whereas another neuronal subset continues to produce melanocortin substances, which restrict food intake.

Equation (14) is used to evaluate pulse rate and complicated diseases such as heart attack. When an object $f1$ places its finger on the data panel, the sensor activates. The result is identified on the input panel. The sensor provides a 5-V direct power source as in Eq. (15).

$$s.t.f1 : \sum_{h_i \in d}^{i} m_i \le m_y \tag{15}$$

The intelligent smart CKD process of client management and monitoring framework is required. The framework suggested $f2$ in Eq. (16) is a framework profited from a fuzzy logic system that has been simple while using it and enforced for creating decisions.

$$f2 : \sum_{g_i \in d}^{i} \alpha_i \le 1 \tag{16}$$

Circulating leptin and insulin suppress appetite besides inhibiting NPY but instead agouti-related peptide (AgRP) manufacturing within the hypothalamus even as increasing the production of monoaminergic protein. Inflammatory mediators cause anorexia by their central behavior. Cytokines restrict gastro-intestinal activity, because metabolic alterations affect the hormonal system, but also modulate the hypothalamic neuropeptide identity, both of which can affect eating patterns.

The $f3$ in Eq. (17) suggests a novel method for organization, as it makes use of both detectable information and a fuzzy decision-making process.

$$f3 : \sum_{g_i \in d}^{i} \beta_i \leq 1 \qquad (17)$$

Desirability is explained in terms of lag time, seeing as f4 in Eq. (18) aims to reduce the lag time of such a power sector, where less time delay was correlated with greater athleticism.

$$f4 : m_i^n \geq 0, \forall i \in d \qquad (18)$$

The d_i strength and endurance values are calculated as in Eq. (19).

$$d_i = \frac{1}{g_i} \qquad (19)$$

Effective and accommodative treatment options for CKD patients are desperately needed. Ghrelin is much more effective than just about every other orexigenic hormone because it increases food intake in small mammals and also in humans. Recent findings support the possible treatment use of ghrelin and also its analogs like a food craving stimulant and an anabolic approach in uremia-associated cachexia, some different kinds of disease-associated cachexia. Ghrelin restricts energy metabolism and may be overcome but may enhance cachectic state via IGF-dependent but also Insulin-like growth factor processes.

4 Experimental Result

Chronic kidney disease (CKD) frequently causes illness and constipation, both of which are associated with a reduced range of life and an increased risk of death. The inflammatory CKD process may influence the development of illness, cachexia, and kidney osteodystrophy, but it is the increased stroke disease in people with CKD that is of concern. Ghrelin appears to be an estrogen synthesized in the stomach. The growth hormone secretagogue receptor GHSR mediates ghrelin's biomedical effects. Ghrelin's potential benefits of food consumption and meal enjoyment ensure that it could be a successful therapy for anorexic CKD patients. Ghrelin showed us by having anti-inflammatory properties in addition to its ability to stimulate food cravings (refer to Fig. 3). The Recognize and Predict Kidney Disease Context of Image Processing in an afferent efferent vessel for the mean and standard deviation, PSNR, and analysis for accuracy in glomerular filtration rate of CKD identified the convoluted tubule bowman capsule using the HFNN algorithm (refer to Table 1).

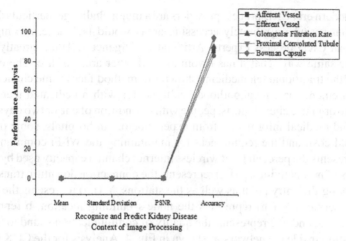

Fig. 3. Performance analysis for the recognition and prediction of kidney disease in the context of image processing

Table 1. Renal function tests analysis for kidney disease identify using hybrid fuzzy neural network algorithm

Parameters	Afferent vessel	Efferent vessel	Glomerular filtration rate	Proximal convoluted tubule	Bowman capsule
Mean	0.5643	0.4534	0.7654	0.7864	0.8658
Standard Deviation	0.2445	0.7563	0.6453	0.8796	0.6756
PSNR	0.6756	0.5564	0.7564	0.9675	0.7564
Accuracy	87.45	84.24	90.46	95.55	96.67

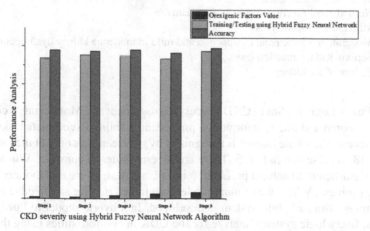

Fig. 4. Analysis of CKD severity using a Hybrid Fuzzy Neural Network Algorithm

In the modern era, CKD process providers are a major challenge, particularly in most-popular countries where remotely accessing areas would lack access to high-quality medicine than CKD process experts. Artificial intelligence (AI) has greatly benefited health in the same way. That it has revolutionized other areas of life. The established structure of the traditional telemedicine showroom method faces some challenges, such as the requirement for a neighborhood health center with a dedicated team, hospital equipment to organise client reports, people with a condition of one or two days in getting treatment and medical information from expert doctors in hospitals, some of the local clinics would cost, and the requirement for maintaining the Wi-Fi communication. in which I represents the percentage of wireless internet channel capacity used by the port to inform users of new activities, g (i,n) represents the connection downturn transformation function among the entry point as well as the stations, Y (i,n) represents the terminal's products or services, g (-n) represents the node's building location, b represents the news team's loss, and σ^2 represents the quality of communication sound to be used for a representation inside the network as shown in Fig. 4. Analysis for the CDK severity in 5 stage (refer Table 2) of training and testing for the CKD severity using Hybrid Fuzzy Neural Network Algorithm to analysis the overall accuracy.

Table 2. Performance result analysis for the CKD severity using hybrid fuzzy neural network algorithm

CKD severity parameter	Value	Training/Testing using Hybrid Fuzzy Neural Networks (%)	Overall accuracy (%)
Stage 1	7 (8.4)	92.12	97.34
Stage 2	7 (8.4)	94.34	96.45
Stage 3	26 (31.3)	93.56	97.35
Stage 4	34 (41)	91,45	95.46
Stage 5	9 (10.8)	96.45	98.67

Stage 1: Normal renal function despite kidney damage
Stage 2: Mild kidney function loss
Stage 3: Moderate to severe renal dysfunction and mild to moderate kidney dysfunction
Stage 4: Serious Kidney function loss
Stage 5: Failure of the kidney.

The Fuzzy Logic for Smart CKD Process Management and Monitoring is character-ized by the command line g_i information processing's ability to complete tasks locally. As an outcome, the whole latency is recognized by g_i researchers only at the local scale, as in Eq. (8) represented in Fig. 5. There are several issues to consider: When a single model is insufficient to solve a problem, more than 2 designs are collaborated to over-come the problem. When two or more models are joined to offer an effective answer to a challenging issue, a hybrid system is developed. In a hybrid model to Fuzzy Neural networks, fuzzy logic systems analyze for the CDK in co-morbidities using the HFNN algorithm to evaluate the hypertension values based on the training and testing (refer to Table 3) in diabetes cerebrovascular disease to evaluate the accuracy.

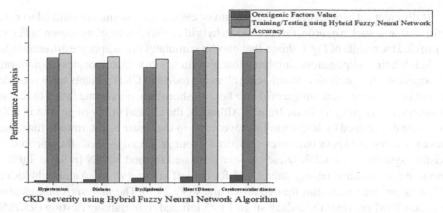

Fig. 5. Analysis for CDK in co-morbidities using hybrid fuzzy neural network algorithm

Table 3. Performance analysis for CDK in co-morbidities using hybrid fuzzy neural network algorithm

Co-morbidities	Value	Training /Testing using Hybrid Fuzzy Neural Networks (%)	Accuracy (%)
Hypertension	78 (94)	89.34	92.34
Diabetes	59 (71.1)	85.53	90.21
Dyslipidemia	73 (88)	82.23	88.34
Ischemic heart disease	24 (28.9)	94.56	96.42
Cerebrovascular disease	5 (6)	93.13	95.34

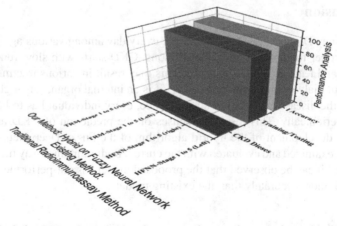

Fig. 6. Analysis for CKD using hybrid on fuzzy neural network comparison with existing method

If different activities, such as with t-norm or even a n_i–conorm, are utilized to reach information to such a neuron, this is called a hybrid artificial neuron, as shown in Eq. (9) to provide the results of Fig. 6 shows that ghrelin stimulates pre-adipocyte differentiation while inhibiting adipogenesis, implying that ghrelin works with adipocytes to encourage adipogenesis. In conclusion, small-scale clinical studies in CKD patients have provided important evidence to encourage evidence here on short-term orexigenic future outcomes of subcutaneous ghrelin administration. Although, the clinical utility of ghrelin in CKD would be determined by long-term improvements in the desire to eat, muscle mass, and function, along with poor outcomes compared to our proposed method. It compared the existing system for the CDK Dieses for our proposed method HFNN (refer to Table 4) providing the training/ testing stage 1 to 5 for the left kidney (98.34%) and right kidney (97.46%) and then evaluating the overall accuracy (99.23%). The analysis for the existing methods TRM provides the kidney stage 1 to 5 left and right training /testing (95.76%) and then evaluate for the overall accuracy (97.46%) it compares to the existing method is best performance result provide for our HFNN methods

Table 4. Comparison result analysis

Algorithm	Kidney stages	CKD	Training/Testing	Accuracy
Hybrid on Fuzzy Deep Neural Network	Stage 1 to 5 (Left)	98.34	97.46	99.23
	Stage 1 to 5 (right)	98.78	97.86	99.34
Existing method: Traditional Radioimmunoassay Method	Stage 1 to 5 (Left)	91.34	95.65	97.46
	Stage 1 to 5 (right)	91.84	95.76	97.56

5 Conclusion

Chronic Kidney Disease (CKD) is increasing every day among various age groups due to lack of proper food, sleep, and other reasons. CKD starts with slow functioning of the kidneys and leads to failed functions. This may result in various treatments for the patients, from dialysis to transplantation. As it is an internal organ, it is highly difficult to diagnose the disease at an earlier stage. Hence, every individual has to have general check-ups periodically. This research focuses on the prediction of CKD at an earlier stage by the development of the hybrid algorithm of the Fuzzy Deep Neural Network model and is examined and evaluated with the current Radioimmunoassay method. From the outcomes, it can be observed that the proposed model has out-performed in disease identification more accurately than the existing model.

References

1. Wang, X., Li, S.: Image saliency prediction by learning deep probability model. Signal Processing: Image Communication, pp. 471–476 (2019). https://doi.org/10.1016/j.image.2019.08.002

2. Rajan, S., Chenniappan, P., Devaraj, S., Madian, N.: Novel deep learning model for facial expression recognition based on maximum boosted CNN and LSTM. IET Image Processing **7**, 1373–1381 (2020). https://doi.org/10.1049/iet-ipr.2019.1188

3. Jwaid, W.M.: Image processing technology and deep learning application: in relation to the context of laser positioning. Journal of Physics: Conference Series **3**, 032130 (2021). https://doi.org/10.1088/1742-6596/1879/3/032130

4. He, J., Lin, J., Duan, M.: Application of machine learning to predict acute kidney disease in patients with sepsis associated acute kidney injury. Frontiers in Medicine (2021). https://doi.org/10.3389/fmed.2021.792974

5. Statement of retraction: based on deep learning in traffic remote sensing image processing to recognize target vehicle. International Journal of Computers and Applications, pp. 1–1, 2021. https://doi.org/10.1080/1206212x.2021.1994767

6. Goshua, A.: Deep-learning model may accurately predict autism diagnosis. Spectrum (2021). https://doi.org/10.53053/nalu6283

7. Datta Gupta, K., Sharma, D.K., Ahmed, S., Gupta, H., Gupta, D., Hsu, C.-H.: A novel lightweight deep learning-based histopathological image classification model for IoMT. Neural Processing Letters (2021). https://doi.org/10.1007/s11063-021-10555-1

8. Lawal, O.M., Zhao, H.: YOLO Fig detection model development using deep learning. IET Image Processing **13**, 3071–3079 (2021). https://doi.org/10.1049/ipr2.12293

9. Kim, Y.-K., Kim, Y.: DiPLIP: distributed parallel processing platform for stream image processing based on deep learning model inference. Electronics **10**, 1664 (2020). https://doi.org/10.3390/electronics9101664

10. Xu, N.: The application of deep learning in image processing is studied based on the reel neural network model. Journal of Physics: Conference Series **3**, 032096 (2021). https://doi.org/10.1088/1742-6596/1881/3/032096

11. Karacan, H., Sevri, M.: A novel data augmentation technique and deep learning model for web application security. IEEE Access 150781–150797 (2021). https://doi.org/10.1109/access.2021.3125785

12. Jahan, S., Hegerty, K., Kark, A., Hale, J., Mallett, A.: SAT-193 clinical audit of the validation of a model to predict progression of chronic kidney disease to end stage kidney disease. Kidney International Reports **7**, S88–S89 (2019). https://doi.org/10.1016/j.ekir.2019.05.227

13. Schwartz, E., O'Nell, K., Alreja, A., Ghuman, A., Anzellotti, S.: Deep networks trained to recognize facial expressions predict ventral face-selective ECoG responses and networks trained to recognize identity. Journal of Vision **9**, 2221 (2021). https://doi.org/10.1167/jov.21.9.2221

14. Sinha, T., Chowdhury, T., Shaw, R.N., Ghosh, A.: Analysis and prediction of COVID-19 confirmed cases using deep learning models: a comparative study. In: Bianchini, M., Piuri, V., Das, S., Shaw, R.N. (eds.) Advanced Computing and Intelligent Technologies. LNNS, vol. 218, pp. 207–218. Springer, Singapore (2022). https://doi.org/10.1007/978-981-16-2164-2_18

15. Sugiyarti, E., Jasmi, K.A., Basiron, B., Huda, M., Shankar, K., Maseleno, A.: Decision support system of scholarship grantee selection using data mining. International Journal of Pure and Applied Mathematics **119**(15), 22392249 (2018)

16. Kusiak, A., Dixon, B., Shah, S.: Predicting survival time for kidney dialysis patients: a data mining approach. Comput. Biol. Med. **35**(4), 311–327 (2005)

17. Gorzaáczany, M.B., RudziĚski, F.: Interpretable and accurate medical data classification–a multi-objective genetic-fuzzy optimization approach. Expert Syst. Appl. **71**, 26–39 (2017)

18. Satheeshkumar, B., Sathiyaprasad, B.: Medical data analysis using feature extraction and classification based on machine learning and metaheuristic optimization algorithm. Applications of Computational Science in Artificial Intelligence **25**, (2022)

19. Kunwar, V., Chandel, K., Sabitha, A.S., Bansal, A.: Chronic kidney disease analysis using data mining classification techniques.. In: Cloud System and Big Data Engineering (Confluence), 6th International Conference, pp. 300–305 (2016)
20. Mridha, K., et al.: Deep learning algorithms are used to automatically detection invasive ducal carcinoma in whole slide images. In: 2021 IEEE 6th International Conference on Computing, Communication and Automation (ICCCA), pp. 123–129 (2021). https://doi.org/10.1109/ICC CA52192.2021.9666302
21. Lu, Y., Yi, S., Zeng, N., Liu, Y., Zhang, Y.: Identification of rice diseases using deep convolutional neural networks. Neurocomputing **267**, 378–384 (2017)
22. Keçeli, A.S., Kaya, A., Keçeli, S.U.: Classification of radiolarian images with hand-crafted and deep features. Comput. Geosci. **109**, 67–74 (2017)
23. Zawbaa, H.M., Emary, E., Parv, B.: Feature selection based on antlion optimization algorithm. In: Complex Systems (WCCS), Third World Conference, pp. 1–7 (2015)
24. Janardhanan, P., Sabika, F.: Effectiveness of Support Vector Machines in Medical Data mining, pp. 25–30 (2015)
25. Rubini, L.J., Eswaran, P.: Generating comparative analysis of early stage prediction of Chronic Kidney Disease. J. Modern Eng. Res. **5**(7), 49–55 (2015)
26. Shankar, K.: Prediction of most risk factors in hepatitis disease using apriori algorithm. Research J. Pharmaceutical Biological And Chemical Sciences **8**, 477–484 (2017)
27. Palimkar, P., Shaw, R.N., Ghosh, A.: Machine learning technique to prognosis diabetes disease: random forest classifier approach. In: Bianchini, M., Piuri, V., Das, S., Shaw, R.N. (eds.) Advanced Computing and Intelligent Technologies. LNNS, vol. 218, pp. 219–244. Springer, Singapore (2022). https://doi.org/10.1007/978-981-16-2164-2_19
28. Shankar, K., et al.: Optimal feature level fusion based ANFIS classifier for brain MRI image classification. Concurrency and Computation: Practice and Experience (2018). https://doi.org/10.1002/cpe.4887
29. AlMuhaideb, S., Menai, M.E.B.: An individualized preprocessing for medical data classification. Procedia Computer Science **82**, 35–42 (2016)

Classification of Adulterated Food Grain Thermal Images Using Convolutional Neural Networks

Vijayakumar Ponnusamy[1], Prateek Anand[2(✉)], and Vishvak Bhatt[3]

[1] Electronics and Communication Engineering, SRM Institute of Science and Technology, Kattankulathur, Kanchipuram, Tamil Nadu, India
vijayakp@srmist.edu.in
[2] Data Science and Business Systems, SRM Institute of Science and Technology, Kanchipuram, Tamil Nadu, India
mathurprateek2001@gmail.com
[3] Networking and Communications, SRM Institute of Science and Technology, Kanchipuram, Tamil Nadu, India

Abstract. Adulteration is a major cause of concern for the food industry pertaining to health of consumers as well as economical value in the market. Rice and paddy being one of the staple diets in India, are of utmost importance when it comes to the detection and treatment of impurities and hence, in this study, various works in the same domain are examined and their limitations are brought to a close with the introduction of a novel methodology. The objective of this proposed approach is to tackle the existing problem of food grain adulteration by applying deep learning based thermal image processing techniques on thermal image samples of various types of rice and paddy grains. The methodology put forth yields an accuracy of 95% in successfully differentiating between pure and impure grains images and hence accomplish the task of adulteration detection.

1 Introduction

Rice and paddy are one of the staple foods and are consumed by more than 3.5 billion people around the globe. With such a high demand in the market, they also turn out to be of great of economic influence because of which fraudulent activities are being devised everyday in the food grain industry, risking the health of consumers. The Food Safety and Standards Authority of India (FSSAI) in its annual public laboratory testing report for 2014–15 mentions that out of the 49,290 samples, nearly one-fifth were found adulterated. Although adulteration is an illegal and unethical practice, the malefactors are continuing it at a large

V. Ponnusamy—Supervised the project and aided in data collection.
P. Anand—Worked on thermal image processing and deep learning based model development.
V. Bhatt—Worked on data manipulation, model creation and testing.

scale, earning huge profits ad even the consumers are overlooking the gravity of this issue because of low pricing of adulterated food grains [1].

We, in this study, aim to present a novel approach of detection of impure food grains by applying CNN based deep learning techniques on individual thermal images of rice and paddy grains. We created the dataset using FLIR T800 by taking thermal images of various types of rice and paddy found in Southern India from three specific distances - 15 cm, 25 cm and 30 cm. After collecting the data, we classified the images as pure and impure; grains of single type and grains mixed with other grains considered as impurities and the second class hence created as impure.

After successfully collecting and bifurcating the dataset, we work on our proposed classification methodology involving a CNN model trained on our dataset, resulting in a classification of thermal images of the considered food grains i.e. pure and impure.

2   Literature Survey

Traditional technologies, when it comes to food grain quality assessment, fail to deliver on an industrial scale. For instance, an inference based quality check process is performed using soaked lime and distinguishes the grains based on their physical properties like color and density during the process [7].

With the further advancement of technology, traditional computer vision techniques involving image processing are being used to check adulteration in commercial rice grains on the basis of factors like aspect size ratio, perimeter and shape [2]. In this process, a suitable region of interest is extracted from the image and the grains are masked out from the background. Such a traditional approach can be used for testing grains in bulk but they lack in terms of accuracy and hence industrial reliability. In a different scenario, different machine learning algorithms were tested and Support Vector Machine(SVM) algorithm was used to distinguish milk from water without any additional reagent. It yielded an accuracy of 89.48% [3].

Later, with the advent of deep learning dealing with thermal images, research has been done for detecting impurities present in food grain samples and using cognitive intelligence provide accurate adulteration testing approaches to the food grain industry [9,13]. Five samples of Asian Rice going by their scientific name Oryza sativa L, were taken as both grains and flour to check for adulteration. Over 63000 images of pure rice and their mixtures were taken for the detection. This system was based on Convolutional Neural Network and gave an accuracy more than 98% [5].

Thermal Imaging to detect adulteration isn't specific to a particular section of food and can also be used for detections in food items like coffee [8] and mutton. The working is based on CNN and this concept used is more accurate but is only concise to checking the adulteration of minced mutton. It involved using 175 samples of minced mutton adulterated in different percentages i.e. 10%, 20%, 30%, 40%, and 50%. Thermal videos were recorded with continuous heating and using the Softmax classifier, a model was created which gave results accurate upto 99.99% for the test samples [12]. A related approach has been taken for adulteration detection in ginger powder, sampled in 7 different categories, which resulted in an accuracy of 99.7% [6]. Another similar work has been done on thermographic images to distinguish between pure and adulterated extra virgin olive oil (EVOO) comprising of less than 8% of different adulterants by weight. CNN models were applied for the use case which yielded accuracy between 97% and 100% [11].

Our presented approach is guided by such worthy literature and we aim at overcoming the limitations of traditional methods, both computational and non-computational as well as improve the accuracy earlier attained by the deep learning based approaches in the domain of thermal image processing.

3 Implementation

3.1 Dataset Creation

In the first and the foremost step, we have taken pictures of different types of rice and paddy grains namely Pulungal Ponni, Karnataka Ponni, Pulumgal, Sonamasori and their mixtures. After collecting the images, we classified them into two different categories - pure and impure based on a simple condition of the grain being lone or mixed with other grains [10] (Fig. 1).

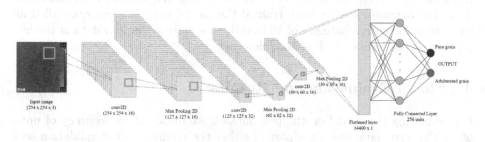

Fig. 1. Flow diagram of CNN

3.2 Dataset Augmentation

An important aspect of our approach is that it does not require a lot of data to move forward. We work with the limited data provided, 36 pure and 12 impure images and augment the images using horizontal flipping, rotation and lateral shifting. This helps us create 10 extra images for every single image, hence giving us a dataset with 396 pure and 528 impure images, which is sufficient enough to train our CNN model.

3.3 Data Preprocessing

In this step, we scale our image in a way that each of its pixel value ranging between 0 and 255, now lie within the range of 0 and 1 as it is computationally easier and effective. We also split our data into three parts - training data (70%), validation data (20%) and test data (10%).

3.4 Model Creation

This is the step in which we create a sequential model [4] using TensorFlow framework consisting of three 2D convolution layers, with ReLU as the activation function, each accompanied by three corresponding max pooling operations. After these operations, we flatten the results and feed them into a dense network performing ReLU activation followed by sigmoid activation.

3.5 Model Compilation

In this step we compile the created model using Adam optimizer and binary cross entropy function for loss computation since we are dealing with binary classification of grain images.

3.6 Model Training

In this step, we train the model on the training data and validate it on validation data. For our use case, we have trained the model using a technique called as early stopping with a patience of 10 iterations, ensuring that our dataset neither overfits not underfits which is possible otherwise.

4 Model Evaluation and Results

On evaluating the model on the test dataset, we obtained an accuracy of upto 95%. This test data was not a part of either the training or the validation sets and comprises of 10% of the total data in consideration. The results obtained on various classification metrics are mentioned in the following table (Table 1):

Table 1. Evaluation metrics

Metrics	Value (in nearest %)
Binary accuracy	95.83
Precision	89.29
Recall	96.15

5 Future Work and Discussion

We have worked on all the popular deep learning components including CNN model, Adam optimizer, Binary Cross Entropy loss function and early stopping and have obtained sufficiently good results for the binary image classification problem in hand. Further work can be done on improving the accuracy of the model, calculating adulteration percentages as well as determining the adulterant, involving much complex approaches.

References

1. FSSAI annual report (2015). https://fssai.gov.in/cms/annual-reports.php
2. Aggarwal, A.K., Mohan, R.: Aspect ratio analysis using image processing for rice grain quality (2010). https://doi.org/10.2202/1556-3758.1788
3. Asefa, B.G., Hagos, L., Kore, T., et al.: Computer vision based detection and quantification of extraneous water in raw milk. https://doi.org/10.21203/rs.3.rs-625039/v1, 06 2021
4. Ekambaram, D., Kumar, V.: Identification of defects in casting products by using a convolutional neural network, June 2022. https://www.researchgate.net/publication/361985340_Identification_of_Defects_in_Casting_Products_by_using_a_Convolutional_Neural_Network
5. Estrada-Pérez, L.V., Pradana-López, S., Pérez-Calabuig, A.M., Mena, M.L., Cancilla, J.C., Torrecilla, J.S.: Thermal imaging of rice grains and flours to design convolutional systems to ensure quality and safety (2021). https://www.sciencedirect.com/science/article/pii/S0956713520304886
6. Jahanbakhshi, A., Abbaspour-Gilandeh, Y., Heidarbeigi, K., Momeny, M.: Detection of fraud in ginger powder using an automatic sorting system based on image processing technique and deep learning (2021). https://www.sciencedirect.com/science/article/pii/S0010482521005588
7. Kumar, R.: Methods for detection of common adulterants in food (2016). https://vikaspedia.in/health/health-campaigns/beware-of-adulteration/methods-for-detection-of-common-adulterants-in-food
8. Chakravartula, S.S.N., Moscetti, R., Bedini, G., Nardella, M., Massantini, R.: Use of convolutional neural network (CNN) combined with FT-NIR spectroscopy to predict food adulteration: a case study on coffee (2022). https://www.sciencedirect.com/science/article/pii/S0956713522000093
9. Rafiq, A., Makroo, H., Sachdev, P., Sharma, S.: Application of computer vision system in food processing- a review, November 2013. https://www.researchgate.net/publication/283503760_Application_of_Computer_Vision_System_in_Food_Processing-_A_Review
10. Sowmya, N., Ponnusamy, V.: Development of spectroscopic sensor system for an IoT application of adulteration identification on milk using machine learning. https://ieeexplore.ieee.org/document/9393967, 2021
11. Torrecilla, J.S., Cancilla, J.C., Pradana-Lopez, S., Perez-Calabuig, A.M.: Detection of adulterations of extra-virgin olive oil by means of infrared thermography, January 202. https://www.researchgate.net/publication/348904072_Detection_of_adulterations_of_extra-virgin_olive_oil_by_means_of_infrared_thermography1

12. Zheng, M., Zhang, Y., Gu, J., Bai, Z., Zhu, R.: Classification and quantification of minced mutton adulteration with pork using thermal imaging and convolutional neural network (2021). https://www.sciencedirect.com/science/article/pii/S0956713521001821
13. Zhu, L., Spachos, P., Pensini, E., Plataniotis, K.N.: Deep learning and machine vision for food processing: a survey (2021). https://www.sciencedirect.com/science/article/pii/S2665927121000228

Distributed Hotel Chain Using Blockchain and Chainlink

Saurabh Yadav[1], Suryansh Rastogi[1], Shubham Soni[1], Prince Kshitij[1],
Nitima Malsa[1]([✉]), Vimal Gupta[1], Ankush Ghosh[2], and Rabindra Nath Shaw[2]

[1] JSS Academy of Technical Education, Noida, India
nitima.malsa@gmail.com
[2] University Center for Research and Development, Chandigarh University, Punjab, India

Abstract. Hospitality industry is very important in our society. This industry can be secured with blockchain technology. The main goal of this chapter is to examine the current blockchain-based hotel chain systems as well as any potential obstacles, with the aim of betterment of hotel chain systems for the future. It also presents a smart contract for the hotel chain distributed application. The research chapter will concentrate on the significance of hotel booking platforms (and hospitality), as these are the two main strategies used by the hotel sector to demonstrate their consideration for and goodwill toward the guest. An explanation of the fundamental components and functions of the blockchain with respect to the hotel reservation system follows. According to this study, hotel management systems enabled by blockchain and chain links might offer different options than conventional hotel reservation systems. The five following categories were used to group the major problems: general, integrity, price-parity agreements, privacy, and a lack of payment options. This study revealed that some issues that are prevalent in the present hotel management systems can be resolved by blockchain technologies. On the other side, the issues with blockchain applications that are commonly highlighted are privacy protection and transaction speed.

Keywords: Blockchain · Hotel · Chain link · Smart contracts · Oracle DeFi

1 Introduction

One of the major issue in the field of travel and hospitality that has not been resolved is the issue faced by small hotel owners from the central authority controlling the industry, which leads to a lack of trust, money fraud, settlement issues, and non-transparency of actions. Additionally, the issues faced by customers are on quick hotel booking, rewards, and quick identification. The application of blockchain technology in the hospitality industry is still in its infancy, and much remains to be learned. Chain-link, which uses oracles and Node operators to integrate off-chain data from the outside world into the blockchain, will also be used by this application.

Despite its relatively young, blockchain technology is one of the most exciting developments in modern digital technology, and it has the ability to profoundly change how transactions are carried out and information is both stored and accessible. The issues that hotel owners and their clients encounter will all be resolved by this application in a distributed, transparent, and immutable manner. The centralized and inaccessible inventory is one of the hospitality industry's biggest concerns. For businesses preserving data is very crucial. Data storage can be expensive as well as inaccessible. Hence, it can be main hurdle in hotel industries. Hence, data can be store securely and safely by using Blockchain technology. Transactions will take less time (peer to peer directly) and they will be less expensive while using blockchain technology, this could attract customers and increase revenue for the hotels.

Blockchain technology is the best option for creating ecosystems without trust. However, the success of the whole implementation cannot be attributed to the blockchain alone. Other protocols help it become the reliable and resilient technology that it is. Due to the decentralization of processing in dense P2P networks and the upkeep of a safe and publicly distributed ledger that provides total transparency over the entire blockchain, blockchain can be applied in trustless networks. Every node has access to the most recent state of the blockchain thanks to the P2P protocol.

A current solution to increase the propulsion of systems employed in several domains is blockchain. Blockchain technology was first and mostly used for keeping track of cryptocurrency transactions. In contrast, new uses and applications have evolved in recent years. Recently, the blockchain-based hotel management system has grown in importance as a potential solution to some issues that might be related to hotel systems. Due to the immutable property of the blockchain, which has made it a decentralised distributed voting system, blockchain-enabled reservation systems have been proposed as the next generation of contemporary electronic reservation systems.

Determining the difficulties that need to be addressed in the creation of a blockchain-based hotel management system is essential in this regard. In order to evaluate the literature and make sense of these issues, we adopted a methodical mapping methodology. The chapter contributes the following: identifying a number of current holes in the hotel management system; exploring the potential of the blockchain idea to enhance reservation systems through an organisation of the key current problems. This study revealed that while privacy protection and transaction speed are usually highlighted issues, blockchain-based hotel reservation systems can prevent data manipulation and integrity issues. The remainder of the essay is structured as follows. We begin by providing an overview of the blockchain idea and the range of available blockchain applications. Then, based on the research, we give the research methodology and a literature evaluation on the blockchain.

1.1 Information on the Blockchain Concept

Satoshi Nakamoto is thought to have created the first blockchain-based system in 2008. It is also obvious that Bitcoin was the first major application of blockchain technology. The idea of a blockchain can be compared to a distributed, open, and secure data book. As a result, the idea can be used not only in the financial and cryptocurrency industries but also in a wide range of other fields where transactions are involved. Although blockchain is well recognized in the cryptocurrency industry, one could legitimately argue that its potential goes much beyond virtual currency. Government agencies as well as private businesses have started experimenting with blockchain. A chain of time blocks connected cryptographically is called a "blockchain." New blocks are added to the existing chain, and the prior block's hash is added to the new block. This chain is immutable and cannot be altered. This blockchain consists As a result, the blockchain enables the development of trust without the requirement for centralized power. Asymmetric encryption, which is slower than symmetric cryptography, is used by blockchain systems.

The peer-to-peer distributed ledger requires a consensus mechanism to be started among the nodes in order to add a block of transactions to it. In addition to ensuring that every node in the network has a duplicate copy of the ledger, the consensus mechanism on the blockchain ensures that all transactions are legitimate and authentic. Numerous distinct consensus algorithms exist. Blockchain infrastructures have typically chosen Proof-of-Work (PoW) and Proof-of-Stake (PoS) models as their preferred consensus techniques [9]. POW is a technique that enables the transactions to be independently and trustworthily validated. The charge is optional and can be exchanged between the participants in the transaction so that it can be forwarded to the users so they can successfully validate it. It might be required in another application scenario, as in the case of Bitcoin. After a block of transactions has been successfully confirmed, the network will provide verifiers with a specified number of coins in addition to a transaction fee. When a user initiates this process, it is known as "mining," which is essentially a transaction that solves a problem. The outcomes of this procedure are simple to confirm but extremely challenging to duplicate. However, POW has a time- and money-consuming process as a drawback. Consuming too much energy is another drawback.

1.2 Blockchain Current Applications

Blockchain applications have started to be incorporated into several sectors' of businesses. Companies attempt to increase the transparency of their management and business operations in this way. Blockchain is thought to deal with a number of security challenges, including fraud and identity management ones. Financial organizations can look into their clients and deal with fraud thanks to blockchain-based solutions. Although the majority of banking and payment systems are suitable for blockchain use cases, there are other industries for which distributed ledger technology can be put to use.

Sustainable logistics management operations and B2B trade are two others very suitable blockchain use cases. By encouraging consumer-producer cooperation, assisting individuals and communities in embracing a more sustainable lifestyle, and assisting businesses in streamlining their resource and reuse procedures, blockchain is playing a rising role in sustainability. Supply chain management can be significantly impacted by blockchain by assuring security, transparency, and traceability while minimizing difficulties. Every transaction in supply chain management is completed on a standard blockchain without the need for a trusted Centre's permission. Following the conclusion of the delivery phase, payments are made automatically. Blockchain can significantly help to increase the entire traceability and security of the items because the transactions are watched by the parties. Thus, even before buying the goods, the client can get precise information on changes in the processes. Improved process visibility, integrity, quicker transactions, and disintermediation are the key advantages.

Blockchain can be applied to other kinds of smart services and internet applications, in addition to possible advantages in the financial industries and supply chain management. The energy industry has also adopted blockchain technology and is currently doing so. It is suggested to plan schemes for efficient electric car charging and local energy trade. In accordance with predefined Internet of Things (IoT) devices, machines can sell and buy energy. Real-time data can be gathered by IoT devices and stored in a blockchain chain. Real-time big data analysis is starting to use it.

Another industry that employs blockchain is insurance. Currently, insurance is based on a trust-based relationship, but in the future, blockchain may be able to address the sporadic error or delays. Another industry with the potential to use blockchain technology is the healthcare sector. In this field, blockchain serves as an effective tool to give key stakeholders like healthcare providers, clinical researchers, pharmacists, and patients secure, quick, and reliable access to electronic medical records.

1.3 Information on Chain Link Concept

Built on Ethereum, Chainlink is a decentralized blockchain oracle network. With the help of the network, tamper-proof data can be easily transferred from off-chain sources to on-chain smart contracts. Its developers assert that by linking the contract directly to real-world data, events, payments, and other inputs, it may be used to verify that a smart contract's specifications are followed in a way that is independent of any of the contract's stakeholders. Any blockchain can safely connect to off-chain data and computing resources thanks to Chainlink's decentralized oracle network, an open-source technology architecture. In order to execute smart contracts, network nodes fetch, validate, and deliver data from various sources onto blockchains. Chainlink can be used for a number of various off-chain calculation tasks, such as a verified random function (VRF) and data feeds, in addition to the transmission of external data to a blockchain.

1.4 Problems Faced on Current Online System

- Incorrect Guest Preferences
- Third-Party Scams
- Mishandled Reservations and Double Bookings
- Money laundering
- Fraud cases
- Evading the taxes like GST, and many service taxes.
- Problem maintaining the record (have chances to lose them due to centralized)
- Slot Management
- Booking Cancellation.

These are the above various problems to encourage make a distributed and immutable hotel chain system (i.e., based on blockchain technology) to fix them.

1.5 Hotel Chain Model

Figure 1 is presenting working model of a hotel chain distributed application. It consists of various functions such as booking, payment service, search and hold service etc. Blockchain deals with hold service, hold manager, the front end of the application, and payment service. Blockchain will work by using smart contracts which will be explained in the following section.

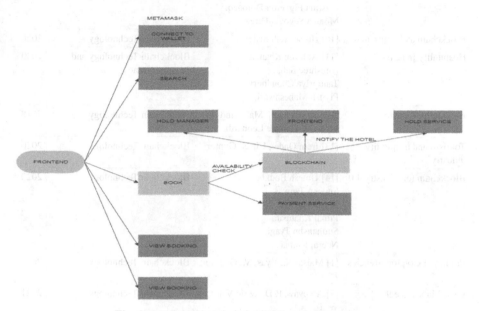

Fig. 1. Model of hotel chain distributed application

2 Literature Survey

Various blockchain platforms are available such as Ethereum, Hyperledger etc. The major application of the blockchain technology was cryptocurrency (Bitcoin) hence, this study Interprets the effects of Bitcoin Pricing on other cryptocurrencies [1, 6].

This emerging technology has many real applications such as academic certificate verification, health care management, identity verification etc. A framework is designed for an academic certificate verification system using blockchain in paper [2, 5]. A smart contract is designed for the academic verification system [3, 4].

The paper [8] presents the framework of blockchain technology in the hotel industry. It also described the technical challenges faced in adopting this technology. Paper [9] discussed identifying the gap in implementing the hotel industry using blockchain.

Chain link is used for adding off-chain data into the blockchain. The proposed framework also presents chain link as a part of this hotel chain system. A survey of chain link oracles usage on Ethereum is presented in the paper [16]. The evolution of decentralized oracle networks is discussed in the paper [15].

The summarized literature survey is presented in Table 1.

Table 1. Summary of literature survey

Applications of blockchain technology	Author	Technology	Year
Hospitality management	[8] Viachaslau Filimonau st.al	Blockchain Technology	2020
Hotel Management	[9] Ma Dolores Flecha -Barrio, Jesús Palomo, Cristina Figueroa-Domecq, Mónica Segovia-Perez	Blockchain Technology	2020
Blockchain and Tourism	[10] Horst Treiblmaier	Blockchain Technology	2020
Hospitality Industry	[11] Abhirup Khanna, Anushree Sah, Tanupriya Choudhury, Piyush Maheshwari,	Blockchain Technology and Cryptocurrency	2020
Hospitality Industry	[12] Tarik Dogru, Makarand Mody, & Christie Leonardi	Blockchain Technology	2018
Tourism and hospitality industry	[13] Irem Onder, Ulrich Gunter	Blockchain Technology	2020
Blockchain for Industry 4.0	[14] Umesh Bodkhe Sudeep Tanwar Karan Parekh Pimal Khanpara Sudhanshu Tyagi Neeraj Kumar	Blockchain Technology	2020
Pricing of Cryptocurrencies	[1] Malsa, N., Vyas, V., Gautam, J	Blockchain Technology	2022
Land Management	[7] Ameyaw, P. D., & de Vries, W. T	Blockchain Technology	2021
Certificate Verification system	[4] Malsa, N., Vyas, V., Gautam, J., Shaw, R.N., Ghosh, A	Framework and Smart Contract for Blockchain using robotics	2021
Academic Certificate Verification	[3] Pathak, S., Gupta, V., Malsa, N., Ghosh, A., Shaw, R.N	Using Ethereum Blockchain Technology	2022
Evolution of decentralized oracle networks	[15] L Breidenbach, C Cachin	Chainlink technology	2021
Chainlink oracles usage on ethereum	[16] M Kaleem, W Shi	Chainlink Technology	2021

3 Implementation

The structure of the rentals (property to be rented) includes its name, city, latitude, longitude, description of facilities, an image of the property, maximum guest occupancy, price per day and the dates for which the property has already been booked along with the owner of the property. Structure rentalsInfo contains three types of data types; string, uint256 and address, all have different purposes as shown in Fig. 2.

```
struct rentalsInfo{

    string name;                    // name of the property
    string city;                    // city in which property is
    string latitude;                //latitude for map
    string longitude;               // longitude for map
    string description1;            // facilities  ex wifi etc
    string description2;            // no. of beds bath toilets etc
    string imageUrl;                //images of property
    uint256 maxGuests;              // max guest allowed
    uint256 pricePerday;            // 24 hour day price
    string[] datesBooked;           // dates for which property has already been booked
    uint256 id;                     // id as its primary key
    address renter;                 // owner of the property
}
```

Fig. 2. Structure of rentals

To rent hotels, the hotel owners and company must first sign a pre-agreement contract (also known as a "smart contract"). Then their property will be listed in the blockchain after proper verification from the company side. Hotel owners need to maintain the decorum of the Brand Name to run their hotels. Customers can book their hotel and the transaction data will be added to the blockchain and the hotel owner will receive the amount at their address. No transaction fees will be charged in case of transaction failed situations.

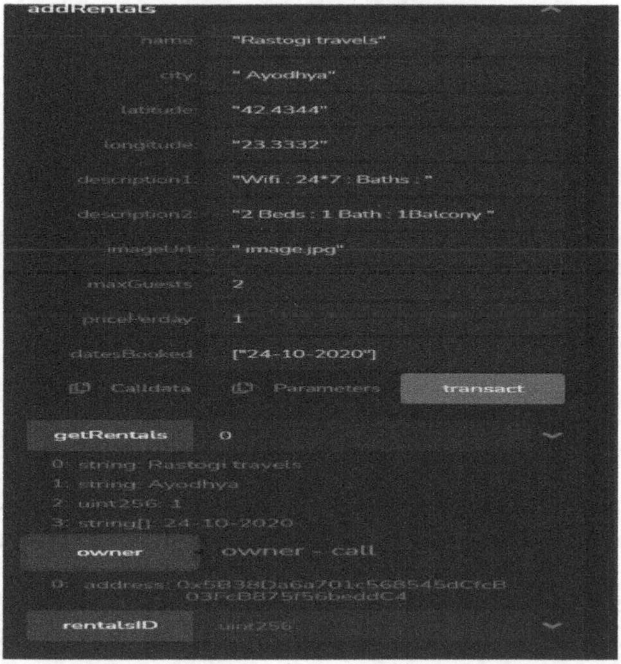

Fig. 3. AddRental functionality

One function AddRental of the model can be seen in Fig. 3. All parameters are given to addRentals function such as name, city, latitude etc. and this rental is added to the rental list (as shown in Fig. 3).

```
function checkBooking( uint256 id,string[] memory newBooking ) private view returns(bool){

          for(uint256 i=0; i < newBooking.length ; i++){
          for(uint256 j=0; j < rentals[id].datesBooked.length ;j++){
              if(keccak256(abi.encodePacked( newBooking[i] )) ==  keccak256(abi.encodePacked(
              rentals[id].datesBooked[j] ))){
                  return false;
              }
          }
      }
      return true;
}


function addBooking(uint256 id,string[] memory newBooking) public payable{


    require( id < counter," NO such rentals exist");
    require( checkBooking(id,newBooking)," Not available for requested date ");
    require( msg.value == (rentals[id].pricePerday * newBooking.length * 1 ether),
    " Please Pay the require ammount");




    for(uint256 i=0; i<newBooking.length ; i++ ){
        rentals[id].datesBooked.push(newBooking[i]);
    }


    payable(owner).transfer(msg.value);
    emit newDatesBooked(newBooking, id, rentals[id].city, rentals[id].imageUrl, msg.sender);
}


 function getRentals(uint256 id) public view returns(string memory ,
     string memory, uint256, string [] memory){
```

Fig. 4. Snapshot for hotel chain code

Events rentalCreated and newDatesBooked are also created. One constructor is also created that ensures that the message sender is the owner. Require () is an error-handling function used to verify that only the instructions written within the require functions will be executed if the condition is true. Different functions addBooking, checkBooking, getRentals are written in the smart contract and they all have specific functions as shown in Fig. 4.

The overview of the smart contract will also contain a function that will lead the customer to check their already booked status in the backend the get Rental() will run.

4   Results

Once the rental details are entered and the rental is added to the rental list. The addBooking function will work and start booking. Figure 4 showing the addBooking results. It shows that booking of Rastogi travels for Ayodhya is done.

The hotel chain application will fix the problems with the conventional hotel chain application by using the Ethereum blockchain and chainlink. As blockchain technology eliminates third parties and enables peer-to-peer transactions, the new application eliminates third party scams. Double bookings are impossible since the Ethereum blockchain solves the double spending problems. The immutability of the underlying blockchain technology lowers fraud situations. The central server that houses all the data in the conventional hotel chain system increases the likelihood of data loss. Data loss risks can be decreased by using a distributed blockchain ledger because the chain is immutable. By using chainlink outsides data can be added to the chain and this will improve the application's utility.

5   Conclusions

Tourism is crucial to a region's wealth and well-being since it promotes job growth, enterprise export revenues, and infrastructure development. Additionally, research has shown how crucial tourism is for creating both forward and backward connections with other economic sectors. Blockchain technology has the potential to significantly revolutionize the travel and tourist industry. A recent technological development called blockchain may be used to increase and strengthen confidence in the travel sector. In this chapter smart contract implementation is done and it is showing booking for a person for Ayodhya. The issue of industry centralization, which affects hotel owners and visitors worldwide, will be remedied by the use of this application. This application will preserve immutability, loyalty, and openness between guests and hotel owners. By using this program, the problem of money laundering and fraud cases will be resolved using blockchain. The application will also fill the technology gap now present in the hospitality sector. This application will also incorporate off-chain data (information from the real world) into blockchain to enhance the user experience for the client. This gives prospective tourists comfort because it demonstrates how technology can foster a relationship of trust between clients and tourism-related developments. The continually enhanced trip booking experience made possible by the traditional centralized paradigm will coexist with the introduction of ground-breaking decentralized capabilities and application cases.

References

1. Malsa, N., Vyas, V., Gautam, J.: Blockchain platforms and interpreting the effects of bitcoin pricing on cryptocurrencies. In: Sharma, T.K., Ahn, C.W., Verma, O.P., Panigrahi, B.K. (eds.) Soft Computing: Theories and Applications. AISC, vol. 1380, pp. 137–147. Springer, Singapore (2022). https://doi.org/10.1007/978-981-16-1740-9_13
2. Pathak, S., Gupta, V., Malsa, N., Ghosh, A., Shaw, R.N.: Blockchain-based academic certificate verification system—a review. In: Shaw, R.N., Das, S., Piuri, V., Bianchini, M. (eds): Advanced Computing and Intelligent Technologies. Lecture Notes in Electrical Engineering, vol 914, pp. 527539 (2022). Springer, Singapore. https://doi.org/10.1007/978-981-19-2980-9_42
3. Pathak, S., Gupta, V., Malsa, N., Ghosh, A., Shaw, R.N.: Smart contract for academic certificate verification using ethereum. In: Shaw, R.N., Das, S., Piuri, V., Bianchini, M. (eds): Advanced Computing and Intelligent Technologies. Lecture Notes in Electrical Engineering, vol 914, pp. 369384 (2022). Springer, Singapore. https://doi.org/10.1007/978-981-19-2980-9_29
4. Malsa, N., Vyas, V., Gautam, J., Shaw, R.N., Ghosh, A.: Framework and smart contract for blockchain enabled certificate verification system using robotics. In: Bianchini, M., Simic, M., Ghosh, A., Shaw, R.N. (eds.) Machine Learning for Robotics Applications. SCI, vol. 960, pp. 125–138. Springer, Singapore (2021). https://doi.org/10.1007/978-981-16-0598-7_10
5. Malsa, N., Vyas, V., Gautam, J., Ghosh, A., Shaw, R.N.: CERTbchain: a step by step approach towards building a blockchain based distributed appliaction for certificate verification system. In: 2021 IEEE 6th International Conference on Computing, Communication and Automation (ICCCA), pp. 800–806 (2021). https://doi.org/10.1109/ICCCA52192.2021.9666311
6. Malsa, N., Vyas, V., Gautam, J.: RMSE calculation of LSTM models for predicting prices of different cryptocurrencies. Int. J. Syst. Assur. Eng. Manag., pp. 19 (2021). https://doi.org/10.1007/s13198-021-01431-1
7. Ameyaw, P. D., de Vries, W. T.: Toward smart land management: land acquisition and the associated challenges in Ghana. a look into a blockchain digital land registry for prospects. Land, 10(3), 239 (2021)
8. Filimonau, V., Naumova, E.: The blockchain technology and the scope of its application in hospitality operations. Int. J. Hosp. Manag. 87, 102383 (2020)
9. Flecha-Barrio, M.D., Palomo, J., Figueroa-Domecq, C., Segovia-Perez, M.:. Blockchain implementation in hotel management. In: Information and Communication Technologies in Tourism, pp. 255–266 (2020). Springer, Cham. https://doi.org/10.1007/978-3-030-36737-4_21

10. Treiblmaier, H.: Blockchain and tourism. Handbook of e-Tourism, 1–21 (2020)
11. Khanna, A., Sah, A., Choudhury, T., Maheshwari, P.: Blockchain technology for the hospitality industry. In: European, Mediterranean, and Middle Eastern Conference on Information Systems, pp. 99–112 (2020). Springer, Cham. https://doi.org/10.1007/978-3-030-63396-7_7
12. Dogru, T., Mody, M., Leonardi, C.: Blockchain Technology & Its Implications for the Hospitality Industry. Boston University (2018)
13. Önder, I., Gunter, U.: Blockchain: Is it the future for the tourism and hospitality industry? Tour. Econ. **28**(2), 291–299 (2022)
14. Bodkhe, U., et al.: Blockchain for industry 4.0: a comprehensive review. IEEE Access **8**, 79764–79800 (2020)
15. Breidenbach, L., et al.: 2.0: Next steps in the evolution of decentralized oracle networks. White paper, Chain-Link (2021)
16. Kaleem, M., Shi, W.: Demystifying Pythia: A Survey of ChainLink Oracles Usage on Ethereum (2021). arXiv preprint arXiv:2101.06781

Accurate Rating System Using Blockchain

B. C. Girish Kumar[1(✉)], Mitul Garg[1], Jagdish Saini[1], Kapil Chauhan[1],
Nitima Malsa[1], and Komal Malsa[2]

[1] Department of Computer Science and Engineering, JSS Academy of Technical Education,
Noida, India
girishkumar@jssaten.ac.in

[2] Department of Computer Science and Engineering, Lingaya's Vidyapeeth, Faridabad, India

Abstract. Most websites' accurate rating systems provide users with product and service ratings. User satisfaction has suffered as a result of a lack of faith and the manipulation of data. Because it communicates with existing accurate rating systems, all score statistics are saved on a central server. As a result, the manager has the ability to remove, all rating data that must be modified and manipulated in order to sway positive feedback on the service or product provider. As a solution to all of the shortcomings of current systems, an accurate rating system based on distributed ledger technologies is proposed in this chapter. Decentralized distributed ledger, with no institution attempting to centralize them. Distributed ledger technologies come in a variety of flavours. Blockchain technology Because it supports smart contracts, it was used in the proposed rating system. The Ethereum platform became selected from among numerous blockchain systems with a public permission network for the proposed accurate rating system. Raters are not permitted to rate in this system unless they make a request to the gadget are permitted to participate in the correct product score process. The Ethereum platform is notable for its smart contract support, which is to be used to create Solidity's rating contract. The TestNet blockchain, on the other hand, can be used in the rating system. Due to the high cost of this method. The proposed rating system was then tested.

Keywords: Accurate · Blockchain · Smart contract · Distributed ledger technologies

1 Introduction

The term "digital transformation" refers to a substantial change in the operation of a company that focuses on transformative technologies. Among the most important transformational technology are the Internet of Things, cloud computing, cell applications, social media, virtual and augmented reality, statistics analysis, synthetic intelligence, and blockchain. [1]. The blockchain era is a form of disbursed ledger era used in digital transformation (DLT) [12]. One of the most significant advantages of blockchain technology is the absence of a central core. Because of the openness of distributed ledger technology as well as the safety of encryption and immutable data flow, this technology has proven to be an excellent tool for facilitating commercial interactions and validating formatives. The blockchain generation is a basic generation that can be configured in a variety of ways based on objectives and business models [2]. The offline system is prohibitively costly, time-consuming, and prone to failure, making rating difficult for those who are unable to attend in person. As a result, accurate rating systems appear because the online system is a viable alternative accurate system that has the ability to remove or at least assist in the removal of the offline system's difficulties and issues. User satisfaction has suffered as a result of a lack of confidence in the integrity and manipulation of data. Yelp, for example, is a website that assists people in finding restaurants.

In addition, based on user feedback, this application rates restaurants and cafés. As a result, customers and users follow Yelp's recommendations for their preferred restaurants and cafés. [3] The SWOT matrix is a strategic planning method used in organizations. This matrix of threats, opportunities, vulnerabilities and strength describes the threats, opportunities, weaknesses, and strengths of a system. The Accurate rating system's SWOT matrix is depicted in Fig. 1. The diagram depicts the system's flaws, which include a lack of transparency, trustworthiness, and privacy. We employ distributed ledger technologies in this study to address the system's lack of transparency and trustworthiness.

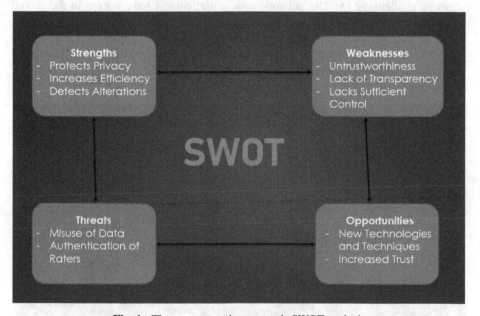

Fig. 1. The accurate rating system's SWOT analysis

1.1 Preliminaries

The phase discusses the essential concepts used in this chapter, which include virtual transformation, disbursed ledger technologies, clever contracts, a correct score device with blockchain, balloting and score device comparisons, the function of blockchain generation in key score device goals, and blockchain generation challenges.

a) **Digital Transformation**

The incorporation of the virtual era into all commercial enterprise fields is known as digital transformation, and it specializes in transforming the way commercial enterprise operations are carried out and pricing is passed on to customers It is also concerned with changing the organizational culture to meet the current challenges [1]. The two are inextricably linked. Cultural elements, on the other hand, that motivate the organization to change quickly in response to changing commercial prospects are required. This is a difficult task.

b) **Distributed Ledger Technologies**

A distributed ledger is a completely shared database that synchronizes the network as a whole, and it is distributed across multiple sites, places organizations. Data can have public witnesses on the distributed ledger, making Cyber-attacks are becoming more challenging [5] The network node's participants have access to the shared network record and a comparable rendition of the records. In addition, any change, in the ledger is versioned when it is modified or added and applied to everyone in a matter of seconds or minutes. It depicts the transition from to a distributed/distributed ledger originating from a centralized network. in Fig. 2:

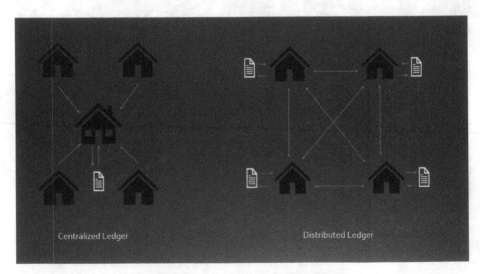

Fig. 2. From centralized to distributed ledger

The issue with attacking the centralized system is solved by DLT. A distributed ledger is what blockchain is that uses novel mechanism. Data and information are encrypted and saved in interconnected blocks.

c) **Smart Contract**

The main feature the contracts are executable without the requirement for faith, removing the necessity of a third party to carry out the contract's various circumstances. Instead of depending on a person who is prone to making blunders either it does what it was intended to do, whether purposefully or unwittingly. at the appropriate time. Initially, all property and agreement situations are encoded and preserved withinside the blockchain. This agreement is replicated and disseminated in several instances by a number of platform nodes. Following processing, the agreement is achieved in line with the phrases indicated. In clever contracts, a man or woman or group can't manage the agreement, and when the agreement's phrases are right, it is fully automated.

To create a smart contract, the following items are required [7, 8]:

1. Contract subject: in order to automatically lock or unlock the contract's services or goods, this programmer must have access to them.
2. Digital signature: Everyone who takes part will sign the contract using their private keys to sign it.
3. Contract terms: Smart contract terms take the shape of a specific sequence of operations that must be completed. These terms must be accepted by all participants.
4. Platform: On the blockchain platform, smart contracts are created and distributed among nodes. Each intelligent contract is made up of several components, including an address, various variables, and input and output functions.

2 Literature Survey

S. no	Year	Author name	Title of the research chapter	Methodology / algorithm	Advantages	Disadvantages	Reference link
1	January 2021	Monir Shaker, Fereidoon Shams Aliee, Reza Fotohi	Online Rating System Development Using Blockchain-Based Completely Distributed Ledger Technology	Distributed Ledger Technology	DLT networks protect against data loss or corruption, increase transparency, and reduce the likelihood of data tampering	Consider inefficiency, the inherent risk of irreversible transactions, and the possibility of a 51% attack	https:// arxiv.org/ abs/2101. 04173

(continued)

(continued)

S. no	Year	Author name	Title of the research chapter	Methodology / algorithm	Advantages	Disadvantages	Reference link
2	20th December, 2020	D. Saveetha and Dr.G. Maragatham	Accurate Customer Reviews on Restaurant Using Blockchain	Smart Contract	Immutability of data, the ability to make contracts and agreements without the parties knowing each other, and the avoidance of potential breach of conditions	The transaction may be lost if one of the parties breaches the contract. The vast majority of smart contracts are not subject to legal oversight or control	https:// www.sem anticscho lar.org/ chapter/ Accurate-Cus tomer-Reviews-on-Restau rant-Using-Saveetha-Maraga tham/840 257cd1 095037 b73e08 4dd2dd d5e68d a40e3d0
3	13th March 2019	K. Salah, A. Alfalasi, M. Alfalasi	A Blockchain-based System for Accurate Consumer Reviews	Ethereum smart contracts and IPFS	Smart contracts do not require confirmation from brokers or other intermediaries, removing the risk of third-party manipulation	The best experience is when the local node is enabled. In some cases, public gateways are too slow. If you want to share it in other ways, you'll need twice as much space	https:// www.res earchg ate.net/ public ation/331 702344
4	8th November 2020	Tanakorn Karode, Warodom Werapun, Tanwa Arpornthip	Blockchain-based Global Travel Review Framework	Smart Contract	Immutability of data, the ability to make contracts and agreements without the parties knowing each other, and the avoidance of potential breach of conditions	If one party breaches the contract, the transaction may be lost. The vast majority of smart contracts are not governed or controlled by law	https:// www.res earchg ate.net/ public ation/344 022802_ Blockc hain-based_ Global_ Travel_ Review_ Fra mework

(continued)

(continued)

S. no	Year	Author name	Title of the research chapter	Methodology / algorithm	Advantages	Disadvantages	Reference link
5	Jan. 27 – 29, 2021	Saveetha.D,Dr.G.Maragatham	Movie Rating System based on Blockchain	Smart Contract	Immutability of data, the ability to make contracts and agreements without the parties knowing each other, and the avoidance of potential breach of conditions	If one party breaches the contract, the transaction may be lost. The vast majority of smart contracts are not governed or controlled by law	https://iee explore. ieee.org/ doc ument/ 9402381
6	26th April 2022	Jitendra Singh Yadav, Narendra Singh Yadav & Akhilesh Kumar Sharma	Security evaluation of clever settlement primarily based totally score and evaluation systems: the perilous kingdom of blockchain-primarily based totally advice practices	Smart Contract Based	Smart contracts have the potential to improve product and material traceability	One significant issue with smart contracts is that, because they are stored on a blockchain, they are pseudonymous	https:// www.tan dfaccu rate.com/ doi/full/ 10.1080/ 095 40091. 2022.206 6065
7	13th May 2019	Yi-Cheng Chen, Shih-Yu Chen, Song-Yu Wu	A Trustworthy E-commerce Business Model Based on a Blockchain-Based Product Grading System	Big-Data Analytics	Customer Acquisition and Retention, Identification of Potential Risks Innovate, Complex Supplier Networks, Cost Optimization, and Efficiency Improvement	Security risk	https://iee explore. ieee.org/ doc ument/ 8713204

Most websites include an online rating system that enables users to give feedback on various goods and services. User happiness has been reduced by user unease with data tampering and inaccuracy. All rating data is stored on the central server, with which all currently used online rating systems interact. As a result, in an effort to favour the service or good supplier, the system manager has the power to change, remove, and modify any rating information. A distributed ledger-based online rating system is proposed in this study as a solution to all the issues with the current ones.

We outline a method for building a secure, reliable, and trusted platform for an online review system with high integrity and resilience using the Ethereum Blockchain, Smart Contracts, and IPFS. We look at the fundamentals of architectural design, the interactions between system components, algorithms, and logic flow. We also show how we put the overall system functions into practise and tested them.

The Ethereum platform is used, which incorporates each the backend and the frontend. This process involves the participation number of users who act as authors and judge. As a result, in this new system, the authors are directed to a page where they can submit their chapter, as well as for the judges to review the chapters and give their approval or disapproval, with the entire process taking place on the Ethereum blockchain system [11]. As communication technology in tourism advances, industry, tourists can now share information about travel destination rankings via their mobile devices. The centralized model is the most widely used method of data sharing. However, because A centralized architecture has several advantages and flaws, it ought to be used through the decentralized structure evolved in this study (TDRS). This study describes a hybrid machine created from 6AsTD as a framework for assessing the degree of achievement of tourism locations and the safety machine based on the China Blockchain era as a statistic-sharing structure among tourists [12].

The current e-trade commercial enterprise version is untrustworthy for plenty of customers, and each consumer is searching for a dependable supplier. Suppliers with various product first-rate may also actually have customers from well-known online retailers like Amazon and Alibaba, which do now no longer use quality grades to assess products. We suggest a blockchain technology (BPGS) system to address massive facts for those enterprise models in this chapter. Because blockchain is a decentralized technology that allows us to speed up product grading. Furthermore, for 51% of attacks detected using the planned BPGS system cannot be implemented unless 51% of e-commerce suppliers and firms agree to it at the same time threatened [13].

Participants in an Energy can be exchanged directly between peers in a peer-to-peer energy system one. A pricing mechanism can hold the rate of exchange among traders beneath control, and a scoring metric can inspire members to behave responsibly. The chapter proposes a peer-to-peer strength buying and selling a version with a blockchain framework to ensure service provider statistics and execution, in addition to a two-tier pricing mechanism to decide the rate of strength transaction prices, and a credit score system [14, 15], as an example Manufacturers can take advantage of this pricing mechanism to save the most money or make the most money, whereas the credit score rating gadget encourages them to enhance their reputation in order to gain a competitive advantage when trading.

Traditional small lending is a brand-new exact database wherein human beings from all around the international can lend cash to the ones in need. The downside of this conventional approach is that there is a possibility of failure of nonpayment much higher than with traditional financing, so the platform must be transparent and dependable. [16].

Communication between IoT gadgets is neither steady nor dependable. There are some protection risks. Existing protection systems are tough to manipulate due to the fact they require extra resources, elevating the general value of the system. IoT devices have the functionality computing power and are incapable of performing complex calculations When requests for services from IoT devices are not detected by a reliable security system. The IoT network relies heavily on service reliability. A system model discussed in this chapter for protecting IoT devices from untrustworthy services is proposed. In the Chinese blockchain, the ranking of service providers is stored.

2.1 Accurate Blockchain-Based Rating System

Transparency, privacy, and validation are the following are the three indicators required for a reliable rating system

a. Transparency: the ultimate outcome must be obvious. As a result, each rater must double-check that their votes were counted.
b. Security: no one can see what the users' ratings are given.
c. Validation: its miles are signed with the user's personal key (score data), and validators can validate it through the usage of the general public key. Ratings should not be manipulated either.

These features can be provided by blockchain [19, 20]. The use of blockchain technology enables decentralized rating validation and counting. The primary benefit of using this method is that it is decentralized, it allows people involved in the network to check the accuracy of various rating stages, and all rating data is saved on network nodes rather than servers [17]. As a result, to control the data, someone needs to first infiltrate all the nodes (computers) concerned in the method and benefit get the right of entry to a huge quantity of particular data though nearly impossible. Furthermore, A rater can easily verify whether or not his or her rating was appropriately entered. Using blockchain technology. Furthermore, any issues with the organization's product or service rating steps are automatically identified for the user. Furthermore, since the monitoring will be carried out by an impartial personnel process, blockchain's transparency facilitates monitoring and the completion of various rating steps. Furthermore, no additional sources or maybe the bodily presence of personnel or raters are required in this method [18].

This aids in Anonymity, obscuring findings, and doing computations on encrypted data are all possibilities. Because of their open-source and decentralized nature these items are absent from other blockchain-related systems. No one can ever change the rating results using this system by manipulating data [19]. Finally, after completing the rating process, users can ensure that their feedback and ratings are entered into the system. Another intention of growing this machine is to comprise information this is complete, accurate, without paradoxes, and without any sort of logical error. In fact, the machine has the functionality of stopping different customers from getting access to its information, with most effectively described customers having access.

3 Methodology

a) **Ethereum**

Ethereum developed a mechanism for creating distributed apps. In some ways, Ethereum is a cryptocurrency that laid the groundwork for developers. as well as a Touring-only blockchain, this means that a system that has infinite resources such as memory, processing power and storage space can run in infinite loops.

b) **Solidity Programming Language**

Solidity is a programming language like C and JavaScript. Solidity is a famous programming language for developing numerous clever contracts. This is the code that allows for decentralized contracts or application execution. Solidity, a brand-new programming language, turned into created through Ethereum, the second-largest cryptocurrency marketplace through valuation. Solidity programming makes use of variables, functions, classes, mathematics operations, string manipulation, and plenty of different concepts.

c) **JavaScript**

JavaScript is a dynamic programming language for computers. It is lightweight and is maximum typically used as an aspect of net pages, in which implementations are executed allowing the customer to interaction with the person and create dynamic sites. It is an object-orientated programming language that may be interpreted. Live Script was the original name for JavaScript, but Because of the popularity of Java, Netscape renamed itself JavaScript.

d) **React.js**

React is a front-end JavaScript library for developing consumer interfaces primarily based totally on UI additives that are unfastened and open-source. Meta (previously Facebook) is managed by a network of individual builders and agencies. Using frameworks such as Next.js, React may be utilized as a basis in the building of single-page, mobile, or server-rendered apps. However, because react is only concerned with dealing with data and displaying it to the DOM, constructing React applications necessitates the usage of extra frameworks for routing. And client-side functionality.

e) **Node.js**

Node.js is a cross-platform programming language that can operate on Windows, Linux, Unix, and Mac OS, and other operating systems. Node.js is a JavaScript run-time environment for the back end. Node.js executes JavaScript code outdoors of an internet browser with the usage of a JavaScript Engine (e.g., the V8 engine). Node.js allows developers to write command line tools and server-side scripting using JavaScript. The server-side scripting functionality generates earlier than the net web page is dispatched to the user's net browser, and dynamic net web page content material is loaded. As a result, Node.js promotes a "JavaScript everywhere" paradigm, bringing web-app improvement around a single programming language instead of separate languages for server-aspect and client-aspect scripts. Node.js' event-pushed shape permits asynchronous I/O. These layout picks are meant to enhance through-put and scalability in internet programs with more than one input/output operation, in addition to in real-time Web applications.

4   Research Methodologies

When a person logs in to the website, she or he chooses and prices a product primarily based totally on the rating system. The clever agreement (smart contract) will then be initiated, and the transaction might be validated; if the validation is positive, a brand-new block might be formed, and the blockchain might be updated; otherwise, the clever agreement will go back to the homepage (Fig. 3).

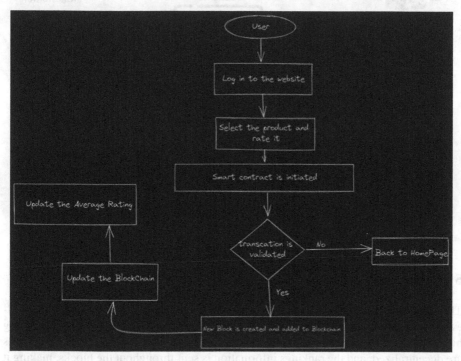

Fig. 3. Flowgraph of accurate rating system

4.1 Proposed Architecture

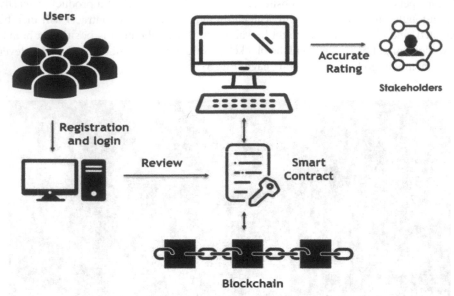

Fig. 4. Rating system architecture proposal

5 Conclusion

This study proposes an accurate Blockchain-based rating system. This method is relevant to all product and carrier issuer websites. Some of the benefits of incorporating blockchain generation into the scoring machine are as follows. Such systems' databases are decentralized, and the rankings information is sent throughout the blocks, making it not possible for absolutely everyone to alternate their, integrity (Fig. 4).

Future Scope
Registered raters' complete rankings exactly as they should be. The issuer of a carrier or product will never be able to persuade or score consequences. Raters' personal information is kept private, and no rater may price the same product more than once. Because the blockchain era prevents statistics from being altered, the outcomes of this scheme can be confirmed. [20]. Furthermore, when using the score clever contract, there are no intermediaries between the rater and the service issuer inside the scoring machine. This research resulted in the introduction of a decentralized score utility based entirely on allotted ledger technologies, one in every of which has become blockchain. Blockchain technology can help you save money by preventing data tampering. This utility has numerous features, including the ability to make rankings credible and citable. Ratings are completed online and precisely by registered raters. A company that provides services or products will never be able to control score results.

Acknowledgement. We'd like to say our heartfelt indebtedness to Mr. Girish Kumar B.C, our mentor and guide, for guiding us with correct approaches and constant feedback. We are also grateful to Mrs. Urvashi Rahul Saxena (coordinator) for performing regular project reviews. Finally, we'd like to thank our group members for inspiring and supporting one another throughout the duration of this project.

References

1. Heavin, C., Power, D.J.: Digital transformation challenges-towards a conceptual decision support guide for managers. J. Decis. Syst. **27**(supplement 1), 38–45 (2018)
2. Zheng, Z., Xie, S., Dai, H., Chen, X., Wang, H.: A primer on blockchain technology, including architecture, consensus, and future trends. In: 2017, the IEEE International Big Data Congress (Bigdata Congress) was held, pp. 557–564 (2017)
3. Yelp (2015). https://www.yelp.co.uk/
4. Kamran, M., Khan, H.U., Nisar, W., Farooq, M., Rehman, S.U.: Blockchain and the Internet of Things: a bibliometric analysis. IEEE. **81**, 106525 (2020)
5. Saad, A., Park, S.Y.: Decentralized directed acyclic graph-based DLT network. In: Proceedings of the International Conference on Omni-Layer Intelligent Systems, pp. 158–163 (2019)
6. Liu, X., Farahani, B., Firouzi, F.: Distributed ledger technology. In: Firouzi, F., Chakrabarty, K., Nassif, S. (eds.) Intelligent Internet of Things, pp. 393–431. Springer, Cham (2020). https://doi.org/10.1007/978-3-030-30367-9_8
7. Aung, Y.N., Tantidham, T.: Ethereum-based emergency service for smart home system: smart contract implementation. In: 2019 21st International Conference on Advanced Communication Technology (ICACT), pp. 147–152 (2019). IEEE
8. Zhang, Y., Kasahara, S., Shen, Y., Jiang, X., Wan, J.: Smart contract-based access control for the internet of things. IEEE Internet Things J. **6**(2), 1594–1605 (2018)
9. Yadav, J.S., Yadav, N.S., Sharma, A.K.: Security analysis of smart contract-based rating and review systems: the perilous state of blockchain-based recommendation practices. **34**(1), 1273–1298 (2022). Received 11 Jan 2022, Accepted 09 Apr 2022
10. Lamba, A., Singh, S., Balvinder, S., Dutta, N., Rela, S.: Mitigating IoT security and privacy challenges using distributed ledger based Blockchain (Dl-BC) Technology. International Journal for Technological Research in Engineering, **4**(8) (2017)
11. Schaufelbühl, A., et al.: EUREKA–a minimal operational prototype of a blockchain-based rating and publishing system. In: 2019 IEEE International Conference on Blockchain and Cryptocurrency (ICBC), pp. 13–14 (2019). IEEE
12. Malsa, N., Vyas, V., Gautam, J., Shaw, R.N., Ghosh, A.: Framework and smart contract for blockchain enabled certificate verification system using robotics. In: Bianchini, M., Simic, M., Ghosh, A., Shaw, R.N. (eds.) Machine Learning for Robotics Applications. SCI, vol. 960, pp. 125–138. Springer, Singapore (2021). https://doi.org/10.1007/978-981-16-0598-7_10
13. Girish Kumar, B.C., Nand, P., Bali, V.: Opportunities and challenges of blockchain technology for tourism industry in future smart society. In: 2022 Fifth International Conference on Computational Intelligence and Communication Technologies (CCICT), pp. 318–323 (2022). https://doi.org/10.1109/CCiCT56684.2022.00065
14. Girish Kumar, B.C., Nand, P., Bali, V.: Review on opportunities and challenges of blockchain technology for tourism industry in future smart society. In: Bali, V., Bhatnagar, V., Lu, J., Banerjee, K. (eds): Decision Analytics for Sustainable Development in Smart Society 5.0. Asset Analytics (2022). Springer, Singapore. https://doi.org/10.1007/978-981-19-1689-2_16

15. Masla, N., Vyas, V., Gautam, J., Shaw, R.N., Ghosh, A.: Reduction in gas cost for blockchain enabled smart contract. In: 2021 IEEE 4th International Conference on Computing, Power and Communication Technologies (GUCON), pp. 1–6 (2021). https://doi.org/10.1109/GUC ON50781.2021.9573701
16. Malsa, N., Vyas, V., Gautam, J.: Blockchain platforms and interpreting the effects of bit-coin pricing on cryptocurrencies. In: Sharma, T.K., Ahn, C.W., Verma, O.P., Panigrahi, B.K. (eds.) Soft Computing: Theories and Applications. AISC, vol. 1380, pp. 137–147. Springer, Singapore (2022). https://doi.org/10.1007/978-981-16-1740-9_13
17. Pathak, S., Gupta, V., Malsa, N., Ghosh, A., Shaw, R.N.: Blockchain-based academic certifi-cate verification system—a review. In: Shaw, R.N., Das, S., Piuri, V., Bianchini, M. (eds): Advanced Computing and Intelligent Technologies. Lecture Notes in Electrical Engineering, vol 914, pp. 527539 (2022). Springer, Singapore. https://doi.org/10.1007/978-981-19-2980-9_42
18. Pathak, S., Gupta, V., Malsa, N., Ghosh, A., Shaw, R.N.: Smart contract for academic cer-tificate verification using ethereum. In: Shaw, R.N., Das, S., Piuri, V., Bianchini, M. (eds): Advanced Computing and Intelligent Technologies. Lecture Notes in Electrical Engineering, vol 914, pp. 369384 (2022). Springer, Singapore. https://doi.org/10.1007/978-981-19-2980-9_29
19. Wu, H.T., Su, Y.J., Hu, W.C.: A study on blockchain-based circular economy credit rating system. In: International Conference on Security with Intelligent Computing and Big-data Services, pp. 339–343 (2017). Springer, Cham. https://doi.org/10.1007/978-3-319-76451-1_32
20. Makhdoom, I., Abolhasan, M., Abbas, H., Ni, W.: The challenges and prospects of blockchain adoption in IoT. J. Network and Computer Appl. **125**, 251–279 (2019)
21. Malsa, N., Vyas, V., Gautam, J., Ghosh, A., Shaw, R.N.: CERTbchain: A step by step approach towards building a blockchain based distributed appliaction for certificate verification system. In: 2021 IEEE 6th International Conference on Computing, Communication and Automation (ICCCA), pp. 800–806 (2021). https://doi.org/10.1109/ICCCA52192.2021.9666311
22. Malsa, N., Vyas, V., Gautam, J.: RMSE calculation of LSTM models for predicting prices of different cryptocurrencies. Int. J. Syst. Assur. Eng. Manag. 19 (2021). https://doi.org/10.1007/s13198-021-01431-1

Approaches to Overcome Human Limitations by an Intelligent Autonomous System with a Level of Consciousness in Reasoning, Decision Making and Problem-Solving Capabilities

A. Jemshia Mirriam(✉), S. Rajashree, M. Nafees Muneera, V. Saranya, and E. Murali

School of Computing, Sathyabama Institute of Science and Technology,
Chennai 600119, Tamil Nadu, India
{jemshia.cse,rajashree.cse,nafeesmuneera.cse,
saranya.cse}@sathyabama.ac.in

Abstract. With the nonstop advancement of software engineering and innovation, PCs are bit by bit applied to numerous fields, including the craftsmanship plan. In this chapter, to work on the effectiveness and far reaching level of craftsmanship plan, the workmanship plan colleague framework was concentrated on the reason of the entire request of craftsmanship plan. In this framework, the main picture preparing innovation is utilized in contemporary workmanship plan, which can clearly lessen the measure of work of the plan staff, and make an agreeable improvement space for the previously mentioned faculty. In any case, right now, the workmanship plan labourers additionally need to work on their own capacity. Development cost assessment has involved a huge piece of examination benefits in development the board. It is exceptionally difficult to assess project costs during various stages since expenses, deals and benefits sum were hard to be assessed precisely, likewise shy of control data, and issues like insightful mistakes among immediate and aberrant expense and undertaking chances. This chapter has fostered a development cost assessment framework dependent on man-made consciousness, conquering the undertaking vulnerabilities through cutting edge and insightful PC organizations. Simultaneously, this chapter additionally contemplates the accessibility of computerized reasoning.

Keywords: Artificial intelligence · Computer artistic design · ANN

1 Introduction

With the emergence and continuous progress of multimedia technology, computers are gradually used in many fields. The computer's powerful and efficient processing function of graphic information makes the development of computer art design more prominent in the design industry. Whether in the graphic design industry, the industrial styling design industry, or animation, film and television design industry, through the use of computers

R. N. Shaw et al. (Eds.): ICACIS 2022, CCIS 1749, pp. 505–516, 2023.
https://doi.org/10.1007/978-3-031-25088-0_45

to carry out computer art design, the graphic design, efficient and accurate engineering drawings, indoor and outdoor renderings, and miscellaneous animation production and film editing can be carried out. In addition, by using scanners, digital cameras, and many other ancillary facilities, static images can be sought, and after processing by multimedia software, a large amount of data and information can be generated to facilitate design. Therefore, computer art design has gradually become a key tool in the design industry.

The spread of computer and Internet technology has led to a broader space for improvement in the design industry, as well as innovation in content and type. Designers can not only use chapter and pen directly, but also use computer aided design software. Compared with the previous design methods, computer aided software is more efficient. Auxiliary software, with its own leading technology advantages, has launched a certain technological innovation in the premise of traditional design [1].

In the design of the basic pattern, it is necessary to construct a new visual image in the two- dimensional plane space with different or the same basic graphics. The flexibility of the design is strong. Even if the same basic graphics are used, they are arranged in different ways within the frame of the picture, and different permutations and combinations can also be formed, and there are many different paintings and effects. Thus, the designer's thinking is demanding. Using the computer technology can not only improve the accuracy of the design, but also use the copy, mirror, rotation and other commands to seek changes and combinations of patterns, thus to further make graphics which can't be made by hand and obviously reduce the amount of labor of designers [2].

Colour is the key part of the design work, and the combination of various colors will bring a variety of visual and psychological feelings. Before the use of computer technology, designers mostly imagine and blend colors in their brains, and in this way, the colors are not completely mastered. Therefore, imagination and reality do not match, so that designers need to carry out much mediation. In carrying out the three-dimensional design, designers need to make spatial imagination, which requires a high spatial imagination ability of designers. However, only through the imagination, the designer's feelings about the work are not clear, and there are some difficulties in stereoscopic design. Computer 3D modeling and rendering technology can show multiple parts and details of an object, allowing the designer to build and modify the form as he looks at the object [3].

Many complicated problems lie ahead for construction industry, including the big challenge for accuracy of construction cost estimation, on account of uncertain costs, sales and profits, that integrated most of research benefits in construction management. IT played a vital role in construction project. Thomas and other people also explained the significance of IT for the high efficiency of construction project [4].

In recent years, civil engineering and construction industry began to consider applying AI technology in construction cost estimation system. Probability calculation may make mistakes with certain proportion during different stages in project, and these costs almost cannot be calculated as "unpredictable costs" or "risk costs" because there are some uncertain elements in project proposal and construction cost estimation, which was caused by inaccurate separation between contractor's technology, funds, loss evaluation, direct and indirect costs, short of analysis, organizing and correct cost estimation methods. All of these factors may result in evaluation error of information, directly or indirectly [5]. Uncertainties, estimated amounts and distinctiveness of project were able to be calculated in cost estimation system, and we can analyze through different stages in project and through actual variable caused by all other parts.

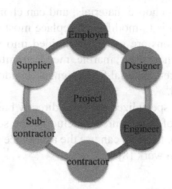

Fig. 1. Parties of a project

As shown in the Fig. 1, there were sponsors, contractors, sub-contractors, suppliers, designers and consultants joining in one project. But all of them stand in different positions and describe different characters so as to hard to estimate the costs during different stages. The cost estimation methods applied in cost estimation could be different with that applied in project implementation [6]. We can estimate costs by means of AI technology in primary stage because of its high uncertainty, and price analysis can be used in planning and implementing period. This chapter has developed a construction cost estimation system based on artificial neural network, combined with fuzzy logic algorithms, which effectively solved the uncertain and fuzzy problems in traditional construction cost estimation and improved accuracy and efficiency to a large extent.

2   Methodology

2.1   System Overall Architecture Design

Before developing computer aided art design system, it is necessary to explore the software requirements and feasibility. The development of computer and Internet technology provides the possibility for intelligent art design system. In this chapter, according to the research status and problems of computer aided design system both at home and abroad, a comprehensive account was carried out. After that, according to the actual situation, the performance requirements and functional requirements of the above system were sorted out. Performance requirements focus on the processing efficiency and design effects of the auxiliary system, and the R & D goals of the above systems generally cover the following sections:

The first is to provide the art designers with the function of constructing art models. The second is to provide the design staff with the choice of design materials. The third is to provide automatic color matching for art designers. The fourth is to provide the automatic extraction function of the design template for the art designer. The fifth is to provide automatic matching function for art designers. The main purpose of the auxiliary system is to provide the designers with an auxiliary system based on the art design, which mainly includes the following aspects:

Art designers are free to choose materials, and can change the materials that have been used, the key in which is to modify and replace most of the material. The above modifications and substitutions are generally divided into two categories. One is the system default material, such as glass, marble, metal, granite, glass, plastic, and so on; the other one is a hand-painted material for designers. In addition, the finished material map can also be adopted [7].

Art designers can create specialized modules directly based on requirements, background changes, and color of light sources, including the scale, radian, and edge type of specific work. In addition, the staff can use the assistance system to view a variety of information about the design work [8].

2.2 Artificial Neural Network

ANN deals with visual data based on human brain and learns to distinguish the objects, which was inspired by biology-- the unit network named as "neuron" in human brain [9]. As shown in the Fig. 2, there is import, hidden and export layer in typical ANN models. They are artificial neurons. And each group of neurons was divided into 3 layers: import, hidden and export layer. At first, neurons in import layer receive information from outer neural networks and send it to hidden layer or export layer. And then, neurons in hidden layer, located between import and export layer, can figure out the information and send it to export layer. At last, export layer figure out the information and offer the results from ANN. Generally, one neuron sets another neuron's output value as input value to figure out. These neurons connect to each other and weight to their connected intensity (Fig. 3).

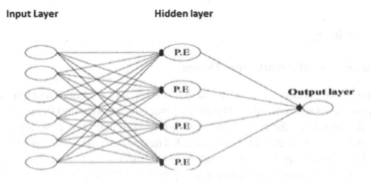

Fig. 2. Neural network structure

In ANN, neurons calculate weight sum imported by other neurons and export it by transfer function, which often transfers function separately according to it's function, learning algorithm, supervised and unsupervised learning. This system chooses Sigmoid function as transfer function [10].

Fig. 3. The structure of neurons

2.3 Fuzzy Logic Algorithm in AI

Fuzzy logic aroused by fuzzy sets is another AI method and its function rudiments are shown in the Fig. 4. The most important feature is that it was suitable to small or missing DS because it need prior conditions less than other estimation methods [11]. Thus, in this project, we combined fuzzy logic algorithm and ANN technology to solve the uncertain and fuzzy problems in construction cost estimation system.

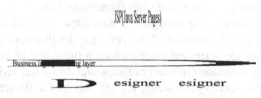

Fig. 4. Fuzzy logic and working system

Generally, we make a decision according to our experience, and the rules in our brain and our intuition. While computer estimation system make such a decision by figuring out the rules form experience and intuition just like the analysis of human brain. Operators do this cluster logic with fuzzy sets of fuzzy logic. When people make a decision, they estimate in a kind of thinking system and conclude according to real conditions. When import and export system were established connection, we use a set of logic expression in fuzzy logic model instead of formulas like transfer function. Computer measures and receives input data by means of reservation function and uses input data in repository to translate language expressions, which is called fuzzy. Before it stops, we made sure the linguistic expression by comparing the specific rules in function library, and linguistic judgment, and finally by real degree logic. All of computer processing results were integrated to a general result sets, which is called fuzzy reasoning[10]. There are linguistic expressions and membership function that represent objective results and supporting degrees, which is called fuzzy output.

2.4 Fuzzy Neural Networks

AI technologies like ANN, fuzzy logic and genetic algorithm have been applied in sub-area of construction management. Fuzzy logic system and ANN have some similar characteristics [4]. Their structure could be changed according to different requirements. Finally, fuzzy logic model and ANN model have been transferred into numerical scheme and calculated by computer procedure. In contrast with traditional models, they are able to work in an uncertain, inaccurate and complex environment. They estimate a function from digital example instead from math description about the output function. ANN, fuzzy logic are value of number in nature, which could be handled by math tools and described by theorem partly [12]. ANN and fuzzy logic are complementary, the former is to fetch information from learning or control system, and the latter is to analyze the language and results of computer, the best way to get their merits and avoid demerits is to integrate them to a new system. For example, we can study rules in a mixed way, and correct them to a better system [13]. FNN was formed by combing ANN and fuzzy logic technology.

After that, we can reconstruct ANN to obtain larger transparency by explaining weight matrix, we also can reduce the subjectivity of fuzzy system by developing automatic parameter adjustment from practical data. Thus, the two systems could be closer to each other because of ANN' larger transparency and fuzzy system's self-adaption. FNN have been solved plenty of problems in many areas by means of human brain simulation. It can also help people to make a decision such as relational equation, objective identification, language processing and sales forecasting [14].

Scripting shared services for both design and software developers allow all software developers to view the content of the software development script. In addition, managers can monitor the script information within the scope of authority, for example, developers of the development team can view and download script information for software development, thereby enhancing the efficiency of software development [6]. Art designers and individual managers are the main players in the auxiliary system can prepare model function. And the auxiliary system can provide design material selection function, environment lighting layout function, design work browsing and development script, information sharing function and so on for designers; in addition, it can also prepare user information management function, script information management function and so on for managers (Fig. 5).

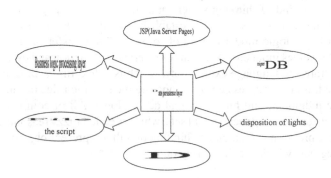

Fig. 5. Designer use case diagram

2.5 The Design of Computer Aided Art Design System

In this chapter, based on the needs of computer aided art design system, research is carried out, and then the use goal of the auxiliary system is determined. In addition, the comprehensive structure of the system and the detailed function of many modules are also designed on the above premise. During the design period, the following requirements should be followed [7]. In the design period, the auxiliary system needs to meet most of the designers' standards for computer aided design system, so as to work independently in the main art design. In addition, it is necessary to ensure the efficiency, stability and reliability of the design, so that the auxiliary system can operate smoothly [8].

Under normal circumstances, in the specific design of auxiliary systems, each function of the system will be modular processing. On the one hand, each module is relatively independent, and is convenient to update and maintain; on the other hand, when some module functions fail, the function of other modules will not be affected. Of course, each module needs an interface for external contacts [9].

The system hierarchy is designed in the computer aided design system. Scripting information sharing platform, essentially based on J2EE technology, is set at the top level of the computer communication network (the application layer) that focuses on JSP technology, HTML technology, and SERVLET technology. The Web server will operate the controlled Web application in accordance with user needs. The hierarchical partitioning diagram of the system is shown in Fig. 6.

From Fig. 6, it can be seen that many levels of the system are separate, and the division of labor is very clear. In addition, many layers of functions are encapsulated and only a unique external interface is prepared. Therefore, when the function of the module changes, as long as the interface type remains unchanged, the auxiliary system can work smoothly, and then improve the system's stability [10]. As for the system network architecture design, according to the user's needs, the network deployment diagram of the assistant system is set up. In addition, for deployment diagrams and auxiliary systems, users can use not only the LAN, but also the Internet to access art design assistance systems. However, it is worth noting that LAN users can use all the functions of the system, while Internet users can only use a small number of functions. And the above arrangement mode is mainly to enhance the security of the system [11].

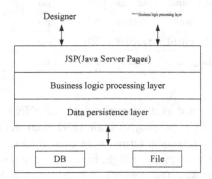

Fig. 6. System hierarchy partition diagram

Within the system function structure, the H3 technology system is used to design computer aided design system, whose goal is to maintain the scalability of the system. First, based on the system, a number of functional modules are divided, so as to facilitate modular research and development. In addition, the utilization of software code can be improved. Figure 4 shows the detailed functional structure of the system. As can be seen from Fig. 4, the functions of the system include system management, work modeling, material setting, lighting layout and sharing of software scripts. The system management module focuses on building, opening, previewing, and saving design works. The above functions are all the key parts of the auxiliary function of art design, and can also be invoked by the program of other modules [4].

To ensure that developers share, query, and download script information, additional databases are designed to complete the management of data information. In carrying out software engineering management, first of all, based on the system needs and the environment, the research is carried out. After that, the database is designed to prepare data storage, review and management services for users. Database design goes through many periods: system requirements research, outline design, system logic structure construction, model analysis and data type design. The main function of the database is to prepare data query and storage services for users and administrators. In addition, in the design period, it is also necessary to consider the compressive strength of database when it is too large. In an integrated system, if the database is out of order, the overall system is paralyzed, and so the capabilities of the database can affect how the system works. The type of information stored in the database can be divided into user's personal information and software script information [12]. The details can be referred to in Table 1.

Table 1. User information data dictionary

Field name	Type	Length	Empty or not
userinfo_id	varchar	20	No
userinfo_pass	varchar	32	No
userinfo_level	int	4	No
userinfo_name	varchar	20	no
userinfo_work	varchar	50	no
userinfo_email	varchar	50	no
userinfo_tel	varchar	20	no

Three factors were elected as the input variable of FNN model: market condition (MC), project complex (PC) and project scale (PS), their definition and value range were shown in table. Six linguistic terms were used to describe the output variable identification (M). There are degrees of high, higher, medium, lower, low and very low, and Initial weighted value was 10%, 8%, 6%, 4%, 2% and 1%. FNN model includes an input with three nodes, an input layer with three membership functions to each input node, a fuzzy reasoning layer with 27 rules and a output layer with a node. Bid sample was produced by simulation program, random assortment of project under uncertain preconditions, and identify expected percent of each project in line with fuzzy reasoning rules, eight supposed project were produced on precondition of rules. In total, 200 bid

Table 2. Three factors of KNN model for mark-up estimation

No	Influencing factors	Definition	Abbr.	Rating scale	Values	Values
1	Market condition	Current construction market	MC	0–0,4 Bad	0.5–0.7 Moderate	0.8–1.0 Good
2	Project complexity	What degree of complexity of the project?	PC	0–4 Low	5–7 Medium	8–10 High
3	Project size	Project size estimated in dollar volume	PS	$0–10 M		

samples were produced for model training and five new samples were produced for model experiment (Table 2).

3 Results and Discussion

In order to ensure the availability of software, the expected use of the software, the smooth operation of the software, and user's best use effect, the software was compared and the performance was tested. The use of testing not only can ensure the full completion of all functions, but also the overall handling of problems in the software [13].

The entity computer is the main organization of the testing work, which mostly conforms to the user's environment at a certain level. Only on the physical computer can the test elements of some hardware, peripherals and their drivers, and multiple-network access environment be reached [14]. In reality, there are many problems that can't be dealt with by using an entity machine as a test machine, for example, many machines configured to operate many system platforms are expensive, and in addition, an environment of problems can't be fully stored. The initiation of the virtual machine can realize the complementarity between the overall and the physical computer. A virtual machine is actually the software running on an entity computer, which can partition the CPU / memory / hard disk resource of an entity computer into one or more virtual machines in accordance with specific rules. In this way, each entity can operate multiple virtual machines, and each virtual machine can be equipped with a separate operating system and application software. The advantages of a virtual machine are: it can operate many operating systems on a single computer, including Windows, Linux, and so on; a virtual PC environment for all Windows applications can be set up to allow a computer to run many platforms in the Windows series; the cost of capital can be reduced by increasing energy efficiency, reducing hardware requirements, and increasing the ratio of servers / administrators; the highest availability and performance of the application can be guaranteed; improved disaster recovery processing scheme is adopted to improve service continuity and achieve high availability.

By performing performance testing scripts, performance data was gathered, which focused on three parts: response time, execution efficiency, and resource utilization. From the point of view of version performance test data, the final conclusion of software performance can't be obtained. In reality, testers perform horizontal and vertical comparisons of performance data to show how good or bad the software is. The horizontal comparison is mainly to compare the performance data of the test software with that of the competing software on the market, usually based on the mainline outgoing version. For competing software, the latest version of the software is the main target. In addition, tests are implemented in the same test environment, so that the overall strength of the software can be mastered in the performance part before sending it out. The vertical comparison is to compare the current version of the test software with the previously tested version of the more stable performance. In general, if the test project does not have anything to do with the network environment, data from the same test machine and the same mirror with the same script is believable. As a result, performance data for previous releases is available for immediate use, so that the performance changes of each version of the software can also be controlled. Depending on the integration and modification of the development section, as well as the expected performance changes of the new functionality, the functional changes to version software can be evaluated. The difference between performance testing and functional testing is that functional testing should be detected in a clean environment, and the test results are valid. However, performance tests are different. Different test machines and different mirror images will lead to differences in the testing environment, so that the test data loses the credibility of the contrast. As a result, each project in the performance test requires a stable test machine and a stable system image. And all items will be divided into multiple testers based on test frequency. At the time of testing, projects on each test machine can be developed together, but the automation of the scripts is required. Performing performance test data is shown in Table 3.

Table 3. Perform performance test data

Degree value and risk level	Data server	Office computer	Network link device	Input/output device	Operating system	Application platform
Membership value	0.3862	0.3656	0.2658	0.1258	0.3268	0.4523
Security level	4	3	3	2	5	4

4 Conclusion

It is hard to estimate costs, profits and risks due to the uncertainty of project during construction cost estimation. If cost engineers have the ability to predict accurately the errors of estimation, they could prepare emergency funds, emergency plans for a rainy day. This chapter studies ANN technology to improve the accuracy of construction cost estimation and to predict estimation errors conveniently by model study. The model hypotheses are more flexible than regressive modelling. At the same time, the construction cost estimation system designed by this chapter adopt fuzzy logic model as costs decision- making.

The results of experiment have shown the effectiveness of ANN model in predicting costs during construction cost estimation. After estimation costs showing, this system is able to extend to practical costs in predicted project, which requires further research to obtain larger samples for improving prediction of model. Future research would seek to integrate AI and probability estimate. Probability estimate model of AI is not to obtain point estimation, but to produce minimum estimation and estimation of most possible, which will provide more useful information for decision-making. Before the software development of the computer aided art design system, the requirement analysis and feasibility analysis of the software must be carried out. In this chapter, the research status and existing problems of the mature computer aided design system both at home and abroad were expounded in detail. In addition, according to the actual situation, the performance requirements analysis and functional requirements analysis of the auxiliary system were summarized, in which, the performance requirements were mainly composed of the processing efficiency and the design effect of the auxiliary system. There are also obvious disadvantages in the design of the auxiliary system. Since then, the auxiliary system is the focus of the analysis direction, and is also the main trend of art design. Now art designers need to pay more attention to the design basis, appreciation level and creativity.

References

1. Bourcier, W.L., Wolery, T.J., Wolfe, T.: A preliminary cost and engineering estimate for desalinating produced formation water associated with carbon dioxide capture and storage. Int. J. Greenhouse Gas Control 5(5), 1319–1328 (2011)
2. Aibinu, A.A., Pasco, T.: The accuracy of pretender building cost estimates in Australia. Construction Manage. Econo. 26(12), 1257–1269 (2008)
3. Narbaev, T.: Analysis of causes of delay and time performance in construction projects. J. Constr. Eng. Manag. 140(1), 999–1003 (2014)
4. Sheta, A.F., Ayesh, A., Rine, D.: Evaluating software cost estimation models using particle swarm optimisation and fuzzy logic for NASA projects: a comparative study. Int. J. Bio-Inspired Computation 2(6), 365–373 (2010)
5. Lin-Yu, Y.U., Sun, W.J., Wang, A.L.: A method of cost estimate based on component software simulation. Computer Simulation 23(12), 93-95 (2006)
6. Montequ, V.R.: Software project cost estimation using AI techniques. Wseas/iasme International Conference on Systems Theory and Scientific Computation. World Scientific and Engineering Academy and Society (WSEAS), pp. 289–293 (2005)
7. Chen, W.H.: Contractor costs of factoring account receivables for a construction project. J. Civ. Eng. Manag. 18(2), 227–234 (2012)
8. Lamprecht, A.-L.: Lessons learned. In: Lamprecht, A.-L. (ed.) User-Level Workflow Design. LNCS, vol. 8311, pp. 141–162. Springer, Heidelberg (2013). https://doi.org/10.1007/978-3-642-45389-2_7
9. Aretoulis, G.N., Kalfakakou, G.P., Seridou, A.A.: Project managers' profile influence on design and implementation of cost monitoring and control systems for construction projects. Int. J. Information Technol. Project Manage. 6(3), 1–25 (2015)
10. Knight, K., Fayek, A.R.: Use of fuzzy logic for predicting design cost overruns on building projects. J. Constr. Eng. Manag. 128(6), 503–512 (2002)

11. Rajawat, A.S., Rawat, R., Shaw, R.N., Ghosh, A.: Cyber physical system fraud analysis by mobile robot. In: Bianchini, M., Simic, M., Ghosh, A., Shaw, R.N. (eds.) Machine Learning for Robotics Applications. SCI, vol. 960, pp. 47–61. Springer, Singapore (2021). https://doi.org/10.1007/978-981-16-0598-7_4
12. Vanhoucke, M., Vereecke, A., Gemmel, P.: The project scheduling game (PSG): simulating time/cost trade-offs in projects. Proj. Manag. J. 36(1), 51–59 (2005)
13. Shi, H., Li, W.: The integrated methodology of rough set theory and artificial neural-network for construction project cost prediction. In: International Symposium on Intelligent Information Technology Application, pp. 60–64 IEEE (2008)
14. Attarzadeh, I., Ow, S.H.: Proposing a new software cost estimation model based on artificial neural networks. In: International Conference on Computer Engineering and Technology, pp. 487–491 (2010)

BBACTFM (Blockchain Based Accurate Contact Tracing Framework Model) for Tourism Industry

B. C. Girish Kumar[1]($\boxtimes$) (iD), Parma Nand[1] (iD), and Vikram Bali[2] (iD)

[1] Computer Science and Engineering, Sharda University, Greater Noida, India
girishkumar@jssaten.ac.in
[2] IMS College of Engineering, Ghaziabad, India

Abstract. Contact tracing is, at its core, a straightforward and logical operation. The testing facility or healthcare facility that performed the test notifies the neighborhood public health department if a person tests positive for any communicable disease (such as COVID-19, omicron). The health department then contacts the sick person and asks them to list any contacts they had for a predetermined amount of time before to the test. The health department then gets in touch with these people to request a test. The process is repeated until all of the patients have tested negative if any of those patients have a positive result. Patients who test positive for a disease are typically informed of how long they must spend in quarantine and are publicly notified after they "recover." Blockchain technology can anonymize patient records and offer higher degrees of protection to maintain the privacy of tourist health details. Since test results are connected to a visitor's public/private key rather than their Personal ID, their name or identity cannot be determined by simply browsing or querying the blockchain. In addition, since every blockchain entry is cryptographically signed, malicious parties are unable to alter a record without also invalidating all future records. Additional controls can be added using identity access management software to restrict what data a user can read on the blockchain. The shortcomings of conventional contact tracing applications would be resolved by our proposed framework, dubbed BBACTFM (Blockchain Based Accurate Contact Tracing Framework Model for Tourism Industry).

Keywords: Blockchain · Covid-19 · Tourism · BCT · Contact tracing · Tourist

1 Introduction

Contact tracking [2] has been widely utilized to stop the transmission of Coronavirus-2019 [1] (COVID-19). It enables the detection, evaluation, and treatment of persons, who have been exposed to COVID-19 [3], preventing the virus's further spread. Today's market's majority of contact tracing methodologies [1], tools, and solutions fall short of providing decentralized, transparent, traceable, irreversible, auditable, secure, and reliable qualities. In this research work, we describe a decentralized blockchain-based COVID-19 contact tracking solution [4]. Contact tracking can significantly lessen the requirement

R. N. Shaw et al. (Eds.): ICACIS 2022, CCIS 1749, pp. 517–532, 2023.
https://doi.org/10.1007/978-3-031-25088-0_46

for a quick pandemic response [5]. We employ the immutable [8] and tamper-proof [9] characteristics of Blockchain to impose trust [6], accountability [3], and transparency [7]. On-chain [10] and off-chain data are linked together using trustworthy and registered oracles. There are no centralized [13] or third-party systems involved, making the users' medical information impervious to invasion, hacking [11], or abuse. Each user's digital medical passports [14] are utilized for registration. The users' whereabouts are updated after a 20-min delay in order to safeguard their privacy. Using Ethereum smart contracts, transactions [8] are carried out on-chain with emitted events and immutable logs. In-depth descriptions of the implemented algorithms and the outcomes of their testing are provided. We examine the suggested approach's security, cost, and privacy aspects to show that it is successful.

Blockchain

A blockchain is a type of distributed ledger that is made up of blocks. Every block contains a collection of transactions that are encrypted [30]. Formal paraphrase Because accountability is distributed across the entire network, the dynamic features of blockchain assist us in making this operation safer and more transparent. In international transactions, a similar effect can occur, increasing trust among all parties involved [6]. The first part of this essay examines the foundations of blockchain technology and highlights the elements that are crucial to comprehending the rest of the implementation. Recognising its limitations and using it in the tourism sector [10]. What features and disadvantages of blockchain could shape the future of the travel and tourism sector? (Table 1).

Table 1. Blockchain characteristics and benefits [3, 5

Areas	Description
Secure transaction	Different encryption methods are supported by the blockchain algorithm to enable safe transactions and reduce the risk of data fraud
Disintermediaries	Blockchain technology reduces the use of intermediaries across industries
Data integrity	Data alteration won't take place
Decentralization	Blockchain is designed without a centralised server, therefore each user's identity is not necessary
Immutability	All users linked to a chain can see data recorded in a blockchain, and all users will have the same view of the data
Transparency	Users can exchange similar master records on the blockchain network, which promotes high user consistency and accuracy
Trust	Blockchain platform enables trustworthiness and security of payment distribution
Accurate-Contact tracing app	A contact tracing tool with blockchain technology can assist to stop the COVID-19 infection from spreading further, which will boost tourism

Contact tracing is, at its core, a straightforward and logical operation [8]. The testing facility or healthcare facility that conducted the test notifies the neighborhood public health agency if a person tests positive for SARS-Cov-2. The health department then contacts the sick person and asks them to list any contacts they had for a predetermined amount of time before to the test. The health department then gets in touch with these people to request a test.

The process is repeated until all of the patients have tested negative if any of those patients have a positive result [9]. Patients who have tested positive for a disease are frequently advised of the length of time they must remain in quarantine and are formally notified after they have "recovered." (Fig. 1).

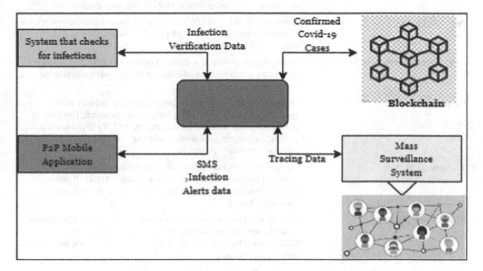

Fig. 1. The information on a blockchain network

The logistical and administrative framework that makes the "test and trace" program possible, however, is not straightforward. Several components are required in order to correctly carry out the aforesaid process:

1) Timely, accurate tests
2) A system that allows for the transfer of patient data from the physician to the public health department and patient contacts workforce to call patients and possible contacts.

2 Literature Review

(Table 2 and 3).

Table 2. Opportunities for coordinating contact as the tourism industry advances in the future smart society (Source: Mbunge, Elliot. 2020).

New innovations [2]	Applications for COVID-19 contact tracing that could be used
Artificial intelligence [3]	The Irish government has declared intentions to use COVID-19, a new system for tracking the body temperatures of those thought to be at risk for heatstroke. It seeks to enable users of Smartphone's, smart watches, smart thermometers, and other devices to check their body temperatures
Internet of Things-IoT [4]	Permit experts to access COVID-19 data for contacts on a continuing basis Remote monitoring of COVID-19 patients in isolation facilities is equivalent to self-isolation
Geographical information systems(GIS) [5]	The movement of patients and contact persons will be tracked in real-time by the GIS, which will also offer data on the epidemic's effects on the local population's health
Big data [6]	Be a part of public welfare data frameworks (HIS) and keep records (portability designs) on a running basis for more research. This links prosperous policymakers to logical screening COVID-19 and resource designation Increase consideration, planning, and correspondence. Support effective video conferencing
Blockchain technology [7]	Confirm and assist Prior to the strategy of leading organizations and managing patients' medication in private offices, COVID-19 patients. Encode economic data as it goes from one centre to the next using a standard architecture
5G Technology [8]	Increase transmission capacity size, administration type, and information transfer rate to provide ongoing access to information enables teleconference between COVID-19 patients, contact persons, and medical services professionals

Table 3. Coordination issues with emerging innovations within COVID-19 contact after exercises (Source: Mbunge, Elliot. 2020) 2020 (Xu, Hao, Lei Zhang)

Source	Challenges	Description
[9]	Asymptomatic individuals	Asymptomatic individuals transmit COVID-19 yet show no symptoms of the infection. Contamination and control issues are present, but they are not particularly committed. This suggests that contact after focusing more on close encounters is likely to be insufficient until clinical testing is complete
[9]	Surfaced significant technical limitations	Users may track down their phone numbers, emails, and other information on the Bitcoin network using the contact tracking software Blue Trace for Bitcoin. The system must be built, installed, configured, and managed by highly skilled professionals.Such professionals are scarce in many parts of the world, making it challenging to find them

(continued)

Table 3. (*continued*)

Source	Challenges	Description
[9, 10]	Absence of supporting data and correspondence	In certain countries, the integration of emerging technologies into healthcare frameworks is still in its infancy. In the COVID-19 pandemic approach, there are no guidelines or a strategy for electronic information assurance. Poorly ICT-developed nations like Chad and the Central African Republic believe it is challenging to allocate limited resources on mechanical improvement
[9]	Socio-economic inequalities	Web connectivity and expensive analytical tools are needed to connect people to high-risk groups, which can be expensive. According to the report, business specialist cooperatives and the affected government can zero rate COVID-19 contact following applications or lower the cost of web information
[9]	Deactivation of mobile phone Wi-Fi and GPS settings	The current contact following applications uses Bluetooth standards, Wi-Fi, and GPS technology to monitor the movements of infected people. The environment, the diversity of conventions, and the parodying of GPS signals can all work against these developments. It is legal for people to customize the association settings on their cell phones
[13]	Issues with standards and interoperability	Contact the Internet of Things and embrace it by using the programmes listed below. Patient and contact information is instantly and continually transferred to the public wellbeing data frameworks. Since these contact-following applications are not universally used, each country must have its own information architecture
[10, 13]	Security risks	Contact-following applications misuse people's information security, secrecy, respectability, and accessibility. They also occasionally link morality to patient protection. When implementing new developments in managing Covid-19, precautions must be taken to prevent health information loss and unauthorized access. The majority of COVID19 contact following applications enables simultaneous access to health data
[10, 13]	Privacy issues	The security of an individual has not been taken into account by wellbeing frameworks while creating contact after arrangements. As they collect, analyze, and approach personal health information including wellbeing conduct, status, travel history, family facilities, and location, some mobile applications infringe on people's privacy
[13]	Political and structural responses	The acceptance of electronic well-being intercessions is significantly impacted by the lack of political will and contribution on the part of state and local governments. Despite the convergence of ICTs, several countries are not focused on further expanding the delivery of medical care. This may be attributed to expenses associated with the setup, reconciliation, and maintenance of emerging technologies

(*continued*)

Table 3. (*continued*)

Source	Challenges	Description
[13]	Ethical and legal risks	The COVID-19 computer applications come in four different varieties. They were created for pandemic management, isolate control, contact and follow-up monitoring, signs testing, and stream demonstrating. By providing little safety to corrupted individuals, these computerized programmes violate general wellness moral standards and information moral standards
[13]	Symptoms checkers	In Spain, accurate and computerized thermometers are used as illustrative reconnaissance tools. Medical services professionals may now collect temperature data from people thanks to accurate thermometers and mobile applications. Manifestation checkers are skilled at screening COVID-19 suspects in crowded areas and emergency situations
[13]	Consent and voluntariness	Applications for contact tracing should allow users to practice assent withdrawal. Although there are obstacles, consent-based information sharing reduces the likelihood of harm. Language barriers, a lack of contact tracing tools, and a lack of the option to refuse consent are all present. Assent withdrawal and COVID-19 regulation must work in unison
[13]	Abuse of contact following applications	The majority of contact tracing applications uses GPS and Bluetooth, which can be used for following by malicious clients. To prevent fake data from being sent to healthcare professionals, contact following applications should incorporate step acknowledgement and other action acknowledgment approaches that involve biometric verification
[13]	Discrimination	Applications for tracking contacts pose a significant risk of segregation, especially for those who have been influenced. Assignment and distribution of COVID-19 assets might be impacted by information from contact following applications. In some settings, this information may lead to segregation and irrational behavior. Both Android and iOS devices can access the app
[9]	Digital divide	In many healthcare systems in certain major lands, like Africa, the advanced separation continues to be a problem. The reconciliation of contact after applications acknowledges that everyone comes. Despite recent improvements, there is still a gap between public access to and use of ICT

3 Proposed System

By using a contact tracing technology built on the blockchain, we hope to stop the spread of COVID-19 infections [1]. To overcome the contact tracing issues, we make use of the inherent qualities of blockchain technology [11]. As a result, the adopted solution respects the user's privacy. It is unchangeable, transparent, and by design, accountability is a feature. Blockchain is a distributed, decentralized [12] shared ledger with unchangeable, tamper-proof logs. Every node in the linked list maintains a local copy of every other node. From supply chain management to e-commerce, blockchain offers a wide range of uses. Blockchain has shown to be a flexible technology that may be applied in a variety of ways to reduce the spread of illnesses in the context of the COVID-19 pandemic [13]. One of the numerous ways that blockchain has shown to be effective in eradicating the pandemic's effects is contact tracing. The use of the Ethereum blockchain and the added programmable logic provided by smart contracts enables the various parties to be open, responsible, and dependable. Third-party servers, centralized systems [14], and identity fraud are all eliminated by our approach. Transparency and trust are enforced through the immutable logs of the distributed ledger. On-chain transactions [15] are all signed by the author of the transaction. As a result, everyone on the chain is responsible for their actions.

We suggest using blockchain to establish a connection between the user/patient and the authorized problem solvers in order to desensitize user ID and location data. Our technique demonstrates superior security and privacy when compared to recently proposed contact tracing [5] solutions, with the added benefits of being battery-friendly and available anywhere. Results indicate viability from both a server and a mobile phone perspective in terms of the necessary resource. In light of the aforementioned difficulties and problems, improved privacy protection, improved contact tracing efficiency, and improved ability to combat false information are needed for the post-pandemic [16] contact tracing. Our blockchain-enabled contact tracing [17], which satisfies both privacy and performance requirements, is presented because we believe that there should be no compromise between privacy and tracing performance.

We think the effectiveness of contact tracing also matters by protecting user privacy [18]. The effectiveness of the tracing network's infection prevention measures, as well as its level of technological sophistication and geographic [19] reach, should be used to evaluate its overall performance. Because they are restricted to a local network, the present decentralized [20] solutions do not affect a larger group of users.

The importance of privacy [1] should be appreciated from the beginning to the finish, and contact tracing [21] requires a whole life cycle solution for privacy. The life cycle of the shared data should be managed at the users' fingertips. Users of contact tracing shall have complete authority to use key management to share and cancel sharing at any moment. Additionally, sensitive user data must only be shared inside a reliable, audited cooperation by public entities. With the use of cryptography [22], the suggested blockchain platform may offer individuals and organizations comprehensive credential management functions.

The user's privacy is protected at all times during the tracing scheme, and the duration of data storage should also be governed by the General Data Protection Regulation (GDPR) [18] and recommendations made by health organizations, such as the World Health Organization (WHO) [23], which suggested a minimum tracing cycle length of 14 days. In other words, generation, sharing, and deposition will all preserve the user's privacy [17] to the fullest extent possible. Nevertheless, due to technological limitations of blockchain, the data cannot be erased from the blockchain but must instead be preserved as cipher text that no one can decipher once the specified amount of time has passed.

4 Tools and Methodologies

Ethereum
You can currently choose from a wide variety of platforms to construct your DApp [24]. They consist of well-known blockchain technologies including Cardano, Hyperledger Fabric, and Ethereum [21]. Ethereum appears [21, 30] to be the greatest option out of all of these due to the vibrant community, useful tools, and online tutorials. Ethereum employs Solidity [8], which is another factor in our decision. Smart contracts and DApps can be developed and deployed using Solidity. You can experiment freely and it is simple to learn.

Using Ethereum, we'll create a basic blockchain application [18, 31]. Ethereum is an open source, decentralized blockchain that supports smart contracts. Second-generation blockchain technology Ethereum offers cutting-edge capabilities like smart contracts [6], Proof-of-Stake [8], and, most crucially, the capacity to develop decentralized applications (DApps).

Ganache
An Ethereum [25] development tool is called Ganache. It enables you to manage, deploy, and create tests, smart contracts, and apps. The high-end development tool Ganache is used to operate your own local blockchain for the creation of both Ethereum and Corda DApps. Ganache is useful during the entire development process.

You can create, implement, and test your projects and smart contracts on the local chain in a deterministic and secure setting. Ganache [8] comes in two "versions," a desktop programme and a command-line utility. The command-line tool, Ganache-CLI, only allows Ethereum [21] development, whereas the desktop application, Ganache UI, offers development for both Corda and Ethereum.

Furthermore, Mac, Windows, and Linux users can use any of Ganache's variants. You should be able to use it using the command-line tool once it has been installed. To create a private Ethereum Blockchain [21] for testing Solidity contracts, utilize Ganache.

Node.js
Our next tool that has to be installed is Node.js [7]. You must install the Node Package Manager [26] in order for the private blockchain to function on your computer. After installation, launch your terminal and enter $node -v. If it starts up, you are ready to go. A distributed [3] database, the blockchain contains all of the data on every node. No central server exists. The remaining nodes will still have the whole blockchain even if

hackers take out one of them. Every node may operate as a ledger for all transactions since it always has the most recent state of the database.

Metamask Ethereum Wallet
We require a wallet that can be used from a browser because we will be working on the Ethereum blockchain. A web browser wallet called Metamask [27] enables communication with the Ethereum blockchain. Once installed, it gives users the ability to hold Ethereum and other ERC-20 tokens, allowing them to send payments to any Ethereum address. Users can utilize a browser extension or mobile app to access their Ethereum wallet [27], which can then be used to connect with decentralized applications. DApps [28] are simply too challenging for many consumers to use. By decreasing the entry barrier to the great world of DApps and delivering the decentralized web to the general public, Metamask aims to change that.

Truffle Framework
The Truffle Framework [27] is the last piece of software we'll set up. The Ethereum Virtual Machine (EVM)-based blockchain development environment, testing framework, and asset pipeline known as Truffle was created with developers in mind. It provides a large selection of tools that you may use to work productively on your DApp. A Solidity programme [28] can be used to create an Ethereum smart contract [21].

Some of the key Truffle Framework [7] features include the following

- Proper smart contract management
- Networking management
- Automated testing
- Development Console
- Script Runner
- Deployment and Migrations
- Client-Side Development.

To install, you need to use the npm [7] command. Simply run the following command in the command line:

$ **npm install − g truffle@5.0.2**

Algorithm-1 Steps to be followed to Use BBACTFM (Blockchain Based Accurate Contact Tracing Framework Model:
Step1:
On his Smartphone, the user first downloads the app from the App or Google store.
Step2:
The user can register using the registration page that appears. If a user is entirely new to the app, he will first need to register and create an account with accurate information.
Step3:
If a person has previously registered, he or she can sign in with their credentials. The user can immediately log in using his information if he has previously registered.
Step4:
The user must enter personal information after logging in or signing up to assist the authorities in securely storing that information for accurate disease[9] detection. In order to track their past locations and the people they've met in the previous seven to fourteen days, the user must grant access to their location.
Step5:
If an infection is found, the information is given to the authorities, who then get in touch with the sick person and asks them to name any individuals they have come into contact with within a certain time frame before the test.
Step6:
The authorities then get in touch with such individuals and ask them to submit to a test. The process is repeated until a set of all patients who underwent negative testing is reached, in case any of those patients had tested positive for the condition. Authorities frequently inform those who have tested positive for the illness of how long they must stay in quarantine and will formally notify them once they have "recovered."

The below Fig. 2.shows the flow of how our proposed system will work in terms of tracing the Covid-19/infection disease for further spreading of diseases. The above steps also gives the clear idea of how to use this accurate contact tracing application to stop further spreading of infected disease (Figs. 2 and 3).

5   Comparative Analysis of Tourist Arrivals in Domestic and International Tourism

A. Analysis of domestic and international tourism (UN World Tourism Organization) (Table 4 and 5, Figs. 4, 5 and 6).
B. Feasibility Study
    Due to the project's minimal cost requirements, it has been determined that it is extremely viable to begin widespread utilization. It is very affordable and simple for regular people to utilize because no actual hardware needs to be bought. It only needs a little installation to get started, so doctors [29] may use it right away.

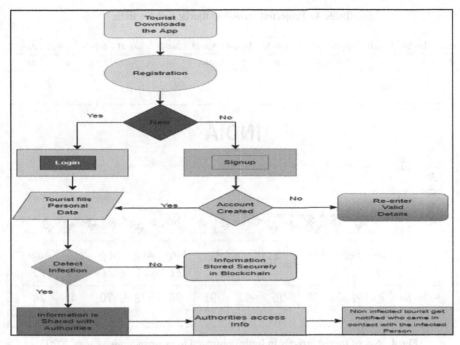

Fig. 2. Flowchart for accurate contact tracing (DApp)

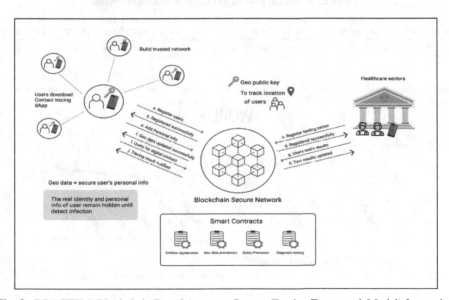

Fig. 3. BBACTFM (Blockchain Based Accurate Contact Tracing Framework Model) for tourism industry

Table 4. Projected growth in tourist arrivals India

India	Jan-20	Feb-20	Apr-20	Jul-20	Oct-20	Jan-20	Apr-21	Jun-21	Aug-21	Sep-21	Jan-22	Aug-22
%	9	7	−100	−98	−96	−92	−91	−96	−78	−70	4	24

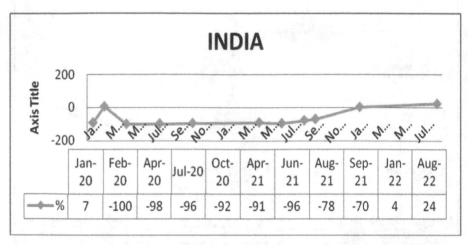

Fig. 4. No. of tourist arrivals in India compared to pre-pandemic year of 2020

Table 5. Projected growth in tourist arrivals worldwide

World	Jan-20	Feb-20	Apr-20	Jul-20	Oct-20	Nov-20	Dec-20	Jan-21	Apr-21	Jun-21	Aug-21	Sep-21	Jan-22	Aug-22
%	1	−14	−97	−79	−82	−85	−89	−86	−85	−77	−63	−63	4	16

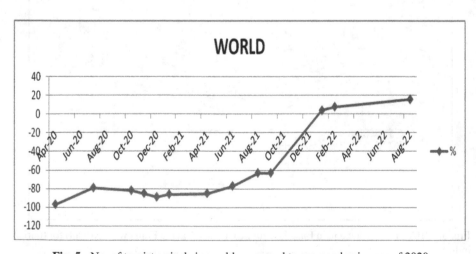

Fig. 5. No. of tourist arrivals in world compared to pre-pandemic year of 2020

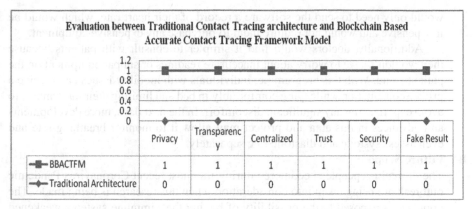

Fig. 6. Comparison chart (0 indicates 'No' 1 indicates 'Yes')

6 Conclusion

The world has been shocked by the COVID-19 epidemic's global effects on human health. Numerous nations were unprepared to combat the pandemic because of how swiftly it spread, which led to needless fatalities. Nations instituted lockdown procedures with varied degrees of rigor as soon as the hospital system started to exhibit signs of overcrowding in order to stop the epidemic from spreading throughout the neighborhood. 32 nations have released smartphone applications that collect data of various kinds to track the movements of people under lockdown and keep tabs on neighborhood relations. A thorough review of 32 countries' worth of apps finds that they collect a lot of user information, which is a severe invasion of privacy. India also released Arogya sethu application but some limitation exists in this App like privacy, Security, trust and other. According to an analysis, the applications gathered information on user symptoms, contact identification, type of contact with COVID/Infection disease positive people, and demographics. As a result, consumers expressed concerns about their privacy and the apps were not well received by them. Our proposed system named BBACTFM (Blockchain Based Accurate Contact Tracing Framework Model) helps with cutting-edge, privacy-preserving COVID-19 and other infection disease contact tracing architecture.

A. Real-World Applications

The difficulties that people encountered during the most recent Coronavirus Pandemic outbreak were taken into consideration when developing this model. The populace is exposed to the possibility of having their immune systems weakened to the point of organ failure as they wait to be exposed to a virus. Due to the ongoing epidemic and the absolute lockdown, many persons with a common cold fever also worried that they had contracted the COVID-19 virus. They also found it difficult to access competent medical care that might allay their concerns.

If properly implemented, this research work could solve every issue that the general public encounters. In order to receive the necessary consultation, patients would only need to send the software a record of their heart rate, which would be inexpensive and would not require them to purchase any expensive equipment.

Additionally, doctors would find it simpler to consult with patients because they wouldn't have to worry about inaccurate readings or subpar equipment on the patient's end. With this programme, individuals with mobility issues can receive a private consultation while lying comfortably in bed and limiting their movements to avoid experiencing any significant discomfort. In the next days, more developments and advances in this area and project may allow it to monitor breathing rate and even assess systolic and diastolic rate separately.

B. **Future Scope**

The difficulties people encountered during the most recent Coronavirus Pandemic outbreak are being taken into consideration when this research is being made. The populace is exposed to the possibility of having their immune systems weakened to the point of organ failure as they wait to be exposed to a virus. Due to the ongoing epidemic and the absolute lockdown, many persons with a common cold fever also worried that they had contracted the COVID-19 virus. They also found it difficult to access competent medical care that might allay their concerns. If properly implemented, this research work could solve every issue that the general public encounters. Since the system is cost-effective and doesn't require any expensive equipment at all, all that would be needed for the required consultation is for the general public to record their heart rate using the software and send it to the appropriate doctors. Additionally, doctors would find it simpler to consult with patients because they wouldn't have to worry about inaccurate readings or subpar equipment on the patient's end.

With this programme, individuals with mobility issues can receive a private consultation while lying comfortably in bed and limiting their movements to avoid experiencing any significant discomfort. In the next days, more developments and advances in this area and project may allow it to monitor breathing rate and even assess systolic and diastolic rate separately.

Benefits of Blockchain. Better Security, Immutability, Efficiency, and Traceability, as well as Greater Transparency [4, 15].

Conflict of Interest. The authors claim that our interests are the same.

Funding. No funding

Ethical Approval. The writers of this work do not limit their research to a single subject or animal.

References

1. Abdul-Raheem, I.: Covid-19 Contact Tracing and Tracking, vol. 7, pp. 2456–4184 (2022). www.ijnrd.org
2. Gurudas Vernekar, A.: Blockchain based water management system. Int. Res. J. Eng. Technol, pp. 7505–7507 (2020). www.irjet.net
3. Pahontu, B., Arsene, D., Predescu, A., Mocanu, M.: Application and challenges of Blockchain technology for real-time operation in a water distribution system. In: 2020 24th Int. Conf. Syst. Theory, Control Comput. ICSTCC 2020 - Proc., pp. 739–744 (2020). https://doi.org/10.1109/ICSTCC50638.2020.9259732
4. Pincheira, M., Vecchio, M., Giaffreda, R., Kanhere, S.S.: Exploiting constrained IoT devices in a trustless blockchain-based water management system. IEEE Int. Conf. Blockchain Cryptocurrency, ICBC 2020 (2020). https://doi.org/10.1109/ICBC48266.2020.9169404
5. Klaine, P.V., Zhang, L., Zhou, B., Sun, Y., Xu, H., Imran, M.: Privacy-preserving contact tracing and public risk assessment using blockchain for COVID-19 pandemic. IEEE Internet Things Mag. 3(3), 58–63 (2020). https://doi.org/10.1109/iotm.0001.2000078
6. Ardito, L., Cerchione, R., Del Vecchio, P., Raguseo, E.: Big data in smart tourism: challenges, issues and opportunities. Curr. Issues Tour. 22(15), 1805–1809 (2019). https://doi.org/10.1080/13683500.2019.1612860
7. Nand, P., Bali, V.: BLOBDBM : Blockchain Based Framework for Decentralized Business model in Tourism industry I. Introduction.
8. Bari, N., Qamar, U., Khalid, A.: Efficient Contact Tracing for pandemics using blockchain. Informatics Med. Unlocked 26, 100742 (2021). https://doi.org/10.1016/j.imu.2021.100742
9. Mbunge, E.: Integrating emerging technologies into COVID-19 contact tracing: Opportunities, challenges and pitfalls. Diabetes Metab. Syndr. Clin. Res. Rev. 14(6), 1631–1636 (2020). https://doi.org/10.1016/j.dsx.2020.08.029
10. Xu, H., Zhang, L., Onireti, O., Fang, Y., Buchanan, W.B., Imran, M.A.: BeepTrace: Blockchain-enabled Privacy-preserving Contact Tracing for COVID-19 Pandemic and Beyond. 8(5), 3915–3929 (2020). https://doi.org/10.1109/jiot.2020.3025953
11. Önder, I., Treiblmaier, H.: Blockchain and tourism: three research propositions. Ann. Tour. Res. 72(C), 180–182 (2018). https://doi.org/10.1016/j.annals.2018.03.005
12. Pillai, B.G., Madhurya, J.A.: A decentralized data privacy for mobile payment using blockchain technology. Int. J. Recent Technol. Eng. 8(6), 5260–5264 (2020). https://doi.org/10.35940/ijrte.f9426.038620
13. Iyengar, K., Upadhyaya, G.K., Vaishya, R., Jain, V.: COVID-19 and applications of smartphone technology in the current pandemic. Diabetes Metab. Syndr. Clin. Res. Rev. 14(5), 733–737 (2020). https://doi.org/10.1016/j.dsx.2020.05.033
14. Tasatanattakool, P., Techapanupreeda, C.: Blockchain: challenges and applications. International Conference Information Networking, pp. 473–475 (2018). https://doi.org/10.1109/ICOIN.2018.8343163
15. Swati, V., Prasad, A.S.: Application of blockchain technology in travel industry. In: 2018 International Conference Circuits System Digital Enterprise Technology ICCSDET, pp. 1–5 (2018). https://doi.org/10.1109/ICCSDET.2018.8821095
16. Seyitoğlu, F., Ivanov, S.: Service robots as a tool for physical distancing in tourism. Curr. Issues Tour. 24(12), 1631–1634 (2021). https://doi.org/10.1080/13683500.2020.1774518
17. Xu, H., Zhang, L., Onireti, O., Fang, Y., Buchanan, W.J., Imran, M.A.: BeepTrace: blockchain-enabled privacy-preserving contact tracing for COVID-19 Pandemic and beyond. IEEE Internet Things J. 8(5), 3915–3929 (2021). https://doi.org/10.1109/JIOT.2020.3025953
18. Oksiiuk, O., Dmyrieva, I.: Security and privacy issues of blockchain technology. In: Proceedings. - 15th International Conference Advanced Trends Radioelectronics Telecommunications

Computer Engineering TCSET, pp. 531–535 (2020). https://doi.org/10.1109/TCSET49122.2020.235489

19. Ricci, L., Di Francesco Maesa, D., Favenza, A., Ferro, E.: Blockchains for covid-19 contact tracing and vaccine support: a systematic review. IEEE Access **9**, 37936–37950 (2021). https://doi.org/10.1109/ACCESS.2021.3063152

20. Xia, W., Chen, X., Song, C.: A framework of blockchain technology in intelligent water management. Front. Environ. Sci. **10**(June), 1–12 (2022). https://doi.org/10.3389/fenvs.2022.909606

21. Hasan, H.R., Salah, K., Jayaraman, R., Yaqoob, I., Omar, M., Ellahham, S.: COVID-19 contact tracing using blockchain. IEEE Access **9**, 62956–62971 (2021). https://doi.org/10.1109/ACCESS.2021.3074753

22. Kassab, M., Destefanis, G.: Blockchain and contact tracing applications for COVID-19: the opportunity and the challenges. In: Proceeding - 2021 IEEE International Conference Software Analysis Evolution Reengineering, SANER, pp. 723–730 (2021). https://doi.org/10.1109/SANER50967.2021.00092

23. Wen, Z., Yu, K., Qi, X.: Blockchain-empowered Contact Tracing for COVID-19 Using Crypto-spatiotemporal Information, pp. 16 (2021)

24. Ozdemir, A.I., Ar, I.M., Erol, I.: Assessment of blockchain applications in travel and tourism industry. Qual. Quant. **54**(5–6), 1549–1563 (2019). https://doi.org/10.1007/s11135-019-00901-w

25. Panchamia, S., Byrappa, D.K.: Passport, VISA and Immigration Management Using Blockchain. Proceeding - 23rd Annual Conference Advanced Computing Communications ADCOM, pp. 8–17 (2017). https://doi.org/10.1109/ADCOM.2017.00009

26. Narendran, S., Pradeep, P., Ramesh, M.V.: An Internet of Things (IoT) based sustainable water management. GHTC 2017 - IEEE Global Humanitarian Technology Conference Proceeding, vol. 2017-Janua, pp. 1–6 (2017). https://doi.org/10.1109/GHTC.2017.8239320

27. Kumar, B.C., Singh, A., Patel, U., Yadav, A., Kumar, A.: Tourist and Hospitality Management using Blockchain Technology. **11**(8), 28670–28672 (2021)

28. Kumar, B.C., Mahesha, A.M., Harsha, K.G.: A Review on Data Storage & Retrieval using Blockchain Technology, **11**(8), 28630–28637 (2021)

29. Işın, A.: Current issues in tourism and hospitality management. Curr. Issues Tour. Hosp. Manag., pp. 193–206 (2019)

30. Girish Kumar, B.C., Nand, P., Bali, V.: Opportunities and challenges of blockchain technology for tourism industry in future smart society. In: 2022 Fifth International Conference on Computational Intelligence and Communication Technologies (CCICT), pp. 318–323 (2022). https://doi.org/10.1109/CCiCT56684.2022.00065

31. Girish Kumar, B.C., Nand, P., Bali, V.: Review on opportunities and challenges of blockchain technology for tourism industry in future smart society. In: Bali, V., Bhatnagar, V., Lu, J., Banerjee, K. (eds): Decision Analytics for Sustainable Development in Smart Society 5.0. Asset Analytics. Springer, Singapore (2022). https://doi.org/10.1007/978-981-19-1689-2_16

Randomized Active Learning to Identify Phishing URL

P. Ponni[1(✉)] and D. Prabha[2]

[1] Department of Computer Science and Engineering,
CMS College of Engineering and Technology, Coimbatore 641032, India
ponniramakrishna@gmail.com
[2] Department of Computer Science and Engineering,
Sri Krishna College of Engineering and Technology, Coimbatore 641008, India
prabha@skcet.ac.in

Abstract. Data analytics is rapidly being employed in cybersecurity concerns, and has been found to be beneficial in situations where large amounts of data and heterogeneity make human assessment by security specialists difficult. Obtaining data with annotations is a tough and well-known restrictive constraint for various supervised security analytics tasks in real-world cyber-security situations using data-driven analytics. Because annotation is largely manual and involves a great deal of expert effort, vast sections of large datasets are frequently left unlabeled. We adopt a randomly ranked feature active learning strategy to create a semi-supervised solution in this research to address this constraint in an applied cyber-security challenge of phishing classification. An early classifier is trained on a slight sample of interpreted data, and then iteratively updated by selecting just relevant samples from a huge pool of unlabeled data that are most likely to effect classifier presentation quickly. Randomly ranked feature Active Learning has a lot of potential in terms of achieving quicker convergence in relationships of classification presentation in a group learning environment, needing even less human annotation labor. Without requiring a significant number of marked training examples to be accessible during training, a helpful feature rank update strategy paired with active learning displays good classification results for labeling phishing/malicious URLs.

Keywords: Active learning · Feature selection · Phishing URL

1 Introduction

Phishing is one of the many sorts of fraud that may be done today, and it is becoming more prevalent. In criminal law, fraud is defined as purposeful deceit carried out only to obtain personal benefit or sully the reputation of an individual. The act of misleading someone into disclosing their personal information, usually with the intent of gaining a financial or personal advantage, can be defined as a fraud in general terms. A blacklisting service has been established by the online security community to identify hazardous websites. Using a variety of techniques such as manual reporting, web crawlers and honeypots in

R. N. Shaw et al. (Eds.): ICACIS 2022, CCIS 1749, pp. 533–539, 2023.
https://doi.org/10.1007/978-3-031-25088-0_47

conjunction with site investigation algorithms, these blacklists are created and updated regularly. Although URL blacklisting takes proven to be effective to a certain extent, that is relatively simple for an invader to trick the system by somewhat altering one or extra components of the URL string to fool the system. Inevitably, many harmful websites are not blacklisted, either because they were discovered too recently, or because they were never or erroneously reviewed by the antivirus software.

To overcome these issues, the most recent detection methodologies for cyber-security analytics in Phishing detection focus on the development of a classifier, which is often done in a supervised environment. The availability of enough data samples from both phishing and benign categories is a critical assumption for the majority of these tasks to achieve satisfactory classification performance in both malicious and benign categories [1]. The work of explaining the vast quantity of data accessible online, on the other hand, is often too time-consuming and needs a significant level of human involvement on the part of security analysts in real-world applications. The understanding of numerous components of the underlying phishing mechanism, surveyed by the attack forms, is necessary to report the problematic with a more discriminatory approach, on the other hand [2]. URL patterns can also be useful in identifying and assessing potentially hazardous behaviors carried out on the internet. Phishing emails can potentially contain harmful software that has the potential to infect a whole company. The difficulties connected through phishing have grown in both strength and impact over time, and this trend is expected to continue. According to the 2011 Symantec research, the year-over-year growth in web attacks is approximately 36 percent, which explains into over 4, 500 new attacks per day, a rate that has significantly exceeded the performance of traditional anti-malware software. In 2007, it is anticipated that the charge of spam organization in the US alone will be 71 billion dollars [3].

A semi-supervised issue formulation for security analytics is proposed in this research, in which a randomly selected quantity of obtainable interpreted training models for security analytics is used to create an early classifier perfect for the problem. Afterward, an iterative model refinement procedure is carried out, in which a human-machine combined technique inside an active learning outline is utilized to slowly update the classifier model iteratively by investigating the unannotated training samples is carried out. In an active learning environment, randomly ranked feature based on randomly selected features is used to identify the phishing URL in a very slight number of unannotated models. That requires human investigation which means to make the learning process quicker. An extra feature ranking technique is offered to assign relative importance to a reduced collection of feature proportions. This process is shown to be effective for the purpose and is described in detail.

In the next sections, you will find the rest of the chapter: Section 2 delivers a brief overview of related revisions. Section 3 explains proposed method. Both the experimental data and the conclusion are presented in Sections 4 and 5, respectively.

2 Related Work

2.1 Phishing URL

A URL-based phishing assault is agreed out by providing malicious URLs to users that appear to be genuine, and then deceiving them into clicking on the malicious link. If an incoming URL is determined to be fraudulent or not fraudulent by examining the URL's many characteristics, it is categorized as phishing or not fraudulent. Several machine learning algorithms are skilled on diverse dataset of URL characteristics [4]. The URL remained sectioned into various tokens, of which organization features were retrieved and used in the classification process. Sequenced relationships among tokens were represented by the features. The authors emphasized that the combination of increased URL segmentation and feature abstraction enhanced the classification frequency when compared to several starting point techniques, as demonstrated by their results [5].

2.2 Active Learning in Phishing URL

A semi-supervised solution to the applied cyber-security tricky of phishing classification is designed using a human-machine concerted approach. An early classifier is trained on a small quantity of explained data, which is formerly slowly updated iteratively by selecting only applicable samples from a huge pool of unlabeled data that are most expected to have an immediate impact on the classifier's performance. According to preliminary results, ranked active learning holds important promise for achieving quicker convergence in terms of organization concert within a batch learning framework, thus needful even less determination from the human annotation process. Active learning combined with a useful feature weight update technique yields hopeful organization performance for classifying phishing/malicious URLs lacking the need for a huge number of annotated training models to be accessible through the training period [6]. The approach can be used to gather phishing data efficiently, generate representations for phishing authentication and finding in real-time, and collect data from multiple sources. Active learning reduced the cost of manual labeling while also creating an ensemble classifier for cleaning up invalid data. They developed a two-stage model for detecting phishing websites that had low false-positive rates and were easy to implement [7]. Optimal feature collection and neural networks are used in this chapter to develop OFS-NN, effective phishing attacks finding model based on best feature selection and neural networks. Then, using the FVV index, an algorithm is developed to select the most advantageous characteristics from phishing URLs and their associated websites. In the end, the particular features are used to train the primary neural network to develop a classifier that can spot phishing attacks [8]. In this chapter, they survey the current trend of online learning and investigate a real-time method to phishing URL detection in the context of web browsing. The model they are using is predominately a lexical model that has been qualified on the output of a robust content-inspection approach. In contrast to earlier work, we do not make usage of host-based features in this project. The feature set is made up of surface-level characteristics that are inevitably derived from URLs and other sources. As demonstrated, a confidence-weighted method can attain a high degree of accurateness in classifying URLs that have never been seen before if the training set is appropriately designed. Thus, a model-based solely on data obtained through URL inspection outperforms content inspection-based systems, and it has the potential to remove many of the expenses and security hazards associated with content inspection-based systems. It is the result of this work that we have a conceptual design for a system that can be deployed with the bare minimum of committed human resources while still achieving a high level of labeling accuracy [9]. Online learning refers to a collection of ml algorithms that are both efficient and scalable. On the contrary to conventional batch learning methods, which assume that all training data are obtainable or accessible to the learning task, online learning continuously updates the predictive models in a sequential manner, making it more suitable for web applications, where training data is frequently delivered in a sequential manner [10]. There has been no proposal for a comprehensive, industry-standard framework for malware detection URLs. With using machine learning techniques in a real-time setting, it is exorbitantly slow to identify malicious URLs on the web. A URL space is legally insane, with phishing URLs outnumber benign URLs by a wide margin. Given that now the URL space is active and changes constantly, it is important to modify the classifier on a regular basis. There is no limit to how large the URL space will grow, which means we will be unable to train on all URLs using traditional batch learning methods [11].

3 Proposed Work

In some cases, samples that are similar to labelled samples are selected by active learning algorithms. As a result, it would not improve the classifier. The distance between a sample and its closest labeled neighbour is used to determine the degree of similarity between a sample and the labeled samples in our proposed approach to measuring similarity. It is dissimilar to other labeled samples if the sample is located a long distance away from its nearest labeled neighbourhood. On the otherhand, if it is similar to the nearby labelled sample, it is likely that there would be at least one set of data in the labelled set that is similar to it. As a result, for manual labelling, we choose the sample that is the furthest away from its nearest labelled neighbourhood.

3.1 Impact of Feature Ranking

The following points observed to understand the importance of the feature ranking [12].

1. An increase in the speed and appropriateness of ranking every feature for a assumed class can significantly improve organization performance.
2. Statistical methods like correlation and dispersion evaluation can aid in the accurate estimation of the rank of a feature within a given class of features.
3. A larger dataset is required for better training rather than simply testing a detection technique on a insignificant dataset.
4. We must use datasets that are representative of current networks in order for the approach to be scalable to holder Big Data as possible.
5. In the framework of URL phishing detection, we must achieve cost-effective classification to remain competitive. The use of parallel computation to select features is therefore likely to be beneficial.

3.2 Algorithm for Randomized Active Learning

Randomly select samples from the phishing dataset and extract the feature that identifies the URL as the phishing URL. Based on the randomly selected samples, the features are ranked.

Step 1: Create an initial training set L by selecting several samples at random from the phishing dataset and using them to build a model.

Step 2: Select a subset of samples from unlabeled phishing dataset U for manual labeling based on a ranked feature. And also calculate the similarity between selected samples.

Calculating distance between the samples x_i for $x_i \in U$

$$div_i = \min_{j=1,2,3...n} \|x_i - x_j\|^2$$

Step 3: L is increased in size by the addition of selected samples, and the classification model is retrained using the new training set (Fig. 1).

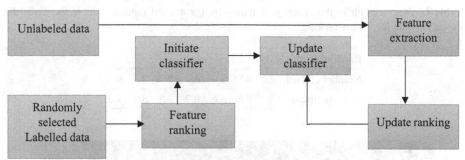

Fig. 1. Randomized active learning

4 Experimental

Initial research examines the impact of random sample selection in a phishing dataset, as well as continuing to work concurrently on the runtime of the feature ranking process. We can see that when we perform a random sample in a dataset, the runtime for a subset of sample selection in a dataset is increased, whereas when we perform a random sample in a dataset, the execution efficiency is reduced. When determining whether a URL is a phishing or non-phishing URL, it is critical to observe how the implementation time changes when the random collection of samples is changed (Table 1 and 2, Figs. 2 and 3).

Table 1. Variation in implementation time due to variation in the quantity of randomly selected samples for fixed partitions

Number of partitions = 6						
Random Sample	10	11	12	13	14	15
Avg exe time (sec)	10.2	10.6	11.1	11.5	12.1	12.6

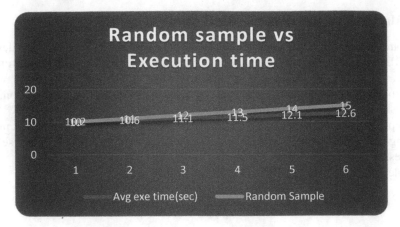

Fig. 2. Random sample vs Execution time

Table 2. The variation in the quantity of partitions for a fixed random sample increases the execution time for feature ranking.

Random sample = 12						
Number of partitions	4	5	6	7	8	9
Avg exe time(sec)	8.5	8.6	8.7	8.8	8.9	9.0

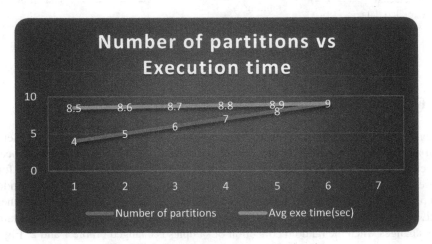

Fig. 3. Number of partitions vs Execution time

In proposed work active learning-based variation in execution time is experimented. The variation in execution based on two criteria. 1. For fixed partition with variation in random sample. 2. For fixed sample with variation in partition. In above two criteria execution time is gradually increased. But accuracy of finding URL phishing is increased because actively updating the features. Similarity based identifying random active learning helps to update the feature rank. Feature ranking will give better accuracy for identifying the phishing URL.

5 Conclusion

In this chapter randomized active learning similarity-based random sampling takes place. Random sampling improved the feature ranking. Based on the feature ranking the accuracy of finding phishing URL is increased. Execution time is slightly increased because of categorized the selection of random sample.

References

1. Korkmaz, M., Sahingoz, O.K., Diri, B.: Detection of phishing websites by using machine learning-based URL analysis. In: 2020 11th International Conference on Computing, Communication and Networking Technologies (ICCCNT). IEEE (2020)
2. Bhattacharjee, S.D., Talukder, A., Al-Shaer, E., Doshi, P.: Prioritized active learning for malicious URL detection using weighted text-based features. IEEE Int. Conference on Intelligence and Security Informatics (ISI) **22**, 107–112 (2017)
3. Ma, J., Saul, L.K., Savage, S., Voelker, G.M.: Beyond blacklists: Learning to detect malicious web sites from suspicious URLs. In: Proceedings of the ACM SIGKDD International Conference on Knowledge Discovery and Data Mining, pp. 1245–1254 (2009)
4. Tang, L., Mahmoud, Q.H.: A survey of machine learning-based solutions for phishing website detection. Machine Learning and Knowledge Extraction **3**(3), 672–694 (2021)
5. Vanhoenshoven, F., et al.: Detecting malicious URLs using machine learning techniques. In: 2016 IEEE Symposium Series on Computational Intelligence (SSCI). IEEE (2016)
6. Rajawat, A.S., Rawat, R., Barhanpurkar, K., Shaw, R.N., Ghosh, A.: Vulnerability analysis at industrial internet of things platform on dark web network using computational intelligence. In: Bansal, J.C., Paprzycki, M., Bianchini, M., Das, S. (eds.) Computationally Intelligent Systems and their Applications. SCI, vol. 950, pp. 39–51. Springer, Singapore (2021). https://doi.org/10.1007/978-981-16-0407-2_4
7. Li, J.-H., Wang, S.-D.: PhishBox: An approach for phishing validation and detection. In: 2017 IEEE 15th Intl Conf on Dependable, Autonomic and Secure Computing, 15th Intl Conf on Pervasive Intelligence and Computing, 3rd Intl Conf on Big Data Intelligence and Computing and Cyber Science and Technology Congress (DASC/PiCom/DataCom/CyberSciTech). IEEE (2017)
8. Zhu, E., et al.: OFS-NN: an effective phishing websites detection model based on optimal feature selection and neural network. IEEE Access **7**, 73271–73284 (2019)
9. Blum, A., et al.: Lexical feature-based phishing URL detection using online learning. In: Proceedings of the 3rd ACM Workshop on Artificial Intelligence and Security (2010)
10. Zhao, P., Hoi, S.C.: Cost-sensitive online active learning with application to malicious URL detection. In: Proceedings of the 19th ACM SIGKDD International Conference on Knowledge Discovery and Data Mining (2013)
11. Sadique, F., et al.: An automated framework for real-time phishing URL detection. In: 2020 10th Annual Computing and Communication Workshop and Conference (CCWC). IEEE (2020)
12. Deka, R.K., Bhattacharyya, D.K., Kalita, J.K.: Active learning to detect DDoS attack using ranked features. Computer Commun. **145**, 203–222 (2019)

Data Analysis on ERP System of Easy-Pay Payment Services

Neha Surpam[✉] and Apeksha Sakhare

G H Raisoni College of Engineering, Nagpur 440016, India
neha23surpam@gmail.com

Abstract. Machine Learning is one of the leading technologies in this generation with unique techniques and problem-solving algorithms which are very helpful to predict the models accurately with higher positivity rates as compare to the less or false positives prediction of any given projects. In this chapter, we can assure that all of the proposed approaches are almost valid and able to detect fraud transactions. Through this chapter, our aim is to show and determine the possibility of balancing the ratio between fraudulent and non-fraudulent transactions. The methods and parameters which have been used to study the project has anticipated after a thorough research and every requirement have been fulfilled to obtain the desired output. Payment fraud detection is the solid example of classification. The datasets have been modelled after analyzing and pre-processing the existing datasets later to differentiate between fraudulent and non-fraudulent transactions. Such predictions can only be determined with the help of Machine Learning as we used along with the relevant algorithms and techniques which was required for the respective chapter. Numerous interpretations have been done, but acquiring 100% accuracy is still cannot be accomplished due to class imbalanced data related to the transactions. To monitor the usual transactions of people is a vast task and so is to track the fare and fraudulent transactions among billion of people. The main goal of this research is to prevent users from performing unusual transactions through unverified sources and to obtain the positive results in terms of data accuracy and data visualization.

Keywords: Machine learning · Fraud detection · Logistic regression · Support vector machine · XG-Boost algorithm

1 Introduction

With the emerging IT World and after having the simplest technologies, the digital payment systems are blooming rapidly, especially the transactions volumes. This chapter mainly focuses on imputing fraud transactions from the general datasets which are acquired from Kaggle.com. The outburst in online and digital transactions has been the solo concern in these times and even harder to prevent.

Fraud detection systems are successful only after extracting the fraudulent transactions from non-fraudulent transactions. The high accuracy and efficiency rate is extremely obliged. The criticality to make sure safe transactions are highly depending

R. N. Shaw et al. (Eds.): ICACIS 2022, CCIS 1749, pp. 540–548, 2023.
https://doi.org/10.1007/978-3-031-25088-0_48

upon the quantity of genuine users. The key challenging task in applying Machine Learning techniques and algorithms in predicting fraudulent transactions is that the highly imbalanced datasets. While a number of the datasets are proven helpful to induce the output as an especially small fraudulent transactions.

In this chapter, we've applied various classification techniques like Support Vector Machine i.e., Linear SVM and Logistic Regression (Fig. 1).

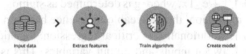

Fig. 1. Flow of the project

2 Methodology

The proposed methodology of our project is solemnly dependent on data visualization after getting the output and after performing certain techniques using pie-charts, histogram and data distribution.

The Supervised and Unsupervised Machine Learning techniques have proven helpful in exaggerating flagged transactions and non-flagged transactions from the given datasets. Similarly, the Semi-Supervised Learning and XG-Boost algorithm has played a key-role in defining the categorical output of the data which results into accurate data at the end of the task (Fig. 2).

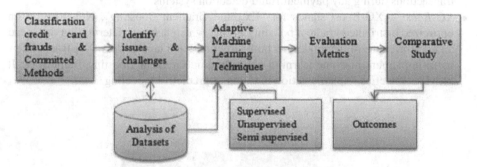

Fig. 2. Architecture diagram of fraud detection system

a) Credit card data is often very imbalanced. A defined sampling approach is a definite requirement.
b) The Fraud and Non-Fraud imbalance can make the use of 'Accuracy' in a Confusion Matrix moderately ineffective.
c) Accurate identification of fraud is often a primary concern so there is a need to look at the statistical measures in improving Recall and Precision.

The purpose of this research is to separate fraud and non-fraud transactions by extracting data within the feature space defined by input transactions. Some of the features used to filter the datasets are as follows:

- *Logistic Regression-* Logistic Regression is employed only the info is categorical. It's helpful in terms of understanding the link between variable quantities or one or more experimental variable. The given hypothesis is –
- h_(x) = g (_T x) = 1/1 + e_Tx, where g is determined as sigmoid function. In between mean and logistic regression, the noticeable difference between them is that they are bounded by 0 and 1. Additionally, as critical regression, logistic regression discards linear relationship between inputs and output variables. This is often accomplished after applying a nonlinear log transformation to the percentages ratio as stated below-

$$Logistic\ Function = 1/(1 + e'x).$$

- *Support Vector Machine* - Support vector machine are often used for both classification and regression problems. The training process aims to see a hyper-plane to mark the extreme points. The decision boundary is called as hyper-plane to segregate n-dimensional spaces. SVMs optimization problem will be characterized by –

$$K(x, z) = \exp(-\frac{||x - z||^2}{2\sigma^2})$$

- *Class weights for imbalanced data-* We can train our model by applying relevant techniques. This technique helps us in classifying fraud samples as compared to non-fraud samples. It is critical to differentiate between fraudulent and non-fraudulent transactions during any payment fraud detection systems.
- *XG-Boost* – XG-Boost stands for "Extreme Gradient Boosting". XG-Boost is an optimized distributed gradient boosting library which helps us determining the speed and performance of the model for both structured and tabular data. XG-Boost helps us to implement machine learning algorithms in Gradient Boosting framework. It provides effective implementation in terms of predictive modeling.

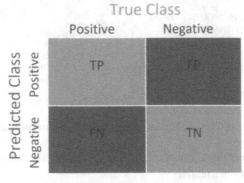

Fig. 3. Confusion matrix

- *Confusion Matrix* A Confusion matrix is largely used for assessing the performance of a classification model, where N is that the number of target classes. It predominantly describes the error made by the classifiers. With the help of confusion matrix, it is easy to predicate different models. It is mandatorily useful for measuring Recall, Precision, Specificity, Accuracy, and most significantly AUC-ROC curves (Fig. 3).

3   Literature Survey and Data Analysis

Here, we are analyzing the information by distributing the datasets and by categorizing the various forms of transactions. We have also performed required Principal Component Analysis to project the proper variance of knowledge in 2-D (dimensional) spaces. The below dataset contains following categories of transactions (Table 1):

Table 1. Financial dataset

Transaction types	Non-fraudulent transactions	Fraudulent transactions	Total
Cash-Ins results	1399285	0	1399274
Cash-outs results	2233385	4117	2237510
Transfers	528814	4098	532908
Debits	41433	0	41433
Payments	2151495	0	2151484
Total	6355408	8214	6362621

Among 6 million transactions, total 8314 transactions are labelled as fraudulent.

Datasets are highly imbalanced with 0:15 percent fraud transactions. By performing two dimensional PCA on subsets for both transactions, we can define the results that can contain fraud transactions – TRANSFERS and CASH-OUTS transactions.

The datasets which we have used consists of categorical and numerical data by dividing it in subsequent features to train the models such as –

- Transaction type of data
- Transaction amount of data
- Sender account balance before transaction of imputed data
- Sender account balance after transaction of imputed data
- Recipient account balance before transaction of imputed data
- Recipient account balance after transaction of imputed data.

The machine learning algorithms which we used are as follows –

1. *Logistic Regression* - Logistic Regression is employed only the info is categorical. It's helpful in terms of understanding the link between variable quantities or one

or more experimental variable. The given hypothesis is – $h\_(x) = g \ (\_T \ x) = 1/1 + e\_Tx$, where g is determined as sigmoid function. In between mean and logistic regression, the noticeable difference between them is that they are bounded by 0 and 1. Additionally, as critical regression, logistic regression discards linear relationship between inputs and output variables.

2. *Random Forest Algorithm* - Random Forest Algorithm technique is being used because it shows the best possible accuracy outcomes as expected. It is carried out along with Regression by categorization to carry out various decision trees.

3. *Data Analysis and Preparation* - Extracting the datasets which have been obtained from the Kaggle.com and analyzing all the data to perform various functionalities to visualize the data and to aim for the determined results by adding up techniques such as Feature Engineering, Data Imputation- to distinguish between valid and invalid data and to remove the null values from the datasets to provide accurate results.

4. *KNN Algorithm* - Various anomaly detection algorithms have exploited the conception of nearest neighbor analysis. Three primary rudiments influence the performance of the KNN algorithm.

- The distance metric used to detect the nearest neighbors.
- The distance rule that's used to classify k nearest neighbors.
- The fresh sample was classified grounded on the number of neighbors it had.

5. *Decision Tree* - The training set is divided into bumps, each of which can contain all or utmost of one data order. Decision Tree is erected by using recursive partitioning to classify the data. Originally, a trait is named and its being the stylish trait to resolve the data. It's resolve by minimizing the contamination at each step. Contamination of a knot is calculated by the entropy of data in the knot. Entropy is a measure of query, in simple words. Entropy of the knot is how important arbitrary data is in that knot.

4   Data Visualization

(Figs. 4, 5, 6, 7)

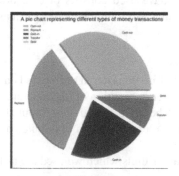

Fig. 4. Types of transactions

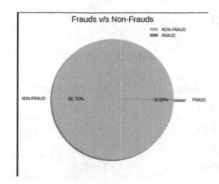

Fig. 5. Fraud and non-fraud transactions

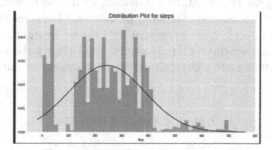

Fig. 6. Plot distribution as per transactions

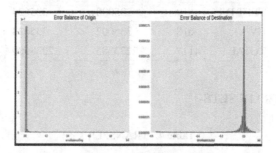

Fig. 7. Error balance origin graph

- DATASET SPLITS STRATEGY AND ACCURACY RESULTS

  Datasets has been divided based on different transaction types, the datasets of TRANS-
  ACTIONS and CASH-OUT columns have been extracted because they can contain high fraudulent transactions. For both types, the datasets are categorize into
  three parts as given- Training-70%, Testing – 15% and for CV-15 %. Stratified
  sampling has been used in creating train/CV/test splits and to provide greater precision
  (Table 2).

RESULTS ON CV SET

Table 2. Transfer

Split DS	Fraudulent	Non-fraudulent	Total
TRAIN DS	2869	370169	373037
CV'S	615	79323	79937
TEST DS	619	9323	79938
TOTAL	4098	528813	532908

After analyzing the TRANSACTIONS dataset, we'll move forward to CASH-OUT's dataset to judge performances by computing metrics Recall and Precisions. For TRANSFERS dataset, the effect is quite prominent for Logistic Regression and Linear algorithms. We use higher weights for fraud samples. Similarly, equal class weights for both the samples are resulting into high recall and precision scores to avoid over-fitting (Table 3, 4, 5).

Table 3. CASH-OUT DATASET

Split DS	Fraudulent	Non-fraudulent	Total
TRAIN DS	2882	1563368	1566252
TEST DS	619	335008	335624
CV's	618	335007	335624
TOTAL	4117	2233385	2238500

RESULTS ON TRAIN SETS-

Table 4. TRANSFER's

Algorithm output	Recall output	Precision output	F1-measure output	AUPRC output
LR ds	0.9957	0.4453	0.6154	0.9205
L-SVM ds	0.9957	0.4434	0.6134	0.9122
SVM with RBF ds	0.9957	0.6034	0.7514	0.9896

Less promising results have been obtained for both the datasets of Cash-outs and Transactions.

Overall, we can see that all of the proposed methods and approaches have been successfully implemented to predict fraudulent transactions which results into high accuracy and low false positives.

Table 5. CASH-OUT'S DATASET

Algorithm output	Recall output	Precision output	F1-measure output	AUPRC output
LR ds	0.9848	0.1542	0.2665	0.7565
L-SVM ds	0.9367	0.1226	0.2116	0.7064
RBF ds	0.9874	0.1356	0.2387	0.7632

The final computing matrices, i.e., Confusion matrices results are as shown below –

a) Logistic Regression:
   PRED

TRUE	-	+
-	78555	767
+	3	614

b) Linear – SVM
   PRED

TRUE	-	+
-	78577	747
+	3	614

c) SVM using KBF Kernel
   PRED

TRUE	-	+
-	78888	438
+	7	606

5   Conclusion

In fraud detection method, we entirely deal with highly imbalanced datasets. In the given selected dataset (Financial), we have shown that all the proposed standpoints are able to determine fraud transactions with mostly accurate results and low false positives results. The respective approaches can be proved highly impactful in terms of detecting fraudulent transactions that every company should try in future to improve the performance of online transactions and payment gateways. We've prescribed this problem by proposing our class weights for imbalanced data. We are able to improve our techniques in future aspects by using algorithms like Decision trees and XG-Boost.

References

1. "Credit Card Fraud Detection Based on Transaction Behaviour –by John Richard D. Kho, Larry A. Vea" published by Proc. of the 2017 IEEE Region 10 Conference (TENCON), Malaysia, November 5–8 (2017)
2. "Survey Paper on Credit Card Fraud Detection by Suman" , Research Scholar, GJUS&T Hisar HCE, Sonepat published by International Journal of Advanced Research in Computer Engineering & Technology (IJARCET) Volume 3 Issue 3 (2014)
3. https://www.mygreatlearning.com/blog/xgboost-algorithm/
4. https://towardsdatascience.com/understanding-confusion-matrix-a9ad42dcfd62
5. https://towardsdatascience.com/fraud-detection-with-graph-analytics-2678e817b69e
6. https://www.altexsoft.com/whitepapers/fraud-detection-how-machine-learningsystems-help-reveal-scams-in-fin-tech-healthcare-and-ecommerce/
7. Lakshmi, S.V.S.S., Kavilla , S.D.: Machine Learning for Credit Card. Fraud Detection System. unpublished [7] N. Malini, Dr. M. Pushpa,"Analysis on Credit Card Fraud Identification Techniques on the basis of KNN and Outlier Detection", Advances in Electrical, Electronics, Information, Communication and Bio-Informatics (AEEICB), 2017 Third International Conference, pp. 255- 258. IEEE
8. Malsa, N., Vyas, V., Gautam, J., Shaw, R.N., Ghosh, A.: Framework and smart contract for blockchain enabled certificate verification system using robotics. In: Bianchini, M., Simic, M., Ghosh, A., Shaw, R.N. (eds.) Machine Learning for Robotics Applications. SCI, vol. 960, pp. 125–138. Springer, Singapore (2021). https://doi.org/10.1007/978-981-16-0598-7_10
9. "Credit Card Fraud Detection Based on Transaction Behavior –by John Richard D. Kho, Larry A. Vea" published by Proc. of the 2017.IEEE Region 10 Conference (TENCON), Malaysia, November 5–8 (2017)
10. Machine Learning For Credit Card Fraud Detection System, Lakshmi S V S , Selvani Deepthi Kavila (2018)

Self-driving Car: Lane Detection and Collision Prevention System

Namrata Singh[1(✉)], Meenakshi Srivastava[2], Sumit Mohan[1], Ashif Ali[1], Varun Kumar Singh[1], and Prashant Singh[1]

[1] Department of Computer Science and Engineering, Sunder Deep Engineering College, Ghaziabad, India
nam2817120@gmail.com

[2] Department of Information Technology, Amity Institute of Information Technology, Amity University, Lucknow, India
msrivastava@lko.amity.edu

Abstract. Self-driving cars or vehicles don't require humans to take control to safely operate the vehicle. Also, popular as autonomous or driverless cars, they combine various sensors and software like radar, lidar, sonar, GPS, odometry, etc. to control, navigate, and drive the vehicle. This chapter presents the working model of the Self-driving Car: Lane detection and Collision prevention system (LDCP System) using machine learning and computer vision. In the LDCP System two processes working simultaneously based on object detection and recognition and human facial expression recognition to hold the responsibility of the car's outer and inner environment to prevent any collision which occurs due to human errors such as lack of concentration or focus. The extraction of information about objects and face(s) is performed by capturing the live video feed through multiple cameras. The implemented algorithm is advanced enough to works in real-time which is for sure can prevent any collisions.

Keywords: Computer vision · Machine learning · Self-driving car · Drowsiness · Yawning · Object detection · Lane detection

1 Introduction

Traffic collisions are the major source of deaths, injuries, and property damage every year throughout the world. "There were 496,762 collisions on the road and railway crossing in 2015."—The National Crime Records Bureau (NCRB) in the report of 2016. "And 148,707 traffic-related deaths." Uttar Pradesh, Maharashtra, and Tamil Nadu are the three top states in India for the highest number of road accidents with 33% of the total in 2015 [1].

The Lane Detection and Collision Prevention System holds the power of machine learning and advanced algorithms which is unique and one of its kind. The combination of algorithms in this system is never used before in any of the vehicles, as it holds the control of the outer as well as the inner environment of the car to protect and save the lives which are priceless in comparison to any other thing in this world.

R. N. Shaw et al. (Eds.): ICACIS 2022, CCIS 1749, pp. 549–562, 2023.
https://doi.org/10.1007/978-3-031-25088-0_49

The system is Technical, Legal, and Cost Feasible. Firstly, the problem of road detection was aroused which was resolved by using the road lanes to detect lanes. And another major problem was that pedestrians and domestic animals are found so frequent on roads which can cause a serious collision, so this problem was resolved by the application of object detection and recognition instead of vehicle recognition only. The system can be classified as an SAE Level 2 system with the additional implementation of the Adaptive Cruise Control System, and the system is suitable for general Indian roads and even for highways with lane markings.

Almost all the software used for the development of the system is open-source and camera/ video recording devices will charge a little cost only.

1.1 Scope Identification

1. How the LDCP system impacts on economy?
2. How the LDCP system impacts on environment?
3. How the LDCP system impacts on industry?
4. How the LDCP system impacts on Society?
5. What are the future scopes?

2 Literature Survey

In recent times many automobile companies are working on autonomous vehicles. In which Tesla, Inc. is on top of the race with developing Tesla Autopilot system classified as an SAE Level 2 system, but the Tesla Autopilot system is specially developed for highways with good lane markings and not for general roads. [2].

Testing of self-driving cars has increased from three in 2017 to 27 in 2018 respectively by Apple. [3, 4].

In 2016 Yandex started to develop self-driving cars. In Feb. 2018, they tested the prototype of a taxi on the streets of Moscow[5]. There are some companies that work on self-driving cars as given – Waymo, BMW, Nissan, Ford, General Motors, Delphi Automotive Systems, Tesla, etc.

Baidu and King Long developed an automated minibus, a 14 seats vehicle without any driving seat. With 100 vehicles produced, 2018 was the first year with commercial automated service in China. [6, 7].

Nawal Alioua, et al. proposed the use of Support Vector Machine (SVM) which is face extraction-based and circular Hough transform (CHT) for mouth detection [8].

In the chapter represented by Tiesheng Wang and Pengfei Shi, the Kalman filter is used to track the face region. Further, the degree of mouth opening is used to determine the yawning [9].

Jabbar, R., et al.[10]. In this paper dlib library is used for face landmarks coordinates detection and later these coordinates are passed to the multilayer perceptron classifier as inputs to train the model. Further, the trained model is used to decide if the driver is drowsy or not.

In [11], Ganlu Deng, Yefu Wu presented the method to detect the curved road lanes using Hough transform.

Vivek Nair and Nadir Charniya [12], Haar cascade classifier, and template matching technique are used for eye and yawn detection. MQ-3 alcohol sensor is used to determine whether the driver is drunk or not.

A. K. Jain [13], lane detection is performed using a trained CNN model over images of road lanes.

In [14], Hough transform technique and Lucas-Kanade optical flow algorithm along with Cumulative density function (CDF) is used for lane detection and vehicle detection.

3 Methodology

A driverless vehicle on road is nothing less than a call for an accident if it is not intelligent. In the LDCP System, two processes are working simultaneously.

3.1 Live Video Capture and Frame Extraction

In the initial stage of the system, the camera will activate to capture the live video from the surrounding. Here, two different cameras are used, one for the car's outer environment and one for the car's inner environment. And the respective frames will be extracted from the live video and will be provided to both processes one and process two respectively as input. Further, in process one, the information is extracted from the frames using computer vision and image processing.

3.2 Lane Detection

Lane detection is the first step of process one and here first the Canny Edge Detector is applied to the extracted frames to detect all the edges along with road lanes edges and then Hough Transformation is applied over the ROI (region of interest) to detect the road lanes (Figs. 1, 2).

Fig. 1. Live frame captured and edge detection using Canny Edge Detector

Fig. 2. Region of interest and road lane detection

3.3 Object Detection

In this phase, the LDCP System detects almost all the objects which can be any vehicle, pedestrians, or animals, etc. present on the road using R-CNN (Region Based Convolutional Neural Network) model on TensorFlow.

3.4 Collision Prevention

Here, the system will ensure to prevent any possible collision from any objects from which there is a chance of collision. The score of the objects which were detected in the object detection phase will be calculated and if there is a chance of collision then the system will raise an alarm for collision alert.

In the second process, the system will monitor the driver for various errors which is most likely to happen.

3.5 Face Landmarks Detection

The objective of the first phase of the second process is to detect the face landmarks by recognizing the eyes and mouth shape from the frames. And this is efficiently done by the dlib face detector which is fast and accurate enough to detect in real-time (Fig. 3).

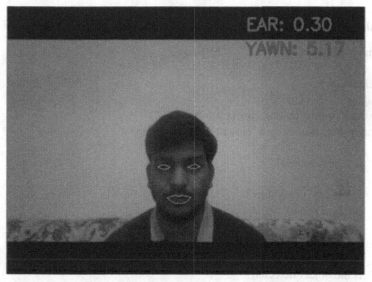

Fig. 3. Face landmarks detection using dlib face detector (with EAR-eye aspect ratio frequency and yawn frequency)

3.6 Drowsiness Detection

Now, the LDCP system will calculate the EAR (Eye Aspect Ratio) of the eyes with the help of landmarks, and if the calculated EAR is less than the threshold EAR for a certain number of consecutive frames then the system will raise an alarm for drowsiness alert.

3.7 Yawn Detection

Here, the calculation will be made to measure the upper and lower lip distance with the help of landmarks detected through dlib. If the calculated distance is more than the threshold value for a certain number of consecutive frames, then the system will raise an alarm for the yawning alert.

3.8 Cellphone Detection

Finally, by using R-CNN the frame will be processed to detect if the driver is using a cellphone or not. If the cellphone is detected, then the system will raise an alarm for cellphone detection.

3.9 Tools

- Software: Python 3, OpenCV, dlib, TensorFlow, NumPy, Matplotlib, PyCharm/ Sublime
- Hardware: RAM: 8 GB DDR4, Processor: Intel Core i5 8th Gen., System type: 64-bit

3.10 Algorithms

Algorithm for First Process

1. Vehicle Active.
2. Capturing live video.
3. Extracting information from each frame.
4-a. Canny edge detection & Hough transformation.

    a. Is lane detected?

        i. If yes: go to step 8
        ii. Else: go to step 3

4-b. R-CNN on TensorFlow.

    a. Is the object detected?

        i. If yes: go to step 5
        ii. Else: go to step 3

5. Distance Calculation.
6. Chances of Collision.

    a. If yes: go to step 7
    b. Else: go to step 3

7. Collision ALERT.
8. Is the vehicle active?

    a. If yes: go to step 3

b. Else: go to step 9

9. Process terminates.

Algorithm for Second Process

1. Vehicle Active.
2. Camera active: capture the driver's face in real-time.
3. Extracting information from each frame.

4-a. Dlib face detector.
4.1. Extract eyes and lips shape.

4.1.1. Calculating eye aspect ratio (EAR).

a. Calculated EAR is less than threshold EAR.

i. If yes: Drowsiness Alert.
ii. Else: go to step 5

4.1.2. Calculating upper and lower lips distance.

a. The calculated distance is greater than the threshold value.

i. If yes: Yawn Alert.
ii. Else: go to step 5

4-b. Cell phone detection using R-CNN on TensorFlow.

a. A cell phone detected.

i. If yes: Cell phone Alert.
ii. Elsc: go to step 5

5. Vehicle active.

a. If yes: go to step 2
b. Else: go to step 6

6. System stop.

3.11 Flow Charts

(Fig. 4, 5)

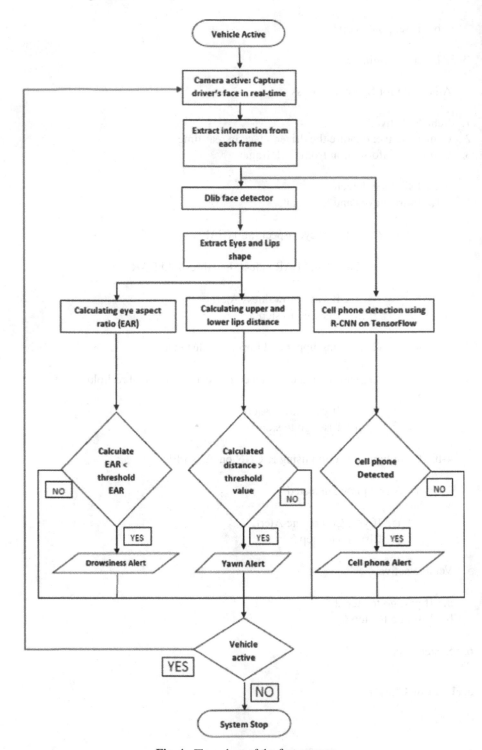

Fig. 4. Flow chart of the first process

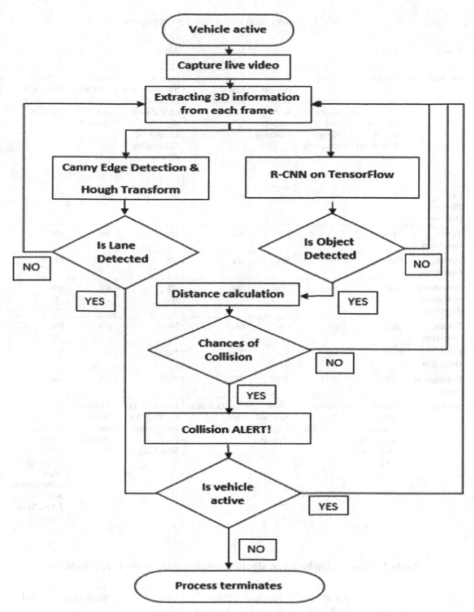

Fig. 5. Flow chart of the second process

Observations
(Table 1, 2)

Table 1. Observation based on relevant papers

Result	Alarm		Alarm	Stops the vehicle	Alarm		
Methodology	Support vector machine (SVM), and Circular Hough Transform (CHT)	Canny edge detection algorithm and Hough transform	Harr cascade along with template matching	Convolutional neural network	Hough transform and Lucas-Kanade optical flow algorithm along with Cumulative density function (CDF)	Kalman filter and degree of mouth opening	Dlib and Multilayer perceptron classifier
Cell Phone Detection	n/a	n/a	n/a	n/a	n/a	n/a	n/a
Yawn Detection	**Yes**	n/a	**Yes**	n/a	n/a	**Yes**	n/a
Drowsy Detection	n/a	n/a	**Yes**	n/a	n/a	n/a	**Yes**
Pedestrian or objects detection	n/a	n/a	n/a	n/a	n/a	n/a	n/a
Vehicle Detection	n/a	n/a	n/a	n/a	**Yes**	n/a	n/a
Lane Detection	n/a	**Yes**	n/a	**Yes**	**Yes**	n/a	n/a
Publication Year	2014	2018	2019	2018	2016	2005	2018
Author	Nawal Alioua, Aouatif Amine, and Mohammed Rziza	Ganlu Deng, Yefu Wu	Vivek Nair and Nadir Charniya	Aditya Kumar Jain	Jyun-Min Dai, Lu-Ting Wu, Huei-Yung Liny, Wen-Lung Tai	Tiesheng Wang and Pengfei Shi	Rateb Jabbar, Khalifa Al-Khalifa, Mohamed Kharbeche, Wael Alhajyaseen, Mohsen Jafari, Shan Jiang

Table 2. Observation based on algorithm implemented in the LDCP System

Lane detection	Vehicle detection	Pedestrian or objects detection	Drowsy detection	Yawn detection	Cell phone detection	Methodology	Result
Yes	Yes	Yes	Yes	Yes	Yes	Canny edge detector and Hough transform R-CNN, dlib	Alarm

4 Results

(Fig. 6, 7, 8, 9, 10 and Table 3)

Fig. 6. Lane, pedestrian, and vehicle detection with alert warning

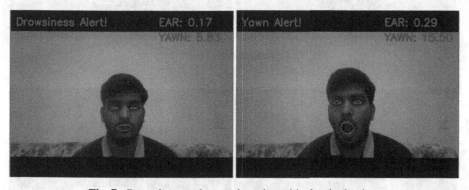

Fig. 7. Drowsiness and yawn detection with alert in daytime

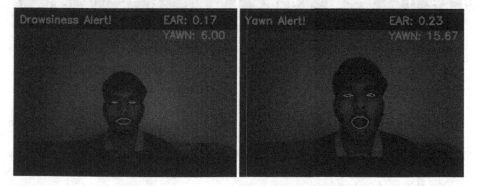

Fig. 8. Drowsiness and yawn detection with alert in nighttime

Table 3. Observation on EAR and yawn frequency

Eyes and mouth in different lighting condition	EAR frequency	Yawn frequency
Closed eyes (in day light)	0.17	5.83
Yawning (in day light)	0.29	15.5
Closed eyes (in night light)	0.17	6.0
Yawning (in night light)	0.23	15.67

Fig. 9. Cell phone detection in daytime

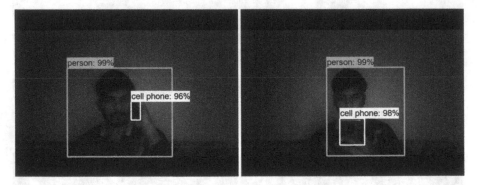

Fig. 10. Cell phone detection in nighttime

5 Discussion

1. **Economic benefits**: Road accidents in India cost $8.2 billion per year, so with a decrement of 5–10% in it the country can save millions of dollars every year.
2. **Energy and environmental impacts**: Automation of trucks is important, not only because of the improved safety aspects of these very heavy vehicles but also due to the ability of fuel savings.

3. **Lower Costs and Related effects**: Reduce the costs of vehicle insurance. Taxi/pooling and car-sharing services, reduce automotive production, Controlling illegal passenger behavior, and Reduction in Crime.
4. **Social benefit**: Every year 1.3 million people are killed worldwide due to road accidents/collisions. By removing manual driving controls from humans, errors such as speeding, drink driving, and distractions occurring within and outside the vehicle will reduce and so leading to a reduction in road fatalities which involves human error.

6 Future Scope

5. **Accessibility for those who cannot drive**: There are many people in Australia who have restricted mobility because of age or disability. So, this problem can be resolved with the availability of fully automated vehicles.
6. **Quicker commute times**: With autonomous cars able to sense other cars around them and communicate with them, bumper-to-bumper traffic jams should be a thing of the past. Along with the implementation of the automatic braking system, driverless cars can travel at a consistent distance which will prevent crashes.
7. **Parking Spaces**: Autonomous taxis could, on the other hand, be used continuously after it has reached its destination leads to reduce in need for parking space.

7 Conclusion

The Lane Detection and Collision Prevention System (LDCP System) proposed in this chapter is advanced and capable enough to save lives by preventing collision which occurs due to human errors. The system is tested under various conditions and all the test results are impressive with high accuracy. All the software implemented in the system is open source which makes it very much cost-efficient. The future work will focus on the implementation of the Adaptive cruise control system to make the car more advance and intelligent.

8 Publications

1. Agrawal R., Singh N. (2020) Lane Detection and Collision Prevention System for Automated Vehicles. In: Iyer B., Rajurkar A., Gudivada V. (eds) Applied Computer Vision and Image Processing. Advances in Intelligent Systems and Computing, vol 1155. Springer, Singapore. https://doi.org/10.1007/978-981-15-4029-5_5

References

1. https://en.wikipedia.org/wiki/Traffic_collisions_in_India
2. https://en.wikipedia.org/wiki/Tesla_Autopilot
3. Krok, A.: Apple increases self-driving test fleet from 3 to 27. Roadshow (2018)
4. Hall, Z.: Apple ramping self-driving car testing, more CA permits than Tesla and Uber. Electrek. Retrieved 21 March 2018 (2018)
5. https://www.vedomosti.ru/technology/news/2018/02/16/751267-yandeks-bespilotnoe
6. "China's first Level 4 self-driving shuttle enters volume production". newatlas.com
7. LLC, Baidu USA (4 July 2018). Baidu Joins Forces with Softbank's SB Drive, King Long to Bring Apollo-Powered Autonomous Buses to Japan. GlobeNewswire News Room
8. Nawal, A., et al.: Driver's fatigue detection based on yawning extraction. International Journal of Vehicular Technology (2014)
9. Soni, A., Dharmacharya, D., Pal, A., Srivastava, V.K., Shaw, R.N., Ghosh, A.: Design of a machine learning-based self-driving car. In: Bianchini, M., Simic, M., Ghosh, A., Shaw, R.N. (eds.) Machine Learning for Robotics Applications. SCI, vol. 960, pp. 139–151. Springer, Singapore (2021). https://doi.org/10.1007/978-981-16-0598-7_11
10. Jabbar, R., et al.: Real-time driver drowsiness detection for android application using deep neural networks techniques. The 9th International Conference on Ambient Systems, Networks, and Technologies, 2018., Procedia Computer Science, Volume 130, pp. 400–407 (2018). https://doi.org/10.1016/j.procs.2018.04.060
11. Biswas, S., Bianchini, M., Shaw, R.N., Ghosh, A.: Prediction of traffic movement for autonomous vehicles. In: Bianchini, M., Simic, M., Ghosh, A., Shaw, R.N. (eds.) Machine Learning for Robotics Applications. SCI, vol. 960, pp. 153–168. Springer, Singapore (2021). https://doi.org/10.1007/978-981-16-0598-7_12
12. Nair, V., Charniya, N.: Drunk driving and drowsiness detection alert system. Int. Conference on ISMAC in Computational Vision and Bio-Eng. **3**, 1191–1207 (2019)
13. Jain, A.K.: Working model of self-driving car using convolutional neural network, Raspberry Pi and Arduino. In: 2018 Second International Conference on Electronics, Communication and Aerospace Technology (ICECA). IEEE, Coimbatore, India (2018)
14. Dai, J.-M., Wu, L.-T., Liny, H.-Y., Tai, W.-L.: A driving assistance system with vision-based vehicle detection techniques. In: 2016 Asia-Pacific Signal and Information Processing Association Annual Summit and Conference (APSIPA). IEEE, Jeju, South Korea (2016)

A Novel Machine Learning Classification Model to Analyze the COVID-19 Pandemic's Impact on Academics: Sentiment Analysis Approach

Sumit Mohan⑩, Varun Kumar Singh⑩, Namrata Singh⑩, Ashif Ali⑩, and Prashant Singh(✉)

Sunder Deep Engineering College, Ghaziabad, AKTU, Lucknow, India
prashant.ert@gmail.com

Abstract. The COVID-19 Pandemic is considered as the worst situation for human beings; it affected people's lives worldwide. Due to this pandemic, the respective government authority announced the lockdown to break the coronavirus chain. The lockdown impacted people's mental health, leading to many psychological issues as well as hampered students' academics. In this chapter we have studied the impacts on students' academics due to lockdown effect. The data has been collected via a google form questionnaire circulated to various educational institutes. Further, we have developed a novel machine learning classifier model called Naïve Bayes-Support Vector Machine for analyzing the data, which utilizes the properties of both classifiers by using a deep learning framework. We have used natural language processing (TextBlob, Stanza and Vader) libraries to label the dataset and applied in the proposed NBSVM method and other machine learning models and classified the sentiments into two categories (Positive vs Negative). We also applied the natural language processing libraries used a topic-modelling technique called Latent Dirichlet Allocation to know the essential topics words of both classes from students' feedback data. The study revealed 83% and 86% accuracy for unigram and bigram, respectively, whereas the precision was 79% and recall 81%. According to NLP libraries' result, approximately 71% of the feedback's sentiment is negative, and only 16% of feedbacks are positive. The proposed model shown that (Naïve Bayes-Support Vector Machine) outperforms the other variants of the Naïve Bayes and support vector machine.

Keywords: COVID-19 · Machine learning · Naïve Bayes · Natural language processing · Sentiment analysis · Support vector machine

1 Introduction

The health experts/scientists/virologists predicted that there will be another wave of COVID-19 worldwide and need to prepare for the upcoming waves, which is a major problem for the education bodies. We faced two COVID-19 waves whereas the second wave was the worst compared to the first one. We saw lot of casualties during the second wave caused by the new coronavirus variant Delta-I. Now we have another coronavirus

© The Author(s), under exclusive license to Springer Nature Switzerland AG 2023
R. N. Shaw et al. (Eds.): ICACIS 2022, CCIS 1749, pp. 563–575, 2023.
https://doi.org/10.1007/978-3-031-25088-0_50

variant (Omicron); therefore, we might have another complete lockdown to break the chain of the virus [1]. Thus, analyzing the previous lockdown and its impact on academics has become essential for the government.

For this reason, we have collected students' feedback from various institutions across the country to study their problems. Due to Covid-19, everything was shut down for a certain period in lockdown. All universities and colleges switched their teaching activities to online mode. This pandemic was a challenging situation for everyone, especially for students and teachers, because everything turned into a virtual mode, so it is more important for universities and colleges to take care of the online teaching process [2]. Thus, feedback from students plays a vital role to get a clear insight into the current teaching process so that colleges and universities can take the appropriate action to provide better online teaching process. Handling the student's opinion manually would be a hectic task because of large-scale data, therefore to tackle this issue, here we have used ML(Machine Learning) models and DL(Deep Learning) models to automatically process student feedback and extract the students' thoughts, emotions, and attitudes [3]. Natural language processing libraries and machine learning algorithms are commonly utilized to remove the thoughts and feelings expressed in opinion writing. The most challenging part is choosing the suitable models and libraries to represent the text's real meaning. So, to extract the accurate sentiment from student feedback datasets, we have used three natural language processing libraries (NLTK Vader, Stanza, and Textblob) and machine learning models.

Emotion may be extracted from a text using sentiment analysis. We can't determine the actual feeling in this feedback since it has two polarities, making it impossible to do a sentiment analysis. For example, "The entire lockdown is beneficial for nature to sustain warming, but that's the worst condition for living creatures" (positive, negative). Therefore, it may be challenging to pick the library or model [4]. This is the method used to extract the text's topics using Latent Dirichlet Allocation. Such studies are essential for improving various interactive online learning platforms by integrating automated feedback analysis. As a result, educational institutions must analyze student feedback on online learning platforms so that both teachers and colleges adequately understand what needs to be modified and strengthened [5]. COVID-19 has impacted every area, particularly in the education sector. The government announced a lockdown to prevent the virus from spreading. Hence, all universities, colleges, and schools stopped offering physical classroom activities. It became virtual (online), which was difficult for students and teachers; this chapter describes the critical academic challenges students faced during the pandemic.

We used Kaggle, google form, social media, and other platforms to gather information from students. Due to the difficulty in determining the exact sentiment of people's opinionated text. Sentiment analysis of people's opinionated text is a decisive factor in deciding something or making the right decision. People are constantly using emoticons in their text to convey their emotions or sum up their sentences, resulting in the absence of several emotions [6] (Fig. 1).

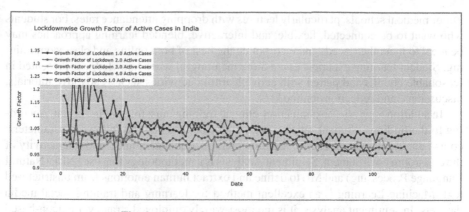

Fig. 1. Growth factor of lockdowns and unlock

2 Related Works

This study proposes a proper utilization of available machine learning model NB (Naïve Bayes), SVM (Support Vector Machine), and RF (Random Forest) for SA (Sentiment Analysis) on Malayalam tweets. In this study, for extracting the features, they used the available machine learning library under the natural language processing library known as NLTK. Compared to other components, all classifiers containing the last two characteristics have been more accurate. The most accurate classifier was the RF classifier using Unigram and Sentiwordnet, which included negation terms, with a 95.6 per cent accuracy [7]. Although MOOCs have gotten much press around the world, academics still do not fully understand what makes students interested in them.

The study has analyzed the vast data gathered from the thousands of students enrolled on the online platform. This data was collected from active learners of MOOCs. For this instance, they analyzed this student's data using machine learning models to get the exact parameters for MOOCs. This study defines MOOC success as students' satisfaction with the course. Satisfied MOOC students will assist a school in reaching out to a larger audience[8]. Their findings indicate that the current scenario is not working well for them and requires more investigation. Most pupils are dissatisfied with online instructional activities; they dislike online classrooms. Respective faculties are not carrying out their responsibilities properly. Making a healthy relationship between students and instructors becomes increasingly essential, and practical teacher training should be mandated to address student issues [9]. The importance of sentiment analysis corresponds to the advancement of the electronic stage, such as computer hacker reviews, discussions of cyber risk studies, malicious movement-based web-based overview journals, smaller scope sites, and informal affiliations related to this research cyber-lawbreakers. Traditional measures of MOOC performance include student completion rate, which is often misleading since many students do not complete the course; for analyzing this situation, they collected some data from the students to get to know the student's satisfaction parameters, for this they applied supervised machine learning model [10]. Before the coronavirus disease 2019 (COVID-19) outbreak, we looked at methods to enhance our university medical programme's student experience and learning outcomes. Questions have been raised concerning the value and manner of pre-clinical content presented in junior medical schools, particularly lectures with dropping attendance rates. For students who want to be connected, flexible, and interactive, blended learning approaches may be ideal to meet their needs and incorporate the best of both online and classroom training. Student learning experiences are more meaningful when knowledge is presented in reasonable chunks and paired with active learning activities such as adaptive tutorials, discussions, and reflections online [11].

In addition to physical examination, clinical training must follow this format. According to the findings, Student satisfaction majorly depends on the following parameters: course duration, content, course, teaching method, doubt clearance, and interactivity of the classroom environment. Sentiment Analysis is a methodology that uses NLP (Natural Language Processing) and ML to define and extract human emotions from unstructured text. Machine Learning is an excellent method for learning and training social media datasets. In sentiment analysis, it is the most widely employed strategy. Lexicon-based and rule-based techniques can both be used with machine learning. This chapter compiles a list most recent studies of sentiment analysis on people's opinionated text [12].

Sentiment for relevant financial markets was extracted at sentence level from ca 3,500 daily newsletters. The model was generally better at classifying up movements than down movements. An economic evaluation of the model and trading behaviours in a realistic investment environment may prove valuable for finance practitioners. All campus-related physical activity has been halted following the World Health Organization's recommendation. Students and academic staff were the focus of this research's review study. 2021 This pandemic lockdown affected the pupils' mental health. Therefore they concentrated on their online teaching difficulties. During this COVI-19 Pandemic, suitable procedures are put in place to guarantee that pupils are not experiencing academic challenges [13].

People post about anything on social media in today's world, whether they're pleased or sad. Millions of individuals everyday use Twitter, Facebook, and Instagram, three of the most popular social media platforms. Over 50 tweets are logged every day, and virtually every second, around 6K tweets are caught. Only Twitter has that many users. Astonishingly, Facebook collects more than 500 terabytes of data every day. It gives people the freedom to express their opinions on every topic, from politics to education to society. Individuals use Twitter to communicate their views on various issues, whether stylish, text-based or emoji-based. If you're a company, you may now use these views as real-time feedback on your product and make decisions based on what others say about it. Thus, users may determine the text message's polarity (negative, neutral, and positive) by analyzing the sentimental polarity (opinions and aims) of a text message or remark. Further research could include and analyze additional textual sources related to macroeconomic variables and the index constituents [14]. This paper presents the results of a systematic examination into newly emergent Covid-19 emotions as stated in user tweets. With our feature's concatenation engineering method, the analysis concludes that ETC is the best performing because textual data, such as tweets, cannot be separated into linearly separable class planes. In the future, we want to focus our efforts on deep learning algorithms to improve their performance on small datasets [15].

Artificial intelligence (AI) has been used in online advertising; therefore, digital marketing has become the tool to reach customers. For this situation, machine learning is the only choice to examine the problem by own learning to reach targeted customers. Many studies have been conducted, so this chapter has proposed a model for targeting the online audience. This research looks at the different machine learning algorithms to find the targeted audience for online ads [16]. On social media, words and phrases express people's opinions about goods and services. Sentiment Analysis is a task in natural language processing that entails extracting sentiment from people's opinionated text, which is essential for decision making., therefore, knowing the people's opinion then it needed to analyze the available opinionated text of peoples for this instance, sentiment analysis comes into mind [17]. Using Apache Spark, they look at alternative sentiment analysis methodologies and methodologies for large Amazon datasets utilizing the Apache Spark data processing engine and found that Linear SVC outperforms NB and logistic regression in terms of performance because Amazon's food data is growing exponentially; traditional solutions cannot keep up. This is verified for both individuals and companies, as well as society as a whole As a result of this study, we were able to determine whether the route behind such material is for sure (+) or negative, depending on whether the touch of a substance carries unique conceptual knowledge and what kind of excited information it imparts [18]. Online social media platforms have led to a rise in opinion mining or sentiment analysis, which extracts users' sentiments or thoughts on any issue. Because it provides so much data in so many different areas, researchers have begun focusing on Twitter. Emotional polarity scores, including positive, negative, and neutral, have been the focus of most current studies in this field. Tweets may convey a wide range of human emotions, including love, hate, fear, sadness, and a host of others. Random Forest and Bi-directional Learning are two machine learning and deep learning approaches discussed in this chapter. To compare the performance of multiple procedures and extract the best findings, LSTM, BERT, and other methods are utilized [19].

A significant degree of clarity when it comes to emotions It was discovered that the BERT-based strategy had the best accuracy, followed by the bidirectional LSTM method and then, ultimately, the remaining model based on data from the Crowd flower project. Finding the most prevalent and essential viewpoints on a particular issue is critical to dynamic analysis. People's feelings towards natural disasters may be studied using a combination of machine learning, statistical modelling, and lexicon-based techniques in this chapter [20]. Twitter is an excellent place to find out what the public thinks about a hot topic. Researchers from Iran's Institute of Medical Sciences utilized the future wheel method to perform a forthcoming study in April 2020. A semi-structured interview was for vice-chancellors of biomedical sciences institutions and university presidents, faculty/staff/health experts/graduates purposefully picked. All of the information was gathered via a series of in-depth interviews. To evaluate the discussions, MAXQDA version 10 software was employed. The impacts were classified into three categories: primary, secondary, and tertiary [21]. In addition, 16 significant impacts, 51 secondary effects, and 24 tertiary effects were found. Stress management and rumour management seminars were also necessary because of the proliferation of rumours regarding particular people' illnesses. Postponement of experimental and vocational courses has a major influence on medical science education, increasing the educational term and delaying students' graduation. This may result in less of a workforce. The lengthening of the faculty hiring process will further worsen this problem. Due to a scarcity of human resources, contingency plans must be drawn up in this regard [22].

3   Statement of the Problem and Aims

Since Sentiment Analysis is the hot topic for today era because it plays a vital role in deciding something, it helps to take the appropriate decision on something; therefore, the accuracy of a classifier is the main problem hence developing a model which can give the correct sentiment classification is the scope of the work in this field. Much work has been done for the same; every day, there is a new library for feature extraction & selection, and there is always be an opportunity for researchers to work on it.

- Developing a model which can classify the sentiment accordingly to student's feedback data
- To propose a novel machine learning classifier using the concept of NB and SVM
- Improving the accuracy of the proposed NBSVM model through hyperparameter tuning.
- Finding the significant keywords from the negative sentiment dataset.

4   Methodology

This section shows the overall work Fig. 2, text preprocessing, Neural Implementation of NBSVM, Feature Selection & Extraction, Algorithm of Proposed Model, Generating Log Count Ratio, Converting Word_ID sequences from DTM, and topic modelling.

4.1   Text Preprocessing

In sentiment analysis, data-preprocessing is essential for unstructured textual data. Data Preprocessing process carrying out the following steps for Sentiment Analysis, Lower Casing, Removal of Punctuations, Stop-Words, Frequent words, Emojis, Emoticons, Stemming & Lemmatization, Emoticons to words translation Emoji to word translation, Spelling correction so these steps must be followed as mentioned earlier, sometimes we do not need to apply all the steps it depends on the use case of data. For instance, in the case of sentiment analysis, we cannot remove the emojis & emoticons because they represent some kinds of the emotion of people.

Lower Casing: by default, it is already done by ML & DL libraries like Sklearn TF-IDF Vectorizer and Keras Tokenizer.

Lemmatization and Stemming: are identical in the context of text preprocessing only difference is because the meaning of that word may not be the same after the stemming process, and also, lemmatization is a bit slower than stemming. Still, in the current scenario, both text preprocessing processes are automatically done by available machine learning and deep learning libraries like NLTK, known as a natural language toolkit. In the same way that is stemming reduces inflected words to their word roots, lemmatization ensures that the root word remains in the dataset. But lemmatization process is quite time-consuming process as compare to stemming. So, we can apply stemming or lemmatization depending on the need for speed.

Conversion of Chat Words: This is a critical text preprocessing step if we are working with chat data. People in conversation use a lot of short words. Therefore, we might find it helpful to lengthen those words for our analysis.

Corrections to Spelling: Spelling correction is another crucial data-preparation step. Text data is prone to misspelling, so we should check for them before proceeding with our study (Fig. 3).

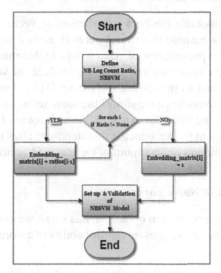

Fig. 2. Flow chart of the proposed model

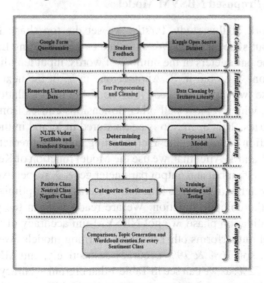

Fig. 3. The proposed methodology

4.2 A Neural Implementation of NBSVM in Keras

NBSVM is working as a text classifier that combines the features of SVB & NB, and it uses a log count ratio instead of word count. It fills a linear model like linear regressor does and Bayes theories. Recent studies show that NBSVM is quite powerful for classifying massive data. This chapter implements this model in a deep learning framework as a neural network like Keras.

4.3 Creating Word_ID Sequences from DTM

Here, we convert the student's feedback one-dimension vector with most filled zeros after preprocessing data because this neural network embedding layer takes words as input and returns scaler representation of given words. In this study, this EL (Embedding Layer) gives LCR (Log Count Ratio) of all given words in the student's feedback data. This EL model works fast as processing rows from DTM (Document Term Matrix); Simultaneously, both approaches have almost the same set of variables, and EL reduces the number of features and variables examined in each round. If the number of words exceeds the maximum length, we truncate this iteration; after this whole process, we calculate the mean, minimum & maximum of the received vector and return it to EL.

4.4 Generating LCR of Naïve Bayes

It is the final stage of the preparation of data. In this stage, we compute the Naïve Bayes Log Count Ration. These ratios represent the probability of a word appearing in a specific document class.

4.5 Defining the Proposed NBSVM Model

It is the actual work of this study. Firstly, we set the top shape for the embedding layer using the Input shape method. We calculate two Embedding Layers using a word embedding with the parameters of the number of words, input length, maximum length, and weights, and one is stored in X. Another one in Y. in the next step, calculate the dot product of these two layers and keep it in the Y. We use the flatten layer function to reshape the vector, which removes all other dimensions entries from the vector except one-dimension entries. This operation is again stored in Y, and in the next step, we use the activation function sigmoid in the Y embedding layer for predicting the probability with the range of -1 and 1. After that, we use the Model function of Keras for creating the layers of the graph with input and output parameter get & X respectively and then finally compilation the model with compile function of Keras, loss, optimizer, and metrics are the arguments of the compile function. We are ready to train the proposed NBSVM model; after the validation phase, we got NBSVM-uni accuracy of 83% and NBSVM-bi 86%; this model outperforms other machine learning models. We got SVM-uni and SVM-bi in comparison 76% & 79% accuracy respectively, and MNB-uni & MNB-bi accuracy is 69% & 72%, as we can see in Table 1 that bigram accuracy is more significant than unigram in this use case, but it may not be identical in some other use cases.

Algorithm: Naïve Bayes-Support Vector Machine

Input: Students Feedback Data
Output: Sentiment (Positive /Neutral/Negative)

Notations: EL=Embedding Layer, LCR= Log Count Ratio, IP=Input
LR= Logistics Regression, DTM= Document Term Matrix, NoW=
Number of Words, NB= Naïve Bayes, WE= Word Embedding, EI=
Embedding Initializer, NP= NumPy, ML= Max-Length

#Defining Ratios of NB Log-Count

```
Define LogCountRatio (DTM, X, Y): Log = DTM [X==Y]
       return [(Log) / (X==Y)]+1
    ratios =np.log[LogCountRatio(DTM, X,1)/ LCR (DTM, X,0))
    ratios = Sqeeze(ratios)
```

 # Algorithm for Defining the model

1: *Begin*
2: *Define* Model (NumofWords, max_len, ratios=NULL):
    # setting Ratios of NB Log-Count for EL
3: **EmbeddingLayer** = insert 0's[Numof Words]
4: *for* each k (1, NumofWords):
5: *if* ratios!=NULL:
    # when we have LCR then this model work as NBSVM
6: EmbeddingLayer[k] = ratios[--k]
7: *End of if*
8: *else:*
    #when we don't provide LCR then this model work as LR
9: EL[k] = 1
10: *End of else*
11: *End of for*
12: **End**

#Set up of the model

```
    get = Input(shape=(max_len,))
    X=WordEmbedding(NoW,1,IPlength=ML,weights =[EL]) (get)
    Y=WordEmbedding(NoW,1,IPlength=ML,EI='glorot_Normal) (get)
    Y = dot product of ( [X, Y], Axis=1)
    Y = Flatten()(Y)
    Y =Activation('Sigmoid')(Y)
    model = Creating layers of graph between [get and Y]
```
Calculating loss function *b/w* predicted & actual values
Optimizing the predicted values
Calculating the Accuracy metrics of NBSVM
Returning the NBSVM model

#Validating the proposed NBSVM Model

```
Validate = Model (NumofWords, MaxLength, Ratio=ratios)
```

Note: Whole Source Code Available at GitHub Repository **Click_Here**

5 Results and Discussions

The proposed Model Naïve Bayes -Support Vector Machine result is quite good than other machine learning models; NBSVM-Bigram gives better accuracy, whereas 71% of the feedback is negative and 13% are neutral. To learn about the negative feedback topic and their words, we used the Latent Dirichlet Allocation topic modelling technique. We categorized the issues into three significant classes problems, solutions, and suggestions. In case of problem topic and negative sentiment class, financial, resources, connectivity, health, practical, electricity, materials, fees, concentration, motivation, mobile data, social-life, and panic are the words. as per findings of these words from the negative sentiment class, we can say that these are the problem words which affected student' life. The frequency of these words is financial, connectivity, resources, and mobile data. Therefore, concerned authorities should focus on these findings and take necessary actions to overcome these problems. At the end of this pandemic, we should take bitter notes on these findings to be ready for the future (Fig. 4).

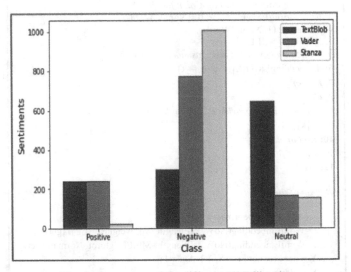

Fig. 4. Percentage of the different NLP libraries

6 Comparison with Existing Machine Learning Models

A comparison of the proposed model is given in Table 1, as we can see that proposed Model NBSVM-Unigram & NBSVM-Bigram accuracy is 83% and 86%, respectively. In contrast, other model's accuracy falls under the NBSVM accuracy. We also analyzed the same dataset with NB and SVM. SVM accuracy is comparable with the proposed model, whereas Naïve Bayes model accuracy is not up to the mark. NBSVM-bigram has the highest accuracy, 86%. In contrast, others have lower than NBSVM on textual student feedback data with an emoticon. Thus, Bigram variant model accuracy is more

Table 1. Comparison between the proposed naïve bayes support vector machine model and other models

Machine Learning (Models)	Accuracy (%)	Precision (%)	Recall (%)
Multinomial Naïve_Bayes-Unigram	69	66	63
Support_Vector_Machine-Unigram	76	73	71
Multinomial Naïve_Bayes-Bigram	72	71	68
Support_Vector_Machine-Bigram	79	77	74
Proposed Model (NBSVM)-Unigram	83	79	81
Proposed Model (NBSVM)-Bigram	86	83	79

remarkable than unigram for this dataset. All data related to this study is available at author's GitHub Repository [23] (Fig. 5, 6).

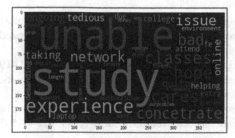

Fig. 5. Word-cloud for the negative sentiment   **Fig. 6.** Word-cloud for the entire dataset

7 Conclusions

As per the outcomes of this study, respective concerned authorities, universities, institutes, and, students community must take a serious note of these findings. The government/ Ministry of education must examine the universities and colleges teaching activities because our study reveals that students are not in favor of online teaching, and also 71% of feedbacks are negative. Therefore, proper examination of online teaching has become compulsory. Hence respective government bodies/vice-chancellor/directors/ chairman should address these problems and take necessary action. Together with humanity, we can fight against this COVID-19 pandemic. Future research is always there because since new frameworks and libraries for sentiment analysis, like we have implemented Naïve Bayes and Support Vector Machine together in Keras. We can apply some other available framework/library for the same use case and get better accuracy than this NBSVM proposed model.

References

1. Mendon, S., Dutta, P., Behl, A., Lessmann, S.: A hybrid approach of machine learning and lexicons to sentiment analysis: enhanced insights from twitter data of natural disasters. Inf. Syst. Front. **23**(5), 1145–1168 (2021). https://doi.org/10.1007/s10796-021-10107-x
2. Abidah, A., Hidaayatullaah, H.N., Simamora, R.M., Fehabutar, D., Mutakinati, L.: The impact of covid-19 to Indonesian education and its relation to the philosophy of "merdeka belajar." Studies in Philosophy of Science Educ. **1**(1), 38–49 (2020)
3. Schleicher, A.: The impact of COVID-19 on education insights from education at a glance (2020). oecd.org website: https://www.oecd.org/education/the-impact-of-covid-19-on-educat ion-insights-education-at-a-glance-2020.pdf
4. Tarkar, P.: Impact of COVID-19 pandemic on education system. International J. Adv. Science Technol. **29**(9), 3812–3814 (2020)
5. Satu, M.S., et al.: Tclustvid: a novel machine learning classification model to investigate topics and sentiment in covid-19 tweets. Knowl.-Based Syst. **226**, 107126 (2021)
6. Ullah, M.A., Marium, S.M., Begum, S.A., Dipa, N.S.: An algorithm and method for sentiment analysis using the text and emoticon. ICT Express **6**(4), 357–360 (2020)
7. Marinoni, G., Van't Land, H., Jensen, T.: The impact of Covid-19 on higher education around the world. IAU Global Survey Report (2020)
8. Hew, K.F., Qiao, C., Tang, Y.: Understanding student engagement in large-scale open online courses: a machine learning facilitated analysis of student's reflections in 18 highly rated MOOCs. Int. Rev. Research in Open and Distributed Learning **19**(3) (2018)
9. Di Pietro, G., Biagi, F., Costa, P., Karpiński, Z., Mazza, J.: The likely impact of COVID-19 on education: Reflections based on the existing literature and recent international datasets, Vol. 30275. Publications Office of the European Union (2020)
10. Kuhfeld, M., Soland, J., Tarasawa, B., Johnson, A., Ruzek, E., Liu, J.: Projecting the potential impact of COVID-19 school closures on academic achievement. Educ. Res. **49**(8), 549–565 (2020)
11. Hew, K.F., Hu, X., Qiao, C., Tang, Y.: What predicts student satisfaction with MOOCs: a gradient boosting trees supervised machine learning and sentiment analysis approach. Comput. Educ. **145**, 103724 (2020)
12. Singh, J., Singh, G., Singh, R.: Optimization of sentiment analysis using machine learning classifiers. HCIS **7**(1), 1–12 (2017)
13. Rustam, F., Khalid, M., Aslam, W., Rupapara, V., Mehmood, A., Choi, G.S.: Performance comparison of supervised machine learning models for Covid-19 tweets sentiment analysis. PLoS ONE **16**(2), e0245909 (2021)
14. Chaturvedi, K., Vishwakarma, D.K., Singh, N.: COVID-19 and its impact on education, social life and mental health of students: a survey. Child Youth Serv. Rev. **121**, 105866 (2021)
15. Chen, T., Peng, L., Jing, B., Wu, C., Yang, J., Cong, G.: The impact of the COVID-19 pandemic on user experience with online education platforms in China. Sustainability **12**(18), 7329 (2020)
16. Sinha, T., Chowdhury, T., Shaw, R.N., Ghosh, A.: Analysis and prediction of COVID-19 confirmed cases using deep learning models: a comparative study. In: Bianchini, M., Piuri, V., Das, S., Shaw, R.N. (eds.) Advanced Computing and Intelligent Technologies. LNNS, vol. 218, pp. 207–218. Springer, Singapore (2022). https://doi.org/10.1007/978-981-16-2164-2_18
17. Arora, A.K., Srinivasan, R.: Impact of pandemic COVID-19 on the teaching–learning process: a study of higher education teachers. Prabandhan: Indian J. Manage. **13**(4), 43–56 (2020)
18. Chauhan, D., Singh, C.: Sentimental analysis on impact of COVID-19 outbreak. In: Agrawal, S., Kumar Gupta, K., H. Chan, J., Agrawal, J., Gupta, M. (eds.) Machine Intelligence and

Smart Systems. AIS, pp. 233–242. Springer, Singapore (2021). https://doi.org/10.1007/978-981-33-4893-6_21

19. Rawat, R., Mahor, V., Chirgaiya, S., Shaw, R.N., Ghosh, A.: Sentiment analysis at online social network for cyber-malicious post reviews using machine learning techniques. In: Bansal, J.C., Paprzycki, M., Bianchini, M., Das, S. (eds.) Computationally Intelligent Systems and their Applications. SCI, vol. 950, pp. 113–130. Springer, Singapore (2021). https://doi.org/10.1007/978-981-16-0407-2_9

20. Qaiser, S.: A comparison of machine learning techniques for sentiment analysis. Turkish J. Computer and Mathematics Educ. (TURCOMAT) 12(3), 1738–1744 (2021)

21. Singh, M., Jakhar, A.K., Pandey, S.: Sentiment analysis on the impact of coronavirus in social life using the BERT model. Soc. Netw. Anal. Min. 11(1), 1–11 (2021). https://doi.org/10.1007/s13278-021-00737-z

22. Van Atteveldt, W., van der Velden, M.A., Boukes, M.: The validity of sentiment analysis: comparing manual annotation, crowd-coding, dictionary approaches, and machine learning algorithms. Commun. Methods Meas. 15(2), 121–140 (2021)

23. https://github.com/SumitMohan/COVID-19-Pandemic-Impact

Implementation of Optimal Leaf Feature Selection-Based Plant Leaf Disease Classification Framework with RNN+GRU Technique

Kalicharan Sahu[✉] and Sonajharia Minz

School of Computer and Systems Sciences, Jawaharlal Nehru University (JNU), New Delhi,
India
kc.ittech@gmail.com

Abstract. Agricultural productivity is the most important factor for supporting the food sources in the populated economy. Therefore, it is highly necessary to solve the disease detection problems that affect the plant agricultural production since it occurs in the natural way. The early disease identification is required for increasing the crop yield in the agricultural sector. The leaf diseases like yellow curved, septoria leaf spot, late blight and bacterial spot are mostly reduced the quality of the crop. Automated techniques have to be developed for classifying the plant diseases and also it supports to take preventive measures to identifying the leaf disease symptoms. Hence, this chapter aims to design the plant leaf disease identification model with efficient deep learning architecture integrated to leaf features to provide the accurate detection results. The input images are collected and utilized for primary stage of processing using the CLAHE technique. Then, the pre-processed images are given into the Leaf segmentation phase, where the appropriate leaf regions are segmented to get accurate classification results. The segmented images are used in the feature extraction phase. Further, the extracted features are considered for choosing the optimal features for classification phase through Fisher Discriminant Analysis (FDA) technique. The optimal features are given into classification phase, in which Recurrent Neural Network (RNN) and Gated Recurrent Units (GRU) are used for performing the leaf disease classification. Experimental analysis reveals that the proposed approach attains better classification performance when considering the analysis with various performance measures.

Keywords: Plant leaf disease classification · Optimal leaf feature selection · Fisher Discriminant Analysis · Recurrent Neural Network · Gated Recurrent Units

1 Introduction

Plant diseases are considered as the most important issues that cause the quality and quantity losses over agricultural production [1]. These losses in production may cause huge negative impact over the production cost and also in the stakeholders gain in

© The Author(s), under exclusive license to Springer Nature Switzerland AG 2023
R. N. Shaw et al. (Eds.): ICACIS 2022, CCIS 1749, pp. 576–592, 2023.
https://doi.org/10.1007/978-3-031-25088-0_51

the agricultural sector [2]. On the other hand, there is an insufficiency in the tools for accurately recognizing the crop diseases. The traditional way of detecting and identifying the plant diseases by visualizing the plant pathologies and farmers for making decisions according to the experiences that may lead to inaccurate results since many of the plant diseases are seem to be relevant in their appearance and symptoms [3]. In addition, their experiences have to be upgraded for next-to-next generations. Inaccurate results in the plant disease may cause inappropriate usage of pesticides that acquires high production cost. These challenges in the traditional detection methods evidences to develop robust and automatic plant disease detection models for supporting farmers particularly for replacing the inexperience and young ones in detecting the plant diseases [4]. Hence, deep learning and machine learning techniques come into the detection models since it has much advancement from the earlier used methods, and it helps to perform early disease detection for preserving the crop at the right time [5].

When utilizing conventional machine learning techniques, the expertise feature extraction and selection techniques are required. It is highly required to develop an efficient feature extraction strategy that should be able to acquire most significant features and pass them into the machine learning classifiers [3]. The considered classifier gets training using the input data and utilizes the trained information for making effective classification results. On the other hand, enhanced results are acquired through deep learning techniques [6], which are also utilized in the image revolutionizing and also for object classification sector. Instead of depending on the handcrafted features, these deep learning techniques are involved as the end-to-end approaches since they perform automatically in order to learn the similar type of features without relying on the expert knowledge [7]. It is highly sufficient in providing better efficiency by extracting the essential feature description using the huge scale of input plant images [8].

Deep learning ensures the great opportunity for the identifiers for detecting the crop diseases at the right time that enhances the accuracy of the plant protection. This also leads to its scope in the field of computer vision over the precision agriculture. The deep learning technique like Convolutional Neural Network (CNN) contains filter size and diver se pooling operations for diagnosing the rice diseases, which improves the accuracy performance [9]. Further, the CNN is also used for detecting the maize disease like northern leaf blight, which overcomes the challenges caused by the limited data off the grown plants. The detection scheme has attained better accuracy. Some of the CNN-based techniques are useful for enhancing the accuracy at some extent, but it requires high number of parameters as well as high training time in convergence that shows negative impacts on the recognition rate [10]. For gaining more identification rate in plant disease, it is required for designing the plant disease recognition framework for attaining more recognition accuracy with minimum parameters.

Most significance of the work is mentioned as below.

- To design an efficient plant disease identification framework with hybrid deep learning strategy with optimal plant leaf disease features to gain more accurate results for taking earlier preventive measures with the right decision.
- To perform the optimal feature selection with FDA to provide optimal leaf disease features for RNN and GRU as the hybrid deep learning model for recognizing the plant diseases in the leaf.

- To examine the developed plant leaf disease identification framework with conventional classifiers using diverse performance metrics.

The rest of the sections in the developed plant disease classification framework are described as follows. In Sect. 2, the existing works of the concerned model are discussed. In Sect. 3, the implemented plant disease diagnosis framework using deep learning technique. In Sect. 4, the leaf segmentation with FCM and feature extraction techniques is used for the identification model. In Sect. 5, the optimal feature selection with FDA and further, classification techniques are used. The results attained and conclusion made for implemented model is correspondingly given in Sects. 6 and 7.

2   Literature Survey

2.1   Related Works

In 2018, Zhang et al. [13] have utilized an enhanced GoogLeNet and Cifar10 frameworks according to deep learning for enhancing the detection accuracy regarding the maize leaf diseases and also has minimized the parameter requirement on the network. Two distinct techniques were employed for training and testing the maize leaf diseases, which was performed through the adjustments over the parameter, varying the pooling fusions, combining the dropout operations and also has minimized the classifiers count. The enhanced techniques were enhanced the disease detection accuracy and also decreased the convergence iterations that has enhanced the recognition efficiency and model training. In 2021, Ahmad et al. [14] have developed the stepwise transfer learning technique for providing the fast convergence that reduced the overfitting and also prevented the negative transfer learning with the considerations of knowledge transfer across domains. This developed model was undergone training and also estimated over two different standard datasets. The developed framework has assured to be with better accuracy on both the datasets.

In 2021, Atila et al. [15] have developed EfficientNet for categorizing the plant disease, and also the efficiency of the framework has been estimated by comparing with the conventional deep learning techniques. This developed framework has been trained with the transfer learning technique. The transfer learning approach has comprised of many layers for training performance. The outcomes have acquired with the test dataset that has more performance rate with the comparison over the other deep learning frameworks.

2.2   Problem Statement

Most of the plant disease diagnosis causes various challenges in identifying different types of diseases as they have relevant appearance and symptoms. So, it is necessary to move towards the deep learning approaches, and some of the deep learning techniques used for diagnosing the plant leaf diseases are mentioned in Table 1. CNN [11] is highly effective in diagnosing the unstructured dataset and also enhances the accuracy rate. Yet, it has utilized with the limited amount of crop affected diseases and minimum number of disease images trained to the network. AlexNet, VGG16, ResNet-50 [12] acquires superior accuracy and does not cause any overfitting problems. Yet, it depends on more amounts of training data for acquiring high robustness. DCNN [13] is used for practical applications since it has better accuracy and rapid speed on detecting the plant diseases when compared to other methods. Still, it is unable to identify the other types of plant diseases with this model. MobileNet [14] ensures effective classification results with plant leaf disease images. Still, it is affected with the prediction of slight or moderate disease affected over the plants. EfficientNet [15] provides the quantifying uncertainty under the valuable background of information, which is sufficient for decisions making. But, it creates minimum confidence scores for both the incorrect and correct samples. Therefore, these challenges push to utilize the advanced deep learning strategy for diagnosing the plant diseases.

Table 1. Features and challenges of existing plant disease diagnosis frameworks

Author [citation]	Methodology	Features	Challenges
Barburiceanu et al. [11]	CNN	• It is highly effective in diagnosing the unstructured dataset and also enhances the accuracy rate	• It has utilized with the limited amount of crop affected diseases and minimum number of disease images trained to the network
Pham et al. [12]	AlexNet, VGG16, ResNet-50	• It acquires superior accuracy and does not cause any overfitting problems	• It depends on more amounts of training data for acquiring high robustness
Zhang et al. [13]	DCNN	• It is used for practical applications since it has better accuracy and rapid speed on detecting the plant diseases when compared to other methods	• It is unable to identify the other types of plant diseases with this model
Ahmad et al. [14]	MobileNet	• It ensures effective classification results with plant leaf disease images	• It is affected with the prediction of slight or moderate disease affected over the plants
Atila et al. [15]	EfficientNet	• It provides the quantifying uncertainty under the valuable background of information, which is sufficient for decisions making	• It creates minimum confidence scores for both the incorrect and correct samples

3 Proposed Plant Disease Classification Architecture

An automated plant leaf disease identification model is developed with hybrid deep learning techniques to provide the accurate detection results using the plant leaf images. The leaf images are gathered from the standard datasets that are split into ten different datasets based on the disease classes. The gathered images are utilized for pre-processing with the CLAHE technique. Then, the pre-processed images are given into the leaf segmentation using FCM approach to gain better and accurate classification outcomes. The segmented images are used in the feature extraction phase for extracting shape features, color features, and texture features. Further, the extracted features are optimal feature selection stage through FDA technique to improve the classification efficiency. The optimal features are given into classification phase, in which hybrid deep learning technique is developed with RNN, and GRU are used for performing the leaf disease classification. An automatic plant disease diagnosis models with deep learning approach is shown in Fig. 1.

3.1 Diverse Plant Disease Datasets

The developed framework utilize the dataset named "New Plant Diseases Dataset", from which ten datasets are generated according to their disease class labels. The input images

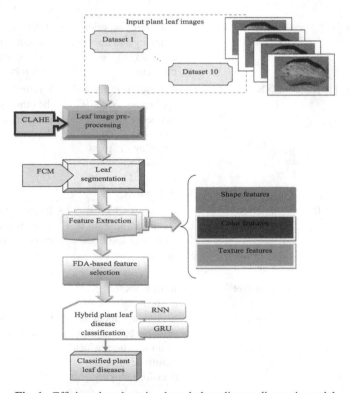

Fig. 1. Efficient deep learning-based plant disease diagnosis model

are obtained through the "10 https://www.kaggle.com/vipoooool/new-plant-diseases-dat aset: access date: 2022–09-06". Here, the dataset is comprised of 87k leaf images under the "healthy and diseased images", that are considered into 38 classes. The implemented plant disease diagnosis framework has generated ten datasets from this dataset, which apple leaf images as the dataset 1, cherry leaf images as the dataset 2, corn leaf images as the dataset 3, grape leaf images as the dataset 4, peach leaf images as the dataset 5, pepper leaf images as the dataset 6, potato leaf images as the dataset 7, strawberry leaf images as the dataset 8, tomato leaf images as the dataset 10 and citrus leaf images as dataset 10 for identifying the diverse classes of leaf diseases.

3.2 Leaf Image Pre-processing

The input images are given into the pre-processing phase, where CLAHE [16] is used for enhancing the fidelity and contrast on the images. This technique requires two steps for processing that are histogram equalization and image intensity adjustment for assuring the information over the input images. The pixels are sorted according to the uniform intensity value with the concept of histogram equalization to enhance the image contrast that is formulated in Eq. (1).

$$HE(xy(py, qy)) = round\left(\frac{cf(xy(py, qy)) - cf_{min}}{(ry \times cy) - cf} \times Ny - 1 \right) \quad (1)$$

Here, the intensities count is indicated by Ny, the present pixel's intensity is indicated by $cf(xy(py, qy))$, the gray level's frequency level is represented by cf, the minimum CDF value is indicated by cf_{min}. The product of pixel count at rows and columns are represented by ry and cy. The contrast improved image is represented by $HE(xy(py, qy))$. The pre-processed image using CLAHE is represented by LI_a^{pre}, where $a = 1, 2, \ldots, A$ and A represents the total pre-processed images.

4 Leaf Image Segmentation and Feature Extraction

The pre-processed images are given into the segmentation process using FCM approach [17]. FCM clustering is considered as the unsupervised clustering approach. It employs one input vectors for diverse clusters based on its objective function that is shown in Eq. (2).

$$Li_{ji} = \sum_{mi=1}^{Ji} \sum_{ni=1}^{Ni} wi_{mi\,ni}^{ji} \|zi_{mi} - fi_{ni}\|^2 \quad (2)$$

Here, the fuzzier at ni^{th} position over d-dimensional data is represented by ji and the clusters ni along with membership degree zi_{mi} that is represented by $wi_{mi\,ni}$. The cluster center at ni^{th} position is indicated by fi_{ni}. The criteria $\|*\|$ shown for indicating the centre similarity and computed data. The membership of $wi_{mi\,ni}$ and the cluster center fi_{ni} are improvised with the tuning over the objective function in an iterative manner. This type of fuzzy portioning is described in Eq. (3).

$$wi_{mi\,ni} = \frac{1}{\sum\limits_{qi=1}^{fi}\left(\frac{\|zi_{ni}-fi_{ni}\|}{\|zi_{ni}-fi_{pi}\|}\right)^{\frac{2}{fi-1}}} \tag{3}$$

$$fi_n i = \frac{\sum\limits_{mi=1}^{Ji} wi_{mi\,ni}^{ji} zi_{ni}}{\sum\limits_{mi=1}^{Ji} wi_{mi\,ni}^{ji}} \tag{4}$$

$$\max_{mi\,ni}\left\{\left\|wi_{mi\,ni}^{qi+1} - wi_{mi\,ni}^{qi}\right\|\right\} < \varepsilon \tag{5}$$

The last iterative process is described in Eq. (5), where the iteration count is indicated by qi and the termination limit stays between $(0, 1)$ that is expressed by ε. The leaf segmentation images from FCM technique is indicated by $LI_a^{seg\_fcm}$.

The leaf features required for the proposed model is obtained through the three different types like shape features through the contour technique, color features through HSV, LAB and YCRCB techniques and texture features through GLCM and LBP techniques.

Leaf Shape Feature Extraction with Contour Technique [18]: This technique executes the shape properties of the input object images, which differentiates the shapes with same region-shape properties as well as with distinct contour shape-based properties. This description is efficient for the applications that have more intraclass variability among shape owing to the object deformations or perspective deformations.

Leaf Color Feature Extraction [19]: Different types of color features such as HSV, LAB and YCbCr are extracted. Color transformation is used for estimating the chromaticity and luminosity layers that is efficient classify the colors based on the human vision system and also provides high efficiency in subjective evaluation of leaf images judgment.

GLCM-Based Texture Feature Extraction [19]*:* This method employs the separated images for acquiring the textural characteristic features belongs to leaves. GLCM obtains the object texture used for representing the pixel arrangement over the "spatial relationship". The object texture is obtained by computing with the co-variance matrix along with the pixel value.

LBP-Based Texture Feature Extraction [20]*:* It is considered as the efficient tool to acquire the texture features, which includes the local intensity variation about the segmented images to ensure the improved discrimination features. The intensity of the segmented images is indicated by Tr over the pixel value as (ar_{dr}, br_{dr}) without considering the center pixel Tr_{cr}. Further, the LBP computation belongs to image pixel

(ar_{dr}, br_{dr}) that is expressed in Eq. (6).

$$lbp(ar_{dr}, br_{dr}) = \sum_{ir=0}^{Ir} tr(Tr_{Ir} - Tr_{Cr})2^{ir},$$

$$where \ tr(ar) = \begin{cases} 1, & ar \geq 0 \\ 0, & otherwise \end{cases}$$

(6)

Here, the center pixel value is indicated by Tr_{cr}, the neighboring value is represented by Tr_{Ir}, the pixel count at the neighborhood is shown by ar_{dr}, and the neighborhood radius is represented by br_{dr}. The extracted shape, color and texture features are together indicated by FeT_f^{cst}.

5   Optimal Deep Learning-Based Classification Model

5.1   Optimal Leaf Image Feature Selection

The concatenated features FeT_f^{cst} are given into optimal feature selection using FDA. This technique is considered as the optimal dimensionality reduction method for enhancing the separability among the data classes. It computes the group of projection vectors that increase the scatter among the classes and at the same time, reducing the scatter among same class. Initially, the training data gets stacked for entire classes into particular matrix $Y \in \Re^{o \times n}$, where the total scatter matrix at j^{th} row over Y together with column vector y_j is determined through Eq. (7).

$$T_s = \sum_{j=1}^{m} (y_j - \bar{y})(y_j - \bar{y})^T$$

(7)

Here, the total mean vector is indicated by $\bar{y}$ and then, consider the matrix Y_j with rows Y for respective classes j that is given in Eq. (8).

$$T_j = \sum_{y_j \in Y_j} (y_j - \bar{y}_j)(y_j - \bar{y}_j)^T$$

(8)

This equation is computed for within-scatter matrix and the class count is assumed to be d, then the derivation can be made by Eq. (9).

$$T_x = \sum_{j=1}^{d} T_j$$

(9)

Above equations shows the derivation for the within-scatter matrix and the between-class scatter matrix is given as Eq. (10).

$$T_c = \sum_{j=1}^{d} m_j (y_j - \bar{y})(y_j - \bar{y})^T$$

(10)

Here, the term m_j indicates the observations count among class j. Further, the observation shows that the total-scatter matrix is computed to be equal to the total sum of within-scatter matrix and between-scatter matrix. FDA vectors are equivalent when compared to the generalized eigenvectors of eigenvalue problem that is given in Eq. (11).

$$T_c z_j = \lambda_j T_z z_j \tag{11}$$

Here, the term λ_j shows the eigenvalues used for indicating the "degree of overall separability among the classes". Also, the norm is generally considered to be $\|z_j\| = 1$. The selected optimal features are indicated by FeT_g^{opt}, where $g = 1, 2, 3, \ldots, G$ and G represent the total number of optimal features from FDA.

5.2 Hybrid Deep Learning-Based Classification Model

In this model, RNN and GRU architecture are integrated for categorizing the plant diseases with the processing of optimal features FeT_g^{opt}. The description of RNN and GRU are given as follows.

RNN [21]: It is designed with collection of neural networks and its functions according to the outcome of the earlier network. This network initializes the arrangement of sequence of input features that made enhancement in identification of variation among the optimal features. The RNN output over the network is computed based on the optimal features that are given by Eq. (12).

$$Sp_{Tp} = Ap_{\tanh}\left(Bp_1 + uSp_{Tp-1} + vZp_{Tp}\right) \tag{12}$$

$$\widehat{O}_{PTp} = Ap_{soft\,max}\left(Bp_2 + wSp_{Tp}\right) \tag{13}$$

Here, the terms Bp_1 and Bp_2 are indicated for the weight vectors, the tanh activation function is denoted by $Ap_{\tanh}$, the softmax activation function is depicted by $Ap_{soft\,max}$, the weight matrices are given by u, v and w and the network state is shown by Sp_{Tp} over the time Tp.

GRU [22]: It has the GRU activation that is indicated as in Eq. (14).

$$br_{vr}^{kr} = \left(1 - ar_{vr}^{kr}\right)br_{vr-1}^{kr} + ar_{vr}^{kr}\tilde{b}r_{vr}^{kr} \tag{14}$$

Here, the GRU activation is indicated by br_{vr}^{kr} at the interval of vr, which is computed between the earlier region br_{vr-1}^{kr} and candidate activation stage $\tilde{b}r_{vr}^{kr}$. The update gate is depicted as in Eq. (15).

$$ar_{vr}^{kr} = \sigma\left(\Pr_{dr} cr_{vr} + Rr_{vr}br_{vr-1}\right)^{kr} \tag{15}$$

Here, the term ar_{vr}^{kr} indicates the update gate and the candidate activation $\tilde{b}r_{vr}^{kr}$ are worked according to Eq. (16).

$$\tilde{b}r_{vr}^{kr} = \tanh(\Pr cr_{vr} + Rr(dr_{vr} * br_{vr-1}))^{kr} \tag{16}$$

The element wise multiplication is given by $*$. The reset gate is formulated in Eq. (17).

$$dr_{vr}^{kr} = \sigma \left(\Pr_{dr} cr_{vr} + Rr_{dr} br_{vr-1} \right)^{kr} \tag{17}$$

Here, the term d_{vv}^{kk} is termed for indicating the reset gate.

Finally, the classification output that is classified different leaf diseases are obtained through averaging function taken between the output of RNN and the output of GRU. This whole classification procedure is given in Fig. 2.

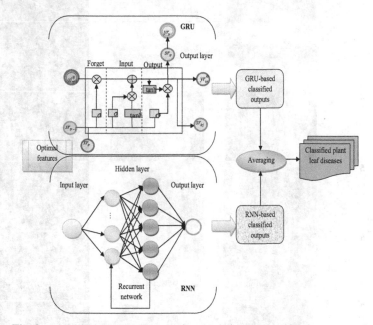

Fig. 2. Hybrid RNN-GRU-based plant leaf disease classification approach

6   Results and Discussions

6.1   Experimental Setup and Performance Metrics

The platform involved for designing the implemented plant disease diagnosis framework was Python. The proposed RNN-GRU estimated its efficiency by comparing with other conventional classifiers like "CNN [11], Long Short Term Memory (LSTM) [23], RNN [21] and GRU [22]".

The implemented plant disease diagnosis framework is tested its efficiency with distinct performance metrics that are given in "https://en.wikipedia.org/wiki/Precision_and_recall".

6.2   Leaf Image Segmentation Results

The FCM-based segmented results of the implemented plant disease diagnosis framework using ten datasets are depicted in Fig. 3.

Dataset description	Original image	Pre-processed image	Segmented image

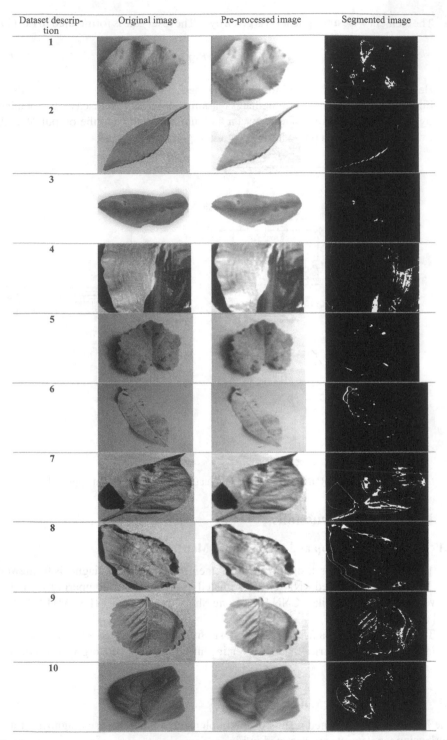

Fig. 3. Segmented Images from FCM mechanism for developed plant disease diagnosis framework

6.3 Efficacy Analysis of Implemented Model

The implemented plant disease diagnosis framework is tested that is given in Table 2 with the consideration of ten datasets. The developed RNN-GRU secures 2.72%, 3.97%, 1.81% and 1.07% better classification results than CNN, LSTM, RNN and GRU, respectively at the dataset 1 analysis. Similarly, the enhanced performance is observed in the proposed RNN-GRU-based plant disease classification approach.

Table 2. Overall estimation on developed plant disease diagnosis framework with different classifiers using ten datasets

Measures	CNN [11]	LSTM [23]	RNN [21]	GRU [22]	RNN-GRU
Dataset 1					
Accuracy	92.62738	91.50798	93.45085	94.13278	95.14925
F1-Score	86.26229	84.375	87.6964	88.89971	90.753
Specificity	92.64025	91.43935	93.48087	94.18425	95.12781
NPV	92.64025	91.43935	93.48087	94.18425	95.12781
FNR	7.41122	8.286155	6.639218	6.021616	4.786413
FPR	7.359753	8.560645	6.519128	5.815749	4.872191
FDR	19.25494	21.87637	17.31996	15.6582	13.30834
Precision	80.74506	78.12363	82.68004	84.3418	86.69166
MCC	81.61157	79.07224	83.54182	85.15767	87.65173
Sensitivity	92.58878	91.71384	93.36078	93.97838	95.21359
Dataset 2					
Accuracy	92.53136	91.33409	93.50057	94.35576	95.09692
F1-Score	92.5271	91.34396	93.50057	94.3718	95.09692
Specificity	92.58837	91.22007	93.50057	94.0707	95.09692
NPV	92.58837	91.22007	93.50057	94.0707	95.09692
FNR	7.525656	8.551881	6.49943	5.359179	4.903079
FPR	7.411631	8.779932	6.49943	5.929304	4.903079
FDR	7.420091	8.759954 ara>	6.49943	5.895692	4.903079
Precision	92.57991	91.24005	93.50057	94.10431	95.09692
MCC	85.06277	82.6684	87.00114	88.71296	90.19384
Sensitivity	92.47434	91.44812	93.50057	94.64082	95.09692
Dataset 3					
Accuracy	92.7422	91.19869	93.53038	94.08867	95.20525
MCC	79.67285	75.76636	81.6549	83.12913	86.10316

(continued)

Table 2. (*continued*)

Measures	CNN [11]	LSTM [23]	RNN [21]	GRU [22]	RNN-GRU
Specificity	92.73399	91.25616	93.55501	94.08867	95.19704
FDR	23.85445	27.77053	21.62534	20.08368	16.78623
FPR	7.26601	8.743842	6.444992	5.91133	4.802956
NPV	92.73399	91.25616	93.55501	94.08867	95.19704
FNR	7.224959	9.031199	6.568144	5.91133	4.761905
F1-Score	83.64175	80.52326	85.24345	86.42534	88.82083
Precision	76.14555	72.22947	78.37466	79.91632	83.21377
Sensitivity	92.77504	90.9688	93.43186	94.08867	95.2381
Dataset 4					
Accuracy	92.59158	91.44341	93.56206	94.17715	95.17496
F1-Score	86.20865	84.21583	87.91378	88.99793	90.79531
Specificity	92.58247	91.48897	93.53016	94.16803	95.1704
NPV	92.58247	91.48897	93.53016	94.16803	95.1704
FNR	7.381083	8.693275	6.342264	5.795517	4.811372
FPR	7.417532	8.511026	6.469838	5.831966	4.829597
FDR	19.37173	21.85307	17.16634	15.66324	13.21037
Precision	80.62827	78.14693	82.83366	84.33676	86.78963
MCC	81.5419	78.84187	83.84137	85.29597	87.70678
Sensitivity	92.61892	91.30672	93.65774	94.20448	95.18863
Dataset 5					
Accuracy	92.49307	91.37119	93.57341	94.12742	95.1662
FDR	19.65401	22.06994	17.0516	15.69796	13.26942
Specificity	92.44691	91.37581	93.59187	94.16436	95.14312
FNR	7.368421	8.642659	6.481994	5.98338	4.764543
FPR	7.553093	8.624192	6.408126	5.835642	4.856879
NPV	92.44691	91.37581	93.59187	94.16436	95.14312
Precision	80.34599	77.93006	82.9484	84.30204	86.73058
F1-Score	86.0525	84.1112	87.91667	88.89471	90.78426
Sensitivity	92.63158	91.35734	93.51801	94.01662	95.23546
MCC	81.33589	78.70534	83.8395	85.15244	87.69377
Dataset 6					

(*continued*)

Table 2. (*continued*)

Measures	CNN [11]	LSTM [23]	RNN [21]	GRU [22]	RNN-GRU
Accuracy	92.64871	91.63861	93.54658	94.10774	95.06173
F1-Score	92.64458	91.65266	93.54295	94.11105	95.06173
Specificity	92.70483	91.47026	93.60269	94.05163	95.06173
NPV	92.70483	91.47026	93.60269	94.05163	95.06173
FNR	7.407407	8.193042	6.50954	5.836139	4.938272
FPR	7.295174	8.529742	6.397306	5.948373	4.938272
FDR	7.303371	8.501119	6.404494	5.941704	4.938272
Precision	92.69663	91.49888	93.59551	94.0583	95.06173
MCC	85.29747	83.27769	87.09321	88.21554	90.12346
Sensitivity	92.59259	91.80696	93.49046	94.16386	95.06173
Dataset 7					
NPV	93.23077	91.58974	93.53846	94.35897	95.07692
Specificity	93.23077	91.58974	93.53846	94.35897	95.07692
Accuracy	92.92308	91.48718	93.53846	94.30769	95.02564
FPR	6.769231	8.410256	6.461538	5.641026	4.923077
FNR	7.384615	8.615385	6.461538	5.74359	5.025641
Precision	93.18885	91.57246	93.53846	94.35318	95.07187
FDR	6.811146	8.427544	6.461538	5.646817	4.928131
Sensitivity	92.61538	91.38462	93.53846	94.25641	94.97436
MCC	85.84778	82.97453	87.07692	88.61543	90.05133
F1-Score	92.90123	91.47844	93.53846	94.30477	95.02309
Dataset 8					
Accuracy	92.61337	91.51473	93.59514	94.08602	95.16129
Sensitivity	92.56662	91.30435	93.82889	94.1094	95.16129
Specificity	92.63675	91.61992	93.47826	94.07433	95.16129
Precision	86.27451	84.49059	87.79528	88.81535	90.76923
FPR	7.363254	8.380084	6.521739	5.925666	4.83871
FNR	7.43338	8.695652	6.171108	5.890603	4.83871
NPV	92.63675	91.61992	93.47826	94.07433	95.16129
FDR	13.72549	15.50941	12.20472	11.18465	9.230769
F1-Score	89.30988	87.76542	90.71186	91.38577	92.91339

(*continued*)

Table 2. (*continued*)

Measures	CNN [11]	LSTM [23]	RNN [21]	GRU [22]	RNN-GRU
MCC	83.79868	81.42869	85.94288	86.97335	89.30045
Dataset 9					
FPR	7.111111	8.888889	6.444444	5.777778	4.777778
Sensitivity	92.55556	91.44444	93.55556	94.22222	95.33333
NPV	92.88889	91.11111	93.55556	94.22222	95.22222
Accuracy	92.72222	91.27778	93.55556	94.22222	95.27778
Precision	92.86511	91.14064	93.55556	94.22222	95.22752
Specificity	92.88889	91.11111	93.55556	94.22222	95.22222
FNR	7.444444	8.555556	6.444444	5.777778	4.666667
F1-Score	92.71007	91.29229	93.55556	94.22222	95.2804
FDR	7.134894	8.859358	6.444444	5.777778	4.772475
MCC	85.44492	82.55601	87.11111	88.44444	90.55561
Dataset 10					
FPR	7.359748	8.598086	6.463104	5.808797	4.866109
Specificity	92.64025	91.40191	93.5369	94.1912	95.13389
Sensitivity	92.51908	91.34133	93.54417	94.22028	95.15812
Accuracy	92.62814	91.39586	93.53762	94.19411	95.13631
FNR	7.480916	8.65867	6.455834	5.779716	4.841876
Precision	58.27724	54.1365	61.659	64.31443	68.48218
NPV	92.64025	91.40191	93.5369	94.1912	95.13389
F1-Score	71.51045	67.9815	74.32631	76.44665	79.64586
MCC	69.90795	66.28155	72.8221	75.00842	78.31105
FDR	41.72276	45.8635	38.341	35.68557	31.51782

7 Conclusion

This chapter has presented an automated plant leaf disease identification model using hybrid deep learning techniques to provide accurate detection results using the plant leaf images. The optimal features were given into classification phase, in which hybrid deep learning technique was developed with RNN and GRU for performing the leaf disease classification. The developed model has obtained 5.2%, 7.4%, 3.38% and 2.19% improved efficiency than CNN, LSTM, RNN and GRU, respectively at the dataset 8 analyses. Therefore, better efficiency was observed in the developed framework in classifying the plant leaf disease when compared to other classification techniques.

References

1. Ferentinos, K.P.: Deep learning models for plant disease detection and diagnosis. Comput. Electron. Agric. **145**, 311–318 (2018)
2. Aasha Nandhini, S., Hemalatha, R., Radha, S., Indumathi, K.: Web enabled plant disease detection system for agricultural applications using WMSN. Wirel. Pers. Commun. **102**, 725–740 (2018)
3. Sachdeva, G., Singh, P., Kaur, P.: Plant leaf disease classification using deep convolutional neural network with Bayesian learning. Mater. Today Proc. **45**(Part 6), 5584–5590 (2021)
4. Tiwari, V., Joshi, R.C., Dutta, M.K.: Dense convolutional neural networks based multiclass plant disease detection and classification using leaf images. Ecol. Inform. **63**, 101289 (2021)
5. Vishnoi, V.K., Kumar, K., Kumar, B.: Plant disease detection using computational intelligence and image processing. J. Plant Dis. Prot. **128**, 19–53 (2021)
6. Gajjar, R., Gajjar, N., Thakor, V.J., Patel, N.P., Ruparelia, S.: Real-time detection and identification of plant leaf diseases using convolutional neural networks on an embedded platform. Vis. Comput. **38**, 2923–2938 (2021). https://doi.org/10.1007/s00371-021-02164-9
7. Saleem, M., Atta, B.M., Ali, Z., Bilal, M.: Laser-induced fluorescence spectroscopy for early disease detection in grapefruit plants. Photochem. Photobiol. Sci. **19**, 713–721 (2020)
8. Raji, S.N., et al.: Detection and classification of mosaic virus disease in cassava plants by proximal sensing of photochemical reflectance index. J. Indian Soc. Remote Sens. **44**, 875–883 (2016)
9. Tuncer, A.: Cost-optimized hybrid convolutional neural networks for detection of plant leaf diseases. J. Ambient Intell. Humaniz. Comput. **12**, 8625–8636 (2021). https://doi.org/10.1007/s12652-021-03289-4
10. Abbas, A., Jain, S., Gour, M., Vankudothu, S.: Tomato plant disease detection using transfer learning with C-GAN synthetic images. Comput. Electron. Agric. **187**, 106279 (2021)
11. Barburiceanu, S., Meza, S., Orza, B., Malutan, R., Terebes, R.: Convolutional neural networks for texture feature extraction. applications to leaf disease classification in precision agriculture. IEEE Access **9**, 160085–160103 (2021)
12. Pham, T.N., Tran, L.V., Dao, S.V.T.: Early Disease classification of mango leaves using feed-forward neural network and hybrid metaheuristic feature selection. IEEE Access **8**, 189960–189973 (2020)
13. Zhang, X., Qiao, Y., Meng, F., Fan, C., Zhang, M.: Identification of maize leaf diseases using improved deep convolutional neural networks. IEEE Access **6**, 30370–30377 (2018)
14. Ahmad, M., Abdullah, M., Moon, H., Han, D.: Plant disease detection in imbalanced datasets using efficient convolutional neural networks with stepwise transfer learning. IEEE Access **9**, 140565–140580 (2021)
15. Atila, Ü., Uçar, M., Akyol, K., Uçar, E.: Plant leaf disease classification using EfficientNet deep learning model. Ecol. Inform. **61**, 101182 (2021)
16. Koonsanit, K., Thongvigitmanee, S., Pongnapang, N., Thajchayapong, P.: Image enhancement on digital x-ray images using N-CLAHE. In: Biomedical Engineering International Conference (BMEiCON), pp. 1–4 (2017)
17. Mridha, K., et.al.: Plant disease detection using web application by neural network. In: 2021 IEEE 6th International Conference on Computing, Communication and Automation (ICCCA), pp. 130–136 (2021). https://doi.org/10.1109/ICCCA52192.2021.9666354
18. Yang, C., Fang, L., Wei, H.: Learning contour-based mid-level representation for shape classification. IEEE Access **8**, 157587–157601 (2020)
19. Mohan Sai, S., Gopichand, G., Vikas Reddy, C., Mona Teja, K.: High accurate unhealthy leaf detection. In: Computer Vision and Pattern Recognition, August 2019

20. Chakraborti, T., Chatterjee, A.: A novel binary adaptive weight GSA based feature selection for face recognition using local gradient patterns, modified census transform, and local binary patterns. Eng. Appl. Artif. Intell. **33**, 80–90 (2014)
21. Wei, Xu., Wang, Q., Chen, R.: Spatio-temporal prediction of crop disease severity for agricultural emergency management based on recurrent neural networks. GeoInformatica **22**, 363–381 (2018)
22. Hu, F., Liu, J., Li, L., Huang, M., Yang, C.: IoT-based epidemic monitoring via improved gated recurrent unit model. IEEE Sens. J. **22**(18), 17439–17446 (2022)
23. Verma, T., Dubey, S.: Prediction of diseased rice plant using video processing and LSTM-simple recurrent neural network with comparative study. Multimed. Tools Appl. **80**, 29267–29298 (2021). https://doi.org/10.1007/s11042-021-10889-x

Smart Lysimeter with Artificial Lighting & Plant Monitoring System

Sujatha Rajkumar, Apoorv Singh[✉], Ayush Ranjan, and Pratyay Halder

Vellore Institute of Technology, Vellore, Tamil Nadu, India
sujatha.r@vit.ac.in, apoorvsinghlko@gmail.com

Abstract. Many Indian people are dependent on farming and agriculture for their daily income. There is a compelling need to investigate effective ways of cultivating crops with the aid of cutting-edge technology because natural resources are running out. This study suggests an automated lysimeter system that monitors a plant's daily water needs and regulates the irrigation pump's operation based on environmental data. In addition to this, an artificial lighting system is proposed consisting of a mixture of different light colours in different proportions. The advantages of growing a plant under this proposed artificial lighting system and in natural sunlight were examined in this study. A plant height measurement was used to track plant growth, and a comparison with a plant growing under normal conditions and in artificial lighting was made.

Keywords: Smart farming · Lysimeter · Soil moisture · Artificial lighting

1 Introduction

The rise of "smart farming" is a result of the Internet of Things (IoT) technology. This has resulted in improvement in crop productivity, an increase in crop yields and a rise in profitability by reducing the carbon footprint. Farmers cultivating crops in remote areas have been able to transmit and communicate data from edge devices to the cloud. This, in turn, has helped in crop water management and sustainable agriculture. Producing high-quality crops while also meeting the rising demand for food has been a big problem for the Indian farmers in the past few years [3]. An improved crop yield is necessary for good production, which in turn necessitates the usage of fertilizers and nutritive products for the crops.

Better plant growth can be achieved with the aid of an automated system, and by giving the consumers a user-friendly interface for remote farmland monitoring. Utilizing sensors correctly is crucial for improving agricultural processes and minimizing the necessity of various environmental resources [2].

R. N. Shaw et al. (Eds.): ICACIS 2022, CCIS 1749, pp. 593–604, 2023.
https://doi.org/10.1007/978-3-031-25088-0_52

The proposed system consists of an ESP8266 Wi-Fi System-on-chip, connected to a resistive Soil Moisture Sensor, a Light Dependent Resistor (LDR), and a Digital Temperature & Humidity Sensor (DHT-11). Using these components, an automated lysimeter can be built, which can help measure and monitor the amount of water lost by a plant by evapotranspiration, as demonstrated in [4]. The system also keeps track of the amount of soil moisture for a given plant over a given time period. This increase or decrease in soil moisture helped us determine the amount of water consumed due to evapotranspiration. The proposed system also gave some useful insights about the plant to the end-user. Essential crop health data and surrounding environment data can be monitored remotely. By combining more sophisticated and less expensive methods, a larger crop can be produced by using water efficiently, i.e., by reducing the amount of wastewater. To aid this, an automated system is implemented wherein the plant-watering process is done based on the sunlight intensity and soil moisture level sensor readings obtained in real-time.

Furthermore, to increase the overall productivity and to analyse the influence of light intensity on plant growth, the efficacy of photosynthetic performance was tested when a mixture of red and blue lights is used to cast light upon the plant, as a source of artificial lighting. Blue-red LEDs (Light Emitting Diodes) resulted in enhanced growth of plants and have demonstrated to be much more beneficial as artificial lighting sources. This artificial lighting system switches to the ON state based on the sunlight intensity. In this manner, the plant can get sufficient light energy to photosynthesize even on a cloudy day. A comparative study was performed between two plants grown at the same time and in the identical environment (temperature, soil type, etc.), one with the proposed system incorporated and the other without the system and analysed the results.

2   Literature Survey

During the initial study, many research articles were discovered, which focused on finding salient solutions aimed to reduce excessive water wastage in agricultural and industrial applications. Numerous solutions and concepts based on the most recent technological concepts have been developed as a result of unfavourable weather conditions and diminishing water supplies, such as in [12]. Owing to the steep rise, the need for a smart agriculture system is growing day by day. In [1], the authors devised a fertilizer mixer system using the ESP32S platform. They worked on an application that runs on smartphones, calculating the formula N-P-K to get the desired mixed fertilizer. Plant vegetative growth is enhanced by an augmented usage of nitrogen in the fertilizer.

In [5], the effectiveness of Long Range Wide Area Network (LoRaWAN), NB-IoT (Narrowband Internet of Things) and Sigfox (the most popular low-power Wide Area Network technologies) were compared and evaluated for a smart farming use case. They concluded that the LoRaWAN method is the most suited due to its low power consumption, long battery life, and very high coverage range.

In [8], using mathematical formulae, the abilities of white LEDs, sunlight, purple LEDs, and blue-red LEDs to promote photosynthesis were assessed. According to the research, when plants are lit with both blue and red lights, photosynthetic performance is at its peak. The learned authors in [11] grew 9 plants in sunlight and 9 plants in a blue-red light environment. They concluded that plants grown in sunlight grew better. However, in the absence of sunlight, artificial lighting is a good alternative to growing plants, given the wavelengths of light are appropriate. In [13], to aid in the growth of the plant, the authors have created a light intensity monitoring system utilising a Raspberry Pi that permits the remote maneuvering of the LED-based lighting mechanism. In [10], to help towards growing some succulents, the authors used red light, blue light and UVB light as scientific supplementary lighting.

In [9] the authors produced a Digi-Farming model that would equip Indian farmers with weather & climatic information, help them use IoT to optimize yield and enable them to learn many new techniques in farming with the help of a website and mobile app.

In [14] the author designed a site-specific irrigation system that reviews the location of the water sprays from GPS and connects them wirelessly to the main network hub. For the results in [6] and [7], the authors came up with a smart greenhouse wherein a few sensors collected data from the crops and used the MQTT protocol to transmit the information to an Android application. The user could also give inputs to control the components.

3 Objectives

We plan to assist the agricultural sector by providing them with information about their field and weather on their mobile phones in an easy to use way. The solution will have a positive impact on productivity by helping to adapt to the smart farming system. Proper use of water can also help to conserve water and understanding the land will lead to better utilization of other nutrients that the farmer brings to the field. The chapter also focuses on an artificial lighting system which will activate when the plant has lack of sunlight like on a cloudy day or in the night.

Our primary goals are:

- To provide farmers a helping hand by providing some insights about their fields.
- To save electricity, water and other bills by automating the process.
- To increase the overall growth of the plant adopting an artificial lighting system for the plants to grow when there is lack of sunlight.

4 Research Methodology

Two identical plants are taken and tested under identical conditions to assess the impact of the proposed methodology on plant growth. The control plant is placed in natural conditions, whereas the latter is equipped with a smart plant monitoring system and artificial lighting. The system is made up of a DHT-11 digital temperature and humidity sensor, a light-dependent resistor (LDR), and resistive soil moisture. The data from the sensors is sent to the microcontroller, which then transmits it to the Blynk IoT cloud platform via the ESP8266 Wi-Fi SoC.

Additionally, soil moisture data is used to control the intensity of the water pump, and illumination data from LDR is used to control the blue and red components in the artificial lighting system. Furthermore, the Webhooks are also fired from Blynk IoT platform whenever the status of pump is changes to notify the user through e-mail via IFTTT software. Eventually, the growth of these two plants is recorded and compared using available data.

5   Theory

The microcontrollers used for this chapter are Arduino UNO and ESP8266 Wi-Fi System-on-Chip (SoC). These microcontrollers are connected to each other to increase the number of analog pins as the ESP8266 Wi-Fi SoC has only one analog pin. The microcontroller is powered by a DC power supply which has the sensors and a water pump connected to it [15]. The DHT-11 sensor, soil moisture sensor and light dependent resistor (LDR) are included in this system. The cloud server receives data from the sensor system, which the user application and web dashboard use to display the data analytics [15]. This data is also used for email alerts.

The digital temperature and humidity sensor (DHT-11) sensor gives an idea about the temperature & humidity around the plant so that it may be decided whether there is a requirement for more water [16]. The light-dependent resistor (LDR) converts light energy into an electrical signal output, which is then used to measure the plant's exposure to sunlight. The cloud platform chosen here is Blynk IoT – which will be used for providing web and application-based dashboards to the end-user. IFTTT was used for sending out email alerts.

Plants thrive in full-spectrum sunlight, which consists of a combination of blue and red wavelengths (400–700 nm) with lower amounts of green, yellow, and infrared wavelengths to help in photosynthesis. The colour of the light is an important aspect in the healthy growth of plants. Light colours are crucial for the plant's healthy growth, even though the availability of carbon dioxide, watering, and a supply of nutrients are equally important. Because chlorophyll mostly absorbs blue and red wavelengths but not green light, plants seem to be green [17].

The light that plants use for photosynthesis is known as photosynthetically active radiation, and it happens to be the same spectrum of light that humans see. By utilising pigments known as chlorophyll, they can absorb light hues, although not all of the spectrum Chlorophylls swiftly absorb various colour combinations to make food and energy for the plant, directly assisting with photosynthesis. Red is preferred by plants up to five times more than blue. Red wavelength supports flowering whereas blue wavelength supports strong stem growth and root development. However, blue has the shortest wavelength of the two and a relatively high amount of energy that can easily harm a plant's growth. As a result, it must be carefully blended with red to prevent overexposure.

The artificial lighting system should ideally contain 80% blue light and 20% red light, hence, the system has incorporated a similar combination through the prototype which has the intensity of red and blue light components in the ratio of 1:5 respectively is utilised. Blue and red are considered the greatest hues for plant growth and development [18].

6 Testing and Analysis

The DHT-11 sensor gives us an idea about the temperature & humidity around the plant so that we can decide whether it requires more water or not. The LDR converts light energy into an electrical signal output, which is then used to measure the plant's exposure to sunlight. The microcontrollers used here are Arduino UNO and Node MCU. The cloud server chosen is Blynk IoT – which will be used for providing webpage and application-based dashboards to the enduser. The artificial lighting system should ideally contain 80% blue light and 20% red light, hence, we have incorporated a similar combination through our LED prototype. Figure 1 shows the system flow diagram for the proposed system.

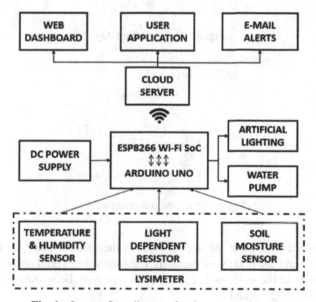

Fig. 1. System flow diagram for the proposed system

7 Results and Discussions

Experimental results were studied and obtained after the successful implementation of the circuitry. The output parameters captured by the sensors in Figs. 2, 3 and 4 on the Blynk IoT website and the corresponding mobile application show the plant data and real-time analytics of the plant.

Fig. 2. Real time temperature

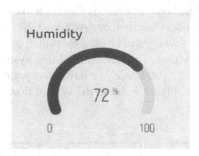

Fig. 3. Real time humidity

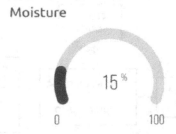

Fig. 4. Real time soil moisture data

This dashboard allows the end user to monitor the humidity, temperature, moisture level of the soil, and the plant's surrounding light intensity. The mobile application as well as the image of the working hardware prototype have been shown to validate the results achieved in Figs. 5 and 6.

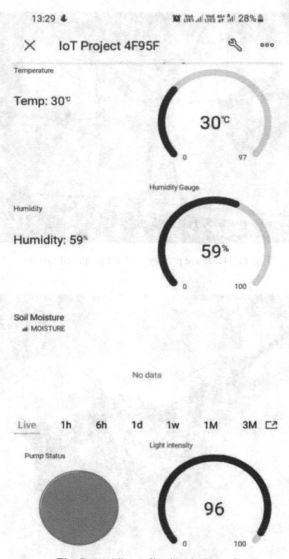

Fig. 5. Mobile application dashboard

Figures 7 and 8 show the implementation of the proposed artificial lighting system designed to work when surrounding light intensity reduces.

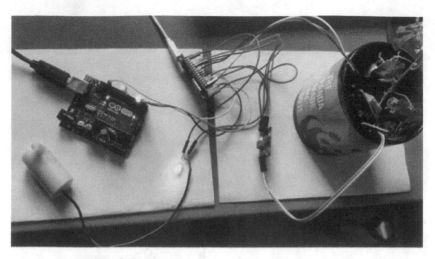

Fig. 6. Hardware prototype of the proposed system

Fig. 7. Artificial lighting OFF (high sunlight)

Comparative analysis of the two plants is done on the basis of the amount of water consumption and the height of the plant with time. Figure 9 shows us that without the system (Plant B), the plant is irrigated with a constant amount of water at fixed intervals of time as it is not dynamic, however, the plant with the system incorporated (Plant A) has dynamic water consumption. It fetches water only when it is necessary, hence, the overall water requirement is less.

Fig. 8. Artificial lighting ON (low sunlight)

Water Consumption with and without Smart System

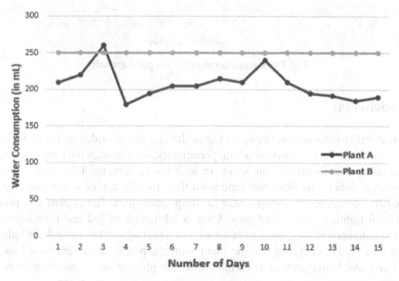

Fig. 9. Comparison of the proposed system with no system

Figure 10 shows us the comparison between the plant heights with (Plant A) and without (Plant B) using the artificial lighting of the system. It is clear from the graph that the plant with the artificial lighting has grown more in the same amount of time as compared to the plant without the system.

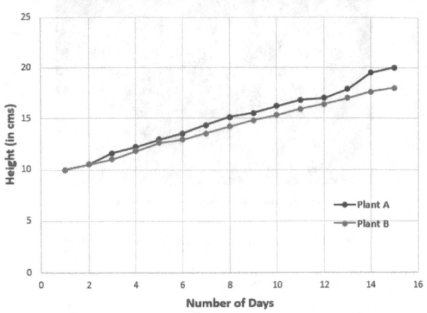

Fig. 10. Comparative graph for plant growth

8 Conclusion

The smart irrigation solution implemented in the chapter provides real-time insights to the user about the various environmental parameters. It automates the irrigation process, thus reducing the manual labour spent. In addition to this, the farmer can also view the historical data of his field over time from their mobile app or web portal. By using this assistive data, they can adopt better farming techniques. The system also proposed an artificial lighting system that provides a combination of red and blue lights. This helped in enhanced plant growth as compared to a plant grown in natural sunlight. This comparative study concludes that the plant with the proposed system used less water overall and had better growth as compared to the plant in the same environment but without the system.

Acknowledgment. This research was supported by the Vellore Institute of Technology. We thank our institute colleagues who gave insight and knowledge that considerably assisted the research. We gratefully acknowledge our professor, Dr. Sujatha R, for her suggestions that significantly enhanced the work and helped with the implementation of IoT. We would also like to express our gratitude to our classmates for contributing their thoughts to this research.

References

1. Chaikhamwang, S., Janthajirakowit, C., Fongmanee, S.: IoT for smart farm: a case study of the fertilizer mixer prototype. In: 2021 Joint International Conference on Digital Arts, Media, and Technology with ECTI Northern Section Conference on Electrical, Electronics, Computer and Telecommunication Engineering, pp. 136–139 (2021)
2. Kempelis, A., Romanovs, A., Patlins, A.: Implementation of machine learning based approach in IoT network prototype. In: 2021 IEEE 9th Workshop on Advances in Information, Electronic and Electrical Engineering (AIEEE), pp. 1–6 (2021). https://doi.org/10.1109/AIEEE54188.2021.9670255
3. Paul Sathiyan, S., Swathi, S., Mariya Sharmini, G.: Automated plant nutrient monitoring system for better plant growth. In: 2021 International Conference on Advances in Electrical, Computing, Communication and Sustainable Technologies (ICAECT), pp. 1–7 (2021). https://doi.org/10.1109/ICAECT49130.2021.9392607
4. Niu, H., Zhao, T., Wei, J., Wang, D., Chen, Y.: Reliable tree-level evapotranspiration estimation of pomegranate trees using lysimeter and UAV multispectral imagery. In: 2021 IEEE Conference on Technologies for Sustainability (SusTech) (2021)
5. Islam, N., Ray, B., Pasandideh, F.: IoT based smart farming: are the LPWAN technologies suitable for remote communication?. In: 2020 IEEE International Conference on Smart Internet of Things (Smart IoT), pp. 270–276 (2020). https://doi.org/10.1109/SmartIoT49966.2020.00048
6. Anghelof, M.M., Suciu, G., Craciunescu, R., Marghescu, C.: Intelligent system for precision agriculture. In: 2020 13th International Conference on Communications (COMM), pp. 407–410 (2020). https://doi.org/10.1109/COMM48946.2020.9141981
7. Eridani, D., Martono, K.T., Hanifah, A.A.: MQTT performance as a message protocol in an IoT based chili crops greenhouse prototyping. In: 2019 4th International Conference on Information Technology, Information Systems and Electrical Engineering (ICITISEE), pp. 184–189 (2019). https://doi.org/10.1109/ICITISEE48480.2019.9003975
8. Shailesh, K.R.: Energy efficient LED lighting design for horticulture. In: 2019 1st International Conference on Advanced Technologies in Intelligent Control, Environment, Computing & Communication Engineering (ICATIECE) (2019)
9. Thakor, H.P., Iyer, S.: Development and analysis of smart digi-farming robust model for production optimization in agriculture. In: 2019 6th International Conference on Computing for Sustainable Global Development (INDIACom), pp. 461–465 (2019)
10. Yue, X., Wang, W., Yang, C., Kang, H., Wang, J., Ma, S.: Intelligent succulent plant management system based on wireless network. In: 2019 IEEE Symposium Series on Computational Intelligence (SSCI), pp. 2863–2868 (2019) https://doi.org/10.1109/SSCI44817.2019.9002935
11. Rangarajan, A.K., Purushothaman, R., Venkatesan, H.S.: Evaluation of Solanum melongena crop performance in artificial LED light source for urban farming. In: 2018 2nd International Conference on I-SMAC (IoT in Social, Mobile, Analytics and Cloud) (I-SMAC), pp. 33–36 (2018). https://doi.org/10.1109/I-SMAC.2018.8653651
12. Putjaika, N., Phusae, S., Chen-Im, A., Phunchongharn, P., Akkarajitsakul, K.: A control system in an intelligent farming by using Arduino technology. In: 2016 Fifth ICT International Student Project Conference (ICT-ISPC), pp. 53–56 (2016). https://doi.org/10.1109/ICT-ISPC.2016.7519234
13. Khot, S.B., Gaikwad, M.S.: Development of cloud-based Light intensity monitoring system for green house using Raspberry Pi. In: 2016 International Conference on Computing Communication Control and automation (ICCUBEA), pp. 1–4 (2016). https://doi.org/10.1109/ICCUBEA.2016.7860128

14. Huneria, H.K., Yadav, P., Shaw, R.N., Saravanan, D., Ghosh, A.: AI and IOT-based model for photovoltaic power generation. In: Mekhilef, S., Favorskaya, M., Pandey, R.K., Shaw, R.N. (eds.) Innovations in Electrical and Electronic Engineering. LNEE, vol. 756, pp. 697–706. Springer, Singapore (2021). https://doi.org/10.1007/978-981-16-0749-3_55

15. Tanveer, A., Choudhary, A., Pal, D., Gupta, R., Husain, F.: Automated farming using microcontroller and sensors. Int. J. Sci. Res. Manage. Stud. 2(1), 21–30 (2015)

16. R Shamshiri, R., et al.: Research and development in agricultural robotics: a perspective of digital farming (2018)

17. Mamatha, M.N., Namratha, S.N.: Design & implementation of indoor farming using automated aquaponics system. In: 2017 IEEE International Conference on Smart Technologies and Management for Computing, Communication, Controls, Energy and Materials (ICSTM), pp. 396–401. IEEE (2017)

18. Dutta Gupta, S., Agarwal, A.: Artificial lighting system for plant growth and development: chronological advancement, working principles, and comparative assessment. In: Dutta Gupta, S. (ed.) Light emitting diodes for agriculture, pp. 1–25. Springer, Singapore (2017). https://doi.org/10.1007/978-981-10-5807-3_1

Automatic Detection and Monitoring of Hate Speech in Online Multi-social Media

Ashwini Kumar(✉) ⓘ, Santosh Kumar, and Vishu Tyagi

Graphic Era Deemed to be University, Dehradun, Uttarakhand, India
ashwinipaul@gmail.com

Abstract. Nowadays, we all want to be a part of social media networks in the internet world. Social media has played a critical role in human interaction in the last decade. Every day people use social media huge in numbers and many unfiltered messages are also being posted on multi-social media. Many hate speeches in these messages target an individual or group. In this context, many government and non-government organizations are concerned about these messages and taking some necessary steps to prevent their impact. In this chapter, we have created an intelligent system named *"HateDetector-a recursive system"* for monitoring and generating alerts on hate speech text for preventive measures on multi-social media with the help of an LSTM-CNN automatic detection model. We have also compared the performance of our LSTM-CNN model with classical machine learning methods in terms of F1 Score, Precision, Recall and, Accuracy.

Keywords: Social media · Hate speech · CNN · LSTM

1 Introduction

In the last decade, online multi-social media has become very popular because people share their information worldwide. Based on the increasing number of people on multi social media, lots of harmful content is widely used by a particular group of people daily. This is a severe issue of online communications of multi-social mediums [9, 10, 16]. Currently, there is no formal definition of hate speech exists in our literature. We consider hating speech to discriminate against a person or group based on religion, race, nationality, gender, or other factors. Many countries and government organizations work on these serious problems and try to find these persons or groups involved in spreading hateful comments on social media [3–6]. To cope with this issue, manually remove hate speech or block the user account. Most researchers work on an automatic detection model in one kind of online social media platform to address the problem of hate speech.

In this chapter, we have studied the various works [7, 11–13, 18, 20–24] on the automatic detection of hate speech. As we have seen, many researchers work on extracting their or existing datasets from social media, especially Twitter. They have developed automatic detection models in various ways/methods which claim to give better accuracy. However, existing models tend to outperform only based on the dataset from which you use social media.

R. N. Shaw et al. (Eds.): ICACIS 2022, CCIS 1749, pp. 605–612, 2023.
https://doi.org/10.1007/978-3-031-25088-0_53

We have collected datasets from multi-social media (Twitter, YouTube, Facebook, gab, and Stormfront); this dataset is what individual researchers have used in their chapters. After collecting the dataset of multi-social media, we combined all the datasets [7, 11–13, 18, 20–24] and created a dataset, now we have a huge corpus that is from multi-social media and is also pre-annotated because researchers have already used these datasets. This combined dataset has two categories, such as hate speech or neither.

This chapter aims to design a new system, *"HateDetector-a recursive system"* that detects and monitors hate speech. As well as it also generates alerts on hateful comments or tweets for preventive measures. In this new system, we have created a deep learning model which will analyze hate speech with the diversification of online multi-social media.

The contributions of our works are summarized below:

1. Our data model for dealing with the diversification of multi-social media data is trained on a large collection of hateful comments.
2. Design a novel system, *"HateDetector-a recursive system"* for monitoring and generating alerts on hate speech text for preventive measures.
3. The new approach uses BiLSTM-CNN-based deep neural networks and its performance is the best among baseline state-of-art methods.

The rest of this chapter is structured as follows: state-of-the-art related work in Sect. 2. Design a novel system along with our BiLSTM–CNN architecture is given in Sect. 3. Analyses the resulting system and compares it against classical machine learning methods in Sect. 4. Finally, the conclusion of our chapter and proposed future work discuss in Sect. 5.

2 Related Work

The authors of [7] discussed hate speech detection tasks using a machine learning approach. The main problem faced while creating an automated model is that it considers the words that are hateful and classifies the sentence as hate speech, but it may or may not be hate speech. The authors did not use the "Bag of words" approach as often this approach [8, 9] leads to false positive, which can misclassify words as hate speech. So instead of this, authors used Porter stemmers for stemming sentences and then to capture the quality of each tweet modified Flesch-Kincaid Grade Level and Flesch Reading Ease scores. This assigns a score to every tweet for classification. The authors of [13] mentioned that the data had been extracted through Reddit with 39800 annotated comments. Dataset is based on the three major classes of slur usage, i.e. DER, APR, NDG and HOM. Around 400 participants were rounded up and split randomly into teams, and each team annotated 1000 comments daily. For derogatory comment detection Perspective API by Conversation, AI was used in a given method.

The authors of [2] collected approximately 20 k tweets against East Asia and criticism of East Asian peoples during Covid-19. They used the pre-trained model to classify tweets into four categories and achieved an F1 score of 0.83. The gap in this chapter is that authors could be implemented using a deep learning approach to enhance the model's performance. The Authors of [14, 15] discussed granular taxonomy for hate speech text. They collected datasets from YouTube, Facebook, and Online news Media and implemented in classical machine-learning approach [25] to detect hateful comments. The authors find the model's performance with an F1 score of 0.79.

Recent approaches have used RNN algorithms (LSTM [1], Bi-LSTM, and GRU) to solve textual data for capturing long-term dependencies to detect hate speech and improve the performance of the proposed model [19, 21].

3 Hate Speech Detection: Implementation and Evaluation

This section discusses the multi-social media heterogeneous dataset and proposes a novel "HateDetector" system for detecting hate speech. We also describe our implementation and experiment evaluation in Sect. 3.3.

3.1 Dataset Description and Pre-processing

We used an existing multi-social media dataset provided by various authors [7, 11–13, 18, 20–24] to evaluate our proposed system shown in Table 1. This heterogeneous annotated dataset contains 0.2 million texts or messages that have been combined all datasets into a single dataset. The classification of our classes in the combined dataset is shown in Table 2.

Table 1. Available multi-social media hate speech corpora

Social media	Dataset	#Tweets/Comments
Twitter	Davidson et al. [7]	24783
	Thomas et al. [22]	7005
	Zampieri et al. [20]	13240
	Ousidhoum et al. [23]	5647
	Golbeck et al. [24]	20360
	Fortuna et al. [21]	45407
Facebook/YouTube	Chung et al. [11]	20186
	Salminen et al. [18]	3222
Gab	Kennedy et al. [12]	22527
Reddit	Karrek et al. [13]	40000
Total Tweets from Multi Social Media		**202377**

Our labeled annotated heterogeneous dataset is processed to normalize texts as follows:

- Remove non-alphanumeric characters, <Question mark>, <Exclamation mark>, and stopwords.

Table 2. Statistics of multi-social media hate speech dataset

Class	Tweets
Hate	113651
Neither	88726
Total	202377

- Remove noise characters i.e. |:;, &amp \.
- \<hastag\>, \<Laughs\>, \<url\>, \<user\>, and \<number\> to replace them with a standard format.
- Convert all texts to lowercase.
- Stemming and Lemmatization

3.2   Overview of a Novel " *HateDetector*" System

We aim to develop a new *"HateDetector-a recursive system"* that can detect hate speech and relies on a correctly annotated multi-social media dataset from our given input sample. The architecture of the proposed method is shown in Fig. 1. We train and detect hate speech with the help of our new system, which is based on Bi LSTM-CNN deep

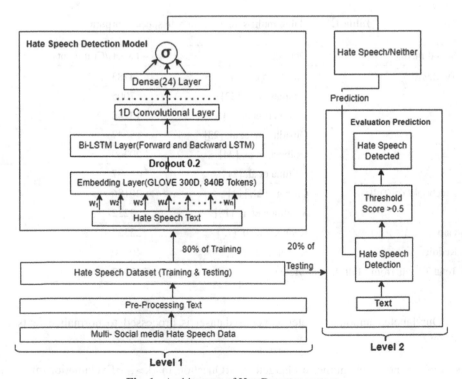

Fig. 1. Architecture of HateDetector system

neural network. After our new model training, it detects whether the new input sample is hate speech or neither. Based on the system "HateDetector", as soon as the social media user sends a message, then our new system will detect whether there is hate speech in that post or not. If the message comes in the hate speech category as a preventive measure, our system will warn the user that the word hate speech has been used in your text, so our advice would be that you remove the hate speech words from your message and then you can send your clean message.

3.3 Experimental Evaluation

In this section, we discuss the functioning of our proposed architecture of *"HateDetector – a recursive system"*. The first step is to collect data from different social media platforms (Twitter, Facebook, YouTube, Reddit, Gab, and Stormfront)) and stored into a single dataset CSV file. These different datasets are used by authors [1–6] in our proposed model. Next, we are pre-processing (Sect. 3.1) our combined single dataset. After Pre-processing, the given dataset, we consider 80% of the training dataset to train our Hate Speech Detection Model (Fig. 1-Level1) and 20% used in validation data for evaluation prediction (Fig. 1-Level2). In Level-1, we use the first layer in our model as a 300-D Glove Embedding Layer (Pre-trained vectors −840B tokens) [17] for our input text/comments and then use the dropout layer (0.2) to avoid overfitting. The values come from the embedding layer assigned to a Bidirectional-LSTM layer (size-64) to read text from both directions (left-to-right and right-to-left). The output of the Bi-LSTM layer fed into a 1-Dimensional Convolutional Layer with 128 filters and size is 4, which further fed into a dense layer (size-24) with the activation function "Relu". The last layer has two outputs to predict whether the given tweet is hate speech or neither, with the help of the sigmoid activation function. Based on Hyper-parameters in our training, we used Adam optimizer and cross entropy loss function with 10 epochs. The details of the parameters used in our proposed model are shown in Table 3.

In Level 2, the input text/new sample is fed into our proposed hate speech detection model (shown in Level 1) to determine whether the sample causes hate speech or not.

Table 3. Details of BiLSTM-CNN model

Layer (type)	Output shape	Param#
Embedding_1 (Embedding)	(None, 120, 300)	32098800
Dropout_1 (Dropout)	(None, 120, 300)	0
Bidirectional_1 (Bidirectional LSTM)	(None, 120, 128)	186880
conv1d_1 (Conv1D)	(None, 117, 128)	65664
dense_2 (Dense)	(None, 117, 24)	3096
dense_3 (Dense)	(None,117, 1)	25

Total params: 32,354,465
Trainable params: 32,354,465
Non-trainable params

If the input sample contains any hate speech, the user is issued a warning to remove or replace this message; otherwise, the message will be classified as hate speech.

4 Results

We have trained our model using the Keras framework with Tensorflow 2.6.0 as the backend, Glove - pre-trained embedding (840B Tokens, 300-Dimension), and the scikit-learn library. After training, the proposed "HateDetector" System performed good results against classic baseline methods for detecting hate speech. Table 4 shows the performance of our novel "HateDetector" System based on Precision, Recall, F1-score, and Accuracy.

Table 4. Performance of our hate speech detection model

HateDetector-a recursive system	Precision	Recall	F1	Accuracy
	0.92	0.92	0.92	0.925

5 Conclusion and Future Work

In this study, we have proposed a novel *"HateDetector-a recursive system"* that leads to competitive performance of multi-social media data and will work in a real-time online environment. Our system used a deep neural network based on BiLSTM and CNN to monitor the hate speech text and the warnings for the users sending the messages fall under the hate speech category. We may optimize and fine-tune different deep-learning models for multi-social media data in future work. We will explore pre-trained models and compare our novel "hate detector" system with other state-of-the-art methods.

References

1. Hochreiter, S., Schmidhuber, J.: LSTM can solve hard long time lag problems. In: Advances in Neural Information Processing Systems, (Neural information processing systems foundation), pp. 473–479 (1997)
2. Vidgen, B., et al.: Detecting east asian prejudice on social media. In: Proceedings of the Fourth Workshop on Online Abuse and Harms, pp. 162–172 (2020)
3. Burnap, P., Williams, M.L.: Cyber hate speech on twitter: an application of machine classification and statistical modeling for policy and decision making. Policy and Internet, pp. 223–242 (2015)
4. Djuric, N., et al.: Hate speech detection with comment embeddings. In: WWW 2015 Companion Proceedings of the 24th International Conference on World Wide Web. Association for Computing Machinery, Inc, pp. 29–30 (2015)

5. Nobata, C., et al.: Abusive language detection in online user content. In: 25th International World Wide Web Conference, WWW 2016. International World Wide Web Conferences Steering Committee, pp. 145–153 (2016)
6. Malmasi, S., Zampieri, M.: Detecting hate speech in social media. In: International Conference Recent Advances in Natural Language Processing, RANLP Association for Computational Linguistics (ACL), pp. 467–472 (2017)
7. Davidson, T., et al.: Automated hate speech detection and the problem of offensive language. In: Proceedings of the 11th International Conference on Web and Social Media, ICWSM 2017, pp. 512–515. AAAI Press (2017)
8. Bird, S., et al.: Natural Language Processing with Python: [Analyzing Text with the Natural Language Toolkit], 1st edn. O'Reilly, Sebastopol, Calif (2009)
9. Waseem, Z., Hovy, D.: Hateful Symbols or Hateful People? Predictive Features for Hate Speech Detection on Twitter. Association for Computational Linguistics (ACL), pp. 88–93 (2016)
10. Zhang, Z., et al.: Hate Speech Detection Using a Convolution-LSTM Based Deep Neural Network. Eurpoean Semantic Web Conference, pp.745–760 (2018)
11. Chung, Y.L., Kuzmenko, E., Tekiroglu, S.S., Guerini, M.: CONAN--Counter Narratives through Nichesourcing: a Multilingual Dataset of Responses to Fight Online Hate Speech. arXiv preprint arXiv:1910.03270. (2019)
12. Kennedy, B., et al.: Introducing the Gab Hate Corpus: defining and applying hate-based rhetoric to social media posts at scale. Lang. Resour. Eval. 1–30 (2021). https://doi.org/10.1007/s10579-021-09569-x
13. Rawat, R., et al.: Sentiment analysis at online social network for cyber-malicious post reviews using machine learning techniques. In: Bansal, J.C., Paprzycki, M., Bianchini, M., Das, S. (eds.) Computationally Intelligent Systems and their Applications. SCI, vol. 950. Springer, Singapore (2021). https://doi.org/10.1007/978-981-16-0407-2_9
14. Salminen, J., et al.: Anatomy of online hate: developing a taxonomy and machine learning models for identifying and classifying hate in online news media. In: Twelfth International AAAI Conference on Web and Social Media (2015)
15. Houlsby, N., et al.: Parameter-efficient transfer learning for NLP. In: 36th International Conference on Machine Learning, ICML 2019, pp. 4944–4953. International Machine Learning Society (IMLS) (2019)
16. Kumar, A., Das, S., Tyagi, V.: Anti Money Laundering detection using Naïve Bayes Classifier. In: 2020 IEEE International Conference on Computing, Power and Communication Technologies (GUCON), pp. 568–572. IEEE (2020)
17. Pennington, J., et al.: GloVe: global vectors for word representation. In: EMNLP 2014 – 2014 Conference on Empirical Methods in Natural Language Processing, Proceedings of the Conference, pp. 1532–1543. Association for Computational Linguistics (ACL) (2014)
18. Salminen, J., Hopf, M., Chowdhury, S.A., Jung, S.-G., Almerekhi, H., Jansen, B.J.: Developing an online hate classifier for multiple social media platforms. HCIS 10(1), 1–34 (2020). https://doi.org/10.1186/s13673-019-0205-6
19. Gambäck, B., Sikdar, U.K.: Using Convolutional Neural Networks to Classify Hate – Speech, pp. 85–90. Association for Computational Linguistics (ACL) (2017)
20. Zampieri, M., et al.: Predicting the type and target of offensive posts in social media. In: NAACL HLT 2019 - 2019 Conference of the North American Chapter of the Association for Computational Linguistics: Human Language Technologies – Proceedings of the Conference. Association for Computational Linguistics (ACL), pp. 1415–1420 (2019)
21. Gautam, J., Atrey, M., Malsa, N., Balyan, A., Shaw, R.N., Ghosh, A.: Twitter Data Sentiment Analysis Using Naive Bayes Classifier and Generation of Heat Map for Analyzing Intensity Geographically. In: Bansal, J.C., Fung, L.C.C., Simic, M., Ghosh, A. (eds.) Advances in

Applications of Data-Driven Computing. AISC, vol. 1319, pp. 129–139. Springer, Singapore (2021). https://doi.org/10.1007/978-981-33-6919-1_10

22. Mandl, T., et al.: Overview of the hasoc track at fire 2019: hate speech and offensive content identification in indo-european languages. In: Proceedings of the 11th Forum for Information Retrieval Evaluation, pp. 14–17 (2019)

23. Ousidhoum, N., Lin, Z., Zhang, H., Song, Y., Yeung, D.Y.: Multi lingual and multi-aspect hate speech analysis. arXiv preprint arXiv:1908.11049 (2019)

24. Golbeck, J., et al.: A large labeled corpus for online harassment research. In: Proceedings of the 2017 ACM on Web Science Conference, pp. 229–233 (2017)

25. Diwakar, M., et al.: Directive clustering contrast-based multi-modality medical image fusion for smart healthcare system. Network Model. Anal. Health Inform. Bioinform. **11**(1), 1–12 (2022). https://doi.org/10.1007/s13721-021-00342-2

Energy Efficient Routing in Wireless Sensor Network for Moving Nodes Using Genetic Algorithm Compared with PSO

Ramisetty Lakshmi Pavan Kumar and Vijayalakshmi[✉]

Department of Electronics and Communication Engineering, Saveetha School of Engineering,
Saveetha Institute of Medical and Technical, Sciences, Saveetha University,
Chennai, Tamil Nadu 602105, India
vijayalakshmi.sse@saveetha.com

Abstract. The objective of the research work is to examine energy-efficient routing in wireless sensor networks for moving nodes by contrasting new evolutionary algorithms with the Particle Swarm Optimization (PSO) Algorithm. Comparative analysis of energy efficient routing is performed by a novel genetic algorithm where there are several samples (N = 10) and a PSO algorithm where there are several samples (N = 10) techniques with pre-test power of 80% using NS2. When routing wireless sensor networks with moving nodes, Various metrics, including delay, energy use, and packet delivery ratio, are used to compare PSO and genetic algorithms. The evolutionary algorithm outperforms the PSO algorithm in these ways in terms of packet delivery ratio, energy usage, and delay. ($p < 0.05$) indicates a statistically significant difference. The research's findings comprised the three metrics of delay, energy consumption and packet delivery ratio. The method shows that the novel Genetic algorithm outperforms the PSO algorithm for wireless sensor network energy-efficient routing for moving nodes by identifying a set of routes that can satisfy the delay restrictions.

Keywords: Novel genetic algorithm · Particle Swarm Optimization (PSO) · Wireless sensor network · Delay · Energy consumption · Packet delivery ratio

1 Introduction

There are many different types of wireless networks, such as mobile ad hoc networks and wireless sensor networks. These networks are devoid of infrastructure and are composed of a group of wireless nodes with several hops that can connect with one another without the help of a centralised administrator. Self-organized connectivity is made possible via MANETs and mobile sensor networks [1]. Numerous factors, including multi-node routing, resource availability, and topology change, should be considered in this regard. To accomplish effective data transfer, it is important to meet the high-performance criteria. All of these challenges must be overcome by a routing system in mobile networks [2]. In a variety of industries, including the military, healthcare, agriculture, environmental monitoring, and many more, wireless sensor networks (WSNs) have demonstrated their

© The Author(s), under exclusive license to Springer Nature Switzerland AG 2023
R. N. Shaw et al. (Eds.): ICACIS 2022, CCIS 1749, pp. 613–621, 2023.
https://doi.org/10.1007/978-3-031-25088-0_54

usefulness [3]. A wireless sensor network is made up of a large number of tiny sensors with communication and sensing capabilities [2, 4]. They are sensors capable of seeing and detecting elements of their immediate environment, and they are also capable of communicating this information to base stations, in order to carry out particular activities.

There have been several research chapters during the past five years, including 387 articles in Science Direct, 426 articles in Google Scholar, and 426 articles in IEEE Xplore. An established routing method known as Ad-hoc On-Demand Multi-Path Distance Vector, chooses routes by looking at the fewest number of hops possible [5]. Because AOMDV offers backup routes in the event of a node failure or channel disconnect, going through the route finding phase is not necessary. Which minimises latency and increases throughput. The AOMDV method, however, does not take the node's energy availability into account. Numerous routing strategies have been suggested to improve network performance [6]. To extend network lifetime and cut down on energy consumption, and reduce packet latency, a dynamic energy ad-hoc on-demand distance vector routing protocol was created. The shortest path with energy-efficient nodes is chosen using the DE-AODV protocol. One of the routing protocols with the longest lifetime is Efficient Power Aware Routing Protocol (EPAR) [6, 7], It is a development of the DSR protocol. EPAR chooses the route with the highest packet capacity at the lowest packet transmission energy consumption. [8] presented Energy Efficient Hierarchical Clustering (EEHC), which lengthens the sensor network's lifespan. Cluster heads, on the other hand, experience overload and power loss more quickly than other nodes as a result of hierarchical clustering.

Due to this issue of high energy consumption in a clustered WSN, one of the main challenges that WSNs confront is the restricted energy source of sensors. In order to address the issue of excessive energy consumption in a clustered WSN, this research work suggests an energy-efficient model. The aim of the research work is to investigate energy-efficient routing in wireless sensor networks for moving nodes by comparing innovative evolutionary algorithms to the Particle Swarm Optimization (PSO) Algorithm.

2   Materials and Methods

The research work was executed in the Wireless Communication lab at Saveetha School of Engineering, Saveetha Institute of Medical and Technical Sciences, Chennai. Particle Swarm Optimization (PSO) algorithms and novel genetic algorithms are basically the two categories under which it is divided. The Novel Genetic Algorithm is in Group 1 with a sample size of 10, and Particle Swarm Optimization is in Group 2. (PSO) method, which also has a sample size of 10. These two algorithms were contrasted in terms of delay, energy use, and packet delivery ratio.

The energy, delay, and packet delivery ratio of Particle Swarm Optimization (PSO) are examined in the sample preparation for group 1 by randomly altering the depth for various time slots in NS2 using aqua-Sim. Network coding is created using NS2 to model routing performance [9, 10]. The technique uses an energy model for acoustic propagation, and at one millisecond intervals, routing metrics are assessed for each node.

Aqua-sim is used to randomly adjust the depth for various time slots in NS2 to test the energy, delay, and packet delivery ratio of the Genetic Algorithm (GA) in the sample preparation for group 2. With the goal of simulating routing performance, NS2 is utilized to develop network coding [9]. An energy model for acoustic propagation is used in the method, and routing metrics are assessed for each node every one millisecond.

2.1 Genetic Algorithm

The GA algorithm has been used on these routes dedicated by AOMDV in order to create new routes with minimal energy usage at nodes. In our algorithm, assume that the initial energy of every node is the same. Following are the six steps of GA:

1. The minimum number of hops used by the AOMDV protocol determines the array of routes (PopSize) that is returned (Genes). In order to create new child routes, the GA will be applied to the set of parent routes in PopSize, as will be explained below.
2. The evaluation of FF is based on the least energy consumed by the PopSize-involved nodes. The elitism strategy eliminates routes with poor fitness levels, leaving only the remaining routes to be used as parents in the GA.
3. By using the crossover approach across the elitism parent routes, new child routes can be created automatically.
4. Utilize Pm to apply the mutation process to the parent and child routes,
5. An effective routes array E should be used to store all feasible parent and child routes.
6. The efficient path is the one that has the highest fitness, so sort the entries of array E in that order. If the chosen route is unsuccessful due to channel disconnection or malfunctioning nodes, other routes in E will be used.

3 Statistical Analysis

The analysis uses IBM SPSS version 21 (Greatorex 2015). It is a statistical programme that is used to analyse data. With a maximum of 10 samples, 10 iterations of the proposed and existing algorithms were carried out, and for each iteration, the Independent Sample T-test result was calculated. The dependent variables are delay, energy, and packet delivery ratio. The performance of suggested and current algorithms based on dependent factors was assessed using independent two-tailed tests by analysing the independent variables, which are the number of particles and population size.

4 Results

The comparative analysis of novel genetic algorithms and particle swarm optimization (PSO) algorithms with the respective parameters include energy consumption, packet delivery ratio, and delay. Genetic algorithms outperform the PSO algorithm in terms of delay, packet delivery ratio, and energy consumption.

Figure 1 depicts the end-to-end delay. The PSO has attained a delay of 19 ms at the 10th node, whereas with the novel genetic algorithm the end-to-end delay has been dropped to 7 ms at the same node. Figure 2 describes the energy consumption attained using the suggested novel genetic algorithm over PSO for a varied number of nodes that ranges from 0 to 10. Despite of the specified algorithm, As the number of nodes grows, increases the overall energy consumption of the network. For instance, in node 10, the total energy consumption of the novel genetic algorithm and PSO attains 8 millijoules and 14 millijoules, respectively. Figure 3 depicts the ratio of delivered packets. This measurement represents the amount of time needed for a data packet to transit from source to destination. The PSO algorithm has attained a packet delivery ratio of 9% at the 10th node, whereas in the novel genetic algorithm, the packet delivery ratio has been increased to 11% at the same node. The mean delay for groups 1 and 2 is compared in Fig. 4. Ggroup 1 is a novel genetic method, and group 2 is a Particle Swarm Optimization (PSO) algorithm. The Novel Genetic algorithm provides less delay than the PSO algorithm. Figure 5 compares the mean packet delivery ratio. (+/− 1SD) for groups 1and 2; The genetic algorithm provides the highest packet delivery ratio than the Particle Swarm Optimization (PSO) algorithm. Figure 6 compares the average energy consumption (+/− 1SD) for groups 1 and 2. The novel genetic algorithm provides less energy consumption than the PSO algorithm.

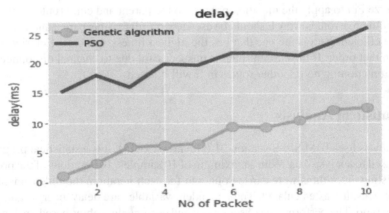

Fig. 1. Shows the comparison between Novel Genetic Algorithm and PSO algorithm for delay with respect to No of Packets in wireless sensor network for moving nodes. X axis: No of Packets, Y axis: Delay.

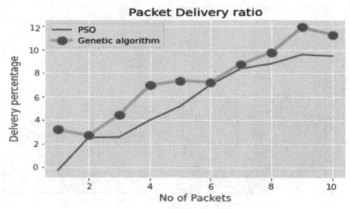

Fig. 2. Represents the comparison between Novel Genetic algorithm and PSO algorithm for Energy Consumption with respect to Energy consumed in wireless sensor networks for moving nodes. X axis: No of Packets, Y axis: Energy Consumed(mj).

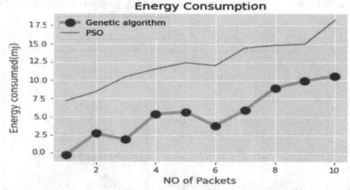

Fig. 3. Represents the Packet Delivery Ratio with respect to No of packets for comparison between Novel Genetic algorithm and PSO algorithm for wireless sensor network for moving nodes. X axis: No of packets, Delivery percentage.

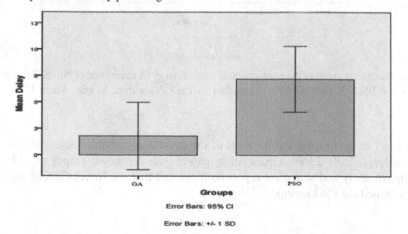

Fig. 4. Barchart represents the comparison of mean Delay of Novel Genetic Algorithm and PSO Algorithm. X axis: Genetic Algorithm vs PSO Algorithm, Y axis: Mean Delay +/−1 SD

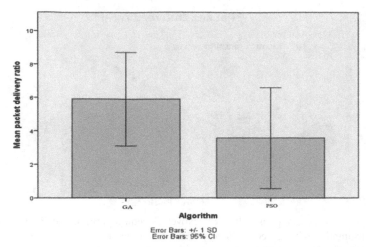

Fig. 5. Barchart represents the comparison of mean packet Delivery Ratio of Novel Genetic Algorithm and PSO. X axis: Genetic Algorithm vs PSO Algorithm, Y axis: Mean Delay +/−1 SD.

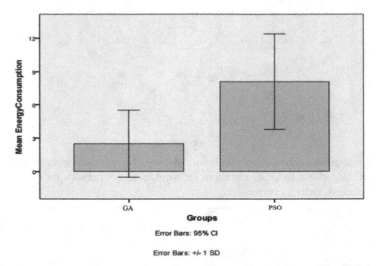

Fig. 6. Barchart represents the comparison of mean Energy Consumption of Novel Genetic Algorithms and PSO. X axis: Genetic Algorithm vs PSO Algorithm, Y axis: Mean Delay +/−1 SD

Table 1 compares the mean values of the dependent variables according to statistical analysis. Table 2 shows association between the dependent output variables. The descriptive study and statistical report both showed that the Novel Genetic algorithm outperformed the PSO method.

Table 1. Represents descriptive statistical comparison of three parameters with respect to number of packets. The mean of delay, energy consumption, and packet delivery ratio for Novel Genetic algorithm have 1.80, 3.40 and 2.10 respectively.

Groups	Parameter	N	Mean	Std. deviation
Genetic algorithm	Delay	10	1.80	3.190
	Energy consumption		3.40	4.274
	Packet delivery ratio		2.10	3.028
PSO	Delay	10	7.20	3.120
	Energy consumption		5.30	3.120
	Packet delivery ratio		8.10	4.306

Table 2. Independent Sample Test for significance and standard error determination for all the three parameters. P value is 0.023(<0.05) considered to be statistically significant and 95% confidence interval was considered.

Levene's test for equality of variables		F	Sig	T-test for equality of mean						
				t	df	Sig. (2-tailed)	Mean diff	Std error	95% Confidence Interval of the difference	
									Lower	Upper
DELAY	Equal variances assumed	0.03	0.03	−3.827	18	.01	−5.40	1.411	−8.365	−2.435
	Equal variances not assumed			−3.827	17.991	.01	−5.40	1.411	−8.365	−2.435
Packet delivery ratio	Equal variances assumed	0.023	0.02	−1.076	18	0.296	−1.800	1.673	−5.316	1.716
	Equal variances not assumed		0.02	−1.076	16.470	0.298	1.800	1.673	−5.339	1.739
Energy consumption	Equal variances assumed	0.025	0.025	−3.364	18	0.003	−5.600	1.665	−9.097	−2.103
	Equal variances not assumed			−3.364	17.150	0.004	−5.600	1.665	−9.126	−2.074

5   Discussion

In this work the energy efficient Routing in a wireless sensor network for moving nodes using a novel genetic algorithm compared with PSO. The novel genetic algorithm outperforms in terms of delay, energy consumption, and packet delivery ratio, according to the simulation results. The novel genetic algorithm has a mean delay of 1.80, a mean energy consumption of 3.40, and a mean packet delivery ratio of 2.10.

Numerous routing approaches have been developed to enhance network performance. The author [11] to reduce packet delays, increase network lifetimes, and save energy, [12]. Presented a cluster head distribution strategy to extend network lifetime and prevent unnecessary redundancy, hence reducing energy dissipation. In [13], In contrast to the variables evaluated during the route discovery process, such as the latency for obtaining the shortest path and the quantity of viable routes. The processing time and energy required by this technology are high. One of the different maximum lifetime routing methods is known as Efficient Power Aware Routing Protocol [7], It is a development of the DSR protocol. In order to maximize packet capacity while using the least amount of energy possible, EPAR selects the route.

The majority of earlier research in the subject of WSN is severely energy-strained; this shows that continually active nodes quickly deplete their power, which explains why the WSN has a short lifespan. a few scheduling techniques [14]. These methods put a sensor node into a sleep state and keep it there for the longest amount of time possible to reduce energy usage. The usage of natural heuristics has been covered in a few recent research. WSN energy usage optimization techniques using artificial intelligence (AI). The challenge of situating the sensor nodes can be resolved, for instance, by employing enhanced virtual force and particle swarm algorithms [15]. With the use of a genetic algorithm, By using the distance, density, energy, and heterogeneous node capability fitness function criteria, the GACHS protocol has been designed to improve the selection of cluster heads (CH) [16].

Nodes in wireless sensor networks are powered by batteries with very little memory and CPU processing capability. Such time-consuming routing techniques might be beyond the capacity of these constrained resources. Therefore, future aspects of this research work can be concentrated on using various bio-inspired optimization strategies and can be evaluated using various parameters.

6   Conclusion

In order to provide moving nodes in wireless sensor networks with energy-efficient routing, a novel genetic algorithm is contrasted with PSO. The simulation results show that the novel genetic algorithm performs better in terms of delay, energy consumption, and packet delivery ratio. The novel genetic algorithm has a mean delay of 1.80, a mean energy consumption of 3.40, and a mean packet delivery ratio of 2.10.

References

1. Femila, L., Marsaline Beno, M.: Optimizing transmission power and energy efficient routing protocol in MANETs. Wireless Pers. Commun. **106**(3), 1041–1056 (2019). https://doi.org/10.1007/s11277-019-06202-7

2. Saritha, V., Venkata Krishna, P., Alagiri, I., Madhu Viswanatham, V., Obaidat, M.S.: Efficient multipath routing protocol with quality of service for mobile ad hoc networks. In: 2018 IEEE International Conference on Communications (ICC) (2018). https://doi.org/10.1109/icc.2018.8422385

3. Gogu, A., Nace, D., Dilo, A., Meratni, N.: Review of optimization problems in wireless sensor networks. Telecommun. Netw. Curr. Status Future Trends (2012). https://doi.org/10.5772/38360

4. Yick, J., Mukherjee, B., Ghosal, D.: Wireless sensor network survey. Comput. Netw. **52**(12), 2292–2330 (2008). https://doi.org/10.1016/j.comnet.2008.04.002

5. Fu, X., Fortino, G., Li, W.: Environment-cognitive multipath routing protocol in wireless sensor networks. In: 2018 IEEE International Conference on Systems, Man, and Cybernetics (SMC) (2018). https://doi.org/10.1109/smc.2018.00471

6. Aashkaar, M., Sharma, P.: Enhanced energy efficient AODV routing protocol for MANET. In: 2016 International Conference on Research Advances in Integrated Navigation Systems (RAINS) (2016). https://doi.org/10.1109/rains.2016.7764376

7. Choudhary, R., Sharma, P.K.: An efficient approach for power aware routing protocol for MANETs using genetic algorithm. In: Rathore, V.S., Worring, M., Mishra, D.K., Joshi, A., Maheshwari, S. (eds.) Emerging Trends in Expert Applications and Security. AISC, vol. 841, pp. 133–138. Springer, Singapore (2019). https://doi.org/10.1007/978-981-13-2285-3_17

8. Pandey, K.K., Saud, B., Kumari, B., Biswas, S.: An energy efficient hierarchical clustering technique for wireless sensor network. In: 2016 Fourth International Conference on Parallel, Distributed and Grid Computing (PDGC) (2016). https://doi.org/10.1109/pdgc.2016.7913184

9. Banerjee, A., et al.: Construction of effective wireless sensor network for smart communication using modified ant colony optimization technique. In: Bianchini, M., Piuri, V., Das, S., Shaw, R.N. (eds.) Advanced Computing and Intelligent Technologies. LNNS, vol. 218, pp. 269–278. Springer, Singapore (2022). https://doi.org/10.1007/978-981-16-2164-2_22

10. Li, Z., Lei, L.: Sensor node deployment in wireless sensor networks based on improved particle swarm optimization. In: 2009 International Conference on Applied Superconductivity and Electromagnetic Devices (2009). https://doi.org/10.1109/asemd.2009.5306655

11. Feng, W., et al.: Joint energy-saving scheduling and secure routing for critical event reporting in wireless sensor networks. IEEE Access **8**, 53281–53292 (2020). https://doi.org/10.1109/access.2020.2981115

12. Paul, A., Sinha, S., Shaw, R.N., Ghosh, A.: A neuro-fuzzy based IDS for internet-integrated WSN. In: Bansal, J.C., Paprzycki, M., Bianchini, M., Das, S. (eds.) Computationally Intelligent Systems and their Applications. SCI, vol. 950, pp. 71–86. Springer, Singapore (2021). https://doi.org/10.1007/978-981-16-0407-2_6

13. Badni, A.B., and Smt Kamala Sri Venkappa M Agadi college of Engineering and Technology: Energy efficiency routing of wireless sensor networks utilizing particle swarm optimization and LEACH protocol Int. J. Eng. Res. Technol. (Ahmedabad) **V9**(06) (2020). https://doi.org/10.17577/ijertv9is060219

14. Burgos, U., Amozarrain, U., Gómez-Calzado, C., Lafuente, A.: Routing in mobile wireless sensor networks: a leader-based approach. Sensors **17**(7), 1587 (2017). https://doi.org/10.3390/s17071587

15. Zungeru, A.M., Seng, K.P., Ang, L.-M., Chia, W.C.: Energy efficiency performance improvements for ant-based routing algorithm in wireless sensor networks. J. Sens. **2013**, 1–17 (2013). https://doi.org/10.1155/2013/759654

16. Nandan, A.S., Singh, S., Awasthi, L.K.: An efficient cluster head election based on optimized genetic algorithm for movable sinks in IoT enabled HWSNs. Appl. Soft Comput. **107**. 107318 (2021). https://doi.org/10.1016/j.asoc.2021.107318

Prediction of Compressive Strength of Green Concrete by Artificial Neural Network

Manvendra Verma[1], Kamal Upreti[2(✉)], Priyanka Dadhich[3], Soumi Ghosh[4], Vishal Khatri[5], and Prashant Singh[6]

[1] Department of Civil Engineering, GLA University, Mathura, Uttar Pradesh, India
manvendra.verma@gla.ac.in
[2] Department of Computer Science and Engineering, Akhilesh Das Gupta Institute of Technology and Management, Delhi, India
kamalurpeti1989@gmail.com
[3] Department of Big Data Analytics, Asia Pacific Institute of Management, Delhi, India
[4] Department of Information Technology, Maharaja Agrasen Institute of Technology, Delhi, India
[5] Department of Computer Science and Engineering, Bhagwan Parshuram Institute of Technology, Delhi, India
vishalkhatri@bpitindia.com
[6] Department of Computer Science and Engineering, Sunder Deep Engineering College, Ghaziabad, India

Abstract. The concrete business has just come out with a brand-new product called geopolymer concrete. Because of its resilience in harsh environments and its high strength, it has the potential to revolutionise the whole construction industry. It is an excellent substitute for the traditional kind of concrete. It outperforms traditional concrete in terms of sustainability, ecology, durability, and economic viability. In this day and age, the use of machine learning strategies is not just the future of the research and development industry, but of all industries. These methods provide predictions about the outcomes by analysing the facts from the past. The process of determining the outcomes or worth of anything in the construction sector is very challenging, time consuming, and arduous. Without having to conduct destructive experiments or take samples, the strength of a mix design may now be more accurately predicted thanks to these procedures. By using deep learning and the random forest method, the purpose of this research is to predict the compressive strength of flyash-based geopolymer concrete. This will be accomplished by comparing the two algorithms with varying degrees of error and coefficient correlation. It has been shown via the use of simulated data that the random forest algorithm is the method that is most suited for making predictions about compressive strength. After the developing a model, the various errors were found for accuracy. The mean absolute error, root mean square error, relative absolute error, and root relative squared error are 3.46%, 5.94%, 64.32%, and 82.97%, respectively for the deep learning predicted compressive strength. The errors provide the proof of model accuracy to predict the compressive strength on the basis of ingredients proportions.

Keywords: Green concrete · Geopolymer concrete · Sustainable · Machine learning · Artificial neural network

© The Author(s), under exclusive license to Springer Nature Switzerland AG 2023
R. N. Shaw et al. (Eds.): ICACIS 2022, CCIS 1749, pp. 622–632, 2023.
https://doi.org/10.1007/978-3-031-25088-0_55

1 Introduction

In this new period, humans are accomplishing a variety of important developmental milestones [1–5]. The evolution of society is contingent upon the development of society's underlying infrastructure [6]. As a result, the building sector plays an important part in the progression of society. When building any kind of construction, concrete is one of the most important building materials to use [7]. Geopolymer concrete is a type of green concrete that completely replaces cement with fly ash, GGBFS, and alkaline solution and works as a binding material [8]. On the other hand, conventional concrete is an everyday and household-usable type of concrete that has been around for the last two to three decades [9, 10]. After water, concrete is the material that has the second highest potential utility on this planet [11]. Cement is the principal binding element in the typical concrete composition, and the manufacturing of one tonne of cement results in the release of approximately one tonne of carbon dioxide into the environment [12]. In geopolymer concrete, fly ash and ground-granulated blast-furnace slag take the role of cement. In concrete, the substance with the highest emission rate is cement [13]. In conclusion, the use of geopolymer concrete can cut ordinary concrete's carbon footprint by around 80% [14].

The release of carbon dioxide has a direct impact on the warming of the planet. Therefore, sustainable development is extremely important for the continued growth of the building industry in the future [15]. The price of geopolymer is significantly lower than that of traditional concrete [16]. It results in a cost reduction of approximately forty percent of the initial amount [17]. Due to the geopolymer concrete's superior strength and longevity, it may be possible to use it in place of traditional concrete in some applications [18]. It is necessary to use an alkaline solution in order to activate the pozzolanic material that will be used in geopolymer concrete in order for it to be able to form bonds [19]. Cement is completely replaced in geopolymer concrete by flyash, slag, or metakaolin, which are all elements of concrete [20]. An alkaline material could be utilised in geopolymer concrete, and some examples include sodium or potassium hydroxides as well as silicates [21]. Reactions and linkages formed by geopolymer concrete are distinct from those formed by conventional concrete [22]. The phrase "geopolymer" derives mostly from the link that is formed as a result of these interactions, and Professor Davidovits was the first person to illustrate this concept [23]. In the laboratory's testing, geopolymer concrete's performance was shown to be superior to that of conventional concrete [24]. This indicates that geopolymer concrete could be an ideal replacement for conventional concrete [25]. It's possible that this is where the green building and construction sector is headed [26].

The strength of geopolymer concrete is impacted by a wide range of characteristics, including both internal and external variables [27]. When it comes to the exterior parameters, the curing kinds, duration, temperature, humidity, and air containment all play significant roles [28]. On the other hand, the internal aspects include the quality of the materials as well as the various compositions [29]. The composition of the binding materials and the size of the particles are important factors in both the initiation of the reaction and the subsequent strengthening of the material; however, the ratios of these factors also play an important role in the ability to control the strength in accordance with the requirements [30]. The addition of slag to the mix results in an increase in the compressive strength of the geopolymer concrete after it has cured under ambient conditions [31]. Because of the higher surface area that is available to them, the finer particles of flyash and slag react quickly, which contributes to an increase in the early strength of the concrete [32]. Additionally, the liquid to binder has a significant part in the reaction, and it is difficult to get strength [33]. Because water is required for and during the initiation of the geopolymer reaction, but it would release during the hardening process, and it is not required in the end reaction products of the geopolymer reaction, the minimum liquid content is required to react with all of the constituents of geopolymer concrete [31]. The optimal amount of liquid that should be included in the composition has a direct bearing on the geopolymer concrete's strength [34]. Because SNF-based superplasticizers are the most ideal for the boding of geopolymer concrete, the selection of the use of those superplasticizers in geopolymer concrete play a significant role in the formation of bonds. When it comes to kickstarting the geopolymer process, the quality and concentration of the alkaline solution are of the utmost importance. The molarity of sodium or potassium hydroxide is directly implicated in the reaction that takes place, and it either raises or lowers the performance and strength of the concrete. The curing temperature and circumstances are also highly successful in achieving the design strength, as seen by the fact that oven-cured samples readily obtained the strength required, as compared to specimens that were cured in ambient settings. In addition to this, the geopolymer concrete is very resistant to harsh weather conditions. Therefore, geopolymer concrete could be the key to achieving sustainable growth in the building sector in the future. Around the globe, geopolymer concrete is used for a variety of purposes in a variety of applications. The Delhi Metro Rail Corporation (DMRC) is now using the usage of geopolymer concrete in the building of tunnels and platforms in the city of Delhi, India.

2 Materials and Method

Fly ash, an alkaline solution (consisting of sodium hydroxide and sodium silicate), coarse aggregates, fine aggregates, a superplasticizer, and water are the components that go into making geopolymer concrete. Prior to the manufacture of concrete on a big scale, the labs always do quality checks to ensure that the raw ingredients are of an acceptable standard. Flyash is almost usually acquired from the chemical industry, while alkaline solution and superplasticizer are brought from the thermal plant that is located closest to the construction site. Both coarse and fine aggregates are sourced from materials that are readily accessible in the area [35–43]. The water is utilised in accordance with the requirements that are necessary in that location. Before 20 to 24 h have passed after the mixing, the alkaline solutions are prepared. Because conventional concrete requires less time to mix in mixers than geopolymer concrete does, it is not possible to manually combine the two types of concrete. There is no doubt that M-sand can be used effectively in geopolymer concrete. Because of the well-graded particles, it produces far better outcomes than regular sand would.

It is vital to design the ratio between the amounts of alumina, silica, and sodium oxide content, thus an XRF test was performed on the flyash or any other pozzolanic materials that were available in order to determine the mineral contents that were present in the raw samples. When the chemicals are obtained from the various industries, the companies will provide the mineral contents or the minimum assay that is contained in the various chemical solutions. In the laboratories, coarse aggregates and fine aggregates were examined to determine their particle sizes, fineness modulus, bulk density, moisture content, silt content, specific gravity, shape, size, elongation index, flakiness index, crushing value, impact value, and abrasion value for coarse aggregates, and particle sizes, fineness modulus, elongation index, flakiness index, specific gravity, shape, size, elongation index, flakiness index, crushing value, impact value Before moving further with the mixed design of the concrete, all of these experiments were carried out.

Techniques that are based on machine learning are very necessary in this day and age. They have significant potential applications in all areas of research and development in the future. The mathematical tools and models serve as the foundation for these strategies. They use a wide variety of different approaches, depending on which ones are most suited to anticipate how the future will unfold. The neural network method is quite well-known, and it is simple to compute and forecast the data based on the data that was previously stored.

Neural networks have the ability to learn complicated patterns because to their use of layers of neurons that mathematically alter the input. The fundamental components of the multilayer perception model are shown in Fig. 1. "Hidden layers" refers to the layers that come between the input and the output of a system. A neural network has the ability to understand correlations between features that other algorithms are unable to simply uncover on their own.

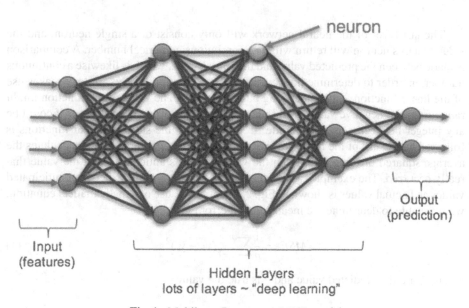

Fig. 1. Multilayer Perceptron (MLP) model

The diagram that was been shown to you is called a Multilayer Perceptron (MLP). A minimum of three layers are required for an MLP, which includes an input layer, a hidden layer, and an output layer. They have a complete network connection; for example, every node in one layer has a weighted connection to every node in the next layer. Deep neural networks are the models used for machine learning that give rise to the phrase "deep learning," which was created to describe the process. This post's objective is to serve as a guide for determining which combination of the final-layer activation function and loss function need to be used in a neural network in accordance with the particular enterprise objective.

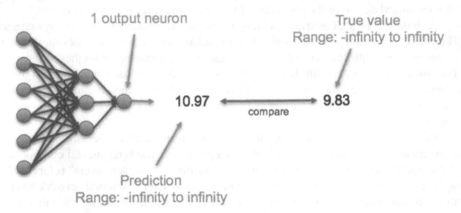

Fig. 2. Picture of comparison between the predicted and true value

The last layer of the neural network will only consist of a single neuron, and the value that this neuron will return will be a continuous numerical number. A comparison is made between the predicted value and the actual value, which is likewise a continuous number, in order to determine how accurate, the prediction is. This strategy makes use of the linear function as its underlying building block. The value of the function might range from the negative value of infinite to the positive value of infinite, or it could be any integer between zero and infinite. In this method, the study of linear functions is followed by the use of the mean squared error mathematical model. This calculates the average squared difference between the value that was anticipated and the value that really occurred. The example of how the mean square error works between anticipated values and actual values is shown in Fig. 2. Through the use of a mathematical equation, we were able to determine the mean squared error (1).

$$MSE = \frac{1}{n} \sum_{i=1}^{n} (y_i - \bar{y}_i)^2 \tag{1}$$

where $\bar{y}_i$ are the predicted value and y is true the value

3 Results and Discussion

In this part, the findings that were discovered via the use of machine learning methods such as multilayer perception or deep learning and the random forest algorithm are discussed. First, maintain the data that was discovered in the labs by the testing that was done on the samples of the geopolymer concrete mix designs, and then put them in MATLAB by initially 70% for the development of model and 30% utilised before the training of the model. In the beginning, the data set consisted of 61 records with 11 elements, all of which were written down in numerical form. The workflow of machine learning approaches is shown as a flow chart in Fig. 3, which can be seen here. Every single approach for machine learning is based on the same principle, but operates in a unique manner depending on a set of factors. It demonstrates the first input characteristics that are made up of basic data in order to create modal, and after selecting the method to construct the model based on the basic data input and target the out data, it displays the first input attributes that are used to produce modal. It's possible that the actual data and the anticipated data will be comparable.

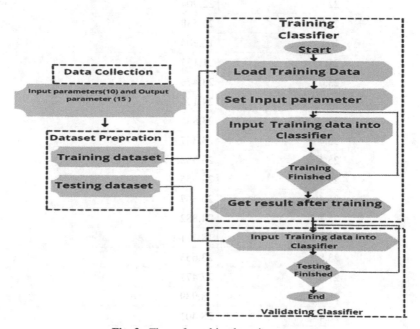

Fig. 3. Flow of machine learning process

These machine learning algorithms each have a unique method of operation that focuses on a certain set of output data in order to make accurate predictions. The whole of the procedure that the deep learning method uses to forecast the output outcomes is seen in Fig. 3. It is a significant part of the job to train the input, output, and data, and it is performed in sequence. During the first phase, it gathers the input data using 11 parameters and produces only one output parameter. Following the completion of the data collection, it would next construct the training data sets, which would comprise the training classifier. The whole procedure of training a data set is included into the training classifier. This procedure begins with loading the input data and is followed by the setting of the input parameters for the data sets. Once that, conclude the data training, then proceed to examine the outcomes after the classifiers have been applied to the trained data sets. The 10folds cross-validation training of data is used in this procedure in order to reduce the amount of error that exists between the projected results and the actual outcomes. This is the whole process of using deep learning to make predictions based on real-world data sets.

Table 1. Compressive strength of both actual and predicted

Actual compressive strength (Mpa)	Predicted compressive strength (Mpa)
21.5	21.48
24.4	24.173
22.9	22.904
21.7	21.538
16.2	16.204
21.3	21.177
23.6	23.47
24.1	24.19
24	23.886
23.4	23.387
25.4	25.388
29.1	28.955
26.4	26.367
25.1	24.882
18.1	18.111
23.8	23.653
27.6	27.477
28.9	28.939
28.4	28.401
27.6	27.588

Compressive strength test findings for geopolymer concrete samples are remarkably close to those discovered using machine learning methods. Table 1 shows a comparison of the compressive strength findings obtained using real, and artificial neural network. Sixty rows of compressive strength data are shown. All predictions for compressive strength were made using deep learning and random forest methods, and the results are shown in three columns per row. The unit of compressive strength is megapascals

(MPa). The range of 25 MPa to 45 MPa is used for the majority of the data. Compressive strength predictions and measurements are compared using the different formulae. The degrees of accuracy (R2, MAE, RMSE, RAE, and RRSE) were computed using the respective mathematical procedures (Eqs. 2–6). The equations' computed error values are shown in Table 2. Included are the relative absolute error and root relative squared error in addition to the neighboring correlation coefficient. There is a clear difference between the mistakes made by random forests algorithm.

$$R^2 = \frac{\left(n \sum x_i y_i - \sum x_i \sum y_i\right)^2}{\left(n \sum x_i^2 - \left(\sum x_i\right)^2\right)\left(n \sum y_i^2 - \left(\sum y_i\right)^2\right)} \tag{2}$$

$$MAE = 1/n \sum_{i=1}^{n} |x_i - y_i| \tag{3}$$

$$RMSE = \sqrt{\left(\frac{1}{n}\right) \sum_{i=1}^{n} |x_i - y_i|^2} \tag{4}$$

$$RAE = \frac{\sum_{i=1}^{n} |x_i - y_i|}{\sum_{i=1}^{n} |x_i - (1/n) \sum_{i=1}^{n} x_i|} \tag{5}$$

$$RRSE = \sqrt{\frac{\sum_{i=1}^{n} (x_i - y_i)^2}{\sum_{i=1}^{n} \left(x_i - (1/n) \sum_{i=1}^{n} x_i\right)^2}} \tag{6}$$

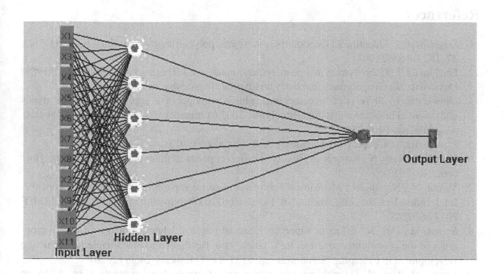

Table 2. Different error between predicted and actual

	Artificial neural network predicted
Correlation coefficient (R^2)	0.7252
MAE	3.4579
RMSE	5.9379
RAE	64.32
RRSE	82.9719

4 Conclusion

The experimental investigation in laboratories, to provide the compressive strength of the specimens for different ingredients proportions. Then, Artificial neural network machine learning techniques is used predict the future compressive strength for different ingredients proportions by developing a model. After the developing a model, the various errors were found for accuracy. The mean absolute error, root mean square error, relative absolute error, and root relative squared error are 3.46%, 5.94%, 64.32%, and 82.97%, respectively for the deep learning predicted compressive strength. The errors provide the proof of model accuracy to predict the compressive strength on the basis of ingredients proportions.

References

1. Davidovits, J., Quentin, S.: Geopolymers inorganic polymeric new materials. J. Therm Anal. **37**, 1633–1656 (1991)
2. Davidovits, J.: Geopolymers and geopolymeric materials. J. Therm. Anal. **35**, 429–441 (1989)
3. Davidovits, J.: Geopolymer Chemistry and Applications. 5th edn. (2020)
4. Davidovits, J.: 30 Years of successes and failures in geopolymer applications. market trends and potential breakthroughs. In: Geopolymer 2002 Conference, 28–29 Oct 2002. Melbourne, Australia, pp. 1–16 (2002)
5. Davidovits, J.: Geopolymer Chemistry & Applications (2015)
6. Verma, M., Dev, N.: Review on Effects of different parameters on behaviour of Geopolymer concrete (2017)
7. Verma, M., Nigam, M.: Mechanical behaviour of self compacting and self curing concrete. Int. J. Innov. Res. Sci. Eng. Technol. **6**, 14361–366 (2017). https://doi.org/10.15680/IJIRSET. 2017.0607245
8. Verma, M., Dev, N.: Effect of superplasticiser on physical, chemical and mechanical properties of the geopolymer concrete. In: Challenges of Resilient and Sustainable Infrastructure Development in Emerging Economies, pp. 1185–1191. Kolkata, India (2020)
9. Verma, M., Dev, N.: Geopolymer concrete: a way of sustainable construction. Int. J. Recent Res. Asp. **5**, 201–205 (2018)
10. Verma, M., Dev, N.: Sodium hydroxide effect on the mechanical properties of flyash-slag based geopolymer concrete. Struct. Concr. **22**, E368–E379 (2021). https://doi.org/10.1002/ suco.202000068

11. Upreti, K., Kumar, N., Alam, M.S., Verma, A., Nandan, M., Gupta, A.K.: Machine Learning-based congestion control routing strategy for healthcare IoT enabled wireless sensor networks. In: 2021 Fourth International Conference on Electrical, Computer and Communication Technologies (ICECCT), pp. 1–6 (2021). https://doi.org/10.1109/ICECCT52121.2021.9616864

12. Upreti, K., Singh, U.K., Jain, R., Kaur, K., Sharma, A.K.: Fuzzy logic based support vector regression (SVR) model for software cost estimation using machine learning. In: Tuba, M., Akashe, S., Joshi, A. (eds.) ICT Systems and Sustainability. LNNS, vol. 321, pp. 917–927. Springer, Singapore (2022). https://doi.org/10.1007/978-981-16-5987-4_90

13. Verma, M., Dev, N.: Effect of ground granulated blast furnace slag and fly ash ratio and the curing conditions on the mechanical properties of geopolymer concrete. Struct. Concr. **23**, 2015–2029 (2022). https://doi.org/10.1002/suco.202000536

14. Verma, M., et al.: Experimental analysis of geopolymer concrete : a sustainable and economic concrete using the cost estimation model. Adv. Mater. Sci. Eng. **2022**, 1–16 (2022). https://doi.org/10.1155/2022/7488254

15. Garg, C., Namdeo, A., Singhal, A., Singh, P., Shaw, R.N., Ghosh, A.: Adaptive fuzzy logic models for the prediction of compressive strength of sustainable concrete. In: Bianchini, M., Piuri, V., Das, S., Shaw, R.N. (eds.) Advanced Computing and Intelligent Technologies. LNNS, vol. 218, pp. 593–605. Springer, Singapore (2022). https://doi.org/10.1007/978-981-16-2164-2_47

16. Verma, M., Dev, N., Rahman, I., Nigam, M., Ahmed, M., Mallick, J.: Geopolymer concrete: a material for sustainable development in Indian construction industries. Curr. Comput. Aided Drug Des. **12**, 514 (2022). https://doi.org/10.3390/cryst12040514

17. Upreti, K., Verma, M.: Prediction of compressive strength of high-volume fly ash concrete using artificial neural network. J. Eng. Res. Appl. **1**, 24–32 (2022). https://doi.org/10.55953/JERA.2022.2104

18. Verma, M.: Experimental investigation on the properties of Geopolymer concrete after replacement of river sand with the M-sand. In: International e-Conference on Sustainable Development & Recent Trends in Civil Engineering, pp. 46–54 (2022)

19. Chouksey, A., Verma, M., Dev, N., Rahman, I., Upreti, K.: An investigation on the effect of curing conditions on the mechanical and microstructural properties of the geopolymer concrete. Mater. Res. Express. **9**, 055003 (2022). https://doi.org/10.1088/2053-1591/ac6be0

20. Upreti, K., et al..: Prediction of mechanical strength by using an artificial neural network and random forest algorithm. J. Nanomater **2022**, 1–12 (2022). https://doi.org/10.1155/2022/7791582

21. Kumar, R., Verma, M., Dev, N.: Investigation of fresh, mechanical, and impact resistance properties of rubberized concrete. In: International e-Conference on Sustainable Development & Recent Trends in Civil Engineering, pp. 88–94 (2022)

22. Verma, M., Juneja, A., Saini, D.: Effect of waste tyre rubber in the concrete. In: International e-Conference on Sustainable Development & Recent Trends in Civil Engineering, 4th–5th January 2022, pp. 99–103 (2022)

23. Kumar, R., Verma, M., Dev, N., Lamba, N.: Influence of chloride and sulfate solution on the long-term durability of modified rubberized concrete. J. Appl. Polym. Sci. 1–15 (2022). https://doi.org/10.1002/app.52880

24. Kumar, M., Shenbagaraman, V.M., Shaw, R.N., Ghosh, A.: Digital transformation in smart manufacturing with industrial robot through predictive data analysis. In: Bianchini, M., Simic, M., Ghosh, A., Shaw, R.N. (eds.) Machine Learning for Robotics Applications. SCI, vol. 960, pp. 85–105. Springer, Singapore (2021). https://doi.org/10.1007/978-981-16-0598-7_8

25. Gupta, A., Gupta, N., Saxena, K.K.: Experimental study of the mechanical and durability properties of Slag and Calcined Clay based geopolymer composite. Adv. Mater. Process. Technol. **00**, 1–15 (2021). https://doi.org/10.1080/2374068X.2021.1948709

26. Gupta, P., Gupta, N., Saxena, K.K., Goyal, S.: Random forest modeling for fly ash-calcined clay geopolymer composite strength detection. J. Compos. Sci. **5** (2021). https://doi.org/10.3390/jcs5100271

27. Gupta, A., Gupta, N., Saxena, K.K.: Mechanical and durability characteristics assessment of geopolymer composite (Gpc) at varying silica fume content. J. Compos. Sci. **5** (2021). https://doi.org/10.3390/JCS5090237

28. Gupta, A.: Investigation of the strength of ground granulated blast furnace slag based geopolymer composite with silica fume. Mater. Today Proc. **44**, 23–28 (2021). https://doi.org/10.1016/j.matpr.2020.06.010

29. Parashar, A.K., Gupta, A.: Investigation of the effect of bagasse ash, hooked steel fibers and glass fibers on the mechanical properties of concrete. Mater. Today Proc. **44**, 801–807 (2021). https://doi.org/10.1016/j.matpr.2020.10.711

30. Bhogayata, A., Dave, S.V., Arora, N.K.: Utilization of expanded clay aggregates in sustainable lightweight geopolymer concrete. J. Mater. Cycles Waste Manage. **22**(6), 1780–1792 (2020). https://doi.org/10.1007/s10163-020-01066-7

31. Ananthi, J., Sengottaiyan, N., Anbukaruppusamy, S., Upreti, K., Dubey, A.K.: Forest fire prediction using IoT and deep learning. Int. J. Adv. Technol. Eng. Explor. **9**, 246–256 (2022). https://doi.org/10.19101/IJATEE.2021.87464

32. Rajawat, A.S., Barhanpurkar, K., Goyal, S.B., Bedi, P., Shaw, R.N., Ghosh, A.: Efficient deep learning for reforming authentic content searching on big data. In: Bianchini, M., Piuri, V., Das, S., Shaw, R.N. (eds.) Advanced Computing and Intelligent Technologies. LNNS, vol. 218, pp. 319–327. Springer, Singapore (2022). https://doi.org/10.1007/978-981-16-2164-2_26

33. Singh, I., Dev, N., Pal, S., Visalakshi, T.: Finite element analysis of impact load on reinforced concrete. In: Ha-Minh, C., Tang, A.M., Bui, T.Q., Vu, X.H., Huynh, D.V.K. (eds.) CIGOS 2021, Emerging Technologies and Applications for Green Infrastructure. LNCE, vol. 203, pp. 265–274. Springer, Singapore (2022). https://doi.org/10.1007/978-981-16-7160-9_26

34. Gautam, J., Atrey, M., Malsa, N., Balyan, A., Shaw, R.N., Ghosh, A.: Twitter data sentiment analysis using naive bayes classifier and generation of heat map for analyzing intensity geographically. In: Bansal, J.C., Fung, L.C.C., Simic, M., Ghosh, A. (eds.) Advances in Applications of Data-Driven Computing. AISC, vol. 1319, pp. 129–139. Springer, Singapore (2021). https://doi.org/10.1007/978-981-33-6919-1_10

35. IS 383 1970: Specification for coarse and fine aggregates from natural sources for concrete. Bur. Indian Stand. 1–20 (1997)

36. IS 2386 (Part II): Methods of test for aggregates for concrete Part II Estimation of deleterious materials and organic impurties. Bur. Indian Stand. 2386 (1998)

37. IS 2386 (Part VIII): Methods of test for aggregates for concrete Part VIII Petrographic examination. Bur. Indian Stand. 2386 (1997)

38. IS 2386 (PartV): Methods of test for aggregates for concrete Part V Soundness. Bur. Indian Stand. (1997)

39. IS 2386 (Part I): Methods of test for aggregates for concrete Part I Particle size and shape. Bur. Indian Stand. 2386 (1997)

40. IS 2386 (Part III): Methods of test for aggregates for concrete Part III Specific gravity, density, voids, absorption and bulking. Bur. Indian Stand. 2386 (1997)

41. IS 2386 (Part VII): Methods of test for aggregates for concrete Part VII Alkali aggregate reactivity. Bur. Indian Stand. (1997)

42. IS 2386 (Part IV): Methods of test for aggregates for concrete Part IV Mechanical Properties. Bur. Indian Stand. 2386 (1997)

43. IS 2386 (Part VI): Methods of test for aggregates for concrete Part VI Measuring mortar making properties of fine aggregate. Bur. Indian Stand. 2386 (1997)

Early-Stage Dementia Detection by Optimize Feature Weights with Ensemble Learning

Tanvi Mahajan[✉] and Jyoti Srivastava

National Institute of Technology, Hamirpur, Himachal Pradesh, India
tanvimahajan003@gmail.com, jyoti.s@nith.ac.in

Abstract. Dementia has become a serious health concern for many people above fifty years. Several types of dementia typically applied and in stages. Past studies have received a report from persons of different ages who have afflicted from long-term memory problems and constantly reflecting because of neuro-degenerative illness. Dementia is defined by irreversible and serious memory loss. Though it is more prevalent in the elder people, an increase in cases among the younger age group has stimulated professionals' interest and inspired them to examine the nerve cells, which an lead to memory lapses and difficulty remembering information stored in memory. Dementia can often be decreased to some extent if identified early enough. Additional tree classifier and Optimize learning are used to extract information from MRI Brain images and characterise dementia at initial point. The hyper-parameters achieved from XGboost were determined in order to explore different forms of mortality risk. Gradient boosting is a method that is frequently used to derive variables from independent to dependent variables, in addition to the derived variables which outcome from this process.

Keywords: Dementia · Alzheimer disease · MRI · Machine learning · Deep learning · Classification

1 Introduction

Dementia is becoming a severe health risk for people over the age of 50 in the modern day. Dementia has grown to be one of the most serious health disorders afflicting adults aged 50 to 70 worldwide. Around 2.5 million people were added to Europe's dementia. Dementia appears to be a neurological disorder characterised by progressive and irreversible memory loss. Although it affects a higher proportion of the elderly than young people, it has piqued the interest of researchers in neuro-disorders related to memory loss. Dementia [1, 28, 11] can assist the patient in regaining some control if detected early. As shown in a review of existing and potential future demo- graphics, there will be over 120 million users with dementia and 75 million with Alzheimer's disease by the year 2050. Alzheimer's disease (AD), the most prevalent form of dementia, is a significant healthcare concern in the 21st century. AD is a chronic, irreversible brain condition characterised by a deterioration in cognitive performance and the absence of a recognized disease-modifying medication [10, 36]. As a result, considerable effort

R. N. Shaw et al. (Eds.): ICACIS 2022, CCIS 1749, pp. 633–648, 2023.
https://doi.org/10.1007/978-3-031-25088-0_56

has been invested on developing procedures for early identification, particularly at pre-symptomatic phases, with the goal of slowing or halting disease development [13, 14, 16, 24]. Sophisticated neuroimaging technologies, like positron emission tomography (PET), magnetic resonance imaging (MRI) have been established and are being utilized to uncover molecular and structural biomarker associated with AD [13]. Major developments in neuroimaging have complicated the integration of massive, multimodal neuro imaging data. As a result, interest in computer-aided machine learning (ML) methodologies for integrative analysis has developed fast. Numerous well-known pattern-based analysis techniques, including support vector machine (SVM), support vector machine recursive feature elimination (SVM-RFE), linear discriminant analysis (LDA), logistic regression (LR), linear program boosting method (LPBM), are being used and possess the potential for early monitoring and detection of AD progression [22]. To implement such ML algorithms, it is necessary to define proper design and architecture or pre-processing processes in advance. Categorization studies utilising ML typically involve 4 phases: feature selection, feature extraction, dimensionality reduction, and method choice based on feature-based categorization. These techniques necessitate specialised knowledge and numerous optimization phases, which can be time demanding. Reproducibility seems to have been a concern with these techniques [17]. For instance, during the feature representation, AD-related features are selected from a variety of neuroimaging modalities in order to generate more informative combinational measures. These character traits could include mean subcortical volumes, grey matter concentrations, brain glucose metabolism, cortical thickness, and cerebellar amyloid-b accumulation in ROIs such as the hippocampus [19].

1.1 Types of Dementia

Dementia represents a composite name for a variety of symptoms that affect one's memory, thinking, and social abilities considerably. Though dementia is still not a single disorder, it can be brought on by a range of different disorders [15].

Alzheimer Dementia: This results in difficulties with language, memory, and logic. 5% of instances begin well before age of 65.

Vascular Dementia: Impairment of judgement, balance, and motor skills. Stroke and heart disease enhance the likelihood of this occurring.

Mixed Dementia: Numerous kinds of dementia are implicated in the symptoms. The condition is more prevalent in adults over the age of 85.

Alzheimer's Disease with Lewy Bodies: As a result of Lewy body proteins. Symptoms may also include hallucinations and sleep disturbances.

Fronto-temporal Dementia: Changes in personality and communication difficulties. The most prevalent age of onset somewhere between 45 and 60 years.

Parkinson's Disease: As the illness advances, it may manifest as dementia symptoms.

Others: Conditions like Creutzfeldt-Jakob disease; depression; and multiple sclerosis are only a few examples.

1.2 Neuroimaging Analysis for Diagnosis of Dementia

Early diagnosis, possible treatments, and sustenance are critical for the patients in the pre-dementia stages/pre-symptomatic of the disease in order to slow deterioration and maintain a high standard of living for as long as possible. Imaging, in instance, can reveal quantitative biomarkers indicative of a specific aetiology and prognosis for dementia [18, 43]. Figure 1 illustrates the many imaging techniques available for such biomarkers, including MRI/PET/SPECT pictures, which have the potential of capturing brain abnormalities and neural vulnerability characteristics associated with dementia.

a. MRI Modalities: MRI generates magnetic waves in order to create 2D o 3D images of the brain's structure without the need of radioactive tracers. It permits the investigators to determine both anatomical and functional problems of the brain, such as dementia. Figure 2 illustrates several sample MRI scans used to diagnose dementia.

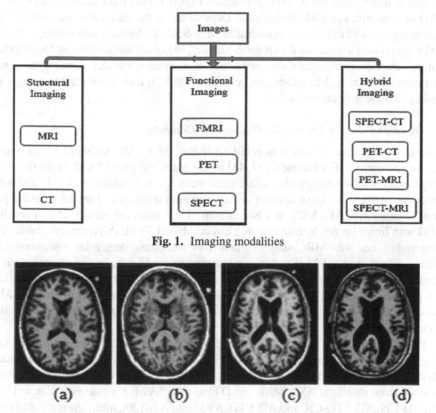

Fig. 1. Imaging modalities

Fig. 2. Healthy MRI scans (a–b) and Alzheimer's disease (c–d) [44]

b. PET modalities: PET stands for Positron Emission Tomography, and it analyses emissions to produce 2D or 3D images of chemical distribution throughout the brain by infusing radiotracers into blood. The primary benefit of PET-based imaging is that oxygen, blood movement, and glycogen absorption in functioning brain tissues can be evidently noticed, indicating the brain's activity and provides a glimpse into its working. Figure 4 depicts some typical PET image processing dementia detection patterns.

c. SPECT Modalities: SPECT, or Single-Photon Emission Computed Tomography imaging, is a fully functioning nuclear imaging technology which records 2D or 3D images of the brain's regional cerebral perfusion using a radioactive tracer or SPECT agent. Figure 5 shows the search patterns of the DLB and NC SPECT modalities.

1.3 Dementia Diagnosis Using Machine Learning Techniques

Neuro-imaging diagnostic for dementia recognition is a lengthy process that takes into account a plethora of variables based on the imaging modality used. Machine Learning [5–7] has the potential to enhance clinical diagnostic decision-making by automatically identifying and forecasting dementia employing neuro-imaging modalities and computer-aided diagnosis (CAD) approaches. Figure 6 illustrates the core step-by-step CAD of dementia using ML techniques. Depending on the parameter selected, images were pre-processed utilising tools such as SPM or SeeCAT. Various statistical approaches [33] were utilised to generate the cross-validation [39], extracted features and appropriate feature selection optimisation was performed to guarantee the techniques were generated correctly. Lastly, ML techniques such as SVM [20] have been used to categorise, predict, and identify dementia.

1) *Traditional ML Techniques for Diagnosing Dementia:*

Numerous works have been conducted with the aid of ML techniques and neuro-imaging modalities. For instance, [47, 48] investigated the use of SVM-based full brain categorisation to autonomously differentiate between individuals with AD and MCI employing MRI and a leave-one-out cross-validation technique. They used ADNI pictures to categorise AD, MCI, and NC in [46]. They analysed various classifiers, like SVM with linear kernel. Recent research has combined SVM, PCA, and ensemble classifier techniques with MRI images to detect or categorise dementias associated with Alzheimer's disease. SVM classification is accomplished by the use of a hyper-plane or a group of hyper-planes in a high-dimensional space [49]. It is a widely used classifier that performs well with sparse training data and has low generalisation error. SVM is indeed the most often used classifier in multivariate classifications and for early detection of dementia (Fig. 3).

In [35], SVM-based classification of initial Alzheimer's disease was performed utilising three brain slices relying on the OASIS MRI dataset. The proposed approach has a 90.66% accuracy rate for premature AD diagnosis [32]. Used voxel-wise feature maps obtained from structural ASL, MRI, and DTI to train SVMs for categorisation of FTD-CN, AD-CN, AD-FTD-CN, and AD-FTD. SVM and A In [20], multi-class classification of MCI, AD cMCI, and NC employing ADNI MRI characteristics was accomplished via ensemble SVM either using a linear or an RBF kernel-based selection technique. With an accuracy of up to 59.1%, the ensemble SVM got better results than the single SVM. [45] evaluated the early diagnosis of AD in a fully automatic CAD relying on SPECT image categorisation via RBF SVM. They discovered that sagittal correlation

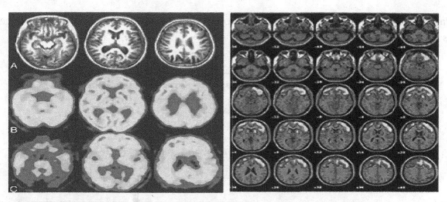

Fig. 3. (a) Numerous PET images of a 77-year-old patient with AD, A) Right Hippocampus, B) FDG-PET and C) PiB accumulation. (b) FDG-PET maps for two bvFTD variants in single subjects [42].

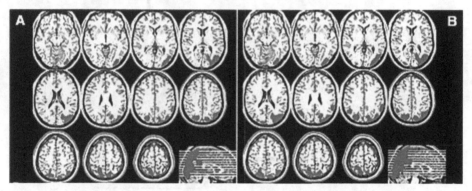

Fig. 4. Employing SPECT scans, a group study of grey matter accumulation in DLB and normal controls [29].

parameters and coronal standard deviation are the most beneficial features for enhancing the system's accuracy by 90.38% when compared to the voxel-as-features (VAF) technique. A personalized diagnostic approach based on SVM and MRI brain information has indeed been suggested in [22], in which bv FTD is classed and estimated in a group comparison and for each subject utilizing brain atrophies from MRI scans out across entire brain and the frontotemporal, insular, and basal ganglia most troubled areas with an overall accuracy of 86.5%.

2) Approaches to Dementia Diagnosis Based on Deep Learning

Deep learning (DL) is a machine learning technology which is used in medical imaging in which the DL employs many layers of non-linear processing information to distinguish feature values in data such as text or images. The primary success of DL [3, 4, 9, 12] is that incredibly accurate mathematical equations may be learned from a big dataset without knowing the internal details of the process. An ANN is the fundamental building block of DL and has been applied in a wide variety of tasks, including medical image analysis. Previously researchers used the Levenberg-Marquardt supervised technique to train a 2-layered feed-forward neural network with sigmoid function to classify images as demented or normal.

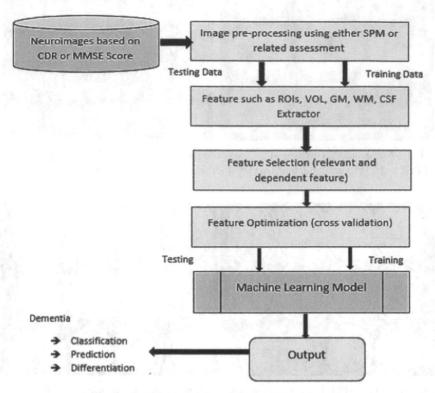

Fig. 5. CAD of dementia employing ML techniques

The Two-Threshold Binary Decomposition methodology converts grayscale photos to binary images. The characteristics were mined via a segmentation-based Fractal Texture Analysis (SFTA) approach. [36] provided a new ensemble learning framework for diagnosing AD and MCI focusing on 4 layered ANN for identifying neuroimaging anomalies of brain PET, MRI, and PET-MRI scan, which handled the feature fusion issue and also the prediction problem concurrently. In [40], researchers used a multi-modal imaging marker called randomised denoising autoencoder marker (rDAM) and ADNI MCI datasets to help predict cognitive and neural declines from amyloid florbetapir PET, structural MRI scans, and FDG-PET to make predictions cognitive and neural decline. While [26] classified AD from mild cognitive impairment (MCI) and cognitive normative (CN) in dementia patients just by using deep neural networks (DNN) and stacked auto-encoder (SAE). [25] proposes a Deep Ensemble Sparse Regression Networks for the prediction and diagnosis of AD and MCI for clinical decisions, which combines two fundamentally different methodologies of deep learning and sparse regression. They tested the proposed approach in an ADNI cohort and found that it performed well in three different classification tasks. In [23], a Deep Belief Network was being used to classify structure-based MRI images in order to detect AD. For image-based pre-processing and feature extraction, researchers evaluated a voxel-based morphometric technique. Their DBN was made up of three hidden units, every having its own set of fine-tuned variables such as momentum, epoch, and the number of nodes in every layer.

2 Related Work

Deepa and Devi [1]. An improved E-TLCNN model is suggested in this study for diagnosing HR employing high-quality fundus pictures. As a consequence, transfer learning is utilised to identify its phases so that the results may be understood accurately. In addition, a novel model called DenseNet has indeed been suggested for classifying features in order to concentrate on severity, like reading AVR and diabetic retinopathy, which may be used to detect diseases. The Kaggle database, which includes train and test, reveals a 96% accuracy in classifying sensitivity. Morshedul Bari Antor et al. [2]. This study offers the results and analyses of multiple ML models for diagnosing dementia. The system was created with the help of the OASIS database. Although the dataset is modest, it contains some noteworthy numbers. Hadeer A. Helaly and colleagues [3]. It made advantage of DL, specifically CNN. The Alzheimer's disease spectrum is classified into four categories. Furthermore, every two-pair category of AD stage has its own binary medical picture categorization system. To identify medical images and diagnose Alzheimer's disease, two approaches are employed. The first method uses basic of CNN architectures to deal with 2-dimensional and 3-dimensional structural and functional brain The technique utilises the transfer learning concept to make use of pre-trained medical picture categorisation models like the VGG19 framework.

Tambe et al. [4]. This chapter proposes a deep CNN that can recognize Alzheimer's disease and differentiate between stages of the disease. Grueso & Viejo-Sobera [5]. This study used PRISMA standards to perform a systematic evaluation of research in which machine learning was used to predict whether individuals with moderate cognitive impairment would acquire AD dementia or stay stable using neuroimaging data. Researchers evaluated 452 studies and chose 116 for qualitative approach after deleting duplicates. Pradhan et al. [6]. This research offers a model that uses brain MRI sample pictures as input and output to assess whether an individual has mild, moderate, or no Alzheimer's disease. For this categorization, the researchers apply the DenseNet169 and VGG19 designs, providing a comparison of which structure offers impressive outcomes. Hemalatha & Renukadevi [7]. This study looks at how different types of ML algorithms can be used to address AD diagnostic challenges. Harsimran Guram [number eight]. This research proposes a classification model for the genesis of brain disease depending on MRI. After that, attention-based transfer learning (extracting variable aspects of designs from MRI scans) has been used to build more accurate predictive patterns, and ultimately, features were taught and utilized to classify fMRI data to produce more accurate predictive patterns. To discover diverse patterns of dementia risk, boost-derived hyper-parameters were obtained and assessed. Salehi et al. [9]. The use of DL in the medical profession is discussed in this chapter.

A comprehensive study of various DL algorithms for diagnosing Alzheimer's disease is conducted, in which such a disease is a degenerative brain disorder that progressively

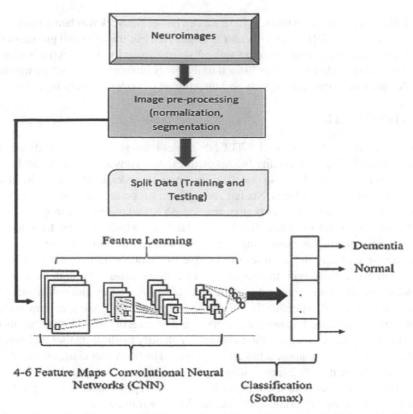

Fig. 6. Softmax classifier using DL Convolutional Neural Network-based hierarchical feature-based learning and classifying for dementia [31, 34].

destroys brain memory, and it is a serious ailment in older persons characterised by dementia. g-Eun Ryu et al. [10]. This chapter offers a dementia risk-based prediction model which is based on XGBoost by extracting derived variables from numericalized dementia statistics and optimising hyper-parameters. With the aid of gradient boosting, the proposed methodology recovers variable importance from conventional independent variables and subsequently produces derivative variables. Daniel Stamate et al. [11]. The aim of this chapter is to analyze ADNI information and calculate its efficacy for developing classification models that differentiate between the categories Mild Cognitive Impairment (MCI), Dementia (DEM), and Cognitively Normal (CN) using three DL models: two Multi-Layer Perceptron (MLP1 and MLP2) models and a Convolutional Bidirectional Long Short-Term Memory (ConvBLSTM) model. Taheo Jo et al. [12]. Researchers conducted a comprehensive evaluation of chapters that used deep learning techniques and neuro imaging data to classify AD diagnostically. Between January 2013 and July 2018, designers conducted a Google Scholar and PubMed search to discover DL studies on AD published in-between Jan'2013 and July'2018. These publications were analysed, appraised, and classified to get appropriate results.

3   The Proposed Method

Algorithm 1:   Conditional -Convolutional segmentation
Input:Dataset with MRI images having labels
Output : Segmented Images

Initialize Parameter W= W_0 and $\theta = \theta_0$

For Each Image I do

For Number of Iteration do

Forward pass of Image pixels

Define the optimize function by Eq(1)

Calculate the optimize Patches by Eq(2)

$Initialize XG - BoostModeling$
$F_0(x) = argmin \sum_{i=1}^{n} L(f_v^{(x)}, \gamma)$

Using L and N for Leaf node and each instance respectively
$\varepsilon(F_0(x)) = \gamma L + \frac{1}{2}\lambda \sum_{i=1}^{L} w_i^2 ..$
For Each Leaf
$W_i = \dfrac{-\sum_{i \in L_i} g_i}{\sum_{i \in N_i} h_i + \gamma}$
Make Classifier Model
$\alpha_2 < -(W_i, \theta)$
Performance $< -\alpha_L$ (Test Set)
Analysis Performance Metrix

$$\in (x) = \phi(xi) + \phi(xi + xj) \tag{1}$$

$\phi(x)$ It's gradient which compute every pixel

$$\phi_u(x) = -\log p(xi) \tag{2}$$

- Step1: Input Dementia Base dataset with different classes Images and preprocess images.
- Step2: Segmented MRI images and extract grey and white matter. On the segmented part apply texture feature-based function.
- Step3: Apply feature weighting using optimization-based approach.
- Step4: According to feature weights define the structure of ensemble learner Xg-Boost.
- Step5: After training the optimize structure of Xg-boost make classifier model and analysis precision, recall and accuracy (Fig. 7).

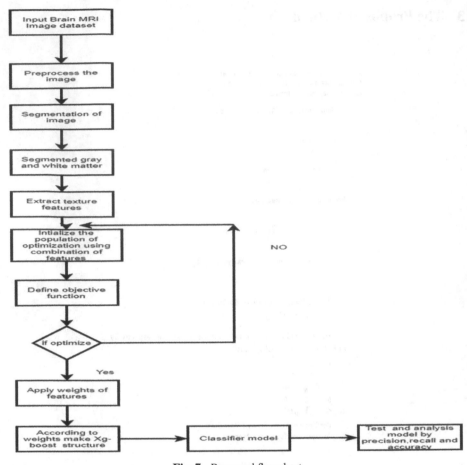

Fig. 7. Proposed flowchart

Accuracy: Defines the images that should be labelled for Meningioma, Glioma, and Pituitary. Equation 3 determines the accuracy of the proposed model.

$$Accuracy = \frac{TP + TN}{TP + TN + FP + FN} \tag{3}$$

In Eq. 3, TP stands for correctly classified positive samples, while TN stands for correctly classified negative samples.

FP represents incorrectly classified samples as correctly classified, and FN represents correctly classified sample data as incorrectly classified.

Specificity: It specifies how many negative samples correctly classified from total negative samples. Specificity is computed using Eq. 4.

$$Specificity = \frac{TN}{TN + FP} \tag{4}$$

Sensitivity: This metrics specifies how many of the actual positive cases we were able to predict correctly with our model. Sensitivity metric is computed using Eq. 5.

$$Sensitivity = \frac{TP}{TP + FN} \tag{5}$$

F-measure: It is used to demonstrate specificity and sensitivity. It only accepts positive samples classified as Meningioma, Glioma, or Pituitary. The F-measure is calculated using Eq. 6.

$$F - measure = \frac{2TP}{2TP + FP + FN} \tag{6}$$

Precision: Precision indicates the correctly predicted cases which actually turned out to be positive.

$$Precision = \frac{TP}{TP + FP} \tag{7}$$

4 Result Analysis

Table 1. Comparison of proposed and existing

Approaches	Accuracy	Precision	Recall	F-score
CNN-existing	52.45	50.12	56.12	54.23
Metaheuristic-XG boost	75.23	76.34	73.45	74.56

Table demonstrates two kinds of techniques i.e., CNN-Existing and Metaheuristic- XG boost in terms of accuracy, precision, recall, and F-score. The accuracy of Metaheuristic-XG boost when compared to CNN-Existing techniques is more i.e., 75.23 and 52.45, respectively. Metaheuristic- XG boost offers a rich precision i.e., 76.34 on contrasting it with CNN-Existing i.e., 50.12. Likewise, both for recall and F-score, the Metaheuristic-XG boost techniques generated considerably better values when compared to CNN-Existing approaches (Fig. 8 and Table 1).

Figure represents the performance metrics of both the given approaches i.e., CNN-Existing and Metaheuristic- XG boost in terms of accuracy, precision, recall, and F-score. When compared to CNN-Existing procedures, Metaheuristic-XG boost strategies produced significantly better results.

The table illustrates four distinct classes in terms of precision, memory, and F-score: Non-Demented, Mild-Demented, Moderate-Demented, and Demented. Mild-Demented (78.34) has the highest precision, followed by Moderate-Demented (75.67), Demented (70.23), and non-Demented (62.34). Similarly, the recall for Mild-Demented individuals (78.34) is high, followed by non-Demented individuals (76.23), Moderate-Demented individuals (75.12), and Demented individuals (72.34). Similarly, the F-score

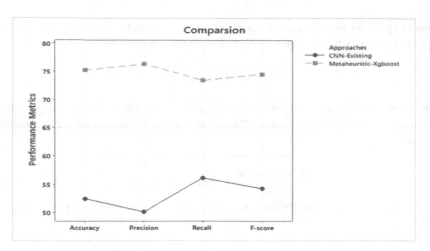

Fig. 8. Comparison of proposed and existing

Table 2. Comparison of class-wise proposed approach

Class	Precision	Recall	F-score
Non-semented	62.34	76.23	78.23
Mild-demented	78.34	78.34	75.12
Moderate-demented	75.67	75.12	70.2
Demented	70.23	72.34	71.23

for non-Demented individuals was high (78.23), followed by Mild-Demented individuals (75.12), Demented individuals (71.23), and Moderate-Demented individuals (70.2) (Fig. 9).

The figure depicts the recommended performance metrics for the proposed technique in terms of precision, recall, and F-score for each class, namely Non-Demented, Mild-Demented, Moderate-Demented, and Demented. The values are plotted according to the table analysed above.

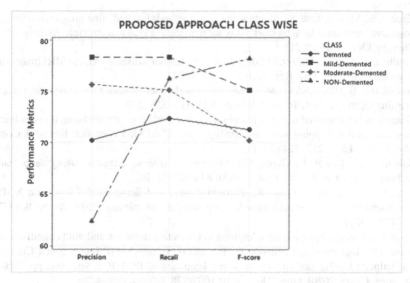

Fig. 9. Comparison of class wise proposed approach

5 Conclusion

The present chapter examined the capacity of machine learning algorithms to distinguish between MRI representations of stable brains, mildly cognitively impaired brains, and brains afflicted by Alzheimer's Disease. Classic machine learning algorithms (i.e., decision trees and rule-based structures), and neural networks, were applied to the standardised ADNI magnetic resonance imaging dataset.

The gradient Boost technique uses optimisation for pre-processing, allowing weak classifier models to learn progressively. The classifier is built using residual classification and gradient descent. Dementia Elderly individuals have a lower death rate than those in other age groups, particularly those above the age of seventy. Precision will improve by 2-3%, while recall will improve by increasing recall and memory efficiency by 5–6%.

References

1. Deepa, N.: E-TLCNN Classification using DenseNet on various features of hypertensive retinopathy (HR) for predicting the accuracy. In 2021 5th International Conference on Intelligent Computing and Control Systems (ICICCS), pp. 1648–1652. IEEE (2021)
2. Bari Antor, M., et al.: A comparative analysis of machine learning algorithms to predict alzheimer's disease. J. Healthcare Eng. **2021** (2021)
3. Helaly, H.A., Badawy, M., Haikal, A.Y.: Deep learning approach for early detection of alzheimer's disease. Cogn. Comput. 1–17 (2021). https://doi.org/10.1007/s12559-021-099 46-2
4. Tambe, P., Saigaonkar, R., Devadiga, N., Chitte, P.H.: Deep learning techniques for effective diagnosis of Alzheimer's disease using MRI images. In: ITM Web of Conferences, vol. 40, p. 03021. EDP Sciences (2021)

5. Grueso, S., Viejo-Sobera, R.: Machine learning methods for predicting progression from mild cognitive impairment to Alzheimer's disease dementia: a systematic review. Alzheimer's Res. Therapy **13**(1), 1–29 (2021)
6. Pradhan, A., Gige, J., Eliazer, M.: detection of alzheimer's disease (AD) in MRI images using deep learning. Int. J. Eng. Res. Technol. **10**(3) (2021)
7. Hemalatha, B., Renukadevi, M.: Analysis of alzheimer disease prediction using machine learning techniques. Inf. Technol. Indust. **9**(1), 519–525 (2021)
8. Guram, M.H.: Improved demntia images detection and classification using transfer learning base convulation mapping with attention layer and XGBOOST classifier. Turkish J. Comput. Math. Educ. **12**(6), 217–224 (2021)
9. Salehi, A.W., Baglat, P., Gupta, G.: Alzheimer's disease diagnosis using deep learning techniques. Int. J. Eng. Adv. Technol **9**(3), 874–880 (2020)
10. Ryu, S.E., Shin, D.H., Chung, K.: Prediction model of dementia risk based on XGBoost using derived variable extraction and hyper parameter optimization. IEEE Access **8**, 177708–177720 (2020)
11. Stamate, D., et al.: Applying deep learning to predicting dementia and mild cognitive impairment. In: Maglogiannis, I., Iliadis, L., Pimenidis, E. (eds.) IFIP International Conference on Artificial Intelligence Applications and Innovations. IFIPAICT, vol. 584, pp. 308–319. Springer, Cham (2020). https://doi.org/10.1007/978-3-030-49186-4_26
12. Jo, T., Nho, K., Saykin, A.J.: Deep learning in Alzheimer's disease: diagnostic classification and prognostic prediction using neuroimaging data. Front. Aging Neurosci. **11**, 220 (2019)
13. Veitch, D.P., Weiner, M.W., Aisen, P.S., Beckett, L.A., Cairns, N.J., Green, R.C., Alzheimer's Disease Neuroimaging Initiative: understanding disease progression and improving Alzheimer's disease clinical trials: recent highlights from the Alzheimer's Disease Neuroimaging Initiative. Alzheimer's & Dementia **15**(1), 106–152 (2019)
14. Goyal, S.B., Bedi, P., Rajawat, A.S., Shaw, R.N., Ghosh, A.: Multi-objective Fuzzy-swarm optimizer for data partitioning. In: Bianchini, M., Piuri, V., Das, S., Shaw, R.N. (eds.) Advanced Computing and Intelligent Technologies. LNNS, vol. 218, pp. 307–318. Springer, Singapore (2022). https://doi.org/10.1007/978-981-16-2164-2_25
15. Types of Dementia. https://www.healthline.com/health/dementia#types
16. Schelke, M.W., et al.: Mechanisms of risk reduction in the clinical practice of Alzheimer's disease prevention. Front. Aging Neurosci. **10**, 96 (2018)
17. Samper-González, J., et al.: Reproducible evaluation of classification methods in Alzheimer's disease: Framework and application to MRI and PET data. Neuroimage **183**, 504–521 (2018)
18. Kumar, A., Das, S., Tyagi, V., Shaw, R.N., Ghosh, A.: Analysis of classifier algorithms to detect anti-money laundering. In: Bansal, J.C., Paprzycki, M., Bianchini, M., Das, S. (eds.) Computationally Intelligent Systems and their Applications. SCI, vol. 950, pp. 143–152. Springer, Singapore (2021). https://doi.org/10.1007/978-981-16-0407-2_11
19. Palimkar, P., Bajaj, V., Mal, A.K., Shaw, R.N., Ghosh, A.: Unique action identifier by using magnetometer, accelerometer and gyroscope: KNN approach. In: Bianchini, M., Piuri, V., Das, S., Shaw, R.N. (eds.) Advanced Computing and Intelligent Technologies. LNNS, vol. 218, pp. 607–631. Springer, Singapore (2022). https://doi.org/10.1007/978-981-16-2164-2_48
20. Sørensen, L., Nielsen, M., Alzheimer's Disease Neuroimaging Initiative: ensemble support vector machine classification of dementia using structural MRI and mini-mental state examination. J. Neurosc. Meth. **302**, 66–74 (2018)
21. Nanni, L., Lumini, A., Zaffonato, N.: Ensemble based on static classifier selection for automated diagnosis of mild cognitive impairment. J. Neurosci. Meth. **302**, 42–46 (2018)
22. Rathore, S., Habes, M., Iftikhar, M.A., Shacklett, A., Davatzikos, C.: A review on neuroimaging-based classification studies and associated feature extraction methods for Alzheimer's disease and its prodromal stages. NeuroImage **155**, 530–548 (2017)

23. Faturrahman, M., Wasito, I., Hanifah, N., Mufidah, R.: Structural MRI classification for Alzheimer's disease detection using deep belief network. In: 2017 11th International Conference on Information & Communication Technology and System (ICTS), pp. 37–42. IEEE (2017)
24. Galvin, J.E.: Prevention of Alzheimer's disease: lessons learned and applied. J. Am. Geriatr. Soc. **65**(10), 2128–2133 (2017)
25. Suk, H.I., Lee, S.W., Shen, D., Alzheimer's Disease Neuroimaging Initiative: deep ensemble learning of sparse regression models for brain disease diagnosis. Med. Image Anal. **37**, 101–113 (2017)
26. Dolph, C.V., Alam, M., Shboul, Z., Samad, M.D., Iftekharuddin, K.M.: Deep learning of texture and structural features for multiclass Alzheimer's disease classification. In: 2017 International Joint Conference on Neural Networks (IJCNN), pp. 2259–2266. IEEE (2017)
27. Kim, J., Lee, B.: Automated discrimination of dementia spectrum disorders using extreme learning machine and structural t1 MRI features. In: 2017 39th Annual International Conference of the IEEE Engineering in Medicine and Biology Society (EMBC), pp. 1990–1993. IEEE (2017)
28. Litjens, G., et al.: A survey on deep learning in medical image analysis. Med. Image Anal. **42**, 60–88 (2017)
29. Imabayashi, E., et al.: Validation of the cingulate island sign with optimized ratios for discriminating dementia with Lewy bodies from Alzheimer's disease using brain perfusion SPECT. Ann. Nucl. Med. **31**(7), 536–543 (2017)
30. Goyal, S.B., Bedi, P., Rajawat, A.S., Shaw, R.N., Ghosh, A.: Smart luminaires for commercial building by application of daylight harvesting systems. In: Bianchini, M., Piuri, V., Das, S., Shaw, R.N. (eds.) Advanced Computing and Intelligent Technologies. LNNS, vol. 218, pp. 293–305. Springer, Singapore (2022). https://doi.org/10.1007/978-981-16-2164-2_24
31. Alkabawi, E.M., Hilal, A.R., Basir, O.A.: Feature abstraction for early detection of multi-type of dementia with sparse auto-encoder. In: 2017 IEEE International Conference on Systems, Man, and Cybernetics (SMC), pp. 3471–3476. IEEE (2017)
32. Bron, E.E.: Multiparametric computer-aided differential diagnosis of alzheimer's disease and frontotemporal dementia using structural and advanced MRI. Eur. Radiol. **27**(8), 3372–3382 (2017)
33. Bron, E.E., et al.: Multiparametric computer-aided differential diagnosis of Alzheimer's disease and frontotemporal dementia using structural and advanced MRI. Eur. Radiol. **27**(8), 3372–3382 (2017)
34. Rajawat, A.S., Barhanpurkar, K., Goyal, S.B., Bedi, P., Shaw, R.N., Ghosh, A.: Efficient deep learning for reforming authentic content searching on big data. In: Bianchini, M., Piuri, V., Das, S., Shaw, R.N. (eds.) Advanced Computing and Intelligent Technologies. LNNS, vol. 218, pp. 319–327. Springer, Singapore (2022). https://doi.org/10.1007/978-981-16-2164-2_26
35. Rabeh, A.B., Benzarti, F., Amiri, H.: Diagnosis of alzheimer diseases in early step using SVM (Support Vector Machine). In: 2016 13th International Conference on Computer Graphics, Imaging and Visualization (CGiV), pp. 364–367. IEEE (2016)
36. Liu, J., Shang, S., Zheng, K., Wen, J.R.: Multi-view ensemble learning for dementia diagnosis from neuroimaging: an artificial neural network approach. Neurocomputing **195**, 112–116 (2016)
37. De Strooper, B., Karran, E.: The cellular phase of Alzheimer's disease. Cell **164**(4), 603–615 (2016)
38. Rajawat, A.S., et al.: Depression detection for elderly people using AI robotic systems leveraging the Nelder–Mead Method. Artificial Intelligence for Future Generation Robotics, pp. 55–70 (2021). https://doi.org/10.1016/B978-0-323-85498-6.00006-X

39. Bron, E.E., Smits, M., Niessen, W.J., Klein, S.: Feature selection based on the SVM weight vector for classification of dementia. IEEE J. Biomed. Health Inform. **19**(5), 1617–1626 (2015)
40. Ithapu, V.K., et al.: Imaging-based enrichment criteria using deep learning algorithms for efficient clinical trials in mild cognitive impairment. Alzheimer's Dementia **11**(12), 1489–1499 (2015)
41. Plis, S.M., et al.: Deep learning for neuroimaging: a validation study. Front. Neurosci. **8**, 229 (2014)
42. Ishii, K.: PET approaches for diagnosis of dementia. Am. J. Neuroradiol. **35**(11), 2030–2038 (2014)
43. Valkanova, V., Ebmeier K.P.: Neuroimaging in dementia. Maturitas **79**(2), 202–208 (2014)
44. Anandh, K.R., Sujatha, C.M., Ramakrishnan, S.: Analysis of ventricles in Alzheimer MR images using coherence enhancing diffusion filter and level set method. In: 2014 International Conference on Informatics, Electronics & Vision (ICIEV), pp. 1–4. IEEE (2014)
45. Ramírez, J., et al.: Computer-aided diagnosis of Alzheimer's type dementia combining support vector machines and discriminant set of features. Inf. Sci. **237**, 59–72 (2013)
46. Rajawat, A.S., Barhanpurkar, K., Shaw, R.N., Ghosh, A.: Risk detection in wireless body sensor networks for health monitoring using hybrid deep learning. In: Mekhilef, S., Favorskaya, M., Pandey, R.K., Shaw, R.N. (eds.) Innovations in Electrical and Electronic Engineering. LNEE, vol. 756, pp. 683–696. Springer, Singapore (2021). https://doi.org/10.1007/978-981-16-0749-3_54
47. Gerardin, E., et al.: Multidimensional classification of hippocampal shape features discriminates Alzheimer's disease and mild cognitive impairment from normal aging. Neuroimage **47**(4), 1476–1486 (2009)
48. Klöppel, S., et al.: Automatic classification of MR scans in Alzheimer's disease. Brain **131**(3), 681–689 (2008)
49. Boser, B.E., Guyon, I.M., Vapnik, V.N.: A training algorithm for optimal margin classifiers. In Proceedings of the Fifth Annual Workshop on Computational Learning Theory, pp. 144–152 (1992)

IoT Enabled an Efficient Vehicle Parking System

Harikesh Singh[1]([✉]), Prashant Singh[2], Mayank Singh[1], K. G. Harsha[1], P. Vinooth[1], and Mukesh Raj[1]

[1] JSS Academy of Technical Education, Noida 201301, UP, India
harikeshsingh@yahoo.co.in, {harshakg,vinooth,
mukeshraj}@jssaten.ac.in
[2] Sunder Deep Engineering College, Ghaziabad 201001, UP, India

Abstract. The parking of vehicles is one of the challenges in all smart cities and people are facing the problem on daily basis and wasting their lot of time to park their valuable vehicle on suitable places. In all parking places many human power involved, but they are still unable to manage at peak hours and people are facing the parking problem regularly. People are paying high amount of parking charges and still looking for proper places to park their vehicle which really frustrate them to search at big places and sometimes leads to traffic jam also. To solve such real problem, the proposed parking system, SCPMS (An IoT based Smart Vehicle Parking Management System) has been developed in which many IoT based sensors will be used for identifying the parking spaces of the vehicle and updated the location of display panel of parking slip counter.

The booking for parking will be based on the availability of spaces and location will be marked in the slip. As a result with less human efforts, the people can easily park their vehicle at suitable place in shortest span of time. The proposed SCPMS system can be easily integrated at required locations for managing large crowds to avoid traffic congestion.

Keywords: Vehicle · Parking · Vehicle · Sensor · IoT · Traffic

1 Introduction

We noticed that with increasing population and increase in purchasing capacity the need for personal transportation has seen a tremendous increase over the years hence the increase for parking spaces at public places such as malls, supermarkets and big housing societies has also increased to provide adequate parking space for the people. With huge parking spaces comes the responsibility to manage it efficiently and conveniently so as to provide fast and easy parking solutions for the users [1].

Currently we see parking facilities hiring assisting staff to help customers who are driving in the facility with finding parking slots. To automate this task so as to minimize and possibly remove human intervention while users park their vehicle, Our system maps the parking slots into a dynamic real time virtual map that updates the parking slot availability as the user parks the vehicle, by sensing the existence of a vehicle in a parking area using Infrared sensors the system updates that particular slot as occupied and then displays it as occupied on the display [2].

As a user enters the facility with the vehicle he/she can look up in the system and see which all slots are occupied and which are available slots in the virtual map and can drive straight to the slot of their choice and then park their vehicle and leave, the system will sense the presence and update the system of the occupied parking slot [3].

In this chapter we will develop a parking system which will use IOT, Arduino, NodeMCU esp8266 wifi module. We will also develop an application for the user to use. Including the NodeMCU esp8266 which is a wifi module and the android application, the user parking slots booked by the user can be monitored from anywhere around the world. By automating this task of locating an available parking slot and guiding the user vehicle to it, we remove unnecessary human interference that was required otherwise for the parking facility. This helps in putting the human force to other tasks and creates a smooth parking facility without the need to appoint multiple assisting help [4].

2 Related Work

Building up a Smart Vehicle Parking System had fluctuating difficulties. Among them was identifying and following vehicles that were entering the parking garage. Our shrewd smart vehicle parking framework was created to give permission for the recognition of a vehicle when placed in the parking area and communicate the required information to the user with the end goal. There have been various tasks chipping away at the same frameworks. Among them were Guangdong AKE Innovation Company Limited, of China [5].

The Guangdong AKE Innovation Company Limited, China is a futuristic venture which manages information procurement and data operation as its centre of innovation and development. This association has created indoor, outdoors and city urban smart vehicle parking frameworks and parking management frameworks. This indoor leaving framework utilizes a module which is ultrasonic and there is a camera as sensor to peruse the item, and vehicle to convey the framework through the RS485 communication cable [6].

The framework measures the data which is accumulated securely from the sensors and showcases the conclusion through RED markers and GREEN markers to the framework clients. A similar thought is implemented in the open air parking framework; the solitary distinction of this chapter is that it extensively uses a sensor which is geomagnetic and distinguishes the difference in magnetic field in that particular allotted territory and conveys the equivalent remotely to the worker giving the current status of parking lot to the client. This smart parking framework utilizes referential sorts of recognition sensors as outside frameworks for checking the accessibility of user parking slots in the whole parking area. The solitary contrast is that the status of the parking area is imparted through the LED lights or transmitted over the internet and it's status can be seen through the user mobile application or a web server by the clients provided for the user [7].

A comparable task had been finished by Smart Vehicle Parking System utilizing IoT [8]. In that chapter they gathered information from the sensor and got the yield through examining and preparing the information. Then Arduino transmits the signal from itself to the servo motor and GSM module which is connected to it which then helps in giving instructions and sending notifications to the user. Every vehicle must have a RFID vehicle so as vehicle enters the parking lot the RFID vehicle of that particular vehicle will be scanned by the reader module which will help in maintaining the authenticity of the user details. Also this will help in giving the information about the available parking slots to the user along with the details of the lot which the user would have registered through a SMS on the registered mobile number of the user [9].

It consists of the Arduino devices and IR sensors. Interaction of users and parking lots will happen via these devices. The second section comprises cloud web services which will interconnect the user and vehicle parking area. All the updates in parking availability happen on the cloud side by side. There is an admin to administer the cloud but the user can check the availability of the slots too. The third section of the chapter architecture is dedicated to the end users. The availability of the user parking spots and the details of the registered slots are sent to the user via SMS. This is done through the GSM module. The user uses the mobile application to interact and find the parking area which is updated at real time because it is connected to the cloud. The user receives notification about the availability of the parking lot. This helps in saving time and fuel [10] (Figs. 1, 2 and 3).

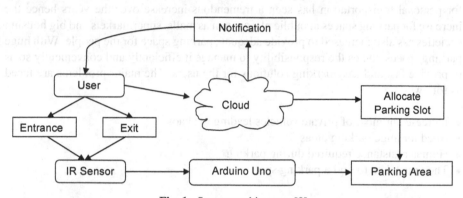

Fig. 1. System architecture [8]

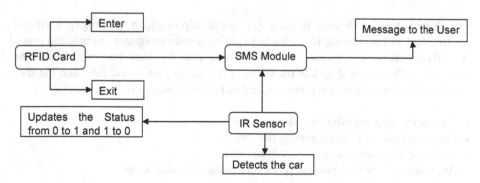

Fig. 2. Hardware architecture [9]

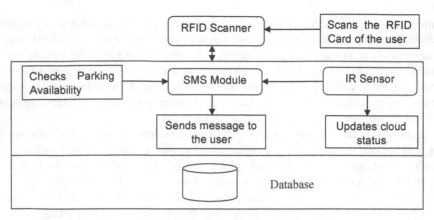

Fig. 3. Software architecture [10]

3 Problem Statement

We noticed that with increasing population and increase in purchasing capacity the need for personal transportation has seen a tremendous increase over the years hence the increase for parking spaces at public places such as malls, supermarkets and big housing societies has also increased to provide adequate parking space for the people. With huge parking spaces comes the responsibility to manage it efficiently and conveniently so as to provide fast and easy parking solutions for the users. The major problems are faced as follows:

- Increased number of private vehicles leading to chaos
- Need for huge parking areas
- Human assistance required during parking
- The time taken to find a parking spot.

4 Objective

Our chapter of a smart vehicle parking system will help to find the parking spot without wasting fuel and wandering in the lot or requiring human resources to guide the users. Also there will be an application for user convenience to check free free slots in the parking lot. The app will update the status of the parking lot in real time and the user can check the location on his phone instead of finding it manually (Fig. 4).

- Generating data regarding the slot vacancy
- Quick parking spot locating using the data
- Reducing the human assistance substantially
- Automating the whole parking procedure in huge parking areas.

Fig. 4. Smart vehicle parking system

5 Proposed Methodology

There are 3 way approaches:

- Using RFID to register the vehicle entry and making payments
- Using IR sensors to register the vehicle presence in a particular parking slot
- Displaying the layout and availability of parking slots in the area.

The parking area is segregated into 2 parking lots.

- Parking A
- Parking B

Every vehicle leaves three spaces &each opening has an infrared sensor integrated in it. For each parking lot we have 1 IR sensor (infrared sensor), therefore there will be a total of 6 IR sensors. Each IR sensor is utilized to identify the presence of a vehicle which comes at that particular parking spot. These IR sensors are connected to Arduino. When a vehicle enters the parking slot, Arduino sends signals to the connected NodeMCU esp8266 wifi module, at that point NodeMCU sends signal to the mobile app through the cloud.

6 Implementation Analysis

6.1 Arduino Board

We will be using an arduino board to convert the input to output. Arduino is a developed reliable open-source platform for electronic development which is very developer friendly in terms of both hardware and software. Then these arduino boards take the inputs from the sensor which is activated whenever a light falls on it or when a finger is put the button or a specific type of message notification and it turns it into desired output which could be turning a device motor on, switching on an LED. The board can be programmed such that it does a particular task on a particular set of instructions which are sent to the microcontroller which is attached to the system. To do the programming on Arduino an IDE is used which facilitates the same [11].

6.2 IR Sensor

An IR sensor which is used to detect the vehicle in this particular chapter. These sensors detect and capture the infrared emitted radiation. These radiations have wavelength greater than 0.7 micrometer There are three male headers in IR sensors named, VCC, GND and OUT(from left to right respectively). We connect the Arduino to the VCC pin of the IR sensor. Ground of the IR sensor is connected to the ground of the arduino. And finally the OUT pin of the IR sensor is connected to IO pins of the arduino [12].

6.3 NodeMCU ESP8266

NodeMCU ESP8266 is a budget friendly, WiFi module which is used to connect chapters of IOT or similar domains, to the internet. The electrical and mechanical equipment which we use today don't have an inbuilt feature to connect to the internet on their own. One can integrate these equipment with NodeMCU ESP8226 to perform many operations like controlling, monitoring etc. which require internet connectivity. NodeMCU ESP8266 can be considered as a System on Chip or SoC. A System on Chip is basically a circuit which integrates and includes every component of the computer or any other electronic device to be used [13].

6.4 Display Unit (LCD)

LCD displays everything on it's screen thus making it a very user friendly device. It has an inbuilt controller which intelligently converts alphabets and digits into their individual ASCII code and then displays it on the screen and the plus point is we don't have to manually specify which LCD combination will light up when a particular alphabet or digit comes [14].

6.5 RFID Tag

In the RFID tag there is an antenna and a microchip through which data is transmitted and received. Sometimes this tag is integrated in a circuit and is called IC. The user codes the RFID tag for whatever purpose he wants. The RFID tags are divided into two types, first is Battery operated tags and second is passive tags. Like the name in battery operated RFID tags there is a battery and a power supply for the tag. If we talk about a passive RFID tag, it uses the electromagnetic energy which the RFID reader transmits to the information. Apart from these two types there is also a battery operated RFID tag available [15].

There are basically three frequencies which a passive RFID tag uses. First is LF (Low frequency) which is in range 125–134 KHz. Second is called HF (High Frequency) range which is around 13.56 MHz and third range is called NFC (Near - Field Communication) which has frequency in the range of 865–960 MHz. NFC is also sometimes referred to as UHF (Ultra High Frequency). There are different tags available with different frequencies.

6.6 Details of Work

The primary stage is to distinguish the left vehicle. For that, one IR sensor will be introduced in each parking lot. The sensor will be introduced before the vehicle, at a height of hundred centimeters from the beginning. The principal stage will be effective when the sensor will recognize the vehicle inside its vicinity.

When an arduino transmits the signal to an IR sensor and those signals are received by IR sensors, then sonic waves are emitted by it. These waves then travel and reach the vehicle standing in the parking lot and are reflected by it. After reflection of these waves they are sensed by IR sensors. Which then tells us if the lot is empty or not. The time elapsed between this process of reflection and sensing highly depends on the distance at which the object (in this case our vehicle) is present with respect to the IR sensor. Sensor then sends a signal to the arduino. The signal sent is in the form of a timing pulse. The timing of this pulse depends on two factors, distance and the program which is uploaded in the module. If after processing the information the distance between sensor and vehicle comes out to be greater than 150 centimeters, it will consider the slot as empty and the red led in the user application is turned to green. And if the distance comes out as less than 150 centimeters then similarly green led turns red in the application. We will be doing the following steps to implement this chapter-

Step-1: Every vehicle leaves three spaces & each opening has an infrared sensor integrated in it.

Step-2: For each parking lot we have 1 IR sensor (infrared sensor), therefore there will be a total of 6 IR sensors.

Step-3: Each IR sensor is utilized to identify the presence of a vehicle which comes at that particular parking spot.

Step-4: These IR sensors are connected to Arduino.

Step-5: When a vehicle enters the parking slot, Arduino sends signals to the connected NodeMCU esp8266 wi-fi module.

Step-6: At that point NodeMCU sends a signal to the mobile app through the cloud.

Step-7: Now the user can see the status of the slots using the app.

Step-8: If any user does not want to use the app, then he/she can go to the parking lot and see the status of the parking lots from the LCD screen which will be present outside the parking lot.

Step-9: When the user enters the parking lot, their RFID tags will be scanned using the RFID scanner.

Step-10: This scanned RFID tag will be used for payment purposes (Fig. 5).

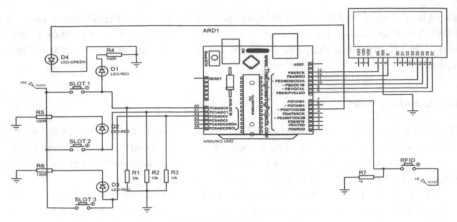

Fig. 5. Circuit diagram

7 Analysis of Results

As a result of the Smart Vehicle Parking system we aim to increase the convenience to the users and save the need to hire helping staff by the parking facility. In simulation, we successfully implemented the Smart Vehicle Parking system which uses RFID. Any vehicle without RFID will not be permitted inside the parking lot. The status of the parking slots will be displayed on the LCD screen in real time.

We further plan on adding some more convenience and advanced features like Automated payment gateway through the vehicles RFID tag, Nearest parking slot navigation assistance, Integrating nearby parking facilities to work in tandem and parking slot booking in advance etc. (Fig. 6).

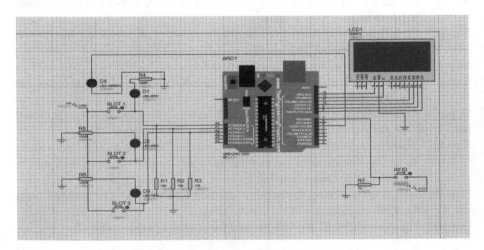

Fig. 6. Proposed smart vehicle parking system

8 Conclusion and Future Scope

Smart vehicle parking systems will successfully help in parking without the help of human assistance and thus increasing the efficiency of the parking facility through automation. In future scope, we would further like to add the following features:

- Automated payment gateway through the vehicles RFID tag
- Nearest parking slot navigation assistance
- Integrating nearby parking facilities to work in tandem.

References

1. Elakya, R., Juhi, S., Pola, A., Namith, R.: Smart parking system using IoT. Int. J. Eng. Adv. Technol. **9**(1), 6091–6095 (2019)
2. Elakya, R., Seth, J., Ashritha, P., Namith, R.: Smart parking system using IoT, global smart parking system market analysis and forecasts 2017 (egypt-business.com) 3. Arduino Uno R3 Development Board-Control Voltage Obstacle Avoidance Reflection Photoelectric Sensor Infrared Alarm Module (2017)
3. Felzenszwalb, P.F., et al.: Object detection with discriminatively trained part-based models. IEEE Trans. Pattern Anal. Mach. Intell. **32**(9), 1627–1645 (2010)
4. Bertone, G.A., Meiksin, Z.H., Carroll, N.L.: Investigation of a capacitance-based displacement transducer. IEEE Trans. Instruments. Meas. **39**, 424–428 (1990)
5. Soni, A., Dharmacharya, D., Pal, A., Srivastava, V.K., Shaw, R.N., Ghosh, A.: Design of a machine learning-based self-driving car. In: Bianchini, M., Simic, M., Ghosh, A., Shaw, R.N. (eds.) Machine Learning for Robotics Applications. SCI, vol. 960, pp. 139–151. Springer, Singapore (2021). https://doi.org/10.1007/978-981-16-0598-7_11
6. Melnyk, P., Djahel, S., Nait-Abdesselam, F.: Towards a smart parking management system for smart cities. In: 2019 IEEE International Smart Cities Conference (ISC2), Casablanca, Morocco, pp. 542–546 (2019). https://doi.org/10.1109/ISC246665.2019.9071740
7. Sadhukhan, P.: An IoT-based e-parking system for smart cities. In: 2017 International Conference on Advances in Computing Communications and Informatics (ICACCI), pp. 1062–1066, September 2017
8. Mejri, N., et al.: Reservation-based multi-objective smart parking approach for smart cities. In: 2016 IEEE International Smart Cities Conference (ISC2), pp. 1–6, September 2016
9. Silar, J., et al.: Smart parking in the smart city application. In: 2018 Smart City Symposium Prague (SCSP), pp. 1–5, May 2018
10. Yan, G., et al.: SmartParking: a secure and intelligent parking system. IEEE Intell. Transp. Syst. Mag. **3**(1), 18–30 (2011)
11. Penttila, K., Keskilammi, M., Sydanheimo, L., Kivikoski, M.: Radio frequency technology for automated manufacturing and logistics control. Int. J. Adv. Manuf. Technol. **31**(1–2), 116–124 (2006)
12. Zhang, L.: An improved approach to security and privacy of RFID application system. In: International Conference on Wireless Communications, Networking and Mobile Computing, (2), pp. 1195–1198 (2005)
13. Biswas, S., Bianchini, M., Shaw, R.N., Ghosh, A.: Prediction of traffic movement for autonomous vehicles. In: Bianchini, M., Simic, M., Ghosh, A., Shaw, R.N. (eds.) Machine Learning for Robotics Applications. SCI, vol. 960, pp. 153–168. Springer, Singapore (2021). https://doi.org/10.1007/978-981-16-0598-7_12

14. Xiao, Y., Yu, S., Wu, K., Ni, Q., Janecek, C., Nordstad, J.: Radio frequency identification: technologies, applications, and research issues. Wiley J. Wireless Commun. Mobile Comput. **7**, 457–472 (2006)
15. Goodrum, P., McLaren, M., Durfee, A.: The application of active radio frequency identification technology for tool tracking on construction job sites. Autom. Constr. **15**(3), 292–302 (2006)

Recommendation Systems for a Group of Users Which Recommend Recent Attention: *Using Hybrid Recommendation Model*

Saurabh Sharma(✉) and Harish Kumar Shakya

Amity University, Gwalior, India
Saurabh.sharma44@gmail.com

Abstract. Group recommendation systems, which deliver items to a group of users, have recently received a lot of interest. Several aggregation and model group recommendation techniques were discussed. On the other hand, group recommendation's cold-start issue has received less attention, severely restricting group recommendation in several crucial areas, such as offline suggestions. In this study, we offer a new deep hybrid framework to address the cold start issue with group event recommendations for a user group. Our framework is the basis for RBM and comprises numerous restricted Boltzmann machines (RBM). The first gathers client preferences as well as high-quality latent data. Context information like location and event structure is used to identify late event aspects. Set up a schedule for the event. To fix the cold-start issue, we tested our proposed framework on two real-world datasets, and the results demonstrate that it outperforms Baseline Group recommendation techniques and efficiently addresses the cold-start issue in group events.

Keywords: Self-attention network · Sequential recommendation · User preference

1 Introduction

Machine learning has a subclass called recommendation engines that often rank or rate people or products. A recommender system, broadly defined, is a system that anticipates the ratings a user would give to a certain item. The user will subsequently be given a ranking of these forecasts.

They are frequently employed by several well-known corporations, like Google, Instagram, Spotify, Amazon, Reddit, Netflix, etc., to boost user and platform engagement. To keep you utilising their platform to listen to music, Spotify, for instance, will suggest tracks that are similar to the ones you've loved or listened to a lot. Based on their information about a user, Amazon uses recommendations to make product suggestions to different consumers.

Recommender systems are frequently viewed as a "black box," and the models developed by these big businesses are not very clear. The recommendations made to the user from the results are frequently items they don't know they need or want until someone suggests them.

Building recommender systems can be done in a variety of ways; some employ formulaic and algorithmic methods like Page Rank, while others use modeling-centric methods like collaborative filtering, content-based methods, link prediction, etc. The complexity of each of these methods can vary, but complexity does not equate to "excellent" performance. Simple strategies and tactics frequently produce the best outcomes. For instance, major corporations like Reddit, Hacker News, and Google have promoted content on their platforms using straightforward, formulaic implementations of recommendation engines.

A recommendation system is a machine learning or artificial intelligence (AI) algorithm that makes suggestions or recommends more products to customers using big data. These may be determined using a variety of parameters, such as previous purchases, search history, demographic data, and other elements. To help people find products and services they might not have found on their own, recommender systems are quite helpful.

Utilizing information obtained from their encounters, recommender systems are trained to comprehend the preferences, prior choices, and characteristics of both people and things. These consist of views, clicks, favourites, and purchases. Recommender systems are a popular among content and product suppliers due to their ability to predict consumer interests and wishes on a highly personalised level. They can direct customers to almost any good or service that piques their interest, including books, movies, health classes, and apparel.

2 Types of Recommendation System

Although there are many different recommender systems and methods, the majority of them fall into three general groups: collaborative filtering, content filtering, and context filtering.

Based on the preferences of many users, collaborative filtering algorithms recommend items (this is the filtering phase) (this is the collaborative part). With the help of previous encounters between users and objects and the similarity of user preference behavior, recommender systems can learn to anticipate future interactions. These recommender systems create a model based on a user's prior actions, such as things previously purchased, ratings given to those items, and similar user decisions. The theory holds that there is a strong likelihood that individuals will choose additional items together in the future if they have already made comparable decisions and purchases, such as choosing a movie. For instance, if a collaborative filtering recommender discovers that you and another user have similar movie preferences, it can suggest a film to you that it has previously discovered that other user enjoys.

Contrarily, content filtering suggests other products that are comparable to the user's choices based on the characteristics or features of an item (this is the content part). This method bases its prediction of the possibility of a new interaction on the closeness of an item's and user's qualities, taking into account the user's age, the cuisine category of a restaurant, and the typical movie review. For instance, if a content filtering recommender notices that you enjoyed the films You've Got Mail and Sleepless in Seattle, it might suggest Joe Versus the Volcano to you if it has the same actors and/or genres.

The benefits of the categories above are combined in hybrid recommender systems to produce a more complete recommending system. Recently, there have been more event-based social networks (such as Meetup1 and Douban Event 2). EBSNs blend online social interactions with offline social contacts by planning and participating in actual events. Finding it relevant to users can be difficult due to the daily volume of events broadcast on EBSNs. An event recommendation system is put forth to address this issue and find the events that are most likely to interest users. Recently, the area of system recommendations has risen to the forefront of the discussion around event recommendations [1–12]. The potential event ideas have a serious issue regarding the new item cold start because they always take place in the future, and no user feedback has been received. As a result, the cold-start problem in event suggestions is not addressed by conventional collaborative filtering techniques.

In a prior study, the cold start problem in the event proposal was facilitated by contextual data, including time, location, and event organizer. Many earlier studies focused only on recommending events to one user at a time, ignoring that users commonly engage in group activities like watching sporting events with friends or picnics with their families. As a result, we must provide group event recommendations—recommendations of events to a group of people. Group recommendation systems have been investigated in numerous fields since individual recommendation techniques cannot directly provide group recommendations. [5–9]. The Group Recommendation System combines individual preferences with group decisions and categorizes aggregation-based techniques into two groups: 1) Member ratings are included in group profiles using preference aggregation (PA) techniques before the CF group methodology is used. [18, 27]; 2) The Recommendation Aggregation (RA) approach first creates recommendations for individual members before aggregating the list for group use. [1, 17] Aggregation-based approaches cannot create a good representation of group preferences because they exclude interactions among group members. Model-based approaches have recently been developed to address this aggregation-based problem. [7, 15, 19] Modern techniques like deep learning and representative learning are used to determine group preferences from the interactions of group members. However, the group's suggestion fell short in its attempt to address the problem of cold starts.

We describe a deep, hybrid approach that uses CRBMs and RBMs to help group event recommendation systems overcome the cold start issue.

We offer new hybrid training and prediction approaches for profound frameworks.

On two EBSN real-world datasets, we perform in-depth tests. The findings show that our suggested framework performs better than simple solutions for groups of various sizes.

The formatting is the same throughout the rest of the document. The relevant research is summarized in the second part. Both the issue and the RBM environment are described in Sect. 3. Section 4 describes the deep hybrid framework, training methodology, and group event recommendation mechanism. The experimental results are presented and discussed in Sect. 5 before the Chapter is concluded in Sect. 6.

2.1 Work Related

One of the most popular forms of group suggestion is aggregation. Yu et al. [27] developed a preference group model for each TV show feature. Pera et al. [18] use content-based methodologies to create group models for recommendation and aggregate group member film tags.

Aggregation approaches like average [19, 27], least misery [17], most admired person [21], and most joyous [14] have been applied to both PA and RA techniques. Various studies have found that the algorithm each person uses and the aggregation strategy they use determine the effect of the aggregation method on the effectiveness of group recommendations [21]. Additionally, aggregation-based methods are still problematic: 1) Individualizing each group member while neglecting their interactions is a hallmark of RA techniques. 2) Due to a lack of user feedback through the aggregation of preferences, developing a group preferences model may be difficult.

To mimic group interaction, some model-based strategies have been developed [7, 8]. Ye et al. generative's model [15] offers a way to consider social influence while modeling group suggestion. A probabilistic model for outlining and advising group activity development procedures is provided by Yuan et al. [8]. DLGR [15] uses several RBMs [11]. As a prerequisite, use group features to simulate the likelihood of choosing a course of action for every group. Cao et al. [8] integrate an attention network with neural collaborative filtering to automatically estimate each member pair's weight from data to get beyond the data sensitivity of traditional aggregation approaches. Event recommendation has grown to be one of the most talked-about subjects in the Recommendation Domain as a result of the popularity of event-based social networks [5, 9, 10, 26].

Some studies only support CF-compliant events, excluding cold-start events brought on by unforeseen circumstances [26]. Quercia et al. [9] concentrate on the problem of user cold-start rather than new problems. Minkov et al. [10] combine the collaborative approach with a content-based strategy based on RankSVM to address cold-start difficulties. Macedo et al. use context-related information, including social ties, location, content, and time to stop cold-start occurrences in EBSNs. On the other hand, those who want to travel together weren't fully investigated. A topic model for evaluating social effects in group recommendations and EBSN data set experiments is provided by Liu et al. [23]. Yuan et al. [19] analyze the EBSN data set model and offer a broad group recommendation themes model, arguing that Liu et al. [23] may not always be right. This study ignores the cold starts in group event suggestions in favor of a narrow focus on group modeling.

3 Preliminary Conferences

This section covers the problem of group event suggestion and some basic principles. Following that, we'll go over the RBMs used to build our deep hybrid architecture.

RBM In general, RBM is an energy-based model with binary visible layer units v 0–1 M and binary hidden layer units h 0–1 N. As shown in Fig. 2, the RBM is represented by an undirected diagram only visible and hidden layer units are connected. Using an energy function, the combined v and h distribution is defined.

$$p(v, n) = \sum \frac{-E(w, hi)}{k} \tag{1}$$

$$p(v, n) = \sum \frac{-E(v, h)}{z} \tag{2}$$

In general, RBM is an energy-based model with binary visible layer units v 0–1 M and binary hidden layer units h 0–1 N. In Fig. 2, the RBM is depicted as an undirected diagram with only visible and buried layer units connected. An energy function defines the combined v and h distribution as follows:

$$P(v_i = 1|h) = s\left(a_i + \sum_{j=1}^{N} W_{ij}h_j\right) \tag{3}$$

$$P(h_j = 1|v) = s(b_j + \sum_{i=1}^{M} v_i W_{ij}) \tag{4}$$

4 Framework Hybrid Deep

Because group interaction is taken into consideration, model group recommendations [15, 16, 19] prefer group models over aggregation-based strategies. However, due to the cold start problem, when users did not respond to the events they advised, these current approaches were not used in Group Event Recommendation. We propose a deep hybrid framework based on RBMs and conditional RBMs. To fix the problem. To recommend future events for groups, this framework may learn high-level features from subsequent events and group features from group members' input.

Joint Modeling and Group Features
The methodology above aims to solve the group event recommendation cold start issue. On the other hand, this method only considers the event profile and disregards how group members and events interact. We combine the CRBM discussed in the preceding part with the RBM double-wing [15], which combines the model group profile and group features with a two-layer collective DBN to tackle this problem. The group profile is connected to a dual RBM wing, while the group features are connected to a different wing. The group and event profiles are represented in the interaction matrix's column and row. For more information on group characteristics, see [15] given an interaction group, a group profile, a group t_g, etc. Let h stand for the group's overall functionality and c for its features. This is the deep hybrid frame in that we propose energy to function.

$$E(c, t, r, h, e) = \frac{||r - a||^2}{2\sigma^2} - t^T Wh + \frac{||t - \delta||}{2\beta^2} - b^T c - c^T Xh - d^T h - r^T Ye - m^T e - f^T Ze \tag{5}$$

$$p(h_{(k)} = 1|c, t) = s(d_k + \sum_{j=1}^{D} c_j X_j k + \sum_{i=1}^{M} t_{(i)} W_i k / \sigma_i) \tag{6}$$

$$p(r_{(i)} = 1|e) = \mathcal{N}(a_i + \sigma_i \sum_{i=1}^{E} e_i Y_{i,l} \sigma_i^2 \tag{7}$$

$$p(t_{(i)} = 1|h) = \mathcal{N}(\delta_i + \beta_j \sum_{k=1}^{E} h_k W_{j,k} \beta_j^2 \tag{8}$$

$$p(e_{(l)} = 1|r,f) = s(m_i + \sum_{i=1}^{M} r_i Y_{il}/\sigma_i + \sum_{q=1}^{F} f_{(q)} Z_{ql}) \tag{9}$$

Figure 2 shows group characteristic biases c, comprehensive characteristic h, and group profile t, which are group characteristic biases c, comprehensive characteristic h, and group profile t, respectively. The standard deviation (r) is expressed in Gaussian visible units. This power function can get every group profile tj, every event profile ri, every full HK, and every event feature el. Model training seeks to estimate the set of model W, X, Y, z, a, d, m, f parameters given the group profile, member profile, and event context information, i.e., the organizer and location. We use greedy layer training based on CD, as stated in the prior paragraph.

Given the group profile, member profile, and event context information, i.e. the organizer and location, model training aims to estimate the set of model W, X, Y, z, a, d, m, f parameters. As the preceding paragraph indicates, we employ greedy layer training based on CD.

Group Recommendation
The group and event profiles can be reconstructed if model parameters are learned.

Sg,e = 1/2(tg,e + re,g) is the ranking for group g and event c. The top-K suggestion list is then generated by classifying Cg for a certain group g by ranking their Sg,e score.

Sg,e = 1/2(tg,e + re,g) is the classification group g and the event c. Then we sort Cg's Sg,e score for the Top-K recommendation list for a certain group g to classify them.

Our tests used two real-world EBSN data sets from Meetup and Douban Event. Users can use the EBSNs to plan, find, and participate in offline events through an online portal. Users can indicate whether or not they plan to attend an EBSN-distributed event by typing "yes" or "no". The Meetup data collection [5] was obtained using the Meetup REST API between January 2010 and April 2014. Only Chicago and Phoenix events are selected for the Meetup databases. Data about events in Beijing and Shanghai between September 2016 and June 2017 was gathered using the Douban API. In two databases, we record contextual information for each event, such as the host, attendees, location, and start time. Before conducting research, data preparation is carried out to lessen the sparsity of data sets. The events between September and December 2016 were taken from the Douban Event dataset. Conference papers show that the trials occurred between January 2013 and December 2014. Users who attend fewer than ten events are also removed from the system to lessen the amount of noisy data. Table 1. displays statistics for Douban Events and the basic data set Meetup.

$$h_j = s(b^h + \sum_{i=1}^{D} c_i X_{ij} + \sum_{k=1}^{M} r_k W_{kj}/\sigma_k) \tag{10}$$

$$e_p = s\left(b_p^e + \sum_{i=1}^{M} r_i Y_{ip} + \sum_{j=1}^{F} f_i Z_{jp}\right) \tag{11}$$

$$p(r_i = 1|e) = \mathcal{N}(\alpha_i + \sigma_i \sum_{t=1}^{E} e_l Y_{i,l}, \sigma_i^2) \tag{12}$$

$$p(t_j = 1|h) = \mathcal{N}(\delta_j + \beta_j \sum_{k=1}^{E} h_k W_{j,k}, \beta_j^2) \tag{13}$$

Assessment techniques: The solution to the cold start problem, which arises when the events to be recommended are still in the future, and the users have little input, is the main challenge in event recommendation, as was mentioned in prior sections. As a result, the main goal of our research is to assess the performance of our strategy and foundational methods in the context of a group event suggestion at the Cold Beginning stage. A realistic group event recommendation scenario is simulated using a time-dependent cross-validation approach [24]. The start time is first indicated before the events are presented in chronological sequence.

Then, based on the event's start time, events are split into four groups, and the following triple cross-validation procedure is utilized. The remaining data is used for testing, and the first half is used for validation training. While the third and fourth parts of the data are used for testing, the first two parts are used for training. In the third validation, the final component is used for testing, while the first three data parts are used for training. Because the new data are more sparse than the previous validation, the efficacy can be evaluated. On the sparsity of various data sets, there exist numerous recommendation algorithms.

We generate synthetic groups for our assessment tests because the majority of data sets don't provide much information about groups. According to numerous group suggestion research, the three forms of synthetic groups are random groups, high-level similarities, and low-level groupings. Random groups, high-level similarities, and low-level groups are the three categories of synthetic groups [8, 10] (Fig. 1).

Due to the limited availability of EBSN data sets, synthetic groups are created based on the shared characteristics of succeeding users [11], with the Pearson correlation coefficient (PCC) being used to measure user similarity.

User distributions in Phoenix, Chicago, Beijing, Shanghai, and other cities. To create enough groups and develop strong similarities when members are more similar than the threshold, we defined a user-to-user similarity threshold. Average user-to-user similarity [27] is our criterion. The following values are for Beijing, Shanghai, Chicago, and Phoenix, respectively: 0.197, 0.192, 0.128, and 0.233. The number of group members, or group size, is set to 2, 3, 4, 5, 6, and 2,000 groups for each group size and data collection. Since huge groups are uncommon in the actual world and group sizes are restricted to six people, it is difficult to identify enough groups that are larger than six people. In these studies, we assess group recommendation systems using reminder and standardized cumulative gain (NDCG). Recall and NDCG is well-liked metrics for assessing recommendation systems and are frequently applied to measure the effectiveness of

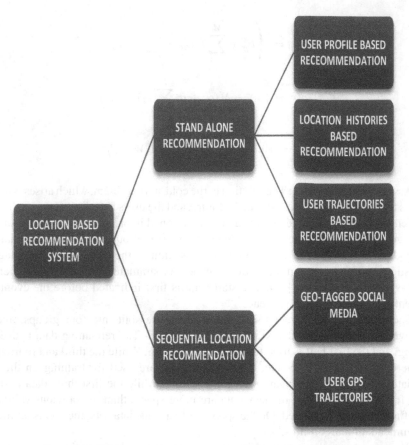

Fig. 1. Location based recommender system

recommendations as a group [1, 10, 26]. Since accuracy is defined as the proportion of events in the list of recommendations with unknown favorable qualities, we do not utilize precision to assess our model.

They measure the recall and NDCG of the group event recommendation technique, which produces a list of k events for each group and computes the recall and NDCG of the group event recommendation approach.

$$Recall@k = \frac{|R_{k \cap T}|}{|T|} \tag{14}$$

where R_k denote the set of events in the recommendation list, T is the set of events in the test set.

$$DCG@k = rel_1 + \sum_{i=2}^{k} \frac{rel_i}{\log(i+1)} \tag{15}$$

$$NDCG@k = \frac{DCG@K}{IDCG@K} \tag{16}$$

5 Comparison Method

We equate our deep hybrid structure to a collective. Since the group event recommendation problem has not been sufficiently explored in the current literature, event recommendation systems and other competing recommendations are not equipped to provide events for a user group. Because we employ several aggregation algorithms [21] that incorporate individual user recommendations in the overall group recommendations, individual event recommendation methods [22] can also be compared to our strategy. In our experiments, we evaluate and contrast the ensuing strategies.

- DLGR [15] is a deep belief advocate collaborative network that uses greater complexity than any prior aggregation-based group advice approach to get high-quality qualities from lower-level features.

A probabilistic generative model for group proposals is COM [19]. Individual decisions and group discussions should influence the collective decision-making process. A COM pre-distribution may contain content information. We use geographic data to recommend our group event task in our COM trials.

- For a set of users, PCGR [20] offers events and locations. Collaborative regression [6] analyzes content data from events and webpages, with assignments and matrix factorization serving as common models.

The goal of HBGG [25] was to give users recommendations for locations. The HBGG model combines social data, group mobility regions, and geographic group themes into one subject. By substituting geographic event coordinates for local geographic coordinates throughout our testing, we employ HBGG to advertise events to users.

For modeling contextual data, such as social interactions, geographic locations, organizers, and textual events, CBPF has adopted Bayesian Poisson [22] as a core unit. To connect the units, a collective matrix factorization strategy is applied. CBPF's recommendations are supplemented with average aggregation approaches to produce group recommendations because it was designed for individual users. We offer a deep hybrid frame called the HDF frame.

Effective Recommendation. The efficiency of our deep hybrid frames and recommendation algorithms on two datasets for group events with turnaround parameters is reported and discussed in this section. Recall and NDCG scores for the Beijing, Shanghai, Chicago, and Phoenix data sets. Recall@k and NDCG@k scores are only displayed when k is set to 5,10,15,20 because users are usually only interested in a few big events, and larger lists of suggestions for top-k recommendations are usually ignored [13, 19, 24].

We notice that HDF recall@10 and NDCG@10 have values of around 0.261 and 0.231, respectively, and that the suggested HDF outperforms previous methods of comparison. Recall@10 shows improvements in DLGR, COM, HBGG, PCGR, and CBPF-AVG of 51.2, 51.2, 4.93, 0.89, 0.088. The following suggestions are being discussed: 1) HDF performs better than HBGG and PCGR in terms of guidelines, illustrating the value of a deep hybrid framework with additional contextual information, such as the organizer and the site. 2) A performance gap between HDF-CBPF-AVG suggests that the hDF's hybrid structure outperforms the aggregation technique of the CBPF-conventional AVG.

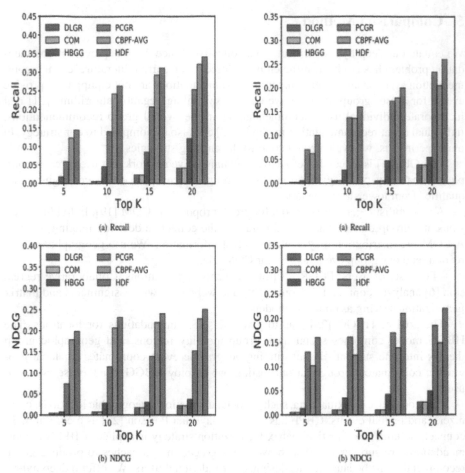

Fig. 2. Top-k performance on Beijing dataset and Shanghai dataset

CBPF-AVG exceeds other base line approaches between comparison methods. The CBPF-AVG shaped several contexts, such as social relations, organizers and locations together, whereas COM and HBGG consider only the geographical influence of venues and only the textual content of events is considered in the PCGR. The recall values and NDCG values when the HDF functions better than other base line approaches in the Shanghai dataset.

The results of the comparison are comparable to those of Beijing and Shanghai. The main distinction is that all approaches outperform the Douban Event dataset on Meetup datasets. In Chicago and Phoenix, for example, HDF hits 0.12 and 0.135 Recall@10, respectively, whereas in Beijing and Shanghai, HDF reaches 0.0261 and 0.16 Recall@10, respectively. Perhaps because the Meetup dataset has less user attendance records than the Douban Event dataset. Table 1. demonstrates that the data set in Chicago has 99.88 percent more sparsity than the data set in Beijing (99.11%). We also notice that the COM,

HBGG, and PCGR perform worse on smaller data sets since less contextual information is supplied.

5.1 Group Different Performance

The influence of different groups' recommendations for group gatherings is examined in this section. The data sets Recall@10 and NDCG@10 for Beijing and Shanghai, respectively, We discover that HDF beats other baselines in Recall@10 and NDCG@10 for the first time, regardless of group size.

HDF's performance in group size lowers by 6 when compared to other techniques. The alternative is that large-group decision-making is exceedingly complex, and existing methodologies make modeling group preference difficult. Recall@10 and NDCG@10 are the most relevant CBPF-AVG baselines. PCGR also uses two more model-based techniques, COM and HBGG, which show that taking into consideration content information is more effective than group mobility and spatial effects of group events.

We also discovered that the recommendation's performance does not decline significantly when applied to large groups. This is because our trials create user-to-user synthetic groups with similar interests.

6 Conclusion

Recommendations play an essential part in EBSNs for a certain group of users. The inherent cold start problem, on the other hand, originates with the group event recommendation. We introduced a deep hybrid framework based on RBM and conditional RBM that addresses the cold start problem by recommending the group event utilizing additional background information from events as result shown in Tables 1 and 2. The specific structure can, for example, integrate conditional RBM events with DLGR group features. Experiments using two real-world EBSN data sets reveal that our proposed HDF outperforms cutting-edge group event approaches. To improve recommendations system, additional contextual data will be incorporated in the future, as well as deeper network structures.

Finally we evaluate our model with Returning common movies and ratings of same for both the users where we have recommendations on the basis of similarity of users with ratings.

Table 1. Recommendation on User Id 50

Movies you should watch are:
[1431 Rocky (1976)
Name: title, dtype: object, 742 African Queen, The (1951)
Name: title, dtype: object, 733 It's a Wonderful Life (1946)
Name: title, dtype: object, 939 Terminator, The (1984)
Name: title, dtype: object, 969 Back to the Future (1985)
Name: title, dtype: object, 510 Silence of the Lambs, The (1991)
Name: title, dtype: object, 1057 Star Trek II: The Wrath of Khan (1982)
Name: title, dtype: object, 1059 Star Trek IV: The Voyage Home (1986)
Name: title, dtype: object, 1939 Matrix, The (1999)
Name: title, dtype: object]

Table 2. Similar users model evaluation

S. No	title_x	userId_x	rating_x	userId_y	rating_y
0	Forrest Gump (1994)	587	4	511	4.5
1	Life Is Beautiful (La Vita Ã¨ bella) (1997)	587	5	511	4.5
2	Matrix, The (1999)	587	4	511	5

References

1. Baker, E.C.: Media Concentration and Democracy: Why Ownership Matters. Cambridge University Press, New York (1998)
2. Beel, J., Genzmehr, M., Langer, S., Nürnberger, A., Gipp, B.: A comparative analysis of offline and online evaluations and discussion of research paper recommender system evaluation. In: Proceedings of the International Workshop on Reproducibility and Replication in Recommender Systems Evaluation (RepSys 2013), pp. 7–14. Association for Computing Machinery, New York, NY, USA (2013). https://doi.org/10.1145/2532508.2532511
3. Bernstein, A., et al.: Diversity in News Recommendations. arXiv preprint arXiv:2005.09495 (2020)
4. Bodó, B.: Selling news to audiences – a qualitative inquiry into the emerging logics of algorithmic news personalization in European quality news media. Digital J. 7(8), 1054–1075 (2019). https://doi.org/10.1080/21670811.2019.1624185
5. Burke, R., Sonboli, N., Ordonez-Gauger, A.: Balanced neighborhoods for multi-sided fairness in recommendation. In: Conference on Fairness, Accountability and Transparency, pp. 202–214 (2018)
6. Castells, P., Hurley, N.J., Vargas, S.: Novelty and diversity in recommender systems. In: Ricci, F., Rokach, L., Shapira, B. (eds.) Recommender systems handbook, pp. 881–918. Springer, Boston, MA (2015). https://doi.org/10.1007/978-1-4899-7637-6_26
7. Chaney, A.J.B., Stewart, B.M., Engelhardt, B.E.: How algorithmic confounding in recommendation systems increases homogeneity and decreases utility. In: Proceedings of the 12th

ACM Conference on Recommender Systems (RecSys 2018), pp. 224–232. Association for Computing Machinery, New York, NY, USA (2018). https://doi.org/10.1145/3240323.324 0370

8. Christians, C.: The Media and Moral Literacy. 62p. (2006)
9. Christians, C., Glasser, T.L., McQuail, D., Nordenstreng, K., White, R.A.: Normative Theories of the Media: Journalism in Democratic Societies. University of Illinois Press, Champaign (2009)
10. Dahlberg, L.: Re-constructing digital democracy: An outline of four 'positions'. New Med. Soc. 13(6), 855–872 (2011). https://doi.org/10.1177/1461444810389569
11. Dillahunt, T.R., Brooks, C.A., Gulati, S.: Detecting and visualizing filter bubbles in Google and Bing. In: Proceedings of the 33rd Annual ACM Conference Extended Abstracts on Human Factors in Computing Systems, pp. 1851–1856 (2015)
12. Dörr, K.N.: Mapping the field of algorithmic journalism. Digital J. 4(6), 700–722 (2016). https://doi.org/10.1080/21670811.2015.1096748
13. Eskens, S., Helberger, N., Moeller, J.: Challenged by news personalisation: five perspectives on the right to receive information. J. Media Law. 9(2), 259–284 (2017). https://doi.org/10. 1080/17577632.2017.1387353
14. Rajawat, A.S., Rawat, R., Barhanpurkar, K., Shaw, R.N., Ghosh, A.: Vulnerability analysis at industrial internet of things platform on dark web network using computational intelligence. In: Bansal, J.C., Paprzycki, M., Bianchini, M., Das, S. (eds.) Computationally Intelligent Systems and their Applications. SCI, vol. 950, pp. 39–51. Springer, Singapore (2021). https:// doi.org/10.1007/978-981-16-0407-2_4
15. Ferree, M.M., Gamson, W.A., Gerhards, J., Rucht, D.: Four models of the public sphere in modern democracies. Theory Soc. 31(3), 289–324 (2002)
16. Bedi, P., Goyal, S.B., Rajawat, A.S., Shaw, R.N., Ghosh, A.: A framework for personalizing atypical web search sessions with concept-based user profiles using selective machine learning techniques. In: Bianchini, M., Piuri, V., Das, S., Shaw, R.N. (eds.) Advanced Computing and Intelligent Technologies. LNNS, vol. 218, pp. 279–291. Springer, Singapore (2022). https:// doi.org/10.1007/978-981-16-2164-2_23
17. Fredrickson, B.L.: Positive emotions broaden and build. In: Advances in Experimental Social Psychology, vol. 47, pp. 1–53. Elsevier (2013)
18. Hanna, A., Denton, E., Smart, A., Smith-Loud, J.: Towards a critical race methodology in algorithmic fairness. In: Proceedings of the 2020 Conference on Fairness, Accountability, and Transparency, pp. 501–512 (2020)
19. Helberger, N.: On the democratic role of news recommenders. Digital J. 7(8), 993–1012 (2019). https://doi.org/10.1080/21670811.2019.1623700
20. Rawat, R., Rajawat, A.S., Mahor, V., Shaw, R.N., Ghosh, A.: Dark Web—onion hidden service discovery and crawling for profiling morphing, unstructured crime and vulnerabilities prediction. In: Mekhilef, S., Favorskaya, M., Pandey, R.K., Shaw, R.N. (eds.) Innovations in Electrical and Electronic Engineering. LNEE, vol. 756, pp. 717–734. Springer, Singapore (2021). https://doi.org/10.1007/978-981-16-0749-3_57
21. Hutto, C.J., Gilbert, E.: Vader: A parsimonious rule-based model for sentiment analysis of social media text. In: Eighth International AAAI Conference on Weblogs and Social Media (2014)
22. Mahor, V., et.al.: Cyber warfare threat categorization on CPS by dark web terrorist. In: 2021 IEEE 4th International Conference on Computing, Power and Communication Technologies (GUCON), pp. 1–6 (2021) https://doi.org/10.1109/GUCON50781.2021.9573994
23. Jannach, D., Jugovac, M.: Measuring the business value of recommender systems. ACM Trans. Manage. Inf. Syst. 10(4), 1–23 (2019). https://doi.org/10.1145/3370082
24. Tandoc Jr, E.C., Thomas, R.J.: The ethics of web analytics. Digital J. 3(2), 243–258 (2015). https://doi.org/10.1080/21670811.2014.909122

25. Kumar, A., Das, S., Tyagi, V., Shaw, R.N., Ghosh, A.: Analysis of classifier algorithms to detect anti-money laundering. In: Bansal, J.C., Paprzycki, M., Bianchini, M., Das, S. (eds.) Computationally Intelligent Systems and their Applications. SCI, vol. 950, pp. 143–152. Springer, Singapore (2021). https://doi.org/10.1007/978-981-16-0407-2_11
26. Karppinen, K.: Uses of democratic theory in media and communication studies. Observation. **7**(3), 1–17 (2013)
27. Keyes, O.: The misgendering machines: Trans/HCI implications of automatic gender recognition. Proc. ACM Human-Comput. Interact. **2**(CSCW), 1–22 (2018). https://doi.org/10.1145/3274357

Face Mask Detection and Recognition with High Accuracy on Live Streaming Video Using Improved Yolo V4 and Comparing with Convolutional Neural Network

Chenjigaram Murugesan Kandan and K. Vidhya[✉]

Department of Electronics and Communication Engineering, Saveetha School of Engineering, Saveetha Institute of Medical and Technical Sciences, Chennai 602105, Tamil Nadu, India
vidhyak.sse@saveetha.com

Abstract. The aim of this research is to detect face masks using Convolutional Neural network (CNN) algorithm and comparing it with the Yolo v4 algorithm. The study includes two groups namely, CNN algorithm and yolo v4 algorithm. The total sample size is 40 with pretest power of 0.8. In order to evaluate how well CNN algorithm methods perform, accuracy values are calculated. Using SPSS software, CNN algorithm method was found to be 92.65% accurate while improved Yolo v4 was found to be 85.87% accurate. 0.000 p(2-tailed) is obtained for the model. Using CNN, it was proved significant improvements to performance than improved Yolo v4.

Keywords: Coronavirus · Artificial Intelligence · Yolo v4 algorithm · Novel intensity feature · CNN algorithm · Face mask

1 Introduction

Many respiratory viruses spread easily through the air, so wearing a face mask is extremely important (Harry 2021). In order to improve the real-time property of object detection, (Choi et al. 2022) a high-speed object detection method based on Artificial Intelligence such as Yolo v4 is recommended. First, it uses two Block modules from the network instead of the two Block modules from Yolo V4 (van Tilborg 2022), reducing computational complexity. (Brown-Beresford et al. 2022) then design additional residual network blocks to extract more feature information for the object and reduce recognition errors. Auxiliary network design uses two consecutive 3×3 convolutions to acquire the receptive field and extract global features. Several applications of face mask detection can be found in the field of Artificial Intelligence such as intelligent control systems, surveillance, smart homes, and autonomous driving, among others (Demoulin et al. 2022).

Over 150 chapters related to this work have been published in IEEE, and more than 100 chapters have been indexed in ScienceDirect. Artificial intelligence techniques aid

---

C. M. Kandan—Research Scholar.

© The Author(s), under exclusive license to Springer Nature Switzerland AG 2023
R. N. Shaw et al. (Eds.): ICACIS 2022, CCIS 1749, pp. 673–681, 2023.
https://doi.org/10.1007/978-3-031-25088-0_59

in the detection of face masks used to protect people from the COVID 19 Coronavirus (Jenstrup et al. 1999). The Internet of Things, a system, or a smart city can use face mask recognition devices to enable public space administrators to enforce the requirement that all visitors should wear masks to reduce risk of coronavirus spread. Face mask detection systems are used among workers to make it confirm wearing of masks, visitor status in supermarkets, Shukla et al. 2021) universities, libraries, etc. Similar place. Some studies have considered the detection of face masks. Convolutional Neural Network (CNN) based Face mask detector that works together to detect faes is suitable for face masks, probably real-time face masks recognition. Yolo v4 with a model Residual network (ResNet) (Klinenberg and Sherman 2021) achieves high detection accuracy in the field of Artificial Intelligence. However, a lightweight version with MobileNet as the backbone (Jia n.d.; Klinenberg and Sherman 2021; Reddy et al. 2021). The problem with the optical model was not resolved and the recognition performance was significantly reduced. Yolo uses neural networks to learn from large amounts of data in the field of Artificial Intelligence. The literature survey shows the detection of face masks using Artificial intelligence principles such as Yolo-v4 method is effective. The output shows that face mask detection using Novel Yolo-v4 has a greater precision value compared to the Novel intensity feature. The ultimate aim of this survey is to have a high gain and performance of the Novel Yolo-V4 algorithm. The experience and expertise of our research team have translated into high-quality publications as a result of our extensive knowledge (Bhavikatti et al. 2021; Karobari et al. 2021; Shanmugam et al. 2021; Sawant et al. 2021; Muthukrishnan 2021; Preethi et al. 2021; Karthigadevi et al. 2021; Bhanu Teja et al. 2021; Veerasimman et al. 2021; Baskar et al. 2021).

The drawback of the existing is lack of performance when there are groups of small objects, because each grid can only detect one object. The goal is to increase the detection accuracy of face masks using CNN algorithm and comparing it with the Yolo v4.

2   Materials and Methods

The proposed work is conducted in the Image Processing Laboratory, Department of Electronics and Communication Engineering at Saveetha School of Engineering. SIMATS, Chennai. CNN algorithm and improved Yolo v4 are 2 groups considered. 40 samples were considered with a pretest power of 0.8 (Tierno and Jr. 2020). Maximum acceptable error is fixed as 0.2 with confidence interval of 95%. Accuracy values are calculated for both the groups and then, the outcomes were compared.

Sample preparation for Group 1 begins with loading the dataset. With several iterations, the accuracy of the CNN algorithm utilizing. Novel intensity feature is determined. Every iteration takes into account 20 samples to increase accuracy. In Group 2 sample preparation the dataset is loaded. The accuracy using Yolo v4 algorithm is found with several iterations. 20 samples are considered for every iteration to improve the accuracy score. Real time images are taken through the webcam that was installed. Matlab toolkit is used for simulation. Using Matlab accuracy values are calculated for both the groups and then results have been compared.

In this work, a profound learning based model for identifying covers over faces in broad daylight spots to diminish local area spread of Coronavirus is introduced. The proposed model proficiently handles fluctuating sorts of impediments in thick circumstances by utilizing troupes of single and two phase locators. The outfit approach helps in accomplishing high exactness as well as further develops identification speed extensively. The high precision of the model is likewise because of exceptionally adjusted facial covering driven dataset accomplished through Random over-examining with information increase over the unique MAFA dataset. Our procedure diminishes the lopsidedness proportion $\rho = 11.82$ (unique) to $\rho = 1.07$.

The acronym YOLO stands for You Only Look Once. Yolo is a cutting-edge, in-the-moment item detection technology. Face recognition Joseph Redmon was the one who created it. A number of things can be recognised by the real-time object recognition system in a single frame. Yolo has undergone changes over time, becoming yolo v2, yolo v3, and yolo v4. YOLO employs a completely unique methodology compared to other earlier detection methods (Tierno and Jr. 2020). Each image is processed by a single neural network. It predicts bounding boxes and probabilities for each zone based on the presence of faces in the image. This bounding box is weighted by the projected probabilities.

In order to forecast the object that will be centered in each grid cell, Yolo divides the input image into a S S grid. Grid cells predict the B bounding boxes and confidence scores for each box. These confidence ratings show how certain the model is that the box contains an object and how precise it believes the box to be in making its prediction. Comparing the Yolo v4 model to classifier-based systems, there are significant benefits. Multiple items can be recognised in a single frame. When testing, it considers the entire image, allowing the global context of the picture to influence its predictions. In contrast to systems like R-CNN that require thousands of evaluations for a single image, it also makes predictions with a single network evaluation.

Statistical Analysis: It is used SPSS software for comparing the accuracy parameters (M. V. Reddy and Venkataswamy Reddy 2019). SPSS software is used to compute the independent sample T-test and group statistics. To calculate the mean, standard deviation, and statistically significant difference between two groups, this software is utilised. In this study, independent variables are the input features such as pixels, and images. The dependent variable's accuracy are the output parameters.

3 Results

Table 1 shows the comparison of the CNN algorithm and Yolo v4 algorithm for the face mask detection. The detection accuracy is 92.65% CNN algorithm with Novel intensity feature and the detection accuracy for the Yolo v4 algorithm is given by 85.37%. Table 2 shows descriptive statistics of accuracy for both the algorithms in the improved Yolo v4 with novel CNN algorithm. Group statistics results mean the CNN algorithm is 92.65% and improved Yolo v4 algorithm is 85.37%, the standard deviation for the CNN algorithm is 1.53 and improved Yolo v4 algorithm is 0.34, the standard error mean for CNN algorithm method is 0.4 and for the improved Yolo v4 is 0.09. Coronavirus The means of the accuracy of CNN algorithm is more compared to improved Yolo v4.

Table 3 shows independent t-test analysis ($p < 0.02$). From this table it is observed that the values of accuracy with the help of spss test and it is categorized into when equality

Table 1. Accuracy of the CNN algorithm and Yolo v4 algorithm respectively. The tabulation gives the accuracy for different samples for CNN (Kanjee 2018) algorithm and Yolo v4 algorithms

S. No	Accuracy (%) using CNN	Accuracy (%) using Yolo v4
1	93.15	84.03
2	94.42	84.54
3	93.25	83.54
4	93.21	83.75
5	94.41	84.64
6	93.28	85.61
7	91.25	84.33
8	93.92	84.95
9	94.59	85.65
10	91.85	83.85
11	92.45	85.82
12	92.07	85.65
13	92.65	84.59
14	93.64	85.65
15	93.56	84.40
16	92.54	85.31
17	92.98	83.12
18	92.54	84.42
19	93.47	83.95
20	93.45	82.31

Table 2. Group statistics show the number of samples taken and mean values of accuracy and standard deviation obtained for 20 samples in case of CNN and Yolo v4 (Tierno and Jr. 2020) using SPSS software

Group		No of samples	Mean	Std. deviation	Std. mean error
Accuracy	CNN algorithm	20	92.6540	1.78120	.398929
	YOLO V4	20	85.3765	0.87175	0.53657

of variance is assumed and when equal variance is assumed not assumed. The CNN algorithm has better accuracy (92.65%)than the improved Yolo v4 algorithm(85.37%) with error bars ±1 SD.

Figure 1 shows the comparison of CNN algorithm with Novel intensity features and improved Yolo v4 algorithms. Comparing algorithms based on independent t-tests also

Table 3. Independent samples test presents the mean difference, standard error difference, and significance of the CNN algorithm and Yolo v4 (Shukla et al. 2021) obtained in SPSS

		Levene's test for equality of variances		T-test for equality of means						95% confidence interval of the difference	
		F	Sig	t	df	Sig (2-tailed)	Mean difference	Std. error diff		lower	upper
Accuracy	Equal variances assumed	0.575	0.453	0.128	38	0.899	0.18250	1.42870		−2.70976	3.07476
	Equal variances not assumed			0.128	37.909	0.899	0.18250	1.42870		−2.70999	3.07499

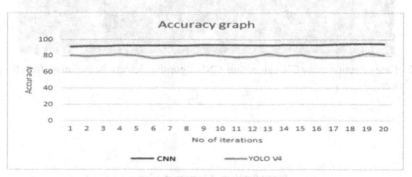

Fig. 1. Accuracy of CNN algorithm and Yolo v4 algorithm are compared for 20 iterations, X-axis: No. of Iterations, Y-axis: Accuracy (%)

reveals statistically significant differences in mean accuracy. The CNN algorithm has better accuracy (92.65%) than the Yolo v4 algorithm (85.37%) with error bars ±1 SD. Face mask detection using Novel texture feature based CNN algorithm is performed and the output obtained is shown in Fig. 2. The two methods are contrasted in a bar graph in Fig. 3, and the mean accuracy value shows a statistically significant difference between the two.

Independent t-test is used for the comparison of two algorithms and a statistically significant difference was noticed with p (sig2-tailed) < 0.05. CNN algorithm obtained 92.65% of accuracy. Therefore, while comparing both the algorithms, the CNN algorithm with novel intensity feature has better accuracy than improved Yolo v4 algorithm and the standard deviation of CNN algorithm with novel intensity feature is slightly better than improved Yolo v4.

Fig. 2. Face detection using CNN algorithm. CNN algorithm detects the face mask from the given input image.

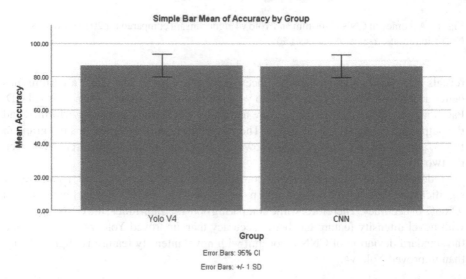

Fig. 3. Graph shows that CNN algorithm has better accuracy compared to Yolo v4 in face mask detection. X-axis: CNN algorithm & Yolo v4 and Y-axis: Mean of Accuracy with ± 1 SD.

4 Discussion

The mean efficiency of the value of the yolo-v4 in group 1 in this study was 85.37% and the CNN algorithm has an optical absorption value of 92.65%. The information from the statistical analysis, including the mean, standard deviation, and standard error mean, is tabulated. Two algorithms are compared using an independent t-test, and a statistically significant difference was found with p (sig2-tailed) lesser than 0.05 compared using an independent t-test, and a statistically significant difference was found with p (sig2-tailed) lesser than 0.05.

CNN learn from a large quantity of data which has an accuracy of 71.78%. Face mask recognition of the proposed system has some difficulty, due to the presence of noise, (Tan et al. 2021; Hoang, n.d.) lack of lighting and blurred images. (Patterson and Gibson 2017). Yolo v4 and other main algorithms such that the accuracy rate can be improved (Jenstrup et al. 1999). CNN detects face mask more accurately in the dim light situations and some filters can be used to reduce the motion of the images (Jenstrup et al. 1999; Shukla et al. 2021). Yolo v4 includes self adversarial training for data augmentation, genetic algorithm to find optimal hyper-parameters, new normalization techniques (Brown-Beresford et al. 2022).

The limitations of this study was that the mask detection is difficult, when the person is wearing a helmet and when the light is dim. As a future scope an advanced algorithms a can be applied for further improvement.

5 Conclusion

The accuracy in detecting Face masks using CNN algorithm method is 92.65% and 85.43% with that of the Yolo v4 algorithm. It is observed that the CNN algorithm algorithm is significantly better in terms of accuracy value compared to the Yolo v4 algorithm for face mask detection.

References

Baskar, M., Renuka Devi, R., Ramkumar, J., Kalyanasundaram, P., Suchithra, M., Amutha, B.: Region centric minutiae propagation measure orient forgery detection with finger print analysis in health care systems Neural Process. Lett. 1–13 (2021). https://doi.org/10.1007/s11063-020-10407-4

Bhanu Teja, N., Devarajan, Y., Mishra, R., Sivasaravanan, S., Thanikaivel Murugan, D.: Detailed analysis on sterculia foetida kernel oil as renewable fuel in compression ignition engine Biomass Convers. Bioref.1–12 (2021). https://doi.org/10.1007/s13399-021-01328-w

Bhavikatti, S.K., et al.: Investigating the antioxidant and cytocompatibility of Mimusops Elengi Linn extract over human gingival fibroblast cells. Int. J. Environ. Res. Public Health **18**(13), 7162 (2021). https://doi.org/10.3390/ijerph18137162

Brown-Beresford, K., Currie, J., Thiruvenkatarajan, V.: The application of a surgical face mask over different oxygen delivery devices; a crossover study of measured end-tidal oxygen concentrations. BMC Anesthesiol. **22**(1), 62 (2022)

Choi, M., Wo, L., Joshi, P., Nugent, A., Thaller, S.R.: Facial flap necrosis from COVID-19 face mask precautions. J. Craniof. Surg. **33**, 1840–1842 (2022). https://doi.org/10.1097/SCS.0000000000008587

Demoulin, B., Duvivier, C., Marchal, F., Demoulin-Alexikova, S.: A physical Analog to assess surgical face mask air flow resistance during tidal ventilation. Front. Physiol. **13**(February), 808588 (2022)

Harry, D.: The Aftermath of Face Mask: Psychology of Who Should Wear Facemask (2021)

Hoang, L.: An Evaluation of VGG16 and YOLO v3 on Hand-Drawn Images (2019). https://doi. org/10.15760/honors.703

Jenstrup, M., Fruergaard, K.O., Mortensen, C.R.: Pollution with nitrous oxide using laryngeal mask or face mask. Acta Anaesthesiol. Scand. **43**, 663–666 (1999). https://doi.org/10.1034/j. 1399-6576.1999.430612.x

Jia, X.: Face Alignment and Face Mask Reasoning for the Images in the Wild (2016). https://doi. org/10.5353/th_991022012289703414

Kanjee, R.: YOLO V3: Robust Deep Learning Object Detection in 1 Hour (2018)

Karobari, M.I., et al.: An in vitro stereomicroscopic evaluation of bioactivity between neo MTA plus, Pro Root MTA, BIODENTINE and glass ionomer cement using dye penetration method. Materials. **14**(12), 3159 (2021). https://doi.org/10.3390/ma14123159

Karthigadevi, G., et al.: Chemico-Nanotreatment methods for the removal of persistent organic pollutants and xenobiotics in water - a review. Biores. Technol. **324**(March), 124678 (2021)

Klinenberg, E., Sherman, M.: Face mask face-offs. Publ. Cult. **33**, 441–466 (2021). https://doi. org/10.1215/08992363-9262919

Chakraborty, A., Chatterjee, S., Majumder, K., Shaw, R.N., Ghosh, A.: A comparative study of myocardial infarction detection from ECG data using machine learning. In: Bianchini, M., Piuri, V., Das, S., Shaw, R.N. (eds.) Advanced Computing and Intelligent Technologies. LNNS, vol. 218, pp. 257–267. Springer, Singapore (2022). https://doi.org/10.1007/978-981-16-2164-2_21

Patterson, J., Gibson, A.: Deep Learning: A Practitioner's Approach. O'Reilly Media, Inc., Sebastopol (2017)

Preethi, K., Auxzilia, K.A., Preethi, G.L., Sekar, D.: Antagomir technology in the treatment of different types of cancer. Epigenomics **13**, 481–484 (2021). https://doi.org/10.2217/epi-2020-0439

Venkatasamy, R.M., Reddy, M.V.: Multivariate Statistical Methods Going Beyond the Linear FPSS. Springer, Cham (2021). https://doi.org/10.1007/978-3-030-81392-5

Reddy, S., Goel, S., Nijhawan, R.: Real-time face mask detection using machine learning/ deep feature-based classifiers for face mask recognition. In: 2021 IEEE Bombay Section Signature Conference (IBSSC) (2021). https://doi.org/10.1109/ibssc53889.2021.9673170

Mukhopadhyay, M., et.al.: Facial emotion recognition based on Textural pattern and convolutional neural network. In: 2021 IEEE 4th International Conference on Computing, Power and Communication Technologies (GUCON), pp. 1–6 (2021). https://doi.org/10.1109/GUCON50781. 2021.9573860

Shanmugam, V., et al.: Circular economy in biocomposite development: state-of-the-art, challenges and emerging trends. Compos. Part C: Open Access **5**(July), 100138 (2021)

Shukla, R.K., Tiwari, A.K., Verma, V.: Identification of with face mask and without face mask using face recognition model. In: 2021 10th International Conference on System Modeling & Advancement in Research Trends (SMART) (2021). https://doi.org/10.1109/smart52563.2021. 9676204

Palimkar, P., Bajaj, V., Mal, A.K., Shaw, R.N., Ghosh, A.: Unique action identifier by using magnetometer, accelerometer and gyroscope: KNN approach. In: Bianchini, M., Piuri, V., Das, S., Shaw, R.N. (eds.) Advanced Computing and Intelligent Technologies. LNNS, vol. 218, pp. 607–631. Springer, Singapore (2022). https://doi.org/10.1007/978-981-16-2164-2_48

Tierno, P.M., Jr.: First, Wear a Face Mask: A Doctor's Guide to Reducing Risk of Infection During the Pandemic and Beyond. Rodale Books (2020)

Sharma, P., Chandan, S., Shaw, R.N., Ghosh, A.: Vibration-based diagnosis of defect embedded in inner raceway of ball bearing using 1D convolutional neural network. In: Artificial Intelligence for Future Generation Robotics, pp. 25–36. Elsevier, Amesterdam (2021). https://doi.org/10.1016/B978-0-323-85498-6.00011-3

Veerasimman, A., et al.: thermal properties of natural fiber sisal based hybrid composites – a brief review. J. Nat. Fibers. **19**, 1–11 (2021)

SMART CITIES: P2P Energy Trading Using Blockchain

Nitima Malsa[1](✉)(ID), Tushar Srivastave[1], Utkarsh Sahni[1], Suraj Garg[1], Ankush Ghosh[2], and Rabindra Nath Shaw[2]

[1] JSS Academy of Technical Education, Noida, UP, India
nitima.malsa@gmail.com
[2] University Center for Research and Development, Chandigarh University, Mohali, Punjab, India

Abstract. This chapter describes a distributed smart grid application for smart cities that enables peer-to-peer energy trading to reduce resource consumption and create a greener, cleaner planet. Future smart cities built with blockchain technology will place a strong emphasis on resource conservation in order to create a greener, cleaner planet. Blockchain has a variety of applications that can help smart cities save more energy. A blockchain-based network, for instance, can be used to track citizens' energy usage. Additionally, residents can exchange surplus electricity for incentives with other members. The chapter evinces a proposed framework for the smart grid. Implementation of work has been done by acutely utilizing blockchain technology as the voguish technology possesses profuse strengths including transparency, open-source, immutability, etc. The paramount part of the microgrid is its controller, implemented by using a smart contract of the blockchain that automatically modulates the smart grid functionality predominantly. Energy producers, consumers, and administrators are indispensable in the system. In this work, the profound implementation including smart contracts has been expounded chronologically. The work is limited by a single smart contract for a single type of grid system. A combination of multiple such types of systems fabricates an absolute smart grid.

Keywords: Blockchain · Ethereum · P2P energy · Remix IDE · Smart city · Smart contract · Smart grid · Sublime Text3

1 Introduction

"Smartness" is not just about installing digital interfaces in traditional infrastructure or streamlining city operations. It also involves intelligently utilizing data and technology to improve decision-making and lifestyle quality. These Smart cities use digital solutions to enhance the use of traditional networks and services. The purpose of smart cities is to increase sustainability, benefit businesses, and enhance residents' quality of life. To create a smart city, three layers must come together.

The first is the technological foundation, which consists of a necessary number of smart devices (such as smart phones and sensors), linked by quickly connected networks. In the second layer of applications, the right tools are needed to convert raw data

© The Author(s), under exclusive license to Springer Nature Switzerland AG 2023
R. N. Shaw et al. (Eds.): ICACIS 2022, CCIS 1749, pp. 682–694, 2023.
https://doi.org/10.1007/978-3-031-25088-0_60

into notifications, insights, and events, and this is where providers of technology and programmers of applications come into the picture.

The public, businesses, and cities using it make up the third layer. Smart cities use their IoT device network and other technologies to enhance livability and promote economic growth.

Successful smart cities follow four steps:

- Data gathering: Smart sensors placed throughout the city collect real-time data.
- Analysis: The process of assessing the information obtained from smart sensors in order to draw pertinent conclusions.
- Communication: The analysis phase's insights are communicated to decision-makers via efficient communication networks.
- Cities act by using the data's information to create solutions, improve operations and asset management, and improve resident quality.

1.1 Blockchain Makes Cities Smarter

There are multiple ways through which cities can be made smarter. Some of them are explained below:

- Better Healthcare:

  A distributed system for patient health records and transparent drug supply chains are being developed using blockchain. The entire diagnosis and treatment process, including financial transactions, may eventually take place over a blockchain as blockchain adoption rises.

  For instance, wearable diagnostic tools can diagnose a patient when AI and blockchain are combined. A medical expert receives the diagnosis after it has been safely shared on a blockchain with them. A smart contract for further treatment can then be started by the patient and the doctor. The smart contract can also be applied to insurance claims. The final benefit of telemedicine is that patients can receive care without having to travel.

- Better Waste management:

  In smart cities, blockchain can contribute to keeping the air clean and hygiene standards high. It can offer real-time tracking of various waste management-related aspects.

  For instance, it can offer transparent, unchangeable data on the quantity of waste collected, the individuals responsible for collecting it, and the methods used for recycling or disposal. Additionally, using blockchain, governments can provide incentives for waste management to encourage cleanliness. Citizens will be encouraged to participate actively as a result, which will improve waste management efforts.

- Education Simplified:

  It takes a lot of time and effort to transfer data between numerous institutions. By producing a centralized, immutable database, blockchain can assist in finding solutions to the issues. On the blockchain network, information can be easily accessed and shared between various academic institutions [1, 2].

  Additionally, since student data cannot be changed due to blockchain's immutability, it will aid in reducing fraud cases like fabricating fake mark sheets.

- P2P Energy Trading:

  Microgrids are, inevitably, reassuring the speculated novel grid structure, a way of expanding and enriching cited technologies possessing an extravagant potential of mitigating or eliminating dissensions, and even allowing their organized expansion and the improvement of upswings.

  A smart grid is a self-contained energy system that serves a distinct geographic area, such as a college campus, a hospital, a commercial Centre, or a neighbourhood [3].

  The smart microgrid concept was offered as a new strategy to merge green and renewable energy technology into the existing power system. Consequently, the smart grid connected to the Internet is profoundly forging an ingenious way to ensure electricity is ubiquitous. The most sought-after goal of these enhancements is to build a sustainable civilization.

Contrary to this, a typical centralized grid system may struggle to integrate and coordinating a lot of growing connections. Consequently, the smart grid is transitioning from a centralized to a decentralized topological state. Blockchain, on the other hand, has several desirable qualities that make it a viable smart grid application. A smart contract is unequivocally accountable for all actions performed in the application that has been prototyped, designed, written, and developed to accomplish this application.

Smartgrids should possess three crucial characteristics which include they should be local, self-contained, and intelligent. Being, they can furnish energy for local customers. Smartgrids are subtly distinguished from central grids on the ground of transmission and distribution lines to expedite central networks to move electricity from power plants over humongous destinations.

Certain bits of aggregated electricity are decimated and evaporated in transmission; delivering power from distance is uneconomical and imprudent. The ruined electricity is speculated to be in orders of 8-15%. A Smartgrid fixes this inefficiency by installing generators close to or inside the building that serves to produce electricity locally (Table 1).

Table 1. Traditional vs. smart grid

Entity	Traditional model	smart grid
Power generators	Centralized	More decentralized
Source of power	Hydrocarbon (natural gas, coal, oil)	Renewable energy
Transaction	Consumers purchase energy from power companies	A direct transaction between generators and consumers
Costing	Government or power company set prices	Every generator can set their price
Payment	Postpaid and prepaid	Prepaid

2 Literature Survey

This section presents a systematic literature review of different blockchain-based energy applications. Table 2 summarizes the contribution, approaches and applications of the studied chapter.

Table 2. A brief overview of blockchain-based solutions for the smart grid

Work	Contribution	Approach	Applications
[4]	A distributed ledger powered by blockchain that stores data from smart meters, which are considered to be energy transactions and can be used to balance the supply and demand of energy	Smart contract, Ethereum platform, and Proof of Stake	Decentralized application management
[5]	Using a permissioned blockchain in the smart grid to guarantee energy security and privacy (traceable and transparent energy usage)	Authorization method, smart contract, and voting-based consensus	Transparent energy usage
[6]	A blockchain-based energy scheduling system that protects privacy framework for energy service providers	Smart contract, and PoS consensus	Demand and supply of energy
[7]	A consortium-based energy blockchain	Smart contract, and PoS consensus	Demand and supply energy
[8]	A blockchain-enabled system deployment for proof-of-concept. Energy price negotiations using private and secure energy transactions	Messaging Streams, PoW, Elliptic Curve Digital Signature Algorithm (ECDSA)	Energy trading
[9]	A blockchain consortium for effective, adaptable, and secure energy trading	PoS, smart contract	Smart grid energy trading
[10]	A blockchain-enabled hierarchical authentication mechanism that rewards EVs and protects privacy in energy transactions over V2G networks	Elliptic curve cryptography (ECC), PBFT consensus algorithm	Energy trading in Vehicle

(continued)

Table 2. (*continued*)

Work	Contribution	Approach	Applications
[11]	A crowdsourced energy system and energy trading model supported by blockchain	Redundant Byzantine Fault Tolerance (RBFT), permissioned blockchain	P2P energy trading, and energy market
[12]	Using blockchain to monitor the smart grid for data transparency between electricity providers and consumers	Smart contract	Smart grid controlling
[13]	A blockchain-based approach combined with contract theory to create a secure framework for charging electric vehicles that includes an innovative energy allocation method and an optimal scheduling algorithm	Reputation-based DBFT consensus, and smart contract	Electric vehicles charging services
[14]	A decentralized, transparent, and privacy-preserving charging coordination system for ESUs like batteries and EVs that runs on the blockchain	Smart contract, Knapsack algorithm	ESUs charging
[15]	To improve the security of transactions between electric vehicles and charging stations, a decentralized security model called LNSC based on blockchain has been developed	A smart contract, elliptic curve cryptography	EVs and their charging
[16]	A blockchain-assisted automated protocol that protects user privacy and searches for the best charging station takes into account both energy prices and the location of EVs	Smart contract	EVs charging management

(*continued*)

Table 2. (*continued*)

Work	Contribution	Approach	Applications
[17]	A blockchain-based proportional-fairness control framework for encouraging distributed energy resources to contribute to microgrid voltage regulation	Smart contract, PoW	Voltage control in microgrid
[18]	A distributed voltage regulation algorithm for a transactive energy system based on the blockchain	Smart contract	Grid operation services
[2]	Decentralized microgrid electricity transactions based on a blockchain and continuous double auction (CDA) allow for independent transactions between distributed generations (DG) and consumers	Multi-signature, PoS	Electricity transactions

3 Implementation

As a fresh approach to integrating green and renewable energy technology into the current electricity infrastructure, the smart grid idea was put out. As a result, the Internet-connected smart grid, also known as the energy Internet, is ingeniously paving the stage for the widespread availability of electricity.

The creation of a sustainable society in smart cities is the most coveted objective of these improvements. A traditional centralized grid system, in contrast, could find it difficult to integrate and manage a huge number of growing connections. As a result, the topological status of the smart grid is changing from centralized to decentralized. On the other hand, blockchain offers a number of advantageous characteristics that make it a workable smart grid application.

Figure 1 depicts the layout of a smart grid framework. The microcontroller is the primary element of the smart grid system. With just a few lines of Python code, the Ethereum library enables microcontrollers to create and sign Ethereum transactions. This gives programmers the ability to leverage Smart Contracts, connect quickly to the Ethereum blockchain, and mashup gadgets with decentralized applications.

This library provides a high-level interface, enabling anyone to start using blockchain and securing any type of distributed application. All acts taken in the application that has been prototyped, created, written, and built to complete this application are without a doubt responsible for a smart contract.

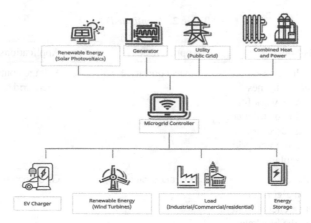

Fig. 1. Design of a local grid framework based on blockchain technology

The distributed grid application smart contract will be further explained in the part that follows:

3.1 Smart Contract for Grid-Distributed Application

Figure 2 depicts the design of a smart contract. The contract's name, data and state variables, constructors, modifiers, and functions are its five main sections. Any valid name may be used as a contact name. The variables that contain the pertinent information are data and state variables. State variables are persistent variables that are kept in contract storage on the blockchain. There can only be one builder listed on a contract. Once a contract has been established, the function Object() { [native code]} code is run in order to initialize the contract state. The completed code is deployed to the blockchain following the execution of the function Object() { [native code]} code. Modifiers are used to change how a function behaves. For instance, to give a function a requirement. The final section of Fig. 2 lists many functions. They are tailored to tasks. For instance, the function approval's () objective is to verify the producer or consumer before each transaction.

Similarly, other functions: production (), demand_elctricity () transfer (), demand_elctricity (), total_consumption (), Get_total_used (), Get_production, Get_total_generation (), Get_information () have their own specific tasks.

A smart contract is a self-executing program that runs and causes events to occur. The sublime text 3 editor is used to create the smart contract. Run, deploy, and test the smart contract functionality using the Remix Ethereum IDE. The smart contract code for distributed grid applications is shown in Fig. 3. Version 0.4.25 of Solidity is compatible with the application.

```
// smart contract name
contract Microgrid_SmartContract
{
.....
.....}
```

```
// variables (data and state) or
structure
address private owner
struct clientinfo
{//contains different variables
..........
}
```

```
//constructor as a special function
that is used to initialize the state
variable
constructor() public {......}
 modirs // to check the condition
require(..)
```

```
// 9 functions
function approval(...)
function production(...)
function transfer(...)
function demand_electricity()
function total_consumption()
function Get_total_used(...)
function Get_production(...)
function Get_total_generation(...)
function Get_information(...)
```

Fig. 2. Design of a smart grid smart contract

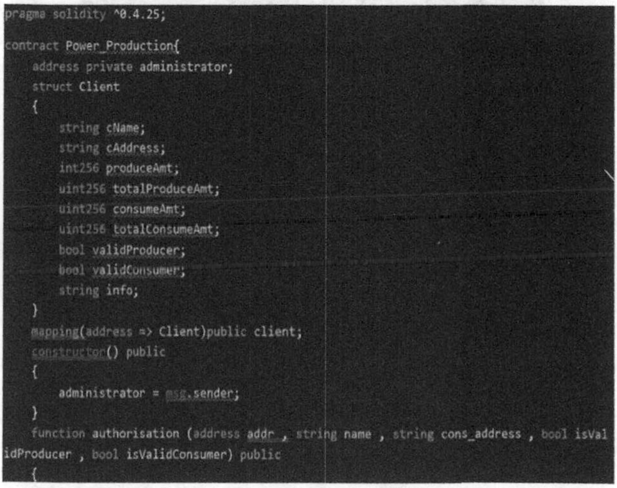

```solidity
pragma solidity ^0.4.25;

contract Power_Production{
    address private administrator;
    struct Client
    {
        string cName;
        string cAddress;
        int256 produceAmt;
        uint256 totalProduceAmt;
        uint256 consumeAmt;
        uint256 totalConsumeAmt;
        bool validProducer;
        bool validConsumer;
        string info;
    }
    mapping(address => Client)public client;
    constructor() public
    {
        administrator = msg.sender;
    }
    function authorisation (address addr , string name , string cons_address , bool isVal
idProducer , bool isValidConsumer) public
    {
```

Fig. 3. Smart contract code for smart grid distributed application

4   Results

This section presents the result of different functions of smart contract (refer to Figs. 4, 5, and 6).

Fig. 4. Authorization and consumeAmount function outputs

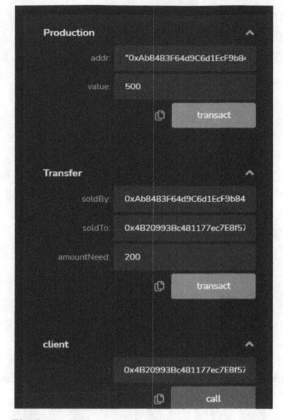

Fig. 5. Production, transfer and client function outputs

Fig. 6. GetInformation, getProduction and GetTotalGeneration function outputs

5 Conclusion

The chapter discusses different blockchain applications in smart city reference. Various applications are healthcare, cryptocurrency, certificate verification systems etc. [19–21]. Electricity is very important for a smart city. Hence, in this chapter, a framework for smart grid application has been designed. Further, a smart contract has been designed and developed for smart grid application. Different function outputs present that all functions of the smart grid application are working properly.

6 Future Scope

We can extend the application by implementing other smart contracts for the smart city such as verifying the education certificates, better waste management in the city and smart healthcare management in the city. In this way, we can make our city smarter. Apart from that they are applicable in financial transactions and reduce the cost of transactions by applying optimizing techniques [22, 23].

References

1. Malsa, N., Vyas, V., Gautam, J., Ghosh, A., Shaw, R.N.: CERTbchain: a step-by-step approach towards building a blockchain based distributed application for certificate verification system. In: 2021 IEEE 6th International Conference on Computing, Communication and Automation (ICCCA), pp. 800–806 (2021)
2. Malsa, N., Vyas, V., Gautam, J., Shaw, R.N., Ghosh, A.: Framework and smart contract for blockchain enabled certificate verification system using robotics. In: Bianchini, M., Simic, M., Ghosh, A., Shaw, R.N. (eds.) Machine Learning for Robotics Applications. SCI, vol. 960, pp. 125–138. Springer, Singapore (2021). https://doi.org/10.1007/978-981-16-0598-7_10
3. Pop, C., Cioara, T., Antal, M., Anghel, I., Salomie, I., Bertoncini, M.: Blockchain based decentralized management of demand response programs in smart energy grids. Sensors **18**(1), 162 (2018)
4. Gai, K., Wu, Y., Zhu, L., Xu, L., Zhang, Y.: Permissioned blockchain and edge computing empowered privacy-preserving smart grid networks. IEEE Internet Things J. **6**(5), 7992–8004 (2019)
5. Tan, S., Wang, X., Jiang, C.: Privacy-preserving energy scheduling for escos based on energy blockchain network. Energies **12**(8), 1530 (2019)
6. Rajawat, A.S., Rawat, R., Barhanpurkar, K., Shaw, R.N., Ghosh, A.: Blockchain-based model for expanding IoT device data security. In: Bansal, J.C., Fung, L.C.C., Simic, M., Ghosh, A. (eds.) Advances in Applications of Data-Driven Computing. AISC, vol. 1319, pp. 61–71. Springer, Singapore (2021). https://doi.org/10.1007/978-981-33-6919-1_5
7. Aitzhan, N.Z., Svetinovic, D.: Security and privacy in decentralized energy trading through multi-signatures, blockchain and anonymous messaging streams. IEEE Trans. Dependable Secur. Comput. **15**(5), 840–852 (2016)
8. Malsa, N., Vyas, V., Gautam, J., Ghosh, A., Shaw, R.N.: CERTbchain: a step by step approach towards building a blockchain based distributed application for certificate verification system. In: 2021 IEEE 6th International Conference on Computing, Communication and Automation (ICCCA), 2021, pp. 800–806 (2021). https://doi.org/10.1109/ICCCA52192.2021.9666311
9. Anwar, A., Goyal, S.B., Ghosh, A.: Tracking clinical trials and enhancement of security & control with blockchain for medical record. In: 2021 IEEE 6th International Conference on Computing, Communication and Automation (ICCCA), 2021, pp. 632–636 (2021). https://doi.org/10.1109/ICCCA52192.2021.9666276
10. Wang, S., Taha, A.F., Wang, J., Kvaternik, K., Hahn, A.: Energy crowdsourcing and peer-to-peer energy trading in blockchain-enabled smart grids. IEEE Trans. Syst. Man Cybern. Syst. **49**(8), 1612–1623 (2019)
11. Wan, J., Li, J., Imran, M., Li, D.: A blockchain-based solution for enhancing security and privacy in smart factory. IEEE Trans. Industr. Inf. **15**(6), 3652–3660 (2019)
12. Su, Z., Wang, Y., Xu, Q., Fei, M., Tian, Y.-C., Zhang, N.: A secure charging scheme for electric vehicles with smart communities in energy blockchain. IEEE Internet Things J. **6**(3), 4601–4613 (2018)
13. Baza, M., Nabil, M., Ismail, M., Mahmoud, M., Serpedin, E., Ashiqur Rahman, M.: Blockchain-based charging coordination mechanism for smart grid energy storage units. In: 2019 IEEE International Conference on Blockchain (Blockchain), pp. 504–509 (2019)
14. Knirsch, F., Unterweger, A., Engel, D.: Privacy-preserving blockchain-based electric vehicle charging with dynamic tariff decisions. Comput. Sci. Res. Dev. **33**(1–2), 71–79 (2017). https://doi.org/10.1007/s00450-017-0348-5
15. Munsing, E., Mather, J., Moura, S.: Blockchains for decentralized optimization of energy resources in microgrid networks. In: 2017 IEEE Conference on Control Technology and Applications (CCTA), pp. 2164–2171. IEEE (2017)

16. Danzi, P., Angjelichinoski, M., Stefanovic, C., Popovski, P.: Distributed proportional-fairness control in microgrids via blockchain smart contracts. In: 2017 IEEE International Conference on Smart Grid Communications (SmartGridComm), pp. 45–51. IEEE (2017)
17. Saxena, S., Farag, H., Turesson, H., Kim, H.M.: Blockchain based grid operation services for transactive energy systems. arXiv preprint arXiv:1907.08725 (2019)
18. Rajawat, A.S., Bedi, P., Goyal, S.B., Shaw, R.N., Ghosh, A., Aggarwal, S.: AI and blockchain for healthcare data security in smart cities. In: Piuri, V., Shaw, R.N., Ghosh, A., Islam, R. (eds.) AI and IoT for Smart City Applications. SCI, vol. 1002, pp. 185–198. Springer, Singapore (2022). https://doi.org/10.1007/978-981-16-7498-3_12
19. Malsa, N., Vyas, V., Gautam, J.: Blockchain platforms and interpreting the effects of bit-coin pricing on cryptocurrencies. In: Sharma, T.K., Ahn, C.W., Verma, O.P., Panigrahi, B.K. (eds.) Soft Computing: Theories and Applications. AISC, vol. 1380, pp. 137–147. Springer, Singapore (2022). https://doi.org/10.1007/978-981-16-1740-9_13
20. Pathak, S., et al.: Blockchain-based academic certificate verification system—a review. In: Advanced Computing and Intelligent Technologies, pp. 527–539 (2022)
21. Pathak, S., Gupta, V., Malsa, N., Ghosh, A., Shaw, R.N.: Smart contract for academic certificate verification using ethereum. In: Shaw, R.N., Das, S., Piuri, V., Bianchini, M. (eds) Advanced Computing and Intelligent Technologies, vol. 914, LNEE, pp. 369–384. Springer, Singapore (2022). https://doi.org/10.1007/978-981-19-2980-9_29
22. Masla, N., et al.: Reduction in gas cost for blockchain enabled smart contract. In: 2021 IEEE 4th International Conference on Computing, Power and Communication Technologies (GUCON). IEEE (2021)
23. Malsa, N., Vyas, V., Gautam, J.: RMSE calculation of LSTM models for predicting prices of different cryptocurrencies Int. J. Syst. Assur. Eng. Manage. 1–9 (2021). https://doi.org/10.1007/s13198-021-01431-1

A Predictive Energy Saving Technique for 5G Network Base Stations

Prashant Shrivastava$^{(\boxtimes)}$ and Sachin Patel

Department of CSE, SAGE University, Indore, M.P, India
prashantaug1@gmail.com

Abstract. In Cellular Network Base Stations data utilization depend on various factors. Data utilization patterns by using Machine Learning (ML) algorithms can be studied. Multiple servers are operational in Base Stations at full capacity to ensure 24 × 7 services however the actual utilization of resources may be less as per the demand for data services in the area. Hence, the server hardware resource allocation can be controlled (linked) as per requirement during the day. To achieve this historical cellular traffic data can be used for identifying trends and patterns which is based on activities in the area. In this chapter, the aim is to design a resource scheduling method based on machine learning and the same can be used for preserving power consumption in cellular base stations. An experimental study between popular ML approaches is done comparing the performance of unsupervised & supervised learning algorithms. Further Long Sort Term Memory (LSTM) & ANN model training is done for predicting future workload for the next 24 h & 7 days. Thus, a scheduling algorithm has been proposed based on a predicted 24-hour workload, and a 7-day workload. This will switch OFF/ON the server hardware processing units in Base Stations based on the requirement, otherwise, in a normal scenario, these server units remain idle and consume power. The experimental data is refereed from the Kaggle repository for 4G (LTE Traffic Prediction). As per the theoretical and basic experimental analysis, we can say that the proposed technique will be able to reduce approx. 25% energy consumption by temporarily switching off the server devices.

Keywords: Traffic prediction · Deep learning algorithm · Machine learning supervised and unsupervised learning

1 Introduction

5G wireless technology will deliver higher data speeds, ultra-low latency, better reliability, massive network capacity and a more uniform user experience to more users. Higher performance and improved efficiency will open opportunity for new applications. 5G speeds will help to create applications which require less response times like near real-time video transmission for sporting events or security applications. In medical field online examinations, robotic surgery will get boost. ML and AI help in 5G networks to be predictive and have proactive approach. By integrating ML into 5G technology, intelligent base stations will be able to communicate faster and can take

R. N. Shaw et al. (Eds.): ICACIS 2022, CCIS 1749, pp. 695–705, 2023.
https://doi.org/10.1007/978-3-031-25088-0_61

decisions for themselves related to optimizations. Mobile devices will be able to create dynamically adaptable clusters based on learned data. This will improve the efficiency, latency, and reliability of network applications. This will involve a large number of new nodes deployment in the network and huge data will be generated for communication between devices. Software-Defined Networking (SDN) is an emerging architecture that is dynamic, manageable, cost-effective, and adaptable, making it ideal for the high-bandwidth, dynamic nature of today's applications. The ML techniques can analyze, group, classify, and forecast. In this chapter, we have studied the recent advancement in 5G applications using machine learning, then a model is proposed for predicting the data traffic in base station by using supervised & unsupervised learning techniques. Based on performance parameters a comparative analysis has been done. Finally, a proactive power optimization technique is proposed based on the predictive scheduling of the base station resources.

2 Related Work

During review of approximate 100 articles from various journals and conferences we selected 23 which were most relevant. Most of the work is related to location prediction, Base Station management & optimization, and feature selection. Work involving power consumption and cost optimization as key issues is also done. Exploring applications to improve the prediction accuracy are also discovered. We also explored articles to find the algorithms and prediction techniques for reference. The summary of the collected literature is presented in Fig. 1.

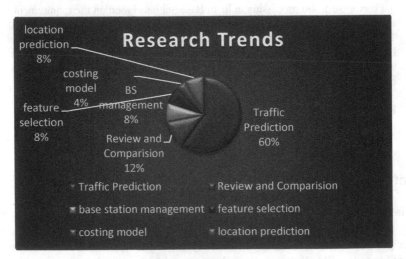

Fig. 1. Research trends

We have also identified the different natures of ML algorithms that are used in designing the required applications. The fractions of the contributions based on different kinds of algorithms used are shown in Fig. 2. In this diagram, we can see that deep learning techniques are utilized frequently now in these days for predictive data modeling. About 45% of applications are utilizing classical machine learning algorithms in terms of supervised and unsupervised learning techniques. In this study, we have investigated both classical techniques as well as deep learning-based techniques for accurate data prediction.

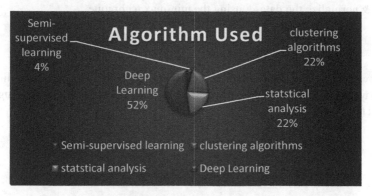

Fig. 2. Types of algorithms used

3 Evaluation of Classical Learning Techniques

We are focusing to compare different classical Machine Learning based prediction model which can accurately forecast the traffic load on base stations. An experimental model is prepared and given in Fig. 3.

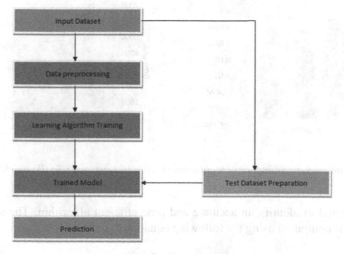

Fig. 3. Flow chart

In this experimental study, we used a dataset obtained from the Kaggle repository which is a wireless LTE network traffic data same was used for training and testing [29]. The entire dataset contains 497545 instances for training, and 9520 instances for validation. Data was for a period of 1-year duration from Oct 2017 to Oct 2018. The parameters were Date, Per Hour, cell name, and data traffic. Figure 4 shows the dataset sample. Data were cleaned and pre-processed. The target was to remove incomplete patterns & normalize the dataset using the min-max technique.

$$normVal = \frac{Value - min}{max - min}$$

Next we trained the different supervised and unsupervised learning models like ANN, SVM, Bays classifier, LR, FCM, SOM and k-means. Separate test & training dataset was used (Table 1).

	Date	Hour	CellName	Traffic
0	10/23/2017 0:00	7	Cell_001803	15.13867
1	10/23/2017 0:00	2	Cell_002303	2.05516
2	10/23/2017 0:00	7	Cell_004083	71.55308
3	10/23/2017 0:00	0	Cell_003781	557.98491
4	10/23/2017 0:00	3	Cell_000112	0.98166

Fig. 4. Data set with variables

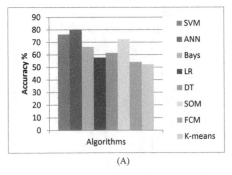 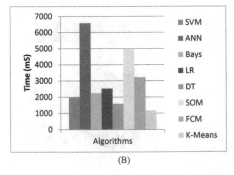

(A)   (B)

Fig. 5. (A) the mean performance of algorithms in terms of Accuracy (%) (B) training time (mS)

We targeted to identify an accurate and time efficient algorithm. The accuracy of algorithms is computed using the following equation

$$Mean\ Accuracy(\%) = 100 - \frac{1}{N}\sum_{i=1}^{N}\frac{|A_i - O_i|}{A_i} \times 100$$

Table 1. Algorithm used for training and testing

Input: Training dataset D, Testing dataset T, Selected learning algorithm L
Output: Predicted Value P, Error rate E

Process:
1. R_n = readTrainingData(D)
2. for(i = 1; i < n; i + +)
    a. if(D_i.elements == null)
        i. Remove(D_i)
    b. else
        i. PR.Add(D_i)
    c. end if
3. end for
4. T_{model} = L.Train(PR)
5. for(j = 0; j < T.length; j + +)
    a. P = T_{model}.Predict(T_j)
    b. E = P − T_{actual_j}
6. end for
7. Return P, E

Table 2. Performance of learning algorithms

S. No.	Algorithm	Accuracy	Time	Memory
1	SVM	76.14%	1961.57 MS	370.76 KB
2	Bays	66.15%	2237.85 MS	370.6 KB
3	Decision Tree	61.34%	1583.14 MS	463.74 KB
4	ANN	79.9%	6670.28 MS	483.4 KB
5	LR	57.64%	2515.14 MS	570.18 KB
6	SOM	72.38%	4983.14 MS	631.74 KB
7	k-Means	52.31%	1162.14 MS	385.28 KB
8	FCM	54.14%	3209.57 MS	555.67 KB

The accuracy is measured in terms of percentage (%) based on the actual and predicted values in Fig. 5 (A). All the algorithms show the similar trends of accuracy but in order ANN, SVM and SOM are giving higher accuracy which is greater than 70%. Results are shown in Table 2.

To compute the time taken for model training the following equation was used.

$$Time\ consumption = End\ time - Start\ Time$$

Results were measured in terms of milliseconds (mS). The time consumption is shown in Fig. 5 (B). While ANN and SOM are taking long training time same is found to be less for Decision Tree and K-Means. We also measured the space complexity of process, i.e the usage of main memory during training

$$Used\ Memory = total\ assigned - total\ free$$

The memory utilization is measured in terms of kilobytes (KB). As per observation SOM, FCM, LR consume higher amount of memory. Decision Tree, Bays and SVM algorithms are memory efficient. In unsupervised learning the k-means is also memory efficient technique. According to the given results in supervised learning SVM and ANN are two accurate algorithms and in unsupervised learning the SOM is having accurate results. However, the time and memory consumption of the SOM algorithm is higher. Finally, the SVM and ANN are time and memory expensive but are preferred due to high accuracy of result as per our requirement. In this section we have investigated the potential of classical ML techniques for workload prediction of cellular network. Next, we have proposed to employ algorithms with traffic load prediction model for different level of predictions.

4   Proposed Energy Efficient Workload Prediction

In this presented work we have aimed to design a predictive power scheduling technique for optimizing the power consumption in cellular base stations. The smart city enables the next generation facility and services therefore a significant number of devices are active by maintaining connectivity and communication among the different other levels of devices. All these devices are consuming a significant amount of power. We are focusing to optimize the power requirement of cellular base stations. However, this is a domain of green computing to minimize and optimizes the network and computing devices power consumption.

In order to prepare a suitable solution, we have proposed a new data model which consists of three phases:

1. **Predicting the trends of the possible workload:** in this phase, we have utilized the historical workload record for analysis. The analysis is performed using the ML algorithms and then after training the workload for the next 24 h and next week will be predicted.
2. **Categorizing the workload on base stations:** in this phase, the predicted workload is categorized in order to describe the workload in terms of low, mid, and high workload.
3. **Providing the schedule for activating and deactivating devices:** in this phase, a power-aware device scheduling algorithm is proposed for implementation.

4.1   Predicting the Trends of Workload

The proposed work is targeted for preparing a computing model which supports the scheduling of base station devices to minimize the power consumption of the base stations. In this context, the LTE dataset available in the Kaggle repository is used for analysis. This dataset consists of a total of 57 base stations. Additionally, for each base station, a one-year traffic load for per hour is available. The preprocessing of data consists of a grouping of the dataed. We first group the data according to the base station's unique ID, then the data is grouped according to date and time. Finally, we have sorted the data according to hours. Then, for simulation and demonstration of the proposed methodology we considered a single base station says ID. Next, we prepare two datasets based on 24 h based grouped data. Next, we train two popular prediction algorithms

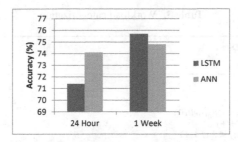

Fig. 6. Predictive accuracy (%)

namely Long Sort Term Memory (LSTM) and Artificial Neural Network (ANN). After training of the models, we made the prediction for one week and one complete day.

The Fig. 6 shows the mean prediction accuracy of both the algorithms. The prediction accuracy of both the algorithms has been measured using the formula discussed in previous section. According to the experimental observations we can see that for predicting the workload for 24 h the ANN provides higher accuracy on the other hand we also identified for one-week long prediction is effectively done by the LSTM.

4.2 Workload Categorization

In order to categorize the workload, we are performing a clustering of the data. But the proposed clustering technique utilizes the single attribute traffic in consideration. Thus, for each hour we calculate the mean of each hour workload. The per hour mean workload is measured based on:

$$W = \frac{1}{N} \sum_{i=1}^{N} w_i$$

where the w_i is defined as the workload of an hour for entire year, thus $w_i = \{w_1, w_2, \ldots, w_{365}\}$, additionally $i = \{1, 2, \ldots, 24\}$. The categorization process of the workload is defined using the following steps in Table 3.

4.3 Scheduling Algorithm

In this phase we are utilizing both the previously measured components thus we use the prediction of the LSTM and ANN. Additionally we make use the categorization of the workloads based on each hour of a day. The Fig. 7 indicates the clustered line which shows the threshold of traffic load and the green line demonstrate the workload predicted.

According to the maximum peak of the workload we provide a red line which demonstrates the maximum traffic can be possible in the base station. Traditionally, if the base station needs to serve then need to power on all the devices thus per hour maximum power is utilized. Let the entire devices will consume X amount of energy per hour, thus for 24 h. The total amount of energy consumption is X*24. But based on the clustered scheduling technique we can reduce the power consumption. In this context the following process is proposed as described in Table 4.

Table 3. Workload categorization

Input: workload dataset D
Output: categorized data C

Process:

1. $R_n = readDataset(D)$
2. $G_{n=24}^{m=365} = GroupData(R_n, CellID)$
3. $for(i = 1; i < n; i + +)$
   a. $for(j = 1; j < m; j + +)$
      i. $w = w + G_i^j$
   b. $end\ for$
   c. $W_i.Add\left(\frac{w}{m}\right)$
4. $end\ for$
5. $dmax = getMax(R_n)$
6. $for(i = 1; i < n; i + +)$
   a. $if(W_i \le dmax * 0.33)$
      i. $C.Add(Low, W_i)$
   b. $else\ if(W_i > dmax * 33\ \&\&\ W_i < dmax * 0.66)$
      i. $C.Add(mid, W_i)$
   c. $else$
      i. $C.Add(High, W_i)$
   d. End if
7. $end\ for$
8. Return C

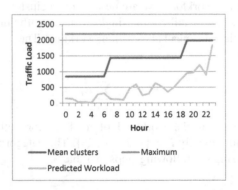

Fig. 7. Clustered load and predicted workload

4.4 Result Analysis

Based on the theoretical and experimental analysis we demonstrate the proposed model can preserve the energy by switch On and Off the additional devices. In both the scenarios i.e., 24 h-based prediction and one week advance prediction based scenarios is compared in Fig. 8 for both the implemented algorithms.

According to the given bar graph we found that the proposed model will able to reduce the power consumption in cellular base station. Moreover for 24 h-based prediction we can preserve approximately 27% of energy using the ANN based algorithm and for the 1-week scenario using LSTM can preserve the 28% of energy.

Table 4. Workload categorization

Input: predicted work load $pw_{N=24}$, categorized mean workload $C = \{high,, mid, low\}$
Output: scheduled power On / Off devices S

Process:

1. $for(i = 1; i < N, i + +)$
   a. $if(pw_i == low)$
      i. $S = TurnOff(D_{total} * 0.66)$
   b. $Else\ if(pw_i == mid)$
      i. $S = TurnOff(D_{total} * 0.33)$
   c. $Else\ if(pw_i == high)$
      i. $S = TurnON(D_{total})$
   d. $end\ if$
2. $end\ for$
3. Return S

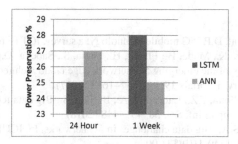

Fig. 8. Power preservation

5 Conclusion and Future Work

The proposed work is an experimental investigation of ML techniques for predicting and preserving the energy consumption in cellular base stations. Thus, the proposed work is motivated towards the green computing to preserve energy consumption in smart cities by reducing power consumption in base stations. Based on the analysis we concluded that the deep learning and ANN based technique provide higher accuracy in prediction of patterns. Finally based on obtained results & with the collected literature and experiments we proposed a three-step power optimization technique for cellular base stations. The first step includes the learning and then prediction of future workload on the different base stations. The next step includes the evaluation of historical records of the Base station to create low, mid and high category of work load based on per hour. The categorized data and the predicted workload are used to schedule the amount of power off machines for individual future hours. Based on experimental and theoretical investigation we found that proposed strategy can preserve approx. 28% of energy consumption as compared to present scenario when Base Station run on full capacity consuming maximum power. The proposed model is effective and promising but still there are some limitations which indicate to improve the proposed model with the following suggestions:

a. Need to investigate more on challenges w.r.t implementation & integration in the real time network scenario with multiple vendor equipment's in the live network. As per forecast how server can be automated to get dynamically switch off & on for specific time period.
b. Analysis is based on time series data, there can be an unpredicted situation, calamity etc. requiring server to get operational immediately with full capacity to meet unexpected surge of load i.e it should come out from OFF mode. This may require manual observation & intervention.
c. With expansion in the network and addition of new Base Stations in the area data utilization pattern of an individual Base Station will change. So continuous monitoring as well as training of model with latest data utilization pattern is must for accurate prediction results.

References

1. Mitra, R.N., Agrawal, D.P.: 5G mobile technology: a survey. ICT Express **1**, 132–137 (2015)
2. Taleb, T., Samdanis, K., Mada, B., Flinck, H., Dutta, S., Sabella, D.: On multi-access edge computing: a survey of the emerging 5G network edge cloud architecture and orchestration. IEEE Commun. Surv. Tutorials **19**(3), 1657–1681 (2017)
3. Oussous, A., Benjelloun, F.Z., Lahcen, A.A., Belfkih, S.: Big data technologies: a survey. J. King Saud Univ. Comput. Inf. Sci. **30**, 431–448 (2018)
4. Rashid, S., Razak, S.A.: Big data challenges in 5G networks. In: ICUFN, pp. 152–157. IEEE (2019). 978-1-7281-1340-1/19/$31.00
5. Álvarez, V.O., Faiza Bouchmal, J.F., Río, M.D.: Trusted 5G vehicular networks blockchains and content-centric networking. IEEE Veh. Technol. Mag. **13**(2), 121–127 (2018)
6. Zanella, A., Bui, N., Castellani, A., Vangelista, L., Zorzi, M.: Internet of Things for smart cities. IEEE Internet Things J. **1**(1), 22–32 (2014)
7. Palattella, M.R., et al.: Internet of Things in the 5G era: enablers, architecture and business models. IEEE J. Sel. CAreas Commun.**34**, 510–527 (2015)
8. Zahariadis, T., Sarakis, L., Voulkidis, A., Karkazis, P., Trakadas, P.: Preventive maintenance of critical infrastructures using 5G networks & drones. In: IEEE AVSS, August 2017, Lecce, Italy (2017). 978-1-5386-2939-0/17/$31.00
9. Wang, X., et al.: Spatio-temporal analysis and prediction of cellular traffic in metropolis. IEEE Trans. Mobile Comput. **18**(9), 2190–2202 (2019). https://doi.org/10.1109/TMC.2018.2870135
10. Li, R., Zhao, Z., Zheng, J., Mei, C., Cai, Y., Zhang, H.: The learning and prediction of application-level traffic data in cellular networks. arXiv:1606.04778v2 [cs.NI], 28 March 2017
11. Huang, C.W., Chiang, C.T., Li, Q.: A study of deep learning networks on mobile traffic forecasting. IEEE (2017). 978-1-5386-3531-5/17/$31.00
12. Banerjee, A., et al.: Building of efficient communication system in smart city using wireless sensor network through hybrid optimization technique. In: Piuri, V., Shaw, R.N., Ghosh, A., Islam, R. (eds.) AI and IoT for Smart City Applications. SCI, vol. 1002, pp. 15–30. Springer, Singapore (2022). https://doi.org/10.1007/978-981-16-7498-3_2
13. Yang, B., Guo, W., Chen, B., Yang, G., Zhang, J.: Estimating mobile traffic demand using Twitter. IEEE Wirel. Commun. Lett. **5**(4), 380–383 (2016)

14. Sultan, K., Ali, H., Zhang, Z.: Call detail records driven anomaly detection and traffic prediction in mobile cellular networks, vol. 6, pp. 2169–3536. IEEE (2018)
15. Dawoud, S., Uzun, A., Gondor, S., Kupper, A.: Optimizing the power consumption of mobile networks based on traffic prediction. In: 2014 IEEE 38th Annual International Computers, Software and Applications Conference (2014). https://doi.org/10.1109/COMPSAC.2014.38
16. Feng, J., Chen, X., Gao, R., Zeng, M., Li, Y.: DeepTP: an end-to-end neural network for mobile cellular traffic prediction. In: IEEE Network. IEEE, November/December 2018. 0890-8044/18/$25.00
17. He, H., Qiao, Y., Gao, S., Yang, J., Guo, J.: Prediction of user mobility pattern on a network traffic analysis platform. In: MobiArch 2015, 7 September 2015, Paris, France. ACM (2015). ISBN 978-1-4503-3695-6/15/09
18. Nie, L., Wang, X., Wan, L., Yu, S., Song, H., Jiang, D.: Network traffic prediction based on deep belief network and spatiotemporal compressive sensing in wireless mesh backbone networks. Hindawi Wirel. Commun. Mobile Comput. **2018**, Article ID 1260860, 10 (2018)
19. Hua, Y., Zhao, Z., Li, R., Chen, X., Liu, Z., Zhang, H.: Traffic prediction based on random connectivity in deep learning with long short-term memory. arXiv:1711.02833v2 [cs.NI], 3 April 2018
20. Smail, G., Weijia, J.: Techno-economic analysis and prediction for the deployment of 5G mobile network. IEEE (2017). 978-1-5090-3672-1/17/$31.00
21. Zhang, C., Zhang, H., Qiao, J., Yuan, D., Zhang, M.: Deep transfer learning for intelligent cellular traffic prediction based on cross-domain big data. IEEE J. Sel. Areas Commun. **37**(6), 1389–1401 (2019)
22. Zhang, S., et al.: Traffic prediction based power saving in cellular networks: a machine learning method. In: © 2017 Association for Computing Machinery. ACM (2017). ISBN 978-1-4503-5490-5/17/11
23. Rajawat, A.S., Bedi, P., Goyal, S.B., Shaw, R.N., Ghosh, A.: Reliability analysis in cyber-physical system using deep learning for smart cities industrial IoT network node. In: Piuri, V., Shaw, R.N., Ghosh, A., Islam, R. (eds.) AI and IoT for Smart City Applications. SCI, vol. 1002, pp. 157–169. Springer, Singapore (2022). https://doi.org/10.1007/978-981-16-7498-3_10
24. Iqbal, M.F., Zahid, M., Habib, D., John, L.K.: Efficient prediction of network traffic for real-time applications. Hindawi J. Comput. Netw. Commun. **2019**, Article ID 4067135, 11 (2019)
25. Azari, A., Papapetrou, P., Denic, S., Peters, G.: User traffic prediction for proactive resource management: learning-powered approaches. arXiv:1906.00951v1 [cs.NI], 9 May 2019
26. Gebrie, H., Farooq, H., Imran, A.: What machine learning predictor performs best for mobility prediction in cellular networks. IEEE (2019). 978-1-7281-2373-8/19/$31.00
27. Chavhan, S., Venkataram, P.: Prediction based traffic management in a metropolitan area. J. Traffic Transp. Eng. (Engl. Ed.) **7**, 447–466 (2020)
28. Zhang, K., Chuai, G., Gao, W., Liu, X., Maimaiti, S., Si, Z.: A new method for traffic fore-casting in urban wireless communication network. EURASIP J. Wirel. Commun. Networking **2019**(1), 1–12 (2019). https://doi.org/10.1186/s13638-019-1392-6
29. Shrivastava, P.: Selection of efficient and accurate prediction algorithm for employing real time 5G data load prediction. In: 2021 IEEE 6th International Conference on Computing, Communication and Automation (ICCCA) (2021)

Cursor Motion Control Using Eye Tracking and Computer Vision

Anshu Kumar Ray[1], Subrata Sahana[1(✉)] ⓘD, Sanjoy Das[2], and Indrani Das[3] ⓘD

[1] Department of Computer Science and Engineering, Sharda University, Greater Noida, India
2020423324.anshu@pg.sharda.ac.in, subrata.sahana@sharda.ac.in
[2] Department of Computer Science, Indira Gandhi National Tribal University-RCM, Kangpokpi, India
[3] Department of Computer Science, Assam University, Silchar, India

Abstract. This research describes an algorithm that performs cursor function while allowing humans and computers to connect without using their hands. It provides a better option to the standard cursor-controlled computer. By using computer vision to scan different facial expressions and matching them to pre-stored expressions, functions can be performed in responses to the movements. That technique is going to allow bodily challenged humans use their face and eye movements to perform cursor tasks. They can lefts-press, rights-press, higher scrolls, and moves pointer lefts and rights. Webcams, numpys, dlibs, but also some few others more fundamental study are all needed by the system.

Keywords: Computers interfaces · Computers visions · Electroencephalogram · Electrocardiograms · Face detection

1 Introduction

In the introduction in 1938 with computer changes the ways [2] today is our times. It was lived past a lot of changes. At first, our tasks was to solves a problem or perform words clarifying it have come such longs ways become all-important part of their real lives, application using technical individual, [3] as surfing it internets, connecting's worlds across socials media, and controlling the big machine in plants utilising a Correct or well-timed processes [6–8, 10]. People with to use his fingertips the cursor and keyboard and eyes to view what is on the display [19]. Connecting them with technologies or makes it computers-compatibles may provide them with a glimmers of optimisms for studying and contribute to their livelihood [12, 14, 16, 18]. Experts are trying find a way to let the disabled engage with computers utilizing signals including electroencephalogram (EEG) from of electrooculogram, brains, and facials muscles signals (EMG) (EOG). Techniques such as limbus, pupils, and retina monitoring, lenses contacts technique, eye, pupils reflect relation, and corneal, pupil reflect connection have also been used [9]. These approaches necessitate its uses of electrodes or a connection which necessitates bodily connections the top, make it impracticable can easily uses computers [7]. This text of voice function, that speaks display, now allows i the blind to use the computer. All

© The Author(s), under exclusive license to Springer Nature Switzerland AG 2023
R. N. Shaw et al. (Eds.): ICACIS 2022, CCIS 1749, pp. 706–714, 2023.
https://doi.org/10.1007/978-3-031-25088-0_62

of the costly technology is used in the technique performed in this chapter. Moreover, any device must create a direct connection with the user [20]. It only allows the It's a computers with a webcams. A simple, quick, or simple solution. The customer's real-time photos are tested using the coder and determines the type of actions to be taken attempting to compare them to previously saved expressions to determines the operations to be carried out and to takes parameters when necessary [6, 12, 19]. For example, when you move the pointer, the relative positions changes. Positions about the internal positions show the cursor's movements directions.

2 Literature Survey

In this paper [1, 2] mainly throws light on developing a computer vision eye motion tracking system and the experiment out in this manners the human can access [2] the computer cursor from his/her eye instead of the olds conventional manners from mouse and keyboard. The paper [3] mainly throws the light on how the techniques which are available today are more sophisticated than 15 years before but they are very from the perfect technique [10]. In this we have looks upon the issues of concerning problems like head movements trackers for sensitivity is not perfect and the equipment's That's far too early for it to lose it calibrate [9]. A small number of people and organizations are unable to use computers. When taking into account the disabilities of the differently abled, [5] it makes more logical to give a readily available computer operating system in this scenario. The human eye can be used to substitute computer and application hardware in some cases [11]. This work used an Internet protocol camera to capture an image of an eye frame for cursor movement. We should first consider the role of in this approach. One by one, a human computer interference system is being implemented [8]. In past, peoples computers interactions system placed mouse or keyboard as in systems components [7]. Those afflicted from a particular illness or condition are unable to use computers [15]. The concept of using computers to control their eyes is extremely useful to people who are handicapped or impaired. Form of controls also avoids need for others to help with the computer [8]. This method will be especially useful for persons who are unable to use their hands and must count on their eyes instead. The cursor's movement is proportional to the pupil's centre. As a result, the first step would be to find the pupil's centre point.

3 Proposed Work

The two most basic mouse operations are mouse clicks and mouse movements [8]. Advanced technology substitutes cursor movements with eye movements with the aid of open Computer Vision [20]. The cursor buttons can be activated by facials motion, blinking eyes, opening mouth, etc. [10] or moving the head. A new camera cursor is included in this variant. That is powered by a Bias face detection using a 3d image algorithm. A personals computer achieves human contact through faster's visual facial tracking due to its configuration tool [20]. Provides a suitable alternative for operation without the use of one's hands. This face scanner is based on a 3D models operate cursor or conduct cursor motions. Estimating help when using a face display contexts because it provides important natural computer interface indications. When used in combination with the time, [6] the camera cursor structure operates as a left click despite the fact that works as a rights clicks events. Real-times eye-gaze assessment technique is uses an eye-controlled cursor to assist impaired [3]. In systems is built idea of accurately detecting and tracking gaze with a low-resolution camera at a reduced cost and without the use of special equipment [2]. The input from the webcam is first supplied into the system, which then detects the face. The system will then keep notes of the face's location as well as its characteristics.

$$EAR = \frac{(p2 - p6) + (p3 - p5)}{2(p1 - p4)} \tag{1}$$

3.1 Methodology

Find a person's face using a face detection technology in this problem [19]. A situation with the mouth and eyeball are caught. When its image is captured to manage cursor function [7] such like lefts-press, rights-press, or cursors movements. Technique does not need any use of special hardware or sensor. It's a system that doesn't require you to use your hands. Really is usefully to people [9]. To start, we must open the lips to enable the cursor control mode. To rotate the cursor left or right, all we must do is rotate our head in the cursor's planned direction of motion as in Eq. 1.

3.2 Implementation

The following procedure was used to achieve mouse movement by pupil and mouth movement:-

A. *Face Detection*

Your client must face its lens in same direction as the camera. Shown in order to display a clean and accurate image Fig. 1. The individual's image is taken with the system's pre-installed webcam and processed with Pythons Fig. 2. Display the picture obtained with a camera.

Dlib offers a pre-trained datasets called iBUG 300-W; it has a total of 68 values map a person's faces [12]. The facial detector recognizes and tracks significant landmarks on a person's face. Figure 3 shows it has a total of 68 values.

B. *Eye Detection*

Eye-Aspect-Ratio is used to detect eyes (EAR). Used it to see if the person's eye in the video frame was flickering or not.

When we go in a clockwise route as indicated in, every eyeball is represented 6 coordinates (p1 − p6), with p1 being [15] p2 − p6 are the positions of the left portion of the eye. Being position properly (Fig. 4).

- p1 − p6 are spots in eye ball
- p2 − p6 or the spacing linking the eyes on the vertical plane is represented by p3 − p5.
- p1 − p4 represents the space linking your eyes on the horizontal plane.

Fig. 1. Eye-mouse configuration on the system

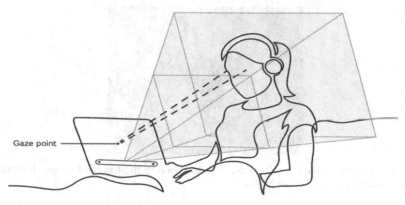

Fig. 2. Images captured using the webcam

As the eyeball is open, the eyeball-aspect-ratio (EAR) is stable, but when the flickering starts, it tends to zero shown in Fig. 5.

C. *Mouth Detection*

The mouth-aspects-ratios (MAR), like the eye-aspect-ratio, is being used to detect [4] if the mouths is open or closed shown in Fig. 6.

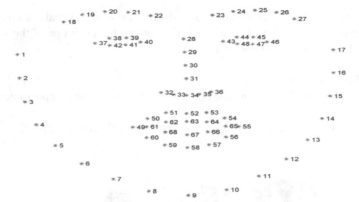

Fig. 3. 68 Facials values points

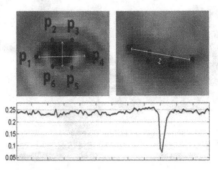

Fig. 4. Eyes are related six face landmarks.

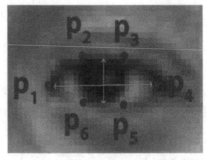

Fig. 5. Eye is open in the top-left corner. Eye is closed in the top-right corner. Bottom: The eyes-Aspects-Ratios above times is plotted.

D. Algorithm

The flowchart depicts the algorithm that was used as shown in Fig. 7.

- At 30 fps, the camera continues to scan for photos. If it identifies a face, [8] it determines not if the facial adjustment system is available activating and deactivate.
- If that's the case, activated, collects for a various directions given by moving his face in line with the orders given.

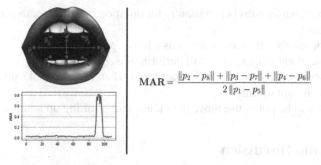

$$MAR = \frac{\|p_2 - p_8\| + \|p_3 - p_7\| + \|p_4 - p_6\|}{2\,\|p_1 - p_5\|}$$

Fig. 6. Mouths-aspects-ratios

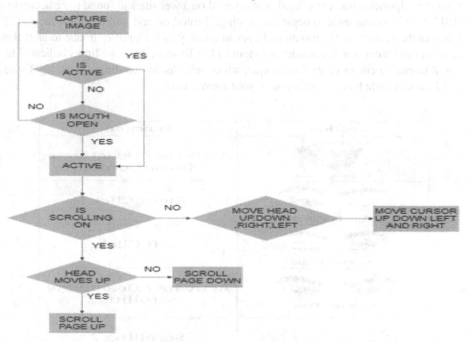

Fig. 7. Flowcharts of the algorithms

- To activate the scrolling feature, [9] he must blink all her eyeballs as her mouth down and up in trying for scroll.
- Customer will just close his eyes to move the cursor.
- To clicking, he'll blink one eye in the position of the mouse he wants to push. [2] He must open his mouse once more to deactivate cursor control.

E. Usage

Figure 8 showed the algorithm's various modes and functions. We discussed the action and its role in this article we used in our algorithm.

- We must open our mouths [4] constantly for duration of time to activate or deactivate mouse control.
- Blinking the user's lefts eyes function as a lefts - press.
- Blinking the client's rights eyes will perform as a right-s press.
- Trying to scroll will be activated or deactivated when the user looks up his or her eye for [18] an amount of time.
- The face would be put to use move the mouse and scrolling up and down.

4   Result and Discussion

When the algorithm was completed, it was tested on a website and found to be accurate. [19] That video was used to begin this testing. Turned on and looking for a face. [12] It marks the borders of the mouth and eyes as quickly as it identifies a face to alert the customer of places it will consider for inputs. [12] To start, open the lip as indicated in Fig. 8 to enable cursor control technique, which will display reading inputs. [2] There will be a rectangle box to notify you of your movements.

Action	Function
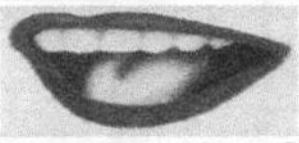 Opening Mouth	Activate / Deactivate Mouse Control
 Right Eye Wink	Right Click
 Left Eye Wink	Left Click
 Squinting Eyes	Activate / Deactivate Scrolling
 Head Movements (Pitch and Yaw)	Scrolling / Cursor Movement

Fig. 8. Activity and its various functions

From the starting place, lines will just be created in the directional movement, showing the distance covered from the center. To move cursor on the screen left or right, all we must do is reposition all heads cursor's the desired course of movement.

We must blink our eye into to the camera to start the scrolling form, [2] which also will display scrolling mode on beginning. You now can move your head from side to side to move the page up and down, accordingly. For lefts-press and rights-press, we should blinking lefts eye and rights eye, accordingly.

- When cursor movement is engaged by open mouths for a given period of time, the pointer moves to the left.
- When cursor control is engaged by open mouth for a given period of time, [3] the cursor moves in the right direction.
- Whenever cursor control is enabled by extending mouths for a particular amount of time, it shows scroll functionality in a negative motion. [12] Staring eyeball also engages timing and scroll options.
- When cursor movement is activated by open lips for a fixed amount of time, and scroll modes is similarly activated by blinking eyes, the scroll function moves upwards.

5 Conclusions

A technology for contactless mouse cursor has been designed and tested [12]. It is simple to use and also has a variety of applications [13]. Simple face-based mouse cursor movements and eye-based modes shifting to allow or disable scroll [10]. To click, I'm blinking. It can be used in a range of methods [2]. It can be applied in the education of physically disabled people because it allows that rather than scribbling, they should text hands. Disabled people would be able find work as a result of this [4]. It can be used in vehicles to monitor the vehicle's idleness by detecting sleepy signals such as blinking [4]. Its also applicable to games and the Internet of Things.

References

1. Shin, G., Chun, J.: Vision-based multimodal human computer interface based on parallel tracking of eye and hand motion. In: 2007 International Conference on Convergence Information Technology (ICCIT 2007), pp. 2443–2448. IEEE, November 2007
2. Ali, N., Khan, N.Y., Imran, A.S.: Controlling mouse through eyes. In: 2007 International Conference on Emerging Technologies, pp. 179–183. IEEE, November 2007
3. Meena, K., Kumar, M., Jangra, M.: Controlling mouse motions using eye tracking using computer vision. In: 2020 4th International Conference on Intelligent Computing and Control Systems (ICICCS), pp. 1001–1005. IEEE, May 2020
4. Ujbányi, T.: Examination of eye-hand coordination using computer mouse and hand tracking cursor control. In: 2018 9th IEEE International Conference on Cognitive Infocommunications (CogInfoCom), pp. 000353–000354. IEEE, August 2018
5. Rose, J., Liu, Y., Awad, A.: Biometric authentication using mouse and eye movement data. In: 2017 IEEE Security and Privacy Workshops (SPW), pp. 47–55. IEEE, May 2017
6. Mohamed, A.W., Koggalage, R.: Control of mouse movements using human facial expressions. In: 2007 Third International Conference on Information and Automation for Sustainability, pp. 13–18. IEEE, December 2007
7. Hegde, V.N., Ullagaddimath, R.S., Kumuda, S.: Low cost eye based human computer interface system (Eye controlled mouse). In: 2016 IEEE Annual India Conference (INDICON), pp. 1–6. IEEE, December 2016
8. Yang, M.H., Ahuja, N.: Detecting human faces in colour images. In: Proceedings 1998 International Conference on Image Processing. ICIP98 (Cat. No. 98CB36269), vol. 1, pp. 127–130. IEEE, October 1998

9. Chau, M., Betke, M.: Real time eye tracking and blink detection with USB cameras. Boston University Computer Science Department (2005)

10. Zheng, N., Paloski, A., Wang, H.: An efficient user verification system via mouse movements. In: Proceedings of the 18th ACM conference on Computer and Communications Security, pp. 139–150, October 2011

11. Ayudhya, C.D.N., Srinark, T.: A method for real-time eye blink detection and its application. In: The 6th International Joint Conference on Computer Science and Software Engineering (JCSSE), pp. 25–30, May 2009

12. Abdulin, E., Komogortsev, O.: User eye fatigue detection via eye movement behavior. In: Proceedings of the 33rd annual ACM Conference Extended Abstracts on Human Factors in Computing Systems, pp. 1265–1270, April 2015

13. Hansen, D.W., Ji, Q.: In the eye of the beholder: a survey of models for eyes and gaze. IEEE Trans. Pattern Anal. Mach. Intell. **32**(3), 478–500 (2009)

14. Kuo, Y.L., Lee, J.S., Kao, S.T.: Eye tracking in visible environment. In: 2009 Fifth International Conference on Intelligent Information Hiding and Multimedia Signal Processing, pp. 114–117. IEEE, September 2009

15. Lakshmi Pavani, M., Bhanu Prakash, A.V., Shwetha Koushik, M.S., Amudha, J., Jyotsna, C.: Navigation through eye-tracking for human–computer interface. In: Satapathy, S.C., Joshi, A. (eds.) Information and Communication Technology for Intelligent Systems. SIST, vol. 107, pp. 575–586. Springer, Singapore (2019). https://doi.org/10.1007/978-981-13-1747-7_56

16. Biswas, P., Langdon, P.: A new interaction technique involving eye gaze tracker and scanning system. In: Proceedings of the 2013 Conference on Eye Tracking South Africa, pp. 67–70, August 2013

17. Swetha, D.L.S., Kishori, P.D., Vaishnavi, G., Rishitha, N., Chowdary, M.M.: Face Cursor Movement Using Open CV (2020)

18. Mehta, S., Dadhich, S., Gumber, S., Jadhav Bhatt, A.: Real-time driver drowsiness detection system using eye aspect ratio and eye closure ratio. In: Proceedings of International Conference on Sustainable Computing in Science, Technology and Management (SUSCOM), Amity University Rajasthan, Jaipur-India, February 2019

19. Mandal, S., et al.: Motion prediction for autonomous vehicles from lyft dataset using deep learning. In: 2020 IEEE 5th International Conference on Computing Communication and Automation (ICCCA), 30–31 October 2020, pp. 768–773 (2020). https://doi.org/10.1109/ICCCA49541.2020.9250790

20. Vasisht, V.S., Joshi, S., Gururaj, C.: Human computer interaction based eye controlled mouse. In: 2019 3rd International conference on Electronics, Communication and Aerospace Technology (ICECA), pp. 362–367. IEEE, June 2019

IoT-Based Control System to Measure, Analyze, and Track Basic Vital Indicators in Patient Healthcare Monitoring System

Kamal Upreti[1]([⊠]), Prashant Vats[2], Mustafizul Haque[3], Adheer A. Goyal[3], Sachin R. Wankhede[4], Prashant Singh[5], Mohammad Shabbir Alam[6], and Mohammad Shahnawaz Nasir[6]

[1] Department of Computer Science and Engineering, Akhilesh Das Gupta Institute of Technology and Management, Delhi, India
kamalupreti1989@gmail.com

[2] Department of IT, Indira Gandhi Delhi Technical University for Women, New Delhi, India

[3] School of Commerce and Management, G H Raisoni University, Dhoda Borgaon, Madhya Pradesh, India

[4] Department of Management Studies, Smt. Kashibai Navale College of Engineering, Savitribai Phule Pune University, Pune, India

[5] Department of Computer Science and Engineering, Sunder Deep Engineering College, Ghaziabad, India

[6] Department of Computer Science, College of Computer Science and IT, Jazan University, Jizan, Saudi Arabia
mnasir@jazanu.edu.sa

Abstract. The construction of a patient tracking system for the bodily temperatures with respiration rate—two essential vital signs—is discussed in this study. The monitoring system was developed utilizing the Arduino Mega 2560 and ESP8266 Wi-Fi Modules on an IoT ecosystem. Each physiological parameters level is determined by two sensor devices, which each uses temperature readings. The aims of the project are to create a healthcare monitoring system which can detect physiological parameters levels, analyze vital sign levels depending on the patient age, offer alerts for problematic conditions, and remotely show data using Android applications. This initiative would reduce the load for nursing professionals and offer a far more practical way to check the condition of each participant's physiological parameters throughout the hospital. The traditional system, which calls for a therapist to visit each patient to monitor their physiological parameters, takes a lot of time. Through installation of Android applications on any Android phone, caregivers using this method could keep an eye on patient condition. By obtaining the information from the system in the shape of a spreadsheet, doctors or nurses can easily evaluate the prior heart rhythm status. When this system's 2 important signs were compared to levels determined by personal inspection or conventional measurement instruments, the findings were remarkably close.

Keywords: Temperature sensors · Insurance · Monitoring · Medical services · Biomedical · CCU surveillance

© The Author(s), under exclusive license to Springer Nature Switzerland AG 2023
R. N. Shaw et al. (Eds.): ICACIS 2022, CCIS 1749, pp. 715–725, 2023.
https://doi.org/10.1007/978-3-031-25088-0_63

1 Introduction

The physicians and caregivers inside hospitals put in long hours to help patients to improve and preserve life. In essence, a nursing must constantly check on individuals who have been taken to the hospital to ensure that nothing bad happens to them. Occasionally there are still too many people that the nursing must watch over at once. The medics still have to visit each hospital emergency room individually today to check on them and assess their condition. The proportion is alarmingly high [1]. To increase the effectiveness of the patient's work, a proposed regime must be created. Overall body of the individual is often measured by using the physiological parameters. Height, stature, heart rate, pulse, core temperature, & respiration rate are indeed the six essential functions [2]. The emphasis of this research is on respiration rate and core temperature. 37 °C is the typical mean core temperature. There really are four basic locations where thermometers are typically used it to monitor body temperatures: the mouths, the perineum, the underarm, and lastly the inner ear. Fever is defined as a rise in normal temperature just above average, whereas hyperthermia is defined as a fall in body temp under 35 °C. The number of breaths an individual takes per second while at repose is known as the respiratory rate or breathing rate. The average breathing rate for each age bracket is shown in Table 1. An individual's typical breathing rate is between 12 and 20 breaths. Therefore, it is thought because having a respiratory rate outside of this region during sleeping is abnormal. The respiratory rate can be impacted by a number of conditions, including asthmatic, nervousness, heart failure, pulmonary illness, and many others [13, 14].

Table 1. The group age, normal age range and their normal respiratory rate

Group age	Age	Normal respiratory rate
1	1 year	30 to 40
2	2–5 years	20 to 40
3	6–10 years	15 to 25
4	11–18 years	15 to 20
5	18–70 years	12 to 20
6	>70 years	15 to 20

Numerous studies have examined patient surveillance systems, incorporating measures of body temperatures and respiration rate [4–7]. By utilizing the temperature readings MLX90614 with LM35 and the ESP8266 as the wireless module again for Arduino Mega 2560 controller, the patient's surveillance system in this research is centered on assessing the respiratory rate (RR) and skin temperature. Additionally, there is indeed a keyboard for the nurses to enter the participant's groups age, as well as a Lcd screen that shows the groups age, skin temperature, breathing rate, and the patient's status, among other crucial pieces of information. Last but not least, the mobile apps in the caregivers' cellphones run on the Blynk Development kit [11, 12].

2   Proposed Methodology

2.1   Healthcare Monitoring Technical Measures

The healthcare monitoring program's schematic diagram for measuring core temperature and respiration rate is shown in Fig. 1. Touchscreen and thermal sensor (LM35 and MLX90614) are being used as interfaces. Two LM35 are being used to measure the participant's respiration rate, whereas a gauge called the MXL90614 is utilized to measure the patient's temperature of the body. Information is then transferred to the Ardino Mega mcu for processing before being output to a Lcd screen and a cellphone. The ESP8266 wi-fi modules is responsible for supporting the data supplied to cellphones. Figure 2 diagram demonstrates how the process works to determine each patient's RR. The stopwatch will begin ticking down for 2 min after the caregiver has entered the age bracket of the individuals (loop counter for 20). Thermocouples 1 (TS1) and 2 (TS2) have begun to function, as well as the system is now able to calculate the temperatures needed for patients respiration and ambient temperature. The two temperatures then were contrasted. The countdown for RR will just go up one if the differential is more than 2 °C. The procedure is carried out over and over till the 20 min are up. Afterwards when, the RR count is multiplied by threefold to get the RR every min (to get the RR for 60 s or one min) [16, 17]. After that, the process is repeated for yet another round.

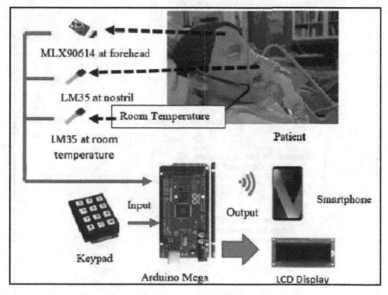

Fig. 1. Patient monitoring equipment schematic representation.

The sources, controllers, and outcomes of the remote monitoring of patients are classified into many categories. These include analog temperature readings, LM35, non-invasive thermal detectors, MLX90614, keypads, Arduino Microcontroller 2560, LCD displays, as well as wi-fi ESP8266 modules. Figure 3 shows the software's Systems Engineering Diagrammatic representation.

2.1.1 Input/Sensors

Thermocouples and a keyboard were used as interfaces. Thermocouples and patients' respiration parameters are detected using two analogue temperature kind LM35 devices. For 2 min, a computation is performed to determine the difference between the two data points. Automated non-contact thermal imaging sensors, model number MLX90614, are the alternative form of temperature probe. The MLX90614 is used to detect the patient's core temperature through the top of the head. In Fig. 4 below, it is depicted. The physician entered the patient's subgroup age using the keyboard. Since the typical respiratory rate varies each age range, the group's age insertion is essential. With the aid of a keyboard, the device can accurately assess a participant's regular respiratory rate within a spectrum while also providing a more accurate indicator or warn regarding the

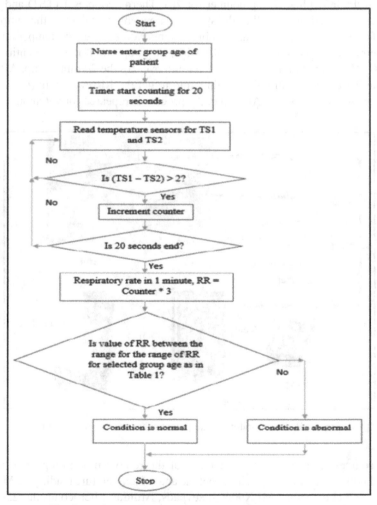

Fig. 2. Software flowchart for respiratory rate calculation.

participant's abnormal condition [15]. The age of the group is displayed in Table 1. The age range for men between the ages of 11 and 18 is equal to that of people older than 70, suggesting that their respiration rates are within another range.

2.1.2 Results

The LCD screen is also one of the program's output port. It's being used to display the participant's core temperature, age group, and rate of breathing values. Furthermore, the LCD showed the participant's state, that was either "regular" or "aberrant" based on calculations the system has made using the data input. Each bit of evidence is displayed in each and every row of the LCD panel because it has four sets. The patient's smartphone's system software (GUI) is another display. The ESP8266 wi-fi shield supports GUI created with the Blynk app.

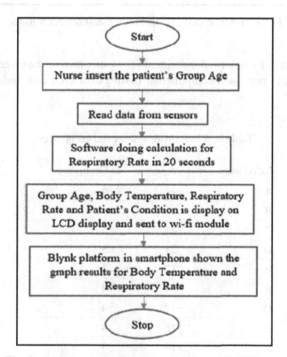

Fig. 3. Systems engineering diagrammatic representation.

3   Proposed Technique's Validation

13 individuals of various ages participated in the research, as shown in Table 2. Every subject is examined three times in succession for every measure. Since not everyone has bronchial or lung issues, the five measurement methods were then utilized to calculate the confidence interval in order to check the accuracy and reliability of the patients

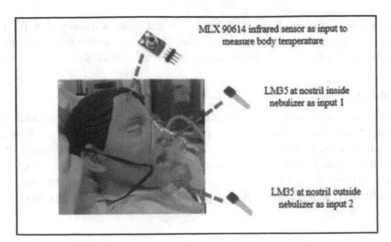

Fig. 4. Position of the temperature measurement sensors.

monitoring program for a normal individual. The outcomes of the research have indeed been separated into two main components: findings for GUI and findings showing on Display screen.

Table 2. The individual ages and group ages.

Individual	Age	Group age
A	23	5
B	23	5
C	21	5
D	21	5
E	17	4
F	17	4
G	17	4
H	16	4
I	10	3
J	8	3
K	8	3
L	4	2
M	3	2

3.1 LCD Screen

The LCD screen that was employed for this research included four rows, the first of which indicated the participants' core body temperature, the next their subgroup ages, the 3rd their calculated respiration rates, and the fourth their conditions. The illustration of outcomes in Fig. 5(a) and (b). An illustration of a participant in a cohort with an age bracket of roughly 11 to 18 years old is shown in Fig. 5(a). The average breathing rate each moment again for population, as shown in Table 1, is lifespan ranges from 15 to 20. The person's status is acceptable because the respiration rate in Fig. 5(a) is within the reasonably expected. Whereas the participant's breathing rate in Fig. 5(b) is less than average.

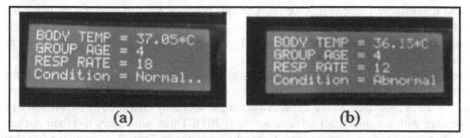

Fig. 5. Provides an illustration of a result for a person in (a) reasonable level and (b) problematic conditions.

3.2 Results in GUI (Blynk Platform)

The ESP8266 component's data was received using the Blynk framework. A cellphone software called Blynk platforms allows a caregiver to keep an eye on clients from a

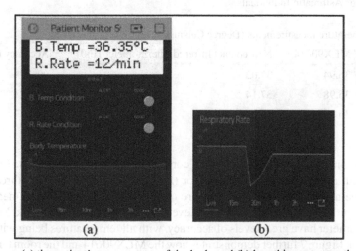

Fig. 6. Shows (a) the patient's temperature of the body and (b) breathing rate together through a graph showing the patient's core temperature and breathing rate, respectively.

faraway. Figure 6 displays acquired data out from ESP8266 on the Blynk product's GUI displays and graphing outcomes. The participant's internal temperature is stable at about 37.5 °C, indicating that the patient's overall health.

4 Experimental Results

For the LCD Screen Utilization for the Project Displayed. The four rows of the LCD utilized for this project displayed the body.

4.1 Evaluation of nonintrusive thermal thermometers and sensing element (MLX90614) for measuring temperature of the body (FI01). 13 people had their core temperature recorded 5 times each 10 min that used a non-contact InfraRed sensor (FI01) and temperature probe (MLX90614). Contrast between median readings by using the chart displays the relationship between both the MLX90614 sensors and the FI01 thermometers for the 13 subjects. As seen in Fig. 7. The intended measurements are set as that of the measurement captured by FI01, and the data along with the result of the proposed methodology is the data acquired by MLX90614 sensor. The average variance for the accuracy of this suggested system was also evaluated using the MLX90614 sensors.

4.2. For bronchial people, a contrast of core temperature measured by the MLX90614 sensors with a non-contact infrared sensor (F101). Three asthmatics had their normal body temperatures measured, and the results are listed in Table 3. Despite the fact that three of these people have asthma, the measurements are unaffected by the body temp measurement because none of individuals have such a fever. As seen in Table 3, both the MLX90614 and thermometer have great levels of accuracy, with all temperatures being within 1% of one another. Figure 7 further demonstrates how the MLX90614 and the room temperature recorded measurements are related to each other.

Table 3. Body temperature comparison between MLX90641 and non-contact infrared thermometer (FI01) for Asthmatic Individuals.

Body temperature measurements (Degree Celsius)			
Patient	MLX90614	Non-contact Infrared Thermometer (FI01)	Accuracy (100%)
X	36.94	37.02	99.78%
Y	36.98	37.14	99.57%
Z	36.98	36.97	99.97%

4.3. For bronchial people, a contrast of core temperature measured by the MLX90614 sensors with a non-contact infrared sensor (F101). Despite the fact that three of these people have asthma, the measurements are unaffected by the body temp measurement because none of individuals have such a fever. As seen in Table 2, both the MLX90614 and thermometer have great levels of accuracy, with all temperatures being within 1% of one another. Figure 7 further demonstrates how the MLX90614 and the room temperature recorded measurements are related to each other.

While the breathing rate assessment doesn't really offer precise and accurate readings, measuring body temp MLX90614 can be said to have reliable data. This is attributable to the fact that the sensors LM35 used it to measure respiration takes considerable time to produce accurate findings and has a lengthy cooling-off period. As a result, the accuracy of the measurement of the respiration rate has been impacted by this issue. By substituting another sensitivity temperature gauge for the LM35 detector, the measurement's accuracy is improved.

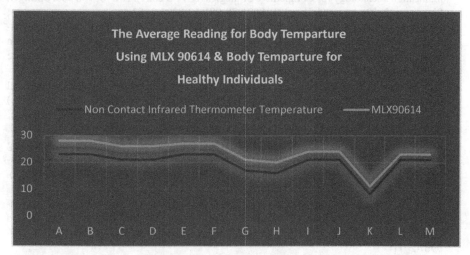

Fig. 7. Compares the overall reading for core temperature from a body thermometers and the MLX90614 device

5   Conclusions

A successful IOT-based health monitoring system was created. The body temperature and breathing patterns may be recorded by this technology, and the measurement values can be remotely communicated to Android apps via the Development kit. Through Android applications, this technology may inform users and caregivers to any emergency situations. The patients result on the Lcd screen don't have many problems, but the mobile apps, whose network issues are crucial to the implementation of Internet of things, have had some unstable outcomes. In order to obtain correct findings for the assessment of breathing rate, the kind of temperature probe used it to monitor breath warmth is also important. Highly sensitive sensors may be utilized in the future to produce better and more accurate results.

References

1. Singh, P., et al.: Cloud-based patient health information exchange system using blockchain technology. In: Kaiser, M.S., Xie, J., Rathore, V.S. (eds.) Information and Communication Technology for Competitive Strategies (ICTCS 2021). LNNS, vol. 401. Springer, Singapore (2021). https://doi.org/10.1007/978-981-19-0098-3_55

2. Sharma, A.K., et al.: An IoT-based temperature measurement platform for a real-time environment using LM35. In: Joshi, A., Mahmud, M., Ragel, R.G. (eds.) Information and Communication Technology for Competitive Strategies (ICTCS 2021). LNNS, vol. 400. Springer, Singapore (2023). https://doi.org/10.1007/978-981-19-0095-2_57

3. Phogat, M., et al.: Identification of MRI-based adenocarcinoma tumours with 3-D convolutionary system. In: Kaiser, M.S., Xie, J., Rathore, V.S. (eds.) Information and Communication Technology for Competitive Strategies (ICTCS 2021). LNNS, vol. 401. Springer, Singapore (2023). https://doi.org/10.1007/978-981-19-0098-3_57

4. Jain, E., et al.: A CNN-based neural network for tumor detection using cellular pathological imaging for lobular carcinoma. In: Choudrie, J., Mahalle, P., Perumal, T., Joshi, A. (eds.) ICT with Intelligent Applications. Smart Innovation, Systems and Technologies, vol. 311. Springer, Singapore (2023). https://doi.org/10.1007/978-981-19-3571-8_51

5. Doja, F., et al.: A comprehensive framework for the IoT-based smart home automation using Blynk. In: Kaiser, M.S., Xie, J., Rathore, V.S. (eds.) Information and communication technology for competitive strategies (ICTCS 2021). LNNS, vol. 401. Springer, Singapore (2023). https://doi.org/10.1007/978-981-19-0098-3_6

6. Gupta, A., et al.: A sustainable green approach to the virtualized environment in cloud computing. In: Zhang, Y.D., Senjyu, T., So-In, C., Joshi, A. (eds.) Smart Trends in Computing and Communications. LNNS, vol 396. Springer, Singapore. https://doi.org/10.1007/978-981-16-9967-2_71

7. Vats, P., Singh, S., Barda, S., Aalam, Z., Mandot, M.: A novel approach for detection of intracranial tumor using image segmentation based on cellular automata. In: Nagar, A.K., Jat, D.S., Marín-Raventós, G., Mishra, D.K. (eds.) Intelligent Sustainable Systems. LNNS, vol. 334, pp. 593–603. Springer, Singapore (2022). https://doi.org/10.1007/978-981-16-6369-7_54

8. Chauhan, K., Gupta, K., Vats, P., Mandot, M.: A comparative study of various wireless network optimization techniques. In: Joshi, A., Mahmud, M., Ragel, R.G., Thakur, N.V. (eds.) Information and Communication Technology for Competitive Strategies (ICTCS 2020). LNNS, vol. 191, pp. 641–652. Springer, Singapore (2022). https://doi.org/10.1007/978-981-16-0739-4_61

9. Vats, P., Aalam, Z., Kaur, S., Kaur, A., Kaur, S.: A Multi-Factorial Code Coverage Based Test Case Selection And Prioritization For Object Oriented Programs. In: Tuba, M., Akashe, S., Joshi, A. (eds.) ICT Systems and Sustainability. AISC, vol. 1270, pp. 721–731. Springer, Singapore (2021). https://doi.org/10.1007/978-981-15-8289-9_69

10. Afreen, Q., et al.: A review of machine learning (ML) in the internet of medical things (IOMT) in the construction of a smart healthcare structure. J. Algebraic Stat. 13(2), 225–231 (2022). https://publishoa.com. ISSN: 1309-3452

11. Upreti, K., et al.: Prediction of mechanical strength by using an artificial neural network and random forest algorithm. J. Nanomaterials (2022). https://doi.org/10.1155/2022/7791582

12. Palimkar, P., Bajaj, V., Mal, A.K., Shaw, R.N., Ghosh, A.: Unique action identifier by using magnetometer, accelerometer and gyroscope: KNN approach. In: Bianchini, M., Piuri, V., Das, S., Shaw, R.N. (eds.) Advanced Computing and Intelligent Technologies. LNNS, vol. 218, pp. 607–631. Springer, Singapore (2022). https://doi.org/10.1007/978-981-16-2164-2_48

13. Haider, M., Upreti, K., Nasir, M., Alam, M., Sharma, A.K.: Addressing image and Poisson noise deconvolution problem using deep learning approaches. Comput. Intell. (2022). https://doi.org/10.1111/coin.12510
14. Alam, M., Jalil, S.Z.A., Upreti, K.: Analyzing recognition of EEG based human attention and emotion using Machine learning. Mater. Today Proc. (2021).https://doi.org/10.1016/j.matpr.2021.10.190
15. Rajawat, A.S., et.al.: Depression detection for elderly people using AI robotic systems leveraging the Nelder–Mead Method. Artif. Intell. Future Gener. Rob., 55–70 (2021). https://doi.org/10.1016/B978-0-323-85498-6.00006-X
16. Sharma, A.K., Upreti, K., Vargis, B.: Experimental performance analysis of load balancing of tasks using honey bee inspired algorithm for resource allocation in cloud environment. Mater. Today Proc. (2020). ISSN 2214 7853. https://doi.org/10.1016/j.matpr.2020.09.359. https://www.sciencedirect.com/science/article/pii/S2214785320370693
17. Upreti, K., Vargis, B.K., Jain, R., Upadhyaya, M.: Analytical study on performance of cloud computing with respect to data security. In: 2021 5th International Conference on Intelligent Computing and Control Systems (ICICCS), pp. 96–101 (2021). https://doi.org/10.1109/ICICCS51141.2021.9432268

A Comprehensive Review on Skin Disease Classification Using Convolutional Neural Network and Support Vector Machine

Shivani Mishra[1], Sonali Satpathy[1], Shrishti Malkani[1], Vikram Yadav[1],
Vimal Gupta[2(✉)], Sur Singh Rawat[2], Nitima Malsa[2], Ankush Ghosh[3],
and Rabindra Nath shaw[3]

[1] Department of Computer Science and Engineering, JSS Academy of Technical Education, Noida 201301, India
[2] Faculty, Department of Computer Science and Engineering, JSS Academy of Technical Education, Noida 201301, India
{vimalgupta,sur.rawat,nitimamalsa}@jssaten.ac.in
[3] University Center for Research and Development, Chandigarh University, Ajeetgarh, Punjab, India

Abstract. Skin illness is one of the most common medical problems that can affect people of all ages, from infants to the elderly. As the diagnosis of skin illnesses totally relies on the expertise of professionals, skin biopsy reports are laborious, time-consuming, and subject to subjectivity; thus, it is required to boost diagnostic accuracy and entail less human effort. It can be challenging to categories skin illnesses because of their eerie resemblances. This study investigates several methods for classifying skin illnesses, such as Deep Learning, Support Vector Machine (SVM) and *Convolutional neural network* (CNN).

Keywords: Convolutional Neural Network (CNN) · Deep learning · Support Vector Machine (SVM)

1 Introduction

Skin problems are among the most common and undertreated diseases in the world. One of the many types of dermatological disorders is skin cancer. There are many different treatment options and prognoses available depending on the kind and stage of each disease. The traditional clinical method used to classify the kind of skin sickness in a preliminary clinical skin cancer screening is visual diagnosis. Skin disease diagnosis is extremely challenging due to the unexplained symptoms of skin disorders, which are a long-lasting and constantly changing process occurring in specific areas of the skin. Numerous indicators are meant to be used in conjunction with the appropriate biological underpinning to diagnose skin illnesses, such as distinct lesion architecture, morphological assortment, scale, colour, and arrangement. It has been demonstrated that, depending on the type of melanoma, people with darker skin tones either have a higher risk rate or a lower death rate than people with lighter skin tones. This is despite the fact that people with darker skin tones are roughly 20 to 30 times more likely to develop melanoma than people with lighter skin tones. Technology can guarantee early detection of many skin disorders, which is essential for efficient treatment in the healthcare sector. Machine learning techniques for disease diagnosis, prediction, and categorization have in certain circumstances yielded outcomes that have outperformed those of human experts when used in conjunction with relevant and reliable data. The use of deep learning to a variety of illnesses utilizing relevant and reliable data. Combining machine learning with deep learning techniques is one of the most popular ways to get the desired outcomes. The models can be trained to treat some serious disorders on their own and may be utilized to diagnose and treat illnesses under the correct medical supervision.

2 Literature Review

Many scholars with an interest in using artificial intelligence to diagnose skin lesions have been working on this recently across a wide range of scientific disciplines. [1] presented a multimodal transformer that combines two encoders for extracting picture information and a decoder for extracting metadata features. The goal of this transformer is to combine images and metadata to classify skin conditions. Despite the fact that it was recognized that the model did not produce better results than earlier methods that did not include MA and SLE. [2] discussed a comparative Study of Multiple CNN Models for the Classification of 23 Skin Illnesses, the model is useful for comparing CNN models on various diseases but is less useful for thoroughly researching a single disease. [3] suggested a deep learning model for skin cancer detection. It was determined that the project required extensive clinical domain expertise. [4] used CNN to classify skin diseases using deep neural networks in order to combat class imbalances in picture classification. It was discovered that the Model performed significantly better than human experts (60–76%). [5] suggested an entropy-based fuzzy topsis algorithm, which evaluated feature selection techniques for illness survival prediction. The accuracy of the model varies depending on the kind of dataset, hence the chapter assists in predicting the strategies to be employed in the models. [6] discussed an artificial intelligence system that uses convolutional neural networks to classify skin diseases. The model used a number of conventional methods with little testing, which resulted in reduced accuracy. [7] in order to categorise the many types of skin diseases, MobileNet V2 is employed, and LSTM is used to improve model performance by preserving feature state information.

It was found that low illumination captures cause the model's prediction accuracy to decline. By using hybrid LBP, GLCM, and DWT algorithms, [8] retrieved features from the examined photos. After that, classification was performed using ANN and FFNN algorithms. The results demonstrated that the ResNet-50 and AlexNet CNN models were outperformed by the ANN and FFNN algorithms.[9] proposed an intelligent system for skin disease prediction that makes use of an SVM algorithm and a modified pre-trained model of a convolutional neural network. The result is based on a pre-trained model that hasn't been altered. [10] examined the various elements influencing the precision of multiclass skin disease classification and covered the application of transfer learning, AlexNet architecture, and data augmentation methods. It was discovered that the accuracy is actually decreased by the usage of various data augmentation approaches. A Step Towards an Intelligent Dermoscopy Device, proposed by [11], is an Adaptive Federated Machine Learning-Based Intelligent System for Skin Disease Detection.[12] discussed the use of dermoscopy images to diagnose skin conditions. The complexity was decreased by combining One-versus-All and convolutional neural networks. Improves Skin-Disease Classification Based on a Customized Loss Function, Balanced Mini-Batch Logic, and Real-Time Image Augmentation [13]. The model combines a deep CNN system with EfficientetB4-CLF to classify a variety of skin disorders.[14] talked about A multi-class, multi-level categorization system that has been built using both conventional machine learning and cutting-edge deep learning techniques. Additionally, the model's application highlights how the number of diseases and their characteristics have expanded in this study as compared to previous studies, and the classification accuracy of some disorders has improved. The methods SVM (Support Vector Machine), KNN (K-nearest Neighbor), and ID3 (Iterative Dichotomiser 3) were used to categorise various skin disorders [15]. (Iterative Dichotomiser 3).

It was established that combining the SVM and KNN algorithms produced superior performance outcomes than doing so independently. [16] provided studies that concentrated on the categorization of facial skin diseases using clinical photos utilizing five popular CNN algorithms that had been trained on ImageNet [9].They are DenseNet121, ResNet-50, Inception-v2, Inception-ResNet-v3, and Inception-v3.It was discovered that the model is significantly more accurate at diagnosing the problem with a single body component than the model for all body components. In addition to a multi-model ensemble method that classified skin diseases using the Gaussian Bayesian (NB), Support Vector Machine (SVM), and K-Nearest Neighbor algorithms, [17] also examined a model for predicting skin disorders using binary classification machine learning. In an open, web-based, multinational diagnostic investigation, [18] examined the diagnostic effectiveness of human readers and machine-learning algorithms for the classification of pigmented skin lesions.

Modern machine-learning classifiers were found to perform better than human specialists at identifying pigmented skin lesions. [19] demonstrated five distinct classification techniques for the diagnosis of skin issues, including machine learning, logistic regression, SVM kernel, naive bayes, random forest, and CNN. The accuracy, mistake rates, and training accuracy of each of the five suggested algorithms have been analyzed. [20] discussed the use of a Deep CNN model to detect skin problems. The model's architecture consists of pre-processing, feature extraction, and classification. The detecting method was developed using SVM and a convolutional neural network (AlexNet) that had already been trained. Table 1 compares the findings of the aforementioned studies.

Table 1. Brief study of state-of –the–art methods

Year	Methods	Algorithm	Advantages	Disadvantages	Future scope of the chapter
2022	[1]	Two encoders are used in the model's construction to separate the image features and metadata features, respectively, and a decoder is used to combine them The Transformer framework served as inspiration for it	On the confidential dataset, the recommended model performed better than other well-known networks with an accuracy of 0.816. On the ISIC 2018 dataset, the recommended method achieves an accuracy of 0.9381 and an AUC of 0.99	The model does not produce better outcomes than earlier approaches that did not include MA and SLE	In this study, a brand-new multimodal Transformer is presented to combine photos and information for the categorization of skin diseases
2022	[2]	Several steps have been taken to establish a computer vision-based system for classifying skin disorders Each image in the DermNet preprocessing step has its size altered in line with the input of each model and via a number of transformation stages in order to increase the number of images in the dataset (rotation, flip, zoom, etc.)	These architectures are used to categorise skin illnesses in order to compare them and choose the best model to create an effective computer-aided diagnosis system for the dermatology sector	This model is useful for comparing CNN models on various diseases, but it cannot be used to fully understand a single condition	DermNet dataset was used to train high-performance CNN architectures like InceptionV4, InceptionV3, DenseNet-201, MobilenetV3, ResNet50, VGG19, ResNext50, NASNetLarge, GoogleNet, and InceptionResNetV2. DermNet dataset contains 19434 images of skin conditions according to 23 groups
2022	[3]	Deep Learning using the Dermoscopic method, which is frequently utilised	Integrate numerous widely-used imaging modalities, incorporate powerful algorithms, and take into account demographic data to make deep learning more credible and acceptable in clinical applications	On a wide scale, clinical domain expertise is needed	Deep learning only applied to tiny

(continued)

Table 1. (*continued*)

Year	Methods	Algorithm	Advantages	Disadvantages	Future scope of the chapter
2022	[4]	Convolutional neural networks can be used to analyse dermoscopic images of skin cancer using a number of cutting-edge CNN models	The model will accurately diagnose 90% of the cases if an accuracy rate of 90% is required. If a 95% accuracy is needed, correctly identifying 70% of the patients will result in the desired results. The model had a diagnosis rate of 99.5% for 40% of the cases, cutting the hospital's burden in half	Only American skin can be utilized for this, and it may be used to identify skin cancer	In comparison to human experts, models performed much better (60–76%). The enormous performance improvement made possible by these new artificial intelligence models in the real world has the potential to save countless lives
2022	[5]	Proposed fuzzy topics method based on entropy	The accuracy of the model varies depending on the kind of dataset, and this study helps to anticipate the strategies to be utilised in the models	When there is just one feature, alternatives may be completed fast, but choosing from a large pool of potential techniques can occasionally be challenging since they have a variety of metrics	It has been proven that feature selection methods based on GR, GA, and IG perform well in the ANN classification technique for enhancing disease survival prediction
2022	[6]	For purposes of classification, the model uses CNN	When compared to other methodologies or techniques in use, the suggested method is effective in terms of diagnostic accuracy	One of the shortcomings of the strategy is that the model is only evaluated on a single dataset The model settles for a close to 88% accuracy because it is unable to achieve a better accuracy	

(*continued*)

Table 1. (*continued*)

Year	Methods	Algorithm	Advantages	Disadvantages	Future scope of the chapter
2021	[7]	The type of skin ailment is classified using MobileNet V2, and the model's performance is improved using LSTM by keeping track of the features' current states	The results show promise, with an accuracy of 85.34% over the real-time photos captured when tested and compared to other approaches In terms of categorization and tracking the development of the tumour growth based on textured-based data, it has been shown that the suggested model has surpassed the competition	When tested on a collection of images taken in dim lighting conditions, the model's accuracy is noticeably reduced to just under 80%	The bidirectional LSTM has the potential to significantly enhance the model's performance The model may be improved further by taking into account the model's potential for self-learning and knowledge acquisition from its earlier experiences
2021	[8]	Combining the LBP, GLCM, and DWT algorithms allowed features to be extracted from the investigated pictures. Then, for classification, ANN and FFNN algorithms were employed	ResNet-50 and AlexNet, two CNN models, were shown to perform worse than ANN and FFNN algorithms All prior techniques only managed accuracy between 89.3% and 60%, while the ANN and ResNet-50 of the proposed system both achieved accuracy of 95.3%	When establishing a diagnosis, the classification algorithms become confused due to the closeness of various illnesses' traits	

(*continued*)

Table 1. (*continued*)

Year	Methods	Algorithm	Advantages	Disadvantages	Future scope of the chapter
2021	[9]	In the suggested system, a modified pre-trained Convolutional neural network model and SVM algorithm were used	By adjusting picture intensities using the histogram equalization method, contrast is enhanced. It's not necessarily necessary to boost the contrast all the time	The outcome is based on a pre-trained model that has undergone little modification	The substantial resemblance between the characteristics of some illnesses, which confounds the classification algorithms while reaching a diagnosis, is one example of the study's limits and difficulties. In the future, it will be necessary to combine deep feature maps with standard methods for extracting features from multiple algorithms
2021	[10]	Transfer learning, the design of AlexNet, and data augmentation methods	In comparison to the four level model and the three level model, accuracy is higher	The use of various data augmentation techniques actually reduces accuracy when compared to applying no augmentation at all, so it should be used with caution	The networks' depths were reduced to make the models more straightforward, and when compared to the three-stage and four-stage models, the two-stage model had the best accuracy. This implies that it is possible to retain skin disease categorization accuracy despite decreasing network depths

(*continued*)

Table 1. (*continued*)

Year	Methods	Algorithm	Advantages	Disadvantages	Future scope of the chapter
2021	[11]	The two types of adaptive ensemble CNN are cloud-based and edge-based	It provides an ongoing increase in classification accuracy by using the adaptation mechanism to provide a more durable solution Both the cloud model and the edge model performance of the suggested framework were good	After adaptation, there is some classification loss when using the clustering-based approach to separate various classes for related characteristics	This study suggested an intelligent dermoscopy tool that medical professionals may utilise to make a clinical diagnosis of skin malignancies
2020	[12]	Two distinct approaches have been suggested to automatically categorise skin diseases: (1) the CNN model alone, and (2) the CNN and oneversusall combo (OVA)	The method has shown extremely promising results in the identification of skin lesions without the use of any filtering or feature extraction The benefit of OVA is that each class' categorization is based on true or untrue statements. As a result, complexity decreased as a result	Only when each class was assessed separately did the accuracy rate values across multiple classifications rise	The proposed approach, known as the combination of CNN and OVA, could be applied to a variety of classification issues in medical imaging
2020	[13]	CNN, Real-time Image Augmentation, Balanced Mini-Batch Logic	On the Test-10 dataset, which consists of 2,453 dermoscopic pictures, the suggested Deep CNN system, in conjunction with EfficientNetB4-CLF, obtained the greatest ACC at 89.97% and Recall at 86.13%	This model cannot be used with a set of common, unbalanced data	A new strategy for classifying multiple skin diseases is proposed using a hybrid approach that combines creating a new loss function with balanced mini-batch logic at the data level, followed by real-time image augmentation

(*continued*)

Table 1. (*continued*)

Year	Methods	Algorithm	Advantages	Disadvantages	Future scope of the chapter
2020	[14]	The Multi-Class Multi-Level (MCML) classification system has been constructed utilising sophisticated deep learning techniques as well as conventional machine learning techniques	The model could be retrained using the fresh data while the training data may be reused thanks to the use of MCML. Additionally, the classification accuracy of several illnesses has improved. In this survey, there are more illnesses and more of their characteristics than in earlier studies	Inconsistencies in the data set caused by various data sources and data collection methods. Another drawback of this research is the	Finding the ideal collection of features requires the extraction of additional features and the use of feature selection algorithms More illnesses might be added to the multi-class categorization of skin lesions, and a mobile-enabled expert system could be created for distant places
2019	[15]	The following algorithms are employed in the suggested system: Support Vector Machine (SVM), K-nearest neighbour (KNN), and ID3 (Iterative Dichotomiser 3)	It offered a quicker and simpler method of detecting diseases, as well as their severity if discovered Better performance results are achieved by this system's combination of SVM and KNN techniques rather than either one alone	The performance of the classification system suffers as a result of the impact of particular classes, which has a negative impact on the system's overall performance	This system can be enhanced in the future to identify and categorise more diseases as well as their severity

(*continued*)

Table 1. (*continued*)

Year	Methods	Algorithm	Advantages	Disadvantages	Future scope of the chapter
2019	[16]	Using ImageNet as a training set, five common CNN methods. ResNet-50, Inception-v3, DenseNet121, Xception, and Inception-ResNet-v2 are the five structures mentioned	In comparison to the model for all body parts, the model can classify the issue with a specific body part with a lot more accuracy	The model can only detect skin conditions on the face since it was only trained on facial photos	The performance of CNN-based facial skin disease diagnostic algorithms will keep getting better thanks to the growing body of face image data illustrating diverse skin conditions and the ongoing development of the network architecture. We think that in the future, patients will employ practical CNN-based apps to maintain the health of their facial skin
2019	[17]	Logistic Regression (LR), Linear Discriminant Analysis (LDA), k-Nearest Neighbor (KNN), Classification and Regression Tree (CART), Gaussian Bayesian (NB), and Support Vector Machine are among the methods for classifying	The model uses four distinct machine algorithms, including two boosting and two bagging techniques, to address the improvement in accuracy It also covers how we are looking at fine-tuning the settings for the most well-known algorithms that have shown potential in spot-checking	The focus of the study, which is comparison-based, is fully on the technical side of it and not on the model's improvement with a primary focus on healthcare. There is no exploration or modification of the dataset	As the chapter compares different algorithms for classifying skin diseases, it can be used as a basis for deciding which algorithm is best for the job at hand

(*continued*)

Table 1. (*continued*)

Year	Methods	Algorithm	Advantages	Disadvantages	Future scope of the chapter
2019	[18]	Human readers' diagnoses were contrasted with those produced by 139 algorithms developed by 77 machine-learning labs	Modern machine-learning classifiers performed better than human experts at identifying pigmented skin lesions	These algorithms' lower performance with out-of-distribution photos might be a potential drawback. Our lack of providing additional information beyond dermatoscopic images—such as anatomical location, age, and sex—despite the fact that these details were equally necessary for the algorithm's creation is a drawback of our work	Future studies may remove the restriction of algorithms' poor performance with regard to out-of-distribution images
2019	[19]	For the purpose of detecting skin diseases, five different classification algorithms—machine learning, logistic regression, SVM kernel, naive bayes, random forest, and CNN—are used	For each of the five suggested methods, accuracy and error rates as well as training accuracy have been calculated. But among the five algorithms, CNN offers more accurate predictions since it is a fully connected neural feed-forward network	The model's scope is kept in check because it concentrates on minor problems like acne rather than serious skin conditions	Future real-time data availability might make it easier to diagnose skin diseases using AI, which has made significant strides recently

(*continued*)

Table 1. (*continued*)

Year	Methods	Algorithm	Advantages	Disadvantages	Future scope of the chapter
2019	[20]	Skin disease detection has been done using the Deep CNN model. The model's architecture consists of feature extraction, preprocessing, and classification	The suggested feature extraction has been carried out using a pre-trained convolutional neural network. Because it is the simplest and most reliable method for utilising the potential of pre-trained deep learning networks	Saudi Arabia serves as the research's context. Thus, the model's effectiveness in the	To identify skin disorders, several extensions and improvements may be applied. Second, mobile devices may be used to identify skin illnesses using methods that may be applied to the dermis layer of the skin. Other contexts might potentially reveal the presence and severity of other illnesses

3   Methodology

The stages that make up this work's approach are as follows:

- Preprocessing
- Feature extraction
- Classification.

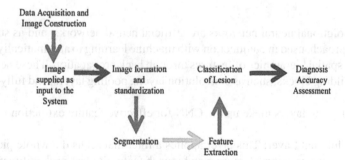

Fig. 1. [21] Flow of the classification methods

3.1   Dataset

[10] Given the magnitude of the dataset and the fact that dermatological data varies due to regional differences, the categorization of skin diseases is a difficult model to handle. The

HAM10000 dataset served as the basis for this model's training. They were originally manually modified to improve visual contrast and colour reproduction, cropped, and centred on the lesion. For the purpose of identifying pigmented skin lesions, the Human Against Machine with 10,000 Training Photos (HAM10000) dataset contains 10,000 training images. The dataset contains photos that were captured, saved, and gathered from various populations using various modalities (Fig. 1).

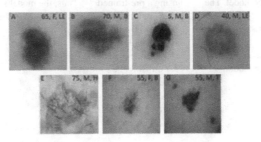

Fig. 2. [22] HAM10000 Dataset for classification

Regarding the diagnostic lesion categories, there were seven distinct classes (Fig. 2):

- Melanocytic Nevi
- Melanoma
- Benign Keratosis-like Lesions
- Basal Cell Carcinoma
- Actinic Keratoses
- Vascular Lesions
- Dermatofibroma.

3.2 CNN

[6, 9] Convolutional neural networks are artificial neural networks, and as such, a deep learning approach, used in conjunction with machine learning to automatically and adaptively learn spatial hierarchies of features through back propagation. These networks use multiple building blocks, such as convolution layers, pooling layers, and fully connected layers (Fig. 3).

The following layers make up the CNN for effective feature extraction in images.:

- 1) Convolutional Layer: This layer applies a filter that scans the whole picture a few pixels at a time, creating a feature map for each feature's class probability predictions.
- 2) The output volume of the conversion layer is sent to a Rectified-Linear Unit (ReLu) layer, which serves as the elementwise activation function (ReLu). Given the input data, the ReLu layer will decide if an input node will "fire." This "fire" indicates if the filters in the convolution layer have picked up a visual characteristic.
- 3) Pooling Layer: A layer that scales down the data generated by the convolution layer while still preserving the most crucial data. Max pooling and average pooling are two different forms of pooling.

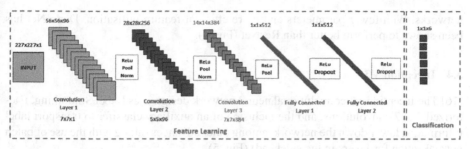

Fig. 3. [23] CNN architecture classifying data sample into seven different skin lesions

- 4) For usage in the next FC layers, the FC Input Layer flattens the outputs of the preceding layer into a single vector.
- 5) The final probabilities are generated by the FC Output Layer, which then determines.

3.3 DenseNet121

[16] A DenseNet is a type of convolutional neural network that makes use of dense connections between layers, as opposed to Dense Blocks, where all layers (with matching feature-map sizes) are linked to one another directly. In order to retain the feed-forward nature, each layer gets additional inputs from all earlier layers and broadcasts its own feature-maps to all following levels. The main objective of DenseNet was to intentionally exacerbate the accuracy reduction caused by the vanishing gradient of high-level neural

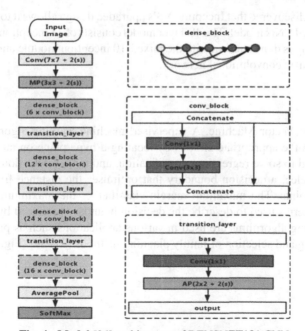

Fig. 4. Model [24] architecture of DENSNET121 CNN

networks. With fewer parameters and more efficient feature utilisation, DenseNet has been shown to perform better than ResNet (Fig. 4).

3.4 Inception V3

[16] The Inception-v3 convolutional neural network design uses Label Smoothing, Factorized 7×7 convolutions, and the inclusion of an auxiliary classifer to transport label information lower down the network, among other advances (along with the use of batch normalisation for layers in the sidehead) (Fig. 5).

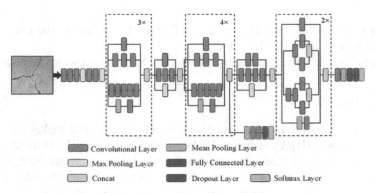

Fig. 5. [25] inception V3 architecture

It has been discovered that Inception V3's upgraded design allows it to perform better than the standard CNN model. The 48-layer model consists of 11 inception model blocks; backward tuning is done starting with the mixed-10 inception module and moving on to the complete basic convolutional network.

3.5 SVM

[9, 19] Support Vector Machine, A supervised machine learning algorithm classifies a test case into the appropriate entities by locating a hyperplane on an n-dimensional plane. It is used to solve regression, classification, and outlier detection issues. Due to its ability to select a decision boundary that optimises the distance from all classes' nearest data points. The maximum margin classifier or the maximum margin hyper plane are two terms used to describe the decision boundary produced by SVMs. Other machine learning algorithms are used in various applications such as price prediction, load forecasting and selection of family planning methods [37–39] (Fig. 6).

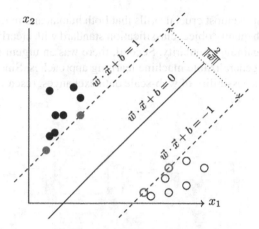

Fig. 6. [26]. SVM classification

3.6 Alexnet

[10] Alexnet is acknowledged as a leading architecture because it won the 2012 Visual Recognition Challenge. This model was created to overcome the limitations of the lenet-5. With the ability to adjust during training, this model was created with eight layers. It receives as input the RGB images. Three max pooling layers and five convolutional layers total eight layers. Due to the layers' complete connectivity, the input's size is fixed. In order to get the best results, it was tuned with unique details like ReLU, which is used to assemble the model (Fig. 7).

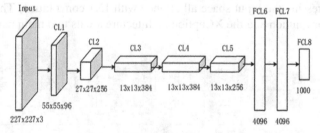

Fig. 7. [27]ALEXNET architecture

3.7 ImageNet

[16] The photos are the project's primary prerequisite for machine learning. For research purposes, the imageNet project offers a sizable database containing millions of photos. It was created for use in experiments with visual object identification software. The ImageNet project was inspired by two critical research gaps in the area of computer vision. The first was the requirement for a well defined North Star problem in computer vision. While there were many pressing issues in the field that needed to be resolved, including image segmentation, stereo vision, and 3D reconstruction, object categorization was

recognised as one of the most crucial skills that both human and machine vision needed to have. Thus, a high quality object classification standard with clearly stated assessment parameters started gaining popularity. Second, there was an urgent need for additional data to allow more generalizable machine learning approaches. Since the advent of the digital age and the accessibility of web-scale data exchanges, researchers in these fields have been active (Fig. 8).

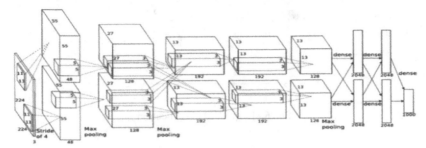

Fig. 8. [28] Architecture of IMAGENET deep CNN model

3.8 Xception

[16] Depthwise separable convolutions are a component of "extreme inception," sometimes referred to as Xception. It beyond the concepts put out in Inception. In Inception, each depth space was first constructed from a different input space using a new set of filters after the initial input was compressed using 1x1convolutions. With Xception, the exact opposite takes place. Instead, it applies the filters to every depth map separately before compressing the input space all at once with 1X1 convolution. The Depth wise Separable Convolution and the XCeption architecture are its two main parts (Fig. 9).

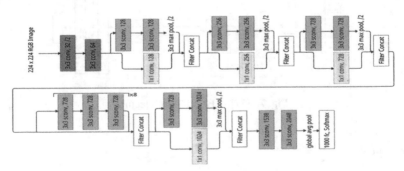

Fig. 9. [29] Architecture of XCEPTION Deep CNN model

3.9 Transfer Learning

[10, 31-36] The machine learning method of transfer learning as shown in the Fig. 10 below uses a model developed for one job as the foundation for another. The learned features are transferred to a second target network that is trained on a target dataset and task in transfer learning after first being applied to a base network that was trained on a base dataset and task. This process is more likely to be successful if the features are generic, that is, applicable to both the base task and the target task. When predictive modelling is being employed and picture data is being used as the input, transfer learning is typically used for classification tasks.

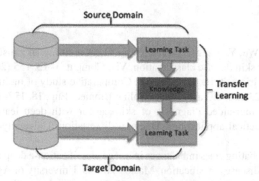

Fig. 10. [30] Work flow of transfer learning

4 Challenges and Future Direction

The device will instantly reveal the results and may use the dermis layer of the skin for the detection. The CNN approach used in the model, which delivers 86% accuracy on 40% of the recovered data, would offer more accuracy. Accurate detection will be improved by future real-time data availability. This model may be used by dermatologists and clinics to distinguish between several disorders with similar symptoms. It might be the basis for a range of photo classification problems in the healthcare sector.

5 Conclusion

This chapter provides a model for skin disease prediction using SVM classification and deep learning techniques. We aim to improve accuracy rates while also being able to predict a lot more diseases than we could with prior models, such as heart disease or stock market forecasts, by making use of deep learning's properties. We compare the effectiveness of several categorization approaches in order to categorise skin disorders into numerous groups. Apply the model to individuals with brown skin, evaluate the model's specificity, and determine the detection rate by combining machine learning and deep learning techniques. Health systems should be in line with particular healthcare demands in order to reduce the disproportionately high burden of skin disease found in the aged, to ensure maximum accuracy in skin disease detection, and to assist therapy.

The two main techniques used are: (1) Support vector machines, often known as SVMs, are among of the most popular supervised learning algorithms used for both classification and regression problems. It is mostly used, nevertheless, in Machine Learning

Classification problems. In order to swiftly categorise new data points in the future, the SVM method aims to construct the ideal decision boundary or line that may split n-dimensional space into classes (2) CNNs, a subset of artificial neural networks used in deep learning, are extensively employed for the identification and classification of objects and images. As a result, Deep Learning employs a CNN to recognise objects in an image.

References

1. Cai, G., Zhu, Y., Wu, Y., Jiang, X., Ye, J., Yang, D.: A multimodal transformer to fuse images and metadata for skin disease classification. Vis. Comput. 1–13, 135 (2022)
2. Aboulmira, A., Hrimech, H., Lachgar, M.: Comparative study of multiple CNN models for classification of 23 skin diseases. Int. J. Online Biomed. Eng. 18, 127–142 (2022)
3. Wang, Y.: Computer-aided diagnosis of skin cancer with deep learning: addressing the challenges of practical applications. Doctoral dissertation, University of British Columbia (2022)
4. Aamodt, E.: Combating class imbalances in image classification-a deep neural network-based method for skin disease classification. Master's thesis, University of Agder (2022)
5. Lalli, M., Amutha, S.: Evaluation of feature selection methods for disease survival prediction using proposed entropy-based topsis technique (2021)
6. Rajpoot, A., Saluja, G., Malsa, N., Gupta, V.: A Pchapter swarm optimization based ANN predictive model for statistical detection of COVID-19. In: Artificial Intelligence in Healthcare, pp. 21–34. Springer, Singapore (2022)
7. Srinivasu, P.N., SivaSai, J.G., Ijaz, M.F., Bhoi, A.K., Kim, W., Kang, J.J.: Classification of skin disease using deep learning neural networks with MobileNet V2 and LSTM. Sensors 21(8), 2852 (2021)
8. Abunadi, I., Senan, E.M.: Deep learning and machine learning techniques of diagnosis dermoscopy images for early detection of skin diseases. Electronics 10(24), 3158 (2021)
9. Elngar, A.A., Kumar, R., Hayat, A., Churi, P.: Intelligent system for skin disease prediction using machine learning. J. Phys. Conf. Ser. 1998(1), 012037 (2021)
10. Fan, J., Kim, J., Jung, I., Lee, Y.: A study on multiple factors affecting the accuracy of multiclass skin disease classification. Appl. Sci. 11(17), 7929 (2021)
11. Hashmani, M.A., Jameel, S.M., Rizvi, S.S.H., Shukla, S.: An adaptive federated machine learning-based intelligent system for skin disease detection: a step toward an intelligent dermoscopy device. Appl. Sci. 11, 2145 (2021)
12. Polat, K., Koc, K.O.: Detection of skin diseases from dermoscopy image using the combination of convolutional neural network and one-versus-all. J. Artif. Intell. Syst. 2, 80–97 (2020). https://doi.org/10.33969/AIS.2020.21006
13. Pham, T.C., Doucet, A., Luong, C.M., Tran, C.T., Hoang, V.D.: Improving skin-disease classification based on customized loss function combined with balanced mini-batch logic and real-time image augmentation. IEEE Access 8, 150725–150737 (2020)
14. Hameed, N., Shabut, A.M., Ghosh, M.K., Hossain, M.A.: Multi-class multi-level classification algorithm for skin lesions classification using machine learning techniques. Expert Syst. Appl. 141, 112961 (2020)
15. Pugazhenthi, V., et al.: Skin disease detection and classification. Int. J. Adv. Eng. Res. Sci. (IJAERS) 6(5), 396–400 (2019)
16. Wu, Z.H.E., et al.: Studies on different CNN algorithms for face skin disease classification based on clinical images. IEEE Access 7, 66505–66511 (2019)

17. Chaurasia, V., Pal, S.: Skin diseases prediction: binary classification machine learning and multi model ensemble techniques. Res. J. Pharm. Technol. **12**(8), 3829–3832 (2019)
18. Mridha, K., et al.: Plant disease detection using web application by neural network. In: 2021 IEEE 6th International Conference on Computing, Communication and Automation (ICCCA), pp. 130–136 (2021). https://doi.org/10.1109/ICCCA52192.2021.9666354
19. Adhikary, A., Majumder, K., Chatterjee, S., Shaw, R.N., Ghosh, A.: Machine learning based approaches in the detection of Parkinson's disease – a comparative study. In: Mekhilef, S., Shaw, R.N., Siano, P. (eds.) ICEEE 2022. LNEE, vol. 894, pp. 774–793. Springer, Singapore (2022). https://doi.org/10.1007/978-981-19-1677-9_68
20. Alenezi, N.S.A.: A method of skin disease detection using image processing and machine learning. Procedia Comput. Sci. **163**, 85–92 (2019)
21. Okuboyejo, D.A., Olugbara, O.O., Odunaike, S.A.: Automating skin disease diagnosis using image classification. In: Proceedings of the World Congress on Engineering and Computer Science, vol. 2, pp. 850–854, October 2013
22. Lucius, M., et al.: Deep neural frameworks improve the accuracy of general practitioners in the classification of pigmented skin lesions. Diagnostics **10**(11), 969 (2020)
23. Aydogdu, M.F., Celik, V., Demirci, M.F.: Comparison of three different CNN architectures for age classification. In: 2017 IEEE 11th International Conference on Semantic Computing (ICSC), pp. 372–377. IEEE, January 2017
24. Ji, Q., Huang, J., He, W., Sun, Y.: Optimized deep convolutional neural networks for identification of macular diseases from optical coherence tomography images. Algorithms **12**(3), 51 (2019)
25. Gupta, V., Bibhu, V.: Deep residual network based brain tumor segmentation and detection with MRI using improved invasive bat algorithm. Multimedia Tools Appl., 1–23 (2022)
26. Malsa, N., Singh, P., Gautam, J., Srivastava, A., Singh, S.P.: Source of treatment selection for different states of India and performance analysis using machine learning algorithms for classification. In: Soft Computing: Theories and Applications, pp. 235–245. Springer, Singapore (2020). https://doi.org/10.1007/978-981-15-4032-5_23
27. Palimkar, P., Shaw, R.N., Ghosh, A.: Machine learning technique to prognosis diabetes disease: random forest classifier approach. In: Bianchini, M., Piuri, V., Das, S., Shaw, R.N. (eds.) Advanced Computing and Intelligent Technologies. LNNS, vol. 218, pp. 219–244. Springer, Singapore (2022). https://doi.org/10.1007/978-981-16-2164-2_19
28. Ann, A.J., Ruiz, C.: Using deep learning for melanoma detection in dermoscopy images. Int. J. Mach. Learn. Comput. **8**(1), 61–68 (2018)
29. Srinivasan, K., et al.: Performance comparison of deep CNN models for detecting driver's distraction. CMC-Comput. Mater. Continua **68**(3), 4109–4124 (2021)
30. Tan, C., Sun, F., Kong, T., Zhang, W., Yang, C., Liu, C.: A survey on deep transfer learning. In: Kůrková, V., Manolopoulos, Y., Hammer, B., Iliadis, L., Maglogiannis, I. (eds.) International Conference on Artificial Neural Networks, pp. 270–279. Springer, Cham, October 2018. https://doi.org/10.1007/978-3-030-01424-7_27
31. Rawat, S.S., Verma, S.K., Kumar, Y.: Infrared small target detection based on non-convex triple tensor factorisation. IET Image Proc. **15**(2), 556–570 (2021)
32. Rawat, S.S., Verma, S.K., Kumar, Y.: Reweighted infrared patch image model for small target detection based on non-convex $\mathscr{L}$p-norm minimisation and TV regularisation. IET Image Proc. **14**(9), 1937–1947 (2020)
33. Rawat, S.S., Alghamdi, S., Kumar, G., Alotaibi, Y., Khalaf, O.I., Verma, L.P.: Infrared small target detection based on partial sum minimization and total variation. Mathematics **10**(4), 671 (2022)
34. Rawat, S.S., Singh, S., Alotaibi, Y., Alghamdi, S., Kumar, G.: Infrared target-background separation based on weighted nuclear norm minimization and robust principal component analysis. Mathematics **10**(16), 2829 (2022)

35. Singh, S., et al.: Hybrid models for breast cancer detection via transfer learning technique (2022)
36. Singh, S.: Deep attention network for pneumonia detection using chest x-ray images (2022)
37. Malsa, N., Vyas, V., Gautam, J.: RMSE calculation of LSTM models for predicting prices of different cryptocurrencies. Int. J. Syst. Assur. Eng. Manag. (2021).https://doi.org/10.1007/s13198-021-01431-1
38. Gupta, P., Malsa, N., Saxena, N., Agarwal, S., Singh, S.P.: Short-term load forecasting using parametric and non-parametric approaches. In: Pant, M., Sharma, T.K., Verma, O.P., Singla, R., Sikander, A. (eds.) Soft Computing: Theories and Applications. AISC, vol. 1053, pp. 747–755. Springer, Singapore (2020). https://doi.org/10.1007/978-981-15-0751-9_68
39. Gautam, J., Malsa, N., Gautam, S., Gaur, N.K., Adhikary, P., Pathak, S.: Selecting a family planning method for various age groups of different states in India. In: 2021 IEEE 4th International Conference on Computing, Power and Communication Technologies (GUCON), pp. 1–6 (2021). https://doi.org/10.1109/GUCON50781.2021.9573825

Optimization of Routing Protocol for Underwater Acoustic Sensor Network Using Modified Lion Algorithm Over DPSO

Y. Yashwanth Reddy and Vijayalakshmi[✉]

Department of Electronics and Communication Engineering, Saveetha School of Engineering,
Saveetha Institute of Medical and Technical Sciences, Saveetha University,
Chennai, Tamil Nadu 602105, India
vijayalakshmi.sse@saveetha.com

Abstract. This chapter aims to develop an Energy Optimization routing protocol to reduce delay, energy usage, and normalised routing overhead in Underwater Acoustic Sensor Networks (UASN) by using the Novel LION Optimization Algorithm instead of the Discrete Particle Swarm Optimization algorithm. A 20 samples were considered for the process in two groups and each group contains 10 samples were collected with pre-test of 80% power. For the group 1 the LION Optimization algorithm is used, whereas Discrete Particle Swarm Optimization algorithm is used in group 2. The measures of average energy consumption, delay, and normalised routing overhead from network were measured through simulation using NS 2 simulator. The statistical analysis of the performance measures was calculated Using SPSS Software. For vigorously varying environmental and geographical topology condition the proposed novel LION optimization algorithm achieve 12% of reduction in delay, provides 20% of energy consumption and achieves 40% of Normalized routing overhead when compared to Discrete Particle Swarm Optimization algorithm. Observed statistical analysis reveals that the significant value of P is less than 0.05 was achieved. The proposed LION Optimization algorithm performs drastically better energy efficiency than DPSO algorithm which changed into determined from simulation results.

Keywords: Under Water Acoustic Sensor Networks (UWASN) · Novel LION optimization algorithm · Discrete Particle Swarm Optimization (DPSO) · Energy consumption · Routing overhead · Delay

1 Introduction

Underwater acoustic sensor networks (UWASN) are essential for keeping an eye on and monitoring different ocean depths. Effective routing algorithms are required for monitoring and surveillance in various maritime conditions and water column fluctuations [1]. Water has a crucial role in the lives of both humans and other animals, as well as in the lives of other species. Because of technological developments, it is now possible to conduct this research in these fields. These sensor nodes have smart processors and smart sensors integrated right into them, which allows them to connect with

© The Author(s), under exclusive license to Springer Nature Switzerland AG 2023
R. N. Shaw et al. (Eds.): ICACIS 2022, CCIS 1749, pp. 747–755, 2023.
https://doi.org/10.1007/978-3-031-25088-0_65

one another. Underwater wireless sensor networks (UWSNs) consist of a large number of autonomous sensors with energy constraints and homogeneous nodes [2]. Effective routing algorithms are required in the various ocean environments and water column variations for monitoring and surveillance applications such as pollution monitoring, underwater exploration [3]. The four ocean environments are pressure, temperature, salinity, and depth. The fluctuations in the water column include dissolved gases, sedimentation drift, rotating and divergent wind stress, and geometric and Doppler effects. It's difficult to transmit data when the water column varies [4] because of the frequently changing water column, which is caused by dissolved gas and rotating and divergent wind stress. Effective methods are required for the prediction or measurement of the parameters of the ocean environment and water column.

Within the lats five years, several research chapters on enhancing the lifetime of underwater Acoustic sensor networks (UWASN) have been published under various in which 120 research articles were published in IEEE Xplore and 350 chapters are published in Google Scholar [5] the evolved work seeks to reduce energy consumption and increase network life. ACO was used to identify the best route between the Channel (CH) and Base Station (BS), considering node degree, residual energy, and distance. The chosen work's superiority in terms of energy usage, living nodes, and dead nodes was ultimately demonstrated in [6]. The chapter [6] proposed a novel algorithm called FF-PUD for selecting the best CHs. It also suggested a new clustering model with the best CHS. Finally, the constructed scheme's performance was assessed by comparing it to other systems in terms of risk, alive nodes, energy, and latency. The work [7] suggested a GECR and GA-based routing method for extending network lifetime and enhancing energy efficiency and [8] have presented a fresh clustering method that chose CHs using GWO. The solutions were optimised for CH selection based on the projected energy use and total node remaining energy.

In major research the factor of internal water column variation and doppler effect in UASN are not considered that leads to early dead nodes, more energy consumption and produces longer delays. Underwater Acoustic Sensor Networks can employ the suggested algorithm to enhance energy usage, reduced delay, and normalised routing overhead by using noval lion optimization algorithm in comparison with DPSO algorithm.

2   Materials and Methods

Buffalo algorithm and PSO algorithm two groups (datasets) with 10 samples each are collected for pretest analysis with pre-test power of 80%, error of 0.5, threshold of 0.05, and confidence level of 95%.

Samples for group 1 are prepared using aqua-sim [8] in NS2 to analyse the energy, latency, and normalised routing overhead of the discrete particle swarm optimization (DPSO) algorithm for various time windows. The network coding is created in NS2 in order to replicate the routing performance. For acoustic propagation, the algorithm employs an energy model, and routing metrics are examined for each node at intervals of one millisecond [8]. The testing setup is carried out using the open-source NS2 software and the aqua-sim patch for an underwater setting. The experimental goals are set forth in the testing process in order to improve energy efficiency and decrease delay. Statistical analysis software is used to gather the data sets from the bash file (ns-allinone-2.35.tar.gz) [8].

The group 2 sample preparation to analyse energy, latency, and normalised routing overhead LION overhead LION optimization technique by randomly adjusting depth for various time intervals was done using aqua-sim NS2. For acoustic propagation, the algorithm employs an energy model, and routing metrics are examined for each node at intervals of one millisecond. Group 1 has a brand-new Lion optimization technique to improve network performance as a whole. The Lion optimization algorithm, which is based on dynamic topology, has the characteristics of quick convergence and periodic convergence.

Modified LION optimization algorithm:

The LOA is a population-based meta heuristic method in which the population of the solution space is initially generated at random. Every single solution in this method is referred to as a Lion. A lion is represented in an N-variable dimensional optimization problem as follows:

$$\text{Lion} = (x1; \ x2; \ x3; x4 \ldots; \ xNvar) \tag{1}$$

Each Lion's cost (fitness value) is calculated by assessing the cost function, as follows:

$$\text{fitness value of lion} = f(\text{Lion}) = f(\ x1; \ x2; \ x3; x4 \ldots; \ xNvar) \tag{2}$$

Npop solutions are created at random in the search space in the first stage. Randomly selected as nomad lions are %N of the created solutions [9]. The remaining population will be split into P prides at random. Every answer in this method has a distinct gender that didn't change throughout optimization.

3 Statistical Analysis

IBM SPSS 27.0.1 [10] was used for statistical comparison of parameters like delay, Energy consumption and Normalized routing overhead. The significance value of the independent t-test was $p < 0.05$ which was done in SPSS Software. The statistical analysis for novel Lion optimization algorithm and Discrete Particle Swarm Optimization (DPSO) algorithm was done. The calculation is performed utilizing G-power 0.8 with a confidence interval of 95%. Because they are reliant on the inputs, the dependent variables are normalised routing overhead, delay, and energy. Particle count and population size are the independent variables used to assess how well new and existing algorithms perform on dependent variables using independent two-tailed tests.

4 Results

The Novel Lion optimization algorithm's simulation results are examined in terms of energy usage, delay, Normalized Routing Overhead for efficient data transfer, and mechanisms for hole identification and repair. The performance of the approach was compared to that of the discrete particle swarm optimization (DPSO) algorithm using an NS2 simulator. The simulation results show Energy consumption is reduced 20% The delay 20%and normalized routing overhead reduced by 5% respectively.

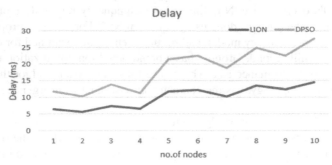

Fig. 1. Shows the comparison between LION optimization algorithm and D PSO algorithm for delay in underwater acoustic sensor network.

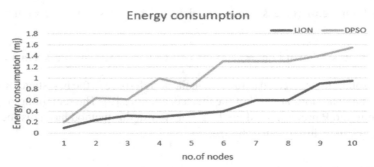

Fig. 2. Shows the comparison between LION optimization algorithm and DPSO algorithm for energy consumption in underwater acoustic sensor network.

The number of nodes required to transfer a data packet from source to destination is depicted in Fig. 1 as the delay. The suggested method, Novel Lion optimization algorithm, is superior since it finds the path between source and destination nodes while relying on the least amount of delay between them. Figure 2 shows how the energy consumption for various algorithms varies. It is described as the total amount of energy used by every node in the network during a specific simulation period. Energy usage grows in tandem with node mobility. Results unambiguously demonstrate that the suggested method consumes less energy than previous approaches. The variation of normalised routing overhead is shown in Fig. 3, the quantity of bytes that the destination has successfully received. Routing protocols saw a decrease in normalised routing overhead as node mobility increased.

Figure 4 shows the comparison of mean delay (±1SD) for group 1 (Novel Lion optimization algorithm) and group 2 (DPSO algorithm). Novel Lion optimization algorithm provides less delay than DPSO algorithm. Figure 5 shows the comparison of mean

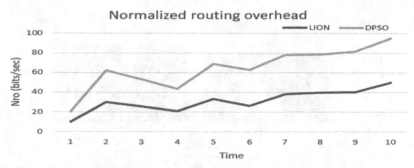

Fig. 3. Shows the comparison between LION optimization algorithm and D PSO algorithm for normalized routing overhead in underwater acoustic sensor network.

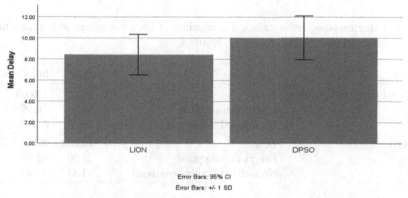

Fig. 4. Barchart-comparison of mean Delay of Lion optimization algorithm and DPSO algorithm. X axis: Lion optimization algorithm vs DPSO algorithm, Y axis: Mean Delay ± 1 SD

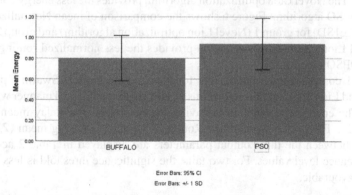

Fig. 5. Barchart-comparison of mean Energy consumption of Lion optimization algorithm and DPSO algorithm axis: Lion optimization algorithm vs DPSO algorithm, Y axis: Mean Energy consumption ± 1 SD.

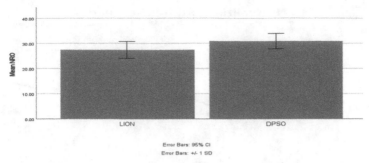

Fig. 6. Barchart-comparison of mean Energy consumption of Lion optimization algorithm and DPSO algorithm. X axis: Lion optimization algorithm vs DPSO algorithm, Y axis: Mean Energy consumption ± 1 SD

Table 1. Represents descriptive statistical comparison of three parameters with respect to time for Lion optimization algorithm and DPSO algorithm.

Groups	Parameter	N	Mean	Std. deviation
LION optimization algorithm	Delay	20	8.762	2.4603
	Energy consumption		50.9	76.56
	Normalized Routing Overhead		26.37	5.275
DPSO	Delay	20	10.602	2.750
	Energy consumption		58.30	42.89
	Normalized Routing overhead		31.84	4.883

energy consumption (±1SD) for group 1 (Novel Lion optimization algorithm) and group 2 (DPSO). The Novel Lion optimization algorithm provides the less energy consumption than the DPSO algorithm. Figure 6 shows the comparison of mean Normalized routing overhead (±1SD) for group 1 (Novel Lion optimization algorithm) and group 2 (DPSO). The Novel Lion optimization algorithm provides the less normalized routing overhead than the DPSO algorithm.

Table 1 compares three parameters for the Discrete Particle Swarm Optimization (DPSO) and Lion optimization algorithms in a descriptive statistical manner with respect to time. The energy consumption is having mean (669.9). The delay mean is having mean (5.62). The packet Normalized Routing Overhead is having mean (27.37). The variations between the three output parameters are displayed in Table 2 according to the significance level values. For two tails, the significance threshold is less than 0.05, which is favourable.

Table 2. The table express the variances between the three output parameters in accordance with the significance level values. (The significance level is less than 0.05 for two tails which is good).

Levene's test for equality of variances		F	sig	T-test for equality of mean							
				t	dif	One side p	Two side p	Mean diff	Standard error	95% confidence interval of the difference Lower upper	
Delay	Equal variances assumed	.053	.028	−1.196	18	.124	.247	−1.395	1.1670	−3.8473	1.0563
	Equal variances not assumed			−1.196	17.781	.124	.247	−1.39550	1.1670	−3.8473	1.0563
Energy consumption	Equal variances assumed	5.141	036	−10.572	18	<.001	<.001	−293.400	27.753	−351.707	−235.09
	Equal variances not assumed			−10.572	14.42	<.001	<.001	−293.400	27.753	−352.86	−233.93
Normalized routing overhead	Equal variances assumed	.222	.036	−1.528	18	.072	.144	−3.4730	2.2731	−8.248	1.3027
	Equal variances not assumed			−1.528	17.89	.072	.144	−3.4730	2.2731	−8.2507	1.3047

5 Discussion

Delay, energy consumption, and normalised routing overhead are just a few of the performance indicators that have been used to measure the networks' performance over extensive research. This study developed a brand-new optimization technique called Lion that complies with energy and delay requirements, and the simulation analysis demonstrates that it outperforms previous approaches even when the network's energy consumption is much reduced. The network lifetime and delay can both be guaranteed to be improved by our comprehensive optimization.

Underwater acoustic sensor networks (UWASN) present a more challenging environment for routing protocol design than terrestrial wireless sensor networks because of the varied transmission media. [11] In order to choose the best forwarder node, the grey wolf optimization technique is applied. The proposed effort extends the lifetime of the network by avoiding the vacuum zone and balancing the energy of the network. The proposed [12] clustering algorithm would dynamically rotate the cluster head while regularly grouping UASNs. The longer network lifetime and decreased energy use are shown by the simulation findings. Additionally, it obtains greater stability [13], since underwater sensors have a finite amount of energy, the majority of UASNs are needed to monitor the underwater 3D environment. To find the best position for SN in underwater communication, [14] a new optimization algorithm called the Sea Lion Optimization (SLO) procedure is suggested. By locating the targeted best position, this method optimally positions the acoustic SNs based on the maximum connectivity rate.

As there is a stringent limit on the amount of energy that can be used in underwater sensor nodes, it is impossible to currently develop an accurate and trustworthy model of energy consumption for underwater sensor nodes and networks. The most critical topic of research is therefore always how to lower the energy consumption of underwater acoustic sensor networks. Future research considers the design of algorithms for dynamically changing topological conditions for improving energy efficiency in various underwater environments.

6   Conclusion

In an underwater acoustic sensor network, a novel Lion optimization algorithm technique was implemented. It outperforms the Discrete Particle Swarm Optimization method in terms of energy consumption, delay, and normalised routing overhead, with reductions of 2 percent, 3%, and 1%, respectively.

References

1. Bhanu Teja, N., Devarajan, Y., Mishra, R., Sivasaravanan, S., Thanikaivel Murugan, D.: Detailed analysis on Sterculia Foetida kernel oil as renewable fuel in compression ignition engine. Biomass Convers. Biorefinery (2021).https://doi.org/10.1007/s13399-021-01328-w
2. Goyal, N., Sapra, L., Sandhu, J.K.: Energy-Efficient Underwater Wireless Communications and Networking. IGI Global (2020)
3. Chen, M., Zhu, D.: Data collection from underwater acoustic sensor networks based on optimization algorithms. Computing **102**(1), 83–104 (2019). https://doi.org/10.1007/s00607-019-00731-6
4. Jin, L., University of Western Australia: Reinforcement Learning Based Energy Efficient Routing Protocols for Underwater Acoustic Wireless Sensor Networks (2012)
5. Rajawat, A.S., Barhanpurkar, K., Shaw, R.N., Ghosh, A.: Risk Detection in wireless body sensor networks for health monitoring using hybrid deep learning. In: Mekhilef, S., Favorskaya, M., Pandey, R.K., Shaw, R.N. (eds.) Innovations in Electrical and Electronic Engineering. LNEE, vol. 756, pp. 683–696. Springer, Singapore (2021). https://doi.org/10.1007/978-981-16-0749-3_54
6. Baskar, M., Renuka Devi, R., Ramkumar, J., Kalyanasundaram, P., Suchithra, M., Amutha, B.: Region centric minutiae propagation measure orient forgery detection with finger print analysis in health care systems. Neural Process. Lett. (2021).https://doi.org/10.1007/s11063-020-10407-4
7. Paul, A., Sinha, S., Shaw, R.N., Ghosh, A.: A neuro-fuzzy based IDS for internet-integrated WSN. In: Bansal, J.C., Paprzycki, M., Bianchini, M., Das, S. (eds.) Computationally Intelligent Systems and their Applications. SCI, vol. 950, pp. 71–86. Springer, Singapore (2021). https://doi.org/10.1007/978-981-16-0407-2_6
8. Banerjee, A., et al.: Construction of effective wireless sensor network for smart communication using modified ant colony optimization technique. In: Bianchini, M., Piuri, V., Das, S., Shaw, R.N. (eds.) Advanced Computing and Intelligent Technologies. LNNS, vol. 218, pp. 269–278. Springer, Singapore (2022). https://doi.org/10.1007/978-981-16-2164-2_22
9. Sathiyaraj, R., Bharathi, A.: An efficient intelligent traffic light control and deviation system for traffic congestion avoidance using multi-agent system. Transport (2019).https://doi.org/10.3846/transport.2019.11115

10. Gola, K.K., Chaurasia, N., Gupta, B., Niranjan, D.S.: Sea lion optimization algorithm based node deployment strategy in underwater acoustic sensor network. Int. J. Commun. Syst. (2021). https://doi.org/10.1002/dac.4723
11. Karthigadevi, G., et al.: Chemico-nanotreatment methods for the removal of persistent organic pollutants and xenobiotics in water - a review. Biores. Technol. 324(March), 124678 (2021)
12. Banerjee, A., et al.: Building of efficient communication system in smart city using wireless sensor network through hybrid optimization technique. In: Piuri, V., Shaw, R.N., Ghosh, A., Islam, R. (eds.) AI and IoT for Smart City Applications. SCI, vol. 1002, pp. 15–30. Springer, Singapore (2022). https://doi.org/10.1007/978-981-16-7498-3_2
13. Bhavikatti, S.K., et al.: Investigating the antioxidant and cytocompatibility of mimusops elengi linn extract over human gingival fibroblast cells. Int. J. Environ. Res. Public Health 18(13) (2021). https://doi.org/10.3390/ijerph18137162

COVID-19 Detection in the Images of Chest CT Scan Using K-NN in Comparison with NB Classifier to Improve the Accuracy

Y. B. Dinesh Govind and B. Anitha Vijayalakshmi[(✉)]

Department of Electronics and Communication Engineering, SIMATS School of Engineering, Saveetha Institute of Medical and Technical Sciences, Chennai, Tamilnadu, India
anithavijayalakshmib.sse@saveetha.com

Abstract. This chapter is about the improvisation in the accuracy in COVID-19 detection using chest CT-scan images through K-Nearest Neighbour (K-NN) compared with Naive-Bayes (NB) classifier. The sample size considered for this detection is 20, for group 1 and 2, where G-power is 0.8. The value of alpha and beta was 0.05 and 0.2 along with a confidence interval at 95%. The K-NN classifier has achieved 95.297% of higher accuracy rate when compared with Naive Bayes classifier 92.087%. The results obtained were considered to be error-free since it was having the significance value of 0.036 ($p < 0.05$). Therefore, in this work K-Nearest Neighbor has performed significantly better than Naive Bayes algorithm in detection of COVID-19.

Keywords: COVID · Novel K-NN · Naive Bayes (NB) classifier · Accuracy rate · CT scan images · Disease

1 Introduction

COVID-19 was caused due to a virus called coronavirus [1, 2]. Coronavirus indications include windedness, fever, migraine, hack, weakness, sore throat, and muscle torment [3]. For the medical practitioner it is a very critical task to identify coronavirus (COVID-19) patients since the spread is very rapid. It is essential to find and avoid those viruses from spreading and treatments for patients. AI predicts COVID and helps to overwhelm the lack of handiness of doctors and physicians in far-off places [4].

Researchers have reported a few works on the use of COVID-19 predictive machine learning and diagnostics over the past three years. More than 180 journal publications, mostly from IEEE, and 60 more chapters from Google scholar are included in this research area, which has been published for more than five years. The classifier of NB has been accepted as a straight forward classifier based on clearly independent- premises from the interpretation of the Bayesian-theorem [5]. Researchers [6] have designed an open-source COVID-19 diagnosis system based on a deep K-NN. To detect COVID-19 from chest X-ray images [7] convolutional neural network frameworks have been proposed. In the work [8] proposed the weighted representation-based and the weighted local

© The Author(s), under exclusive license to Springer Nature Switzerland AG 2023
R. N. Shaw et al. (Eds.): ICACIS 2022, CCIS 1749, pp. 756–763, 2023.
https://doi.org/10.1007/978-3-031-25088-0_66

mean representation-based k-nearest neighbor rule. Our team has extensive knowledge and research experience that has translated into high quality publications [9–18].

The main problem with the existing NB method is that the accuracy depends on the data quality and the extrapolation period is unhurried due to the large amount of information. To rectify the problem, this chapter introduces a technique in detecting COVID-19 disease by utilizing the K-NN in comparison with the NB classifier. The work suggests K-NN to produce better accuracy than the existing NB classifier.

2 Materials and Methods

In this chapter, the database was taken from Kaggle containing an X-ray scan of the chest. It includes 3 stages such as standard scanning, pneumonia scanning and COVID-19 scans. The modified database contains 550 complete scans in which 200 scans of the general population, 200 scans of pneumonia patients and 150 scans of COVID-19 are infected. Two groups are considered and 20 samples for each group, total samples considered are 40. 75% of the database is involved in training and remaining in testing. The NB classifier novel K-NN belongs to group 1 and 2 and has the confidence interval at 95% [19].

2.1 NB and K-NN

NB is a famous classifier that has been applied in a few spaces, for example, climate anticipating, bioinformatics, picture and example acknowledgment, and clinical determination. NB permits each component to contribute towards the order choice both similarly and freely of different highlights. Albeit such straightforwardness increments computational effectiveness, it at times makes NB deficient with certifiable conditions. Consider about $V = \{v_1, v_2, v_3, \ldots v_n\}$ to be a bunch of highlight vectors of another thing NI to be characterized and $T = \{t_1, t_2, t_3, \ldots t_m\}$ be a set of target classes. The likelihood of another thing being in class nc_j utilizing NB is given by

$$Target(NI) = arg\ arg\ \max_{t_j \in T}[P(t_j|V] \tag{1}$$

$$Target(NI) = arg\ arg\ \max_{t_j \in T}\left[\frac{P(V) \times P(t_j)}{P(V)}\right] \tag{2}$$

where, $P(V)$ is the contingent likelihood of class t_j given the element vector V (additionally called back likelihood), $P(V)$ is the restrictive likelihood of class V given the class t_j (likewise called probability), and $P(t_j)$ is the earlier likelihood of class t_j.

2.2 Statistical Analysis

For statistical implementation, the software tool used here is IBM SPSS (Statistical Package for the Social Sciences) V26.0 [20]. The independent sample T test was performed. Dependent variables are accuracy and independent variables are K-NN and NB classifiers.

3 Results

The K-NN accuracy rate is 95.297% and for the NB Classifier is 92.087%. Figure 1 shows the sample input image for COVID-19 from chest CT Scan Images by using K-NN classifier in comparison with NB classifier.

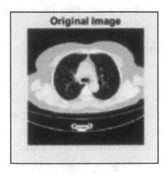

Fig. 1. Sample input image

Figure 2 shows the linearization segmented image for detection of skin cancer cells by using K-NN classifier in comparison with NB classifier. The final classification output as shown in Fig. 3 for detecting COVID-19 using K-NN classifier in comparison with NB classifier.

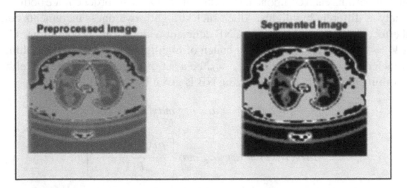

Fig. 2. Preprocessed image and Linearization segmented image

Figure 4 portrays the output measure for performance improvement using the K-NN classifier in comparison with the NB classifier. Figure 5 shows the bar graph for accuracy rate K-NN compared with NB Classifier.

Table 1 portrays the evaluation metrics of comparison of K-NN and NB classifiers. The accuracy rate of K-NN is 95.297% and NB has 92.087%. In all aspects of parameters K-NN provides better performance compared with the NB of a performance improvement with enhanced accuracy rate.

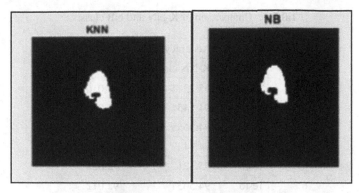

Fig. 3. Final output image

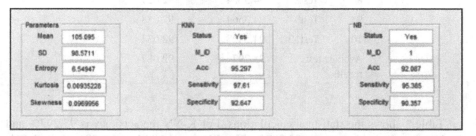

Fig. 4. Output measure for performance improvement in detection of COVID-19

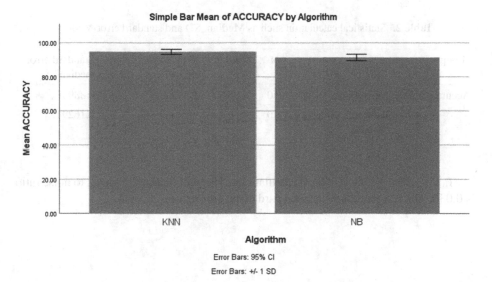

Fig. 5. Simple Bar graph for K-NN classifier accuracy NB Classifier

Table 1. Comparison of K-NN and NB classifier

Si. No	Test size	Accuracy rate	
		K-NN classifier	NB classifier
1	Test1	95.2343	92.010
2	Test2	94.5454	92.0323
3	Test3	94.3655	92.0533
4	Test4	94.3432	92.0282
5	Test5	95.1212	92.023
6	Test6	94.5654	92.012
7	Test7	94.3567	92.085
8	Test8	94.3664	92.029
9	Test9	94.3564	92.058
10	Test10	94.5423	92.034
Average test results		95.297	92.087

Table 2 shows the statistical calculations. For K-NN the accuracy is 95.297% and for NB the obtained output is 92.087%. The SD for K-NN is 0.24029 and for NB is 1.89293. The Standard Error Median of K-NN is 0.16291 and NB is 0.88938.

Table 2. Statistical calculation such as Median, SD and standard error Median

Group		N	Median	Standard deviation (SD)	Standard error median
Accuracy rate	Naive Bayes (NB)	10	92.087	1.89293	0.88938
	K-Nearest Neighbor (K-NN)	10	95.297	0.24029	0.16291

Table 3 displays the statistical calculations. The significance for signal to noise ratio is 0.036. The tests results with a standard error difference of 0.0675.

Table 3. Group variances results

Group		Levene's test		t-test for equality of medians						
		F	Sig.	t	df	Sig. (2-tailed)	Median difference	Std. error difference	95% Confidence interval (Lower)	95% Confidence interval (Upper)
Accuracy	Equal variances assumed	8.672	0.036	17.893	18	.000	11.67484	0.67485	11.78495	13.67833
	Equal variances not assumed			17.183	12.564	.000	11.01123	0.21828	10.21224	12.01823

4 Results

K-NN provides better accuracy output when compared to the NB classifier. K-NN is a powerful technique to classify human misbehavior activity. The accuracy result produced by K-NN 95.297% is better than the NB classifier with accuracy of 92.087%. K-NN can significantly improve classification accuracy and time efficiency. This shows that the maximum accuracy is obtained quickly in the K-NN classifier.

On the occurrence of asymptomatic infection the research was done, and it was found 15.8% in children [21]. The signs of COVID-19 are having lesser senses of taste and smell [22]. Another work [23] is about the transmission of the disease. Based on the objective function and the number of hidden layers will vary. It was [24] learnt about the diagnosis of COVID-19 viral disease.

The K-NN algorithm is a distance based classifier. The limitation is that it deploys heuristic in finding its decision, and it's sensitive to the K value, which makes the analysis complex. In future COVID-19 may be identified by using machine learning to make the process simple and enhance the accuracy in detecting the disease.

5 Conclusion

The proposed model K-Nearest Neighbor (K-NN) exhibits better performance than Naive Bayes (NB), in terms of accuracy. The accuracy of K-Nearest Neighbor (K-NN) is 95.297% and it is higher than Naive Bayes (NB) whose accuracy rate is 92.087%. K-NN shows significant performance improvement in detection of COVID-19 with an improved accuracy rate of 95.297%.

References

1. Barstugan, M., Ozkaya, U., Ozturk, S.: Coronavirus (COVID-19) classification using CT images by machine learning methods. arXiv [cs.CV]. http://arxiv.org/abs/2003.09424 (2020)
2. Shaban, W.M., Rabie, A.H., Saleh, A.I., Abo-Elsoud, M.A.: A new COVID-19 patients detection strategy (CPDS) based on hybrid feature selection and enhanced KNN classifier. Knowl. Based Syst. **205**, 106270 (2020)

3. Huang, C., et al.: Clinical features of patients infected with 2019 novel coronavirus in Wuhan, China. Lancet **395**(10223), 497–506 (2020). https://doi.org/10.1016/s0140-6736(20)30183-5

4. Ye, J., Lin, C., Liu, J., Ai, Z., Zhang, G.: Systematic summary and analysis of Chinese HVAC guidelines coping with COVID-19. Indoor Built Environ. **31**(5), 1176–1192 (2022)

5. Dai, Y., Sun, H.: The naive Bayes text classification algorithm based on rough set in the cloud platform. J. Chem. Pharm. Res. **6**(7), 1636–1643 (2014)

6. Wang, L., Lin, Z.Q., Wong, A.: COVID-Net: a tailored deep convolutional neural network design for detection of COVID-19 cases from chest X-ray images. Sci. Rep. **10**(1), 19549 (2020)

7. Narin, A., Kaya, C., Pamuk, Z.: Automatic detection of coronavirus disease (COVID-19) using X-ray images and deep convolutional neural networks. Pattern Anal. Appl. **24**(3), 1207–1220 (2021). https://doi.org/10.1007/s10044-021-00984-y

8. Gou, J., Qiu, W., Yi, Z., Shen, X., Zhan, Y., Ou, W.: Locality constrained representation-based K-nearest neighbor classification. Knowl. Based Syst. **167**, 38–52 (2019)

9. Bhavikatti, S.K., et al.: Investigating the antioxidant and cytocompatibility of mimusops elengi linn extract over human gingival fibroblast cells. Int. J. Environ. Res. Public Health **18**(13) (2021). https://doi.org/10.3390/ijerph18137162

10. Karobari, M.I., et al.: An In Vitro stereomicroscopic evaluation of bioactivity between neo MTA plus, pro root MTA, BIODENTINE & glass ionomer cement using dye penetration method. Materials **14**(12) (2021). https://doi.org/10.3390/ma14123159

11. Shanmugam, V., et al.: Circular economy in biocomposite development: state-of-the-art, challenges and emerging trends. Compos. Part C Open Access **5**, 100138 (2021)

12. Sawant, K., et al.: Dentinal microcracks after root canal instrumentation using instruments manufactured with different NiTi alloys and the SAF system: a systematic review. NATO Adv. Sci. Inst. Ser. E Appl. Sci. **11**(11), 4984 (2021)

13. Muthukrishnan, L.: Nanotechnology for cleaner leather production: a review. Environ. Chem. Lett. **19**(3), 2527–2549 (2021)

14. Preethi, K.A., Auxzilia Preethi, K., Lakshmanan, G., Sekar, D.: Antagomir technology in the treatment of different types of cancer. Epigenomics **13**(7), 481–484 (2021). https://doi.org/10.2217/epi-2020-0439

15. Karthigadevi, G., et al.: Chemico-nanotreatment methods for the removal of persistent organic pollutants and xenobiotics in water - a review. Bioresour. Technol. **324**, 124678 (2021)

16. Sinha, T., Chowdhury, T., Shaw, R.N., Ghosh, A.: Analysis and prediction of COVID-19 confirmed cases using deep learning models: a comparative study. In: Bianchini, M., Piuri, V., Das, S., Shaw, R.N. (eds.) Advanced Computing and Intelligent Technologies. LNNS, vol. 218, pp. 207–218. Springer, Singapore (2022). https://doi.org/10.1007/978-981-16-2164-2_18

17. Veerasimman, A., et al.: Thermal properties of natural fiber sisal based hybrid composites – a brief review. J. Nat. Fibers, 1–11 (2021)

18. Baskar, M., Renuka Devi, R., Ramkumar, J., Kalyanasundaram, P., Suchithra, M., Amutha, B.: Region centric minutiae propagation measure orient forgery detection with finger print analysis in health care systems. Neural Process. Lett. (2021). https://doi.org/10.1007/s11063-020-10407-4

19. Afify, H.M., Darwish, A., Mohammed, K.K., Hassanien, A.E.: An automated CAD system of CT chest images for COVID-19 based on genetic algorithm and K-nearest neighbor classifier. Ingénierie des Systèmes d Inf. **25**(5), 589–594 (2020)

20. Palimkar, P., et al.: Unique action identifier by using magnetometer, accelerometer and gyroscope: KNN approach. In: Bianchini, M., Piuri, V., Das, S., Shaw, R.N. (eds.) Advanced Computing and Intelligent Technologies. LNNS, vol. 218. Springer, Singapore (2022). https://doi.org/10.1007/978-981-16-2164-2_48X

21. Lu, X., et al.: SARS-CoV-2 infection in children. N. Engl. J. Med. **382**(17), 1663–1665 (2020)
22. Russell, B., Moss, C., Rigg, A., Hopkins, C., Papa, S., Van Hemelrijck, M.: Anosmia and ageusia are emerging as symptoms in patients with COVID-19: what does the current evidence say? Ecancermedical Sci. **14**, ed98 (2020)
23. Li, L., et al.: Propagation analysis and prediction of the COVID-19. Infect. Dis. Model **5**, 282–292 (2020)
24. Yavuz, Ü., Dudak, M.N.: Classification of covid-19 dataset with some machine learning methods. J. Amasya University Inst. Sci. Technol. **1**(1), 30–37 (2020)

Deep Learning Based Dynamic Object Addition to Video Instances for Creating Synthetic Data

Yadhu Vamsi Chinthada[✉] and S. Adarsh

Department of Electronics and Communication Engineering,
Amrita School of Engineering, Amrita Vishwa Vidyapeetham, Coimbatore, India
yvamsich@gmail.com, s_adarsh@cb.amrita.edu

Abstract. Progressing towards the age of Autonomous driving, realistic data is necessary for maximum driving scenarios is required for creating Advanced Driver-Assistance System (ADAS) models that can persevere through our widely unpredictable day-to-day travel. So we intend to generate synthetic data that can be utilized well by the ADAS models and also keep it closer to the real-world scenarios. Using Deep Learning concepts, image synthesizing methods, and video-to-video synthesizing methods together with the available real-world data we have created synthetic data. Generative Adversarial Neural Networks (GANs) based models were previously used for static level object manipulations on benchmark datasets. Here, the idea is to enhance this aspect to adding dynamic objects (like cars, pedestrians, etc.) to real-world scenarios from the Cityscapes dataset. Then by using a pre-trained Mask-RCNN, we have done the object detection on the generated synthetic data and have evaluated the output.

Keywords: Generative Adversarial Networks (GANs) · Regions with Convolution Neural Network (R-CNN) · Semantic Region Adaptive Normalization (SEAN) · Spatially-Adaptive Normalization (SPADE)

1 Introduction

Test-driving the vehicles is one way to validate them before they are given to the end consumer but what levels of test-driving can be sufficient to get to the conclusion on the safety aspect. How much effort and information is required to know if the autonomous driving vehicle is reliable or not; can be availed from the report of RAND Corporation [1]. Autonomous vehicles sometimes have to be intensively driven for several million or even many billions of miles based on the context of reliability in the aspect of injuries and fatalities. Even under the assumptions of rigorous testing, the current fleets of vehicles will take hundreds of years to drive these miles. So we can understand that it is not feasible to get all the data from various geographies of the world as it can be a time-consuming process and can also prove to be costly to attain such data. This problem, therefore, leads to the development of synthetic data that can replicate the real world and can fill the gaps in the path leading to Autonomous driving. There are many simulator tools like CARLA [2] available in the field that can try to curb the reality gap with the capability of generating large trainable datasets but the ultimate results appear non-realistic and worlds apart. Deep Neural Networks especially Generative Adversarial neural networks (GANs) are recently playing a major role to solve the problems in such realistic applications with the help of good adaptive Normalization techniques. In this aspect, NVIDIA has been working on several image synthesizing and video-to-video techniques that deal with semantic segmentation and their photo-realistic output in various manners. As a continuation of the work done by NVIDIA, some models were able to generate synthetic realistic data that included scenarios that dealt with the addition of static objects to the real-world image datasets. Therefore the current idea is to search for possible inputs to the generator of our GAN model that uses Semantic Region-based Adaptive Normalization and generate output that has a dynamic object added to it. Further, to evaluate the model, the generated output frames or images can be given to a pre-trained neural network (that has been trained on real-world data), and get the objects identified successfully as real entities.

2 Literature Survey

In the context of picture-to-picture conversions and video-to-video synthesis aspects, few research works have been explored in the recent past and it has been observed that over time there is an enhancement in the kind of works that were performed.

In order to check whether synthetic data is really a solution to migrate from the real-world data and achieve improvements in the current deep learning-based ADAS algorithms, the work done by B. Jelic et al. [3] stands as evidence of work to the question that was mentioned in their title. Both Real data and synthetic data were taken in certain ratios in various combinations and given to two deep learning object detectors to check the functionality of the virtual data. On a set of real world test images about twelve detectors were tested in total and the outcome was satisfactory because they could achieve a striking point for better performance when a specific ratio of real and synthetic entities was used.

Using Generative adversarial Neural networks (GANs) to work on the realistic application was the idea to proceed further wherein the work done by Ting-Chun Wang et al. [4] the model helped to understand the relation to converting a semantic level image to a photorealistic image of good resolution. Through this work, it is understood that without any pre-trained networks or hand-crafted losses it is possible to synthesize photo-realistic images of high resolution.

The further interest is to understand how the input source that is made up of a set of semantic segmentation maps in order is mapped to a video output that is photo-realistic. The output video should exactly portray the content from the input video. It was evident from the work done by T C Wang et al. [5] that video-to-video kind of synthesis is one such method of approach to progress with generative adversarial neural networks.

Through their next work [6] in this relevant aspect, they have tried to bring about improvements in this context by making the model learn a mapping that is agnostic of subject and converts a sample image and a semantic video into a photorealistic video. In their consequent work [7], they have tried to improve the video-to-video synthesis in the aspect of view consistency and long-term consistency.

Rajat K Soni, in his work [8] has tried to create such realistic data from the segmentation maps using a model that is based on GANs and incorporated the flow embedding technique FlowNet 2.0 [9] to get a consistent result. The scenarios which were generated are relevant to ADAS applications and they include creating an extension to the road, converting a tree into a building, and building into a tree. The object manipulations that were done through this work were on static level conversions.

In this work, taking the above models and configuration into consideration, we have tried to perform dynamic object addition like a car or a pedestrian to the scenarios and generate the relevant photo-realistic output. Since we are trying to add an object from the real world that was earlier not present in the scenario, we have tried to evaluate the output with the help of a Mask-RCNN neural network that has been pre-trained on the COCO dataset.

In further sections the chapter describes the following aspects: Section 3 covers the methodology used to arrive at the output whereas Sect. 4 covers the scenarios and results. Section 5 covers the conclusions and future scope.

3   Methodology

We are trying to use the Generative Adversarial Neural networks (GANs) based model which makes it obvious that new data instances are generated from the data that we have used earlier to train the model. GANs produce the required real output by creating a fake one with the combined help of the generator and discriminator.

In the training model, the Image Encoder takes the pre-processed image, encodes the same into two vectors, and then for a normal Gaussian distribution these two vectors are used as the standard deviation and mean. Later from this Gaussian distribution, a random vector is sampled and concatenated with the feeder Semantic Map to form the generator input. Although training of GANs requires simultaneous training of generator and discriminator for every epoch, each of them is kept constant while training the other. Figure 1 below depicts the architecture of the system in total.

The model tries to address the problem that would arise due to temporal coherence over a long time by considering SPADE [10] (Spatially-Adaptive) Normalization, including depth and guiding the image with semantic and flow inputs. This is where we see the flow input embedding to the generator to address the consistency between the frames. With the use of special SPADE blocks, the given generative adversarial neural network model is working. The input to the generator here consists of the one-hot encoded semantic segmentation map which generally means that each of the available classes is linked to the one-hot encoded map. Further, depth-concatenation of all these maps takes place.

The model is also based on Semantic Region Adaptive Normalization (SEAN) [11] which is used along with the existing video synthesizing methods. In SPADE, we modify batch normalization in a particular way that for every pixel present in the feature map we try to learn numerous sets of parameters, instead of picking a channel and learning a solo set of parameters from it. The same is done by directly equalling the number of pixels with the total number of batch norm parameters by increasing the latter. These video-to-video synthesis methods generate the photo-realistic outputs based on previous frames and their flow maps. With fully connected layers at the end, the discriminator works as a classification network that produces a unique output between 1 and 0, as to how realistic the image appears to the network. As a result, to get the "realisticness" score of the image, the output feature map is averaged. Here, it utilizes the Patch GAN [12] architecture through which different synthesized and real images of different resolutions are taken and each of them is given to the discriminator depending upon the size of the patch. It implies that the discriminator will classify the input patches as fake or real to obtain an output that would be consistent throughout. The objective functions used for the model are similar to the ones that were used in the work [8] where the feature extractor loss, hinge loss and flow loss form the base equations. The Flow loss is again sub-divided into loss corresponding to the ground truth, warp loss, and mask loss which are a part of the FlowNet2.0 [9] architecture.

For the testing part, the required set of images is pre-processed which indicates that images of only one size and aspect ratio are used to train the GAN. It refers that after training, the model is guaranteed to perform well only with images of the same size as that on which it has been trained on. The expected output can considerably degrade if the image used during validation is either too small or too large.

There are different ways of evaluating GANs both qualitatively and quantitatively. Normally by inspecting the images and situation we can conclude the type of measure to be used for the evaluation. In this case, the object being added is not present in the scenario previously and also the scenarios are intended for training the ADAS models. The object should be detected properly by the ego vehicle as well as the other objects in the scenario. So instead of using some mathematical measures for evaluation, the individual frames with dynamically added objects were given to a pre-trained neural network to identify the different objects along with the original objects of the scene.

For evaluation, different predominantly used instance segmentation networks were explored and Mask RCNN [13] was chosen to be trained. Since the added objects were boundary masked with the help of tools and then added to the scenario Mask RCNN is used to detect the object along with its boundaries

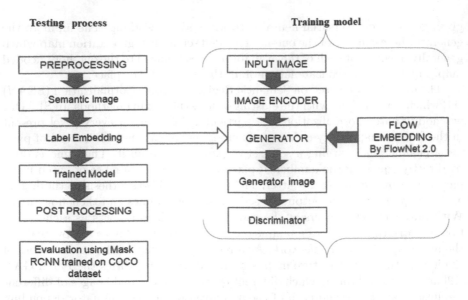

Fig. 1. The architecture of the system

with scores. Therefore the model has been trained on the Microsoft COCO [14] dataset which has about 91 different labeled classes.

4   Results and Analysis

The scenarios that are considered here are in the form of a video from the Cityscapes [15] dataset that has a straight road recorded from the camera of the ego vehicle and which has about 30 frames of images. The idea here is to add the dynamic object which is here a car and a pedestrian as two different cases, in front of the vehicle as an instance to some of the frames based on the scenario. Google Colaboratory was used as a platform to train and validate the current model because it is open to all users and has the support of GPU. Henceforth, for generating this scenario we need the segmentation maps of the entire sequence from the cityscapes dataset. So as a part of pre-processing, the entire objects from a set of input images use many to one color mapping to get the required semantic segmentation maps.

In the Fig. 2, we can see the comparison of four consecutive video frames from the generated output of the desired scenario. Towards the left, we have the color coded segmentation maps of the input 8-bit grey scale segmentation map with the inserted object (car). In the middle we have the original video frames from the Cityscapes dataset. On the right, we have the photo-realistic generated output with the dynamic object car added into the scenario. Since, cars are the most frequently seen objects in the training scenarios the generated output is clearly added. But we still do not have the control over the color of the car added.

Similar to the depicted output above, in Fig. 3 we can see four frames of the scene where the dynamic object added is a pedestrian. It is observed that the model is yet undertrained with the number of people and their movements in the training data thereby making the person unrealistic with appearance. The model has been trained on 15 video sequences of different lengths and various situations of traffic and people for about 120 epochs. For the kind of synthetic data that is being tried to be modified, it requires a large number of object classes and a wide variety of situations to capture the individual object from one case and add it to the other. This is also the reason that the colors, textures, and other attributes that add up to the detailing of the object are not under the control of the scenario maker. The detailing may include a vehicle trying to give an indicator signal before turning on a road, the kind of traffic signboard that should appear in a situation, and the variation of the size of the vehicle based upon whether it is speeding or slowing down concerning the vehicle under control, etc., are all to be learned by the model from huge amounts of available live data and it might also need an additional machine learning-based concept enhancements and applications to the current level of the model. Once the model is up to these marks then there can be better photo-realistic results and also better scenarios can be generated.

The resultant output of the scenarios that were generated and depicted in Fig. 2 and Fig. 3 was evaluated by passing them through the Mask RCNN network which was trained with the real-world Microsoft COCO dataset and then for each of the frames object identification was done. In the below-shown Fig. 4, we can see that the additionally added object (the car) from the first scenario was detected successfully along with the other objects in the instance with a high score. The prediction was very good because training data had more car scenarios and also COCO dataset has good amount of car class objects for Mask RCNN to detect the object properly. The boundary boxes were also satisfactory indicating that the object masking was also done well in such a way that both the models could recognize the object properly.

In Fig. 5, we can see that evaluation has been done for the case where a pedestrian is trying to cross the road and we can see that with a 99% prediction score, the model was able to detect the person in the frame along with the other objects.

Options to Automate

The scenarios that have been shown here were also tried to be automated in the following different ways but each one of them had its respective limitations because of which we could not take it up to the next level but they could be explored further in future works:

Using Simulation Tools: The main aim of our model is to provide photo-realism by creating synthetic data which should be a real-world experience rather than simulated video game graphics that are worlds apart. Simulation tools [16] can be able to serve the purpose up to an extent in the above aspect. We need

Segmentation map of input   Original Image   Generated Output

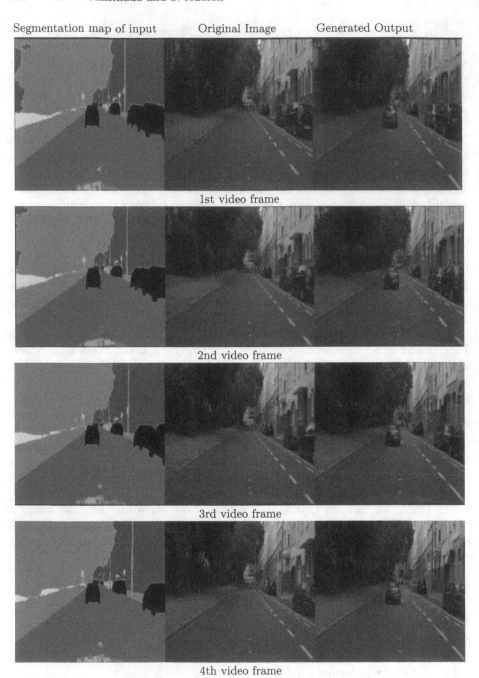

1st video frame

2nd video frame

3rd video frame

4th video frame

Fig. 2. Scenario generated by adding a car.

Segmentation map of input   Original Image   Generated Output

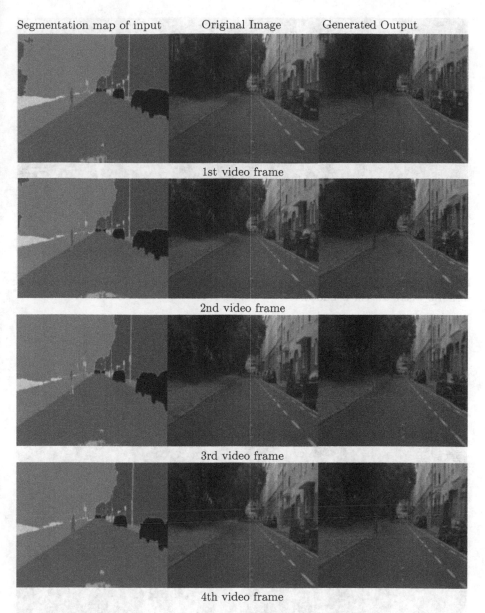

1st video frame

2nd video frame

3rd video frame

4th video frame

Fig. 3. Generated Scenario of a pedestrian is trying to cross the road in front of the car.

to create the required scenario replicating the original scenario with the help of a few simulator tools like MATLAB [17], CARLA, IPG CAR Maker, NVIDIA DRIVE Sim, etc., and then feed the segmentation maps of the output video to this trained model.

Fig. 4. Object identification is done with Mask RCNN forone of the frames from the scenario where the car is added.

Fig. 5. Object detection done with Mask RCNN for one of the frames from the scenario where a pedestrian is trying to cross the road.

In MATLAB we have the "Driving Scenario Designer" application in which various kinds of roads and actor models can be created using a drag-and-drop interface and the scenario can be visualized in a 3D viewer. There are also toolboxes available in MATLAB to visualize the semantic segmentation and the depth of the data that is captured from a camera sensor. By somehow making combined use of these tools, the segmentation maps need to be created for the scenarios that were earlier mentioned.

In the same way, driving scenarios can also be created using the tools available from IPG CAR Maker software. Later the designed scenario can be retrieved in the form of a 3D visualization video which somehow needs to be worked upon for the required depth and color maps that will help and generate the semantic segmentation maps. IPG CAR Maker also provides realistic 3D visualization through its tool "MovieNX" where weather effects and light conditions of various seasons can also be induced. One other open-source urban driving simulation tool is CARLA (Car Learning to Act) with high-end graphics which can be used similarly as depicted above. NVIDIA DRIVE Sim - also comes under the same line of virtual reality designers which is a high fidelity end-to-end simulation platform.

Pixel Allocation: The two-dimensional pixel coordinates of the location as to where the new object needs to be identified along with its dimensions and alignments. Later with the help of python scripts and the information of the coordinates the addition needs to be done to the semantic segmentation maps of the available scenario. But this method can be preferably tried for short duration videos or videos with fewer complexities happening in a short time. Therefore it cannot be adapted to the longer sequence videos. It can be tougher to be implemented on curvy roads and turnings.

Deep Learning Techniques: We need to know the additional deep learning algorithms which can understand the context and then try to add the object to the instance, similar to the work done by Donghoon Lee et al. [18] in their paper. In our case, since we know the type of object to be added and also the precise location of it in the image, we can try to generate our required photo-realistic output through the supervised path. In trying to do so we can get the intermediary semantic segmentation map for a single frame of the scenario. Further for all the frames of the video sequence, these maps could probably be attained and then be interfaced with the current model. Since our model uses FlowNet 2.0 for continuity between the video frames, the output video which is generated is expected to be photo-realistic and consistent.

Concerning the optical flow consistency as well some new techniques and architectures have emerged recently like RAFT (Recurrent All pairs Field Transforms) [19], Spy-Net (Spatial pyramids Network) [20], PWC-Net (Pyramids Warping and Cost Volume-based Network) [21] and so on. Each of them has its functionalities, pros, and cons and therefore has to be chosen based on the level of requirement.

Once we would be able to create large amounts of such synthetic data then we can use it for the improvement of already existing rear-view camera applications like in [24] by incorporating object detection and distance estimation methods that are done through the works [22,23].

5   Conclusion and Future-Scope

The prime objective of the work is to extend the present state of the art for static level object manipulations to dynamic object level of addition keeping in mind the photo-realistic output and it has been satisfactorily achieved. To increase the level of realistic features of the added objects the model needs more and a good amount of training on a huge quantity of data and a wide variety of scenarios. The current level of manual addition of the scenarios can be explored for automation through the various kinds of available methods that were described in the Results and Analysis section for future developments.

References

1. Kalra, N., Susan, M.: Paddock Driving to Safety: How Many Miles of Driving Would It Take to Demonstrate Autonomous Vehicle Reliability?. RAND Corporation, Santa Monica (2016)
2. Dosovitskiy, A., Ros, G., Codevilla, F., Lépez, A., Koltun, V.: CARLA: an open urban driving simulator, arXiv, no. CoRL, pp. 1–16 (2017)
3. Jelic, B., Grbic, R., Vranjes, M., Mijic, D.: Can we replace real-world with synthetic data in deep learning-based ADAS algorithm development? IEEE Consum. Electron. Mag. https://doi.org/10.1109/MCE.2021.3083206
4. Wang, T.C., Liu, M.Y., Zhu, J.Y., Tao, A., Kautz, J., Catanzaro, B.: High-resolution image synthesis and semantic manipulation with conditional GANs. Proc. IEEE Comput. Soc. Conf. Comput. Vis. Pattern Recognit., 8798–8807 (2018). https://doi.org/10.1109/CVPR.2018.00917
5. Wang, T.C., et al.: Video-to-video synthesis. In: Advances in Neural Information Processing Systems, vol. 2018, pp. 1144–1156 (2018)
6. Wang, T.C., Liu, M.Y., Tao, A., Liu, G., Kautz, J., Catanzaro, B.: Few-shot video-to-video synthesis, arXiv (2019)
7. Mallya, A., Wang, T.-C., Sapra, K., Liu, M.-Y.: World-consistent video-to-video synthesis. In: Vedaldi, A., Bischof, H., Brox, T., Frahm, J.-M. (eds.) ECCV 2020. LNCS, vol. 12353, pp. 359–378. Springer, Cham (2020). https://doi.org/10.1007/978-3-030-58598-3_22
8. Soni, R.K., Nair, B.B.: Deep learning-based approach to generate realistic data for ADAS applications. In: 2021 5th International Conference on Computer, Communication and Signal Processing (ICCCSP), pp. 1–5 (2021). https://doi.org/10.1109/ICCCSP52374.2021.9465529
9. Ilg, E., Mayer, N., Saikia, T., Keuper, M., Dosovitskiy, A., Brox, T.: FlowNet 2.0: evolution of optical flow estimation with deep networks. In: Proceedings - 30th IEEE Conference on Computer Vision and Pattern Recognition, pp. 1647–1655 (2017). https://doi.org/10.1109/CVPR.2017.179
10. Park, T., Liu, M.Y., Wang, T.C., Zhu, J.Y.: Semantic image synthesis with spatially-adaptive normalization. In: Proceedings IEEE Conference on Computer Vision and Pattern Recognition, pp. 2332–2341 (2019). https://doi.org/10.1109/CVPR.2019.00244

11. Zhu, P., Abdal, R., Qin, Y., Wonka, P.: SEAN: image synthesis with semantic region-adaptive normalization. In: IEEE/CVF Conference on Computer Vision and Pattern Recognition (CVPR) 2020, pp. 5103–5112 (2020). https://doi.org/10.1109/CVPR42600.2020.00515

12. Isola, P., Zhu, J.Y., Zhou, T., Efros, A.A.: Image-to-image translation with conditional adversarial networks. In: Proceedings 30th IEEE Conference on Computer Vision and Pattern Recognition, CVPR 2017, pp. 5967–5976 (2017). https://doi.org/10.1109/CVPR.2017.632

13. He, K., Gkioxari, G., Dollar, P., Girshick, R.: Mask RCNN. arXiv:1703.06870v3 [cs.CV], 24 January 2018

14. Lin, T.-Y., et al.: Microsoft COCO: common objects in context. arXiv:1405.0312v3 [cs.CV], 21 February 2015

15. Cordts, M., et al.: The cityscapes dataset for semantic urban scene understanding. In: Proceedings of the IEEE Computer Society Conference on Computer Vision and Pattern Recognition, pp. 3213–3223 (2016). https://doi.org/10.1109/CVPR.2016.350

16. Fadaie, J.G.: The state of modeling, simulation, and data utilization within industry- an autonomous vehicles perspective. arXiv:1910.06075 [cs.CV], 7 October 2019

17. MathWorks, "MATLAB Overview," MATLAB Product Documentation (2020)

18. Lee,D., Liu, S., Gu, J., Liu, M.-Y., Yang, M.-H., Kautz, J.: Context-aware synthesis and placement of object instances. In: 32nd Conference on Neural Information Processing Systems (NeurIPS 2018), Montréal, Canada (2018)

19. Teed, Z., Deng, J.: RAFT: recurrent all-pairs field transforms for optical flow. arXiv: 2003.12039v3 [cs.CV], 25 August 2020

20. Ranjan, A., Black, M.J.: Optical flow estimation using a spatial pyramid network. arXiv: 1611.00850v2 [cs.CV], 21 November 2016

21. Sun, D., Yang, X., Liu, M.-Y., Kautz, J.: PWC-Net: CNNs for optical flow using pyramid, warping, and cost volume. arXiv:1709.02371v3 [cs.CV], 25 June 2018

22. Emani, S., Soman, K.P., Sajith Variyar, V.V., Adarsh, S.: Obstacle detection and distance estimation for autonomous electric vehicle using stereo vision and DNN. In: Wang, J., Reddy, G., Prasad, V., Reddy, V. (eds.) Soft Computing and Signal Processing. Advances in Intelligent Systems and Computing, vol. 898, Springer, Singapore (2019)

23. Mukherjee, A., Adarsh, S., Ramachandran, K.I.: ROS-based pedestrian detection and distance estimation algorithm using stereo vision, leddar and CNN. In: Satapathy, S., Bhateja, V., Janakiramaiah, B., Chen, Y.W. (eds.) Intelligent System Design. Advances in Intelligent Systems and Computing, vol. 1171. Springer, Singapore (2021)

24. Dunna, S., Nair, B.B., Panda, M.K.: A deep learning based system for fast detection of obstacles using rear-view camera under parking scenarios. In: IEEE International Power and Renewable Energy Conference (IPRECON) 2021, pp. 1–7 (2021). https://doi.org/10.1109/IPRECON52453.2021.9640804

Improved Accuracy in Speech Recognition System for Detection of Covid-19 Using K Nearest Neighbour and Comparing with Artificial Neural Network

Rallapalli Jhansi and G. Uganya[✉]

Department of Wireless Communication Systems, SIMATS School of Engineering, SIMATS, Chennai, India
uganyag.sse@saveetha.com

Abstract. The objective of this research is to recognize the speech signals for identifying the Covid-19 using K Nearest Neighbour (KNN) and comparing accuracy with an Artificial Neural Network (ANN). Speech recognition using KNN is considered as group 1 and Artificial Neural Network is considered as group 2, where each group has 20 samples. ANN is a machine learning program in which the input is processed by numerous elements and produces the output based on predefined functions. KNN is defined to find the relations between the query and pick the value closest to the query. These groups were analyzed by an independent sample T-test with 5% of alpha, and 80% of pretest power. ANN and KNN achieve an accuracy of 83.5% and 91.49% respectively (significance < 0.05). This analysis observed that KNN has significantly higher accuracy than ANN.

Keywords: Machine learning · Innovative speech recognition · Covid-19 detection · K nearest neighbour · Artificial neural network · Statistical analysis

1 Introduction

Machine learning is a growing technology that lets computers behave like people and learn more as they encounter more data [7]. Initially, most of the research with respect to automatic speech recognition is developed for secure applications. Further, attention is also motivated towards home applications also [24]. Several researches were inspired by the Coronavirus (COVID-19) pandemic. Some symptoms are linked to the respiratory system's function, which affects speech output. A set of fluent speech signals and three speech disturbances was transformed using principal component analysis [4]. The existence of acoustic biomarkers in modalities such as cough, breathing, and speech sounds can provide quick, non-contact, and low-cost testing. COVID-19 detection technique based on breath, voice, and cough signals. In order to train the network, audio signals were used [5]. Machine learning can be used in applications of voice recognition, data analytics, image recognition, and traffic prediction [27].

© The Author(s), under exclusive license to Springer Nature Switzerland AG 2023
R. N. Shaw et al. (Eds.): ICACIS 2022, CCIS 1749, pp. 776–784, 2023.
https://doi.org/10.1007/978-3-031-25088-0_68

In the past 5 years, chapters related to this research have been around 50 chapters published in IEEE Explore and over 650 chapters in Google Scholar on accuracy of speech recognition systems using KNN. Most relevant chapter in this research is to make COVID-19 identification easier using a bio-inspired method to optimize the conversion scale in the frequency domain and the frequency range of the filter bank in speech signal. The speech signal processing tools are used to provide aid and relief to those affected by the Coronavirus [22]. Even a machine learning based Covid-19 detection classifier can be used to find the difference between the positive cough and negative-healthy cough through the speech recording [18]. Each sentence is represented as a super vector of Mel filter bank features for the short term [28]. These characteristics are used to train a two-class classifier that can distinguish COVID-19 speech from normal speech. Speech enhancement algorithms are used to improve classification performance [6]. Our team published much higher quality publications due to their research experience [1–3, 9, 10, 15, 17, 20, 21, 26].

Several algorithms are available in speech recognition systems. But these systems do not give proper detection of Covid-19 in an accurate manner. so, this research is to implement an innovative speech recognition using the K-Nearest Neighbour by comparing its accuracy with the Artificial Neural Network.

2 Materials and Methods

The research work was carried out in the "Machine Learning Lab", Wireless Communication Systems, SSE, SIMATS for which to conduct research on classification of information collected from an open dataset available on the internet (Kaggle.com). Two groups were made with 20 samples in each group, group 1 was KNN and group 2 was ANN [4].

2.1 K-Nearest Neighbour

K-Nearest Neighbour is a technique of supervised machine learning used for both classification and regression problems [12]. It is used to identify hidden characteristics of information and classify the collected data into known labels. K value was assigned as any integer. In the training phase KNN identified data and their characteristics such as age, principal, designation to provide a complete description. It is a lazy adaptive algorithm due to its lack of training phase [23]. If K-value was increased then accuracy also increased.

2.2 Artificial Neural Network

Individual words spoken by different persons are used as input speech signals in the system developed by the researchers. It then extracts what are known as amplitude modulation (AM) spectrogram features, which are basically sound-specific characteristics. The model's retrieved properties are then utilized to train an artificial neural network to detect human speech [16]. The Artificial Neural Network learns to predict single words in new samples of human speech after being trained on a vast library of audio files. Individual speakers' voices are processed based on their continuous speech waveform dispersion using a combination of artificial neural network frameworks (ANN). The decision system determines the recognized speakers by measuring the goodness of match of speech feature frames of the detected speaker from the Artificial Neural Network using correlation coefficient analysis.

2.3 Statistical Analysis

The IBM SPSS software was used to statistically analyze the data in terms of mean, SD, SEM, and mean difference, and significance [19]. Graphical representation was created by fetching the accuracy rate of the both groups in the data. "Independent sample T-test" was conducted for the KNN and ANN. All the data were statistically analyzed after obtaining the raw data. In this work, the dependent variable is accuracy. Independent variables are age, gender, and voice.

3 Results

The covid-19 detection using speech recognition enhancement with the use of K nearest Neighbour algorithm and Artificial Neural Network with a sample size of 20 in each group. Table 1 shows the obtained accuracy data of KNN and ANN model.

Table 2 shows the sample size (N = 20), including the Mean accuracy of KNN is 91%, with a SD of 0.269 and the SER as 0.060. The Mean accuracy of the ANN is around 83% with a SD of 0.299 and the SER as 0.066. Independent sample T-test is shown Table 3, where the significance level obtained is 0.03 which is lesser than that p < 0.05.

Figure 1 shows the speech recognition count analysis chart of PCR test results vs trained values in the KNN. Figure 2 shows the speech recognition analysis chart of the outcomes in the ANN respectively. Figure 3 shows the measurement of accuracy using KNN and ANN for prediction and speech recognition. Based on color, pattern, an accuracy of K Nearest Neighbour is 75.68% and an accuracy of Artificial Neural Network is 70.45%.

Figure 4 shows the simple bar graph for the mean of the accuracy of the respective groups. The accuracy of the KNN based innovative speech recognition has a mean accuracy of 91.49% and the mean accuracy of ANN is around 83.5%. It is clear that the obtained value of accuracy in the KNN is higher than the ANN based algorithm with a significance value of 0.03 which is less than 5% level of significance.

Table 1. Accuracy of innovation speech recognition using KNN and ANN for 20 samples. KNN achieves an accuracy of 91%.

S.no	Group 1 (KNN) Accuracy (%)	Group 2 (ANN) Accuracy (%)
1	91.05	83.11
2	91.32	83.32
3	91.53	83.67
4	91.29	83.43
5	91.92	83.94
6	91.84	83.58
7	91.73	83.76
8	91.18	83.17
9	91.29	83.89
10	91.90	83.29
11	91.23	84.30
12	91.46	83.13
13	91.92	83.38
14	91.26	83.47
15	91.43	83.59
16	91.67	83.68
17	91.39	83.38
18	91.29	83.47
19	91.48	83.82
20	91.83	83.79

Table 2. Group Statistical analysis of KNN and ANN for Covid-19 detection. KNN achieved an accurate speech prediction of 91.49% and the ANN achieved an accurate prediction of 83.5%.

	Group name	No. of samples	Mean accuracy	SD	SEM
Accuracy	KNN	20	91.49	.26931	.06022
	ANN	20	83.5	.29912	.06689

* SD-Standard Deviation, SER-Standard Error Mean

Table 3. Statistical analysis of an Independent Sample T-Test of KNN and ANN with confidence interval 95%. Obtained significance value is 0.03 which is (p < 0.05).

		"Levene's test for Equality of Variances"		"T-test"						
		Freq.	P < 0.05	t	df	Sig.(2-tailed	Mean diff	Std. error diff	Lower	Upper
Accuracy	"Equal variances assumed"	.059	.03	88	38	.000	7.99	.09	7.80	8.172
	"Equal not variances assumed"			88	37.5	.000	7.99	.09	7.80	8.172

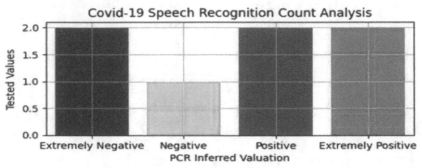

Fig. 1. Covid-19 speech recognition count analysis chart of PCR test results vs trained values in the KNN.

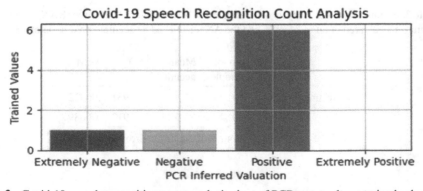

Fig. 2. Covid-19 speech recognition count analysis chart of PCR test results vs trained values in the ANN.

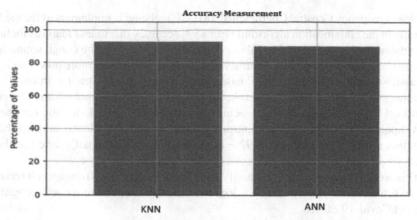

Fig. 3. Accuracy measurement of speech recognition and prediction using KNN and ANN. KNN achieves an accuracy of 91.49%.

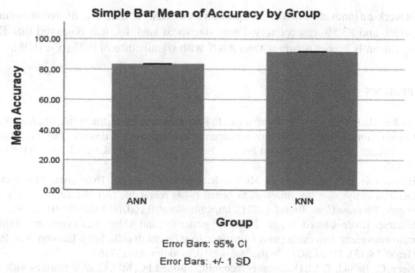

Fig. 4. Bar graph of "Mean Accuracy" of KNN and ANN. X-axis: KNN vs ANN. Y-axis: Mean accuracy of detection.

4 Discussion

In this work, the obtained mean accuracy value of the KNN based innovative speech recognition is 91.49% whereas the ANN has an accuracy around 83.5%. The results are statistically analyzed using SPSS software and the obtained results are tabulated. From statistical analysis, it is observed that the KNN is having significantly higher accuracy than ANN. The obtained "significance" (p) is 0.03 which is less than the 5%.

"Mel Frequency Cepstral Coefficients" (MFCC) scheme is implemented for the best outcome in the classification algorithm with 85% accuracy due to less features included in the dataset [11]. K-Nearest Neighbour classifier firstly detects the cough sound from elements based on modules with accuracy of 83% [14]. But it takes more power and time to classify the datasets [8]. An MLP based speech recognition is used with two layers including input and hidden which has same size as well as an output softmax layer, to perform ANN on the dataset which achieves an accuracy of 93% due the features of Pitch, Spectral Flux, and Spectral Entropy [25]. Convolutional Neural network-based prediction achieved an accuracy of 92% by ignoring the voice signal's time variability [13].

This work takes more time to classify the Covid-19 detection from speech recognition. In future, it can be extended to reduce the time consumption in speech recognition to detect Covid-19 earlier.

5   Conclusion

In this work, an innovative speech recognition using KNN and ANN achieved an accuracy of 91.49% and 83.5% respectively. From statistical analysis, it is observed that KNN has significantly higher accuracy than ANN with significance of 0.03 ($p < 0.05$).

References

1. Baskar, M., Renuka Devi, R., Ramkumar, J., Kalyanasundaram, P., Suchithra, M., Amutha, B.: Region centric minutiae propagation measure orient forgery detection with finger print analysis in health care systems. Neural Process. Lett. (2021). https://doi.org/10.1007/s11063-020-10407-4.

2. Bhanu Teja, N., Devarajan, Y., Mishra, R., Sivasaravanan, S., Thanikaivel Murugan, D.: Detailed analysis on sterculia foetida kernel oil as renewable fuel in compression ignition engine. Biomass Conv. Bioref. (2021). https://doi.org/10.1007/s13399-021-01328-w.

3. Shaeesta Khaleelahmed, B., et al.: Investigating the antioxidant and cytocompatibility of mimusops elengi linn extract over human gingival fibroblast cells. Int. J. Environ. Res. Public Health 18(13), 7162 (2021). https://doi.org/10.3390/ijerph18137162

4. Neha, C., Isshiki, T., Li, D.: Speaker recognition using LPC, MFCC, ZCR features with ANN and SVM classifier for large input database. In: 2019 IEEE 4th International Conference on Computer and Communication Systems (ICCCS). IEEE. (2019). https://doi.org/10.1109/ccoms.2019.8821751

5. Chen, X.-Y., Zhu, Q.-S., Zhang, J., Rong Dai, L.: Supervised and self-supervised pretraining based COVID-19 detection using acoustic Breathing/Cough/Speech Signals (2022). http://arxiv.org/abs/2201.08934

6. Dong, M., Huang, X., Bo, X.: Unsupervised speech recognition through spike-timing-dependent plasticity in a convolutional spiking neural network. PLoS ONE 13(11), e0204596 (2018)

7. Echle, A., et al.: Artificial intelligence for detection of microsatellite instability in colorectal cancer-a multicentric analysis of a pre-screening tool for clinical application. ESMO Open 7(2), 100400 (2022)

8. Mohammad Zafar, I., Faiz, M.F.I.: Active surveillance for COVID-19 through artificial intelligence using real-time speech-recognition mobile application. In: 2020 IEEE International Conference on Consumer Electronics - Taiwan (ICCE-Taiwan). IEEE. (2020). https://doi.org/10.1109/icce-taiwan49838.2020.9258276

9. Mohmed Isaqali, K., et al.: An in vitro stereomicroscopic evaluation of bioactivity between Neo MTA Plus, Pro Root MTA, BIODENTINE & glass ionomer cement using dye penetration method. Materials **14**(12), 3159 (2021). https://doi.org/10.3390/ma14123159

10. Karthigadevi, G., et al.: Chemico-nanotreatment methods for the removal of persistent organic pollutants and xenobiotics in water - a review. Biores. Technol. **324**(March), 124678 (2021)

11. Khamlich, S., Khamlich, F., Atouf, I., Benrabh, M.: Performance evaluation and implementations of MFCC, SVM and MLP algorithms in the FPGA board. Int. J. Electr. Comput. Eng. Syst. **12**(3), 139–153 (2021)

12. Gaoyuan, L., Zhao, H., Fan, F., Liu, G., Xu, Q., Nazir, S.: An enhanced intrusion detection model based on improved kNN in WSNs. Sensors **22**(4), 1407 (2022). https://doi.org/10.3390/s22041407

13. Sinha, T., Chowdhury, T., Shaw, R.N., Ghosh, A.: Analysis and prediction of COVID-19 confirmed cases using deep learning models: a comparative study. In: Bianchini, M., Piuri, V., Das, S., Shaw, R.N. (eds.) Advanced Computing and Intelligent Technologies. Lecture Notes in Networks and Systems, vol. 218, pp. 207–218. Springer, Singapore (2022). https://doi.org/10.1007/978-981-16-2164-2_18

14. Mesut, M.: Diagnosis of COVID-19 and non-COVID-19 patients by classifying only a single cough sound. Neural Comput. Appl. **33**, 1–12 (2021)

15. Muthukrishnan, L.: Nanotechnology for cleaner leather production: a review. Environ. Chem. Lett. **19**(3), 2527–2549 (2021)

16. Nalini, N., Sabitha, K., Chitra, S., Viswanathan, P., Menon, V.P.: Histopathological and lipid changes in experimental colon cancer: effect of coconut kernal (Cocos Nucifera Linn.) and (Capsicum Annum Linn.) red chilli powder. Indian J. Exp. Biol. **35**(9), 964–971 (1997)

17. Preethi, K., Auxzilia, K.A., Preethi, G.L., Sekar, D.: Antagomir technology in the treatment of different types of cancer. Epigenomics (2021). https://doi.org/10.2217/epi-2020-0439

18. Kumar, A., Das, S., Tyagi, V., Shaw, R.N., Ghosh, A.: Analysis of classifier algorithms to detect anti-money laundering. In: Bansal, J.C., Paprzycki, M., Bianchini, M., Das, S. (eds.) Computationally Intelligent Systems and their Applications. Studies in Computational Intelligence, vol. 950, pp. 143–152. Springer, Singapore (2021). https://doi.org/10.1007/978-981-16-0407-2_11

19. Sarantakos, S.: Getting to know your SPSS. Quant. Data Anal. (2007). https://doi.org/10.1007/978-1-137-03825-8_2

20. Sawant, K., et al.: Dentinal microcracks after root canal instrumentation using instruments manufactured with different NiTi Alloys and the SAF system: a systematic review. NATO Adv. Sci. Inst. Ser. E Appl. Sci. **11**(11), 4984 (2021)

21. Shanmugam, V., et al.: Circular economy in biocomposite development: state-of-the-art, challenges and emerging trends. Compos. Part C: Open Access **5**, 100138 (2021)

22. Naeem, S.: Intelligent Credit Scoring: Building and Implementing Better Credit Risk Scorecards. 2nd edn. Wiley, Hoboken (2017)

23. Chaohong, S., Li, X.: Cost-sensitive KNN algorithm for cancer prediction based on entropy analysis. Entropy **24**(2), 253 (2022). https://doi.org/10.3390/e24020253

24. Subbarao, M.V., Padavala, A.K., Harika, K.D.: Performance analysis of speech command recognition using support vector machine classifiers. In: Gu, J., Dey, R., Adhikary, N. (eds.) Communication and Control for Robotic Systems. Smart Innovation, Systems and Technologies, vol 229. Springer, Singapore (2022). https://doi.org/10.1007/978-981-16-1777-5_19

25. Tsai, K.-T., Chien, T.-W., Lin, J.-K., Yeh, Y.-T., Chou, W.: Comparison of prediction accuracies between mathematical models to make projections of confirmed cases during the COVID-19 pandamic by Country/region. Medicine **100**(50), e28134 (2021)
26. Arumugaprabu, V.: Thermal properties of natural fiber sisal based hybrid composites – a brief review. J. Nat. Fibers, **19**(12), 4696–4706 (2021)
27. Vijayaraj, N., Uganya, G., Balasaraswathi, M., Sivasankaran, V., Baskar, R., Syed Fiaz, A.S.: Efficient Resource Allocation Using Multilayer Neural Network in Cloud Environment. Sensor Data Analysis and Management: The Role of DeepLearning (2021). https://books.google.com/books?hl=en&lr=&id=zd5FEAAAQBAJ&oi=fnd&pg=PA1&dq=uganya&ots=3emskyK6w3&sig=NY6TRR_ziTAbhz8i0lky5_fCnQM
28. Webber, C.: Howard, Ann [real Name Ann Pauline Giles, Née Swadling] (1934–2014), Singer. Oxf. Dictionary Nat. Biography (2018). https://doi.org/10.1093/odnb/9780198614128.013.108499

Role of Artificial Intelligence in the Screening of Neoplastic Oral Lesions

Paarangi Chawla[✉] and Partha Roy

Department of Biosciences and Bioengineering, Indian Institute of Technology, Roorkee, Roorkee, Uttarakhand, India
paarangichawla@hotmail.com, partha.roy@bt.iitr.ac.in

Abstract. Oral cancer is one of the most common cancers worldwide and more prevalent in India due to a variety of carcinogenic irritants, both inhaled and chewed, leading to more than 50,000 deaths annually. It not only causes loss of precious lives but morbidity due to oral cancers and the exuberant cost of treatment is a financial burden to patients and the state. When identified early, in benign, oral potentially malignant, or even in early stages of malignant disease, the 5-year survival rate of more than 80% can be expected. As early detection is the most important key to improved prognosis, the development of Artificial intelligence-based image recognition at Primary and Secondary healthcare centers is of paramount importance. In this study, we have explored the potential of Deep learning-based application to identify and segregate normal, benign, oral potentially malignant lesions and malignant lesions. This application offers great potential for a non-invasive technique for the early detection of oral neoplastic lesions.

Keywords: Oral Cancers · Malignant lesions · Oral potentially malignant disease · Artificial intelligence · Deep Learning · Convolutional Neural Networks

1 Introduction

Worldwide, oral cancer is the sixth [1] most common cancer. India is the second country having the highest number of oral cancers, contributing to one-third of total oral cancer cases in the world. Smoking, tobacco consumption including smokeless tobacco, betel nut chewing, alcohol consumption, poor oral hygiene, and viral infections like human papillomavirus are the risk factors contributing to oral cancers. As with all cancers, early detection and diagnosis is the key to a good outcome. In many cases, malignant lesions are preceded by benign, premalignant lesions which include oral sub-mucosal fibrosis (OSMF), Leukoplakia, Erythroplakia, and Melanoplakia. Early detection at the benign and premalignant stages can help to thwart progression into the malignant stage. The diagnostic tools required to make the diagnosis of oral neoplastic lesions include clinical examination, biopsy, and histopathology, radiological scans including, MRI, CT, PET scan, and fluorescent imaging, and biomarkers. Developing countries, including India, lack infrastructure for early diagnosis at the level of primary and secondary care centers, leading to delay in diagnosis and poor prognosis. Artificial Intelligence and Machine Learning can help in early diagnosis at the primary care center level and even predict prognosis. AI works in two phases, the first phase involves training, and the second involves testing.

Recent advances in AI, ML and Deep Learning, and medical image analysis have now made it possible to detect lesions at the premalignant or potentially malignant stage to improve early diagnosis and prognosis. ML is a branch of AI that can gather information and then predict new data with previously learnt information. DL is a subfield of ML to achieve even higher accuracy of information.

In this study, we aim to explore the potential application of artificial intelligence and Deep Learning in oral cancer screening.

2 Materials and Methods

Images of the oral mucosa, whether normal, oral potentially malignant lesions and malignant lesions were retrieved from publicly available sources using search engines (https:// images.google.com [2], https://yandex.com/images/ [3]) from the last 12 years. The period chosen was when AI and ML were evolving in learning and detection techniques. The images were corroborated with the help of a head and neck surgeon to ensure optimal identification.

The images (Appendix) were then arranged in order of normal, benign/ potentially malignant lesions and malignant lesions. The Oral Potentially Malignant (OPML) lesions and malignant lesions were then bounded in polygons. Our final database was of 329 images (Table 1), out of which 80% (263) were kept for training and 20% (66) for testing and validation (Fig. 1). AI and ML were then used to identify the lesions so that the "normal" and the "lesions" are learnt such that Deep Learning can be used to identify and diagnose the captured lesions.

Table 1. Distribution of the image set of 329 images amongst Normal Oral Mucosa, Premalignant and Malignant lesions and how many images were kept for training and testing in each lesion class.

Number of Images for classification experiments according to lesion class and dataset type				
Image Classification	Normal Oral Mucosa	Oral Potentially Malignant Lesion	Malignant	Total
Training	30	121	112	263
Testing	8	30	28	66
Total	38	151	140	329

Convolutional Neural Network (CNN) [4] in Deep Learning was employed for image identification. It combines localization and classification and that is why it stands out as a state-art algorithm for image detection in real-time. Repeated training was carried out to improve and enhance object detection and precision.

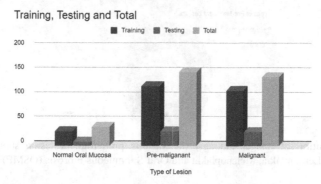

Fig. 1. Total number of images kept for training and testing in Normal Oral Mucosa, Premalignant and Malignant lesions

3 Results

Medical image analysis [5] aims to aid clinicians in making the diagnostic and treatment process more efficient. The tremendous development in the data-centric areas such as computer vision shows that Deep Learning methods could be the most suitable technique for this purpose. In Deep Learning, a **convolutional neural network** (**CNN**, or **ConvNet**) is a class of artificial neural networks most commonly applied to analyze visual imagery.

In our series of 329 cases, all cases were first validated with the help of a head and neck surgeon and then classified into three categories, normal, oral potentially malignant, and malignant/carcinoma lesions.

The oral potentially malignant cases included Leukoplakia [6], Melanoplakia [7], Erythroplakia [8], and Oral Submucous Fibrosis (OSMF) [9] (Table 2, Fig. 2).

Table 2. Number of images of the various pre-malignant subtypes

Number of Images of the various Pre-malignant subtypes			
Type of Premalignant Lesion	Number of images		
	Training	Testing	Total
Erythroplakia	40	2	42
Melanoplakia	14	4	18
Leukoplakia	47	15	62
Oral SubMucous Fibrosis	20	9	29
Total	**121**	**30**	**151**

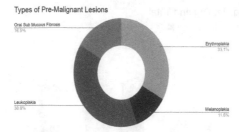

Fig. 2. Distribution of images amongst the various premalignant lesion subtypes, namely Erythroplakia, Leukoplakia, Melanoplakia and Oral Submucous Fibrosis (OSMF)

Deep learning [10] was employed with the convolutional backbone for the lesion identification task. Some of the images used for testing and training of the CNN are given in the Appendix.

The study revealed that CNN had the ability of 87.5% in correctly identifying normal oral mucosa. For premalignant lesions, CNN was 63.3% accurate and for malignant lesions, it was 75% accurate, making overall accuracy of 72% in distinguishing normal oral mucosa, premalignant and malignant lesions (Table 3).

Table 3. Accuracy of CNN in detecting the normal oral mucosa, premalignant and malignant lesion

	Normal	Premalignant	Malignant	Total
Total number of images	8	30	28	66
Number of images identified correctly	7	19	21	47
Percentage of images identified correctly	87.5%	63.3%	75%	72%

4 Discussion

Uncontrolled growth of cells which may spread and invade surrounding and distant tissues, is what is called Cancer. Oral cancers constitute the second-largest category of cancers affecting the Indian population. Tobacco consumption in the form of smoking, be it bidi, hookah, cigarette, or even reverse smoking, is one of the prime factors for oral cancers. Tobacco chewing in the form of Khaini, Zarda, Paan, Paan Masala, beetal areca nut chewing, constitute a category of carcinogenic factors only seen in the Indian Subcontinent.

In India, over 75,000 new cases of oral cancer and over 50,000 deaths are reported annually [11]. The reason for concern is that around 70% of cases in India are reported in advanced stages. Due to late-stage detection of oral cancers, the 5-year survival rate in India is a poor 20%, as compared to 54% in the USA.

In many cases, malignant lesions are preceded by premalignant lesions which include Leukoplakia, Melanoplakia, Erythroplakia, and Oral Submucous Fibrosis (OSMF).

Early identification of oral lesions in premalignant/ OPMD and in early stages of malignant cancers is the key to improving prognosis. In a country like India where tertiary level health care is not available in nearly 70% of districts, it becomes important that identification, detection, and screening facilities are improved at primary and secondary health care levels. Here comes the importance of Machine Learning and Deep Learning, which may be employed at primary and secondary health care levels for image identification and screening of cases and early referral to a tertiary care center.

Here comes the role of medical image analysis. What our eyes see, the brain processes it, stores it and can later recall it. Medical image analysis is supposed to solve the same problem by analyzing these medical images. The aim is to gather as much information from the medical images, store it and improve recalling ability of the system. In recent years medical image analysis using Deep Learning has become a leading research area in most countries. Scientists are now exploring the use of neural networks to analyze, store and improve the recalling ability of Deep Learning.

The use of Medical Image analysis in diagnostics is ever increasing both in radiodiagnosis and in pathology. In the field of pathology, medical image analysis can be used both for gross image of the lesion as well as for microscopic image of histopathology of the lesion. Improved data storage, data analysis and data recalling is required to improve the medical image analysis capability of Deep Learning, which is now fast emerging as the best tool suited for this purpose. As discussed earlier, just like brain, Deep Learning has capability to mimic brain to analyze and recall images.

In the gross medical images, the lesion is cropped and bounded in polygons for the model to gather maximum information. As more and more images become available, the data is bound to grow. Here in comes the role of Deep Learning to analyze, segregate and store the relevant information. Amongst all machine learning technologies, only Deep Learning is capable of handling this kind of raw data. Deep Learning extracts the required properties of the image and is able to recall in future. A number of good platforms of deep learning came up but the best technique to solve the problem of medical image analysis for gross lesions, histopathology and radiological images is Convolutional Neural Networks.

Deep learning is an offshoot of machine learning, which has the inherent capacity to handle and store linear and other non-linear data in an abstract manner. The medical image analysis depends upon a perfect blend of color recognition and best possible resolution. Many Deep Learning applications like Deep Belief Networks (DBNs), Restricted Boltzmann Machine (RBM), Auto-encoders, and stacked Auto-encoders were used to achieve this purpose but Deep Convolutional Neural Networks were found to be best suited as they had the inherent capacity of image and video recognition, raw data analysis, storage and recall ability. With the ever growing data of medical images, image cropping and bounding of the required lesions with polygons were employed to improve segregation capacity of the Deep learning model. With multiple training, the recall capacity of the model grows. As the resolution of the images is improving, so with multiple training, the image identification and discriminative ability of the CNN is also improving.

In a country like India, such an improved identification ability will help healthcare workers in primary and secondary health care centers to identify premalignant and malignant lesions as early as possible for an improved prognosis.

In our study, we had an accuracy of 72%, with the highest accuracy of 76%, in detecting premalignant and malignant lesions. Similar studies done in the past by Gizem Tanriver et al. [12] have reported the highest accuracy of 87% for detecting oral cancers. An overview by Hanya Mahmood et al. [13] reported the role of artificial intelligence in head and neck cancers. As more data will be available, these techniques are expected to give even higher accuracy and reliability in detecting and segregating oral lesions.

5 Conclusion

In a country like India, Artificial Intelligence and Machine Learning can play a great role in the early detection of Oral Potentially Malignant Disorders (OPMD) and malignant lesions to improve prognosis. More parameters like histopathology, immunochemistry, fluorescence-staining, and radiological scanning improve diagnosis but image analysis alone can initiate and speed up the diagnosis and screening and can improve prognosis.

This study presents the potential application of Deep Learning algorithms for the identification of oral lesions like premalignant lesions (i.e., Leukoplakia, Erythroplakia, Melanoplakia, and OSMF) and malignant lesions, and normal oral mucosa. It is envisaged that the proposed model paves the way for a low-cost, non-invasive, and easy-to-use tool that can support the screening process and improve early detection of OPMD and malignant oral cancers. A larger dataset with more images of premalignant and malignant lesions can bring greater benefit to this model and thus it will be the focus of future research.

Appendix

Images of Normal Oral Mucosa (a), Premalignant lesions [Erythroplakia (b), Leukoplakia (c), Melanoplakia (d), OSMF (e)] and Malignant lesions (f,g,h).

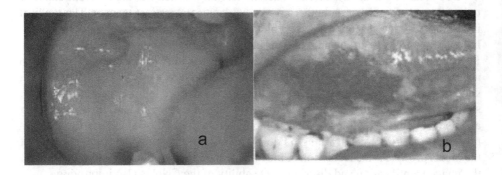

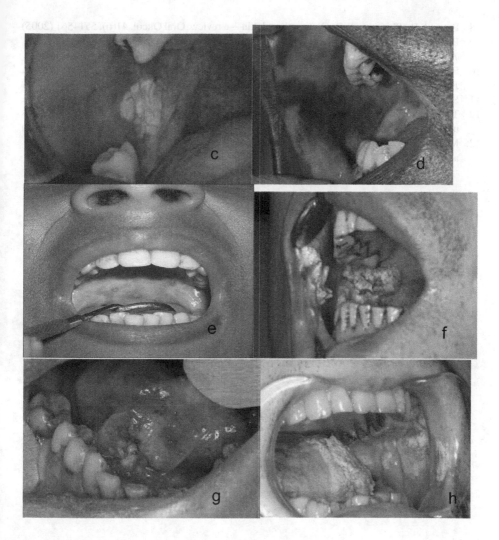

References

1. Borse, V., Konwar, A.N., Buragohain, P.: "Oral cancer diagnosis and perspectives in India." Sens. Int. **1**, 100046 (2020)
2. https://images.google.com
3. https://yandex.com/images/
4. Kayalibay, B., Jensen, G., Smagt, P.V.D.: CNN-based segmentation of medical imaging data. arXiv preprint arXiv:1701.03056 (2017)
5. Suzuki, K.: Overview of deep learning in medical imaging. Radiol. Phys. Technol. **10**(3), 257–273 (2017). https://doi.org/10.1007/s12194-017-0406-5
6. Van der Waal, I., et al.: Oral leukoplakia: a clinicopathological review. Oral Oncol. **33**(5), 291–301 (1997)
7. Wang, Y.: Melanoplakia of the oral mucosa. Zhonghua kou Qiang yi xue za zhi= Zhonghua Kouqiang Yixue Zazhi Chin. J. Stomatology **25**(1), 2–4 (1990)

8. Peter, A.R., Philipsen, H.P.: Oral erythroplakia—a review. Oral Oncol. **41**(6), 551–561 (2005)
9. Pindborg, J.J., Sirsat, S.M.: Oral submucous fibrosis. Oral Surg. Oral Med. Oral Pathol. **22**(6), 764–779 (1966)
10. Fourcade, A., Khonsari, R.H.: Deep learning in medical image analysis: a third eye for doctors. J. Stomatology Oral Maxillofac. Surg. **120**(4), 279–288 (2019)
11. Silverman, J.R.S.: Early diagnosis of oral cancer. Cancer **62** S1, 1796–1799 (1988)
12. Tanriver, G., Tekkesin, M.S., Ergen, O.: Automated detection and classification of oral lesions using deep learning to detect oral potentially malignant disorders. Cancers **13**(11), 2766 (2021)
13. Mahmood, H., et al.: Artificial Intelligence-based methods in head and neck cancer diagnosis: an overview. Br. J. Cancer **124**(12), 1934–1940 (2021)

Author Index

Printed in the United States
by Baker & Taylor Publisher Services